NOVELL'S®

Guide to Storage Area Networks and Novell® Cluster Services™

NOVELL'S®

Guide to Storage Area Networks and Novell® Cluster Services™

STEPHEN C. PAYNE AND ROBERT WIPFEL

Novell Press, San Jose

Novell's® Guide to Storage Area Networks and Novell® Cluster Services
Published by
Hungry Minds, Inc.
909 Third Avenue
New York, NY 10022
www.hungryminds.com

Library of Congress Control Number: 2001092916

ISBN: 0-7645-3581-1

Printed in the United States of America

10 9 8 7 6 5 4 3 2 1

1B/QZ/RR/QR/IN

Distributed in the United States by Hungry Minds, Inc.

Distributed by CDG Books Canada Inc. for Canada; by Transworld Publishers Limited in the United Kingdom; by IDG Norge Books for Norway; by IDG Sweden Books for Sweden; by IDG Books Australia Publishing Corporation Pty. Ltd. for Australia and New Zealand; by TransQuest Publishers Pte Ltd. for Singapore, Malaysia, Thailand, Indonesia, and Hong Kong; by Gotop Information Inc. for Taiwan; by ICG Muse, Inc. for Japan; by Intersoft for South Africa; by Eyrolles for France; by International Thomson Publishing for Germany, Austria, and Switzerland; by Distribuidora Cuspide for Argentina; by LR International for Brazil; by Galileo Libros for Chile; by Ediciones ZETA S.C.R. Ltda. for Peru; by WS Computer Publishing Corporation, Inc., for the Philippines; by Contemporanea de Ediciones for Venezuela; by Express Computer Distributors for the Caribbean and West Indies; by Micronesia Media Distributor, Inc. for Micronesia; by Chips Computadoras S.A. de C.V. for Mexico; by Editorial Norma de Panama S.A. for Panama; by American Bookshops for Finland.

For general information on Hungry Minds' products and services please contact our Customer Care department within the U.S. at 800-762-2974, outside the U.S. at 317-572-3993 or fax 317-572-4002.

For sales inquiries and reseller information, including discounts, premium and bulk quantity sales, and foreign-language translations, please contact our Customer Care department at 800-434-3422, fax 317-572-4002 or write to Hungry Minds, Inc., Attn: Customer Care Department, 10475 Crosspoint Boulevard, Indianapolis, IN 46256.

For information on licensing foreign or domestic rights, please contact our Sub-Rights Customer Care department at 212-884-5000.

For information on using Hungry Minds' products and services in the classroom or for ordering examination copies, please contact our Educational Sales department at 800-434-2086 or fax 317-572-4005.

For press review copies, author interviews, or other publicity information, please contact our Public Relations department at 317-572-3168 or fax 317-572-4168.

For authorization to photocopy items for corporate, personal, or educational use, please contact Copyright Clearance Center, 222 Rosewood Drive, Danvers, MA 01923, or fax 978-750-4470.

Ryan Johnson, Publisher, Novell Press, Novell, Inc.
Novell Press is a trademark and the Novell Press logo is a registered trademark of Novell, Inc.

Welcome to Novell Press

Novell Press, the world's leading provider of networking books, is the premier source for the most timely and useful information in the networking industry. Novell Press books cover fundamental networking issues as they emerge — from today's Novell and third-party products to the concepts and strategies that will guide the industry's future. The result is a broad spectrum of titles for the benefit of those involved in networking at any level: end user, department administrator, developer, systems manager, or network architect.

Novell Press books are written by experts with the full participation of Novell's technical, managerial, and marketing staff. The books are exhaustively reviewed by Novell's own technicians and are published only on the basis of final released software, never on pre-released versions.

Novell Press at Hungry Minds is an exciting partnership between two companies at the forefront of the knowledge and communications revolution. The Press is implementing an ambitious publishing program to develop new networking titles centered on the current versions of NetWare, GroupWise, ZENworks, DirXML, and networking integration products.

Novell Press books are translated into several languages and sold throughout the world.

Ryan Johnson
Publisher
Novell Press, Novell, Inc.

About the Authors

Stephen C. Payne is a Novell consultant in the Northern California Branch, assigned to the Cluster Services Practice, Net Directory Outside the Firewall Practice, and the GroupWise Pros team. He is a frequent speaker on clustering at Novell's annual Brainshare technical conference and is the author of the June 2001 AppNote "Configuring a Fault-Tolerant Messaging System Using GroupWise 5.5 and Novell Cluster Services." Stephen was one of several consultants that developed and revised the Novell Consulting methodology for implementing Novell Cluster Services and participates on the Novell Consulting GroupWise methodology team related to the High Available Messaging component. Stephen has successfully implemented Novell Cluster Services at several Novell clients and has received public success stories related to these implementations.

Stephen has spent the last nine years designing and implementing networking solutions for clients, as well as teaching Novell and Microsoft authorized education courses. He helped develop the Novell Consulting course on Novell Cluster Services and the Novell Education Novell Cluster Services Seminar and periodically facilitates these courses for internal and external clients. Stephen's specialties include Project Management, all aspects of NDS and eDirectory, Novell Cluster Services, Novell Account Manager (formerly NDS for NT and NDS Corporate Edition), GroupWise, Novell Portal Services, ZENworks, TCP/IP, SLP, LDAP, NetWare upgrades, and BorderManager.

A Novell President's Award Winner in 2000, **Robert Wipfel** is a software engineer consultant in Novell's Storage Services Group and is the architect and technical lead for the Novell Cluster Services product. His current projects include Cluster Services for NetWare 6 and research for future products. Robert is a frequent speaker on clustering and SANs at Novell's annual Brainshare technical conference.

Robert has spent the last 15 years researching, designing, and implementing various parallel computer systems. In the U.K., Robert spent 2 years using parallel processing techniques to research the machine vision problem. He was responsible for a systems product line that integrated VAX/VMS with Transputer-based parallel processing arrays. He then spent 5 years at INMOS, where he helped design and implement an operating system and distributed-file system for a campus area network of Transputer-based workstations (one of the first ever real production SANs). He also was a member of a European Community–funded research team that ported the Chorus-distributed operating system to Transputer family processors. Robert joined Unisys (in Salt Lake City, Utah) to help the company enter the commercial parallel processing market in collaboration with Intel's Scientific Super-Computer Division. During his 3 years at Unisys, Robert worked on a distributed, single-system image variant of the UNIX SVR4 operating system and on projects in collaboration with Oracle Corporation's Massively Parallel Processor (MPP) division.

Novell Press

Publisher
Ryan Johnson

Hungry Minds

Acquisitions Editor
Katie Feltman

Project Editor
Kevin Kent

Technical Editor
Stuart Proffitt

Copy Editors
Jennifer Mario
Gabrielle Chosney

Editorial Managers
Ami Frank Sullivan
Kyle Looper

**Senior Vice President,
Technical Publishing**
Richard Swadley

Vice President and Publisher
Mary Bednarek

Project Coordinator
Nancee Reeves

Graphics and Production Specialists
Gabriele McCann
Jill Piscitelli
Jacque Schneider
Betty Schulte
Erin Zeltner

Quality Control Technicians
David Faust
Andy Hollandbeck
Susan Moritz
Linda Quigley

Proofreading and Indexing
TECHBOOKS Production Services

To Angie, Jeffrey, Anthony, and Sarah

To my parents and Colonel Limbaugh — see, I'm not really functionally illiterate!

Stephen Payne

To Da Yang, Mia, Max, Otto, Monika, and Monica

Robert Wipfel

Foreword

Everywhere we look, networks matter. They are becoming the centerpiece of every computing activity and are transforming every aspect of commerce, government, society, and daily life. As a result of its rapid growth and global reach, the Internet has become a catalyst for rethinking business strategies and processes. Businesses are forced to compete on traditional and digital fronts, with new competitors, in new ways. They must use interactions with customers, partners, and employees as opportunities to drive revenue, increase productivity, and enhance service with greater speed and cost-effectiveness via the Internet. Competitive advantage in this perpetually changing "Net economy" is increasingly defined by the speed with which an organization can respond to these opportunities and competitive threats.

Success in the Net economy now rests upon the network in all its forms— including intranets, extranets, and the Internet. The role of the network is rapidly evolving from a medium that provides connectivity and information sharing to one that serves as the new, strategic platform for IT and business. In this role, the network and the software that advances its capabilities must become increasingly powerful and universal to securely power applications inside, outside, and between organizations.

Networking software began with the sharing of files and printers within local area networks (LANs) and evolved into the management of wide area networks (WANs) that enabled enterprise-class computing. The addition of intranets, extranets, and the Internet has resulted in multiple internal and external networks for employees, partners, and customers. At Novell, we envision a world in which all types of networks—intranets, the Internet and extranets; corporate and public; wired to wireless—work together as *one Net* to simplify the complexities of eBusiness and provide the power and flexibility organizations need to succeed in the Net economy.

In *Novell's Guide to Storage Area Networks and Novell Cluster Services*, Robert Wipfel and Stephen C. Payne clearly explain how the unification of networking principles and traditional server attached storage architectures has created a new class of network—the Storage Area Network (SAN). Novell Cluster Services is software that runs on a number of commodity server nodes and enables a single system image—the illusion of a single highly available and scalable system. Nodes are connected to two kinds of networks — the traditional client/server local area network and the new Storage Area Network. Clustering software enables high availability of access to network services and SAN resident data. Clusters represent the appropriate metaphor for achieving Novell's one Net vision, where local area networks and Storage Area Networks operate seamlessly and are managed as one.

Because success in the Net economy now rests upon the network, the combination of Storage Area Networks and Novell Cluster Services software represents a powerful solution to those who want to achieve highly available network services and access to information — a primary requirement for many businesses in the Net economy.

In writing this book, Robert and Stephen drew from their wealth of knowledge covering both system architecture and practical deployment. Robert is Novell's architect for high availability and a principal developer of the Cluster Services product. Stephen is a senior consultant within Novell's consulting practice and is responsible for many cluster implementations and customer success stories. Their combined, yet diverse, experience has resulted in a book that is as theoretically solid as it is practical.

Novell's Guide to Storage Area Networks and Novell Cluster Services is a valuable reference for anyone interested in the theory and operation of Storage Area Networks and Novell Cluster Services software — a technology combination Novell calls *clustered SANs*. Equally important, Robert and Stephen's book is a useful, practical desktop reference for anyone responsible for implementing or supporting Novell clustered SANs.

Storage Area Networks are becoming the benchmark standard way to manage ever-increasing amounts of mission-critical eCommerce data. In the federated global economy, electronic respite no longer exists; information must be available at all times and across international time zones. Therefore, high availability of network services and data is paramount and can be achieved by decoupling servers from storage via Storage Area Networks. Clustering software ensures that mission-critical eCommerce processes survive the failure of physical server elements through automated restart on alternate servers. Clustered SANs can be considered the twenty-first century mainframe — a powerful architecture that is ideally suited to hosting nonstop global eCommerce.

Dr. Eric Schmidt,

Chairman of the Board, Novell, Inc.

Preface

Novell's *Guide to Storage Area Networks and Novell Cluster Services* is your guide to understanding and implementing Novell Cluster Services and Storage Area Networks (SANs). By reading this book, you will learn both the theoretical and practical aspects of SANs and clusters and how they are related. We call this combination *clustered SANs*. This book provides the information and instructions for setting up a clustered SAN using NetWare servers and Storage Area Network devices. By implementing a clustered SAN, you enable high availability of access to network services and data and reduce the impact and cost of downtime incurred by your company. You can also dramatically reduce the complexity and cost of managing individual server storage resources by consolidating storage for all your servers and dynamically adjusting the allocation of storage to servers as a function of consumption and demand.

Reading this book will help you learn about Novell Cluster Services and how to implement many Novell applications in a highly available configuration. In addition, you will explore the methods necessary to apply the theoretical ideas and practical advice to other applications that aren't specifically covered here or in Novell's documentation.

Who This Book Is For

This book is written for anyone interested in — or responsible for — designing, planning, setting up, or maintaining NetWare server clusters and Storage Area Networks. If you are a system architect, administrator, support technician, CNE, or consultant, this book gives you the skills you need to understand how to design, install, and operate a Novell clustered SAN. If you are in management and want to understand the latest high availability and storage technologies and strategies, this book is also designed for you. Use this book to build your company's network computing strategy around highly available clustered SANs.

This book is unique because it is written from the two entirely different perspectives of its authors: Robert Wipfel — the architect and lead engineer of the Novell Cluster Services product — and Stephen C. Payne — a principal in Novell Consulting's cluster practice. From their two unique perspectives comes this book's well-developed content, which includes solid theory, detailed engineering information, direct cluster implementation information, and customer experience.

How This Book Is Organized

This book is organized into two main parts, covering both theory and practice:

▸ *Part I: Exploring Storage Area Networks and Novell Cluster Services* — Part I describes the theory — related concepts and terminology — of Storage Area Networks, high availability, and Cluster Services. Part I provides a foundation for the key concepts you need to know to work with and deploy clustered SANs and includes a thorough description of the architecture of Novell's Cluster Services product.

▸ *Part II: Applying Novell Cluster Services with Network Applications* — In Part II, you put your clustered SAN theory to practical use. It includes complete chapters on how to plan, install, configure, and manage a Novell Cluster Services SAN and also provides the information necessary to work with external shared disk storage. You learn how to apply your knowledge with various Novell applications and services for high availability failover. These chapters contain the practical information you will need to create, configure, and operate a clustered SAN. Furthermore, a case studies chapter provides examples of five real-world clustered SANs that are in full production at Novell customer sites.

In addition to Parts I and II, the book contains two appendixes. The first appendix is a compendium of available third-party Storage Area Network solutions for NetWare — hardware and software products that work with NetWare and Novell Cluster Services. The second appendix contains checklists that can help you to quickly configure cluster resources. These checklists provide an excellent supplementary resource to remind you of the steps previously covered in many of the chapters, without going into extensive detail about them.

What Software Versions Are Covered

This book primarily focuses on the current shipping version of Novell Cluster Services — Novell Cluster Services version 1.01 for NetWare 5.*x*. At the time of this writing, Novell Cluster Services 1.01 support pack 2 (SP2) was recently released. Where instructions or information are SP2-specific, the text specifically notes the dependency.

This book was primarily written assuming NetWare 5.1 with Support Pack 2A. At the time this book was completed, Support Pack 3 (SP3) for NetWare 5.1 was released. Where instructions or information is SP3-specific, the text specifically notes the dependency. In addition, some of the Notes, Tips, and Warnings covered in this book may have been fixed with the release of SP3, and, where possible, the text has tried to reflect those fixes.

The next major version is Novell Cluster Services version 1.6 for NetWare 6, and it should be stressed that the majority of this book applies equally to both versions of the product. Still, there are obviously new features in version 1.6, so an entire chapter is dedicated to Novell Cluster Services version 1.6 for NetWare 6. This chapter also includes detailed information on how to upgrade a NetWare 5.x cluster running Cluster Services version 1.01 to NetWare 6 running Cluster Services 1.6. Therefore, by design, this book is useful when working with both versions of Novell Cluster Services software for NetWare 5 or NetWare 6.

Features of the Book

Novell's Guide to Storage Area Networks and Novell Cluster Services has a few features to help you locate important information.

The Cluster Failover Classification Index

Because different types of applications and network services behave differently when running in a cluster configuration, this book offers a *cluster failover classification index*. The primary consideration of this index is what happens when a clustered server fails and applications or network services are automatically restarted on surviving servers. The amount of time this takes is very much a function of the application or network service and how well it recovers from server failure when restarted. Another important factor is to what extent a server failure causes noticeable disruption from the perspective of clients using an application or service running on the server. Is the Cluster Services–initiated restart of failed services completely transparent to users, and, if not, to what extent will the impact of a failed or otherwise unavailable server be noticed by users? In practice, actual results vary depending on the type of client, the application or network service, and what the client was doing at the precise time the server failed. For example, when they notice a failure to communicate with a server, some clients automatically enter a recovery mode and attempt to reconnect on behalf of the user.

The cluster failover classification index, offered at the end of most of the practical chapters, is intended to offer a baseline metric for how well different application or network services function when being restarted after server failure. The index has the following three qualitative elements:

- *Transparency* — How transparent is the automatic restart process? What is the worst the user may be subjected to on restart? For example, will the client software automatically reconnect to a new cluster server and replay any pending operations that were in progress at the time of failure? An application that is very transparent will allow for a failover or migration with almost no noticeable impact at the client (or impact that occurs only if the client performs a specific action during the migration), while applications that are nontransparent will require some sort of end-user intervention such as logging out and logging back in to the network.

- *Active/Active or Active/Passive* — Can cluster servers run multiple instances of the same service type on the same server and can an instance of a service type be restarted on a new server if that server is already running a different copy of the same service type (thus making failover/migration faster)? All cluster nodes are Active/Active in the sense that they can all provide services. This matrix refers to the actual service — if the service can be actively running on each node in the failover path, and all it has to do to failover or migrate is start an instance (or bind an IP address), then it is considered Active/Active. If the service can run on only one node in the failover path, and must completely start up upon failover or migration, then that service is considered Active/Passive. Most services that are Active/Active may also be configured as Active/Passive.

- *Time to failover* — On average, how long does it take to restart an application or network service on another server should the server currently hosting the resource unexpectedly fail?

The following is an example of a Cluster Failover Classification Index.

CLUSTER FAILOVER CLASSIFICATION INDEX	
Transparency	Very transparent
Active/Active or Active/Passive	Either
Time to failover	Both configurations are very fast, typically taking a few tens of seconds to failover

Icons

Several icons are used throughout the book to flag certain text for your attention:

The Cross-Reference icon points you to other places to get more information about a topic.

X-REF

When something stands apart from the general discussion or bears a bit more explanation, your eyes will be drawn to it by a Note icon.

NOTE

A Tip is a helpful piece of advice that comes from the authors' experience and makes a procedure or process described in the book much easier to perform.

TIP

Warnings are issued when something you do (or don't do) is likely to have serious consequences.

WARNING

Acknowledgments

A very special thanks to my family for putting up with all the nights and weekends that I spent working on "the book." Your support and understanding made this book possible.

Special thanks to Robert Wipfel and Stuart Proffitt for believing that we could get this done and for turning our idea into reality.

Thanks to Ed Hanley, Matt Weisberg, Hylton Leigh, Courtney Elliott, Mike Robinson, Stuart Thompson, Jill Boogaard, Howard Tayler, Ralph Tse, Jon Christensen, and Patti Brooks for all of the GroupWise input and feedback — your patience with my endless queries, as well as the continued improvements in GroupWise to support Novell Cluster Services, is greatly appreciated.

Thanks to Howard Shapiro and Jeff Fawcett for providing the training and the opportunity to participate on the Cluster Practice, as well as the support in this endeavor.

Thanks to Robert Wipfel, Ranjan Gupta, Alexander Danoyan, Kelli Frame, Brad Christensen, Dan Lawyer Brad Young, Ed Hart, and Blair Merrell — you produced an awesome product that truly fulfills our client's needs for high availability.

And thanks to Kathy Takayama and Eric Wing for your valuable feedback and encouragement through this process.

— *Stephen C. Payne*

My biggest thanks go to Da Yang Wipfel for her encouragement, enthusiasm, support, and understanding. I am indeed very lucky.

Next, to Stephen Payne — I would not have written this book unless you had suggested the idea and led the way. Your dedication to everything you do has been inspirational.

Special and warm thanks to my friends and members of the Orion team: Alexander Danoyan, Kelli Frame, Ranjan Gupta, Ed Hart, and Blair Merrell. We did it — none of this would have been possible without you. To Changju Gao, welcome to the team!

Thanks also to Michael Bryant, Brad Christensen, Dan Lawyer, and Brad Young.

I owe a big debt of gratitude to Eric Schmidt and Craig Miller. Thanks for your support and for believing in the Orion team.

To LaMont Leavitt, Jim Rohan, and Jawaad Tariq — thanks for making the product solid.

Thanks also to Chris Beck, Patti Brooks, Brad Dayley, Calvin Dickson, Courtney Elliot, Todd Grant, Jeff Hawkins, Allen Jack, Linda Kennard, Markus J. Krauss, Robert Kumiega, Simon Lidgett, David Mair, John Mauzy, Jim Norman, Phil Oswald, Greg Pachner, Vandana Rungta, Ahmad Sadeghpour, Dominick Sciusco, Karl-Heinz Schuh, Randy Stokes, Paul Taysom, Ralph Tse, Scott Villinski, and Steve Whitehouse. And to Brian Petersen — thanks for putting early versions of Cluster Services to a real-world test.

— *Robert Wipfel*

We both would like to acknowledge the assistance of the many talented individuals who have contributed to the creation of this book. In particular, we thank the staff of Hungry Minds for their patience and understanding, and for keeping us on track to get the book finished. Many thanks to Kevin Kent, our project editor, who turned chapters into a book. Thanks also to Katie Feltman, our acquisitions editor, and our copy editors, Jennifer Mario and Gabrielle Chosney. And a big thanks to Stuart Proffitt, who did the technical editing.

To Novell's system and support engineers and Novell Consulting Cluster Practice, whose enthusiasm and dedication to our customers make it all worthwhile — keep e-mailing!

Thanks to Novell's partners who understand and are enthusiastic about clustered SANs.

Most of all, our appreciation goes to Novell's customers, who are running the best clustering product and Net Services operating system available. We exist to serve you.

Contents at a Glance

Contents

Exploring Storage Area Networks and Novell Cluster Services

## CHAPTER I

Introducing Storage Area Networks and Novell Cluster Services

At first glance, it might appear that this book is about two completely unrelated topics:

- ▸ Storage Area Networks
- ▸ Novell Cluster Services

Storage Area Networks (SANs) are a relatively new technology and the topic of significant industry interest and discussion. In contrast, clustering is a technology that most people associate with big expensive mainframes.

Why might you be interested in either of these topics? Why should you be interested in a book dedicated to the powerful combination of Storage Area Networks and Novell's Cluster Services product for NetWare? Read on to find out.

▸ . . . . ◂

Introducing Clustered SANs

In a matter of only a few years, the computer industry has experienced dramatic advances that commodity microelectronics and fiber optic bandwidth has enabled. Consider your first experience with a computer. The increases in performance, capacity, and bandwidth since then are nothing less than astonishing. The end of the twentieth century was defined by "Y2K" and the conscious realization that humanity is totally dependent on computers. The twenty-first century is perhaps the dawn of the "always-on" information age, defined by worldwide integrated digital communications, personal processing, and dense storage capacity.

Many people own and carry personal communication and computing devices. Almost everyone has an online digital identity. A large percentage of the population has come to expect digital information on demand. This has been a natural evolution. Hardly anyone pays attention to telephone or electricity outlets, and everyone has come to implicitly require similar levels of service from information utilities. But one difference between electricity and information is everyone collectively both consumes and produces digital information on a very large scale. Historical comparisons also indicate the rate of acceptance and subsequent dependence on information is greater than electrification.

How much disk space does it take to transmit an e-mail with attachments to 10 people? Unlike a human conversation, e-mails are a persistent form of communication. It's often easier to type a brief e-mail than it is to walk down the hallway to exchange verbally generated sound waves. If the recipient isn't physically present to receive the sound waves, the waves are lost. Not so with an e-mail message—

e-mails sit in electronic queues waiting to be delivered. And while written words are a simple form of information, digital voice, images, and video enable much richer expression and representation. If your e-mail attachment is a video clip, how much more disk space is consumed?

Figure 1.1 illustrates the conflicting demands made of today's information systems and the identifiable trend over preceding years. Two primary factors are depicted by the graph. First, the amount of persistent storage required to hold digital information of all kinds is growing exponentially. Information is almost never discarded, and the rate of production is increasing. Second, access to stored digital information is required on demand all the time. This equates to a decreasing trend in tolerance to system downtime.

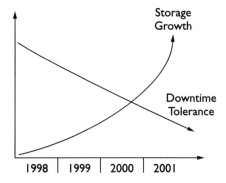

FIGURE 1.1 *The conflicting demands made on today's information systems*

Systems that enable secure scalable storage and online access 24 hours a day, 7 days a week are in high demand. Before the advent of client/server local area networks and the subsequent global expansion to the Internet, "big iron" mainframes enabled fault tolerance for those customers with sufficiently mission-critical applications that could warrant the extremely high cost of deployment. Mainframe architectures pioneered high availability with dual or triple modular redundancy. The techniques of combining redundant processing and I/O elements were developed and mainframe *clusters* became the benchmark standard way to achieve reliable computerization of business processes.

As mainframes were displaced with cheaper personal computers and decentralized local area networks, clustering techniques continued to be applied in situations that required better than the default level of client/server reliability.

The ideas carried forward, but the cost of implementation has remained high until very recently. The effect of mass-market "burn-in" of commodity microprocessor-based servers has increased overall system reliability at the hardware level. Server hardware has evolved through several processor and I/O bus generations. During the same period, software complexity has also grown in at least two dimensions. Self-contained monolithic applications have largely ceased to exist. They were replaced by modular object-oriented applications.

Modular components enabled single applications to be broken down into autonomous distributed application entities that run across multiple servers. The intrinsic complexity of individual software components and their network interrelations has increased. The essential usefulness provided by monolithic applications is no longer associated with an individual computer. The trend is a proliferation of network services — applications are hosted by networks, not clearly identifiable servers attached to networks. Most recently, the artificial barriers of private and public local and wide area networks have given way to the anarchy of the Internet and the mobility of wireless devices. Network services are now free to distribute themselves across worldwide geographies and through previously closed electronic borders. In this transparent global computer age, the key questions become the following: Where is the data, and how is secure, readily available access to the data guaranteed?

Storage Area Networks (SANs) are the product of applying core networking principles to conventional storage. The result is an architecture optimized for high-performance disk I/O that also retains the flexible topologies, scalability, and dynamic behavior of networks. Storage Area Networks enable a network-like topology that interconnects many servers to many storage devices. SANs combine the flexibility, manageability, and scalability of networks with the high bandwidth and reliability of mainframe-class data I/O channels.

The role of servers with respect to disk data is radically altered in a Storage Area Network. Disks are relocated to a centralized location where any server can access them. This completely changes the classic computer architecture relationship between servers and storage. Servers, in fact, become less important in the overall scheme of things and lose their individuality in the process. Servers are anonymous — they simply represent the place that data and processing coincide to get work done. Storage is promoted to a central position, whereas processing becomes peripheral.

The creation of the Fibre Channel standard and the almost exclusive deployment of Fibre Channel as a storage networking technology are primary factors that have enabled large-scale commodity clustering. Shared disk clusters are a direct consequence of Storage Area Network hardware. SANs provide the infrastructure to share physical access to disk data between servers and independent of specific servers. They enable any server to access any data at any time. This capability is a fundamental requirement for clusters.

Clusters are collections of compute elements that function as a single logical computer with the goal of increasing overall system availability, scalability, and capacity. Storage Area Networks provide a unified physical disk subsystem for *single system image* clusters comprising many servers attached to many disks. The result is perhaps what can be considered a twenty-first century mainframe-class computing platform — an architecture that is well suited to hosting dependable network services and enormous amounts of easily managed digital information.

Why Clusters and Storage Area Networks? Clustered SANs enable the following:

▸ *High availability of network services with multiple paths between application components and shared data.* Any-to-any connectivity enables the combination of more servers, more storage, and more options for relocating applications in the event of server failure. The result is a lower cost of availability and management than traditional methods.

▸ *Unified management of relocatable network services and data.* You manage individual network services and their corresponding data sets in a manner that is entirely independent of transient servers. You can replace or upgrade individual servers without affecting the intrinsic ability of the cluster to host network services and enable access to application-specific data. In the event of a server becoming unavailable due to hardware or software failure, network services and SAN resident data are recombined elsewhere on the cluster.

▸ *Online dynamic reconfiguration of storage and server resources.* You add both storage and servers while the cluster is online. This further increases availability by masking individual server maintenance. Because the traditional bond between host server and direct attached storage is broken in a clustered SAN, the complexity and, therefore, the cost of managing increasing amounts of server storage is reduced. Storage resources are centrally provisioned via the SAN and allocated to individual servers on demand. Gone are the days of having one server run out of storage while another has an abundant supply.

Introducing Novell Cluster Services

Novell designed Cluster Services to be scalable from two node shared SCSI cluster configurations up to large-scale multi-node Storage Area Networks. Novell Cluster Services for NetWare is a server-clustering system you can use to ensure high availability and manageability of critical network resources, including data (volumes), applications, server licenses, and services. It is a multinode, Novell Directory Services (NDS)–enabled clustering product for NetWare 5 and NetWare 6 that supports failover, failback, and migration (static load balancing) of individually managed cluster resources.

Novell Cluster Services delivers higher levels of availability than other Intel-based clustering systems: You can provide true multinode clustering with support for up to 32 server nodes in a cluster. In addition, Novell Cluster Services does not require any proprietary hardware; you can install it on off-the-shelf Intel architecture servers and generic Storage Area Networks. Other benefits include the following:

> ▸ *Fan-out failover* — This is the process of moving cluster resources from one failed node to multiple (different) surviving nodes, thus spreading the work out among the survivors. Applications and services can be distributed to multiple surviving servers to prevent an overload of any single cluster node. Multinode failover support allows users continued access to their resources, even in the event of major failures where more than one node in the cluster goes down. With Novell Cluster Services, you can cluster up to 32 active NetWare servers. If one or more of the cluster nodes fail, any surviving nodes in the cluster can take over for those that failed. The surviving cluster nodes remount the failed nodes' volumes and restart any applications or network services the failed nodes provided.

> ▸ *Transparent client reconnect* — You can automatically and transparently reconnect clients from a failed cluster node to a surviving one. Users' drive mappings are preserved when their volumes are remounted on a surviving server. Additionally, many server-based applications can be configured so that when a cluster-node failure occurs, transactions proceed uninterrupted by the failure and unnoticed by the user.

> ▸ *Downtime elimination* — You can provide users with access to network resources provided by a cluster even during routine maintenance or

shutdowns of individual NetWare servers within the cluster. Before shutting down a server for maintenance, you migrate that server's resources to another NetWare server in the cluster. As a result, users experience minimal interruption of access to or service from the network resources provided by the cluster.

▶ *Dynamic additions of new capacity* — When you need to add a new node or storage to the cluster, you can add it without having to shut down other cluster nodes or adjust running cluster resource configurations. This further ensures continuous network service availability during significant maintenance.

▶ *Designed for Storage Area Networks* — Clustered nodes share access to data resident on a SAN (or other type of shared disk system) so that if one node in the cluster fails, the services and data it provided are seamlessly handled by another node in the cluster. Cluster Services enables fine-grained storage virtualization through block-level management and allocation of disk access to servers. At the default SAN layer, only individual disks can be selectively presented to servers. By using Cluster Services, you control multiple server access to SAN disks at the volume (file system) layer.

▶ *Single point of administration* — Novell Cluster Services leverages the power of NDS, taking advantage of its single-point-of-administration capabilities. Cluster resource information, protocols, and polices are maintained in NDS cluster containers and objects and are managed through ConsoleOne, Novell's Java-based management tool. The Novell Cluster Services installation programs run from a client workstation that automatically deploys the Novell Cluster Services software to all network servers targeted to become nodes in the cluster. You do not have to physically go to each network server in the cluster to install the software.

Since the first beta release of Novell Cluster Services in March 1999, the product has evolved in step with Storage Area Network advances. A brief timeline of product versions and corresponding SAN capabilities follows.

NOTE
Novell has changed the name of the Cluster Services product twice. For the 1.0 release, it was called Novell Cluster Services; then it changed names to NetWare Cluster Services. The name has now changed back again.

▸ *October 1999* — Cluster Services 1.0 product release with support for up to eight nodes on fibre channel arbitrated loop Storage Area Networks. Received the Best of Show award at NetWorld+Interop, Atlanta, Georgia.

▸ *November 1999* — Three clusters deployed at COMDEX/Fall to demonstrate the availability and scalability of Storage Area Networks by hosting 300,000 users on the conference e-mail and Internet systems.

The details of the COMDEX clusters are included in the case studies presented in Chapter 21.

X-REF

▸ *March 2000* — Cluster Services 1.01 product release with support for up to 32 nodes on multistage fibre channel fabric–based Storage Area Networks. Featured during a keynote at Novell's annual Brainshare conference in Salt Lake City, Utah. Out of 32 nodes, seven randomly selected nodes were powered down. A video clip streaming from a cluster volume continued to play uninterrupted on the overhead monitors viewed by the conference audience.

▸ *March 2001* — Support for dual-path redundant fibre channel fabrics, third-party volume snapshots, and geographically distributed data and disaster tolerance. More applications support cluster failover.

▸ *August 2001* — Novell Cluster Services 1.6 for NetWare 6 released to beta customers.

Where to Find More Information on Clustered SANs

When you have finished reading this book, check the following Web links for additional information on Novell Cluster Services and Storage Area Networks:

▸ The Novell Web site at `www.novell.com/products/clusters/ncs/`

▸ Novell's online cluster user documentation at `www.novell.com/documentation/lg/ncs/index.html`

▶ Novell's Cluster Support Forum at `http://support-forums.
novell.com/group/novell.support.high-availability.
cluster-services/tmainSupport.tpt/@overview@0@F@15@T,D@All`

▶ The Storage Networking Industry Association at `www.snia.org`

Summary

The perhaps unlikely combination of Storage Area Networks and Novell Cluster Services is the subject of this book. In this introductory chapter, you read about the dramatic advances in microelectronics and fiber optic digital communications that led to the always-on information age and how Novell Clustered SANs are well suited to hosting dependable network services and enormous amounts of easily managed digital information. Novell Cluster Services for NetWare is a server-clustering system you can use to ensure high availability and manageability of critical network resources, including data (volumes), applications, and services. Since 1999, the Cluster Services product has matured in step with commodity Storage Area Networks. At the time of this writing, Novell Cluster Services is the only directory-enabled 32-node clustering product on the market and is in daily use at many Novell customer sites.

Exploring and Implementing Storage Area Networks

The essential properties of Storage Area Networks are defined in this chapter. You first learn about traditional storage mechanisms and the classic NetWare file server architecture. Then the chapter explains the shortcomings of direct attached storage and presents a case for storage networks.

Fibre Channel — the most widely used Storage Area Network (SAN) technology — is introduced in this chapter, as are the fibre channel protocol layers from the bottom physical layer to the top-most protocol-mapping layer. Network addressing, naming, and fibre channel network topologies are covered in this chapter as well.

You learn about storage virtualization by inspecting layers of the disk I/O stack as it exists between target disk devices, extended across storage networks, to file servers. SAN port zoning and logical unit number (LUN)-level masking are defined in this context.

Throughout this chapter, the application of SANs in the NetWare file server environment is considered. The chapter concludes with a discussion of NetWare-specific SAN implementation considerations.

Introducing Storage Area Networks

Electronic storage is an implicit function of computers. You use a computer to store data. You don't really think about data storage without thinking about computers. Perhaps this is because you remember that classic computer architecture books describe processing as central, whereas storage is merely peripheral to the main action. For the most part, standard computer architecture, comprising CPU, memory, and peripheral I/O, hasn't radically changed since it was invented. These three core elements have all experienced amazing advances, but their relationship remains the same. Computers consist of CPUs that process data and peripheral devices that store data.

Figure 2.1 illustrates the classic computer architecture. The central processing unit (CPU) is connected to memory via a memory bus. A bridge chip provides a path from the CPU to I/O devices. The storage devices are attached to an I/O bus via a device-specific adapter. Data travels from the CPU over the memory bus, through the bridge, and onto the I/O bus. A device adapter receives the data and relays it over an I/O channel to the device. The entire data path is short and data bits travel in parallel over multiconductor buses. Data buses are 8, 16, 32, or 64 bits wide.

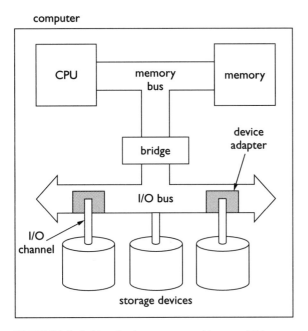

computer

CPU

memory bus

memory

device adapter

bridge

I/O bus

I/O channel

storage devices

FIGURE 2.1 *The classic computer architecture: CPU, memory, and I/O peripherals*

Data has always been more valuable than processing. If you lose your data, no amount of processing can reconstruct it for you. It's gone. Historically, important data was stored on expensive mainframes. Mainframes pioneered reliable storage architectures like intelligent storage coprocessors, fast data I/O channels, and mirrored disks.

Figure 2.2 depicts the organization of an IBM 370 mainframe. The three core elements, CPU, memory, and I/O, are interconnected by buses and I/O channels. Special-purpose I/O coprocessors offload some of the processing related to storage management. The gap between central processing and storage devices is wider than a conventional Intel architecture server.

Inexpensive, fast CPUs and local area networks (LANs) revolutionized the computing world, which had previously relied on mainframe computing, by creating the open systems client/server model. Processing moved from the central mainframe to client computers. Proprietary mainframes were replaced with cheaper shared file or application servers. Clients and servers exchanged data over networks using standard protocols.

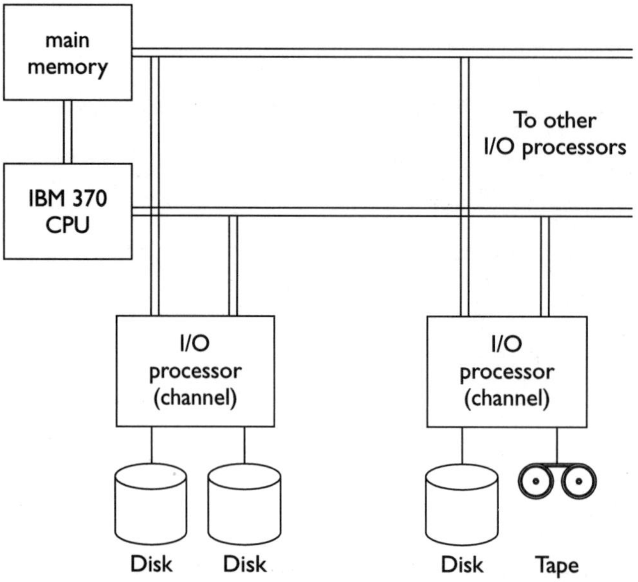

FIGURE 2.2 *The IBM 370 mainframe, featuring distinct storage coprocessors and I/O channels*

Today, everyone's data is still just as important, and you all have a lot more of it. You generate and work with data on personal computers. You share data via common file or e-mail servers that also enable centralized storage management and data protection.

Figure 2.3 illustrates the familiar client/server model: personal computers connected to a file server via a local area network. When you store data on your personal computer or laptop, it isn't as safe or well managed as it is when it's copied to a file server. The file server offers storage, security, and data protection services to clients. Even in the now-standard client/server model, file servers retain the classic computer architecture. The file server in Figure 2.3 has access to its disks over a private I/O channel. Clients communicate with the file server using file access protocols over a public local area network. The file server, transparent to clients, manipulates data on its disks. Users work with files, the file server works with disks. Only the file server has direct access to its disks.

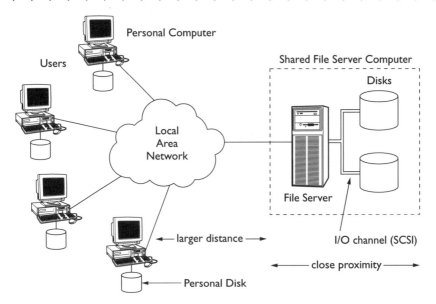

FIGURE 2.3 *Client/server computing: PCs, local area network, and a file server*

Examining Client/Server File I/O

Clients use a network file access protocol like Novell's NetWare Core Protocol (NCP) to access files on a file server. File servers translate client file access requests into disk operations. The most popular and widely used disk I/O channel today is SCSI (Small Computer System Interface). Just like mainframe I/O channels, SCSI is a block-level I/O protocol. I/O *initiators* (servers) use SCSI to transfer data blocks over a parallel data bus to and from I/O *targets* (disks). These details aren't visible to clients that use network file protocols to access files on servers.

NOTE

Because servers are directly attached to their disks via a SCSI bus, this storage organization is usually called *direct attached storage* (DAS).

Table 2.1 lists some of the differences between Ethernet local area networks and SCSI I/O channels.

TABLE 2.1		
Differences between Ethernet LANs and SCSI I/O Channels		
FEATURE	ETHERNET	SCSI
Bandwidth	100MBits/sec	160MB/sec
Distance	100 meters	25 meters
Data reliability	Low	High
Number of devices	Thousands	16
Data path	Serial	Parallel bus

SCSI Addressing

The two kinds of parallel SCSI are named after their comparative databus widths:

▶ *Narrow* — 8-bit data bus. Enables a maximum of eight devices, including the initiator.

▶ *Wide* — 16-bit data bus. Enables a maximum of 16 devices, including the initiator.

Wide Ultra SCSI and Wide Ultra2 SCSI are variants of wide SCSI. They have 16-bit data buses.

NOTE

Target devices are addressed by SCSI bus ID. Because the initiator takes one ID, 7 target device IDs are available on narrow SCSI, and 15 target device IDs are available on wide SCSI. Each device can expand the addressing possibilities further by presenting a number of logical unit numbers (LUNs). Each device ID can have a maximum of eight LUNs. For example, a server-based RAID controller is addressed via one target ID, but can present up to eight disks each with a different logical unit number.

SCSI Limitations

SCSI is popular, but with the increased demands on data storage and availability of access to data, it is starting to show some limitations:

▶ *Scalability* — SCSI was originally intended to support devices in a small computer system — the SCS in SCSI. The number of available target addresses is limited, which means the number of devices you can attach to a single server is limited to the same degree. Even though SCSI has evolved through several versions, its classic computer parallel bus implementation is not keeping up with the demands of enterprise data storage.

▸ *Accessibility* — Even with its addressing limitations, SCSI can support a large amount of data when you consider the capacity of individual disk drives. A single SCSI controller can address fifteen 36GB drives — approximately half a terabyte of storage. If the server fails, a lot of data will become unavailable to clients. The SCSI specification does support multiple initiators enabling more than one server to access the same disk over a shared SCSI bus, but the maximum number of servers is typically limited to two. Data buses just aren't as good at sharing as networks.

▸ *Proximity* — Because of distance limits imposed by the electrical properties of SCSI's parallel data bus–based implementation, SCSI disks have to be located near the servers they are attached to. This further reinforces the classic computer architecture — central processor and direct attached storage — making it difficult to share disks with other servers. And if disaster strikes, both the server and its disks can be lost if they are physically close to each other.

▸ *Provisioning* — Once SCSI disks are plugged into a server's drive bay, they are rarely moved. If you attach a new 36GB drive to a server and use only a few gigabytes initially, the free disk space is permanently reserved for that server's exclusive future use. Suppose you have a second server that has run out of disk space. The free space sitting unused in the first server is wasted — it can't be used where it is really needed. This problem is called *misprovisioned storage* and is a side effect of the relationship between host file server and bus-based disk access. Some companies have hundreds of gigabytes of misprovisioned storage attached to file servers that don't need it and are forced to purchase even more disks for other servers that do need it.

All these limitations reveal the weaknesses that SCSI and the standard client/server approach to storage have, particularly to the demands of enterprise data storage. Another solution is needed to meet the demands of future data storage.

Defining Storage Area Networks

Storage Area Networks (SANs) are the products of applying core networking principles to conventional storage. The result is an architecture optimized for high-performance disk I/O that also retains the flexible topologies, scalability, and dynamic behavior of networks. Figure 2.4 defines a Storage Area Network: a network-like topology that interconnects many servers to many storage devices. SANs combine the flexibility, manageability, and scalability of networks with the high bandwidth and reliability of mainframe-class data I/O channels.

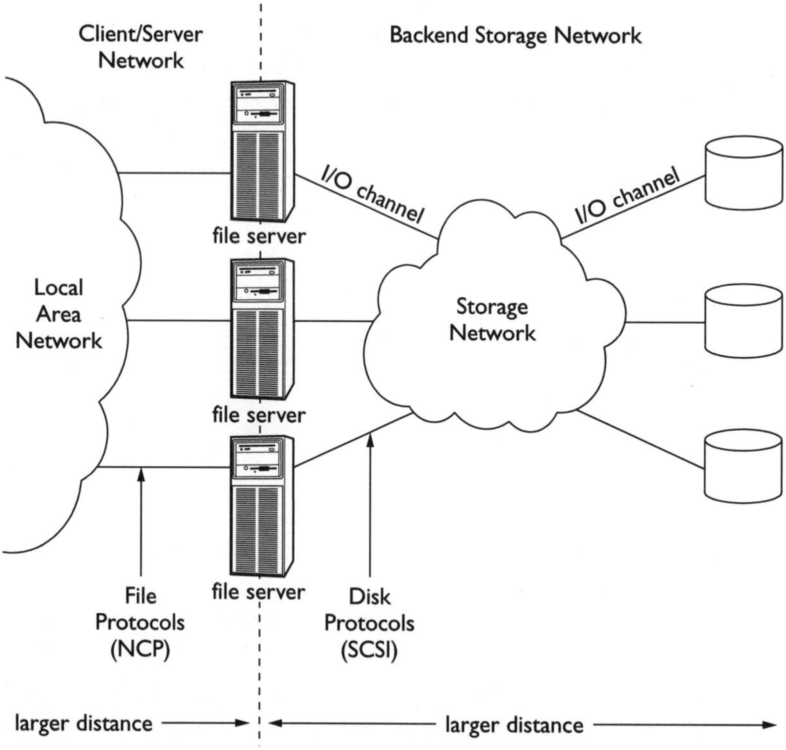

FIGURE 2.4 *A Storage Area Network (SAN) with interconnected servers and storage devices*

Servers are attached to two distinct networks. The backend Storage Area Network connects multiple servers to multiple storage devices. In the backend network, file servers function as clients of storage devices. They use existing disk protocols to access data blocks on remote disks. Distances between servers and disks are extended to network-scale proximity so that, for example, servers need not even be located in the same building as disks. The front-end network is unchanged: It is the traditional client/server LAN used by clients to access file servers. From the perspective of LAN clients, it doesn't matter whether a server is attached to a SAN or has dedicated SCSI bus disk drives. Clients continue to access files using network file protocols.

Applying Network Principles to Storage

Local area networking has many valuable attributes that are desirable in a storage environment:

- *Dynamic discovery* — Devices can be attached to the network and discovered without affecting the ongoing interactions of existing devices. We have become accustomed to attaching a device to a network port and then figuring out how to get it "connected" later. Making additional storage capacity generally available to servers should also be a simple task.

- *Flexible topologies and cabling* — Wiring up a LAN is much easier than wiring a SCSI drive array. You have many options for creating a LAN topology. RJ45 network jacks are much more robust and less failure prone than 68-pin SCSI connectors. You don't have to consider cable strain relief when attaching an Ethernet cable, for example. Network cables are cheaper and longer than SCSI cables. Networking is considered a plug and play technology, while storage is generally thought of as more complex to configure than a LAN.

- *Serial transmission* — Sending data as a bit stream down a single wire instead of multiple bits down multiple electrical conductors in the same clock cycle is proving to be an extremely cost effective and reliable way to transfer data of any kind. Data buses have too many problems with signal and clock skew to extend very far beyond the server enclosure.

Decoupling Storage from Servers

The role of servers with respect to disk data is radically altered in a Storage Area Network. Disks are relocated to a centralized location, where any server can access them. This completely changes the classic computer architecture relationship between servers and storage. Servers can no longer assume they are the only initiator of I/O to devices visible via their I/O buses, and can no longer assume exclusive ownership. Servers, in fact, become less important in the overall scheme of things and lose their individuality in the process. Servers are anonymous — they simply represent the place that data and processing coincide to get work done. Storage is promoted to a central position, whereas processing is peripheral.

Decoupling storage from servers results in the following benefits:

▶ *Availability* — If a server should fail, any data it was interacting with remains available via the SAN. Any other server can access the same disks and take over the processing of the failed server on behalf of network clients.

▶ *Provisioning* — Because servers no longer have exclusive ownership of disks and the space (both used and unused) on those disks, no single server can ever run out of disk space if free space exists. All disks are centrally pooled and available to any server. With appropriate software, you can achieve extremely dynamic multiserver disk space allocation and storage management.

▶ *Data protection* — It's easier to protect data when it's centrally located and independent of servers. Servers can't interfere with access to data during backup windows. When disks and backup devices are intelligent peers of servers, they can connect to each other to back up data independent of data processing by servers.

High availability and dynamic storage management are both features of Novell Cluster Services and are a major topic of this book.

NOTE

SAN Storage Devices

Disks are housed in external storage cabinets called storage arrays or Just a Bunch of Disks (JBOD). The terms *storage array*, *drive array*, *RAID array*, and *JBOD* tend to be used interchangeably. A JBOD is what the acronym suggests — a cabinet with just a bunch of (regular) disk drives accessible to servers on the SAN. There is little to no built-in intelligence. At the opposite end of the spectrum, some storage arrays contain numerous embedded CPUs and RAID controllers, and have extensive fault-tolerant data path features. These SAN disk I/O complexes can support terabytes of storage and hundreds of servers.

Appendix A lists many of the SAN storage solutions available for NetWare.

X-REF

Storage Area Networks don't intrinsically improve the standard data protection options. Individual disk drives can and still do fail whether directly attached to a server or located in a SAN storage array. However, RAID-style disk redundancy is provided in external storage arrays in a manner identical to server/direct-attached storage. Individual disk failures are masked via redundancy. When you use RAID in a server with direct attached disks, you dedicate a hot spare disk for that server. Every server running RAID with direct attached disks has its own spare disk. Centralized RAID processing in a SAN storage array enables better redundancy because hot spares aren't exclusively reserved for each server; instead, they are available to replace any failed drive independent of servers. The ratio of spare drives to data drives is smaller. Failures will still happen, but centralized RAID processing helps provide a level of redundancy that amortizes the failures and reduces the number of spare drives you need to achieve an equivalent level of redundancy for all your servers.

Contrasting Network Attached Storage

You've examined definitions of direct attached storage (DAS) and Storage Area Networks (SANs). To do proper justice to the current storage scene, one more acronym should be discussed, Network Attached Storage (NAS). NAS is a simplified file server. In a diagram, it would look identical to the classic NetWare file server. NAS boxes have direct attached disk drives and attach to local area networks. Only two features distinguish network-attached storage from special-purpose file servers like NetWare:

▶ *Appliance form factor* — NAS boxes don't have keyboards or screens. They are designed to be as easy to install and use as a washing machine. You plug an NAS box into the LAN and power it on. Given a few simple parameters, it auto configures by probing its environment. NAS boxes are really simple to set up and operate. You manage them via a Web browser and IP address.

▶ *Multiprotocol* — NAS is protocol independent. LAN clients access files using their native network file protocol. For UNIX clients, this is NFS (Network File System). For Microsoft Windows clients, it's CIFS (Common Internet File System). UNIX and Windows clients can share files via a single NAS appliance. Clients also share a single authentication namespace, allowing file access rights to propagate to either side. Windows and UNIX clients respect their native access methods.

Network attached storage sounds like storage Nirvana, but there are, of course, some limitations. The problems are mostly similar to those of direct attached storage. For example, when an appliance runs out of disk space, you typically have two ways to increase capacity:

▶ *Buy another NAS box.* Some vendors won't let you open up their appliance box unless you don't care about invalidating the warranty. So you have to buy another appliance.

▶ *Purchase additional disks.* You buy disks from the original NAS vendor and add them to the appliance. Some NAS boxes feature modular drive bays that simplify this expansion task.

When you deploy an additional NAS appliance, it's equivalent to installing another file server on the LAN. You don't get better data availability or storage provisioning. You do get a new file server name and a place to save files. Disks are physically located inside each NAS box, where they remain exclusively owned and are never shared. Some NAS products are intended for small business or departmental file sharing, which is easier to set up and use than a traditional file server. Very inexpensive NAS products contain EIDE drives with no RAID protection. They are considered disposable; if the NAS box fails, all the data is gone and you purchase a replacement. Other higher-end NAS products combine the block level sharing enabled by SANs with the multiple file protocol access offered by NAS in order to improve data availability and storage provisioning while also retaining the flexibility of multiple protocol access to shared files.

NOTE **Novell's NetDevice is a departmental NAS product and Novell's Native File Access Pack (NFAP) enables multi-protocol file sharing for NetWare SANs. At the time of this writing, the NFAP product includes NFS, CIFS and AppleTalk Filing Protocol (AFP) protocols and all are enabled for failover on NetWare 5.x or NetWare 6 clustered SANs.**

Introducing Fibre Channel

Fibre Channel is a networking technology developed by industry groups working under the American National Standards Institute (ANSI) T11X3 committee (http://www.t11.org). *Fibre Channel* defines a number of standards corresponding to the various layers of a complete multilayered communication stack. Separate specifications exist at each layer to define physical attributes like media and mechanicals, data encoding on the wire, and flow control, for example. A number of separate specifications exist for mapping upper-layer protocols, such as IP, SCSI-3, and VIA, to Fibre Channel. Fibre Channel technology has become synonymous with storage area networking because it is primarily used to transport SCSI-3 disk I/O between servers and storage devices. Most of the storage area networks in use at the time of this writing are constructed from Fibre Channel products. This does not mean Fibre Channel is the only storage networking solution; rather, Fibre Channel has established itself as a commodity storage technology and is, therefore, the current de facto standard for SANs.

NOTE **Considerable confusion exists about the spelling of *Fibre Channel*. The spelling was intentionally corrupted to differentiate Fibre Channel from fiber-optic networking. This is ironic, since Fibre Channel can operate over fiber.**

Fibre Channel is a relatively recent technology that integrates high-performance, reliable, channel-based data I/O with network-oriented, serial link–based communications. The result enables mainframe class channel I/O throughput and reliability at prices and connectivity approaching that of commodity local area network technology. Flexible interconnection of PC-based servers and storage devices using plug-n-play cabling and offering very high-performance reliable data transfer is achieved. You can build relatively inexpensive computer systems from PC-based servers and fibre channel networking components that resemble the exotic mainframe architectures of the past. The revolution in microprocessors that enabled desktop supercomputing is matched by integrated serial network communications and high-performance reliable data I/O.

A number of requirements guided the development of fibre channel, including:

▶ *Bandwidth* — The base specification enables 100MB per second. Double-rate implementations are continuing to appear and bandwidth is expected to at least double again in the near future.

▶ *Flexible topologies* — Three topologies are supported: point-to-point, fabric, and arbitrated loop. *Point-to-point* is a direct link between two devices. *Fabric* mirrors the packet-switching network topologies of ATM or Ethernet. *Arbitrated loop* is a ring topology like IBM's token ring. Figure 2.5 illustrates these three fibre channel topologies. Fibre channel devices are annotated with an *N* character (for *node*).

▶ *Reliability* — Although considered a networking technology, fibre channel was designed to exhibit a very low bit error rate (BER) to obviate the need for the kind of complicated higher-layer retransmission protocols found in classic network protocols stacks. The result is a hardware transport mechanism that's as reliable as short distance data bus paths in traditional I/O architectures.

point to point

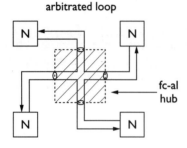

device
nodes

arbitrated loop

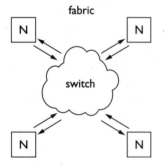

fc-al
hub

fabric

switch

FIGURE 2.5 *Fibre Channel topologies: point-to-point, arbitrated loop, and fabric*

▶ *Cost* — Fibre channel is intended to be low cost. This requirement existed at all levels of the specification development, from cable connectors to switch devices. The goal was to make fibre channel as ubiquitous as traditional networking.

▶ *Protocol support* — Enable a number of existing protocols to layer over the fibre channel transport. The specifications describe mappings for IP, SCSI-3, ESCON, and VIA.

▶ *Industry support* — Fibre channel products should interoperate cleanly and be available from a cross section of industry sources, including major software, disk drive, computer, storage, and adapter companies.

Fibre Channel Layers

Fibre channel is a layered protocol. These layers and their functions are listed in Table 2.2.

T A B L E 2.2		
Fibre Channel Layers and Functions		
LAYER	FUNCTION	EXAMPLE
FC-4	Upper-level protocol mapping	SCSI-3, IP
FC-3	Common services	Striping over multiple paths
FC-2	Link service	Fabric login
	Signalling protocol	Frames, sequences, and exchanges
		Port types
		End-to-end flow control
		Segmentation and reassembly
FC-AL	Arbitrated loop	Loop arbitration and fairness
		Loop initialization
		Physical address assignment
		Opening and closing communication, enabling/disabling loop ports
FC-1	Transmission protocol	8-bit/10-bit encoding for byte
		Ordered sets for frame bounds, low-level flow control and link management
		Error monitoring
		Port states
FC-0	Physical interface	Transmitters and receivers
	Media	Link bandwidth
		Optical or electrical cables
		Connectors

Physical Characteristics

Fibre channel can run over copper or optical media. The different media are described in the next few sections, but in both cases, the current full-speed link is clocked at 1.0625 GBits per second. Data is transmitted serially using the standard 8-bit/10-bit code. With a standard frame size of 2048 bytes and a typical overhead per frame of 120 bytes, the full-speed link enables around 100MB per second unidirectional data bandwidth. Compare this with Wide Ultra2 SCSI, which achieves 80MB per second over a parallel bus. Disk drive companies now manufacture disks with integrated fibre channel controller chips and small form factor copper connectors. This enables direct connection of disks to a fibre channel network at 100MB per second in both directions.

Fiber   Multimode fiber-optic cable carries short-wavelength laser light and enables a maximum link distance of 500 meters. Single-mode fiber-optic cable carries long-wavelength laser light over a maximum distance of 10 km. Imagine a server accessing a disk drive that is located 10 km away — it's possible with fibre channel. The cable connector has two fiber lenses: one for data in, the other for data out.

WARNING   The bend radius of fiber-optic cable should not exceed three inches. Be careful when running fiber around your data center.

Copper   There are also two kinds of copper media. Intracabinet copper cable is designed to link devices inside a cabinet. Its maximum distance is 13 meters. Intercabinet copper cable is designed for longer distances between cabinets in datacenter environments. It enables a maximum distance of 30 meters. Copper connectors are either DB-9 form factor, or a new connector called high-speed serial direct connect (HSSDC).

GBICs   Fibre channel is a serial communication technology: Data travels in bit-serial fashion. Computers process data in parallel bytes, or 32-bit words. When data reaches a computer, it has to be converted from serial to parallel form by a device called a deserializer. Similarly, parallel data leaving a computer has to be serialized for transmission. When the network media is copper, the serializer/deserializer (SERDES) chip simply converts electrical bits to bytes and vice versa. When the network media is fiber, a fiber-optic transceiver converts light into electrical signals.

The actual physical connection to a host computer occurs via a device called a gigabit interface converter (GBIC). GBICs are hot swappable and modular, enabling plug-n-play live attachment of devices to the fibre channel network.

Ports and Topologies

All fibre channel network topologies use the same standard connectors — whether copper or fiber-optic, the physical connection to the network is the same. The logical connection, however, varies with topology type. Communicating devices are called *nodes* — disks and servers are both considered nodes in the fibre channel specifications. A node can support a number of network connections; each connection is made through a node port. Fibre channel specifies a number of different port types. The main ones are listed in Table 2.3.

TABLE 2.3

Fibre Channel Port Types and Functions

PORT TYPE	FUNCTION
N_Port	Node port, used to connect a node to any network topology.
F_Port	When a node connects to a fabric via a switch, the opposite end of the cable is a Fabric (F) port.
NL_Port	When a node connects to an arbitrated loop via a hub, the end of its cable becomes a Node Loop (NL) port.
FL_Port	When a node connects to an arbitrated loop via a switch, the opposite end of the cable is a Fabric Loop (FL) port.
E_Port	Expansion port, used to connect fabric switches to other switches.

Figure 2.6 illustrates the relationship between device nodes, ports, network topologies, and enabling network devices: loop hubs and fabric switches. Point-to-point topologies comprise two nodes connected via a single cable. Each node has a single N_Port. Multiple nodes form an arbitrated loop via their NL_Ports when connected to a fibre channel loop hub. When a node's N_Port is connected to a fabric, the opposite end of the cable attaches to an F_Port. F_Ports are located inside fabric switch devices.

All devices on a fibre channel arbitrated loop share the bandwidth of a single 100MB per second link. Arbitrated loop is similar to traditional token ring–based local area networking. The arbitration protocol ensures fairness between competing devices. Loop devices are connected to a fibre channel hub. Think of a hub as a loop inside a box. Each link has an input and output path and is attached to the hub. Internal to the hub, an input path is connected to the next output path, and so on. The loop path exists inside the hub. External cables attach devices to hub connectors. You are *cascading* hubs when you connect one hub to another. More devices can be connected, but the network topology remains a loop and is limited by the single-link bandwidth.

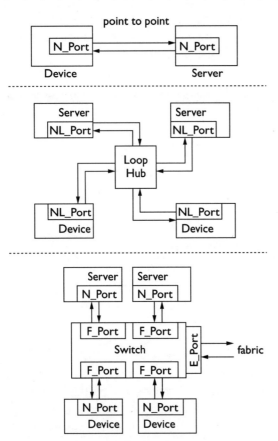

FIGURE 2.6 *Fibre channel device nodes, ports, topologies, and network devices*

Fabrics enable greater overall network bandwidth. Multiple devices transfer data at full link speed through a fibre channel switch. A single fibre channel switch and its attached devices is considered a fabric. Multiple switches are cascaded to create large fabrics with thousands of attached devices.

A good way to describe the difference between fibre channel arbitrated loop and fabric topologies is to offer the analogy of comparing an Ethernet hub to a switch-based LAN. Hubs are slower than switches because all devices share one link's worth of bandwidth.

TIP

Names and Addresses

The Institute of Electrical and Electronics Engineers (IEEE) is responsible for assigning unique addresses to fibre channel equipment. These addresses are just like the unique MAC addresses assigned to Ethernet cards. Every device node is given a unique world wide name (WWN), an 8-byte identifier assigned by the manufacturer of the device. World wide names uniquely identify every device on the network. This capability is important and enables high-layer storage management software to selectively control device access. (More on this topic appears later in this chapter, in the section "LUN Masking".)

In addition to its statically assigned name, fibre channel devices are dynamically assigned a 24-bit port address (N_Port ID). Device port IDs are used for network routing rather than the longer world wide names. 24 bits worth of address space enables addressing for more than 16 million devices in the fibre channel network.

A device that connects to a fibre channel arbitrated loop via an NL_Port also has 24-bit port address. The upper two bytes of the port address are set to zero if there isn't a switch connection to an external network. This is called a *private loop topology*, because the single loop creates its own network. The lower byte of a 24-bit NL_Port address is called the *Arbitrated Loop Physical Address* (AL_PA). 8 bits worth of address space enables addressing for a maximum of 127 devices on a single arbitrated loop.

Upper-Layer Protocols

Existing protocols like SCSI and IP are mapped to the top of the fibre channel protocol stack at layer FC-4. They are considered upper-layer protocols (ULPs) in the fibre channel specifications. An FC-4 mapping layer defines the steps required to perform the functions defined by an upper-layer protocol over a fibre channel network. For example, the standard SCSI command and data operations define exchanges of formatted data blocks that are independent of any particular physical transport. To run over fibre channel, SCSI operations are mapped to generic FC-4 informational units — containers for transporting upper-layer protocol data across the network.

Fibre Channel Storage Area Networks

The most widely deployed upper-layer protocol on fibre channel networks is SCSI. It is so widespread that the possibility of running any other protocol has practically been forgotten. Most purchases of fibre channel networks are made specifically for SCSI storage applications. It should come as no surprise, then, that fibre channel and Storage Area Networks have, therefore, become synonymous. When most people talk about SANs today, they are implicitly discussing fibre channel technology.

A fibre channel–based Storage Area Network comprises the following components:

- ▸ Servers with a fibre channel host bus adapter

- ▸ Fibre channel cables, connectors, and network devices

- ▸ Fibre channel or legacy SCSI storage devices

Servers are typically the initiators of disk I/O, whereas storage devices are the targets. SCSI command and data packets are exchanged between initiators and targets across the fibre channel network. SCSI data can travel great distances across a fibre channel network, compared to the length data is able to travel via a traditional SCSI cable, and neither performance nor latency are sacrificed. When equipped with a fibre channel adapter and appropriate device driver software, most server operating systems really can't tell the difference between a disk attached to a 25-meter parallel SCSI cable versus a disk 500 meters distant on the other side of the fibre channel network. Unlike the restrictions of parallel bus–based SCSI implementations, any initiator can transmit an I/O request to any target device on fibre channel. Fibre channel enables millions of devices and thousands of simultaneous data exchanges. Fibre channel really enables you to have a storage network.

Fibre Channel SAN Devices

So far, fibre channel devices have been discussed only in general terms. Listed here are actual devices you might purchase to implement a fibre channel SAN:

- ▸ *Host Bus Adapter (HBA)* — This is an I/O adapter card you plug into a server, most likely a 32- or 64-bit PCI card. It's a cross between a network interface card (NIC) and a SCSI adapter. You plug an optical or copper cable into the adapter card.

▶ *Loop Hub*— This is an arbitrated loop inside a device with a number of external connectors. Servers and storage devices attach to the hub. The number of ports on a typical hub can range from 4 to 14. With a seven-port hub, you can attach six servers and one storage array, for example. Loop hubs are simple devices. They contain only electrical bypass circuitry to enable/disable ports as devices are added or removed. Loop hubs are the least expensive fibre channel network device.

▶ *Switched Hub*— This is a device that presents the illusion of an arbitrated loop to external devices. Internally, a switched hub has active electronic components that enable greater total throughput than a single fibre channel link-based loop. A switched hub is a hybrid device that offers greater bandwidth than loops, but not full fibre channel fabric functionality. Switched hubs are more expensive than loop hubs, but cheaper than switches.

▶ *Fabric Switch*— This is a device that functions as a switching element of a fibre channel fabric. Fabric switches contain ASIC-based high-performance switching cores that enable nonblocking switching of fibre channel packets. Switches feature 8, 16, 32, or more fibre channel port connectors. Multiple switches are cascaded using interswitch links between switch expansion ports to create large fabrics containing hundreds of device ports. Switched fabrics enable multiple I/O paths. If a switch or fibre channel link should fail, an alternate path through the fabric is used instead. Switches are generally the most expensive kind of network device, but their cost is decreasing.

▶ *Router (also called a Fibre-to-SCSI Bridge)* — This is a device that routes SCSI packets between fibre channel and classic SCSI buses. It's a box with classic 68-pin SCSI connectors on one side and fibre channel connectors on the other. You use a router to connect an existing SCSI-based storage device to a fibre channel SAN. Many existing tape libraries and robotic jukeboxes have only SCSI connectors. Routers enable attachment of legacy SCSI devices to fibre channel.

▶ *Storage Array* — This is a cabinet that contains disk drives. You attach it to the network by connecting one end of a cable to a fabric switch or loop hub port, and the other end to a port integrated with the storage array hardware. Some storage arrays have fibre channel disks wired up internally in a private loop configuration with one port exposed for external network attachment. They are called Just a Bunch of Disks (JBODs). Other arrays have integrated RAID controller logic and internal SCSI disks. The controller has a fibre channel port for external network attachment. Internally, SCSI requests are received over fibre channels and translated into classic SCSI bus operations. The advantage of these hybrid fibre channel/SCSI storage arrays is that you can reuse existing disk drives. A hybrid storage array might have many independent SCSI buses and disk drives. For example, a storage array might enable two fibre channel ports for external network attachment and contain four separate SCSI buses, each with 15 disk devices. In this hypothetical storage array product, you would have 60 disk drives accessible via two network ports. If each disk has a capacity of 36GB, the single storage array enables 2TB of shared network storage.

▶ *Tape Device* — Tape backup devices aren't new and aren't fundamentally different when used on a fibre channel SAN. A number of tape device vendors sell existing tape units with optional built-in fibre channel ports that enable direct attachment to a SAN. Some vendors accomplish this by embedding a fibre channel to a SCSI router inside their product. The external connection is via a fibre channel port, but an embedded internal router converts fibre channel into SCSI bus transfers to a SCSI tape device. This works by receiving SCSI packets from the SAN and re-issuing them to the SCSI bus. Data is returned by copying from the SCSI bus into a SCSI packet and sending it back over the SAN to the initiator. The router and tape device are integrated in a single enclosure.

All of these devices enable the transportation of SCSI packets between servers and storage devices. The mechanism used to ensure the right data gets delivered to the correct device is described in the next section — that is, how traditional SCSI device addressing is mapped to Fibre Channel.

SCSI Addressing on Fibre Channel

SCSI-level device addressing doesn't fundamentally change when SCSI protocol is transported over fibre channel, but it does expand. An initiator of I/O has to identify a target device by ID and logical unit number. Because fibre channel is a network technology, an initiator must direct its request to the network port that exposes the desired SCSI disk. Therefore, fibre channel ports add a third element to the overall network disk address scheme. Fibre channel storage is addressed via three address components:

▸ Fibre channel port ID

▸ SCSI device ID

▸ SCSI logical unit number

The result is virtually unlimited scalability.

Redundant Topologies

With many more devices accessible over fibre channel than are available over a single SCSI bus, it would be unfortunate if the technology didn't enable any kind of fault tolerance. You can imagine, for example, that a single switch fault might cause a total network failure — many servers would be affected because none would be able to access remote storage devices. Such a problem would be a much more widespread failure than would be experienced if a single server with direct attached disks failed. Fortunately, fibre channel is designed to support network redundancy. Redundancy is enabled at a number of points:

▸ *Server attachment* — Multiple HBAs can be attached to each server, enabling multiple I/O paths from server to network. If one path should fail, become disconnected, or otherwise become nonfunctional, the alternate path can take over on behalf of the server. Multiple HBAs also offer the opportunity to load balance I/O over many I/O paths.

▸ *Redundant network paths* — Multiple fabric switches can be cascaded to enable multiple redundant network paths. At least two paths exist from any server to any device. Should any network link fail or become disconnected, the fabric will detect link failure and automatically switch to an alternate path. Fabric topologies can also be designed to eliminate individual switch elements as single points of failure. If a switch should fail, other switches provide any-to-any alternative paths. None of the possible server-to-device paths are affected if a switch should fail.

▸ *Redundant storage array controllers* — Just like it's possible to install multiple HBAs into a server, an individual storage array can support multiple controllers and network attachments. If a controller should fail, a secondary controller, also attached to the fibre channel network, can take over. Controller failover doesn't affect I/O from servers to disks inside the storage array.

Long Haul Connectivity

Fibre channel SANs do allow connectivity over long distances; however, there is a trade-off that comes with the capability. The maximum distance of single mode optical cable is 10 km. When distances greater than 10 km are required, bridging over Wave Division Multiplexing (WDM) or Asynchronous Transfer Mode (ATM) is possible. But with longer distances comes longer latency. A single SCSI disk I/O will take as long as it takes the corresponding request and response packets to travel the network.

Attaching NetWare Servers to Fibre Channel SANs

NetWare is the classic network (storage) operating system (NOS). Attaching a NetWare server to a fibre channel Storage Area Network requires three steps:

1. Purchase and install a fibre channel host bus adapter.

2. Install and load the vendor's host bus adapter device driver software.

3. Type LIST DEVICES at the server console to confirm that the server can "see" the storage (optional).

The LIST DEVICES command returns a list of all SCSI devices accessible to the server via its disk adapters. The list includes all direct attached disks accessible over local SCSI buses and all disks reachable over the SAN. As far as NetWare is concerned, there is no difference between a locally attached disk and a remote disk located in a fibre channel network storage array. Both kinds of disks are managed using standard NetWare disk and file system management software. Any standard fibre channel storage array will work with NetWare. All standard fibre channel storage arrays enable block-level SCSI disk access and are completely independent of server operating system software or software vendor.

Appendix A lists fibre channel SAN devices that are certified for use with NetWare.

X-REF

Fibre channel host bus adapters are controlled via server device driver software. On NetWare, the standard NetWare Peripheral Architecture (NWPA) supports fibre channel devices. HBA vendors supply disk driver software with their adapter hardware. Disk driver software is certified by Novell or by the host bus adapter vendor. NetWare drivers exist for point-to-point, fibre channel arbitrated loop and switched fabric topologies.

For example, CPQFC.HAM is the NWPA-compliant device driver for Compaq's fibre channel host bus adapter. Figure 2.7 shows the result of loading CPQFC.HAM on a NetWare server. The server contains two HBAs and both are detected when the driver loads. In Figure 2.7, the adapters located in slots 2 and 3 are activated. As you can see, the figure shows the result of typing the LIST DEVICES command at the server console and lists a number of devices. By recognizing device hardware names, it's possible to distinguish locally attached from SAN disks. The disks called NFT in SAN are the SAN disks.

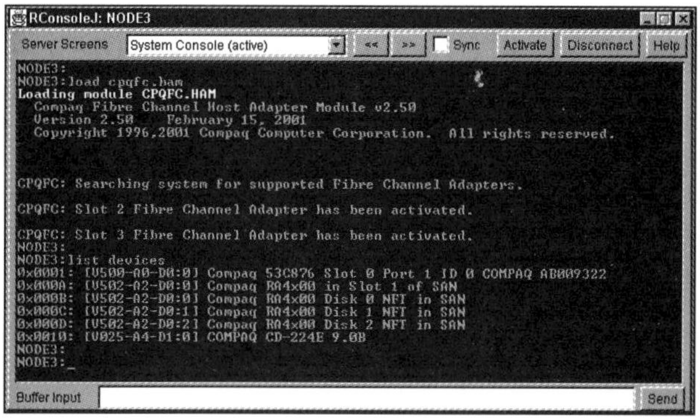

FIGURE 2.7 *Loading a fibre channel device driver and listing SAN devices*

Internet Protocol Storage Area Networks

Before moving on to storage virtualization concepts, it's appropriate to mention that fibre channel is not the only kind of Storage Area Network. It just happens to be the most widely deployed and known implementation of integrated networking and storage at the time of writing. Currently, there is significant industry interest in development of products that enable SCSI over IP networks. This combines the remote SCSI disk methods of fibre channel with IP as a disk I/O transport. One advantage of SCSI over IP is the reusability of existing IP-based network infrastructure. However, most existing LAN infrastructure is entirely unsuitable for SCSI-based disk I/O. The idea that file protocol operations and SCSI disk blocks will travel over the same 100MBits/sec. Ethernet wire is a little far-fetched. Traditional client/server LANs and the new server to remote disk traffic will not mix very well on the same wire. LAN traffic is bursty and packet-oriented, while disk I/O works best when data block can stream across a link. What's likely is the development of integrated Ethernet switching devices that support backbone LAN traffic and storage over the same physical media but isolate that traffic to different network segments. Fibre channel proponents argue that backbone LAN traffic should travel over the fibre channel network since it was designed as a generic network transport. This healthy industry debate continues but it really is no more than a discussion of wiring details — how to transport SCSI packets from one place to another.

Virtualizing Storage Resources

Computer scientists like *virtualization* — the art of illusion applied at every level of computer architecture to enable benefits otherwise not possible. Computers have virtual memory: From the perspective of applications, virtual memory is the appearance of more available memory than physically exists. Virtual reality is a combination of electronic, mechanical, and processor devices that trick humans into believing they exist in an alternative physical world.

The storage industry is no stranger to virtualization. Virtual disks present the illusion of a single large disk drive actually made from RAID. Virtual disks enable better fault protection and I/O performance than physical disks. As of the writing of this book, almost every SAN product vendor is touting virtualization as the next hot SAN feature. The problem is that there isn't one common definition of SAN virtualization. SAN vendors use virtualization terminology in different ways.

Many opportunities exist to invent new virtualization of storage network functions. We offer Novell's perspective on storage virtualization in the framework of the classic NetWare file server. Consider the diagram in Figure 2.8. It illustrates the file server disk I/O stack. At the bottom is a physical disk drive located inside a fibre channel SAN storage array. It is addressed via fibre channel N_Port ID, SCSI ID, and LUN. At the top is a NetWare server running file system, volume manager, and device driver software. The SAN is in the middle. There are multiple levels of virtualization. File systems and volume managers hide details of virtual disks, and virtual disks hide details of physical disks. Storage networks hide details of the physical path that disk blocks (SCSI commands and data packets) travel between servers and disks.

NOTE | **In a nutshell, the responsibility of the SAN is to enable access to disk blocks on logical units. A logical unit is a disk — a contiguous array of disk blocks. Servers issue block-level I/O requests to LUNs. The SAN transports disk blocks between servers and remote LUNs.**

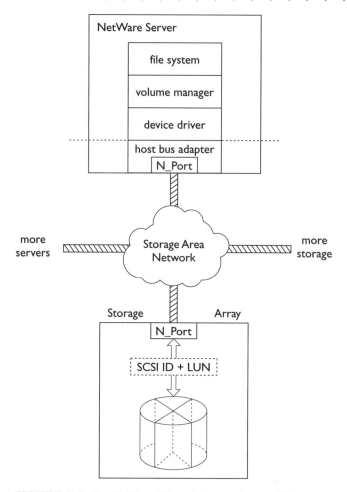

FIGURE 2.8 *The NetWare I/O stack elongated over a SAN*

In order to issue an I/O request to a LUN, a server must send its SCSI request packet to the fibre channel N_Port that owns the LUN. The SCSI packet is encapsulated in a fibre channel protocol unit and delivered to the correct N_Port by the SAN. This delivers the SCSI packet to a storage array port. The SCSI packet contains the target device ID and logical unit number. The storage array hardware uses conventional SCSI addressing to forward the request to the correct target device and LUN. Response data flows in the opposite direction. Note the following points of interest about this SAN disk I/O path:

▸ A single storage array N_Port may present access to multiple LUNs. That is, I/O to any LUN in the storage array must be sent to the same N_Port ID.

▸ If a storage array has an alternate N_Port, the same device addressed via its logical unit may be visible via either N_Port. That is, a server can send a packet to either N_Port ID to address the same LUN.

▸ Any server with a connection to the fibre channel network can perform disk I/O on any device inside a storage array, simply by formatting an appropriate SCSI packet containing the target ID and logical unit number and then sending it to the appropriate N_Port ID. At the lowest hardware level, all disks are shared by all servers attached to the SAN. The original fibre channel specifications do not describe any security mechanisms. If you attach a server to fibre channel SAN, it can do I/O to any device. Security is a problem left for higher-layer software to solve, as discussed later in the sections titled, "Port Zones and LUN Masking."

Virtual Disks

A virtual disk is an illusion presented by a hardware RAID controller or software volume manager. A number of physical disks are combined by an aggregation function. Input to the aggregation function are a number of physical disks. Output is a single virtual disk. There are a number of aggregation functions. For example, the mirroring function takes two or more physical disks as input and outputs a single virtual disk. The capacity of the virtual disk is the same as each input disk. The purpose of this aggregation function is to enable fault tolerance. An I/O issued to a mirrored virtual disk copies data blocks to each of the underlying physical disks. The conventional name given to this is RAID level 1: disk mirroring. Other more complex disk aggregation functions exist as classified by the RAID levels. For example, RAID level 5 is a function of distributed input disks and an error-correcting parity disk. The output is a fault tolerant virtual disk.

In all cases, the output of a disk aggregation function is a virtual disk. Disk virtualization typically occurs in one of two places:

▸ In a SAN storage array as a result of RAID controller firmware.

▸ In a SAN attached server as a result of volume manager software.

When virtualized by server software, input disks can be taken from any SAN storage array. For example, a server-based mirroring aggregation function can take as input one disk from one storage array and a second disk from a different storage array. When virtualized by a storage array RAID controller, the input disks are private to the storage array. Only the output virtual disk is accessible to servers on the SAN.

Port Zones

Consider a SAN comprising two servers and a storage array. Suppose one server is running NetWare and the other is running Windows NT. When either server boots and loads its device driver, it will detect all devices available in the storage array. Neither server is aware of the other server. While they both share access to the SAN, they are not running the same operating system and do not share any common software. This is trouble. The Windows NT server has software that typically grabs all available storage devices and stamps them with a Windows-specific disk signature. Of course, the NetWare server will similarly grab all available devices for its use if instructed to do so by a system administrator. You now have a fight. Both servers remain unaware of one another but nonetheless write data to shared disks in a manner that corrupts operating system–specific data structures for both servers.

At the fibre channel SAN level, disks are accessed via block-level protocols. The NetWare and Windows NT operating systems have different file system software and so they write data structures to disks that aren't understood by the opposing operating system. This is because there is no standard block-level layout for file systems: NetWare and Windows manage disks differently. Before the advent of storage networking, such conflicts were never a problem. Operating systems for servers with direct attached disks safely assumed they were the only entity able to write to the disks. A NetWare server and a Windows NT server with direct attached disks did not access the disks inside the other server. The assumption of exclusive disk ownership by traditional operating system software is invalidated on Storage Area Networks. All SAN attached servers have equal access to all disk devices — disks are shared at the network level. The SAN doesn't have any knowledge of what operating systems are running on each server. All the SAN does is transport disk blocks to and from devices. Disk blocks are formatted differently according to operating system software, but this is neither visible nor understood at the SAN layer.

Even if multiple servers with access to shared disks are running the same operating system, NetWare or Windows NT, disk corruption will still occur. Traditional operating system software assumes it can access any disk the server has access to. Two (or more) servers running the same operating system software will corrupt the contents of shared disks just as readily as two (or more) servers running different operating systems. Two solutions to this uncoordinated shared disk problem exist:

▸ Prevent sharing by partitioning data and assigning different data partitions to different servers.

▸ Allow sharing by adapting operating system software to explicitly understand the concept of disks shared by multiple servers. Server clustering software enables the block-level sharing of disks between multiple servers.

Figure 2.9 provides an example of the partitioned SAN solution using a feature of fabric switches called *port zoning*. The SAN is partitioned into two separate partitions called *port zones*. On the left is the NetWare port zone, "Port Zone A." It contains a NetWare server and a storage array. The port zone contains two ports—two switch ports that connect the NetWare server and its storage array to the switch. The second port zone, "Port Zone B," contains the Windows NT server and its storage array. The fabric switch controls port zoning. It guarantees that fibre channel packets can travel only between ports configured in the same zone. Any other port not configured in the same port zone cannot transmit or receive data to the zoned ports.

Fabric switch port zones enable the dynamic configuration and reconfiguration of so-called "islands of data." You can attach servers running different operating systems to the same SAN by configuring storage devices and the servers into separate port zones. No Windows NT server will ever be allowed access to a NetWare server's storage array as enforced by the SAN switch. It is possible to configure port zones that span ports in multiple switches of a fabric. For example, if you have a fabric with five fibre channel switches, it's possible to create a single port zone that includes ports from all five switches.

NOTE

A device port is configured to be part of one port zone. Port zones are mutually exclusive. If you draw a diagram of a fibre channel fabric with a number of port zones, none overlap.

The main problem with port zoning is the granularity of data partitioning. A single fibre channel port can enable access to hundreds of device LUNs. For example, suppose you have a storage array with a single fibre channel port. Further suppose you had created 50 virtual disks using the storage array's embedded RAID controller. Each virtual disk is identified via a SCSI ID and logical unit number. The problem is that all 50 virtual disks are accessible to servers through one fibre channel port. The port can be part of only one port zone. This means that all 50 LUNs have to be configured in the same port zone. Whatever server is in the same port zone will have access to all 50 LUNs. You cannot split LUNs between different servers using port zones.

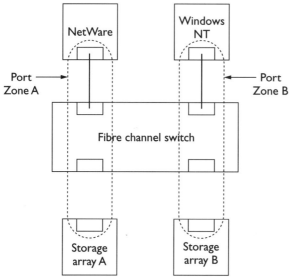

FIGURE 2.9 *A partitioned SAN with servers running different OSes and shared storage*

To configure a port zone, you use a fabric switch vendor's software to create a zone and then identify the switch ports to include in the zone. The port zoning configuration software is typically graphical, enabling you to drag and drop port IDs from a diagram of a switch into the port zone.

SAN port zoning is entirely operating system independent. All of the NetWare certified fibre channel switches listed in Appendix A support port zoning.

NOTE

Port zones are sometimes called virtual SANs. A single physical SAN with a number of port zones defines an identical number of virtual SANs. Virtual SANs are entirely separate and distinct from one another. No I/O can flow between port zones, across virtual SAN boundaries.

LUN Masking

LUN masking solves the granularity problem of port zoning. Instead of creating a port zone, all servers are allowed access to all ports corresponding to any LUN they have an interest in accessing. This means that all LUNs accessible through a given port are accessible to all the servers. LUN masking is intelligent software that selectively presents LUNs to assigned servers. The name comes from the notion that LUNs are masked from view of servers that are not permitted access to them. LUN masking happens one layer above port zoning in the SAN disk I/O stack. Three kinds of LUN masking are available:

- ▸ Storage array LUN masking

- ▸ HBA device driver LUN masking

- ▸ SAN appliance LUN masking

Figure 2.10 illustrates the concept of LUN masking. The diagram shows a fibre channel fabric with a single storage array and multiple servers. All servers share access to all ports (there is no port zoning) and so all LUNs (devices 0, 1, 2, and 3) are accessible behind the storage array's port. LUN masking makes individual LUNs available to select servers while simultaneously masking the same LUN from view of other servers. In Figure 2.10, the NetWare server has access to LUNs 0 and 2, and LUNs 1 and 3 are masked. The NT server has access to LUNs 1 and 3, and LUNs 0 and 2 are masked. Both servers safely share the same SAN storage array and enjoy nonconflicting access to separate LUNs.

Storage Array LUN Masking

The storage array firmware implements LUN masking by preventing a server from issuing I/O to a LUN if access to that LUN has not been specifically granted to the server. The configuration of server-to-LUN assignment is done using storage array specific configuration software and is held centrally in the storage array.

HBA Device Driver LUN Masking

Suppose your storage array doesn't support LUN masking; an alternative is to mask LUNs via the server-side HBA device driver. The device driver has access to all LUNs available through a storage array fibre channel port. The device driver can, therefore, provide the same function as storage array LUN masking firmware. The device driver prevents presentation of certain LUNs to higher-layer operating system software if the server the device driver is running on hasn't been granted access to the LUN.

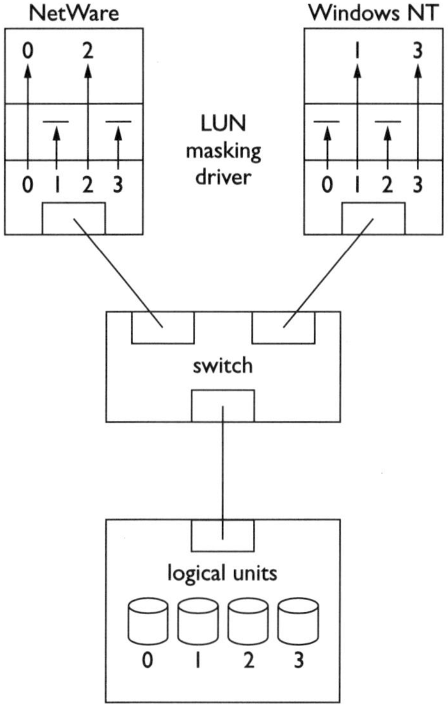

FIGURE 2.10 *LUN masking selectively enables access to LUNs for specific servers.*

This solution assumes some trust is involved. If a server isn't running a LUN masking device driver or is for some reason ignoring its configuration, then it may find itself with access to LUNs it should not have access to. The operating system software above the device driver is unaware that LUN masking is occurring beneath it. For device driver–based LUN masking to work properly, all device drivers running on all servers must share access to one copy of the overall LUN mask configuration. It's no use having one server run a LUN masking driver if that server's LUN mask is inconsistent compared to other servers. For example, a LUN is only exclusively accessible by a single server when only that server lists the LUN in its configuration.

Suppose you want to assign a LUN from a failed server to another server. To do this, you configure the other server to make the new LUN available to it. It would be unfortunate if the failed server still listed the same LUN when it rebooted. Both servers now have access to the same LUN. Unless the LUN masking information is stored externally to all servers and they all download the same consistent LUN masking information when booting, you may find some servers with access to LUNs they should not have. The risk is data corruption.

Reliable device driver–based LUN masking is achievable only under the condition that every server attached to the SAN is guaranteed to run the same device driver software and the LUN masking information is consistently available to all servers. If this can't be guaranteed, then a combination of port zoning and LUN masking is a good alternative to zone out any servers that cannot for whatever reason obey the LUN masking rules.

SAN Appliance LUN Masking

The third LUN masking solution depends neither on special device drivers nor special storage array firmware. A LUN masking SAN appliance is a data block forwarding device that functions as both an initiator and target of SCSI I/O on the SAN. It is a target of I/O for front-end servers by pretending to look like a storage array. It acts as an initiator of I/O to real back-end storage arrays.

LUN masking is implemented inside the SAN appliance. It has access to all LUNs on the back-end storage arrays, but it selectively presents LUNs to certain servers by itself, pretending to be a storage array. The logic is identical to that implemented by storage array LUN masking firmware. The SAN appliance virtualizes multiple back-end storage arrays by presenting the illusion of a new virtual storage array to the servers. If your back-end storage is inexpensive fibre channel JBODs with no embedded intelligence, SAN appliances are a good way to enable LUN masking.

The problem with SAN appliances is they sit right in the data path. All I/O for all servers has to pass through the appliance to reach the actual back-end storage. This is both a performance bottleneck and a huge single point failure. The solution to both problems is to deploy SAN appliances in failover pairs. If one appliance should fail, the other will take over. Performance is improved by partitioning LUNs over multiple appliances so one appliance handles a subset of all LUNs.

Configuring LUN Masks

Specific servers are identified via their host bus adapter fibre channel port world wide name (WWN). Whether LUN masking is implemented by a storage array or by servers running LUN-masking HBA device driver software, you enable access to LUNs via the server's world wide name. Using the SAN vendor's LUN masking software, you select your server's WWN, then select the LUNs to assign to it. This is much more selective than port zoning.

LUN masking software enables many kinds of server-to-LUN associations. For example, you can set up individual LUNs to be exclusively accessed by one server to emulate a direct attached disk. This is a one-to-one mapping of server to LUN. Or you can configure individual LUNs to be accessible to all the servers in a server cluster configuration where device sharing is managed by higher-layer cluster software. Further, the assignment of LUNs to servers is very dynamic. With a click of your mouse, you can take a LUN away from one server and assign it to another one. This enables extremely flexible storage management.

LUN masking is a SAN feature that is entirely operating system independent. Many of the NetWare-certified SAN products listed in Appendix A support LUN masking.

Creating File Systems on LUNs

You have examined the ways individual LUNs are made accessible to server operating system software. The result in all cases is what appears to be a regular disk drive. At this level of the disk I/O stack, NetWare consumes LUNs just like regular disk drives. To NetWare, a LUN presented to it via a SAN is no different than a LUN on a local SCSI bus. A LUN is simply a contiguous array of disk blocks.

NetWare consumes LUNs to make file systems. The diagram in Figure 2.11 depicts the disk I/O stack as it exists inside a NetWare server. LUNs are presented to NetWare by the SAN. Each LUN is considered to be a regular disk drive. NetWare formats each LUN according to the standard IBM DOS specification. A LUN can have up to four DOS partitions. Multiple DOS partitions from multiple LUNs are used to create Novell Storage Services (NSS) storage groups. Storage groups can therefore span many underlying LUNs. At the top of the figure, NSS file system volumes are created from storage groups. They contain classic NetWare folders and files. To mount an NSS file system volume, a NetWare server must have block-level disk I/O access to all of the underlying LUNs that comprise the volume.

Note how NetWare optionally uses a single LUN to create multiple file system volumes. The traditional limit of four DOS partitions per LUN is eliminated with NSS's integrated volume management software. This is also considered virtualization of storage resources at a layer above individual SAN-level LUN access. You can create multiple NSS file system volumes inside one LUN, or you can create NSS file system volumes that span multiple LUNs. The file system software figures out which blocks to access from what LUNs.

Chapter 9 contains detailed information on how to create NSS volumes on shared LUNs. You will also find a discussion of the trade-off between storage array LUN virtualization and NetWare's storage group–based disk virtualization.

X-REF

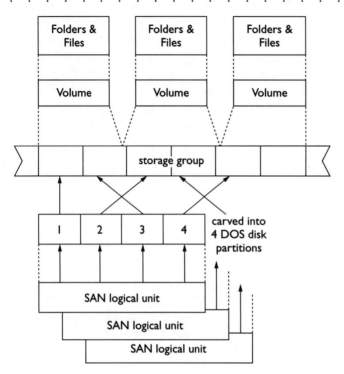

FIGURE 2.11 *The NetWare disk I/O stack as it exists above SAN-presented LUNs*

Intra/Sub-LUN Sharing with Cluster Software

Suppose a single LUN contains multiple volumes. How does the file system running simultaneously on multiple servers share access to the same LUN? For example, you might want to access a volume via one server and a different volume on the same LUN via a different server. The solution is in the domain of host operating system software. Multiserver block-level access to the same LUN is possible only if distributed software running across all servers coordinates their collective shared disk I/O activity.

Novell Cluster Services software enables this functionality for NetWare SANs. With Novell Cluster Services, you set up your SAN LUN masking so that all servers in a cluster configuration are granted access to a set of shared LUNs dedicated to the cluster. Which server actually accesses blocks on a LUN at any given time is a function of Cluster Services software. This enables even finer grained virtualization than is possible with LUN masking. Multiple NetWare servers share access to LUNs at the intra/sub-LUN level.

This is very useful in situations when SAN resident LUN masking or storage array LUN limitations restrict the number of available LUNs. Without cluster software enabled intra/sub-LUN level access, servers are restricted to *whole* LUN access only — LUNs cannot be simultaneously accessed by more than one server at a time without risking data corruption.

Clustering software enables the immediate failover of disk access from one server to another because all servers already have the necessary access to all LUNs. You aren't required to manually adjust a LUN mask to switch a LUN from one server to another. Rapid takeover of LUN access is important for high availability. Any number of clustered servers can take over for a failed server by remounting file system volumes directly from shared LUNs.

With NetWare, it's possible to resize a volume while it's online. With Cluster Services software, it's possible to manage the cluster's storage as though it's owned by a single server. Intra/sub-LUN sharing enables online storage reconfiguration via any server attached to the SAN. The addition of new servers or storage devices to a Novell Cluster Services cluster configuration doesn't require existing servers be rebooted. NetWare servers refresh their view of available storage dynamically, therefore increasing overall system availability.

X-REF

By decoupling storage from servers, SANs intrinsically promote high availability. This is the topic of Chapter 3.

Implementing NetWare Storage Area Networks

There are many reasons for implementing a NetWare SAN. Perhaps your company is consolidating its storage resources in an enterprise-wide storage network to enable simplified storage management for a number of disparate servers and server operating systems. In this case, your NetWare servers will attach to a Storage Area Network shared by servers running a variety of other operating systems.

Alternatively, you might be implementing your company's first SAN dedicated to your NetWare servers or server cluster. Your reasons for doing this might include providing high availability with Cluster Services software — for example, the ability to down servers for maintenance or upgrades without interrupting access to data or services. If you are consolidating a large number of small servers into fewer bigger servers, high availability is probably important to you. When servers are consolidated into fewer bigger machines, downtime of a single machine can affect more users.

Improving your file server backup strategy is another reason for deploying a SAN. With SAN tape devices, data need not travel over the LAN to be backed up to tape. Or you may require the kind of online backup enabled by storage array snapshot hardware.

Another goal might be disk drive inventory cost reductions realized from centralized storage resource pooling for all servers. With Cluster Services software, you enable fine-grained allocation of storage to NetWare servers at the sub-LUN level, making for extremely dynamic online provisioning of storage resources to servers. Spare storage capacity isn't locked up in servers that don't need it while other servers starve for space.

Designing NetWare Storage Area Networks

These are some of the things you should take into consideration when designing a NetWare SAN:

- ▶ Choosing loop or fabric

- ▶ Implementing server attachment

- ▶ Achieving high availability

- ▶ Enabling data protection

Choosing Loop or Fabric

Fibre channel hubs are cheaper than switches but restrict performance to a single link's worth of bandwidth. In general, we recommend you use arbitrated loop to attach no more than four NetWare servers and external storage. More than four servers necessitate a fabric-based SAN. If your NetWare servers are being installed into an existing SAN, you may not have any control over topology decisions. Larger heterogeneous SANs are usually fabric-based, however. You attach your servers to unused fibre channel switch ports or expand the existing SAN by purchasing a new switch.

Implementing Server Attachment

Install a host bus adapter into each of your servers and load the device driver. Some NetWare drivers require you to set special command-line switches to enable access to multiple LUNs. The HBA vendor usually provides this information in a README document with the hardware. You can also find driver setup information on Novell's or the HBA vendor's Web site.

Connecting to an existing SAN requires coordination of port zones or LUN masking to ensure the new servers have access to only the storage reserved for their use. Shared storage is allocated in whole LUNs — you will need to work with storage array configuration software to create LUNs for your servers. You will also need to know the fibre channel world wide name of each host bus adapter's fibre channel port when working with LUN-masking software.

If you are creating a dedicated SAN for a server cluster, then you don't need to worry about port zoning or LUN masking. These virtualization layers are unnecessary when a single cluster defines all the servers and storage in your SAN. You use the cluster software to manage access to your shared disks. If you are sharing a single storage array between two or more clusters, then zoning or LUN masking is necessary to partition storage for each cluster. Servers running in different clusters aren't able to coordinate their relative disk accesses, and this creates the same problem that exists when individual servers have uncoordinated access to the same disks. You'll need to partition and assign storage to each cluster separately. Within the boundary defined by the servers in each cluster, no SAN-level partitioning of data is necessary.

Achieving High Availability

Consider installing multiple HBAs in your servers for added redundancy (assuming the HBA vendor supports this feature). Also use redundant fabric switches and storage array controllers. The goal in designing systems for high availability is to eliminate single point of failure. No single switch or fibre channel cable failure should prevent a server from accessing network storage. Use Novell Cluster Services software to coordinate sub-LUN level access to shared storage.

Enabling Data Protection

Data protection is an important aspect of SAN design and is enabled in various ways:

- ▶ RAID

- ▶ Backup and restore

- ▶ Remote mirroring

- ▶ Hardware snapshot

RAID   Most SAN storage arrays have built-in RAID controllers. Use RAID to protect against individual drive failures. Many options are available for configuring RAID on SAN storage arrays, and some products are so sophisticated that entire books are dedicated to their configuration and management. The tools you use to configure RAID are supplied by the storage array vendor. Some tools run on NetWare, but typically you use software that runs on a Windows NT workstation to manage SAN storage. Web browser–based and storage array–specific interfaces are also available.

Backup and Restore   Backup and restore is an important part of NetWare SAN design and deployment.

Backing up NetWare data held on Storage Area Networks is the topic of Chapter 17.

X-REF

Consider the location of tape devices relative to servers on the SAN. Tape devices typically cannot be shared by more than one server at a time, so you will need to use LUN masking to assign ownership of tape devices to designated backup servers. If you have a NetWare server with an existing integrated tape device, it can be used to back up any SAN data by selectively granting that server access to whatever data needs to be backed up over the SAN. Cluster software is a good alternative to LUN masking, because it enables any clustered server to mount any NetWare volume independent of LUN access. Volumes are backed up by mounting them on the server that has the tape device.

Remote Mirroring   Remote mirroring is an option provided by some storage array vendors for disaster recovery. Data is mirrored between separate storage arrays in different locations. This is transparent to NetWare servers that do normal I/O to virtual disks in the storage array. Embedded storage array software mirrors data blocks between arrays. If a storage array should become inaccessible for whatever reason, the secondary storage array contains an exact copy of the data and takes over.

Hardware Snapshot   Again as a function of your storage array, it's possible to create clone copies of NetWare file system volumes. With two identical clone copies of the same NetWare volume, you can take a logical snapshot of the volume by separating the clones. One clone copy is taken offline to be backed up, while the other clone remains accessible to NetWare.

Managing NetWare Storage Area Networks

Managing a SAN is a task comparable in scope to managing a local area network. It is a systems administration activity that requires the monitoring and management of multiple storage network components. You use software and management interfaces from different vendors depending on the SAN products you purchase. The main areas of SAN management are:

▶ *Servers and server clusters* — If you are attaching individual NetWare servers to a SAN, you manage them no differently than you manage standalone NetWare servers with direct attached disks. Each server is granted access to separate storage with LUN masking or port zoning software. Managing a cluster of servers attached to a SAN is the topic of the remainder of this book.

▶ *Network connectivity* — Fibre channel switch devices are managed via Telnet command line or graphical user interface. Most switch vendors provide management tools for mapping out the storage network and identifying failed links or disabled ports. You typically use the same software to configure switch port zones. Depending on your switch's configuration, it may also be possible to configure your switches to send SNMP alerts or other kinds of notification corresponding to storage network events. You use these alerts to identify failed components before further potential failures cause disk data path outages and prevent servers from accessing storage devices.

Novell Directory Service (NDS) also has a role in Fibre Channel management. It is possible, for example, to configure the Gadzoox Capellix Fibre Channel switch via NDS. This enables replication of switch configuration, such as port zones in NDS, so that a switch can be replaced with a new switch independent of its configuration data. The new switch can download configuration from NDS. NDS is also well-suited for describing devices and their interrelationships in large storage area networks.

▶ *Storage array hardware* — How you manage disks in your storage array is a function of tools provided by the storage array vendor. You create LUNs to be consumed by NetWare servers.

X-REF

Chapter 9 provides a guide to managing NetWare volumes on shared disks.

Summary

This chapter covered the essential properties of Storage Area Networks. The chapter first discussed traditional storage mechanisms and the classic NetWare file server architecture. You then learned about the shortcomings of direct attached storage and were presented a case for storage networks.

Fibre channels are the most widely used SAN technology. This chapter covered the fibre channel protocol layers from the bottom physical layer to the topmost protocol-mapping layer. Network addressing, naming, and fibre channel network topologies were covered in this chapter as well.

You learned about storage virtualization by inspecting layers of the disk I/O stack as it exists between target disk devices extended across storage networks to file servers. SAN port zoning and LUN-level masking were defined in this context.

Throughout this chapter, the application of Storage Area Networks in the NetWare file server environment was considered. The chapter concluded with a discussion of NetWare-specific Storage Area Network implementation considerations. Commodity storage area networking enables commodity server clusters. The decoupling of storage from servers is a key factor that changes the role of servers with respect to specific data. Any server may access any data. A reciprocal relationship also exists between SANs and Clusters. Without appropriate software, SANs are essentially unmanaged. Any server can access any data, whether intentional or not. Clustering provides an excellent metaphor for aggregating a number of servers and associated storage devices into a single management domain — the cluster. Within this *clustered-SAN* domain, important new benefits are realized:

- *Availability* — If a server should fail, any data it was interacting with remains available via the SAN. Any other server can access the same disks and take over the processing of the failed server.

- *Provisioning* — Because servers no longer have exclusive ownership of disks and the space (both used and unused) on those disks, no single server can ever run out of disk space if free space exists.

- *Data protection* — It's easier to protect data when it's centrally located and independent of servers. Servers can't interfere with access to data during backup windows. Data can be mirrored to remote locations for disaster recovery.

## CHAPTER 3

Achieving High Availability

This chapter is about the issue of the availability of your systems. It defines system availability and what constitutes a highly available system. You examine the levels of availability and formula for calculating availability, as well as take a close look at the costs of availability — the cost of unavailable systems and the cost of achieving high availability. This leads to a discussion about some of the reasons why systems become unavailable. Finally, the chapter presents holistic methods for achieving high availability in the real world.

Defining High Availability

When you power on your computer and log in to the network, a myriad of components function together to make everything work as desired, so that you can access files, read e-mail, or surf the Web. Similarly, when business processes are computer-based, they too depend on multiple interrelated systems to perform a number of predetermined tasks. To exchange and access information, collaborate, purchase products online, or simply function in the modern computerized society, you invariably access systems that are outside of your immediate control and are more often than not physically located hundreds of miles away from your screen and keyboard. The characters you type on your keyboard might travel halfway across the world to reach a computer running in the darkness of a foreign time zone. Computers are running all over the world, all the time, and some of them are participating in providing the always-on service you have come to expect. In theory, at least, the systems you work with, either directly or indirectly, are available to serve you on demand.

If only such on-demand availability were true all the time. In the real world, it's extremely likely that at least one of the components you depend on for always-on service isn't on. How many times have you come to work in the morning only to discover that you cannot log in, or that the files you need to share with a colleague aren't accessible because the file server is down? When systems don't do what they're supposed to do, there is an impact. The impact can vary from minor inconvenience suffered by an individual to the widespread disruption of business operations, affecting thousands of customers and potentially losing millions of dollars of revenue for a company.

Humans are dependent on technology, on computers. Economies are dependent on computers. The world comprises millions of networked computers. When a computer stops doing what it is supposed to be doing, someone, somewhere, notices.

When a system stops performing the task it was intended for, the system is said to be *unavailable*. Your file server is down; you can't access your files. Your files are unavailable. If your file server is performing normally, but the network is down, your files are also unavailable. System failures lead to unavailability. Services once provided by a now failed system are no longer provided.

Availability is the opposite of unavailability. When you want access to your files, they are there, ready and waiting for your attention. But suppose you want access to your files in the middle of the night when the file server is down for an upgrade. Perhaps you forgot to copy an important file onto your laptop and you want to download it before leaving town on a business trip. The file server is down, so your file is unavailable. However, if you wait for a few hours until the system administrator has finished whatever maintenance work is being done, your file would become available. Availability is a dynamic quality. Its effects vary at different times.

The level of availability increases in importance when greater demands are made of an unavailable system, and the impact is experienced profoundly by those making the demands. Availability and impact are inversely proportional quantities. More availability equates to less impact. But impact can be a very elusive quality. Impact is experienced only when demands are made of an unavailable system. Suppose you had already copied the files you needed for your business trip. You don't need to access your file server, so it can remain unavailable all night for all you care. The impact of unavailability is zero because there is no demand. On the other hand, suppose your entire team is working late to complete a critical project and your system administrator unwittingly takes the file server down for maintenance. Impact is much greater in this scenario. It's virtually impossible to predict when demands on a system will be made and so it's correspondingly difficult to forecast impact when a system is unavailable. Planning system accessibility around varying demands is little more than guesswork at best, especially when access patterns are a function of worldwide usage. Murphy's law usually applies: if a system is unavailable, it's a reasonably safe bet that it's down at the worst possible moment from the perspective of those consuming its services.

The impact of unavailable systems on those trying to access them can be emotional, financial, and in some cases, even life threatening. You expect computers to behave like another familiar and crucial technology — the telephone system. When you pick up the phone, you hear a dial tone. Accordingly, when you work with computers, you expect them to be up and running. This expectation covers a broad spectrum of what computers do and is usually expressed at a high level.

You want access to your files. One thousand colleagues may also want access to their files at the same moment. No one is thinking in terms of file servers, network packets, or disks. Instead, everyone just expects his or her files to be available.

In short, availability of systems is what enables work to be done. It is a qualitative property. Availability and its impact are related to the demand for availability, and this relationship is dynamic, because demand is dynamic and often unpredictable.

What is high availability? The computer industry has a habit of inventing terminology that promotes the perceived value of new products over previous generations. Most agree that a highly available system is more available than a regular system. The perception is that current systems aren't available enough, so highly available systems are better — they are more available. Historically, mainframes were considered to be highly available, whereas PC-based systems were less available. That perception was based on the fact that mainframes failed less often than PC networks. Today, however, the industry talks about the potential feasibility of achieving mainframe-class computing with commodity Intel architecture (PC-based) servers.

NOTE

Mainframes have complex fault tolerant architectures comprising multiple redundant hardware components that function in lockstep. If a hardware component fails, another immediately takes over and continues processing. Similar duplex principles are applied to mainframe software, resulting in mirrored processing and state replication. Hardware fault tolerance protects against hardware faults and enables uninterrupted processing, but cannot recover from faulty software. Mainframes achieve reliability with fault tolerant hardware and many years of rigorous software testing. They cost millions of dollars as a result. But if your network fails, mainframes are no more available than your PC. Availability is holistic.

Three recent trends have emerged:

▶ The demand for high availability is increasing. Humans and businesses are more reliant on computers and less tolerant of downtime. Worldwide consumer-to-business (C2B) and business-to-business (B2B) systems function in realtime and support large-scale populations. System unavailability has a greater impact.

► Highly available distributed systems built from off-the-shelf, PC-based components are replacing mainframes. Modern applications run on networks of PCs, not centralized mainframes. High-performance networking is ubiquitous and gigahertz multiprocessor Intel architecture servers have reached a commodity scale of economy. For example, you can purchase the latest state-of-the-art server motherboard at most electronics stores across the country.

► More and more applications are considered mission-critical elements of overall business operations. For example, not many years ago, e-mail was merely a tool for exchanging messages with friends or colleagues. Today, electronic collaboration is often part of a critical revenue-generating business process. It's clear from these trends that the issue of availability is getting only more important as people and businesses become more invested in their technological infrastructures. There is a larger audience for highly available systems. But these systems function as a sum of their parts. A system that comprises a number of separate components each contributing to an overall service is only as available as its weakest link. Availability converges on the least common denominator. If the entire system depends on a single component, the overall service it provides can be no more available than that component.

Perhaps the best definition of unavailability is the one put forth by Alan Wood of Tandem Computers — Tandem is considered one of the pioneering fault-tolerant computer companies. In his presentation "Availability in the Real World" at the IEEE Computer Society's 27th Annual International Symposium on Fault Tolerant Computing (June 24th, 1997) Wood said, "It's not just the hardware. It's not just the software. It's anything that causes a customer to think their application [or data] is unavailable."

Levels of Availability

So far this chapter has managed to avoid being specific about the very question it raises, "How available is highly available?" Though the industry hasn't attempted to define standards in this area, it is possible to define availability at a number of discrete levels. Novell, for example, defines Server Fault Tolerance (SFT) levels for increasing degrees of fault protection. NetWare SFT2 enables protection against disk failure by mirroring disks in a server. SFT3 enables protection against server hardware failure by mirroring the operating system state between pairs of master/slave servers and was designed for an era when hardware was more unreliable than software and software less complex than it is today.

The definitions that follow focus on server hardware. But remember, the least available component determines overall availability. If you have reliable server hardware but a poor LAN configuration, the weakest link is your LAN, and it will determine your level of availability.

Common-Off-the-Shelf (COTS) Availability

This level of availability is what you might expect from a common-off-the-shelf (COTS) server with no special availability options. You pay a basic price for a basic server, which has no built-in redundancy features such as dual power supplies or cooling fans. Disk storage is likely to consist of high-quality drives, but no RAID functionality. If a hardware component fails, the server also fails. It might take a few days to replace the bad component or to simply purchase a brand new server. Whatever data you stored on the server's disk drives will be unavailable during this period. If a disk drive fails, you will lose data unless you have an adequate backup strategy. If you replace a failed COTS server, you have to somehow recover your data. This might require moving disks from a failed machine to another machine and figuring out how to make the contained data available to users. If a single disk contains both user data and an operating system, this can be complicated. If only the boot disk has failed, you may be able to rebuild the server from emergency system repair disks, if you have them. If you are replacing failed data drives, you will probably have to restore data from backup tape. None of these activities can be accomplished very quickly. And while you are working hard to repair hardware, users are experiencing extended periods of server unavailability.

Better than COTS Availability

By spending more money, you can purchase a level of availability better than COTS. A more expensive high-end server will feature dual power supplies, dual cooling fans, dual network interface cards (NICs), and a Redundant Array of Inexpensive Disks (RAID) disk controller. Redundant hardware protects against a number of potential faults, enabling the server to continue running when faults do occur. A power supply, cooling fan, or disk drive failure won't bring the server down. Your data is protected via RAID.

A single fault doesn't affect availability. Assuming you realize that the server has experienced a fault and you replace the faulty component in time, a second fault also won't affect availability. You keep on replacing components as they fail. In most cases, replacing a failed disk drive or faulty power supply doesn't require that the server be powered down to perform the repair. But if you do have to power down or reboot a server, it is unavailable for that period of time. Even with some redundant hardware, standard Intel architecture servers are not fully fault tolerant. Unlike mainframe architectures, standard Intel servers do not support redundant CPUs, for example. Though these kinds of chip-level component failures are rare, it is not unheard of for CPU or memory controllers to go bad. Accidents with coffee mugs in the machine room also cause chips to fry.

In general, RAID ensures that your data is protected against a single drive fault. You replace the bad drive with a new one, and the RAID controller rebuilds it. The rebuild process usually happens in quiet I/O periods. Though it would be rare to experience a second fault, if a second drive did fail before the first one had been rebuilt, you would lose data. Restoring data from tape can be time consuming and typically keeps a server I/O bound until the restore is complete. Finally, if you do have to move RAID disks from one server to another, it is important that you reinstall them correctly. Accidental shuffling of disks in drive slots can render a RAID-set unusable. None of these manual recovery steps help increase availability.

Repairing servers takes time, and the system is unavailable during this period. Meanwhile, users experience the resultant effects of system unavailability when they try to access the system.

High Availability: Multiple Redundant COTS

By deploying multiple COTS servers in a clustered SAN configuration, it is possible to mask the availability of individual servers. If one server becomes unavailable, another can step in and take its place. It doesn't matter how long it might take to repair the failed server, because it is no longer preventing access to data or services. Any of the other servers can take over its position. Data remains available via the Storage Area Network and disks are better protected in a fully redundant centralized storage array. Any server can access any disk without having to manually shuffle disks in drive slots.

The result of multiple server redundancy is that overall system availability is not dominated by individual server availability. When redundancy masks failure, no impact is felt by users. Just like a RAID enables protection against disk faults, clusters enable protection against server failure. Large server clusters protect against multiple server failures. You amortize the risk over multiple servers. You can think of a cluster as a Redundant Array of Inexpensive Servers (RAIS). Individual servers need not be expensive or intrinsically highly available. Why spend your money on dual power supplies or cooling fans when you could purchase an additional inexpensive COTS server and enable equivalent availability while also gaining additional capacity?

Measuring Availability

An often-touted availability metric is number-of-nines. You may have read a marketing white paper that promises "three-nines" worth of availability. What does this mean? Considering percentages, if a system is 100 percent available, then, by definition, it can never be unavailable. A 100 percent available system cannot be more available; it is as highly available as it can possibly be.

A constantly available system is probably achievable, but at a dollar cost most organizations are unlikely to be able to justify. The extra percentage points aren't worth the expense. See "The Costs of Availability" section later in this chapter for more on the issue of cost.

The number-of-nines availability metric defines a scale of availability fractionally below the theoretical maximum 100 percent. Table 3.1 defines the number-of-nines availability scale from one-nine to six-nines. Two-nines is approximately equivalent to COTS availability. Four-nines is roughly equivalent to multiple server COTS availability and is the minimum level required to be considered highly available.

TABLE 3.1

Number-of-Nines Availability Scale

NUMBER OF NINES	PERCENTAGE UPTIME	PERCENTAGE DOWNTIME	DOWNTIME PER YEAR	DOWNTIME PER WEEK
1	90%	10%	36.5 days	16 hours, 50 minutes
2	99%	1%	3.65 days	1 hour, 41 minutes
3	99.9%	0.1%	8 hours, 45 minutes	10 minutes, 5 seconds
4	99.99%	0.01%	52.5 minutes	1 minute
5	99.999%	0.001%	5.25 minutes	6 seconds
6	99.9999%	0.0001%	31.5 seconds	0.6 seconds

As you move down the table, from one-nine to six-nines, the amount of downtime decreases. At six-nines of availability, a system is unavailable for only 31.5 seconds each year. That's a very small amount of time when you think how long it takes your personal computer to reboot. Most PCs take at least a couple of minutes to reboot. If you have to reboot your PC every week, you are probably experiencing no more than three-nines availability. Each reboot takes two minutes. One reboot per week will cost you 100 minutes per year — greater than three-nines but less than four-nines of availability. Because you are the only user of your PC, the impact of downtime is less than that of a weekly server reboot that affects many more users. Number-of-nines availability is a useful metric, but it is only a partial metric in measuring availability, as it doesn't adequately account for the important considerations of the impact or costs of unavailability.

Calculating Availability

The textbook equation for availability is a function of two variables:

▸ *Mean Time Between Failure (MTBF)* — The statistical mean (average) time for a component to fail. A server vendor may quote a MTBF of 50,000 hours for an off-the-shelf server. Given a sufficiently large sample of servers, the server vendor has calculated that the average life of a server is 50,000 hours. Some servers may fail much earlier. Other servers may last much longer. MTBF is an average. MTBF is also considered the average continuous *uptime* of a system.

▸ *Mean Time To Repair (MTTR)* — The statistical mean (average) time to repair or recover from a failure. This is the amount of time it takes to repair a failed system and return it to service. Again, this is an average quantity. Depending on the nature of the failure, repair time can vary dramatically. MTTR is also considered the average *downtime* of a system.

From MTBF and MTTR, an availability percentage is calculated as follows:

Availability = MTBF ÷ (MTBF + MTTR)
Availability = Uptime ÷ (Uptime + Downtime)

This equation exhibits some basic fractional behavior:

▸ As MTTR approaches zero, availability is simply MTBF ÷ MTBF. It doesn't matter what value MTBF has, the equation cancels out. Availability trends toward 100 percent.

▸ If MTBF is much larger than MTTR, MTBF + MTTR is approximately the same as MTBF. Again, the equation cancels out and availability trends toward 100 percent.

Therefore, in general, availability increases with fewer failures and faster recovery. For example, suppose you have a system rated at 10,000 hours of MTBF. If it takes five hours to repair, availability is 99.95 percent. If instead it takes 30 seconds to repair, availability is 99.9999 percent. Larger MTBF ratings result in fewer failures. But if the time to repair any failure is negligible compared to the failure rate, availability will always be high.

By deploying multiple redundant servers, the repair time actually becomes irrelevant. Remember, the system is only truly unavailable from the perspective of the consumers of the service it provides. If another server steps in and quickly takes over for the failed server, the time to repair the server doesn't affect the availability equation. The system is unavailable only for as long as it takes to detect failure and switch processing to another server. When running Cluster Services software, MTTR is more accurately defined as the time it takes Cluster Services to switch over processing. Once the switch over completes, your users can continue working. The system is highly available from your users' perspective. Which server your users are using is irrelevant as long as the service remains available. This is a key point. Users of systems care about accessibility of critical services, not the specific physical server that happens to be providing the service. If a server fails, it doesn't matter how long it takes to repair or whether it is even repaired at all. The provision of critical services is quickly and automatically shifted elsewhere. A failed server no longer has any impact on the overall availability equation, and server failures are masked by redundancy. When servers do fail, they can be repaired whenever convenient. The system continues to provide its service to consumers using other servers.

The Costs of Availability

Two financial costs are associated with high availability:

▸ The cost of not implementing high availability

▸ The cost of implementing high availability

The Costs of Not Implementing High Availability

The cost of not implementing high availability is equivalent to the cost of downtime. If a system is unavailable, what impact does this have? The answer depends as always on what the system is used for. Who or what business processes will be affected by downtime? Table 3.2 lists results from a 1996 survey (conducted by Dataquest and published on September 30, 1996, in their journal *Perspective*) of the average dollar cost of downtime per hour across a spectrum of industry and business operations. In some industry sectors, the cost of not implementing high availability is staggering.

TABLE 3.2

Average Downtime Cost Per Hour

INDUSTRY	BUSINESS OPERATION	AVERAGE DOWNTIME COST PER HOUR
Financial	Brokerage operations	$6.45 million
Financial	Credit card authorization	$2.6 million
Media	Pay-per-view TV	$150,000
Retail	Home shopping TV	$113,000
Retail	Home catalog sales	$90,000
Transportation	Airline reservations	$89,500
Media	Telephone ticket sales	$69,000
Transportation	Package shipping	$28,000
Finance	ATM fees	$14,500

Novell's Information Services and Technology (IS&T) department has devised a formula to calculate the real cost of downtime in actual dollars:

$$\text{Frequency} \times \text{Magnitude} \times \text{Duration} = \$ \text{ Cost of Downtime}$$

Frequency *Frequency* is the number of times a problem occurs that results in service downtime. For example, if by applying a server patch a problem is prevented from recurring, then the frequency of that problem becomes zero. No more downtime is experienced, and the future dollar cost is zero. A one-time dollar cost is incurred every time downtime occurs. Over a period of time, the cost of downtime is a product of the cost of each incident.

Magnitude   *Magnitude* is the weighted number representing the impact that downtime has on the production environment. Some examples of factors that determine magnitude are the following:

▶ *Number of users affected* — How many users will be unable to work while the system is unavailable? If the entire company is affected, the magnitude is high.

▶ *Operations affected* — What operations are affected? Does downtime impact a critical business operation? The number of users may be small, but the financial impact might be large, so the magnitude value is correspondingly large.

Duration   *Duration* is the period of time a service is unavailable. It's similar to MTTR. Duration is the actual amount of time it takes to restore a service to operation. Duration has a direct impact on the cost of downtime. If the service can be quickly restarted on a redundant server masking an otherwise lengthy server repair time, duration is negligible, and the cost of downtime is reduced.

The Costs of Implementing High Availability

Highly available systems and processes cost more money and are more complex than less available systems. The cost of implementing high availability comprises capital and operations expenditure. When you analyze the cost of downtime (not implementing high availability), you are actually performing financial risk analysis. The motivating consideration is how much money is lost to the organization when systems are down. In a balance sheet style of analysis, the savings achieved from reducing downtime can be used to justify purchases or projects aimed at increasing availability. The cost of implementing high availability is usually a one-time expense, whereas downtime costs are recurring costs. Highly available systems usually pay for themselves over the first few years of investment.

In some situations, the factors motivating high availability aren't financial. The cost of downtime isn't a spreadsheet dollar amount; the cost is direct human impact. Emergency 911 call center processing, for example, has to be highly available.

When you implement high availability, you need to evaluate your return on investment. How much money are you spending? How much money are you saving? You should also consider risk factors. Spending on high availability is like purchasing an insurance plan. You get more coverage by spending more money, but do you really need that extra coverage? Don't buy expensive dual-redundant everything hardware if you don't really need it, or if you can achieve the same level of availability via other methods.

Analyzing Unavailability

Why do systems become unavailable? Some of the reasons are obvious, others not so. If someone trips over or removes a power cord by accident, an electrical component will stop functioning. If the power cord is connected to a network switch or server, the impact is large. If you crawl under your desk and remove the power cord you thought was attached to your printer, but it was, in fact, connected to your desktop PC, then you will experience the impact of losing work on your PC. This is a silly example, but experience has shown that many reasons exist for unplanned downtime, and some are more bizarre than others.

Systems are also unavailable during periods of planned downtime. Application or operating system software often cannot be upgraded without a server reboot. You cannot install additional memory into a live Intel architecture server. It's conceivable that some users may fail to observe a corporate-wide upgrade e-mail and attempt to access a server that is down for maintenance. Understanding the multiple causes of unavailability helps you to avoid it.

NOTE

For Novell's annual Brainshare technical conference in Australia, Novell engineers set up a four-server cluster to demonstrate Cluster Services software. Unplanned downtime was simulated by randomly powering off individual servers. Client workstations automatically reconnected to alternate servers, demonstrating the value of rapid service restart. In this failure simulation, servers were restarted by simply reapplying power. All four servers were installed in a rack. During the conference, someone inadvertently left a soda can sitting on top of the rack. Disaster eventually struck. The soda can tipped over and its contents drained through cooling holes. The top-most server drowned in soda and failed. The other three servers survived and continued running. Client workstations reconnected to them and continued to run the demo. The drowned server was so badly damaged it had to be returned. It took days to repair it, but the cluster continued to provide service to clients without it.

In 1995, the IEEE Computer Society published a report on the causes of downtime. Figure 3.1 summarizes the analysis. Software failures were and today still are the major reason for unavailability. Forty percent of system failures are caused by software-related issues. Planned downtime comes next at 30 percent.

The planned downtime statistic assumes users were warned in advance of the planned downtime and impact was therefore reduced. But if systems are required to be available 24 hours a day, 7 days a week, then planned downtime is disruptive. People and hardware failures are the two next largest causes of unplanned downtime.

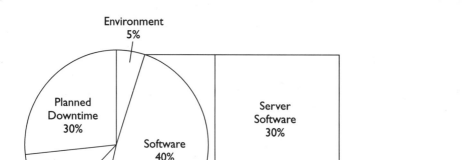

FIGURE 3.1 *Summarizing the IEEE Computer Society survey on the reasons for downtime*

Software Failures

Software failures are the primary cause of system downtime. Failures are caused by design errors, algorithmic or scaling problems, bad assumptions, or unexpected hardware layer interaction. Software failure can cause, among other things, the following kinds of downtime:

- ▸ Broadcast packet storm

- ▸ Server lockup or abnormal end (ABEND)

- ▸ File system corruption

- ▸ Bad router algorithm

- ▸ Client failure while locking a server resource

Planned Downtime

Systems are unavailable when taken down for any of the following kinds of scheduled maintenance, upgrade, or configuration change:

- ▶ Hardware upgrade

- ▶ New software release

- ▶ Patch

- ▶ Bug fix

People-Based Failures

People can cause unintentional downtime due to accidents, inexperience, poor procedures, or malice:

- ▶ Wrong cable pulled

- ▶ Duplicate IP address

- ▶ Data not backed up

- ▶ Application unloaded

- ▶ Accidents with soda cans

Hardware Failures

Systems become unavailable when hardware fails. Downtime is caused by physical faults or hardware component failures of any kind, including:

- ▶ Failed CPU

- ▶ Failed network switch

Environmental Factors

This category includes downtime caused by the following:

- ▶ Power or cooling system failures

- ▶ Failures of external network connections

- ► Natural disasters
- ► Accidents
- ► Terrorism

There are many factors conspiring against your systems, and even the best traditional practices are not sufficient to achieve the levels of availability now demanded by most organizations. New techniques are needed to ensure that services and data remain available.

Implementing High Availability

You implement high availability with appropriate hardware, software, and operating procedures. High availability is achieved via a combination of best practices and attention to detail. High availability cannot be achieved by simply installing a high availability product if other important factors are neglected. High availability is an ongoing operational strategy. For example, if you don't continuously monitor uptime statistics, how will you be certain you have improved the availability of your systems?

Eliminating Weak Links

Always remember the weakest link. Your system is only as available as its weakest link. A single point of failure (SPOF) is a single component whose failure will cause downtime. Servers, disks, and network devices are all potential single points of failure and, therefore, represent weak links in your overall system. You eliminate single points of failure via redundancy:

- ► *RAID* — Use redundant disks to protect against disk failure.

- ► *Clusters* — Use multiple servers to protect against server failure. Cluster software enables dynamic unattended restart of failed services on surviving servers.

- ► *SANs* — Use Storage Area Networks to decouple disks from servers, enabling any server to access any disk. Cluster software enables dynamic assignment of storage to servers without requiring manual reconfiguration.

▸ *LANs* — Use redundant devices and topologies to protect against link failure.

▸ *Power* — Use Uninterruptible Power Supplies (UPSs) to protect against power outages.

Network services can also represent single points of failure. Examples include DHCP and DNS. You eliminate network service single points of failure via redundancy:

▸ Configure primary and secondary service providers.

▸ Use cluster software to restart critical network services on surviving servers.

Reducing Server Downtime

You improve overall availability by reducing unnecessary server downtime. You can do many things to avoid server downtime, including the following:

▸ *Apply the latest OS patches to the server* — Many server stability issues are resolved by installing an OS patch. Your server may be suffering from a known issue for which a patch is readily available.

▸ *Update applications on the server* — Not all bugs are found in applications before they are released. Updated version patches and new releases of products are created as new bugs are found and fixed. You should try to keep all applications up-to-date even if you are not experiencing problems with them.

▸ *Update device drivers on the server* — Hardware vendors continue to fix bugs and performance problems with their device drivers long after the original drivers were shipped. You should try to keep all drivers up-to-date even if you are not experiencing hardware problems.

▸ *Keep ample memory in the server* — Over time, the demands of a server may increase. Make sure your server has enough memory resources to handle the load even during peak access times.

▸ *Keep free space on the SYS volume* — NetWare servers can go down when the SYS volume runs out of space. Make certain your server always has enough disk space on the SYS volume to handle the load, even during peak access times.

▶ *Use restartable address spaces* — By running an application in the context of a restartable protected address space, software faults that would otherwise halt the server are isolated. The offending application is terminated and unloaded from memory. The optional restart feature enables automatic restart so that the application can be returned to service.

For more information on restartable address spaces, refer to Novell Technical Information Document (TID) 10022134, "How to use protected and virtual memory in NW5", at http://support.novell.com.

X-REF

▶ *Use journaled file systems for fast volume mount* — Novell's Storage Services file system mounts volumes immediately, virtually eliminating time to repair.

The Novell Press book *Novell's Guide to Resolving Critical Server Issues* by Richard Jensen and Brad W. Daley (published by Hungry Minds, Inc., 1998) is an excellent reference for understanding how to minimize NetWare server downtime.

X-REF

Following Best Practices

A number of documented well-proven best practices exist that you should always follow. Consider these best practices an entry requirement for high availability. Attaining high availability is unlikely if they aren't an intrinsic part of daily operations. Best practices represent the foundation upon which high availability is achieved.

▶ *Follow a strict backup schedule* — If data isn't backed up on a strict schedule, data will inevitably be lost eventually.

Storage Area Networks enable a number of new methods for backing up data. Chapter 17 describes various backup solutions for clusters.

X-REF

▶ *Automate frequently occurring tasks* — Mistakes are likely to occur during mundane or repetitive tasks. If administration tasks can be automated, the risk of an accident that causes downtime is reduced.

▶ *Document the system and keep paper copies* — If a system component fails, you will need to know exactly what it affects. For example, it is good practice to keep a paper copy of IP addresses to server names for your organization.

▶ *Don't experiment on production servers* — Use a test system to experiment with configuration settings or new software. Never do this on a production server. Only after the test system is stable should you consider releasing changes to production servers. Also, try to limit the potential scope of bad software or hardware by rolling out new releases to a limited number of early adopters. Use clustering to enable partitioning of production and test servers in a common SAN. Failures are then isolated in the test partition.

▶ *Use certified software and hardware* — Hardware and software companies spend a lot of time and money testing and certifying their products on the NetWare OS.

▶ *Run regular server and network health checks and review logs* — Server and network health checks ensure that your system is functioning properly and help isolate problems before they become widespread. Error log files often contain early warnings of problems that can ultimately cause downtime.

Online Configuration

Select hardware and software that enables online configuration. Planned downtime can be reduced if systems are configured or reconfigured while online. Cluster software and Storage Area Networks enable services and data to be migrated to alternate servers, thereby freeing up individual servers for maintenance. The second largest cause of unavailability is planned downtime. If you can perform rolling maintenance by migrating services from one server to the next, you negate the effect that planned downtime has on the overall availability equation.

Summary

This chapter defined system availability and what constitutes a highly available system. You looked at the various levels of availability and formulas for calculating availability. You also surveyed the costs of availability — both the costs of unavailable systems and the costs of achieving high availability. Some of the primary reasons systems become unavailable were analyzed in this chapter.

Finally, the chapter introduced you to holistic methods for achieving high availability in the real world. Implementing a combination of Cluster Services software and a storage area network is one of the best ways to increase overall service and data availability. However, you will fail to improve availability if this is all you do. Do not mistakenly assume that by deploying Cluster Services software, availability will immediately improve. You must understand the causes of downtime in general and in your environment in order to design an appropriate solution. Installing Cluster Services into a poorly maintained environment will not solve existing problems. For example, if your NDS tree or local area network is unstable, neither Cluster Services nor a storage area network will make it any better. High availability is a rigorous discipline and you must exercise attention to detail in order to increase availability.

With a knowledge about why systems fail and what can be done, use Cluster Services and a storage area network as your primary strategy for increasing availability, but do not forget the other elements that surround your clustered SAN. Remember, your system is only as available as its weakest link.

## CHAPTER 4

Examining Novell Cluster Services Architecture

In this chapter, you learn Novell's key clustering concepts and corresponding terminology. This understanding prepares you to apply general principles, such as active/active or active/passive failover, to specific application setup on clusters. After reading this chapter, you'll also be prepared to configure these applications in a Novell cluster, which is covered in detail in Part II of this book.

Storage area networks and server clusters are symbiotic. Storage area networks decouple disks from servers, allowing any server to access any disk, and Cluster Services provides high availability of access to NetWare volumes. This chapter examines cluster hardware and software — that is, the organization of servers and storage devices and the essential Novell Cluster Services software components. It discusses Novell's philosophy toward high availability and the principles guiding the design of the Cluster Services software. Finally, you'll also find a step-by-step example of Cluster Services operation in this chapter.

Understanding the Key Concepts

Figure 4.1 depicts a typical Novell Cluster Services cluster configuration: four NetWare servers (S1, S2, S3, and S4) are attached to a Fibre Channel Storage Area Network (SAN). Client workstations attach to servers via the LAN. All four servers have disk I/O access to shared disks. The disks are located in an external storage array together with an embedded RAID controller. You use storage array management software to carve physical disk drives into virtual disks. Each virtual disk has a logical unit number (LUN). A number of RAID configuration options are available to protect data against physical disk failure. You centrally manage your collective storage resources for all SAN attached servers by configuring storage array RAID to satisfy your performance or fault tolerance goals. Storage area networks enable a great deal of flexibility regarding the number of servers you can attach to the network and the amount and type of storage your servers can access.

On the server side, a Fibre Channel host bus adapter (HBA) driver provides a standard SCSI command set–based interface. Servers are peers at the disk driver level — they all have equal access to the entire set of LUNs presented by storage arrays in the storage area network. Any server can issue a read or write request to any LUN at any time and this arrangement helps to increase overall system availability by eliminating individual servers as potential single points of failure. Any server can access disk data on behalf of clients attached to the local area network.

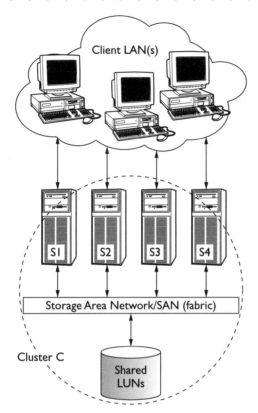

FIGURE 4.1 *A four-server Novell Cluster Services cluster*

Every server also has a local boot disk and SYS volume and runs the NetWare operating system from these direct attached disks. If a server is physically detached from the storage area network, it still functions as a regular standalone NetWare server. The base operating system functionality is not altered when the server is clustered. Servers that run an independent operating system are immune from the failures of other servers running the same operating system. This creates the notion of server-based fault isolation — if one server is experiencing a problem with its operating system or application software, it cannot affect other servers running the same software. Even though the cluster presents the illusion of a single server, the individual server elements function independently and, more importantly, they fail independently. At the operating system layer, servers fail independently of one another. The local SYS volume is what gives each server its independent personality — its name and network address. It's also the volume that contains the base operating system software files. This means that a problem with a server's SYS volume — for example, running out of log file space or accidentally deleting a critical OS file — affects only one server. If that server subsequently fails, the cause of the failure is isolated and affects no other servers.

The use of non-local SYS volumes as an option is discussed in Chapter 6.

X-REF

Benefits of Clustering a SAN

Clustering servers on a SAN offers two primary benefits:

- ▶ High availability
- ▶ Hardware consolidation

High Availability

By clustering servers on a SAN, you can achieve high availability of access to data. If a client accesses data on a NetWare volume via one server and that server fails or becomes disconnected from the LAN, the *exact same* data is available to the client through any of the other servers attached to the SAN. All servers have access to all the data. So the client simply has to reconnect to one of the other servers.

Further, this benefit applies equally to server-side applications and network services. If a server is running software loaded from and accessing data on a shared volume and that server fails, any other server can restart the software by mounting the exact same shared volume and then loading the application software from it. Upon restart, the application or network service will find its *exact same* data also intact on the same shared volume. When application software and data are stored together on a shared volume, any server can mount the volume and run the software from the volume. Once application software is running on a server, it can then access its data from the same volume that it was loaded from. Cluster Services ensures that applications and network services are highly available by quickly restarting them on other cluster servers. In the same way that storage area networks decouple disk drives from servers, Cluster Services software decouples applications and network services from specific servers, thereby allowing them to run on any of the available servers.

Hardware Consolidation

Disk drives are no longer statically dedicated to individual servers when in a SAN. They are consolidated into a central location where they can be assigned to whichever servers need disk space. Gone are the days of having to balance disk space utilization by physically removing drives from one server and installing them in a second server or even purchasing a third server. Free disk space can be reserved in the SAN and assigned to servers on demand. Since data is located centrally in the SAN, access to a specific server is not required to back up the data on the SAN. An appropriately placed Fibre Channel tape drive can back up data from any disk device. Any server or tape drive attached to the SAN can access any shared disk. Fixed assignment of storage to servers is eliminated.

An equally important effect of decoupling storage from specific servers de-emphasizes the role of any particular server. Servers become less special-purpose and less dedicated to any particular task. This consolidation allows you to think of a server as a transient location for running an application, providing network service, or presenting client/server access to shared disk data. Individual servers, therefore, become somewhat anonymous in the overall network. If one server provides access to e-mail data one day and another server provides access to the same e-mail the next, it really doesn't matter that much to clients or users of the data. They are more interested in their e-mail than in what server is providing access to it. The resulting freedom to dynamically assign and reassign applications and network services to servers affords you the opportunity to continuously adjust which servers run what applications and network services, as a function of fluctuating network and server load conditions. By attaching common, off-the-shelf server hardware to a shared disk SAN, you can assign any suitable server any given application or network service. If server upgrade or replacement is necessary, you can easily migrate application or network services to other servers. The more servers you configure on your SAN, the more flexibility your cluster affords you. Consider the benefit of being able to upgrade servers without affecting your network services or users' access to data, for example.

Defining a Cluster by its Access to SAN Disks

You can create two basic kinds of SAN: *homogeneous* and *heterogeneous*. If you dedicate your storage area network entirely to the NetWare servers so that all shared disks are made accessible to all NetWare servers, you are creating a homogeneous SAN. If you partition the SAN through zoning or other SAN virtualization mechanisms to allow additional servers running other operating systems to also access shared disks, you are creating a heterogeneous SAN.

A *Novell Cluster* is defined as a collection of NetWare servers and the shared disks the servers have been granted access to via the SAN. A small cluster can comprise two NetWare servers and a dedicated external drive array. This cluster is defined by the entire SAN because it has access to all the external storage. Larger clusters can contain up to 32 NetWare servers and the shared disk storage contained in a number of external drive arrays. If no other servers are attached to the SAN except the clustered NetWare servers, then this cluster is also defined by the SAN in this case. Both of these examples are considered homogeneous SANs because only NetWare servers are attached to the SAN and all the servers are clustered together. The servers and the SAN define the cluster.

When a NetWare server cluster is attached to a heterogeneous SAN, you must ensure only your NetWare servers have access to their assigned shared disks, via SAN zoning or other SAN virtualization. In these larger SAN configurations, it is typical for NetWare servers to share the SAN with other types of servers. Storage must be partitioned so that shared disks are assigned only to your NetWare servers or to other servers, but not to both types of servers at the same time. If the SAN is incorrectly configured and the same shared disk is accessed by servers running different operating systems, it will be corrupted. If two or more servers are running different operating systems and they access the same shared disk, none of the servers will be aware of the others, and data corruption will result as servers write to the same shared disk in a conflicting way. Any number of servers can be attached to the storage network in order to access mutually exclusive sets of shared disks. In yet more complex SANs, you create a number of clusters, each cluster defined by its servers and assigned shared disks. Different clusters are assigned access to different sets of disks. Again, however, single disks cannot be shared between different clusters, just as servers running different operating systems or those running the same operating system without clustering software cannot share the same disk.

WARNING **At the SAN level, individual shared disks are usually assigned to individual servers in a one-to-one, mutually exclusive fashion. This is done to prevent servers from corrupting a disk in use by other servers. Even if the servers are running the same operating system, without clustering software there is also no way to coordinate all servers to avoid conflicting disk access.**

Cluster Services software eliminates some of these sharing difficulties by coordinating access to storage at a level above individual disks on the SAN — the level known as the volume level. At this next higher cluster level, Cluster Services software coordinates multiple server access to NetWare volumes located on shared disks — NetWare servers are dynamically granted access to file system volumes during cluster operation. Because the cluster software controls disk access at the volume level, all cluster servers are assigned access to all the disks for that cluster at the SAN level, and the cluster software manages volume-level disk access for all servers in the cluster. Shared disk NetWare volumes are mounted by clustered servers. If a server fails, other servers can remount its volumes. You can create many volumes, but only one server can mount any given volume at a time. However, different servers can mount different volumes. A single server can mount many different volumes. Which server mounts a particular volume and under what circumstances is controlled by cluster software. Using the Cluster Services management console, you configure policy settings to associate volumes with servers. By creating rules that govern which servers will automatically mount and remount volumes should a server fail, you decide where volumes are mounted.

Creating a Cluster

You create a cluster by installing Novell Cluster Services software on a group of NetWare servers. Clustering software connects the servers, thereafter called nodes, which then function essentially like a single system — the cluster.

X-REF

Installing Novell Cluster Services is covered in detail in Chapter 6.

Novell Cluster Services comprises a number of NetWare Loadable Modules (NLMs). Every cluster node receives the cluster NLMs during cluster installation. Cluster Services is a layered software product and is installed over the base NetWare operating system.

To create a cluster, all nodes must have SAN-level access to whatever shared disks are assigned to the cluster. All nodes must also be attached to at least one common IP subnet on the LAN. Clustering software uses the LAN and SAN to coordinate the actions of multiple nodes. Cluster Services is a distributed application that runs across all nodes in your cluster using both the LAN and SAN for internode communication.

Configuring a Cluster

Cluster configuration is held in Novell Directory Services (NDS). The base NDS schema is extended to support clustering. Clusters are represented by NDS container objects and contain a number of nodes. The use of NDS permits centrally managed configuration. That means no configuration files or Registry settings need to be individually managed for each cluster node; all nodes share access to directory-held configuration information for the entire cluster. You can create any number of clusters and configure each one separately via the same NDS tree. The power of NDS is its ability to manage network resources independent of individual servers. Through the process of NDS replica synchronization, Cluster configuration information held in NDS remains accessible if servers fail. By applying NDS to the management of Novell Cluster Services, Novell has created a highly available cluster configuration repository that doesn't require administrators to manage individual NetWare servers. Instead, you centrally manage clusters via NDS. Because each cluster is represented by a number of corresponding NDS objects, you manage all of your clusters from a single workstation with access to NDS.

X-REF

You can find out more about planning a Cluster Services configuration in Chapter 5.

Managing a Cluster

Novell Cluster Services clusters are centrally managed with ConsoleOne and cluster-specific ConsoleOne snapins. From a single ConsoleOne management workstation, you monitor and manage all of your clusters, as well as all of your nodes within each cluster. This centralized management approach is enabled via NDS. You don't have to launch multiple copies of the same tool in order to manage different clusters. Instead, you use ConsoleOne and browse your NDS tree for the cluster you want to manage. Because all of your clusters' configuration information is held in NDS, you browse the NDS tree from a single workstation in order to manage any cluster.

Figure 4.2 provides an example of the central management that ConsoleOne and its snapins offer. This figure shows ConsoleOne running the Cluster Services snapins. The console reveals three nodes in the cluster named CLUSTER, which are named NODE1, NODE2, and NODE3. The cluster runs a number of cluster resources across its three nodes. DHCP and DNS services run as cluster resources, and four VOL_SERVER resources provide the NetWare file system service on four NetWare volumes.

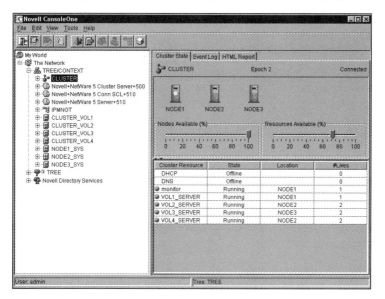

FIGURE 4.2 *Managing a Cluster Services cluster with ConsoleOne*

X-REF

Chapter 7 goes into more depth about managing Novell Cluster Services and using ConsoleOne for administering clusters.

Goals of Cluster Services

Novell designed the Cluster Services product to satisfy the following three goals:

▸ Increasing availability

▸ Simplifying manageability

▸ Supporting online scalability

Increasing Availability

By aggregating multiple nodes into a single cluster, you increase overall service level availability. If a node fails, you can mask repair time by quickly restarting its applications or network services on other nodes in the cluster. When more nodes are supported, more flexibility exists to manage failures by restarting services across any of the surviving nodes.

With this in mind, it's easy to see that Novell's design criteria for Cluster Services targeted large-scale multinode clusters and storage area networks early in the product development cycle. This enables you to start out with two-node clusters and quickly grow into larger configuration for total redundancy. Planning for high availability is easier when you have the flexibility afforded by multiple clustered servers.

A related product goal allows you to use any type of server hardware for your cluster nodes. Cluster nodes do not all need to be equivalent — they may have different amounts of memory or varying numbers of CPUs. This freedom to pick and choose server hardware enables flexible cluster configurations by allowing you to use whatever server hardware you may have at hand, and in the event of server failure, doesn't limit your server replacement options. You don't, for example, have to replace a failed server with an identically configured one. Of course, your servers must still meet the requirements for the operating system and applications you plan to run on them.

Simplifying Manageability

For those in the position of managing servers and storage, a cluster provides a useful metaphor for managing servers and shared storage as a single entity. You can manage your shared storage with any server. Any server can run any application or network service. You use the cluster to manage both servers and storage as a single system. Think of the cluster as a very large and very reliable single computer with lots of disk space. This idea is called Single System Image (SSI).

But such manageability gains don't benefit only the administrator. Another of Novell's criteria when creating Cluster Services was to design SSI from the perspective of both administrators and users of the cluster. Users see the simplified manageability in the form of highly available network services independent of individual servers. Users log in to a single network directory tree rather than an individual server that may or may not be available, and they access applications, network services, or files on volumes independent of individual server availability. From the perspective of users, the cluster appears to be a very reliable single server — one that is always available.

Supporting Multiple Dimension, Online Scalability

Clusters can be scaled in multiple dimensions. You can add servers or storage to scale processing, bandwidth, or storage capacity. Scalability should also be highly available. When you add servers or storage to your cluster, you should not be required to shut down or restart services to reconfigure the system to take advantage of the new hardware. Novell's goal was to achieve online scaling — the ability to expand the capacity of the cluster in various dimensions dynamically, while servers and services are running.

Defining Cluster Resources

A *cluster resource* is a server entity managed by cluster software. A Novell Cluster Services cluster resource is anything that can be run on a NetWare server. In the networked client/server environment, cluster resources provide service to clients in a manner that insulates clients from knowing the actual server providing the service. This property is called *location transparency* and is essential for clustering. If a cluster resource is present on one node and that node subsequently fails, location transparency ensures that when the cluster resource is restarted on a different node, network clients will be able to access the service without incurring any administrative overhead or manual reconfiguration. You simply access the service just as you always have, regardless of which server is hosting the service. If the location of a cluster resource changes, it is transparent to clients of the corresponding service.

An example of a cluster resource is a cluster volume — the NetWare file system service, for example. NetWare clients connect to the server hosting the volume — the server that provides the NetWare file system service. A combination of NDS presentation and virtualization of the host server for that volume provides the location transparency of the NetWare file system service. This example is examined in more detail later in this chapter.

Cluster resources can comprise any of the following cluster resource elements:

▸ Secondary IP addresses

▸ Shared disk volumes

▸ Applications or services

Secondary IP Addresses

An IP address is a network address that clients use to connect to a server. When a NetWare server is installed, it is allocated a unique name and IP address. This is called the *primary address* of the server. In most cases, clients do not care about particular servers; rather, they connect to a server to reach a service hosted by that server. It is more appropriate to think of the primary IP address of a server as actually being the address of services hosted by the server. The client determines the primary IP address and then connects to the server matching that IP address.

This is static. For any given service, clients always connect to the same server via its primary IP address. This arrangement assumes the same server always hosts the same services.

Addressing Services Rather than Servers   Users generally think of accessing a well-known server in order to access a service hosted by that server. You often hear people talk about their home file server or their mail server, for example. To think in terms of clusters, you need to alter this conventional thinking. Instead of focusing on the host server, think about accessing a service via its service address. With this minor shift in emphasis, location transparency and clustering is possible. You always access your service via its service address, regardless of which server is actually hosting the service and its attendant service address.

This is possible by associating services with secondary IP addresses. Although a server's primary IP address never changes once assigned, it is possible to dynamically bind a secondary IP address to any physical server in the cluster. Each secondary IP address provides a constant network address that clients use to connect to a corresponding service. Instead of working with well-known servers, you work with well-known service addresses. For the sake of convenience, just as you assign human-friendly names to servers, you can assign human-friendly names to service addresses.

When a client looks up a service by name, one of several name-to-address resolution mechanisms can be used depending on the client and the service being looked up. The result is always the same — an IP address is returned to the client. To achieve location transparency in a cluster, the name-to-address resolver is configured to return a secondary IP address. Whether an address is primary or secondary makes no difference to the name-to-address resolution mechanism. An IP address is simply an IP address. Several name-to-address resolvers exist, including Domain Name System (DNS), Service Location Protocol (SLP), and Novell Directory Services (NDS). Also, the client- or server-side HOSTS file contains a textual list of names and corresponding IP addresses.

Secondary IP addresses are a critical element of cluster resources. They provide the location-transparent presence for network services. You configure unique secondary IP addresses for each of your cluster resources so that all cluster resources have the freedom to be assigned to physical servers independent of one another. For example, you might allocate a secondary IP address for your GroupWise post office service and a different secondary IP address for your Web server service. In so doing, neither service is statically bound to any particular physical server. Clients of the GroupWise post office connect to its dedicated secondary IP address, and you point your Web browser at the IP address corresponding to the Web server service. Whether both services are running on the same physical server or on two different physical servers is transparent to clients. All the clients need to know are the service addresses, or names assigned to the addresses.

TCP/IP and ARP Moving a secondary IP address from one server to another is possible thanks to the Address Resolution Protocol (ARP). When a client initiates a TCP connection, it provides a target IP address. To send packets to the server that has the secondary IP address bound, the IP protocol uses ARP to convert the IP address into the hardware MAC address corresponding to the network interface card (NIC) in the server. ARP uses subnet broadcast packets to request the conversion of an IP address into a MAC address. The server that recognizes the IP address as one it has bound will respond to the requesting client with its MAC address. Once a MAC address is learned, clients use caches to keep hold of IP address–to–MAC address mappings.

Suppose a cluster node binds a secondary IP address as part of a cluster resource. Clients of the corresponding service will use ARP to locate and connect to the service. In the event the node fails, another cluster node will restart the cluster resource, including binding the secondary IP address. This changes the mapping of the IP address from the old node's MAC address to the new node's MAC address. However, because clients cache the IP-to-MAC-address mapping, you may wonder how clients know the address mapping has changed. When the new node binds the same secondary IP address, it broadcasts an IP-to-MAC-address mapping packet to the network. The ARP protocol requires that all clients update their cache whenever an existing entry is invalidated by the reception of a new mapping packet. When the client next sends a packet to the IP address, the IP protocol sends it to the new MAC address, and therefore to the new node.

Shared Disk Volumes

By virtue of decoupling shared disks from specific servers via the storage area network, volumes created on shared disks also exhibit the required location transparency property. Any server can mount any volume.

Further, shared disk volumes also represent an essential element of cluster resources. They provide the persistent storage for applications and network services. When an application is configured to store its software, configuration, and data files on a shared disk volume, it can run on any server. A cluster resource that requires a shared disk volume first mounts the volume, then loads the application software from it. The software runs from the volume and provides a network service storing whatever data it works with on the same volume. For example, consider the GroupWise application. By installing the GroupWise NLMs on a shared disk volume, any server can run GroupWise simply by mounting the shared disk volume and loading the GroupWise NLMs. When the GroupWise NLMs and the GroupWise database are stored on the same shared disk volume, everything that defines the GroupWise mail application — software code and data — can failover as single unit.

Applications or Services

An application or network service is simply software loaded on a NetWare server, such as a collection of NetWare Loadable Modules (NLMs) or Java-based software. The code itself can be loaded from the SYS volume or a shared disk volume. The code is always the same no matter what server it runs on — this is an obvious example of location transparency. If you want to avoid installing the same application on every node in your cluster, you can install its code to a shared disk volume.

NOTE **For some applications, this may not be possible if the installation program doesn't allow you to select a volume other than the server's SYS volume. For other applications, the NetWare installation can copy application code to the SYS volume of all nodes in your cluster, by default.**

When an application can be configured to function the same way no matter what server its code is loaded on, then it has location transparency. The application's data or configuration determines its behavior. If the configuration files can be stored on a shared disk rather than on a particular server's SYS volume, then any server can provide the same functionality simply by loading the same code and having it reference the shared disk held configuration. If the application is directory enabled, its configuration may be held in the distributed NDS database and therefore accessible to any server in the cluster.

For example, network services like DHCP or DNS use NDS to store configuration and service-level data and may run on any server with access to NDS. An application such as GroupWise is configured with a combination of NDS held data and simple text files. GroupWise can run on any server in the cluster, assuming its configuration information is available to those servers. In most cases, the configuration data is represented by a few text files, and it's relatively simple to replicate files between servers in the cluster. The application's actual data files cannot be replicated and therefore must be stored on shared disk volumes.

Combining Cluster Resource Elements

Most cluster resources follow the same basic pattern: secondary IP address, shared disk volume, and application or network service code that provides access to the shared data according to a client access protocol. Taken together, a cluster resource's elements represent a unit of processing that is assigned to an individual node in the cluster. If that node fails, the cluster resource comprising all its individual elements is restarted on another node in the cluster. Network clients that access a cluster resource in client/server fashion will be able to do so regardless of what node hosts the cluster resource.

Load and Unload Scripts   Resource elements are combined in load and unload scripts. Every cluster resource has a load and an unload script. Both scripts are held in NDS. The *load script* contains the commands necessary to bring a resource online — to start it running. The *unload script* has the opposite purpose. It contains the commands used to shut down a resource. You specify the load and unload scripts when you create a cluster resource.

Because most cluster resources follow a similar pattern, Cluster Services provides default templates that contain commands commonly used in load and unload scripts. Cluster resource templates demonstrate the load and unload script commands used to bind/unbind secondary IP addresses and mount/dismount shared disk volumes, for example.

Specifying Dependencies between Resource Elements   Using scripts, you specify the relative dependencies of resource elements. You will usually want to bind a secondary IP address before starting the application that uses the IP address, for example. You can achieve the desired dependencies between resource elements by ordering the commands in your cluster resource's load and unload scripts.

Defining Failover and Failback

You create cluster resources and assign them to different cluster nodes. Cluster resources are individually managed by following the NDS held policies you configure with the Cluster Services management console of ConsoleOne. One of the most important policies is the *preferred nodes list*. Each cluster resource has its own preferred nodes list. This is a priority-ordered list of cluster nodes that the resource has been configured to run on. The first entry in the list is called the *most preferred node*. A cluster resource will always run on its most preferred node if it's available. In a steady state cluster, each cluster node may run a number of cluster resources. You design the preferred nodes list to balance your cluster resources across the cluster.

Failover

What happens if a cluster node unexpectedly fails? Cluster Services detects the failure and determines what cluster resources were running on the now failed node. The node's failure implies that any cluster resources running on it also failed. For each failed cluster resource, Cluster Services uses the preferred nodes list to select another node in the cluster for the resource to be restarted on. This process of restarting a cluster resource on its next most preferred node is called *failover*. Cluster resources are restarted on a node by executing the commands in their load script.

Failback

If a cluster resource had failed over to another node and its most preferred node becomes available again later, the cluster resource can be migrated back to its most preferred node. This process is called *failback* and is an optional policy setting for each cluster resource. Failback involves shutting down the cluster resource where it is running and restarting it again on its most preferred node. Commands in the unload script are used to shut down a running cluster resource. And commands in the load script are used to start it back up on its most preferred node.

Migration

You can manually migrate a cluster resource from one node to any other node in its preferred nodes list. You might do this to balance the load of the cluster by identifying a busy server and migrating some of its cluster resources to less busy servers. Cluster resource migration is similar to failback and involves shutting down the cluster resource where it is running and restarting it again on the node you select.

Client-Side Impact of Failover

The client-side impact of a failover depends on the application or network service run by the cluster resource and what clients are accessing it. Different clients exhibit different reconnect behavior when their services are restarted. Some clients are more transparent to users than others when reconnecting to the service.

If the cluster resource represents an instance of a NetWare file system service, for example, clients become disconnected from their mapped drives and have to reconnect. Novell client software does this automatically without requiring the user to log in again or otherwise take manual steps to regain access to the service.

See Chapter 9 for a description of what the Novell Clients for Windows 95, 98, Me, and NT do when a cluster volume fails over.

X-REF

Defining Cluster Membership

At any particular time, the nodes you installed into your cluster may not all be available. Some might be down for routine maintenance. Others might have failed. Cluster Services constantly monitors each node, keeping track of dynamic cluster membership. Cluster membership is the subset of installed nodes that are currently available and ready to run cluster resources. As long as at least one node is installed, the cluster remains available. Each cluster node may be in one of three states, which are listed in Table 4.1.

TABLE 4.1

Cluster Node States

NODE STATE	DESCRIPTION
Joined	Node joined the cluster membership and is eligible to run cluster resources.
Left	Node left the cluster membership and is no longer eligible to run cluster resources.
Failed	Node failed and was cast out of the cluster membership by the surviving cluster nodes.

All available nodes in the cluster form a consensus about one another's states and the collective state of the cluster. This list of available nodes together with a cluster-wide membership version number defines the current cluster membership.

If a cluster node boots and the cluster is already running, the booting node *joins* the existing cluster. A cluster node may also voluntarily *leave* the existing cluster, when, for example, it is shut down.

When a node joins or leaves the cluster, the cluster membership is updated to reflect the change of state. A joining node increases the cluster membership by one node. A leaving node decreases the cluster membership by one node. When the cluster membership changes, the cluster membership version number is also incremented. This number is called the cluster *epoch* — it's a count of the number of times the cluster membership has changed since the cluster was first formed. Multiple nodes may simultaneously join or leave the cluster membership in a single incremental epoch change.

If a node voluntarily leaves the cluster, any cluster resources it may be running are first shut down. The cluster resources are then restarted on their next most preferred nodes.

If a node fails, Cluster Services running across the surviving nodes detects the failure and removes the node from the current cluster membership. This is called a *cast out*. It is similar to a node leave, except any cluster resources that were running on the failed node will also have failed and are restarted on their next most preferred node.

Forming a Cluster

Suppose you rebooted all your NetWare servers and now they are running NetWare and loading Cluster Services software. When a node starts running the cluster software, it executes the console command `cluster join` to join the cluster. Cluster Services attempts to locate an existing cluster to join. At boot time, no cluster exists, as all servers are in the same position of trying to locate an existing cluster. If a node cannot find any existing cluster members, the protocols that govern cluster membership eventually form a new cluster containing just the booting node. Once it declares itself a single node cluster, other nodes can join it and increase the cluster membership. At boot time, nodes race to be the first node to form the cluster. If every node declared itself the winner and formed a cluster, you would end up with lots of small clusters, and each would assert ownership of any shared cluster resources, such as shared disk volumes. You must remember the rule that different clusters cannot access the same shared disk and that this situation has to be avoided. Two or more nodes cannot form their own separate clusters at boot or any other time.

The solution to this problem is coordinated by the shared cluster services disk partition. This is a small, dedicated disk partition located on one of the SAN's shared disks. It is automatically created during Cluster Services installation. The cluster services disk partition is used to implement an atomic cluster-wide lock. To declare a cluster, a node must first acquire the cluster lock. This is an atomic operation: If two or more nodes attempt to acquire the lock at the same time, only one of them will succeed and the others will fail. Failure to acquire the lock signals an existing cluster. The other nodes simply join the cluster membership formed by the first node to acquire the cluster lock.

Master Node

The node that first forms a cluster is called the *master node*. The master node manages cluster membership by surveying the state of the other nodes, known as *slave nodes*. If a slave node fails, the master node updates the cluster membership and, using a two-phase commit protocol, distributes the new membership information across the remaining nodes. If the master node fails, one of the slave nodes is elected the master and takes over its responsibilities.

Membership Quorum

Cluster resources are started on nodes only after the cluster membership reaches *quorum*. Quorum is triggered when a configurable number of nodes has joined the cluster or after a configurable amount of time elapses measured from the time the cluster was first formed. Quorum ensures that a sufficient number of cluster nodes are allowed to become available at boot time, before cluster resources are started on their most preferred nodes. Without the concept of cluster membership quorum, all cluster resources might be started on the first node to form the cluster.

Heartbeats

Once a node has successfully joined a cluster, it participates in a distributed failure detection algorithm. Node failure is detected by external monitoring of a continuous heartbeat signal. If the observed heartbeat stops, the monitoring nodes will infer that the monitored node has failed.

Heartbeats are small IP packets. Each node periodically transmits its own heartbeat packet while simultaneously monitoring the heartbeat packets received from other nodes. The heartbeat period is tunable. If a heartbeat is not observed after a tunable threshold period of time, the next phase of the failure detection algorithm is executed.

It is not necessary for all nodes to monitor all other nodes to achieve total coverage. The master node's heartbeat packets are broadcast to all the slaves. Each slave unicasts its heartbeat packets to the master node. The master node monitors all the slaves, and all the slave nodes monitor the master.

Every node also emits a heartbeat signal by periodically incrementing a counter value stored in a per-node sector of the shared cluster services disk partition. Each node reads all the sectors, before writing its own.

The tunable parameters that control heartbeat period and failure detection thresholds are described in Chapter 7.

X-REF

By default, LAN heartbeat packets are transmitted at the rate of one per second. Disk heartbeat I/Os occur at the rate of half the threshold value, one disk heartbeat every four seconds (the default threshold is eight seconds).

Failure detection and the next phase of the algorithm are triggered by the continuous loss of LAN heartbeat packets for a period of time equal to or greater than the threshold parameter. Nodes that remain in contact execute the next phase of the algorithm; master and slave nodes communicate over the LAN to commit a new cluster membership across all nodes. This involves a number of packet exchanges between master and slave nodes. A new master node may be elected during this phase. The final phase of the algorithm compares heartbeat and other information found on the shared cluster services disk partition.

When a node fails, its heartbeat stops. The surviving nodes commit a new cluster membership and then execute failovers by restarting cluster resources. This is done under the assumption that a failed node, because it failed, can no longer have ownership of shared resources. This makes it possible for the surviving nodes to assert ownership of failed resources by remounting shared disk volumes or binding secondary IP addresses, for example.

Mutually exclusive ownership of cluster resources is enforced by Cluster Services software. Only one node can own any given cluster resource at a time, and all cluster nodes maintain consistent agreement. Failed nodes are removed from the cluster and subsequently ignored. A failed node can participate in the cluster again only by rerunning the `cluster join` protocol. This usually happens during server boot. If a node has not executed the `cluster join` protocol, it cannot interact with shared resources.

Split Brains and Poison Pills

If a single node or group of nodes somehow becomes isolated from other nodes, a condition called cluster *split brain* results. Consider a two-node example: If the LAN heartbeat packets from master to slave and slave to master are lost, the master will assume the slave failed. Conversely, the slave will assume the master failed. Both nodes will execute the next phase of the algorithm and both will commit a new cluster membership that excludes the opposite node. Two independent one-node clusters will be formed, and neither cluster will be aware of the existence of the other. If this condition is allowed to persist, each cluster will failover the resources of the other. Since both clusters retain access to shared disks via the SAN, corruption will occur when both clusters mount the same volumes.

In theory, split brain conditions are rare. But they can occur if the LAN experiences a hard fault such as a NIC, hub, or switch hardware failure. In these cases, you can avoid split brains by deploying dual redundant LAN segments.

But if a split brain condition does occur, it must be prevented. The final phase of the algorithm achieves this. Before propagating the new cluster membership to higher layer recovery software, the failure detection algorithm running on all cluster nodes inspects the cluster services disk partition. Only one side of the split brain survives this phase. The other side will be forced to shut down. The safest way to ensure that nodes in the losing side of the split brain cannot corrupt shared state in the future of the winning side is to have them eat a *poison pill*. A poison pill is an intentional server abormal-end (ABEND). Options to force an orderly shut down of losing nodes are limited. Winning nodes must ensure that losing nodes have relinquished control of shared resources before they can safely proceed. This requires communication over a LAN that has apparently failed. The winning side is therefore unable to use the LAN to instruct the losing side to shut down. Even if the winning side could send instructions to the losing side, perhaps over the storage area network as an alternative, it would then have to wait for the losing side to complete its shutdown. While the losing side is shutting down, the winning side has to wait until the losing side is complete and has signaled it is finished. This completion signal also requires an operational communication channel. How long should the winning side wait for the completion signal before moving forward? Suppose the losing side subsequently fails before sending its completion signal — will the winning side wait forever? These issues are resolved by forcing an immediate shutdown of the losing side so that the winning side may immediately proceed. The faster this happens, the less interruption there is for network clients that are accessing the services that have to failover from the losing side to the winning side.

The process that selects winners versus losers is called the *split brain tie breaker*. If there are more nodes on one side of the split versus the other side, the majority side will always win. In the case of a dead heat (an equal number of nodes on both sides), the tie breaker will select the side that contains the previous master node. Remember, in a split brain condition, there are two or more clusters and therefore multiple master nodes. In the special case of a two-node cluster split brain, if NIC link status can be determined, then the node with good LAN connectivity will win. The other node will lose.

The philosophy engrained in these algorithms is intended to increase overall service level availability. This may not be immediately apparent. In normal circumstances, LAN failures cause split brains. If LAN failure cannot be masked with redundant hardware, a node that loses contact with other nodes because of NIC failure, for example, has also lost contact with its clients. Clients, therefore, experience service outage. Instead of allowing this service outage to occur, it is considered a better policy to force the failover of cluster resources to connected nodes that clients can reach over the LAN, even if this means that a semifunctional node will eat a poison pill. This method may seem drastic, but it allows service to continue without outage, thus increasing overall service availability. These algorithms are intended to increase overall availability at the expense of individual servers and enable a tradeoff to be made when designing a cluster. You can eliminate the potential single points of failure that cause network or SAN I/O path failure with redundant hardware—dual NICs or dual Fibre Channel HBAs. You can also deploy an additional server in anticipation of a poison pill induced failover. In either case, the goal is to eliminate the effect of potential single points of failure.

Defining Active/Active and Active/Passive

Novell Cluster Services is a fully *active/active* multinode clustering solution: All nodes are able to run cluster resources, and cluster resources can failover to any node. In an *active/passive* cluster, some nodes are designated *standby nodes* and are considered passive compared to the other active nodes. In normal operation, a standby or passive node does no useful work. It sits idly waiting for a failure. When a failure occurs, a standby node becomes active by taking over the work of a failed active node.

The designation of active/active or active/passive is also applicable to nodes from the perspective of specific cluster resource types. For example, suppose you set up a cluster to provide a highly available NetWare file system service. You might assign every node a different cluster volume, and each volume would be set up to failover to any node. In normal operation, each node is active with respect to the NetWare file system service because each node is providing that service. If any node should fail, its cluster resources will failover to other nodes that are already providing the NetWare file system service for other cluster resources. This is also considered active/active failover.

In contrast, an example of an active/passive cluster resource is IBM WebSphere. You might set up a single cluster resource to run IBM WebSphere. The WebSphere resource will run on only one node at a time—its active node. All other nodes are passive with respect to the WebSphere service.

 Some applications or network services can be configured only for active/ passive failover. That is, if a node is already running an instance of the service, it cannot run an additional instance of the same service.

NOTE

Understanding Cluster Volume Resources

Cluster volume resources represent instances of the NetWare file system service. They comprise a secondary IP address and a shared disk NSS volume. But how do NetWare clients locate and then connect to the correct node running a cluster volume resource?

In nonclustered NetWare networks, regular NetWare volumes have a host NCP server. *Cluster volumes* also have a dedicated host — a *virtual NCP server*. This NDS object contains a network address attribute set to an IP address (a service address) dedicated to the cluster volume. The IP address is dynamically bound to the physical server that mounts the volume. Novell calls this *instantiating a virtual server on a physical server*. You can achieve location transparency of the NetWare file system service by virtualizing the host NCP server and setting its network address to a dedicated IP address.

Figure 4.3 illustrates the relationship between NDS volume and host server objects. The traditional volume/server relationship is shown in the upper left-hand corner. When a volume is created, its corresponding NDS Volume object is linked to an NCP server object via the Host Server attribute. This linkage implicitly assumes only one server can be the host for a volume. When an existing volume is clustered-enabled, the traditional relationship is modified. A new cluster volume resource, with load and unload scripts, policies and preferred nodes attributes, is created under the cluster container object. The IP address you supply to cluster enable a volume is copied into a new NCP server object called a *virtual server*. The existing NDS volume object has its Host Server attribute modified to point at the new virtual NCP server. The new virtual NCP server object has links that point back to the cluster container and the cluster volume resource.

Suppose a shared disk volume called VOL is created on a server named S1 in cluster C. By default, the corresponding NDS volume object would be named S1_VOL. To *cluster enable* this volume, ConsoleOne automatically takes the following steps:

1. Create a new (virtual) NCP server object, named C_VOL_SERVER.

2. Set the new NCP server object's network address attribute to a dedicated IP address you define.

3. Create a new cluster volume resource object, named VOL_SERVER.

4. Rename the original volume object to C_VOL and change its host server attribute to C_VOL_SERVER.

Once ConsoleOne has taken these steps, users running the Novell client software can access files on cluster-enabled volumes just like regular NetWare volumes even when volumes are failed over from one node to another. The relationship between volume and host server is kept intact, but the traditional host server is replaced with a virtual NCP server. This is transparent to the Novell client software, as explained in the sections that follow.

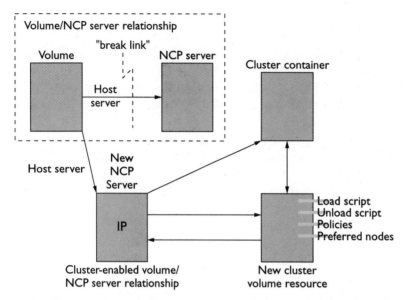

FIGURE 4.3 *The NDS relationship for cluster volumes and virtual NCP servers*

Naming Virtual Servers

The NetWare client traverses the NDS volume/host NCP server relationship in the same manner for regular or cluster volumes. It cannot tell the difference between physical or virtual servers. The client uses NDS to resolve a volume to its host server address. After connecting to a server, one of the first NCP requests a client will make is to get the server name and other parameters. Cluster Services intercepts NCPs that reference the server name and substitutes the virtual server name. In the example mentioned in the "Understanding Cluster Volume Resources" section, the name returned to the requesting client would be C_VOL_SERVER. The client thinks it is connected to a NetWare file server called C_VOL_SERVER no matter what physical server the virtual server is instantiated on.

NetWare Client Reconnect

Under the modified NDS relationship that links cluster volumes to host virtual NCP servers, transparent client-side reconnect is enabled via existing reconnect logic in Novell's Client32 and NT NetWare clients. If a connection to a server is lost, the client will attempt to reconnect to the server's network address, assuming either a transient network outage or a server reboot. The client does not return to its name-to-address resolver; it simply caches the network address in a connection structure and attempts to reconnect to the same address. The NetWare client reconnects to what it thinks is the same physical server — the virtual NCP server. In fact, the client will reconnect to whatever cluster node the cluster volume resource and its secondary IP address failover to.

Volume Identifiers

Mounted volumes occupy an entry in the server mount table identified by a volume identifier — an index into the mount table. The NetWare clients (Client32 and NT) cache these volume identifiers. On reconnect, the client assumes it can reuse cached identifiers to access the same volumes. This requires that volume identifiers remain constant no matter which server the corresponding volume is mounted on. Accordingly, volume identifiers have cluster-wide scope — they are location transparent. Each cluster volume is mounted by specifying its unique volume identifier.

Migrating File System Trustee Assignments

Unlike volume identifiers, file system trustee assignments, however, are not location transparent. When a trustee is added to a file system object, a 32-bit value with local server scope is stamped into the file system. This has long been a problem for NetWare backup and the transportability of removal media. One cannot take a physical volume containing trustee assignments and attach it to a different server. The embedded trustee IDs on the volume are valid only on the server that created them.

Cluster Services solves this problem with a trustee migration utility called TRUSTMIG. TRUSTMIG tracks fully distinguished names (FDNs) of NDS trustees and their corresponding local IDs. When a volume is moved from one server to another, the entire file system is scanned, and IDs are converted. The FDNs have network scope. The IDs do not. The time it takes to convert all the IDs on a volume is somewhere between a function of the number of unique IDs and the number of files. A volume with a large number of trustee IDs can take a few minutes to convert. The volume is not accessible to clients during this process, because access via a stale trustee ID represents a potential security breach.

▶ · ◀

Expanding Cluster Services Components

Figure 4.4 depicts the Cluster Services architecture.

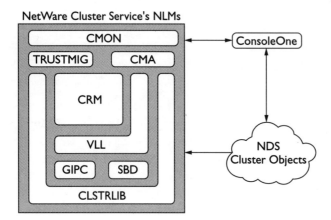

FIGURE 4.4 *Cluster Services architecture*

Cluster configuration data is centrally held in Novell Directory Services (NDS). It is managed via a workstation running ConsoleOne and the Cluster Services snapins. Each server runs a collection of NetWare Loadable Modules that comprise the Cluster Services software. The Cluster Services architecture can be broken down into two main sections:

- Cluster Services NDS schema
- Cluster Services NLMs

Cluster Services NDS Schema

The Cluster Services installation extends the base NDS schema with object class and attribute definitions that represent cluster configuration. These NDS objects store information on each cluster, including the cluster's properties, nodes, cluster resources, and associated properties. The NDS object classes defined by the Cluster Services schema (and shown in Figure 4.5) are as follows:

- Cluster Container
- Cluster Node

▸ Cluster Resource

▸ Resource Template

▸ Volume Resource

Cluster Services NDS Schema

```
┌─────────────────────┐
│  Cluster Container   │
└─────────────────────┘
      │
      │    ┌──────────────────────┐
      ├────│    Cluster Node       │
      │    └──────────────────────┘
      │    ┌──────────────────────┐
      ├────│   Cluster Resource    │
      │    └──────────────────────┘
      │    ┌──────────────────────┐
      ├────│   Resource Template   │
      │    └──────────────────────┘
      │    ┌──────────────────────┐
      └────│   Volume Resource     │
           └──────────────────────┘
```

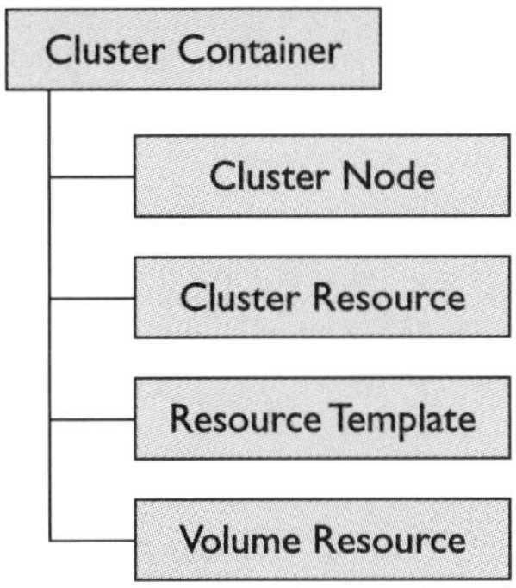

FIGURE 4.5 *The Cluster Services NDS schema*

Cluster Container

An NDS cluster container object represents each cluster of nodes on the network. As the name suggests, a cluster container supports NDS containment. A cluster contains all cluster-specific NDS objects that represent the nodes and cluster resources of the cluster. The cluster container also comprises cluster-wide configuration parameters that control cluster quorum, cluster membership protocol parameters, and the cluster management port settings.

Cluster Node

Each NetWare server installed in a cluster has a corresponding cluster node object created under the cluster container. The cluster node object stores the node number, the TCP/IP address of the node used for cluster heartbeat packets, and a pointer to the NCP server object. A cluster node object functions as an alias for the NCP server that it represents.

Cluster Resource

A cluster resource object is created for every unique application or network service that will run on a cluster's nodes. The cluster resource object holds configuration information for individual cluster resources, including preferred node lists that define which nodes a cluster resource is assigned to as well as the ones it should failover to. Other configurable properties maintained by cluster resource objects are load and unload scripts and failover and failback settings.

Resource Template

Resource template objects are identical to cluster resource objects except they cannot be run on cluster nodes. Novell supplies a number of preconfigured resource templates when you install a cluster. These objects have load and unload scripts that contain the commands necessary to run a subset of Novell's standard applications and network services on cluster nodes. When you create a cluster resource object, you have the option to inherit properties from a resource template. You then customize the cluster resource by editing its properties to suit your configuration.

Volume Resource

The volume resource object is a special kind of cluster resource. It represents an instance of the NetWare file system service. When you cluster enable a volume, a volume resource is created under the cluster container. Its load and unload scripts are automatically generated with the commands necessary to mount the volume and bind the secondary IP address and virtual NCP server name, in the load script, and commands to unbind the IP address and virtual NCP server name, and dismount the volume, in the unload script. Because volume resources represent an instance of the NetWare file system service, they are linked to the corresponding virtual NCP server and volume objects.

NetWare Loadable Modules

When you install a cluster, the following NLMs are copied to the SYS volume of each server in the cluster:

- Cluster library (CLSTRLIB.NLM)

- Group interprocess communication (GIPC.NLM)

- Split brain detector/Split brain detector library (SBD.NLM/SBDLIB.NLM)

- Virtual Interface Architecture link layer (VLL.NLM)

- Cluster resource manager (CRM.NLM)

- Cluster management agent (CMA.NLM)

- Cluster monitor (CMON.NLM)

- Trustee migration tool (TRUSTMIG.NLM)

Figure 4.6 illustrates the functional relationship between the Cluster Services NLMs, which is discussed more extensively in the next several sections. Each node installed in a cluster runs the core NetWare OS plus the same collection of Cluster Services NLMs.

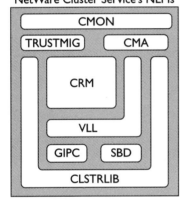

NetWare Cluster Service's NLMs

FIGURE 4.6 *Layering of cluster services NLMs*

Cluster Library

The cluster library (CLSTRLIB) provides the interface between Cluster Services and NDS. Other Cluster Services modules use the cluster library to read cluster configuration information from NDS. Each node has to read its own identity and the identity and network addresses of other nodes installed in the same cluster. Cluster membership heartbeat and other parameters are also read from NDS. On the cluster master node, the cluster resource manager (CRM) uses the cluster library to read-in the configuration of all cluster resources from NDS.

Group Interprocess Communication

The group interprocess communication module (GIPC) contains the core cluster membership protocols and provides the following two services to higher layer cluster modules:

- Cluster membership
- Atomic message multicast

The cluster membership service uses the heartbeat protocol to keep track of available nodes as they join or leave the cluster. The GIPC protocols work to form consensus across the total collection of available nodes. Membership events are generated when the cluster membership changes. The algorithm involves exchanging a number of packets over the common IP subnet that connects all the nodes. The protocol executes in phases, moving to the next phase only when all nodes are in agreement.

The atomic multicast message service underpins the cluster membership protocol and also provides a generic cluster communication mechanism. The cluster resource manager is an NLM that runs on all nodes. It uses the multicast message service to communicate with its peers running across the cluster. The semantics of atomic multicast provide for an all or nothing style of communication. If a node sends a multicast message to its peers, GIPC guarantees that either all nodes in the current cluster membership receive the same message or none will. Furthermore, atomic multicast also ensures that all messages are received in the same order across all nodes. For example, if one node sends a message at the same time another node sends its message, then GIPC will guarantee that all nodes either receive the first message, then the second, or vice versa. This protocol property is called *virtual synchrony*. Cluster communication is ordered and relative to membership changes.

Split Brain Detector

As part of its cluster membership protocols, Cluster Services uses a patented split brain detector (SBD) to ensure that split brain conditions (as explained earlier in this chapter) are detected and prevented. The SBD relies on the clustered nodes' connection to the cluster services disk partition as an alternate communication channel. This is a small dedicated disk partition located on shared disk and accessible to all nodes. The cluster services disk partition contains each node's view of the cluster membership. Each node in the cluster has its own area of this partition in which it records its version of the cluster's membership. Every node has read/write access to its section of the partition, but only read access to those portions belonging to the other nodes. When a membership change occurs, the SBD running on all nodes examines the cluster services disk partition for any inconsistencies between the memberships recorded by the different nodes. SBD also provides a cluster-wide atomic lock mechanism used to coordinate multiple nodes when racing to form a cluster.

Virtual Interface Architecture Link Layer

The Virtual Interface Architecture link layer (VLL) is an infrastructure module that integrates GIPC and SBD and provides an application programming interface (API) in the style of the industry standard VI Architecture. VI Architecture and its programming interface, called VIPL, define an industry standard for high-performance cluster communication. Novell adopted and extended VIPL. Multicast messages are exchanged programmatically using VIPL functions.

VLL is also responsible for handling node join and leave by coordinating with other cluster modules.

Cluster Resource Manager

The cluster resource manager (CRM) is layered above GIPC and CLSTRLIB. It reads cluster resource information from NDS and builds internal data structures representative of each one. CRM uses GIPC-provided cluster membership and multicast services to execute a distributed, event-driven, finite state machine. Nodes change state when they either join or leave the cluster. Cluster resources change state when they are loaded on one node or restarted on another. The cluster resource manager receives cluster membership events and responds by restarting cluster resources on the nodes identified by their individually configured preferred nodes and failover and failback policies. The state of all cluster resources is replicated across all nodes using algorithms based on the exchange of atomic multicast messages. If any node should fail, surviving nodes continue from this up-to-date view of overall cluster status. Cluster resource managers on separate nodes are able to execute various algorithmic steps in parallel. Suppose, for example, a node was running two cluster resources and then failed. If the preferred nodes lists of each cluster resource identify different failover nodes, the cluster resource manager may immediately start restarting the failed cluster resources on both nodes. In this and many other examples, the CRM doesn't need to further communicate to coordinate failover because all nodes maintain consensus agreement.

Table 4.2 lists the various states that the cluster resource manager tracks for cluster resources.

TABLE 4.2

Cluster Resource States

RESOURCE STATE	DESCRIPTION
Unassigned	Unable to run on any cluster node currently in the cluster membership given its preferred nodes list
Offline	Shut down
Loading	Load script is being executed on a cluster node
Unloading	Unload script is being executed on a cluster node
Comatose	Runtime failure detected
Running	Normal operational state: running on a cluster node
Alert	Requires administrator intervention
NDS Sync	Waiting for NDS to synchronize configuration changes
Quorum Wait	Waiting for the cluster membership to reach quorum

Another important function provided by the cluster resource manager is the cluster-wide distributed lock service. The lock service is used to manage the location of shared disk volumes, ensuring that only one node is allowed to activate any particular volume at a time. The distributed lock service is fault tolerant. If a node fails, any distributed locks it might have been holding at the time are automatically released so that other nodes can acquire them.

Cluster Management Agent

The cluster management agent (CMA) functions as a cluster management proxy for ConsoleOne. It uses a TCP/IP-based asynchronous protocol between the cluster and the client workstation running ConsoleOne. ConsoleOne interacts with the CMA to facilitate control of individual cluster resources and to monitor and display the cluster's current cluster membership and cluster resource states. The CMA interacts with VLL and CRM to determine what cluster nodes are active, and to control the state of all resources. When you click the ConsoleOne screen to offline a cluster resource, the ConsoleOne cluster snapin sends a cluster resource offline message to the cluster via the CMA.

Cluster Monitor

The cluster monitor (CMON) is a server-side cluster monitor tool. It shows the current cluster membership and epoch number.

Trustee Migration Tool

The trustee migration tool (TRUSTMIG) is responsible for migrating embedded trustee assignments on cluster-enabled volumes during failover. It also watches for new trustee assignments created on cluster-enabled volumes, or modifications made to existing ones in order to maintain a database of trustee identifiers and fully distinguished trustee object names. This database is used to migrate trustee identifiers.

For more details on TRUSTMIG, see Chapter 9.

X-REF

Detailing Cluster Services Operation

To solidify your understanding of the Novell Cluster Services architecture, consider an example of how its modules work.

Suppose you have a three-node cluster with nodes A, B, and C in a SAN configuration. Further suppose that a GroupWise cluster resource is running on node A. The policies you created in NDS dictate that when node A fails, node B should restart GroupWise and remount the GroupWise data volume, which is located on the SAN.

Now, suppose node A fails. Here's how Cluster Services behaves in this situation:

1. Cluster Services immediately affects a failover of the cluster resources that were running on node A.

2. When node A fails, the GIPC modules on the surviving nodes, nodes B and C, notice that node A has not transmitted heartbeat packets during the defined timeout period. The GIPC modules on nodes B and C exchange messages with their respective VLL modules regarding this suspected failure.

3. The VLL modules send a message to the SBD modules, which check the SAN and find that node A is no longer updating the cluster services partition. The SBD modules send a message to the VLL modules, confirming that node A has failed. After nodes B and C reach consensus regarding that failure, the VLL modules on nodes B and C send event notification of node A's failure to the CRM modules.

4. The CRM modules on nodes B and C check the cluster resource data they read from NDS via CLSTRLIB when the cluster first started. These CRM modules find that node B is responsible for restarting node A's cluster resources. Accordingly, node C does nothing, and node B begins the failover process by running the load script for the GroupWise cluster resource. This load script contains commands to mount the GroupWise data volume, bind a secondary IP address, and then start the GroupWise post office agent and the message transfer agent.

5. Before running the load script for GroupWise, the CRM on node B sends multicast messages to all of the other nodes in the cluster (in this case, just node C), explaining that node B is loading the GroupWise cluster resource. The moment that GroupWise is running, node B sends another message to all other nodes informing them of this change of state from Loading to Running.

6. These state-change messages are sent to all nodes in a cluster before changes are made to any cluster resource. All nodes must then commit to the change by using the same two-phase commit algorithm that the GIPC module uses to agree upon a suspected node failure. That is, the state change has to be made by all of the nodes in the cluster and can never be made on just one node alone.

In this way, Cluster Services ensures that all nodes are always aware of the current state of the cluster and its resources. Cluster Services also ensures that one node cannot attempt to take over a resource without committing that change across the entire cluster. Because all nodes are always aware of the state of the cluster and its resources, all nodes know exactly what is happening. For example, by apprising node C of what node B is doing, node B ensures that if something goes wrong while it is running the load script for GroupWise, node C will know exactly what happened and will be able to take over.

7. GroupWise is now running on node B.

In this example, if you did not have a cluster and your company's GroupWise server failed, you would probably spend several hours restoring GroupWise on another server. You might also have to respond to complaints from users whose productivity depends on the ability to send and receive e-mail during the day.

With Cluster Services, however, most users won't even notice if node A fails. Cluster Services moves the secondary IP address associated with the GroupWise service to the failover server, node B. GroupWise client software simply uses the same IP address to reconnect to what appears to be the same GroupWise server. After the failover is completed, users can read their e-mail messages without having to log in again and without having lost anything.

Summary

Hopefully, this examination of the ideas, jargon, and architecture of Novell Cluster Services and clustering in general helped give you a sense of how this all fits together (and benefits you as an administrator). This chapter introduced you to key cluster concepts and terminology. With that conceptual foundation in place, you were introduced to Novell Cluster Services architecture from both a hardware and software perspective. A discussion of the relationship between clusters and storage area networks led to an exploration of how to combine them to provide high availability and greater consolidation of server and storage resources. Finally, an examination of the primary Cluster Services components led to an explanation about how they interact and work for you.

## CHAPTER 5

Planning Novell Cluster Services Configuration

This chapter covers the basic pre-Novell Cluster Services installation requirements, such as the minimum hardware and software requirements, cluster heartbeat planning requirements, protocol requirements, and general IP name resolution requirements. Next, you get basic planning recommendations for NSS volumes, as well as NSS tuning guidelines, and plans to migrate existing volumes into the cluster. In the third section of this chapter, you learn post–Novell Cluster Services installation guidelines, including help with planning your resource requirements, planning for "application partitioning," and planning a test lab.

Planning for Novell Cluster Services

Planning your Novell Cluster Services deployment requires planning your hardware, software, and application configurations. In addition to these obvious components, you must also plan for several not-so-obvious considerations, such as your TCP/IP infrastructure, support for the cluster protocols, and TCP/IP name resolution.

Novell Cluster Services Hardware Requirements

Novell Cluster Services itself does not add additional hardware requirements beyond the requirements of the operating system.

Novell Cluster Services requires the following:

- ▶ 128MB RAM (but 256MB is recommended for NetWare 5.1)

- ▶ A dedicated (nonshared) disk for each server's SYS volume, either locally to each server, or properly zoned in the SAN so that each server can access only its own SYS volume

- ▶ A shared disk of at least 20MB for the Novell Cluster Services cluster partition used for split brain detection

TIP The actual size of the cluster partition depends on the size of the virtual disk that you install it on. In some cases, this size may actually exceed 17MB. You should, therefore, install clustering prior to partitioning your shared storage—this way, the cluster partition will take what it needs and leave you the rest for data.

Though the overhead for Novell Cluster Services is very light, you must also consider the applications that you plan on installing into the cluster when determining the actual hardware requirements. When planning your hardware, plan for the maximum allowable failure that your company requires you to maintain. For example, if you are implementing a 10-node cluster, and your requirement is that all resources must be available even if four nodes were to fail, then you should plan your hardware requirements based on six servers servicing all the applications in your cluster.

Understanding NSS Requirements

Novell Cluster Services requires that all shared volumes be configured using the NSS file system. The NSS file system benefits clustering with its rapid mount, dismount, and repair times, which are critical for the rapid migration or failover of a volume from one node to the next node.

It is technically possible to use a traditional volume in a cluster (though this is not supported by Novell), but the trustee migration and repair utilities will not function on traditional volumes, which means that any file system trustees will be lost when the volume is migrated. In addition, Novell Cluster Services does not provide protection against two servers mounting the same traditional volume, which makes it much more likely that you will inadvertently cause data corruption by mounting the same volume on two different servers.

Novell Cluster Services also requires that the versions of NSS be identical on all nodes in the cluster. Each operating system support pack for NetWare 5.x has added additional NSS functionality, and this functionality must be the same on each node that can access the same cluster volume. Many of these patches might make modifications to the volume structure itself, and mounting a volume with a higher support pack on a lower revision of NSS may cause the system to "repair" the volume, which in turn would corrupt it.

Planning the Heartbeat Network

Novell Cluster Services requires a single subnet to use for the Cluster Services communication protocols. Although this subnet does not need to be dedicated just for Novell Cluster Services, each node in the cluster must have an interface attached to this subnet, as the clustering protocols are nonroutable.

When you plan the heartbeat network, choose to have either a dedicated subnet just for the clustering communications or to run the clustering communications on the same subnet as your production traffic.

These Cluster Services protocols are discussed in Chapter 4.

X-REF

Because the pros and cons of a heartbeat network take on different levels of importance to different customers, it isn't possible to give one blanket recommendation that works for everyone. You must weigh the pros and cons in your own environment and determine whether or not to implement a dedicated heartbeat network.

One of the key benefits of a dedicated heartbeat network is that it isolates traffic, which protects the cluster nodes from false poison pills due to congestion on your LAN. On the other hand, some issues you should be concerned about if you choose to have a dedicated heartbeat network include:

- *Management complications* — ConsoleOne must have a route to the heartbeat network to manage the cluster state. This is accomplished by enabling routing on the cluster nodes.

- *Production LAN card failures not detected* — On a heartbeat network, if the primary LAN card on the server fails, the cluster does not notice, and the node is not removed even though it no longer provides resources.

- *Extra component which could fail* — If the heartbeat LAN card fails, the node is removed from the cluster even though communications to the clients are still ongoing and valid.

As a general rule, if you know that your public network is never saturated, you might prefer to use the production network as your heartbeat network. Keep in mind that it takes only eight seconds of saturation to prevent the connectionless heartbeat packets from getting through. Then you will have "false" poison pill ABENDs on one or more servers. These ABENDs can be very frustrating to troubleshoot, particularly if the saturation occurs sporadically.

Novell Cluster Services Software Requirements

Novell Cluster Services has the following software requirements:

▶ All servers must have NetWare 5.0 with Support Pack 4 or later, or NetWare 5.1.

Though technically not required for Novell Cluster Services, NetWare 5.1 Support Pack 3 has significant NSS and Novell Cluster Services enhancements.

TIP

▶ All servers must be in the same NDS tree.

▶ All servers must have Novell Licensing Services version 5.02 or later.

▶ All servers must have TCP/IP enabled, and at least one interface on the same TCP/IP subnet.

▶ NSS should be properly tuned for performance.

See Novell Support TID 10012765 for NSS tuning recommendations.

TIP

Understanding Novell Cluster Services Protocol Requirements

Novell Cluster Services requires TCP/IP on all cluster nodes, and at the client workstation for all clustered applications. Additionally, all nodes in the cluster must have one subnet in common for the heartbeat and ConsoleOne management communications protocols.

The gory details of these protocols are discussed in Chapter 4.

X-REF

Since the cluster protocols are nonroutable protocols, all cluster nodes must share a common TCP/IP subnet for the cluster communications. The network interface that each node uses for cluster-related communications is stored in the cluster node object, as shown in Figure 5.1.

The network interface for each node is also stored as a property of the cluster object. You can find this on the Cluster Protocol Internals property page of the cluster object using ConsoleOne.

TIP

▶ · ◀

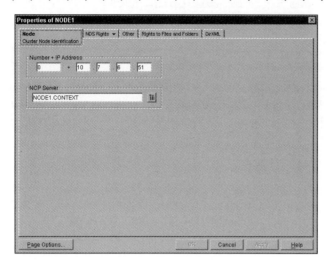

FIGURE 5.1 *Cluster communications interface*

Although all nodes must have a subnet in common, that does not mean that all interfaces on each cluster node must reside on the same IP subnet. It is possible to have multiple interfaces in each cluster node and have these interfaces (except the cluster interface) on different subnets. If you choose to implement a cluster in this manner, you must plan your resources carefully; you can bind a secondary IP address to a server only if that server's primary IP address is on that particular subnet. For example, if a cluster-enabled volume has a secondary IP address of 10.7.5.106 (subnet mask 255.255.255.0), and you try to migrate it to a server that does not have a primary IP address on the 10.7.5 subnet, the resource will go into a comatose state.

Each resource in your cluster requires its own secondary TCP/IP address. This includes each volume that you cluster-enable for fault tolerant file system access. Since each of these resource addresses must be on the same IP subnet as the host server, you must plan your subnets and resources carefully to ensure that you have enough addresses in your subnet for all the resources you plan on clustering, and to allow for future resources you might cluster.

If you combine multiple components into a single cluster resource, each of these components can utilize the same TCP/IP address. For example, if you have an application that requires a cluster-enabled volume, you can also use the TCP/IP address of the cluster-enabled volume for your application. Just remember that all the components that rely on that address need to be configured in a single cluster resource — all components that rely on a specific address must go where that address goes.

If you have applications that depend on other applications running before they can run, you must combine them into a single cluster resource, since there is currently no way to make a cluster resource depend on another cluster resource. If you are combining them into a single resource anyway, consider using a single IP address for both applications.

For example, suppose that you are using a cluster-enabled volume for GroupWise, and you plan to have a single GroupWise resource for both a Message Transfer Agent (MTA) and a Post Office Agent (POA). When you cluster enable the volume, you assign an IP address of 10.7.5.130. You can also use this same TCP/IP address for the MTA and the POA. If you later decide that you want the POA to run as a separate resource, you would have to create a new shared volume to move the Post Office directory structure to and you would have to configure a new cluster resource with another TCP/IP address. You would also need to modify all of the appropriate parameters in GroupWise to accommodate this change.

Understanding Name Resolution in NetWare and Pure-IP

Novell Cluster Services requires NetWare 5.*x* servers and TCP/IP-based connections. Since all of your cluster resources require TCP/IP connections, understanding TCP/IP name resolution to properly set up your name resolution and troubleshoot it when things go wrong is important.

Any time you have a failure connecting to a cluster resource via a name, try connecting or pinging the TCP/IP address of the resource. If you can connect to the TCP/IP address but not the name, you have a name resolution issue.

With IPX, there is rarely a problem finding resources — you ask for a list, and there everything is! With IPX, every server and every router automatically tells the world about everything it knows. TCP/IP does not take this active approach to advertising resources, so you will not necessarily see everything on the network, even if it is properly configured.

Figure 5.2 shows the Novell Client's Protocol Preferences tab. The sections that follow briefly discuss each of these resolution methods and how they relate to finding Novell Cluster Services resources.

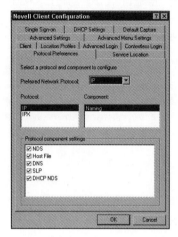

FIGURE 5.2 *Novell Client Configuration Protocol Preferences tab*

Using NDS as a Name Resolution Method

NDS is a valid name resolution protocol that resolves names to IP and/or IPX addresses. However, when using NDS as a name resolution protocol, you must remember to consider context in the resolution process. Suppose you want to resolve the virtual server CLUSTER_PUB_SERVER.CONTEXT using NDS. If your current context is USERS.CONTEXT, and you try to resolve CLUSTER_PUB_SERVER, you will not be successful! That is because NDS works only for short name resolution (that is, not for the entire distinguished name of the resource) if the user's current context is the same as the resource context.

More commonly, you will use NDS to resolve an NDS volume object. In the previous PUB example, suppose you wish to map your F: drive to the cluster-enabled PUB volume, in the PUBLIC directory. If your NDS volume object is CLUSTER_PUB, and it is in the CONTEXT container, you can issue the following MAP command:

```
MAP F: = .CLUSTER_PUB.CONTEXT:\PUBLIC
```

Mapping drives to the NDS volume object is the preferred method with Novell Cluster Services. Using this method provides the best automatic client reconnection performance.

Using the HOSTS File as a Name Resolution Method

The next available IP name resolution method is the HOSTS (or NWHOST) file. For Windows 9x clients, create a NWHOST file in the \NOVELL\CLIENT32 directory with your TCP/IP name–to–IP address mappings. For Windows NT or Windows

2000, use the standard HOSTS file in \WINNT\SYSTEM32\DRIVERS\ETC for these mappings. Using HOSTS files at client workstations is tedious and difficult to maintain on all workstations and, therefore, is not the preferred method for TCP/IP name resolution (except perhaps for the administrator's workstation).

If you decide to maintain HOSTS files for users, you can use Novell's ZENworks to easily distribute the updated files.

TIP

NetWare servers can also use a HOSTS file for IP name resolution. Whenever you cluster enable a volume, it is a good practice to add the virtual NCP server to the HOSTS file of all servers in the cluster. Modify the SYS:ETC\ HOSTS file by adding each virtual server in your cluster, as shown in Figure 5.3. This allows each server to quickly resolve the virtual server names to TCP/IP addresses without needing to query DNS. Since the virtual server IP addresses should not be changing frequently anyway, maintaining the HOSTS files on your cluster nodes should not be too "administrative-intensive".

```
hosts - Notepad
File  Edit  Format  Help
10.7.5.51    NODE1.CLUSTER.PAYNENET.COM   NODE1
10.7.5.52    NODE2.CLUSTER.PAYNENET.COM   NODE2
10.7.5.53    NODE3.CLUSTER.PAYNENET.COM   NODE3

10.7.5.101   CLUSTER_PUB_SERVER.CLUSTER.PAYNENET.COM   CLUSTER_PUB_SERVER
10.7.5.102   CLUSTER_APPS_SERVER.CLUSTER.PAYNENET.COM  CLUSTER_APPS_SERVER
10.7.5.103   CLUSTER_USERS_SERVER.CLUSTER.PAYNENET.COM CLUSTER_USERS_SERVER

10.7.5.105   CLUSTER_NDPS_SERVER.CLUSTER.PAYNENET.COM  CLUSTER_NDPS_SERVER

10.7.5.106   CLUSTER_GW1_SERVER.CLUSTER.PAYNENET.COM   CLUSTER_GW1_SERVER
10.7.5.108   CLUSTER_GW3_SERVER.CLUSTER.PAYNENET.COM   CLUSTER_GW3_SERVER
10.7.5.109   CLUSTER_GW4_SERVER.CLUSTER.PAYNENET.COM   CLUSTER_GW4_SERVER
10.7.5.110   CLUSTER_GW5_SERVER.CLUSTER.PAYNENET.COM   CLUSTER_GW5_SERVER
10.7.5.111   CLUSTER_GW6_SERVER.CLUSTER.PAYNENET.COM   CLUSTER_GW6_SERVER
10.7.5.112   CLUSTER_GWGWIA_SERVER.CLUSTER.PAYNENET.COM  CLUSTER_GWGWIA_SERVER
10.7.5.113   CLUSTER_GWWEB_SERVER.CLUSTER.PAYNENET.COM CLUSTER_GWWEB_SERVER
```

FIGURE 5.3 *Sample NetWare server HOSTS file*

Ultimately, the HOSTS file method is recommended for servers and administrative workstations as a good backup to DNS, but not recommended for the masses at the client workstations.

Using DNS as a Name Resolution Method

Perhaps the most common IP name resolution option is Domain Name Service (DNS). As with the HOSTS file, it is a good practice to place all of your virtual servers into DNS, as well as any cluster resources that users connect to using a name. Assuming that your client workstations are in the same DNS zone as your resources (or that they have the resource zone in their DNS search suffix), this will provide short name resolution to the resources using DNS.

However, placing virtual servers in DNS requires that your DNS server support the underscore (_) character, which may or may not be the case.

The next version of Novell Cluster Services will allow you to name your virtual servers however you want, so you will be able to avoid this issue.

NOTE

Also note that the DNS entry does not need to match the actual resource. For example, you can put CLUSTER-PUB in DNS using the TCP/IP address of the CLUSTER_PUB_SERVER virtual server. Clients can then map drives using the DNS name.

For short name resolution to work using DNS, the client workstation must either belong to the same DNS zone as the resource (examples of DNS zones include consulting.novell.com or education.novell.com), or the resource zone must be configured in the client's DNS suffix search path. For example, if your client workstation's host name is host.consulting.novell.com, but all of the cluster resources were configured in the resources.novell.com DNS zone, you would not be successful using short names via DNS unless you added resources.novell.com to your client's DNS suffix search order.

With the virtual servers configured in DNS, the clients can use DNS to map drives using UNC paths. For example:

MAP F: = \\CLUSTER_PUB_SERVER.CLUSTER.COM\PUB\PUBLIC

Or, assuming the client's DNS zone is the same as the resource:

MAP F: = \\CLUSTER_PUB_SERVER\PUB\PUBLIC

Or, with the example mentioned earlier in this section where the DNS entry doesn't match the resource (in this case, the DNS entry is configured with a host name of CLUSTER-PUB.CLUSTER.COM):

MAP F: = \\CLUSTER-PUB.CLUSTER.COM\PUB\PUBLIC

DNS is a critical name resolution method, and should be utilized in any TCP/IP environment. You should always add all of your NetWare 5.x servers into your DNS zone, as well as all of your virtual servers and resources that support DNS resolution.

Using SLP as a Name Resolution Method

NetWare 5.x uses the IETF standard Service Location Protocol (RFC 2165) to advertise service information across TCP/IP-based networks. SLP does for a

TCP/IP network what SAP does for an IPX network, thus providing short name resolution of TCP/IP-based resources within your network. If you wish to populate Network Neighborhood with the same TCP/IP resources that you are used to seeing with IPX, you need to utilize SLP.

Applying CVSBIND to Achieve SLP Propagation

Novell Cluster Services versions 1.0 and 1.01 do not propagate virtual server information into SLP by default.

The next version of clustering will automatically add this support.

NOTE

If you wish to propagate virtual server information to SLP, download the CVSBIND utility (http://support.novell.com/cgi-bin/search/searchtid.cgi?/2957434.htm). After installing the utility according to the included directions, you add the following command to your cluster load scripts:

```
CVSBIND ADD <NAME> <IP ADDRESS>
```

where *<NAME>* represents the name of the virtual server and *<IP ADDRESS>* is the address of this virtual server. This command adds the virtual server into the bindery.novell SLP service within your existing SLP infrastructure.

To your unload scripts, you add the following command:

```
CVSBIND DEL <NAME> <IP ADDRESS>
```

The primary advantage of using CVSBIND is that it gives you TCP/IP short name resolution regardless of a user's context or DNS zone. This allows UNC paths to be valid using only the short names of the virtual server.

We strongly recommend using CVSBIND for all cluster-enabled volume resources, as TCP/IP name resolution of your virtual servers is critical for any connections to these virtual servers.

DHCP NDS

This option is not actually a name resolution method, but enabling it tells the client to utilize Dynamic Host Configuration Protocol (DHCP) to receive SLP information including the SLP Directory Agent (DA), SLP Scope(s), and Compatibility Mode Migration Agents.

For more information on Service Location Protocol, SLP DA, Scopes, and Migration Agents, see Novell TID 10062474.

TIP

Novell Cluster Services Client Requirements

Novell Cluster Services requires the following Novell client software with NetWare Core Protocol (NCP) over TCP/IP support:

▶ The Novell client must be version 3.1 with Support Pack 2 or later for Windows 95/98, or 4.6 with Support Pack 2 or later for Windows NT. These versions of the client are included on the Cluster Services installation CD.

▶ The administrative workstation must have ConsoleOne version 1.2b or later with the Cluster Services snapins installed. The Cluster Services snapins are included on the Cluster Services installation CD.

If you are running anything prior to the above client versions, the Novell client must be tuned for cluster performance as listed in Table 5.1. With the newer clients, the client software automatically detects whether it is connected to a cluster and modifies its behavior accordingly, without any tuning required.

T A B L E 5.1

Recommended Client Tuning Parameters to Support NCS

WINDOWS 95/98	WINDOWS NT/2000
On the Advanced Settings tab:	**On the Advanced Settings tab:**
Auto Reconnect Level = 3	Auto Reconnect = on
Auto Reconnect Timeout = default	
Handle Net Errors = on	**On the Protocol Preferences tab:**
Name Cache Level = 0	Preferred Network Protocol = IP
Net Status Timeout = 60	Protocol Component Settings = NDS
NetWare Protocol = NDS	

The workstation you use to manage Novell Cluster Services must meet the above requirements, as well as have ConsoleOne version 1.2b or later with the Novell Cluster Services snapins installed. When you install ConsoleOne from the Novell Cluster Services installation CD, it automatically installs the Novell Cluster Services snapins.

Once you have a workstation with the snapins installed, you can easily copy these snapins to another workstation with ConsoleOne installed. To do this, copy the following two directories to the corresponding directories on the desired workstation:

```
C:\NOVELL\ConsoleOne\1.2\resources\NetWareClusterServices
```

```
C:\NOVELL\ConsoleOne\1.2\snapins\NetWareClusterServices
```

You can also copy these directories to the following location on the SYS volume so that the server-based ConsoleOne will have the Cluster Services snapins:

```
SYS:\PUBLIC\MGMT\ConsoleOne\1.2\resources\NetWareClusterServices
```

```
SYS:\PUBLIC\MGMT\ConsoleOne\1.2\snapins\NetWareClusterServices
```

Planning the Volumes

Novell Cluster Services requires that the shared storage utilize NSS volumes for all cluster resources. Each cluster resource that requires shared storage should have its own NSS volume for data, and if the application allows, its application files (NLMs). By storing the application files on the shared storage instead of each server's SYS volume, you can configure a cluster resource to run completely from the SAN, which allows you to easily reconfigure which nodes are available to service that resource.

In a shared disk environment under NetWare Cluster Services, NSS volumes can be either cluster-enabled volumes or standard shared volumes. Both volume types can fail over to another node, but the method for doing so differs. When planning your volumes, you must decide which type of volume your application will require.

Using Standard Shared Volumes

A standard shared volume is an NSS volume on the shared storage that any cluster node can activate and mount for use by an application running on that node. Typically, standard shared volumes are sufficient for applications that handle the application data on behalf of the user — such as Novell Enterprise Web Server. A standard shared volume does not need an NDS volume object associated with it, although by default it will have one based on the node you used to create it. If you need an NDS volume object, then you actually need a cluster-enabled volume instead of a standard shared volume.

TIP

To avoid confusion, delete the NDS volume object associated with the shared volume. Since this volume is available to any of the cluster nodes in the resource preferred nodes list, it is not logical to have the NDS volume object associated with any specific node, and this may cause confusion to administrators.

Although the term *shared volumes* is being used here, it is important to understand that from a pure clustering terminology perspective, these volumes are classified as *share nothing* volumes. What does this mean? The volumes are shared in the sense that any node in the cluster can activate and mount that volume, at which time it can access the data on the volume. They are share nothing volumes because only one server in the cluster can access the volume at any one time.

If any two servers were to access the same volume at the same time and write data to it, file system corruption would occur. The Novell Cluster Services software prevents any node in the cluster from activating the same shared volume at the same time. However, it does not prevent a server that is not part of the cluster, or even a server that is part of a different cluster but is also attached to the same SAN, from activating the same volume.

Deciding When to Cluster Enable Your Shared Volumes

If users need to be able to retain drive mappings to certain volumes in the event of node failure, the volume in question must be cluster enabled. Additionally, cluster-enabled volumes must be used for any application that uses a specific server name in its operation (for example, applications that reference data locations using the server name as part of the directory path, such as a UNC path).

Unlike standard server volumes, cluster-enabled volumes are not permanently bound to any one physical server. They do not have hard ties to a specific physical server, but are bound to a virtual NCP server that acts as a proxy for the hosting server.

Since users and applications see only the relationship between the cluster-enabled volume and the virtual NCP server, they are shielded from knowing about node failures. When a node failure occurs, cluster-enabled volumes can provide uninterrupted service to users and applications.

When a volume is cluster-enabled, three NDS objects are created:

▶ *Cluster volume* — Represents the cluster-enabled volume.

▶ *Cluster volume resource* — Maintains the load and unload scripts for the cluster-enabled volume.

▶ *Cluster virtual server* — Represents the virtual NCP server for the cluster-enabled volume.

Cluster-enabled volumes have properties similar to other cluster resources. Network administrators can specify the nodes that will be eligible to mount a cluster-enabled volume, as well as its preferred node. Like all cluster resources, the cluster-enabled volumes also have their own load and unload scripts.

Each cluster-enabled volume has a unique IP address assigned to its virtual NCP server. Clients attach to the virtual NCP server address, and the IP address is assigned to the cluster node that is currently serving the volume resource.

With cluster-enabled volumes, users can map drives using the name of the cluster-enabled volume and its virtual NCP server. This allows the drive mappings to remain valid when volumes fail over to different nodes in the cluster.

Finally, transparent client reconnect requires cluster-enabled volumes. (Transparent client reconnect preserves users' drive mappings when their volumes are remounted on a surviving server after the node they are on fails. It also supports open files and file locks on Windows 95/98 clients.)

Planning for Fan-Out-Failover

So, how many standard shared volumes and cluster-enabled volumes do you need? How big should these volumes be? Well, the answer, of course, is it depends!

With the ability to store up to 8 trillion files and single files up to 8TB, a single NSS volume may be able to handle all of your company's data needs. So, should you just create one volume? The answer, of course, is no.

The general rule for planning your volumes is to create more small volumes as opposed to fewer large volumes. The goal is to maximize the ability for the cluster to support Fan-Out-Failover. If a single node hosts four volumes and fails, these four volumes can potentially go to four different cluster nodes. In this case, each node would pick up an incrementally small additional load. If instead you had one volume four times as large, then one server would have to take the entire load of this single volume.

Of course, it isn't really the size of the volume that adds the load; rather, the load is added to the I/O of the server based on how many client connections to the volume there are. Because size does not predict load, it isn't possible to give a single recommendation as to how big to make your volumes to support Fan-Out-Failover. You must analyze your environment to determine how you can best optimize the client I/O to the volumes, and divide this load based on the size of your cluster. Get an idea as to the amount of failure your cluster is designed to accommodate (that is, must you be able to efficiently service your user community if one, two, three, or more servers fail?). Based on this business rule, plan the number of volumes appropriate to fan out the load, however many servers fail.

Planning for Trustee Migration

File system trustees are stored on each server based on NDS object IDs. With NetWare 5.x, these object IDs are server-centric — each server has a different object ID for the same NDS object. Because these IDs are server-centric, if you migrate a volume from one server to another, you must also migrate the trustees' object IDs. Note that it is not the object IDs that migrate, but rather the trustee information. Any other dependency on object IDs will not be migrated when the volume moves.

NOTE

File ownership is also based on object IDs. Because of the time required to migrate ownership on each individual file, it is not technically feasible to migrate ownership information and still have migration occur rapidly enough for automatic client reconnection.

The time it takes TRUSTMIG.NLM to convert all the IDs on a volume is a function of the number of unique trustee IDs and the number of files on the volume. Therefore, to minimize the time it takes for a trustee migration to occur, you must minimize the number of unique trustee IDs and/or the number of files on the volume. Based on our experience, the number of trustees on the volume has significantly more impact on trustee migration time than does the number of files on the volume.

No hard and fast rules exist for how many files or how many trustees you can have on a given volume and still have acceptable trustee migration speeds. However, we have found that a conservative guideline of 750 unique trustees per volume will consistently perform trustee migration acceptably. Proper NSS tuning significantly improves trustee migration performance and allows scaling far beyond 750 trustees per volume.

TIP

NetWare 6 will replace the server-centric object IDs with Globally Unique Identifiers. This will remove the need to migrate trustees or ownership attributes.

NSS Tuning

Since you will be using NSS for your cluster data volumes (the SYS volumes still require the traditional file system until NetWare 6 is released), it is important that you tune the servers for optimal NSS performance. This is important not only for speed in data access, but also for TRUSTMIG.NLM performance.

NetWare 5.x default installations are tuned for the traditional file system. NSS does not utilize memory for caching in the same manner as the traditional file system and, therefore, requires different SET parameter modifications to obtain enhanced performance. Failure to tune the server for NSS will most likely result in poor performance.

NSS does not use directory cache buffers, as does the traditional file system, so tuning cache buffer parameters will not help performance. NSS has its own caching parameters that you can set during the loading of the NSS modules (in the AUTOEXEC.NCF file). The following are parameters that tune the performance of NSS:

- ▸ Cachebalance
- ▸ Fileflushtimer
- ▸ Bufferflushtimer
- ▸ Closedfilecachesize
- ▸ Allocahead

Cachebalance determines the amount of memory reserved for NSS to use for file cache. The default for NetWare 5.x is just 10 percent, which is not sufficient in a cluster configuration. Increasing it to 80 percent or 90 percent gives NSS close to the same performance as the legacy file system for typical file access. In theory, you should tune this percentage to the percentage of total volume space taken for NSS volumes to total volume space (that is, 10GB traditional and 90GB NSS produces a parameter of 90 percent). However, this also takes memory away from the memory pool that NLM and Java applications utilize, so you must allow sufficient memory for the applications that you are running. Also, most server health monitoring tools (including Novell's Web-based monitoring tool PORTAL.NLM) do not account for the allocation of RAM to NSS and, therefore, report the server as needing more RAM based on the percentage allocated.

TIP

Tuning the Cachebalance **is the single most important factor in tuning NSS. You will notice the largest performance boost by increasing the memory allocated to NSS for caching—all other parameters will incrementally increase performance. The default of 10 percent is nowhere near adequate for a system designed with NSS volumes.**

Fileflushtimer and Bufferflushtimer parameters control the writing of metadata (NSS control information that describes user data, such as volume free space lists, directory entries, file attributes, and so on) to disk. Increasing them from their defaults may help caching performance up to a certain point, but increasing them too much causes a "throttling" problem, which could decrease performance. The performance you get from these parameters depends somewhat on the processor and disk speed of your system. Setting each of these parameters to 75 will improve NSS performance in many systems, but if it decreases performance in your system, throttle it back down toward 50.

Closedfilecachesize determines how many closed files are kept in cache. With sufficient memory, set this to 50,000 and modify as necessary from there.

Allocahead is used to allocate extra blocks ahead of time in anticipation of new files being larger than the 4K-block size. This improves performance for larger files at the cost of performance for small files. If you know most of the files will be small, disable Allocahead.

NOTE

NSS does not allow you to control the block size on the volume and always utilizes 4K blocks. However, the algorithm used for NSS does not incur the performance penalty typically associated with this small block size.

To activate each of these parameters, you must issue them during the initial load of NSS. For example, place the following command in the AUTOEXEC.NCF file:

```
NSS /AutoDeactivateVolume=All /Cachebalance=80 /Fileflushtimer=75
/Bufferflushtimer=75 /Closedfilecachesize=8192 /Allocahead=0
```

Planning to Migrate Existing Volumes into the Cluster

When you plan to migrate existing volumes into a cluster, take the uncompressed file size into consideration. NetWare 5.*x* does not support compression on NSS volumes, so if your volumes are currently compressed, you need significantly larger volumes in the SAN to accommodate the volumes once they are uncompressed. To determine how much space you need to accommodate your existing files, you can use the command line utility NDIR.EXE or volume properties using NetWare Administrator.

TID 2937820 explains the process for using NDIR to compute volume space saved by compression.

TIP

Once you have determined the disk space required, you need to decide which method to use to get the files to the destination. You can move the files with any of the following:

▸ Backup and restore

▸ Third-party backup software that includes a volume copy feature

▸ Novell's Upgrade Wizard utility

Whatever method you use to migrate data from traditional volumes to NSS, be sure that you force decompression of compressed files. We have seen cases where the backup software doesn't seem to realize that the volume doesn't support compression, and it moves the files in a compressed format. When you try to access the files, you then find that they are corrupt. Novell's Upgrade Wizard is a free utility (found at www.novell.com/download) that does a very good job migrating volumes from NetWare 4.x to NetWare 5.x servers. Also, if you want, you can migrate just the volumes without migrating all the server information, but you need to back up and restore the trustees if you don't use the Upgrade Wizard to its completion (which automatically renames your NetWare 5.x server to match the old NetWare 4.x server).

Planning for Clustered Applications

Novell Cluster Services software has a very small footprint on your systems and does not add to the hardware requirements beyond the NetWare operating system. So capacity planning in your cluster largely involves planning for the resources that will be running in the cluster.

Planning Resource Requirements

The key to planning the hardware in your cluster is understanding the hardware requirements of each application and how these applications will work together on the same server. Placing multiple applications that are processor bound on the same server will not produce as desirable a result as mixing an I/O-bound application with a processor-bound application.

When sizing your servers, once again first start with defining what level of failure your company is willing to accept. If you are building a 10-node cluster and you must be fully operational even if four nodes fail, then your capacity planning should involve planning all your applications to run on six nodes. If you plan for optimal performance based on 10 nodes, performance degradation begins as soon as a single node fails.

Resource requirements is an area where the flexibility of Novell Cluster Services really pays off. By increasing the number of servers in a cluster, you decrease the individual hardware requirements for each server. In a two-node cluster, each server must be powerful enough to handle the entire load of the cluster in the event that one of the servers fails, whereas a four-node cluster means that each server must be able to handle its normal load, plus 25 percent of the total cluster load in the event of a single server failure.

Next, you need to factor in the expected growth of each of the services and how this will affect the resources used by the cluster. If you know that your user community is rapidly growing, make sure you factor in substantially increased storage, processor, and memory. This is perhaps the hardest event to plan for, but vitally important. It is better to over-engineer now than go back in six months needing more hardware.

Application Partitioning

Application partitioning is the process of dividing your cluster up into logical groups of nodes that host similar applications. For example, in a 32-node cluster, you may choose to use eight nodes primarily for GroupWise, two for NDPS, two for backup, eight for Web Services such as DNS, DHCP, database applications, and Servlet engines, eight for file system access, and four for ZENworks (see Figure 5.4).

Cluster nodes need not be identical hardware. You can mix and match different processors, RAM, and even hardware vendors within the same cluster. Application partitioning helps you make the best use of the servers in your cluster. Assume you have a database application that requires multiple CPUs and significantly more RAM than most other applications in your cluster. By partitioning this database to a set of servers designated for database applications, you can designate a portion of your cluster to be available for these databases and purchase higher-end machines to suit this need. For the remaining nodes in the cluster, you can spend a bit less money and purchase less horsepower.

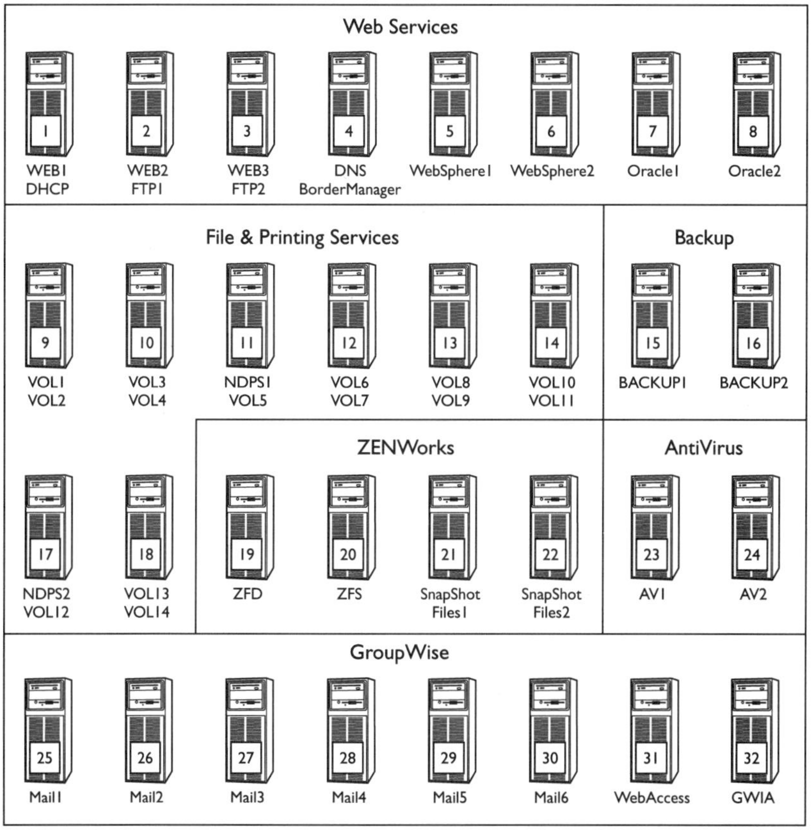

FIGURE 5.4 *Example of application partitioning*

Another benefit of application partitioning is in management. Some applications may require some files on the SYS volume in addition to files that can be installed to the shared volume. For example, the Novell Enterprise Web Server and Novell Distributed Print Services both have SYS volume dependencies. By partitioning these applications to specific nodes, you need to install this software only to a portion of your cluster, and network administrators will have a logical method of knowing which servers are designated for these types of resources.

Clients that utilize multiple subnets for the cluster realize another benefit of application partitioning. Recall that only the cluster communication address for each node must be on the same subnet; it is possible to have each server's "production" address exist on a different subnet than the cluster communications. However, when a cluster resource migrates from one node to another, the secondary IP address used for that resource must correspond to a subnet to which the node has a primary IP address bound. Clients with too many resources for a single TCP/IP subnet (or for other reasons) may decide to span multiple subnets with the cluster, but each application partition would reside in the same TCP/IP subnet. Without application partitioning, it would be much more difficult to plan resources across these multiple subnets. By partitioning, you can easily keep the GroupWise services on a messaging subnet, the Web Services on an Internet subnet, and so on without doing extensive planning to make sure that your resources will be valid on all of the nodes in the failover path.

Yet another reason to partition your applications is to isolate software errors. If you have four nodes designated for a third-party database application and you later apply a patch that causes this application to ABEND the server, by partitioning your applications you restrict your fault to those four servers.

32-Node ABEND

Novell Consulting was called in to assist a hardware vendor in setting up a 32-node cluster for Brainshare 2000. The demo was planned using application partitioning, with all nodes providing services, but groups of nodes designated for specific services.

As the demo was progressing, the hardware vendor wanted to be able to demonstrate that the partitioning was not required, and requested that a single application have all 32 nodes in the failover path. To accommodate this, Novell Consulting set up a new NDPS resource and made this available to all 32 nodes. However, the system was running a version of NDPS prior to the "cluster-friendly" NDPS modifications, which resulted in the NDPS Manager ABENDing the server. When the resource was brought online, all 32 nodes took their turn ABENDing.

This is an excellent lesson on why you should partition your applications within the cluster and how you can avoid taking down an entire cluster with one errant NLM. It also speaks to the need to test your applications in a test lab (like this was) prior to implementing them in production.

Planning a Test Lab

If you have existing resources that you wish to migrate to a cluster, you must not only plan how to cluster the resource, but also how to get the existing resource into the cluster and highly available. Perhaps the most important key to success in doing this is proper testing in a lab.

Many clients utilize the new SAN as their test lab prior to installing Novell Cluster Services into production. This procedure works great for the initial installation, but leaves you with no lab once your cluster is in production. Since it is vitally important that you thoroughly test any application prior to introducing it into your production cluster, you must have a test lab in which to test your applications.

One option is to zone off a portion of your SAN and allow only test machines to see the test portion of your SAN. In this manner, you won't have a test machine causing a live production node to fail, or worse yet a cascading failure through multiple nodes due to some software incompatibility.

In the best-case scenario, you would have another SAN for your test lab, a SAN completely isolated from your production SAN so that there is no chance that anything you do in testing affects production users. The next-best scenario to having an isolated test SAN is to use a portion of the production SAN zoned off so that the test servers can't see the LUNs on the production SAN. However, both of these scenarios require more Fibre Channel cards, Fibre cable, Fibre switch ports, and so on, which can raise the cost of the test lab beyond what your company may be willing to spend.

If this happens to you, there is another option to create a basic test lab without spending your entire IT budget. You can create a shared SCSI test lab for substantially less money, although you'll be limited to two nodes and you will not have as robust a solution. In fact, if you don't use Y cables with external termination, you had better not power off one of the boxes, or the entire SCSI bus will be invalid and your second node will lose its shared storage also.

WARNING **This setup is for a test lab only and is not robust enough for a production environment. Though the major hardware vendors sell shared SCSI solutions that are robust enough for a production environment, using this solution will not produce acceptable results for any purpose beyond a lab.**

To set up the shared SCSI test lab, you need two SCSI adapters (preferably the same make and model, although this isn't actually required). The example built for this book used a test lab with two Adaptec 2940U2 controllers. Configure each adapter to use a different SCSI ID — set one to 6, and the other to 7.

Next, you need an external SCSI drive. If you don't have an external SCSI drive, you can buy an external drive case and place an internal drive in it. In fact, you can find external cases that hold up to three internal drives for under $200. Each drive must be configured for a unique SCSI ID (you've already used ID 6 and 7, so use 0, 1, and 2).

Ideally, use SCSI Y cables (see Figure 5.5), so that one end plugs to the hard drive cabinet and the other plugs to the SCSI card, with a Y to an external terminator (this may actually be built into the cable). The Y cables are not required and are also difficult to find. The advantage of using them is that the SCSI bus will still be terminated even if one of the SCSI adapter cards loses power. If you are using Y cables, make sure that the hard drives and the SCSI adapter cards have termination disabled.

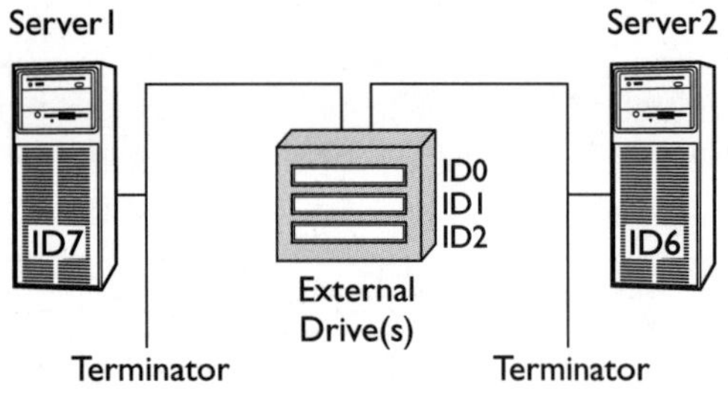

Server1   Server2

ID7   ID0   ID1   ID2   ID6

External Drive(s)

Terminator   Terminator

FIGURE 5.5 *Shared SCSI using Y cables*

If you don't use Y cables, you must enable termination on the SCSI adapters (auto termination may also work) and disable termination on any hard drives. Remember, you can't have any device terminated in the middle of the SCSI chain, and in this case, you are using multiple initiators (each computer's SCSI card), with the hard drives in the middle of one SCSI chain.

Depending on the cards, you may have to make some modifications in the SCSI card BIOS settings. The following settings will generally be successful:

- *Plug and Play SCSI IDs* — Disabled

- *Parity* — Enabled

- *Disconnection* — Disabled

► *Send Start Unit CMD* — Disabled

► *BIOS* — Disabled

► *Reset SCSI bus at Init* — Disabled

If you are not using Y cables, the secret to making this work is to boot the first computer and to not load SERVER.EXE. Next, boot the second machine and let the server start on this one. Let it come all the way up until the server has completed loading all the startup modules. Next, start the server on the first machine. If you lose power to either machine, you will lose the SCSI bus and have to start all over again.

WARNING

If you try to load both servers at once, you will see a loop of each server reporting that the SCSI bus was reset by a third party. This loop will end when you down the servers. You may also want to remove the LDNCS **command from the** AUTOEXEC.NCF **so that you can start both servers before loading Novell Cluster Services.**

► · ◄

Summary

This chapter covered the basic pre-NCS installation requirements, such as the minimum hardware and software requirements, cluster heartbeat planning requirements, protocol requirements, and general IP name resolution requirements. Next, you examined basic recommendations for planning the NSS volumes, for tuning NSS, and for planning NSS migration. The third section of this chapter explored post-NCS installation guidelines for resource requirements, application partitioning, and test lab setup.

This survey of configuration planning issues prepares you to plan for many commonly overlooked issues. By properly planning your hardware, software, and applications before you begin installing your cluster, you greatly increase your chance of success the first time around.

## CHAPTER 6

Installing Novell Cluster Services

This chapter covers the Novell Cluster Services installation process, with a special focus on critical success factors. From preinstallation considerations through main installation, and even into an examination of how to install ConsoleOne and the Novell Cluster Services snapins, this chapter moves you steadily through the steps you'll need to take to install Cluster Services. Additionally, the chapter reviews how to copy the Novell Cluster Services snapins to other workstations and servers so that you can administer the cluster from other ConsoleOne installations, including the NetWare server X-Windows version of ConsoleOne.

This chapter also investigates some postinstallation tasks that relate to the installation process: adding a new node to the cluster, removing a node from the cluster, adding a new network for the cluster heartbeat, and uninstalling Novell Cluster Services.

Installing Novell Cluster Services

Novell Cluster Services is installed from a client workstation to all servers in the cluster at one time. Novell Cluster Services has the following minimum requirements:

- A minimum of two NetWare 5.x servers

- A minimum of 128MB of RAM on each server

- A dedicated disk (not shared) for the SYS volume

- NetWare 5.0 with Support Pack 3A or higher, or NetWare 5.1

TIP

Though Novell Cluster Services RAM requirements do not exceed the operating system requirements, remember that these requirements do not account for the applications running on the cluster. Plan your resource requirements around the applications running on the server, as well as the requirements of any additional applications that may run on the server due to a failure of another node in the cluster.

Using Nonlocal SYS Volumes

Depending on the hardware used, you might be able to use the SAN for the server's SYS volume. This still requires that each server have its own dedicated SYS volume, which must be configured in the SAN as a virtual disk. Once you configure the virtual disk, you must zone this off (using the hardware manufacturer's instructions) so that only the designated server has access to this virtual disk.

Once the disk is zoned, you must configure this virtual disk to appear as logical device 0 to the server that will use it. Some vendor applications require a dedicated Fibre Channel card for this purpose. Additionally, the Fibre Channel card must have its BIOS enabled, which functions similarly to booting from a SCSI controller.

In this manner, the server's DOS partition and SYS volume can be stored on the SAN. This allows for a relatively easy transition to new server hardware should the server fail or need upgrading. Xiotech, EMC, and Compaq all currently have solutions that allow for nonlocal SYS volumes.

Novell Cluster Services Preinstallation Checklist

Installing Novell Cluster Services is straightforward once you have the hardware properly configured. The installation program is a Java application that runs from a client workstation. For best results, use a high-end workstation with plenty of RAM for the installation.

For more information about hardware solutions, refer to Appendix A.

X-REF

You should not start the installation process until the hardware is properly configured on all servers that will be in the cluster, and after you've verified that all servers are able to see all of the shared storage.

Prior to installing Novell Cluster Services, use the following checklist to verify readiness. Do not start the installation until this list is complete.

1. Ensure that the following base requirements for Novell Cluster Services are met:

- Either NetWare 5.0 with SP3A or above, or NetWare 5.1 is installed.

WARNING

Novell does not support mixed NetWare 5.0 and NetWare 5.1 clusters, or clusters that are not all at the same Operating System Support Pack revision.

- TCP/IP is installed — Each server must have one interface on a common TCP/IP subnet for the heartbeat network.

- Servers all reside in the same NDS tree.

- The current Novell client is installed on the workstation you will use to install Novell Cluster Services. At a minimum, you must use the version of the Novell client that is shipped on the Novell Cluster Services CD (for example, Windows 95/98 client version 3.1 with Support Pack 2).

- ConsoleOne is installed from the Novell Cluster Services CD-ROM onto the installation workstation.

2. Ensure that the NDS tree is healthy for installation. Prior to the installation of Novell Cluster Services, perform a minimal NDS health check that includes the following:

- Check synchronization status — NDS is a loosely consistent database. To ensure consistency, NDS synchronizes periodically. This process ensures that all replicas contain identical information. Verifying NDS synchronization will help ensure that the schema update performed by the installation program will succeed. To check the synchronization status, enter **LOAD DSREPAIR** at the server console. When DSREPAIR opens, select *Report Synchronization Status*. The synchronization status check should return with no errors.

- Check time synchronization — Checking NDS time synchronization is important because the replication process uses timestamps to keep track of the order in which particular NDS events occur. (An NDS event occurs when you create, modify, or delete an NDS object or property.) Verifying time synchronization helps ensure that the schema update performed by the installation program will succeed. To check the synchronization status, enter **LOAD DSREPAIR** at the server console. When DSREPAIR opens, select *Time Synchronization*. The time synchronization check should return with no errors.

3. Verify storage configuration:

- Bind the Logical Unit Numbers (LUNs) according to manufacturer specifications.

- Check to verify that each server has the correct host bus adapter (HBA) driver installed.

TIP

A large percentage of problems with Novell Cluster Services involve using the incorrect driver for the HBA, or the wrong HBA for the system. You must ensure that the driver matches the topology — using a Point-to-Point driver with a Fibre Channel Arbitrated Loop (FC-AL) HBA will not work! Also, in some cases the HBA was designed for one specific operating system, and it is not certified for NetWare.

- Type `List Devices` from each server console to ensure that the same LUNs can be seen by each server.

- Verify that proper communications occur between the installation PC and each server within the cluster. You can accomplish this in one of two ways: Either use Windows Explorer and map a drive to the SYS volume of each server (this method is preferred, since this creates an NCP connection to each server, which will be over TCP/IP assuming the server only binds TCP/IP), or PING each server's TCP/IP address.

Installing Novell Cluster Services

Once you are sure that all servers in the cluster are properly configured in the SAN and that you have met the requirements of the preinstallation checklist, you are ready to install Novell Cluster Services.

Novell Cluster Services is installed from a workstation. Ensure that this is a high-end workstation with plenty of memory to run the Java-based installation. Be certain that you have an IP connection with every server in the cluster and that all these servers can see the shared storage (use the `List Devices` command at the server console). Then follow these steps:

1. Insert the Novell Cluster Services CD-ROM and run INSTALL.EXE. The NetWare Cluster Services for NetWare 5 Installation dialog box appears.

2. Click Next to begin the installation. The License Agreement Terms and Conditions dialog box appears.

3. Read and accept the license agreement by clicking Accept.

4. In the Novell Cluster Services Action dialog box, make sure Create a New Cluster is selected, and click Next to continue.

5. In the NCS Cluster Selection dialog box shown in Figure 6.1, do the following:

   a. In the Cluster Object Name field, enter a name for the Cluster.

TIP

It's a good idea to use uppercase characters for the cluster name. The cluster name will be used as part of the virtual server name for any cluster-enabled volume. Some applications (such as NDPS) will not recognize lowercase server names as valid. Once named, you currently cannot change the name of the cluster.

   b. In the Directory Services Tree field, enter your NDS tree name.

   c. In the Directory Services Context field, enter or browse to the context in which you wish to create the cluster object.

   d. Click Next to continue.

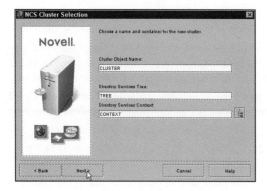

FIGURE 6.1 *NCS Cluster Selection dialog box*

6. Enter authentication credentials and a password. Then wait for the schema to be extended.

7. In the NCS Cluster Node Modification dialog box, shown in Figure 6.2, do the following:

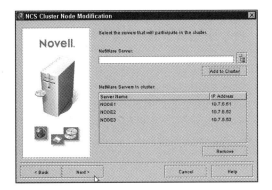

FIGURE 6.2 *NCS Cluster Node Modification dialog box*

a. In the NetWare Server field, either enter the server name or browse and select the NetWare server to add to the cluster, and then click the Add to Cluster button. The installation program will then communicate with the designated server and add it to the NetWare Servers in the cluster list.

TIP

The order in which you add these servers to the list will determine the Node numbers used by Novell Cluster Services. If you have a preference as to which server becomes NODE 1, make sure this is the first node that you add here. Though you can change this later, it is much easier to control here.

b. If the server has multiple network cards bound, you will receive a Select an IP Address dialog box that shows all TCP/IP addresses bound to the server. If you receive this dialog box, select the IP address to use for the heartbeat network, as shown in Figure 6.3, and then click OK. You will be prompted for this address only once, as the installation program will automatically determine the proper address for all subsequent nodes since the heartbeat interface must be on the same TCP/IP subnet.

    c. Repeat Step A for each node you wish to add to the cluster.

    d. After all nodes have been added, click Next to continue.

FIGURE 6.3 *The Select IP Address dialog box*

8. When you add a node to the cluster, Novell Cluster Services installation will verify IP communications to the node, read the devices this node sees, and verify Novell License Service (NLS) installation.

9. Wait for the licensing services to be verified. When this verification is complete, the NCS Shared Media Selection dialog box appears.

10. In the NCS Shared Media Selection dialog box shown in Figure 6.4, do the following:

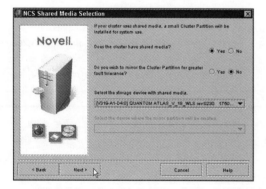

FIGURE 6.4 *NCS Shared Media Selection dialog box*

a. If using shared storage, select Yes for "Does the cluster have shared media?".

b. If using shared media, the drop-down box under "Select the storage device with shared media" should list the SAN devices that all servers have in common. If you do not see a device that you expected to appear here, then at least one server does not see this device. If this is the case, exit the installation and resolve the issue before continuing.

c. If desired, you can also mirror the Split Brain Partition (SBP) by selecting Yes to "Do you wish to mirror the Cluster Partition for greater fault tolerance?".

d. If you are mirroring the SBP to another storage device, then the drop-down box in the "Select the device where the mirror partition will be created" field should show you all the SAN devices that all servers see (except the storage selected above for the SBP). Select the device on which you wish to mirror the SBP.

e. Click Next to continue.

11. Choose either to have Novell Cluster Services automatically reboot all cluster nodes after installation or manually reboot by choosing "Don't reboot newly added or upgraded servers after installation". Then click Next to continue.

WARNING

Try not to reboot more than five nodes at the same time; otherwise, the nodes may lock the Cluster Services partition and may not be able to unlock it, thereby preventing the starting of the cluster.

12. Browse to the location of the Novell Cluster Services licenses, and click Next to continue installation.

13. From the summary screen, select Finish to finish the installation.

14. Novell Cluster Services will make the final determination if the installation requirements are met.

15. When the installation is complete, either click View to view the README file, or click Close to end the installation.

16. Restart each server in the cluster and verify that all nodes join the cluster by viewing the Cluster Membership Monitor screen (see Figure 6.5) on each server console.

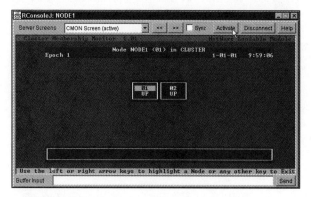

FIGURE 6.5 *The Cluster Membership Monitor screen*

Installing ConsoleOne and the Novell Cluster Services Snapins

Novell Cluster Services requires ConsoleOne for all administrative functions. To administer Novell Cluster Services, you must install ConsoleOne 1.2b or later and install the Cluster Services snapins.

Installing ConsoleOne

Installing ConsoleOne from the Novell Cluster Services installation CD will install both ConsoleOne and the Cluster Services snapins. If you already have ConsoleOne installed, the installation program will detect this and give you the option of either reinstalling everything, or just installing the snapins.

WARNING

The Cluster Services snapins do not function properly from the Windows workstation when using version 1.2c of ConsoleOne. Symptoms of using version 1.2c of ConsoleOne include ConsoleOne's locking up, most notably when accessing streams files such as the load and unload scripts. Though version 1.2c of ConsoleOne does not have any issues when run from the server, the workstation should either use the 1.2b version from the Novell Cluster Services installation CD, or 1.2d or later versions from the Novell Web site.

To install ConsoleOne, follow these steps:

1. Insert the Novell Cluster Services CD into a workstation. Browse to the ConsoleOneInstall directory, and run SETUP.EXE.

2. From the drop-down box, select the language to install.

3. Click Next to continue the installation.

4. Review the license agreement, and click Yes to accept and continue the installation.

5. Browse to where you want to install ConsoleOne. If you wish to install ConsoleOne for server console use, install it to `SYS:PUBLIC\MGMT\CONSOLEONE\1.2`. For workstation installation, installing ConsoleOne to the local hard drive improves performance.

6. If prompted to replace ConsoleOne, either select Yes to replace the existing version, or select No to install only the Cluster Services snapins.

7. Enter the desired program folders for the ConsoleOne icons.

8. Review the installation options, and select Next to continue. ConsoleOne installation will now copy the applicable files.

9. When the installation is complete, click Finish.

Copying the Novell Cluster Services Snapins

Once the Cluster Services snapins are installed, you can copy the snapins to other versions of ConsoleOne without running the installation again. If you installed ConsoleOne to the default location, the snapins will reside in two subdirectory locations:

- `C:\NOVELL\ConsoleOne\1.2\resources\NetWareClusterServices`
- `C:\NOVELL\ConsoleOne\1.2\snapins\NetWareClusterServices`

To apply the snapins to another machine, copy these subdirectories to the corresponding structure on the destination machine. To enable the server version of ConsoleOne, you can install ConsoleOne to the `SYS:\PUBLIC\MGMT\ConsoleOne\1.2` location, or simply copy the snapins from your local installation to the corresponding directory structure on the server.

Adding a New Novell Cluster Services Node

When you install a new NetWare 5.*x* server into the SAN, it is vitally important that the server not be attached to the SAN during the server installation routine. When you perform a new installation, the NetWare 5.*x* installation program by default prompts the user to delete all NetWare partitions that it detects. If the administrator is not careful, all data on the SAN can be destroyed.

Install new servers with the Fibre Channel card installed into the server, but not connected to the SAN. Do not connect the server to the SAN until the server is fully patched, after you have verified you are using the correct HBA driver for the Fibre Channel card.

After the server has been installed and patched, attach the server to the SAN and run the Novell Cluster Services installation program, selecting the option to add a node to the cluster. Refer back to the preinstallation checklist earlier in this chapter for the items you should check before installing — as they also apply to adding a new node.

Once you have run the installation program and added the new node, restart it to have it properly join the cluster. Finally, modify all of your resources to include this newly added node in the failover paths. Depending on the applications in your cluster, you might also need to install other applications (such as NDPS and the Enterprise Web Server) to have the necessary NLMs on the SYS volume.

Adding a New Volume to a Cluster

With Novell Cluster Services 1.01 and newer versions, you can create an NSS volume and have this volume immediately available to other nodes in the cluster. However, it is not always apparent that the volume is available. Entering **NSS VOLUMES** at the server console on nodes where the volume was not created generally will not show these volumes as existing.

When this occurs, you can restart NSS, or you can enter **NSS /ACTIVATE=<Volume>**, where **<Volume>** is the name of the newly created volume. The volume should activate even though **NSS VOLUMES** did not show it as available. Once activated, you can enter the **NSS VOLUMES** command and see the newly added volume.

TIP

Novell recommends that most NSS volume operations occur with only one node running and the other nodes down. This recommendation stems from the danger of performing an NSS operation on a server that doesn't have the current view of the NSS partitions and volumes. If you choose to

disregard this recommendation, designate a single node to use for all NSS operations. Though this does not protect you against all dangers, it does improve the chances that the server performing the NSS operation will have the current view of the storage. NetWare 5.1 Support Pack 3 in conjunction with Novell Cluster Services Support Pack 2 provides a mechanism to update all nodes of volume operations done on any node in the cluster. Even so, it is still a good idea to perform all of your volume operations from a designated node, just to error on the safe side.

Novell recommends that you perform a CLUSTER LEAVE and a DOWN on all nodes in the cluster except one prior to adding an additional volume. The reason for this is the danger of adding a new volume from NODE 1 and then adding another new volume from NODE 2 before it recognizes that the free space no longer exists. It is possible for two servers to attempt to allocate the same space for two different volumes, which will cause corruption.

Adding Space to an Existing Cluster Volume

To add free space to an existing volume (whether cluster-enabled or not), you may need to first offline the resource that uses the volume, and deactivate the volume. Failure to offline the volume prior to expanding may result in file system corruption. (Novell is aware of this issue and has fixed it with NetWare 5.1 Support Pack 3.)

Do not modify volume sizes with the volumes online unless you have applied NetWare 5.1 Support Pack 3 or later with Novell Cluster Services Support Pack 2 or later.

WARNING

When NSS loads, it automatically "loads" all existing NSS volume information into memory. If you expand a volume on one node in the cluster, then migrate (or fail) this to another cluster node that reads the volume information prior to the expansion, the new node will read the volume as corrupt and attempt to repair it. Since it does not have the current volume information, it will repair the volume with stale information, which will cause file system corruption (Novell is currently working on a patch for this issue as well). Based on these facts, use the following procedure to expand an existing volume:

1. Execute a CLUSTER DOWN to bring down the cluster.

2. Execute a DOWN command on every node except one. If you have an NDS master replica of the cluster partition in the cluster, it is best to select that server as the server to remain online.

3. Perform the volume operation on the remaining node.

4. Bring the other servers back online.

These procedures might be more dramatic than desired, but they do ensure data integrity. It would also be possible to perform this operation with the other nodes online and NSS unloaded (in a cluster-leave state); then you would reload NSS and rejoin the cluster after the volume operation.

NOTE   At the time of this writing, Novell is aware of the issues regarding expanding an NSS volume while it is active, and has corrected this issue with NetWare 5.1 Support Pack 3 and Novell Cluster Services Support Pack 2. If you have not yet applied these patches, be sure you don't perform volume-sizing operations while the volume is online.

Removing a Novell Cluster Services Node

To remove a cluster node without uninstalling Novell Cluster Services from the entire cluster, follow these steps:

1. On the server you wish to remove from the cluster, type `Cluster Leave` at the server console prompt.

2. On the server you wish to remove from the cluster, type `ULDNCS` at the server console prompt.

3. Remove the `LDNCS` statement from the server's `AUTOEXEC.NCF` file.

TIP   Review the node number of the node you are about to remove. If you later decide to reinstall clustering on this node, you can have it resume its role by reusing this number and its IP address.

4. Launch ConsoleOne, and browse to the container that contains the Cluster object. Select the Cluster object in the left pane of ConsoleOne.

5. In the right pane of ConsoleOne, right-click the Cluster Node object representing the node you wish to remove, then click Delete NDS Object (as shown in Figure 6.6).

▶ · ◀

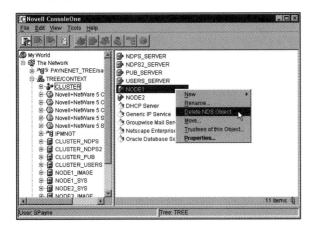

FIGURE 6.6 *Select and delete the Cluster Node object.*

6. Delete the following NLMs and files from the server you are removing in the SYS:SYSTEM directory:

- CLSTRLIB.NLM

- GIPC.NLM

- SBD.NLM

- SBDLIB.NLM

- CRM.NLM

- CMA.NLM

- TRUSTMIG.NLM

- CMON.NLM

- LDNSC.NCF

- ULDNCS.NCF

- _LDNCS.NCF

- _ULDNSC.NCF

- VLL.NLM

- TRUSTOOL.NLM

7. Review all of your cluster resources and modify the assigned nodes as required to account for the node you removed.

8. Remove the node's connection to the shared storage.

WARNING If you remove a server from the cluster, but the server still has access to the SAN, you face the danger of this server mounting a volume while another server has it mounted. Novell Cluster Services prevents cluster nodes from mounting a volume while another cluster node has it mounted, but does not protect against noncluster nodes. If two servers mount and write to the same volume concurrently, file system corruption *will* occur. We strongly recommend preventing the server (or any server without Novell Cluster Services installed) from accessing the shared storage if you remove it from the cluster.

Removing a Volume from a Cluster

Just as the other nodes will not know when an NSS volume is resized, they will also be unaware of the deletion of an NSS volume on the SAN. To avoid that problem, the recommended procedure for deleting a cluster-enabled volume is as follows:

1. Execute a CLUSTER DOWN on one server in the cluster to bring down the cluster.

2. Execute a DOWN command on every node except one. If you have an NDS master replica of the cluster partition in the cluster, it is best to choose that server as the server to remain online.

3. Using NSS Menu or NWCONFIG.NLM, delete the NSS volume (optionally, you may want to release ownership as well if you will not be later assigning the free space to another NSS volume).

4. Using ConsoleOne, delete the cluster resource object for the cluster-enabled volume. This will also delete the Virtual NCP Server and the NDS Volume object.

5. Bring the other servers back online.

While it is rare to delete volumes from a cluster (volumes seem to grow and grow, but rarely shrink), following this procedure will safely remove a cluster-enabled volume resource and its NSS volume, allowing you to reuse this space for another purpose.

Adding or Changing a Heartbeat Network after Novell Cluster Services Installation

The easiest way to configure the heartbeat network is to have both the heartbeat and the production network cards bound when installing Novell Cluster Services. When the installation program detects multiple IP addresses bound to the same server, it will prompt you to select which address (subnet) will be used for the heartbeat network and automatically configure the cluster parameters on all nodes for this subnet.

If you didn't configure the heartbeat network when you installed Novell Cluster Services, it is possible to change this after installation. To change the heartbeat network, follow these steps:

1. At the server console prompt from one node in the cluster, type CLUSTER DOWN.

2. Launch ConsoleOne and browse to the context that contains your cluster container object.

3. Select the cluster container object in the left pane and then right-click the first cluster node on the right pane and select Details. The Cluster Node Properties screen appears (see Figure 6.7).

4. Modify the IP address of the node (be sure to keep the node number the same) to reflect the new address to be used for the heartbeat network.

5. Repeat steps 2 through 4 for each node in the cluster.

6. Right-click the cluster container object, then select Details.

7. Select the Protocol tab, and then select Cluster Protocol Internals. The Cluster Protocol Internals page appears (see Figure 6.8).

8. In the "# Node number + IP address mapping table" section, verify that all nodes reflect the modified heartbeat network. If required, modify these parameters, and then click OK.

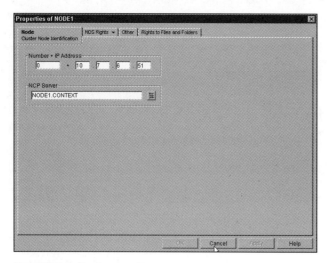

FIGURE 6.7 *Cluster Node properties*

9. At each server console prompt, enter CLUSTER JOIN to restart the cluster using the new heartbeat network.

Properties of CLUSTER

| Quorum | **Protocol** | ▼ | Port | NDS Rights | ▼ | Other | Rights to Files and Folders |

Cluster Protocol Internals

```
# CICP Protocol Parameters
# Generated by Orion GUI at Sun Nov 26 14:39:52 PST 2000

panning clusterid -145318271

heartbeat rate_usecs 1000000
censustaker tolerance 8000000
sequencer master_watchdog 1000000
sequencer slave_watchdog 8000000
sequencer retrans_max 30

# Node number + IP address mapping table

nodeid 10.7.6.51 0
nodeid 10.7.6.52 1

# End of CICP Protocol Parameters
```

| OK | Cancel | Apply | Help |

FIGURE 6.8 *Cluster Protocol Internals page*

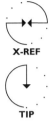

X-REF

For more information about Novell Cluster Services heartbeats, refer to Chapters 4 and 5.

TIP

The IP forwarding interference with client reconnections was resolved with NetWare 5.1 Support Pack 2A or later—if you are using the current NetWare Support Pack, you may safely enable IP forwarding on your cluster nodes. However, many administrators still prefer not to enable IP forwarding on a server that does not need to route. Why add the overhead to support routing if not needed?

Should You Have a Dedicated Heartbeat Network?

A question often asked is whether or not a heartbeat network should be configured. The easy answer to this question is "it depends." Choosing to include a heartbeat network involves many factors, and each environment has different criteria that you need to consider when making a decision.

Currently, Novell Cluster Services will perform the heartbeat only on a single subnet (future versions of the software will allow multiple heartbeat networks). Because you can heartbeat over only one network card, using a heartbeat network will not detect a fault in the nonheartbeat network's NIC. Many administrators find this unacceptable and do not use a heartbeat network based on this fact alone.

Another drawback to the heartbeat network is that the ConsoleOne cluster administration workstation must either be on the heartbeat network or at a minimum have a configured route to the heartbeat network. Since the heartbeat network is typically a dedicated network connected only to the cluster nodes, this would require that at least one node has IP forwarding enabled. Since enabling IP forwarding can interfere with client reconnections, such an arrangement can affect the automatic failover of drive mappings, and provides another reason why many choose to avoid a heartbeat network.

Because of these reasons, you, too, might decide to implement Novell Cluster Services without a heartbeat network. However, after implementing, you may find that the production LAN becomes too saturated at times, which prevents the heartbeat packets from reaching their destinations, which in turn causes false poison pills. The greater the number of clients connecting to the cluster, the more likely this event will occur, and the more likely you will require a heartbeat network.

Uninstalling Novell Cluster Services

Uninstalling Novell Cluster Services is relatively easy, but does have major ramifications when shared storage is used. Novell Cluster Services 1.01 and later versions include a feature that prevents two servers from mounting the same volume at the same time (as long as the clustering software is running, even if the node has not joined the cluster). This multimount protection is critical for ensuring data integrity—if two servers write to the same volume while both servers have it mounted, data corruption will occur.

If you uninstall Novell Cluster Services, you will lose this multimount protection, and you should take other precautions to prevent mounting the same volume on multiple servers. Perhaps the best way to do this is by using zoning at the switch, which would allow only specific servers to see specific virtual disks on the shared storage. This requires prior planning—if you set the SAN up as a single virtual disk with multiple volumes, it is too late to think about zoning!

If you still wish to uninstall Novell Cluster Services from all nodes in the cluster, follow the steps in the section titled "Removing a Novell Cluster Services Node," earlier in this chapter, on each node in the cluster. Next, delete all remaining NDS objects for the cluster, including the cluster container.

Once you have fully removed Novell Cluster Services, you will probably want to determine which servers will host the volumes in the SAN. You will need to mount these volumes on the appropriate nodes, then use NWCONFIG.NLM to upgrade mounted volumes into the Directory to re-create the NDS volume objects for the volumes. To help prevent multiple mounts of these volumes, modify the AUTOEXEC.NCF files on each server to include the NSS /AutoDeactivateVolume= All command and remove the MOUNT ALL command. Then add the appropriate commands to activate and mount only the appropriate volumes for the appropriate server.

WARNING We know of several sites that made the decision to use a SAN without Novell Cluster Services, even knowing the risk of data corruption by multiple mounts of the volumes. Several of these sites inadvertently caused data corruption even though they were aware of this danger. We strongly recommend using Novell Cluster Services or zoning to prevent multiple servers from mounting the same volumes.

Summary

In this chapter, you learned the hardware and software installation prerequisites for Novell Cluster Services. You learned how to install Novell Cluster Services, the Novell Cluster Services ConsoleOne snapins, and how to copy these snapins for use at other workstations or from the server. Finally, we covered postinstallation tasks, such as adding or removing a node from the cluster, and uninstalling Novell Cluster Services. Taken together, these steps should help you both prepare for and execute your own installation of Novell Cluster Services.

## CHAPTER 7

Managing Novell Cluster Services

Once you know the basics about Novell Cluster Services, you are ready for this chapter, which leads you through managing the cluster using ConsoleOne and the various clustering console commands.

Chapter 6 explains how to install Novell Cluster Services and ConsoleOne with the clustering snapins. Installation is obviously a prerequisite for managing your cluster, so if you haven't already installed your cluster and ConsoleOne (with the snapins), you probably want to do so before going through this chapter.

The chapter begins by walking you through the ConsoleOne interface, starting with the Cluster Container object and the cluster-wide configuration options. The chapter covers the various states the cluster can be in, and what these states signify, as well as how to document your cluster-wide configuration. Next, the chapter discusses the NDS management of your cluster node objects, and why you might need to modify your node configuration.

After you learn about managing your cluster and nodes, you explore how to manage the actual cluster resources. This includes an explanation of the resource states, and what these states signify.

The chapter concludes with several command-line (server) console commands you use in conjunction with Novell Cluster Services and the optional clustering statistical tools available to help monitor your cluster heartbeat performance.

Using ConsoleOne to Manage the Cluster

You perform the vast majority of your cluster management using Novell's ConsoleOne utility. Novell Cluster Services ships with version 1.2b of ConsoleOne, but it is highly recommended that you upgrade to at least version 1.2d (Version 1.2d.1, dated 11/30/2000, was used for much of the writing of this book.) Version 1.2d contains many enhancements—most importantly, a major performance increase. Version 1.2d also fixes a problem found in 1.2c that causes the application to crash when writing to streams files, such as the load and unload scripts. If you install ConsoleOne using the Novell Cluster Services CD, and then upgrade to the latest version from www.novell.com/download, your Cluster Services snapins will remain intact. Or, you can follow the instructions in Chapter 6 to apply the snapins after you already have a later version of ConsoleOne installed.

Perhaps the best advice we can give you regarding learning how to manage your cluster is that Novell Cluster Services is "not your typical NetWare." Seasoned network administrators must fight the urge to go to the server console and "fix" any problems—you must get used to using ConsoleOne to manage your cluster resources. Novell Cluster Services assumes that the resources are in the state, on the cluster, that the software put them in—it does not continually monitor for manual interventions and adjust for them.

One example that illustrates this point is an administrator who manually migrates volumes from one server to another. This administrator thinks, "Hmm, all I need to do is dismount the volume, deactivate the volume, remove the IP address, then do the reverse on the server I want to move the volume to." Unfortunately, he or she forgets some of the cluster commands, such as the NUDP command, which tells the server to answer calls for the virtual server, or even more importantly, the TRUSTMIG command. Suddenly, the administrator discovers he or she has no trustee assignments—all because he or she forgot to migrate the trustees! This is perhaps the number one cause of the cluster "losing all trustees"—an administrator manually moves a volume, doesn't migrate the trustees, and then the software cannot automatically migrate the trustees.

Never manually migrate any resources once they are configured in the cluster. Always use ConsoleOne to move resources.

TIP

Additionally, if you manually migrate a resource without using ConsoleOne, then the cluster no longer has an accurate view of where the resources are. If the node you migrate the resource to fails, the resource is not automatically started on another node, since the cluster does not think it was affected.

So, you promise to always use ConsoleOne to manage your resources, right?

Managing Cluster-Wide Parameters

The Cluster Container object for your cluster holds many cluster-wide configuration parameters, which control aspects such as the heartbeat interval and tolerance, the node IP addresses, and so on. This section of the chapter discusses all of the configuration options of the cluster container. To begin configuring any of these parameters, launch ConsoleOne, browse for your Cluster Container object, right-click it, and then select Properties.

See Chapter 4 for a detailed discussion of the Novell Cluster Services architecture and parameters.

X-REF

Configuring the Quorum Trigger Properties

Quorum triggers tell the cluster when it is allowed to begin starting the cluster resources once a specific (configurable) portion of the cluster is brought online or a specific amount of time (configurable) passes. The purpose of configuring a quorum is to prevent the first node that joins the cluster from starting all of the cluster resources before the other cluster nodes have had a chance to join the cluster. Quorum consists of two components: quorum membership and quorum timeout, which are discussed in the next two sections. Quorum is considered reached when the first of these two components has been met. Both of these parameters are configured on the Quorum Properties page of the Cluster Container object, as shown in Figure 7.1.

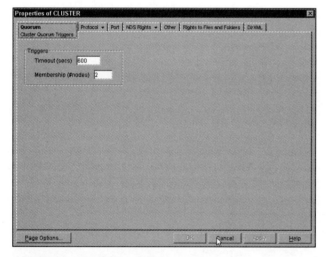

FIGURE 7.1 *Quorum properties*

Remember that quorum matters only when the entire cluster is stopped and then restarted. If three nodes leave the cluster (even if that leaves the remaining nodes below the configured quorum), when these nodes rejoin the cluster quorum is irrelevant because the cluster is still running. Because quorum matters only when the cluster is restarted, any change you make to the quorum parameters doesn't actually take effect until you restart the entire cluster. That doesn't mean that you must immediately restart the cluster when you change the quorum properties — they will be considered the next time the cluster is restarted.

Setting Quorum Membership   The *quorum membership* is the number of nodes that must join the cluster before cluster resources are allowed to load. The value of the quorum membership defaults to the number of nodes you had when you first installed the cluster—if you installed a five-node cluster, the quorum membership is set to five, meaning resources will not start until all five nodes join the cluster (or until quorum timeout is reached).

You should always leave the quorum membership at a value greater than one to prevent one node from starting all of the cluster resources. Typically, you should configure the quorum membership to be equal to the number of nodes in the cluster so that when the cluster starts, all resources start on their preferred node.

Setting Quorum Timeout   *Quorum timeout* specifies the amount of time the cluster waits to reach quorum membership before it starts the cluster resources anyway. Once the timeout has been reached, the nodes that have joined the cluster start loading the cluster resources even if the quorum membership has not yet been achieved.

For example, if you have a 32-node cluster with the quorum set to 32 and the quorum timeout left at the default of 60 seconds, resources will begin loading after 60 seconds even if only three nodes have joined the cluster.

Though Novell does not have an official recommendation for the quorum timeout, in most environments, 60 seconds is not sufficient. If you have a five-node cluster and you need to restart all five nodes, you probably won't be able to restart the five nodes within a minute of each other (it's easy to get distracted somewhere in the middle of restarting clusters), which means that the timeout will pass too soon. You may want to try something like 300 seconds. Remember, setting quorum timeout this way does not mean that the resources won't start for five minutes—it only means that if the quorum membership is not achieved within five minutes, then the resources start. If the quorum membership is achieved in one minute, then the resources will at that time—they don't wait for the timeout.

Configuring the Cluster Protocol Properties

Several parameters make up the Cluster Protocol or heartbeat settings. All of these protocol properties are configured in the Cluster Container object, on the Protocol Properties page shown in Figure 7.2.

The Heartbeat Setting   As discussed in Chapter 4, each of the slave nodes sends a unicast packet to the master node telling the master that they are alive. This packet is called the *heartbeat*, and the frequency of these packets is configured as the *heartbeat parameter*. Under most circumstances, leave this set to the default of one second.

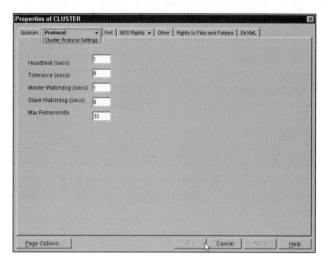

FIGURE 7.2 *Cluster Protocol properties page*

The Tolerance Setting   The *tolerance setting* tells the master node how long to wait between hearing from a slave node before assuming the node has failed and beginning the process of verifying that the node has failed and removing it from the cluster. The tolerance setting is also used to compute how often the nodes perform a heartbeat to the shared storage — they will heartbeat to the storage at a rate equal to one-half of the tolerance setting.

Never set the tolerance lower than the heartbeat! If this is done at one client, it makes it impossible for any node except the master to stay in the cluster. The tolerance does not specify how many missed packets to

WARNING   **wait, but rather a time in seconds.**

The Master Watchdog Setting   As discussed in Chapter 4, the master node sends a multicast packet to all slave nodes informing them that it is alive. The Master Watchdog setting tells the master node how often to send this packet. Typically, this is set to the same interval as the heartbeat setting.

The Slave Watchdog Setting   Perhaps this setting should have been called the Master Watchdog Tolerance, as it tells the slave nodes how tolerant they should be in receiving the master watchdog packet before they start the process of verifying that the master has failed, ejecting it from the cluster, and voting for a new master.

NOTE   It really isn't a fair vote—the new master node is selected based on its heartbeat IP address. When the master node fails, the node in the remaining cluster that has the highest TCP/IP address will become the new master.

The Max Retransmits Setting   The Max Retransmits setting controls the maximum number of multicasts the GIPC process attempts during the two-phase commit process to receive the required ACK (acknowledgement) from all nodes before it gives up and tells all the nodes not to commit the transaction.

Viewing the Cluster Internals Page

The information shown on the Cluster Internals page is computed from settings set elsewhere in the cluster, and should be treated as read-only information. The following sections briefly discuss the information on this page, but it's recommended that you don't actually change any configurations here. Figure 7.3 shows a sample Cluster Protocol Internals page.

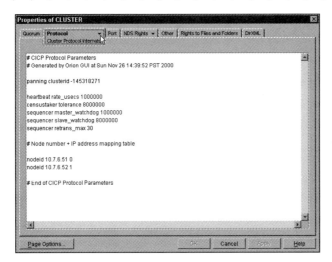

FIGURE 7.3 *Cluster Protocol Internals page*

panning clusterID   The `panning clusterID` is the unique identifier for this particular cluster. It is used by the cluster protocols to determine which cluster the communications pertain to in the event there are multiple clusters on the same subnet.

heartbeat rate_usecs This is calculated based on the Heartbeat setting configured on the Protocol page. The heartbeat rate is the interval in which the slave nodes send their unicast "I'm alive" packets to the master node.

censustaker tolerance This is calculated based on the Tolerance Setting configured on the Protocol page. The censustaker tolerance is the amount of time the master node will wait between hearing from a slave node and assuming the slave node has stopped responding.

sequencer master_watchdog This is calculated based on the Master Watchdog setting configured on the Protocol page. This is the interval in which the master sends its multicast packets to the slave nodes, telling them it is alive.

sequencer slave_watchdog This is calculated based on the Slave Watchdog setting configured on the Protocol page. This is the amount of time the slave nodes will wait to hear from the master node before they assume that the master has stopped responding.

sequencer retrans_max This is calculated based on the Max Retransmits setting configured on the Protocol page. This setting controls the maximum number of multicasts that the GIPC process attempts during the two-phase commit process to receive and acknowledge before backing out an incomplete transaction.

nodeid The `nodeids` show each cluster node's TCP/IP address used for the heartbeat, as well as a node number (beginning at 0). The information here is taken from the cluster node objects — if you change the information on a cluster node object, it will be reflected here as well.

TIP

If you change a node number, you must manually go back through all of your resource assignments and modify the assigned nodes. For example, if you change what was node 3 to be node 4, and you go back to the resources that specified node 3, they will not reflect the change you just made to the node numbers. This might result in resources not being available because the nodes they are now assigned to don't have the right support files.

Modifying the Cluster Management TCP Port

By default, Novell Cluster Services uses port 7023 for the cluster services communications. As long as you don't have some other resource on one of the nodes using this port, you should not have any reason to change the port number. However, should you need to change this, it is configured on the Cluster Container object, on the Port property page, as shown in Figure 7.4.

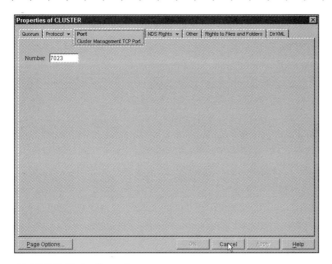

FIGURE 7.4 *Cluster Port property page*

Monitoring Cluster States

ConsoleOne offers two views of the cluster container. So far this chapter has discussed the configuration done using the default Console View, which allows you to configure the cluster resources, cluster nodes, and cluster container. The second view is the Cluster State View, which allows you to actually manage where the resources are running in the cluster, as well as view the current state of the cluster and its resources.

To change to Cluster State View, select the Cluster Container object, then from the menu, select View ⇨ Cluster State. The Cluster State View is divided into three sections, as shown in Figure 7.5.

The left pane shows the NDS tree view, although if you click any of the objects in this pane, ConsoleOne will select that object and automatically change back to the Console View.

The upper-right pane is the status pane, which graphically shows the state of the cluster, all nodes in the cluster, and the percentage of nodes and resources that are currently available.

A green node with a yellow dot in it signifies the current cluster master node.

NOTE

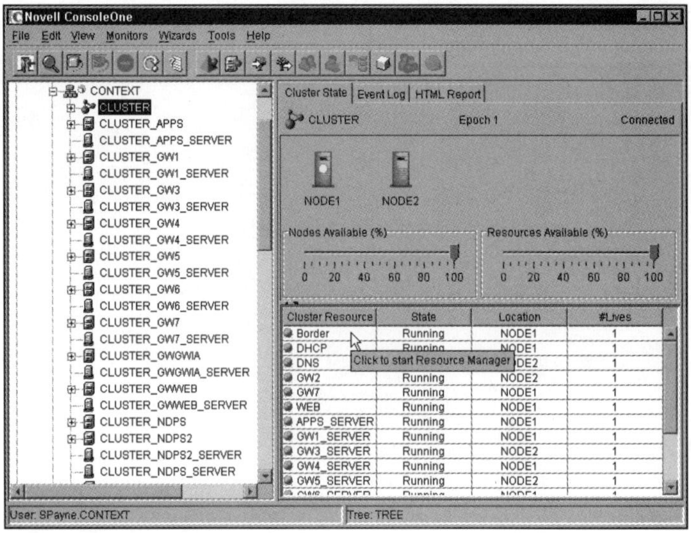

FIGURE 7.5 *Cluster State View*

The cluster nodes can be in any one of the three states shown in Table 7.1.

TABLE 7.1		
Cluster Node States		
STATE	**ICON COLOR**	**DESCRIPTION**
Normal/Joined	Green	This is the normal operating condition for a cluster node, and signifies that the node is available to run cluster resources.
Failed	Red	The cluster node experienced a failure.
Left	Gray	The node has not joined the cluster, or it has left the cluster. The node is not available to service cluster resources.

The lower-right pane shows each cluster resource, the state of that resource, the node the resource is currently active on (if applicable), and the number of lives that resource has (or the number of times the resource has been started on any node since the cluster has been running).

The Cluster State View also has three properties pages, including the cluster state, the event log, and the HTML report. You find the tabs for these in the upper-right pane of the Cluster State View.

Viewing/Printing the Activity Log

To view the Activity log, click the Event Log tab in the upper-right pane of the Cluster State View, shown in Figure 7.6. You cannot directly print from this view, but you can click the Save button to save this view as an HTML file, which you can later print.

► · ◄

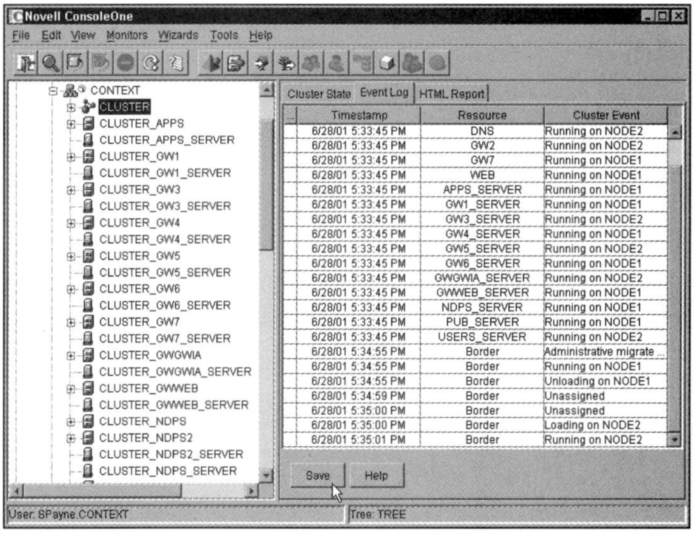

FIGURE 7.6 *Event Log View*

Viewing/Printing All Cluster Configurations

To view the entire cluster configuration, including the configuration of all cluster resources, click the HTML Report tab in the upper-right pane of the Cluster State View, shown in Figure 7.7. You cannot directly print from this view, but you can click the Save button to save this view as an HTML file, which you can later print. The HTML file includes hyperlinks so that you can quickly browse between various components of the report.

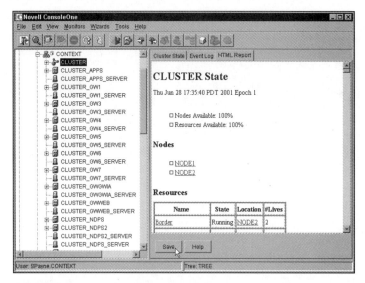

FIGURE 7.7 *HTML Report View*

TIP

Any time you add or modify a cluster resource, be sure to print the HTML Report—this provides an excellent way to document the configuration of your cluster.

Using ConsoleOne to Manage Cluster Nodes

Each cluster node object represents a single node of the cluster and has two attributes that you might want to modify—the node number and the node IP address. To modify these, right-click the cluster node object, then select Properties. In the Node page shown in Figure 7.8, you can modify the node number or IP address as desired, then click OK.

NOTE

The cluster node object is located in the cluster container and looks just like an NCP server object with an added red dot.

If you change the node address of a cluster node, you must manually modify all of the cluster resources that were assigned to this node. The cluster does not dynamically update the cluster resources to reflect the node number change made here.

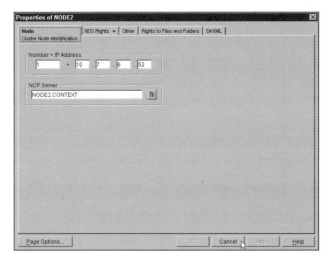

FIGURE 7.8 *Cluster Node properties*

Before you renumber your cluster, be sure you understand the consequences to your cluster resources when changing the node number.

WARNING

The IP address reflected in the cluster node object is the address used for the cluster heartbeat protocols. If you wish to change the subnet used for the heartbeat, you must modify the node address for all nodes in the cluster to reflect this change, and then restart the cluster.

Using ConsoleOne to Manage Resources

Once your resources are configured, you utilize ConsoleOne to manage the resources in your cluster. Managing resources includes (but is not limited to) the following four tasks:

▸ Monitoring resource states
▸ Bringing a resource online

▸ Bringing a resource offline

▸ Migrating resources to a different node

Monitoring Resource States

Figure 7.5 showed you the Cluster State View using ConsoleOne. This is the view that you use to manage the resource states. Cluster resource states are visible in the lower-right of the Cluster State View, and Table 7.2 shows the nine possible states your resources can have.

TABLE 7.2

Cluster Resource States

RESOURCE STATE	DESCRIPTION
Unassigned	All of the cluster nodes that the resource is assigned to are not currently available.
Offline	The resource has been shut down by an administrator.
Loading	The cluster load script is currently executing.
Unloading	The cluster unload script is currently executing.
Comatose	A runtime failure has been detected, generally during either the load or unload script execution.
Running	This is the normal operational condition — the resource is currently running on one of the cluster nodes.
Alert	The resource is awaiting administrative intervention. This generally occurs when failover or failback is set to manual.
NDS Sync	The resource is waiting for NDS to synchronize a change to the resource and for the master node to notify the slave nodes of the NDS change.
Quorum Wait	The resource is waiting for the cluster to achieve quorum.

Bringing a Resource Online

If the cluster resource is in the offline state, you can bring the resource online by performing the following steps:

1. From the Cluster State View, click the resource to start the cluster resource manager. The Resource Manager dialog box appears.

2. Click the online button. The Resource Manager dialog box will go away, and the cluster resource should go from the loading state to the online state.

The resource automatically starts on its most preferred node, or the node that appears first in the node list.

Bringing a Resource Offline

If the cluster resource is Running or Comatose, you can bring the resource offline by performing the following steps:

1. From the Cluster State View, click the resource to start the cluster resource manager.

2. From the Cluster Resource Manager dialog box, click the offline button.

Migrating Resources to a Different Node

If the cluster resource is in the Running state, you can migrate the resource to a different node by performing the following steps:

1. From the Cluster State View, click the resource to start the cluster resource manager.

2. From the Cluster Resource Manager dialog box, shown in Figure 7.9, select one of the available nodes in the list.

FIGURE 7.9 *Cluster Resource Manager dialog box*

NOTE

Only the nodes in the resource preferred node list that are currently in the Normal/Joined state appear in the Resource Manager dialog box. If there is only one node available, your list will only include that node.

3. Click the Migrate button.

Using Novell Cluster Services Server Console Commands

In addition to the management functions in ConsoleOne, there are many console commands that you might need to use to manage your cluster. These include the following categories of commands:

- Cluster commands
- NUDP commands
- CVSBIND commands
- Split Brain Detector (SBD) commands
- TCP/IP commands
- Novell Storage Services (NSS) commands
- Trustee ID Migration (TRUSTMIG) commands
- TRUSTOOL commands

This section briefly lists and discusses each of these types of commands.

Cluster Commands

Five different cluster commands are available: HELP CLUSTER, CLUSTER DOWN, CLUSTER LEAVE, CLUSTER JOIN, and CLUSTER VIEW. In addition, several tracing commands are available to help trace various activities at the VI Architecture Link Layer (VIA) of the cluster architecture.

HELP CLUSTER

The HELP CLUSTER command simply displays all of the CLUSTER commands available to the administrator.

CLUSTER DOWN

The CLUSTER DOWN command takes all nodes out of the cluster. This has the same effect as typing CLUSTER LEAVE on all nodes at the same time. This does not actually down the servers, but simply takes them out of the cluster membership. Although this is executed on only one node in the cluster, because all nodes perform a cluster leave, all resources are brought offline without being migrated to any other node.

CLUSTER LEAVE

The CLUSTER LEAVE command takes a node out of the cluster. All resources running on the node are migrated to other nodes before the command completes. The server DOWN command implicitly calls CLUSTER LEAVE if the server is a member of the cluster, so anytime you DOWN a cluster node, it first performs the CLUSTER LEAVE process.

CLUSTER JOIN

The CLUSTER JOIN command requests that a node join the cluster. Once a member of the cluster, it becomes eligible to execute cluster resources.

CLUSTER VIEW

The CLUSTER VIEW command displays the current cluster membership, as shown in Figure 7.10.

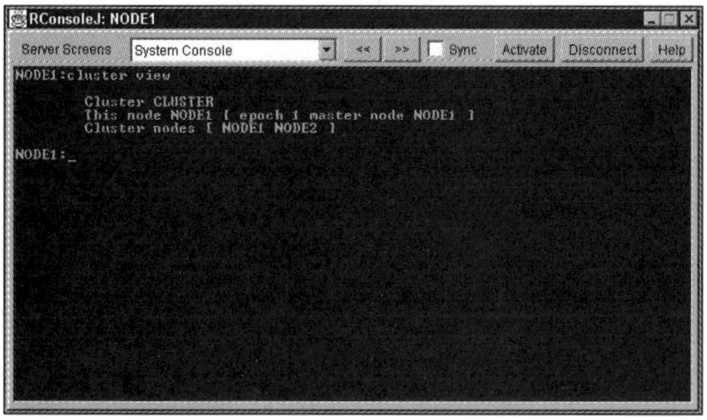

FIGURE 7.10 *CLUSTER VIEW command*

CLUSTER TRACE SBD ON|OFF

The `CLUSTER TRACE SBD ON|OFF` command causes the cluster VLL module to echo Split Brain Detection information to the server console. This reflects information that is sent from the SBD module up to the VI Architecture Link Layer (VIA).

CLUSTER TRACE MCAST ON|OFF

The `CLUSTER TRACE MCAST ON|OFF` command causes the cluster to echo multicast events to the server console.

CLUSTER TRACE GIPC ON|OFF

The `CLUSTER TRACE GIPC ON|OFF` command causes the cluster to echo GIPC events to the server console.

CLUSTER TRACE ON|OFF

The `CLUSTER TRACE ON|OFF` command causes the cluster to echo general cluster events to the server console.

CLUSTER VLL GROUPS

The `CLUSTER VLL GROUPS` command causes the cluster to display a list of clustering multicast groups and status information.

CLUSTER VLL STATS

The `CLUSTER VLL STATS` command causes the cluster to display VLL multicast statistics.

NUDP Commands

The NUDP process causes a physical server to answer requests made for virtual file servers. These commands are typically executed in cluster resource load and unload scripts and are automatically added to the cluster resource that is created when you create a cluster-enabled volume. The commands are required if you wish to have clients automatically retain their drive mappings to cluster-enabled volumes when the volume is migrated to a different node in the cluster.

TIP

Currently there can only be a single virtual server assigned to each cluster-enabled volume. You cannot use multiple NUDP commands to bind multiple virtual servers to the same resource.

NUDP ADD *VirtualServerName IPAddress*

The NUDP ADD `VirtualServerName IPAddress` command binds the virtual server named `VirtualServerName` to this physical server with the IP address specified. For example:

NUDP ADD CLUSTER_GW1_SERVER 10.7.5.105

This command causes the physical server that the command is executed on to respond to IP address 10.7.5.105 (which must be bound to the server) using the virtual server named CLUSTER_GW1_SERVER.

NUDP DEL *VirtualServerName IPAddress*

The NUDP DEL `VirtualServerName IPAddress` command unbinds the virtual server named `VirtualServerName` from this physical server with the IP address specified. For example:

NUDP DEL CLUSTER_GW1_SERVER 10.7.5.105

This command causes the physical server that the command is executed on to stop responding to IP address 10.7.5.105 using the virtual server named CLUSTER_GW1_SERVER.

NUPD DISPLAY

The NUPD DISPLAY command displays all the virtual servers bound to the physical server it is executed on.

CVSBIND Commands

Novell Cluster Services versions 1.0 and 1.01 do not propagate virtual server information into SLP by default (the next version of clustering will automatically add this support). Where the NUDP command tells the server to answer a virtual server request, the CVSBIND command actually causes the virtual server to be advertised via SLP.

We strongly recommend using CVSBIND for all of your cluster-enabled volumes. The primary advantage of using CVSBIND is that it will give you TCP/IP short name resolution regardless of user context or DNS zone. This allows UNC paths to be valid using only the short names of the virtual server.

If you wish to propagate virtual server information to SLP, download the CVSBIND (http://support.novell.com/cgi-bin/search/searchtid.cgi?/ 2957434.htm) utility. After installing the utility according to the instructions, the CVSBIND commands will be available.

CVSBIND ADD   This command adds the virtual server into the bindery.novell SLP service within your existing SLP infrastructure. For example:

```
CVSBIND ADD <NAME> <IP ADDRESS>
```

where `<NAME>` represents the name of the virtual server, and `<IP ADDRESS>` is the address of this virtual server.

CVSBIND DEL   The `CVSBIND DEL Name IPAddress` command stops advertising the virtual server named *Name* from SLP. For example:

```
CVSBIND DEL <NAME> <IP ADDRESS>
```

where `<NAME>` represents the name of the virtual server, and `<IP ADDRESS>` is the address of this virtual server.

Split Brain Detector Commands

Novell Cluster Services provides two Split Brain Detector (SBD) commands to view the Split Brain Detector partition status: `SBD VIEW` and `SBD VIEW ALL`. In addition, there is an `SBD TRACE` command, which echoes SBD information to the server console screen.

SBD VIEW

The `SBD VIEW` command displays the scratch pad area used by the SBD module assigned to this cluster node.

SBD VIEW ALL

The `SBD VIEW ALL` command displays the scratch pad area used by the SBD module to detect split brains. This command can be used to verify that an SBD module is operational on this node and/or remote nodes.

SBD TRACE

The `SBD TRACE` command displays SBD activity to the server console screen. This is information seen by the SBD module running on the cluster node.

TCP/IP Address Commands

Though these TCP/IP Address commands are not new commands implemented just for Novell Cluster Services, they are commands that you will use extensively in cluster resource load and unload scripts, and that you may need to execute at the server console.

ADD SECONDARY IPADDRESS *IPAddress*

The `ADD SECONDARY IPADDRESS` *IPAddress* command binds the specified secondary IP address to this server. For example:

```
ADD SECONDARY IPADDRESS 10.7.5.105
```

DEL SECONDARY IPADDRESS *IPAddress*

The `DEL SECONDARY IPADDRESS` *IPAddress* command unbinds the specified secondary IP address from this server. For example:

```
DEL SECONDARY IPADDRESS 10.7.5.105
```

DISPLAY SECONDARY IPADDRESS

The `DISPLAY SECONDARY IPADDRESS` command displays all secondary IP addresses bound to this server, listed based on the server's primary IP addresses.

SET ALLOW IP ADDRESS DUPLICATES = ON|OFF

The `SET ALLOW IP ADDRESS DUPLICATES = ON|OFF` command allows or disallows duplicate IP addresses on the IP subnet this server is attached to. By allowing duplicate IP addresses, the server binds IP addresses and activates them, even if it detects the address is already in use on the network.

Novell Storage Services Commands

The Novell Storage Services (NSS) commands are typically utilized in the cluster resource load and unload scripts, but will also be used as you first set up new cluster resources.

NSS /?

The `NSS /?` command displays the NSS help screen with all available NSS commands.

NSS /Activate=*VolumeName*

The `NSS /Activate=`*VolumeName* command activates this volume. Such activation must be done before the volume can be mounted and cannot be performed if any other node in the cluster already has the volume activated.

NSS /Deactivate=*VolumeName*

The `NSS /Deactivate=`*VolumeName* command deactivates this volume, making it unavailable for the `MOUNT` command. If the volume is already mounted, this command will automatically dismount the volume first.

DISMOUNT *VolumeName* /FORCE

The `DISMOUNT VolumeName /FORCE` command forcefully dismounts a volume, overriding its normal check for open files. You will not be prompted in the event that there are files open — they will automatically be closed (not gracefully) in the process.

MOUNT *VolumeName* VOLID=*n*

The `MOUNT VolumeName VOLID=n` command mounts a volume with a volume ID. This command forces the same volume ID on each server.

TIP

Volume IDs are required to support the automatic client reconnect process, since the clients remember the volume ID as part of the reconnection routine. You must also make sure that no two cluster-enabled volumes use the same volume ID, or the client will have problems when mapping drives and reconnecting to the volume.

VMVOLUMES

The `VMVOLUMES` command displays all currently mounted volumes on the server along with their assigned volume ID and status.

Trustee ID Migration Commands

Administrators typically won't use these commands directly. These commands are used in autogenerated cluster volume load scripts when you cluster enable a volume.

TRUSTMIG *VolumeName* watch

The `TRUSTMIG VolumeName watch` command migrates the trustees to the volume, and then watches for trustee ID updates on the volume named `VolumeName`.

TRUSTMIG *VolumeName* unwatch

The `TRUSTMIG VolumeName unwatch` command disables watching for trustee ID updates on the volume named `VolumeName`.

TRUSTMIG *VolumeName* migrate

The `TRUSTMIG VolumeName migrate` command migrates only the trustee IDs on the volume `VolumeName`, but does not enable the watcher process.

TRUSTMIG List

The `TRUSTMIG List` command lists all the volumes being watched by `TRUSTMIG` on this server.

TRUSTOOL Commands

Novell Cluster Services provides a command-line utility TRUSTOOL.NLM to assist in documenting and fixing trustee problems. The TRUSTOOL commands are not automatically added to any resource load or unload script, but are manually called by an administrator.

TRUSTOOL *VolumeName* dump

The TRUSTOOL *VolumeName* dump command dumps information about trustee IDs for the volume *VolumeName*.

TRUSTOOL *VolumeName* fix

The TRUSTOOL *VolumeName* fix command builds a repair (NCF) script file for the volume *VolumeName*.

Using the Novell Cluster Services Statistical Tools

Novell provides a set of Cluster Services statistical tools that help you debug problems with the heartbeat. These tools are currently available as an optional download that must be manually applied to each node in the cluster. NetWare 6 will have these tools built into the clustering software.

To use the statistical tools, first download and install the tools using the instructions found in Novell TID 2957678. Then back up and replace the following NLMs:

- ▸ CLSTRLIB.NLM

- ▸ GIPC.NLM

- ▸ SBD.NLM

- ▸ VLL.NLM

Once you've installed the statistical tools and restarted the cluster, the following new commands will be available:

- ▸ CLUSTER_START CLEARSTATS

- ▸ CLUSTER_START DISPLAYSTATS

CLUSTER_START CLEARSTATS

This command clears the current statistics and starts monitoring again. Each time a cluster node leaves and rejoins the cluster, you will want to retype this command to get a correct view of the statistics (this will not be necessary with NetWare 6), as the average times will not be computed correctly otherwise.

CLUSTER_START DISPLAYSTATS

This command displays the current statistics of the servers.

Analyzing the Statistics

Figure 7.11 shows a sample cluster statistics display. Take a closer look at this display while we describe each section.

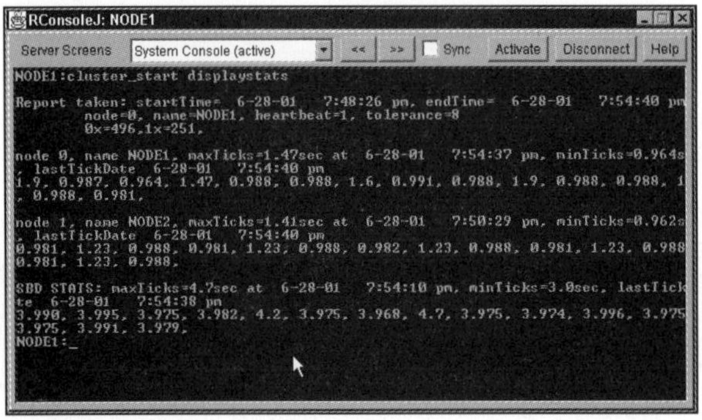

FIGURE 7.11 *Cluster statistics*

The first section of the display provides various general statistics, including the following:

▸ The report statistics were last reset or started on June 28 at 7:48:26 p.m.

▸ The report was run June 28 at 7:54 p.m.

▸ The report was run on cluster node "0," which was the server named "NODE1."

Remember that cluster node numbering starts at 0.

▸ The cluster is set to heartbeat every second, with a tolerance of eight seconds.

TIP

▶ Since the statistical tools were running, the 0x histogram was 496 at the time the report was run. This means that the statistical tool counted 496 times where the heartbeat occurred between 0 and 1 times the heartbeat rate (currently set to one). In other words, during the statistical measuring, there were 496 times that the heartbeat occurred between 0 and 1 second.

▶ Since the statistical tools were running, the 1x histogram was 251 at the time the report was run. This means that the statistical tool counted 251 times where the heartbeat occurred between 1 times and 2 times the heartbeat rate (currently set to one). In other words, during the statistical measuring, there were 251 times that the heartbeat occurred between 1 and 2 seconds.

▶ Since 3x is not listed, there were no occurrences of heartbeats that occurred more than twice the current heartbeat rate.

The goal in analyzing this first section of the report is to verify that the heartbeat parameters are what you expect them to be, and to confirm that you aren't having any heartbeats beyond the "1x" tolerance. You want all of your heartbeats to occur at 0x or 1x, and no slower.

Next, turn to the second section of the report. Since you are viewing this from NODE 0 (the server named NODE1), you see statistics that this node is counting on itself. Reviewing this section tells you the following:

▶ The longest time between any two ticks on this node during the statistical period was 1.47 seconds.

NOTE **The current version of the statistical tool may not report the max ticks correctly. Notice in Figure 7.11 that the max tics is 1.47, yet there was one tick of 1.9 during the interval shown. Novell is aware of this issue, and will be fixing it in a future version of the tool.**

▶ The shortest time between any two ticks on this node during the statistical period was 0.964 seconds.

▶ The last two lines of this section list the last tick counts before the report was run. The last 16 tick counts when this report was run start with a 1.9-second tick count and end with a .981-second tick count. (Note: The report in this example was run when only 15 counts had been performed. However, the statistical tools will report the last 16 counts.)

The current version of the clustering statistical tools does not properly account for nodes leaving and rejoining the cluster and requires that you reset the statistics when a node comes and goes.

Analyzing this section tells us that this server had several occasions where the heartbeat took significantly longer than one second. Since this is reporting on this node itself, LAN traffic does not account for the delays greater than one second. Seeing that this number approaches two on many occasions, you can assume that this server might have too much to do to keep up with the heartbeats (this is true, since this server was running NDPS, six GroupWise resources, BorderManager, DNS, DHCP, and five volume resources at the time the report was run). If you see the heartbeat approaching one half of the heartbeat tolerance, you should strongly consider offloading some processes from the server. For example, with the heartbeat tolerance set at the default of eight seconds, if you see the heartbeat approaching four seconds, it is time to start figuring out how to better distribute your resources.

The next section of this report shows the heartbeat information for the second node of the cluster (this was done in a two-node cluster). From this section, you can tell the following:

▸ The longest time between any two ticks on this node during the statistical period was 1.41 seconds.

▸ The shortest time between any two ticks on this node during the statistical period was 0.962 seconds.

▸ The last two lines of this section list the last tick counts before the report was run. The last 16 tick counts when this report was run start with a .981-second tick count and end with a .988-second tick count. (Note: The report in this example was run when only 15 counts had been performed. The statistical tools will report the last 16 counts.)

Since this section is reporting on a remote node, LAN traffic can interfere in these statistics due to collisions causing missed packets. Comparing these statistics to the heartbeats of the local node can help determine if a LAN communications issue is interfering in your heartbeat traffic. Since the remote node appears to be heartbeating even better than the current node, you can conclude that for this short statistical period, LAN traffic was not a problem for your heartbeat.

The last section of this report shows us the heartbeat to the shared storage. Recall that the servers should perform a heartbeat to the storage at one half of the LAN heartbeat tolerance. From the first section of the report, you can see a tolerance setting of 8, which tells us we should have an SBD heartbeat every 4 seconds. This section of the report tells you the following:

- ▶ The longest time between any two ticks to the SAN during the statistical period was 4.7 seconds.

- ▶ The shortest time between any two ticks to the SAN during the statistical period was 3.0 seconds.

- ▶ The third and fourth lines of this section list the last tick counts before the report was run. The last 16 tick counts when this report was run begin with a tick count of 3.990 seconds and end with a tick count of 3.979 seconds. (Note: The report in this example was run when only 15 counts had been performed. The statistical tools will report the last 16 counts.)

Based on these statistics, you can conclude that the SBD heartbeat also appears to be healthy.

Since this example was run from a two-node cluster, all nodes in the cluster are visible from any node. In practice, however, the statistical tool will show you this node's heartbeat information, and the master node's heartbeats. So the master node will always show you all nodes in the cluster, whereas the slave nodes will show only themselves and the master.

You can use the statistical tool to help determine if you have a LAN-related performance problem, or if you have some CPU hog issues on the server that are preventing its own heartbeat from occurring at the proper intervals. In general, if you see any of these statistics appearing at more than 50 percent of their expected interval, you should research this further to determine the cause. For example, if your SBD expected interval is 4, and you see SBD ticks greater than 6 (4 + (50% × 4)), then you should investigate further.

Summary

This chapter walked you through the ConsoleOne interface, starting with the Cluster Container object and the cluster-wide configuration options. It discussed the various states the cluster can be in, and what these states signify. You also learned how to document your cluster-wide configuration, as well as your history of cluster events.

Next, the chapter discussed the NDS management of your cluster node objects, and why you might need to modify your node configuration. You learned about managing the actual cluster resources, including resource states, and what these states signify.

The chapter concluded with several command-line (server) console commands you use in conjunction with Novell Cluster Services, and the optional clustering statistical tools available to help you monitor your cluster heartbeat performance.

By understanding all of the management configuration parameters, you can better know what to tune and how to tune it. Now that you understand the basics of Novell Cluster Services, and the ConsoleOne management interface and management options, you are ready to move on to creating the cluster resources.

## CHAPTER 8

Creating Cluster Resources

This chapter continues the transition from the theoretical aspects of Novell Cluster Services to their practical implementation. It is the first in a series of chapters dealing with configuring applications in a cluster. This chapter focuses on the general process, and how to go about configuring an application that is not documented anywhere. The following chapters provide more details about how to configure many of the most popular applications that Novell customers wish to cluster.

This chapter covers creating cluster resources. You begin by learning about the Cluster Resource Template objects, including how to create a cluster resource using a template, as well as how to create your own custom template for later use.

Next, you explore the cluster resource properties, including the load and unload scripts; startup, failover, and failback modes; and the preferred nodes list.

Finally, this chapter looks at the basics of how to create a cluster resource for applications that Novell and this book have not documented. You learn the criteria by which you determine whether an application should be configured in a cluster, as well as philosophies of how to cluster enable and test your custom application.

Creating Cluster Resources

For most cluster resources, before you create a cluster resource, you should first create an NSS volume on the shared storage. When you install an application, you specify the shared volume as the location for the application data. If your application allows, you can also specify the volume on the shared storage as the location for the application executable files. By running the application and the data from the shared storage, you can install the application once, and assign it to any node in the cluster, thereby ensuring location transparency for your application. This chapter assumes that you have already created the shared volume prior to creating the cluster resource.

Chapter 9 discusses the process of creating volumes on the shared storage in great detail.

X-REF

You have three ways to create a cluster resource:

▶ Creating a resource using a cluster resource template

▸ Creating a resource without a cluster resource template

▸ Creating a cluster-enabled volume

Each of these methods is discussed in the following sections.

Using the Cluster Resource Templates

Novell Cluster Services provides five different preconfigured resource templates that include the basic commands necessary for clustering specific applications. Table 8.1 describes these preconfigured resource templates.

T A B L E 8.1

Cluster Resource Templates

TEMPLATE	VERSION OF NOVELL CLUSTER SERVICES INCLUDED	DESCRIPTION
Generic IP Service	1.0	This template contains only the most basic commands for creating your own cluster resource.
GroupWise Mail Server	1.0	This template contains the basic GroupWise commands for creating a GroupWise resource without using a cluster-enabled volume or protected memory.
Netscape Enterprise Server	1.0	This template contains the commands for creating an Active/Passive Web server resource.
Oracle Database Server	1.0	This template contains the commands for creating an Oracle 8 database resource.
DHCP Server	1.01	This template contains the basic commands for creating a clustered DHCP server (without using an IP Helper address).

You can modify the preconfigured resource templates, and you can also create new resource templates for any application that you expect to create multiple resources with. These templates also appear as part of the cluster HTML report, which you can use to document your cluster.

X-REF

The cluster HTML report is covered in Chapter 7.

To create a cluster resource using a resource template, follow these steps:

I. Launch ConsoleOne, and select your Cluster Container object.

2. Right-click your cluster container, then select New ⇨ Object.

3. From the New Object dialog box shown in Figure 8.1, select NCS:Cluster Resource, then click OK.

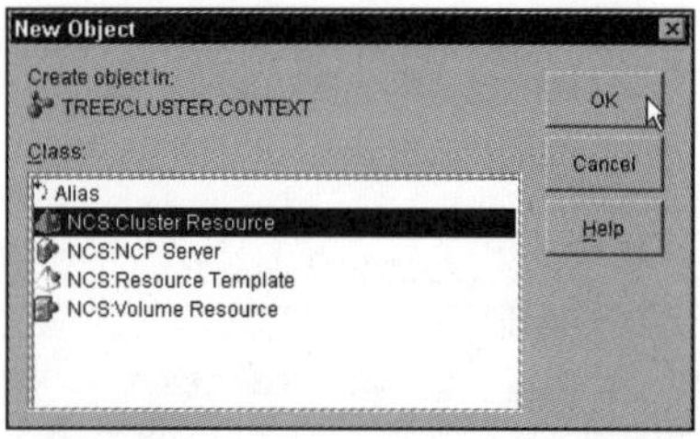

New Object

Create object in:
TREE/CLUSTER.CONTEXT

OK

Class:

Alias
NCS:Cluster Resource
NCS:NCP Server
NCS:Resource Template
NCS:Volume Resource

Cancel

Help

FIGURE 8.1 *New Object dialog box*

4. From the New Cluster Resource dialog box shown in Figure 8.2, do the following:

a. Enter a name for the resource in the Cluster Resource Name field.

b. Click the Browse button in the Inherit From Template field, and then browse the NDS tree for the template you wish to apply to this new resource.

c. Select the Define Additional Properties box.

d. Click the Create button.

FIGURE 8.2 *New Cluster Resource dialog box*

5. Modify the load scripts, unload scripts, nodes, and cluster resource policies as desired for this resource. These policies are described later in this chapter.

TIP

The cluster resource you create based on the included templates must be altered to work for your specific environment. The preconfigured resource templates contain generic volume names and IP addresses that you must modify to fit your application.

Creating a Resource without Using a Cluster Resource Template

Most applications that you may wish to cluster do not have a preconfigured resource template. Creating a resource without a template requires virtually the same procedure as using a template, but it does not include the convenience of having the generic application commands preconfigured for you.

To create a cluster resource without using a resource template, perform the following steps:

1. Launch ConsoleOne, and select your Cluster Container object.

2. Right-click your cluster container, then select New ➪ Object.

3. From the New Object dialog box (shown in Figure 8.1), select NCS:Cluster Resource, and then click OK.

4. From the New Cluster Resource dialog box, shown in Figure 8.3, do the following:

a. Enter a name for the resource in the Cluster Resource Name field.

    b. Select the Define Additional Properties box.

    c. Click the Create button.

FIGURE 8.3 *New Cluster Resource dialog box*

5. Modify the load scripts, unload scripts, nodes, and cluster resource policies as desired for this resource. These policies are described later in this chapter.

TIP

Typically, creating the cluster resource is the last step in clustering an application. Before creating the resource object, install and configure the application on each node that will be in the failover path, and test the application on each node. Once you are satisfied with the application behavior, create the resource object. If the application doesn't work before you create the resource object, it probably won't work from the cluster either.

Creating Cluster-Enabled Volumes

Under certain conditions, your application requires a cluster-enabled volume to function properly in a cluster. Some of the situations that require cluster-enabled volumes include the following:

▶ Applications that access their data using a UNC path, which includes a server name

▶ Clients that access data through a drive mapping

▶ Clients that access data through a UNC path, which includes a server name

One example of an application that requires a cluster-enabled volume is Novell Distributed Print Services (NDPS), since the Broker and the Manager access their data via UNC paths.

X-REF

Applying Novell Cluster Services to NDPS is covered extensively in Chapter 10.

To cluster enable a volume, you must first create an NSS volume. This process is described in detail in Chapter 9. You might also want to mount the volume and upgrade it into the NDS directory before you cluster enable it.

TIP

When you create a new NSS volume using NWCONFIG, **the volume ID is not written to the volume because it is not mounted. Mounting it and upgrading it into the directory properly writes the volume ID to the volume and NDS. To our knowledge, NDPS is the only application that must have this information, although it is quite likely that other applications also depend on this information. Therefore, it's recommended that you complete this process on all NSS volumes you create.**

To cluster enable a volume, follow these steps:

1. Launch ConsoleOne, and select your Cluster Container object.

2. Right-click your cluster container, then select New ⇨ Object.

3. From the New Object dialog box (shown in Figure 8.1), select NCS:Volume Resource, and then click OK.

4. In the New Cluster Volume dialog box, shown in Figure 8.4, browse to the volume you created for the resource and enter the secondary IP address to use for this resource. Select Define Additional Properties, and then click Create.

FIGURE 8.4 *New Cluster Volume dialog box*

5. Using ConsoleOne, select the Cluster object and then change to the Cluster State View by selecting View ⇨ Cluster State from the menu.

6. Click once on the cluster resource to start the Cluster Resource Manager.

TIP

Before onlining a cluster resource, it is a good idea to make sure that the volume is not already mounted somewhere in the cluster, and that no server has the IP address already bound. Many times you will manually mount the volume and bind the IP address to install the application — just don't forget to dismount and unbind before onlining the resource or your resource will go to a Comatose state.

7. Click the Online button to start the resource.

You may want to watch the server console on the node that you are activating the resource on. Thus, if there is a load failure, you can see any error messages on the server console screen and quickly know where to fix the problem based on the error message(s) returned.

Adding Your Commands to the Cluster-Enabled Volume Resource

Because Novell Cluster Services does not give you the ability to make one resource dependent on another resource, you must configure all dependent applications as a single cluster resource. This means that if you have an application that requires a cluster-enabled volume, all of the commands for that application must be contained in the load and unload scripts of the cluster-enabled volume resource.

After you create the cluster-enabled volume, place all of the commands to start your application in the load script of the cluster-enabled volume resource. These commands should typically be placed at the end of the script so that the volume comes online before the resource actually starts. In effect, you are building your required dependencies into the load script.

Next, place all the commands to stop your application in the unload script of the cluster-enabled volume resource. These commands should typically be placed at the beginning of the unload script before the existing commands for the cluster-enabled volume. This way, you unload the application before you take away the data volume.

Creating/Modifying Cluster Resource Templates

Simply editing any of the preconfigured cluster resource template properties and saving the changes easily modifies the preconfigured cluster template. You may decide that the preconfigured templates should be modified prior to use, such as by converting the Netscape Enterprise Server template from the Active/Passive configuration to an Active/Active server or by adding the protected memory commands to the GroupWise templates.

X-REF

Netscape Enterprise Web Server is discussed in Chapter 13.

In addition, you can create your own resource template objects for any resource you desire. This is very useful for custom applications, once you have determined all the proper commands necessary to cluster additional services.

To create a cluster resource template, follow these steps:

1. Launch ConsoleOne, and select your Cluster Container object.

2. Right-click your cluster container, then select New ⇨ Object.

3. From the New Object dialog box shown in Figure 8.5, select NCS:Resource Template, then click OK.

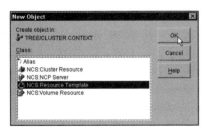

FIGURE 8.5 *New Object dialog box*

4. From the New Cluster Resource dialog box shown in Figure 8.6, do the following:

    a. Enter a name for the template in the Cluster Resource Name field.

b. If desired, click the Browse button in the Inherit From Template field, and then browse the NDS tree for the template you wish to apply to this new resource template. This allows you to create a template based on an existing template object.

c. Select the Define Additional Properties box.

d. Click the Create button.

FIGURE 8.6 *New Cluster Resource dialog box*

5. Modify the load scripts, unload scripts, nodes, and cluster resource policies as desired for this resource. These policies are described later in this chapter.

Discussing Resource Policies

Resource policies control the behavior of individual resources when the resource is started, stopped, or migrated to another node in the cluster. These policies include the following:

- ▸ Load scripts
- ▸ Unload scripts
- ▸ Startup mode
- ▸ Failover mode

> ▸ Failback mode

> ▸ Preferred nodes list

Each of these policies is discussed in the following sections.

Load and Unload Scripts

Load and unload scripts contain the commands necessary to start and stop the clustered resource. They are analogous to NCF files that are executed automatically when a resource loads or unloads. Thus, they can contain any command (NetWare console command) that you would typically use in NCF files.

Load Scripts

The Load Script policy contains a list of commands to be executed on the target node any time the cluster resource is started. Figure 8.7 shows a sample cluster resource load script from a DNS server resource.

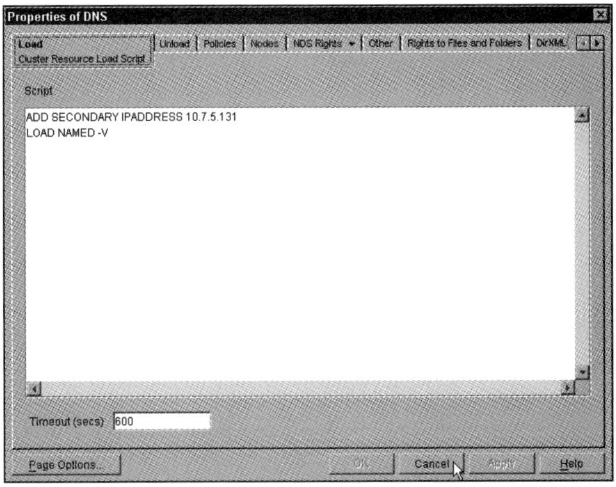

FIGURE 8.7 *Sample cluster resource load script*

The first line of the load script binds a secondary IP address to the node that executes it. This is the address, in this case, that will be used for a DNS server resource.

The second line of the load script calls the NAMED.NLM module and tells it to load in the verbose mode.

The timeout setting is left to the default of 600 seconds. If the load script does not complete within the 600-second timeout, then the resource will go into a comatose resource state.

Unload Scripts

Unload scripts contain all of the commands necessary to stop the clustered application on the current node. These scripts are executed any time you take a resource offline, or any time you migrate a resource from one node to another node in the cluster. Figure 8.8 shows a sample cluster resource unload script for the same DNS resource referenced in the preceding section.

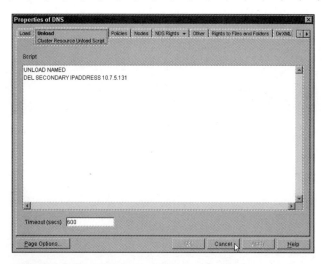

FIGURE 8.8 *Sample cluster resource unload script*

The first line in the unload script unloads the NAMED.NLM module. The second line in the unload script unbinds the secondary IP address used for the DNS service from this server. The timeout of 600 seconds specifies how long the unload script has to execute before the resource changes to a comatose state.

It is important to unload services in the reverse order that your load scripts load them. If you follow this methodology, you avoid the issue of "pulling the rug out from under an application. For example, GroupWise cannot cleanly shut down its database if the volume the database is on is no longer mounted.

Startup, Failover, and Failback Modes

The Policies page of the cluster resource specifies how the resource behaves in the cluster. Figure 8.9 shows all of the cluster resource policies available.

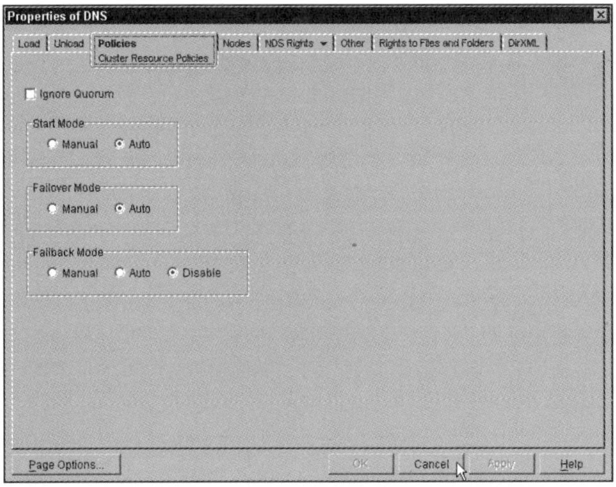

FIGURE 8.9 *Sample cluster resource policies page*

Ignore Quorum

Selecting Ignore Quorum for a cluster resource tells the cluster that this resource is so important that it should not wait for quorum to be achieved before starting. If you enable the Ignore Quorum setting, the resource automatically starts on the first node in its preferred nodes list that joins the cluster, regardless of node order.

Start Mode

Cluster resources have one of two start modes: manual or automatic. When set to automatic, the cluster resource automatically starts on its preferred node any time the cluster is restarted.

Setting the start mode to manual causes the resource to go into an Alert state any time the cluster is restarted. In the Alert state, ConsoleOne shows the resource as an alert and presents a dialog box asking if you wish to start the cluster resource. Since this mode requires manual intervention to start the service, it is not recommended that you use the manual mode unless you have a specific reason to do so.

Failover Mode

Cluster resources have one of two failover modes: manual or automatic. When set to automatic, the cluster resource automatically starts on its next most preferred node (the topmost node that is available in the resource's cluster resource preferred nodes list) any time the node that the resource is running on fails. This provides the best possible failover behavior because no manual intervention is necessary to make the service available on the next node. This is the preferred (and default) configuration for almost all cluster resources.

Setting the failover mode to manual causes the resource to go into an Alert state any time the cluster node the resource was running on fails. In the Alert state, ConsoleOne shows the resource as an alert and presents a dialog box asking if you wish to start the cluster resource on the next most preferred node. Since this mode requires manual intervention to restart the service, it is not recommended that you use the manual mode unless you have a specific reason to do so. Using a manual failover mode almost guarantees that automatic client reconnection will not occur, since odds are it will take the administrator longer to determine that there is an issue than it will for in-use applications to timeout their connections.

Failback Mode

The Failback Mode policy instructs the cluster resource what to do should its most preferred node come back online and rejoin the cluster. Failback mode has three options: manual, auto, or disable, with the default being disable.

When failback is set to manual, should the resource's most preferred node come back online and rejoin the cluster, the resource will go into an Alert state. The Alert state will show on ConsoleOne, which asks the administrator if the resource should be moved back to its preferred node. Until the administrator acknowledges this message, the resource remains where it is running.

When failback is set to auto, the cluster resource will automatically failback to its most preferred node any time it comes back online and rejoins the cluster. No prompting is provided prior to automatically migrating the resource, and no warning is given to the administrator or the users. Though this mode is beneficial for scheduling backup and antivirus scanning jobs, it's not recommended because there is no way to know if the problem that caused the node to leave the cluster was fixed prior to moving the resource back to it. For example, if you have a situation that periodically causes ABENDs on a particular node, it is better to leave the resource running on a different node than it is to automatically move it back to a node that may not be stable.

When failback is set to disable, no action is taken by the cluster resource when its most preferred node comes back online and rejoins the cluster. This is the default setting, and is also the recommended setting under most circumstances.

Cluster Resource Preferred Nodes List

The failover order (also known as the *preferred nodes* list, or the *available nodes* list; see Figure 8.10) determines the order in which the resource migrates to cluster nodes in the event of node failures. The topmost node in the Assigned column is known as the most preferred node, or the resource default node. This is the node that the resource starts on when the cluster is restarted, or when the resource is onlined after being offlined.

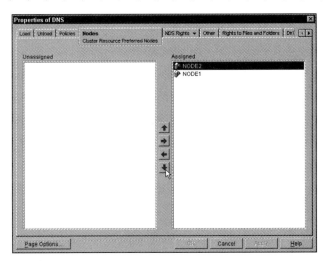

FIGURE 8.10 *Sample cluster Preferred Nodes page*

You can add an unassigned node to the resource by selecting it in the Unassigned column, then clicking the right-facing blue arrow. Conversely, you can take an assigned node and unassign it by selecting it in the Assigned column, then clicking the left blue arrow.

To change the preference order of the resource, select the node that you wish to modify in the Assigned column, then click the up or down blue arrow to change the order in which it appears in the lists. The topmost node is the most preferred node, and the bottommost node is the least preferred node for this resource.

Cluster Enabling Applications

Novell Cluster Services provides preconfigured resource templates for many common applications you might choose to cluster. In addition, this book provides detailed information on how to cluster various applications. However, just because certain applications are included in this book does not mean that these are the only applications that you can cluster.

The two major keys to clustering an application are understanding your application and thoroughly testing your configuration. You must know how to properly start and stop your application, and then apply this knowledge to the resource load and unload scripts.

A common misconception of Novell Cluster Services is that the application must be cluster aware to be configured in a cluster. This is not at all true — almost any application or service can be cluster enabled providing the following are true:

- ▶ The application is TCP/IP-based.

- ▶ The TCP/IP address can be specified during or after installation (in other words, it doesn't default to the primary bound IP address of the server).

- ▶ Data location can be controlled (non-SYS: volume dependent for the data, even if the application itself has SYS: volume dependencies).

- ▶ The server name is not hard coded into the application code or data.

- ▶ The application or service can be loaded and unloaded without user intervention through an NCF file or LOAD/UNLOAD command.

- ▶ The application, or the way the client connects to the application, does not require UNC paths.

TIP

If UNC paths are used by the application, you can still cluster enable the application by cluster enabling the data volume and using the UNC path through the virtual server.

Every application needs to be tested within a cluster before deployment into production, as client behavior and results vary.

Reviewing Keys to Cluster Enabling New Applications

It would not be possible for Novell to configure, test, and document every application that you may decide you wish to cluster. In fact, just configuring, testing, and documenting the Novell applications that can be configured in a cluster is a daunting task, and no one has documented every Novell or third-party application that can be clustered. For example, the following Novell products can be clustered, although no public documentation on these applications exists at the time of this writing:

- NIMS

- Novell's iFolders

- BTRIEVE

- AFP Services

So, must you wait for Novell to document an application before you can cluster it? Of course not! However, you need to thoroughly test the application and test the client behavior during a migration and during a server failure. Test anything you can think of, and then get the end users who will use that application involved and test anything that they can think of.

Since it is impossible to give exact steps as to how to cluster an undocumented application, here are a few general guidelines to help you get started:

- When installing the application, try to install the modules to the shared volume.

- Document the exact commands to start and stop your application.

- Verify with the application vendor that the application is supported on NSS volumes.

- Determine and document how the application handles a server failure — understand how resilient the application will be and how data integrity is maintained.

- Determine how the application finds its data and its application files. You may need to add a search command for the application directory or cluster enable the volume if the application uses UNC paths.

▶ Check on Novell's support forums by using an NNTP client and attaching to `support-forums.novell.com`, and subscribing to the `novell.support.high-availability.cluster.services` forum. Post a general question to the group and see what experience/scar tissue other Novell users have to share.

▶ Determine how the clients connect to the application. Client/server using TCP/IP is the preferred method, and drive mappings are the least-preferred method.

▶ Determine your SYS volume dependencies. If there are any, you must install the application on each node in the preferred nodes list.

▶ Test, test, and yes, test some more!

Configuring Combination Resources

You may find that your application has multiple components that combine to form the single service. If these applications do not depend on each other to load, you may be able to split the application up into multiple cluster resources and achieve the greatest level of fan out failover. For example, with GroupWise, you can configure a single cluster resource for the Message Transfer Agent (MTA) and another resource for the Post Office Agent (POA). If you find that your application has subcomponents that depend on each other, and that one must be started before another can load, you must combine these subcomponents or applications into a single cluster resource. The load and unload scripts must reflect any dependencies. You might also find that some modules must fully initialize before others can load, so you may need to add delay commands into the load script to allow dependent modules to load. Or you may have to add delay commands into your unload scripts to allow one application to unload before another starts to unload.

Summary

In this chapter, you learned about creating cluster resources. You examined the Cluster Resource Template objects, including how to create a cluster resource using a template, as well as how to create your own custom template for later use or to modify existing templates to meet your needs.

You explored the various cluster resource properties, including the load and unload scripts; startup, failover, and failback modes; and the preferred nodes list. Finally, the chapter discussed the basics of how to create a cluster resource for applications that Novell and this book have not documented.

Now that you have a general idea how to create cluster resources, you will learn all about NSS volumes and how they work with your shared storage in a cluster. Following the storage, you will learn step-by-step procedures about how to cluster the most popular applications. By reading the specific application instructions and applying the knowledge from this chapter, you should be able to cluster many other applications even if you can't find someone else that has documented all the ins and outs for you.

## PART II

Applying Novell Cluster Services with Network Applications

Working with Shared Disk NSS Volumes

Because your cluster nodes are all attached to a shared disk SAN, storage configuration and volume management are a little more involved than working with disks attached to a standalone, nonclustered server. This chapter helps increase your expertise by exploring how to work with shared disk storage and Novell Storage Services (NSS) volumes. This material helps you learn how to use the standard NetWare storage and volume management tools to configure your SAN shared disks and explains how to create and modify NSS volumes on shared disks. The concept of cluster-enabled volumes is introduced in this chapter. You work with the ConsoleOne Cluster Services snapins to cluster enable volumes for automatic failover and consider how to set up your NetWare clients to access files on cluster-enabled volumes. You'll also find a detailed step-by-step description of what happens during a volume failover. Finally, this chapter closes with some essential tips for ensuring the availability and performance of your cluster's data on shared disk volumes.

Understanding Direct Attach and Shared Disk Interfaces

Each of your cluster nodes has at least two kinds of disk interfaces:

- Direct attach SCSI or EIDE host bus adapter (HBA)
- Shared SCSI or Fibre Channel HBA, required for clustering

A *direct attach disk interface* connects a server to its boot disk. This is the server's C: drive. It contains the server's DOS boot partition and \NWSERVER directory. Depending how you installed NetWare, the boot disk probably also contains the SYS volume. Or, another direct attach disk may contain SYS. Direct attach disks are dedicated to the server they are physically connected to and cannot be accessed by any other server.

A *shared SCSI* or *Fibre Channel disk interface* is required for clustering. They connect servers to shared disks. Shared disks are located in a separate physical disk array chassis and are accessible by every node in your cluster.

Figure 9.1 depicts the difference between direct attach and shared disks. Each server has its own private direct attach disk (the local disks shown in the figure) that contains a DOS boot partition, a \NWSERVER directory, and a SYS volume. Data on direct attach disks cannot be shared. However, by definition, shared disks are accessible to every server. They are located in a separate disk array chassis and are connected to each server over a SAN or shared SCSI bus. A cluster is defined by a number of servers that share access to disks on a SAN.

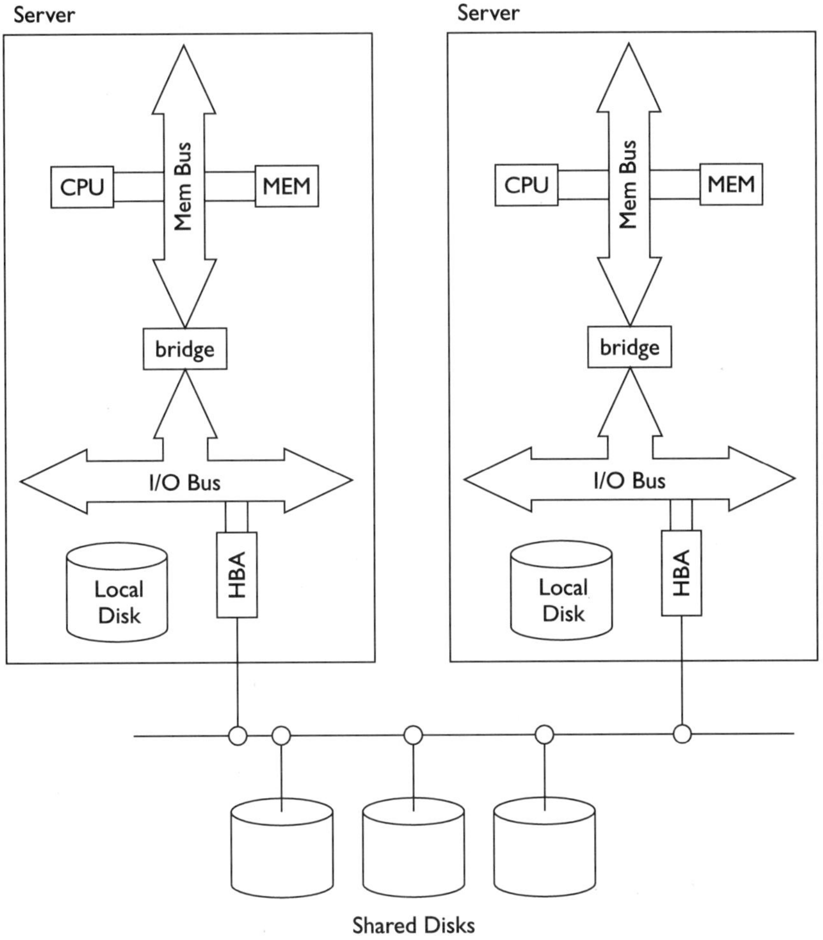

FIGURE 9.1 *Servers with both direct attach and shared disks*

TIP

Aim to reduce the amount of direct attach disk space you use. Data kept on direct attach disks is not highly available. If a server fails, its data cannot be accessed or quickly recovered if it's stored on direct attach disks. Limit your use of direct attach disk space to the DOS boot partition, the \NWSERVER **directory, and a default SYS volume, and store your applications and data on shared disks instead.**

Distinguishing Direct Attach Disks from Shared Disks

NetWare does not distinguish direct attach disks from shared disks. To NetWare, a disk is just a disk whether it's physically contained in a server or in a separate disk array chassis. But when you work with storage and volumes, distinguishing between direct attach and shared disks is very important. Because shared disks are accessible to any server, only volumes created on shared disks can failover from one cluster node to another. In practice, this means you need to recognize the names of your shared disks. You can do this using the LIST DEVICES command. Figure 9.2 shows the result of entering the LIST DEVICES command at a server console.

FIGURE 9.2 *Result of the LIST DEVICES command*

TIP

Consider using the SCAN FOR NEW DEVICES **command before running the** LIST DEVICES **command to ensure your server has a current view of available storage devices. For example, if you power up your shared disk array after starting the server, you need to scan for new devices.**

Figure 9.2 lists a number of devices. By checking device names and knowing what disk hardware you are working with, it is possible to distinguish direct attach from shared disks. In this case, the following devices are shared disks:

```
[V502-A3-D0:0] Compaq RA4x00 Disk 0 NFT in SAN

[V502-A3-D0:1] Compaq RA4x00 Disk 1 NFT in SAN
```

The other devices are direct attach disks or CD-ROMs.

Disk device names have two components, separated by a colon character. The first part, before the colon, is the target device name. The second is a logical unit number. In this example, the target device name is identical for both shared disks — V502-A3-D0. The logical unit number identifies one disk from another on the same target device. The shared disk "Disk 0" is logical unit number 0 on target device V502-A3-D0. Shared disk "Disk 1" is logical unit number 1 on the same target device. Both disks are known to be shared because the corresponding vendor-specific device name — Compaq RA4x00 — is recognized as a Fibre Channel storage array.

TIP

The best way to distinguish shared from local disks is to know your storage hardware and its corresponding vendor-specific device names.

Configuring Shared Disks

Configuring your shared disks involves learning how to use a third party–supplied disk array configuration tool. Tools usually come bundled with your shared disk array hardware. Depending on your desired disk fault tolerance or performance requirements, you select a RAID level and create a number of RAID sets. You can, for example, decide to employ RAID level 5 for distributed parity redundancy and combine a number of physical disks into a single *RAID set* — also called a *virtual disk*. Your shared disk array presents its (virtual) disks to each attached server.

NOTE

There are many popular forms of standard disk terminology. *RAID set* and *virtual disk* are used interchangeably. A RAID set is an aggregation of physical disks that creates the illusion of a single physical disk. Hence the alternate term — virtual disk. *Logical unit number* (LUN) is another term often used to describe a RAID set. But a logical unit number does not necessarily imply a RAID set. Rather, it is a standard way to identify disks presented via the same target device. Accordingly, a LUN can be either a physical or virtual disk.

If your disk array configuration tool runs on NetWare, shut down all servers except the one running the configuration tool. When the other servers are booted, they will automatically scan for new devices and detect the shared disks. If your disk array configuration tool runs on a Windows NT workstation, you need not have any NetWare servers up and running. Use the disk array configuration tool to set up your shared disk storage and then bring up your NetWare servers.

WARNING

Be careful when configuring shared disks. If your servers are actively using the disk array when it is being configured, you risk data loss. Shared disk array configuration usually requires that your servers be shut down. Consult your disk array documentation for advice.

Working with Novell Storage Services Volumes on Shared Disks

Novell Storage Services (NSS) is Novell's advanced 64-bit journaled file system for NetWare 5.x and beyond. NSS is designed to eliminate the scalability and availability restrictions of the Traditional NetWare File (TFS) system. With NSS, you can store large files and large numbers of files while providing rapid access to your data — all without degrading system performance. Volumes can be mounted in seconds rather than in minutes or even hours, regardless of their size. NSS gives you all these capabilities on servers with virtually any amount of memory. NSS mounts any size volume with as little as 1MB of memory and delivers higher performance on systems configured with more memory.

This flexibility enables volume failover in a cluster. By eliminating rigid memory requirements, NSS volumes are free to failover from node to node even where other volumes are already mounted. The speed with which NSS volumes can be mounted ensures that they are brought online quickly and, after a failover, transparently in most cases to users of the NetWare client accessing their files. For these reasons, NSS is required by Novell Cluster Services and offers you many other advantages, including:

- The ability to store larger files — up to 8 terabytes.

- The ability to store large numbers of files on an NSS volume — up to 8 trillion.

- The ability to have up to 1,000,000 files open simultaneously.

▸ Rapid access to data regardless of file size — any size file can be opened in the same amount of time.

▸ The ability to mount many more NSS volumes on a server — up to 255 depending on the NetWare Loadable Module and any physical limitations.

▸ NSS volumes that mount and verify themselves rapidly. Any size volume can be recovered and mounted in seconds if cleanly dismounted.

▸ 64-bit file system, as opposed to 32-bit.

▸ Memory usage that is not a linear relationship to the volume size — very large volumes can be mounted with almost the same amount of memory as small volumes.

▸ Salvage that can be enabled on a volume-by-volume basis.

▸ Full CD-ROM support for ISO9660 and Macintosh HFS formats, which includes automatic mounting using CDROM.NLM. The new CDROM.NLM, along with NSS, makes it much faster and easier to mount your CD-ROM than it has been in the past.

▸ DOS FAT partitions that can be made available dynamically as NSS volumes.

▸ The ability to mount NSS volumes with only 1MB of available RAM.

▸ Faster error recovery — NSS volume errors are logged quickly.

▸ The ability to define new name spaces (in addition to DOS, Macintosh, LONG, and UNIX/NFS).

▸ The ability to store a large object or large numbers of objects without degrading system performance — no matter how large a volume, directory, or file is, NSS still performs well.

Because the Traditional File System (TFS) wasn't designed for rapid crash recovery, Cluster Services does not support TFS volumes on shared disks. Novell decided against integrating Cluster Services and TFS because achieving high availability through rapid volume remount on failover nodes isn't possible using TFS — it takes too long to remount a TFS volume after a server crash. TFS also isn't well-suited to the scale of storage management required in enterprise SAN environments. Novell's Cluster Services and Storage Services products are designed to enable integrated high availability and online storage management that scales to enterprise storage area networks.

Running Novell Storage Services

Chapter 4 discusses the fact that if two or more NetWare servers are attached to a shared disk SAN and they are not all running Cluster Services software, it is possible to corrupt shared disk volumes. Suppose your SAN is configured so that two or more servers have access to shared disks. One server modifying shared disk data blocks may be unaware that a second server is also reading or writing data blocks on the same disks. Both servers believe they have exclusive access to whatever disk storage is presented to them, and if they both modify the same disk blocks, volume corruption may occur. Cluster Services eliminates this potential for conflict by coordinating the activities of multiple cluster nodes attached to your shared disk SAN.

WARNING

If you attach a NetWare server to your shared disk SAN and it is not running Cluster Services software, you run the risk of corrupting your volumes. Also, when you install NetWare on a new server, ensure that the server is not attached to your shared disk SAN until you are ready to install Cluster Services software. If you leave the server attached to the SAN and if you allow it to do so, the NetWare server install has the potential to delete shared disk partitions. You can also use SAN port zoning or LUN masking to prevent access to shared disks until you are ready to install Cluster Services.

NSS guarantees that it will never read or write a volume's underlying shared disks if the volume is not in the ACTIVE or MAINTENANCE state. Cluster Services ensures that only one cluster node at a time can ever place a volume into either of these states. Thus by employing NSS in a cluster, you prevent a node from reading or writing to a volume if the volume is in the ACTIVE or MAINTENANCE state on a different node. At any instant in time, individual volumes are in the ACTIVE state on only one cluster node, but different nodes can activate different volumes.

Table 9.1 lists the different NSS volume states and their meanings.

T A B L E 9.1	
NSS Volume States	

STATE	MEANING
ACTIVE	Volume is active and can be mounted.
DEACTIVE	Volume is deactive and cannot be mounted.
MAINTENANCE	Volume is enabled for verify or rebuild.

During Cluster Services installation, each server's AUTOEXEC.NCF file is modified as shown in Figure 9.3.

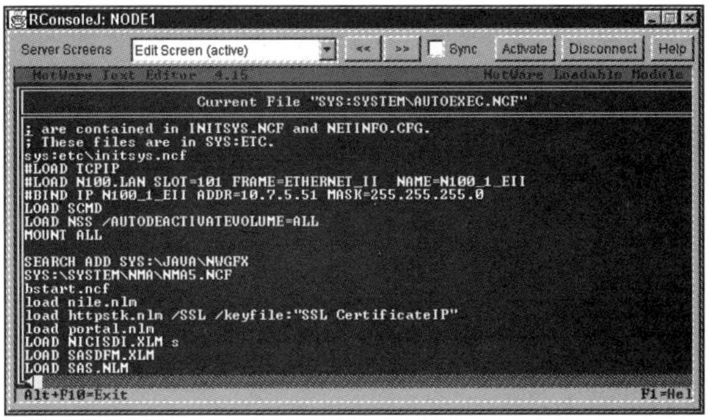

RConsoleJ: NODE1

Server Screens Edit Screen (active)   ▼   <<   >>   ☐ Sync   Activate   Disconnect   Help

NetWare Text Editor 4.15   NetWare Loadable Module

                    Current File "SYS:SYSTEM\AUTOEXEC.NCF"
; are contained in INITSYS.NCF and NETINFO.CFG.
; These Files are in SYS:ETC.
sys:etc\initsys.ncf
#LOAD TCPIP
#LOAD N100.LAN SLOT=101 FRAME=ETHERNET_II NAME=N100_1_EII
#BIND IP N100_1_EII ADDR=10.7.5.51 MASK=255.255.255.0
LOAD SCMD
LOAD NSS /AUTODEACTIVATEVOLUME=ALL
MOUNT ALL

SEARCH ADD SYS:\JAVA\NWGFX
SYS:\SYSTEM\NMA\NMA5.NCF
bstart.ncf
load nile.nlm
load httpstk.nln /SSL /keyfile:"SSL CertificateIP"
load portal.nln
LOAD NICISDI.XLM s
LOAD SASDFM.XLM
LOAD SAS.NLM

Alt+F10=Exit   F1=Help

FIGURE 9.3 *AUTOEXEC.NCF modified during Cluster Services installation*

Halfway down the screen in Figure 9.3, the command used to LOAD (and start) NSS is modified with the option /AUTODEACTIVATEVOLUME=ALL. This ensures that all NSS volumes are initially set to the DEACTIVE state.

WARNING

Make certain you have only one command to load NSS in your AUTOEXEC.NCF **file and that the** /AUTODEACTIVATEVOLUME=ALL **option is always present. If the option is not present, you run the risk of shared disk NSS volumes being mounted by the** MOUNT ALL **command before Cluster Services software loads. This sequence of events could possibly lead to data corruption if two or more servers mount the same volume.**

The subsequent MOUNT ALL command will ignore deactive NSS volumes and mount all Traditional File System (TFS) volumes. To prevent the accidental mounting of shared disk volumes should Cluster Services software not be present or loaded, we recommend you delete the MOUNT ALL command altogether. Its presence in the AUTOEXEC.NCF file doesn't serve any useful purpose in a cluster. Volume SYS is the only volume located on direct attach disks and it is automatically mounted during NetWare boot, before the commands in the AUTOEXEC.NCF file are executed. Unless you have other volumes on direct attach disks, which we recommend against, the MOUNT ALL command is redundant and can be eliminated.

WARNING **Since Cluster Services does not support shared disk TFS volumes, avoid creating TFS volumes on shared disks. If you don't avoid TFS volumes, the** MOUNT ALL **command, when run by multiple servers, will cause all the servers to mount the same TFS volumes, which can cause volume corruption.**

Avoid mounting shared disk NSS volumes from your AUTOEXEC.NCF file, because doing so would tie them to specific cluster nodes and prevent Cluster Services from managing failover. In the following sections, you learn how to create and cluster enable NSS volumes so they are mounted automatically by Cluster Services on the specific cluster nodes you configure. Although it is not recommended, if you have created an NSS volume on direct attach disks, you can add a command to mount it in the AUTOEXEC.NCF file.

Near the end of the AUTOEXEC.NCF file, you'll find the command used to load Cluster Services software. This command, LDNCS, is shown in Figure 9.4. Once Cluster Services is loaded, you have complete management and protection of NSS volumes on shared disks.

FIGURE 9.4 *AUTOEXEC.NCF loads Cluster Services software near the end.*

TIP **For successful operation of Cluster Services and your shared disk NSS volumes, avoid changing the relative ordering of the NSS and Cluster Services startup commands in your** AUTOEXEC.NCF **file and ensure the NSS** AUTODEACTIVATEVOLUME=ALL **option is always present.**

NSS Disk Partitions

Every disk, whether virtual or physical, direct attach or shared, must be initialized with the standard IBM disk format. This allows a maximum of four disk partitions. You initialize and create partitions on your shared disks the same way you do on direct attach disks, using the NWCONFIG utility. Newly created RAID sets are unformatted. When browsing your disks with NWCONFIG, you are prompted to confirm initialization if an unformatted disk is encountered. NWCONFIG formats the disk by creating an empty partition table at the head of the disk.

NSS scans each of your disks to find contiguous areas of unpartitioned free space and lists each free space area as a separate storage deposit. This terminology is intended to suggest the idea of disk space being deposited into a storage bank operated by NSS. From the list of storage deposits, you select how much space you want NSS to claim ownership of. When NSS claims unpartitioned free space on a disk, it becomes an NSS managed object, and the storage is deposited with NSS. From NSS managed objects, you can create storage groups and NSS volumes.

NOTE

A disk has free space if it contains unpartitioned contiguous data blocks and if there is at least one unused partition table entry. Even if a disk has free data blocks, it may not have any free space if all four of its partition table entries are in use. Conversely, it is possible to consume an entire disk with a single partition that uses every data block on the disk. When NSS claims ownership of unpartitioned free space, it creates an NSS partition on the disk. NSS uses the partition type 0x69 to mark its disk partitions. You cannot resize a disk partition after it's been created. If you later discover the size is wrong, you have to delete and then recreate the partition.

NSS Storage Groups and Volumes

Once NSS has claimed ownership of free space and created managed objects, you can create storage groups and NSS volumes. Two kinds of managed objects exist: Single and Group.

A Single object is really just a single NSS disk partition with a different name. Its size cannot be changed, and it can only be used to create a single, fixed-size NSS volume. A storage Group object is a single object that has been upgraded. It is possible to create any number of volumes in a storage group, and storage groups can be combined to expand the size of volumes. Because of this flexibility, using storage groups to create NSS volumes is the recommended course of action. Single objects are intended for simple configurations where expandability is not important and volumes do not need to span multiple disks. On a shared disk SAN, you will want to use storage groups to help manage multiple disks and ensure that your volumes are expandable if you add disks. Storage groups also enable the best upgrade path from NetWare 5.x clusters to NetWare 6 clusters. *Figure 9.5* depicts three shared disks with unpartitioned free space claimed by NSS.

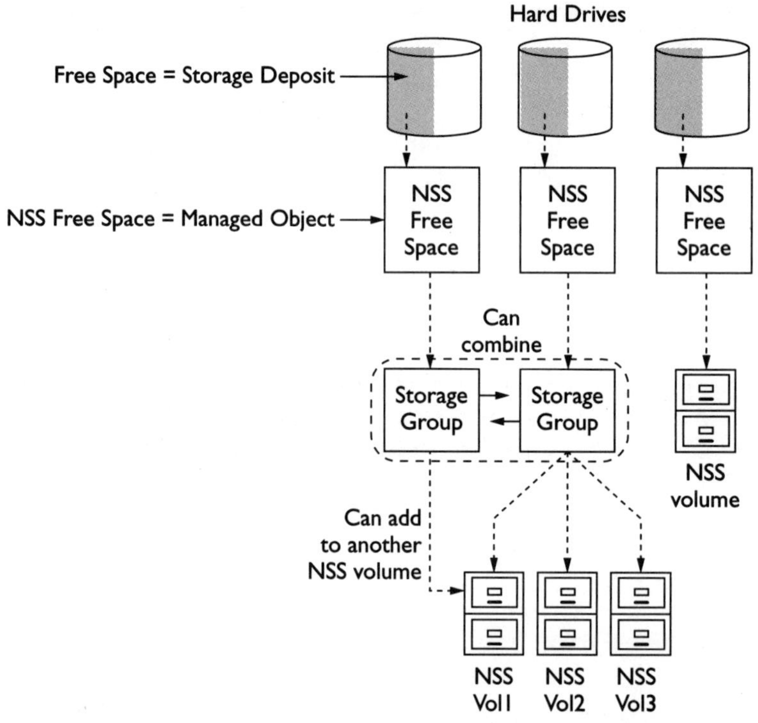

FIGURE 9.5 *Shared disks, NSS partitions, storage groups, and volumes*

In Figure 9.5, NSS claims the unpartitioned free space by creating an NSS partition on each of three shared disks. This creates three managed objects, one per disk. Two storage groups are created from the first two managed objects. The third managed object is a single object and is used to create a single NSS volume. This volume cannot be expanded unless it is destroyed (along with all of its data) and its single managed object is upgraded into a storage group and then added to the other storage groups. From one of the storage groups, three volumes are created and the remaining storage group is combined with the other storage group to expand the size of Vol1.

Using NWCONFIG with NSS

You use the NetWare Configuration utility, NWCONFIG, to manage NSS storage. Here is a review of the NWCONFIG utility and a tour of the main points of navigation through the NSS specific portions of the NWCONFIG menus.

X-REF

You can find detailed instructions for creating a shared disk NSS volume in the "Creating a Storage Group" and "Creating a Volume" sections, later in this chapter.

At the server console, enter **NWCONFIG** and press Enter to launch the NetWare configuration utility. Select NSS Disk Options, then press Enter to display the Available NSS Options menu. This is the starting point for working with the NSS-specific portions of the NWCONFIG utility. You have two main choices from the Available NSS Options menu:

▶ *Storage* — Storage allows you to view and prepare free space for NSS configuration. It contains the following options: Update provider information, Assign ownership, Release ownership, and View free space. If you choose Update provider information, NSS scans your disks to find free space and lists the free space on each disk as a separate storage object. You can also view free space. Once NSS has claimed free space, you can create your storage groups and NSS volumes.

▶ *NSS Volume Options* — NSS Volume Options allow you to create one or more NSS volumes. The volume options are: Create, Modify, Delete, and View volumes. To create multiple NSS volumes in one storage group, first create the storage group by selecting Create ⇨ Storage Group. You then select Create ⇨ NSS Volume, a managed object marked Group, the volume size, and the name. For additional NSS volumes, select NSS Volume again and repeat the steps, segmenting your volumes according to how much space you have in your storage group and the desired size of your volumes.

NOTE

You can also use the NSS administration menu to create NSS volumes. To start the NSS administration menu, type nss /menu **at the server console. NSS menu provides more or less the same features as** NWCONFIG. **If you create volumes from** NWCONFIG, **they are automatically placed into NDS, but not if you use the NSS administration menu. You must use NWAdmin or ConsoleOne to add volume objects to the NDS tree if you're creating volumes with NSS menu.**

Creating NSS Volumes

To create a shared disk NSS volume, follow these steps:

▶ Create a storage group out of unpartitioned free space on a shared disk.

▶ Create a volume out of free space taken from a shared disk storage group.

WARNING

Unless you are running Novell Cluster Services version 1.01 SP2 or later, the steps to create a volume should be performed on only one node in the cluster. Novell Technical Support recommends downing the other nodes in the cluster prior to creating an additional volume, which guarantees that all nodes register the creation of a new volume on shared disks.

If you are not running Novell Cluster Services version 1.01 SP2, the other nodes do not immediately recognize the newly created volume when you type **NSS VOLUMES** at their corresponding server console prompt. Even though they will not show the volume, if you migrate the volume to them, they will refresh their view when the NSS /ACTIVATE=<VolumeName> command is executed, and they will be able to activate and mount the volume. The danger lies in creating another new volume from one of the other cluster nodes before that node recognizes that the free space has already been allocated, which would cause it to attempt to allocate the same space for its volume and lead to data corruption. You can avoid this problem by always performing volume operations on the same node, or upgrading your cluster software to Novell Cluster Services 1.01 SP2 or later. If you are running SP2 or later, you can create storage groups and volumes on any node and all nodes are automatically refreshed. In either case, the actual steps to create volumes are identical.

Before creating your first shared disk NSS volume, you should ensure that space exists on one of your shared disks for the Cluster Services partition. This partition is created automatically during Cluster Services installation. If you plan to create volumes on your shared disks before installing Cluster Services, then you should reserve space for a disk partition on one of your shared disks. If you have already installed Cluster Services, a partition has already been created for you.

The amount of space you need to reserve for the Cluster Services partition is calculated as follows. Disk geometry comprises heads, sectors per track, and cylinders. DOS type partitions must lie on a cylinder boundary. A cylinder is a number of heads multiplied by sectors per track. This is the minimum size of a disk partition. In most shared disk SANs with large disks, the geometry is

63 heads and 255 sectors per track. The minimum space you should reserve for the Cluster Services partition is 63 multiplied by 255 sectors = 16,065 sectors. With a fixed 512-byte sector size, this equates (16,065 × 512) to 8MB. In practice, we recommend you reserve at least 16MB on one of your shared disks for the Cluster Services partition.

Ideally, you should create shared disk NSS volumes after installing Cluster Services.

TIP

Know Your Shared Disks

Becoming familiar with your shared disks before creating storage groups or volumes is administration time that is well spent. Use NWCONFIG and select Standard Disk Options ⇨ Modify disk partitions and Hot Fix. You won't configure anything from this screen, but the information presented helps correlate use of your shared disks with the storage objects NSS displays on its configuration screens. Figure 9.6 shows the disk devices listed when you select Modify disk partitions and Hot Fix.

► • ◄

```
RConsoleJ: NODE1                                              _ □ ×
Server Screens   NWConfig Screen (active)   ▼   <<   >>  □ Sync  Activate  Disconnect  Help
NetWare Configuration

┌─────────────────────────────────────────────────────────────┐
│                    Configuration Options                       │
│ D├─────────────────────────────────┬──────────────────────────┤
│ S│     Available Disk Options       │d network drivers>        │
│ N│                                  │artitions/volumes>        │
│ L│ Modify disk partitions and Hot Fix│ge and volumes>          │
│  │ Mirror/Unmirror disk partitions  │licenses>                 │
│  ├─────────────────────────────────┴──────────────────────────┤
│  │                    Available Devices                         │
│  │ Device #1 [V500-A0-D0:0] Compaq 53C876 Slot 0 Port 1 ID 0 COMPAQ AB00932 │
│  │ Device #E [V502-A3-D0:0] Compaq RA4x00 Disk 0 NFT in SAN     │
│  │ Device #F [V502-A3-D0:1] Compaq RA4x00 Disk 1 NFT in SAN     │
│  └──────────────────────────────────────────────────────────┘ │
│                                                                 │
│ Highlight a disk drive and press <Enter>.                       │
│ Press <Esc> to return to the previous menu.                     │
└─────────────────────────────────────────────────────────────┘
```

FIGURE 9.6 *Using the Modify disk partitions and Hot Fix screen to display shared disks*

In Figure 9.6, NWCONFIG lists two shared disks in its Available Devices screen. These are the same devices displayed by entering the LIST DEVICES command at the server console. The corresponding shared disk device names are:

```
V502-A3-D0:0 - Compaq RA4x00 Disk 0 NFT in SAN

V502-A3-D0:1 - Compaq RA4x00 Disk 1 NFT in SAN
```

Make note of the device names corresponding to your shared disks, as you will need them later when creating NSS storage groups and volumes.

TIP

If you select one of your shared disks, its partitions will be displayed. Figure 9.7 lists the partitions on the shared disk named Disk 0.

FIGURE 9.7 *Disk 0 contains the Cluster Services partition and free space.*

If you aren't sure which of your devices are shared disks, you can try entering the LIST DEVICES **command at several of your server console screens. Your shared disks should be listed by every server attached to the shared disk array. Use this method to ignore devices listed only by one server. By definition, a disk cannot be a shared disk if it's visible to only one server. Be careful, however, because this method isn't foolproof; if you have not configured your shared disk driver correctly, or physically connected your server to the shared disk SAN, you may not see the shared disks you expect.**

TIP

Figure 9.7 shows that Disk 0 has a single partition. This shared disk happens to be the shared disk chosen by the Cluster Services install for the reserved Cluster Services partition. The Cluster Services partition has a size of 8MB. The rest of the shared disk is 17355.9MB of unpartitioned free space.

Figure 9.8 shows the result of inspecting the second shared disk called Disk 1. This has 17363.9MB of unpartitioned free space. It is completely empty. Disk 0 and Disk 1 are physically identical — both are 18.2GB 10,000 RPM Ultra-SCSI drives. Disk 1 has 8MB more free space than Disk 0, because Disk 0 contains the 8MB Cluster Services partition.

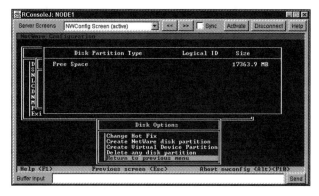

FIGURE 9.8 *Disk 1 has 17,363.9MB of unpartitioned free space and is completely empty.*

TIP

In addition to the list of shared disk device names you keep, also take note of how much free space is on each shared disk. The combination of device names and free space makes it easier to identify specific shared disks when using NWCONFIG **to create NSS storage groups and volumes. The size of free space displayed by the Disk Partition screen should be identical to available free space displayed by the NSS Storage ⇨ View free space screen.**

Creating a Storage Group

To create a storage group, you need to do two things:

- ▶ Claim ownership of unpartitioned free space on a shared disk (this will deposit a single storage object with NSS)

- ▶ Create a storage group from the single object.

TIP

Verify that NSS successfully detects the same amount of available free space as shown in the NWCONFIG Standard Disk Options menu. Using NWCONFIG, select NSS Disk Options ⇨ Storage ⇨ View free space, and tally the address and size of free space. Figure 9.9 lists two free space objects corresponding to shared disks Disk 0 and Disk 1 that are displayed on the NSS Available Free Space screen.

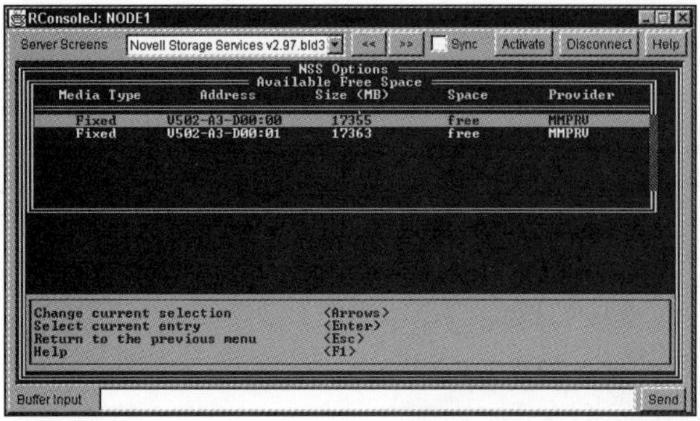

FIGURE 9.9 *The NSS Available Free Space screen lists available free space objects.*

In this example, the two free space objects correspond to shared disks Disk 0 and Disk 1, as shown in Table 9.2.

TABLE 9.2

Disk, Address, and Size

DISK	ADDRESS	SIZE (MB)
Disk 0	V502-A3-D00:00	17,355
Disk 1	V502-A3-D00:01	17,363

Before creating a storage group, you must first claim ownership of free space:

1. At the root NSS Available Options menu, select Storage ⇨ Assign ownership.

2. Select the free space object you wish to claim and hit Enter.

3. You are prompted to enter a size in megabytes. By default, NSS will claim the entire free space. If you want to reserve an area of unpartitioned free space on your disk, specify a smaller size now. You might, for example, want to reduce this value by 16MB to ensure there is space on the disk for the Cluster Services partition if you haven't already installed Cluster Services. Enter the desired size of your storage deposit, as shown in Figure 9.10.

4. Hit Enter and then confirm the operation.

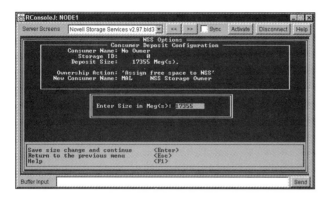

FIGURE 9.10 *Specify how much unpartitioned free space is assigned to NSS.*

NSS creates a new NSS disk partition of the size you specified, on your shared disk. The corresponding free space is deposited with NSS and you now have what NSS considers to be a single managed storage object. You can verify that NSS created a disk partition by returning to the Standard Disk Options ⇨ Modify disk partitions and Hot Fix screen. Figure 9.11 confirms that NSS has successfully created a new disk partition as a result of the assign ownership operation just completed.

FIGURE 9.11 *A new NSS disk partition is created when you assign ownership.*

To create a storage group from your single object, follow these steps:

1. Select NSS Disk Options ⇨ NSS Volume Options.

2. Log in to NDS as a user with sufficient rights to create the storage group.

3. Select Create ⇨ Storage Group. Your newly created single storage object is displayed on this screen, along with other objects.

4. Select your single object and hit Enter. Figure 9.12 shows the final confirmation required to create a storage group. In this example, 17,354MB of shared disk space corresponding to your single object is being assigned to the NSS storage group manager.

NOTE
To create a storage group, NSS reserves a small amount of space in your single object. The size of the resulting storage group is approximately 1MB less than that of the original single object. NSS uses the reserved space for internal management purposes.

FIGURE 9.12 *Creating a storage group converts a single object to a group object.*

Creating a Volume

You can create any number of volumes in a storage group as long as space is available. You can also extend the size of a volume by allocating additional space from any of your storage groups, effectively merging storage groups together.

When you create a volume in a storage group, you specify a size and a name. NSS requires that you select an existing storage group and specify a size that fits the available free space in that group. If you need to create a volume larger than the space available in any one of your storage groups, you can extend its size later by consuming space from other groups. Storage groups allow you to span volumes over a number of shared disks.

Follow these steps to create a volume in a storage group:

1. Select NSS Disk Options ⇨ NSS Volume Options.

2. Log in to NDS as a user with sufficient rights to create the storage group.

3. Select Create ⇨ NSS Volume. Free space available in your storage groups is listed, as shown in Figure 9.13. (Figure 9.13 lists two storage groups. One is 8MB larger than the other. The Address column identifies the corresponding disk devices.) Select the storage group you want to use to create the volume.

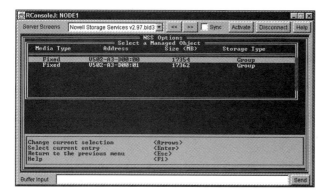

FIGURE 9.13 *When creating a volume, first select a storage group.*

4. Specify a size for the new volume in megabytes. Figure 9.14 shows a 1,000MB volume being created.

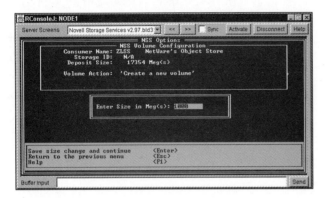

FIGURE 9.14 *Then specify a size for the new volume in megabytes.*

5. Specify a name for the volume, as in Figure 9.15. The new volume is called VOL1.

FIGURE 9.15 *Finally, type a name for the new volume.*

6. Hit Enter, and NSS creates a new volume, taking 1,000MB of free space from your storage group.

If you do the math (17,354 − 1,000 = 16,354MB of free space), you can see how much free space is still available for you to use to create other volumes. A new volume object is also created in NDS with a name derived from the physical server and volume names: NODE1_VOL1. This naming follows a standard convention: *ServerName_VolumeName*. Because you can create shared disk NSS volumes from any server in your cluster, the server name part of your NDS volume objects inherit the name of the server you used to create your volumes.

Managing NSS Volumes

Shared disk NSS volumes work the same as regular NSS volumes, with the following differences:

- ▸ To mount a shared disk NSS volume on a cluster node, the volume must first be activated. It must be placed in the ACTIVE state before it is mounted.

- ▸ To activate a shared disk NSS volume on a cluster node, the cluster node must be in the JOINED state. The cluster node must be a member of the cluster. If the cluster node is not a member of the cluster, the request to activate the volume fails.

- ▸ If a shared disk NSS volume is in the ACTIVE state on a cluster node, the volume cannot be activated by another cluster node. A request to activate the volume on a different cluster node will fail.

- ▸ To dismount a shared disk NSS volume so it can be mounted by another cluster node, the volume must be deactivated. It must be placed in the DEACTIVE state after it is dismounted.

- ▸ If a cluster node leaves the cluster, the cluster node will automatically deactivate all its shared disk NSS volumes.

- ▸ If a cluster node fails, other cluster nodes are allowed to activate any shared disk NSS volume that the failed cluster node may have activated and mounted before it failed.

Mounting a Volume

To mount a volume, enter the following commands, as shown in Figure 9.16 (volume VOL1 is mounted by cluster node NODE1):

```
NSS /ACTIVATE=volume_name
MOUNT volume_name
```

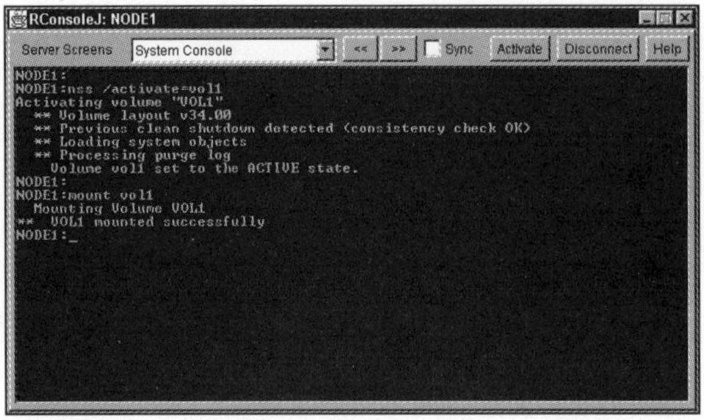

FIGURE 9.16 *Mounting a volume*

If you omit the NSS /ACTIVATE **command and mount a volume in the DEACTIVE state, NSS activates the volume automatically.**

TIP

Cluster Services guarantees you cannot mount a shared disk volume on more than one of your cluster nodes at the same time. You can try this for yourself. Go to the server console of another cluster node and try mounting the same volume. You receive the error shown in Figure 9.17.

FIGURE 9.17 *Cluster Services prevents a shared disk volume from being mounted by more than one cluster node.*

Dismounting a Volume

To dismount a volume, enter the following commands, as shown in Figure 9.18:

```
DISMOUNT volume_name
```

```
NSS /DEACTIVATE=volume_name
```

FIGURE 9.18 *Dismounting a volume*

If you omit the DISMOUNT **command and deactivate a volume that is mounted, NetWare dismounts the volume automatically.**

TIP

Listing Volume States

To list the state of your shared disk NSS volumes, enter the following command, as shown in Figure 9.19 (VOL1 is shown in the DEACTIVE state on cluster node NODE1):

```
nss volumes
```

When you type NSS VOLUMES **at a server console, NSS will display an additional volume named NSS_Admin. This is an internal in-memory volume provided by NSS for management purposes. NSS_Admin does not exist on any physical disk.**

NOTE

FIGURE 9.19 *Listing the state of volumes*

Cluster Enabling NSS Volumes

Cluster enabling a shared disk NSS volume is a procedure that configures the volume to be accessible using a standard Novell NetWare client regardless of which physical cluster node has the volume mounted. Once a shared disk NSS volume is cluster enabled, you can use your NetWare client to access files on the volume without needing to know which cluster node has the volume mounted at that time. If a cluster node fails or leaves the cluster, another cluster node will automatically remount the volume, and the NetWare client will reconnect to the new node. This enables continuous access to data and isolates users from server failure. Cluster enabling a volume masks all details of which cluster node is providing access to the volume so that any cluster node can mount the volume in unexpected server failure or maintenance situations. Because shared disk NSS volumes are physically decoupled from servers, when a volume fails over from one cluster node to another, the exact same data is made available when the volume is remounted and the NetWare client reconnects.

TIP
You do not need to cluster enable a shared disk NSS volume if files on the volume will not be accessed by the NetWare client. This may be the case if you intend to use the volume for Web server or database files. This kind of data is accessed using data-specific clients such as a Web browser or a client-side database utility.

You access and map drives to cluster-enabled volumes just like any other NetWare volume. This section contains instructions for cluster enabling shared disk NSS volumes and shows you how to use the standard Novell NetWare client to access files and map drives.

TIP

Using the NetWare client, you can access files on a shared disk NSS volume by browsing to the server that currently has the volume mounted and selecting the volume. However, this practice is problematic because you have no way of knowing which cluster node has the volume mounted at any given instant in time. Suppose, for example, you browse to cluster node NODE1, select volume VOL1, and map a drive. If cluster node NODE1 fails and volume VOL1 fails over to another cluster node, your NetWare client will lose its connection, and you will not know which of your other cluster nodes remounted the volume. But if you always map to the virtual NCP server/volume, you will always have access to the volume you mapped to. Cluster enabling shared disk NSS volumes is the recommended way to manage access to files on a cluster.

To cluster enable a shared disk NSS volume, you use the Cluster Services snapins for ConsoleOne. To cluster enable a volume, follow these steps:

1. Using ConsoleOne, select your cluster container object and click the New Cluster Volume button, or select File ➪ New ➪ Cluster ➪ New Cluster Volume. Your cluster container object must be highlighted, as in Figure 9.20, to enable the New Cluster Volume button. Click the button to open the New Cluster Volume dialog box.

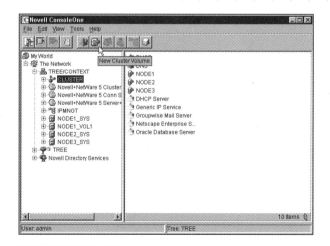

FIGURE 9.20 *Select the cluster container object.*

2. From the New Cluster Volume dialog box, shown in Figure 9.21, click the Volume button to browse the NDS tree and select the volume object corresponding to your shared disk NSS volume. You can also enter the fully distinguished NDS name of your volume object if you know it. It does not matter which cluster node you used to create the volume so long as there is a corresponding NDS volume object.

FIGURE 9.21 *Cluster enable a volume using the New Cluster Volume dialog box.*

Figure 9.22 shows the Select Object (Type: Volume) dialog box that appears when you click the Browse button. Select a volume object and then click OK.

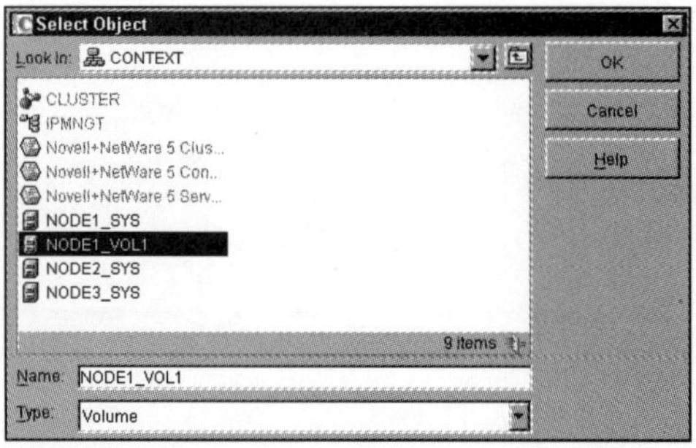

FIGURE 9.22 *Select a volume object using the Select Object (Type: Volume) dialog box.*

3. Back in the New Cluster Volume dialog box, specify a unique unused IP address. This IP address is the service address for the cluster-enabled volume and is entered as shown in Figure 9.23.

FIGURE 9.23 *Enter a unique IP address to complete the New Cluster Volume dialog box.*

4. Once you have completed the New Cluster Volume dialog box, click the Create button to cluster enable your shared disk NSS volume. ConsoleOne shows your cluster-enabled volume, as shown in Figure 9.24. The results of cluster enabling your shared disk NSS volume include:

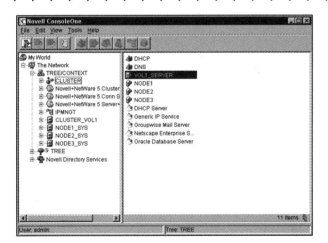

FIGURE 9.24 *The results of cluster enabling a volume*

- A new cluster volume resource object is created in the cluster container. VOL1_SERVER in Figure 9.24 is the new cluster volume resource object.

- The original NDS volume object is renamed to eliminate the server name dependency by replacing the server name part, with the cluster name. Figure 9.24 shows NODE1_VOL1 renamed to CLUSTER_VOL1.

- ConsoleOne also creates a new virtual NCP server object. (See Chapter 4 for an in-depth discussion of this object.) The virtual NCP server object name in this example is CLUSTER_VOL1_SERVER. Its network address is set to the IP address that you specified in the New Cluster Volume dialog box.

Congratulations! You have now cluster enabled your shared disk NSS volume.

Bringing a Cluster Volume Resource Online

Your newly created cluster volume resource must be online before NetWare clients can access the corresponding volume. Cluster Services executes the commands contained in the cluster volume resource load script to online the resource. ConsoleOne generates these commands automatically. Figure 9.25 shows the load script for the cluster volume resource, which you can view by right-clicking the cluster volume resource object, selecting Properties, and then selecting the Load tab.

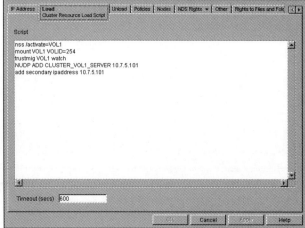

FIGURE 9.25 *Cluster volume resource load script*

WARNING **Ensure the shared disk NSS volume is deactivated before you online the cluster volume resource. If the volume is already in the ACTIVE state, the cluster volume resource load script will fail when it tries to activate the same volume. If this happens, ConsoleOne will show the cluster volume resource entering the Comatose state. To resolve this, you have to offline the cluster volume resource and then online it again.**

In this example of a load script, Cluster Services executes the following steps to online a cluster volume resource:

I. `nss /activate=VOL1`

Activates the shared disk NSS volume VOL1.

2. `mount VOL1 VOLID=254`

Mounts the volume with a fixed unique volume identifier. Each cluster-enabled volume is automatically assigned a unique volume identifier in descending order from 254 to 2 inclusive.

3. `trustmig VOL1 watch`

Migrates trustee identifiers and enables trustee watching. NDS trustee IDs embedded in the volume are translated to match the local server. This step scans the volume and translates all IDs.

4. `NUDP ADD CLUSTER_VOL1_SERVER 10.7.5.101`

Instantiates the cluster volume's virtual NCP server and IP address. Just like a regular volume, a cluster-enabled volume has a host NCP server. A virtual NCP server is instantiated on a physical NCP server and emulates the host server for its corresponding cluster-enabled volume. NetWare clients connect to a physical server via the virtual server IP address and believe they are connected to a server identified by the virtual server name, not the actual physical name. Because virtual NCP server names are constant regardless of which physical server they are instantiated on, a NetWare client connecting to a cluster-enabled volume will always receive the same file server name.

5. `add secondary ipaddress 10.7.5.101`

Adds the virtual NCP server's IP address as a secondary IP address. This command dynamically adds the IP address to the physical server so NetWare clients can access the cluster-enabled volume by connecting to its corresponding virtual NCP server IP address.

WARNING If you edit the cluster volume resource load script, be sure to retain the ordering of the automatically generated commands. The ADD SECONDARY IPADDRESS command used to add the virtual NCP server's IP address must always follow the TRUSTMIG command. If the order of these two commands is reversed, NetWare clients might be able to connect and access files on the volume before trustee IDs are completely processed.

To online the cluster volume resource, follow these steps:

1. In ConsoleOne, select View ⇨ Cluster State. The cluster volume resource VOL1_SERVER, shown in Figure 9.26, is in the offline state when first created.

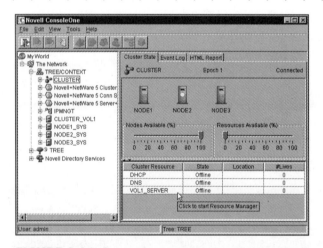

FIGURE 9.26 *Cluster volume resources are created in the offline state.*

2. Click the cluster volume resource to start the Cluster Resource Manager dialog box. Your choices are Online, Cancel, or Help, as shown in Figure 9.27. Click the Online button to start the cluster volume resource.

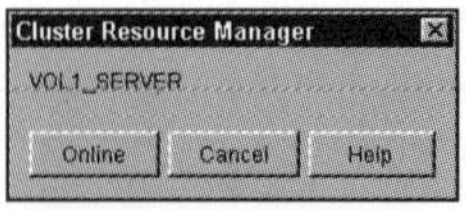

FIGURE 9.27 *Click the Online button to start the cluster volume resource.*

3. Cluster Services executes the commands in the cluster volume resource load script on the cluster node determined by the current cluster membership and the preferred nodes list. By default, this is the first node configured in your cluster, as shown in Figure 9.28.

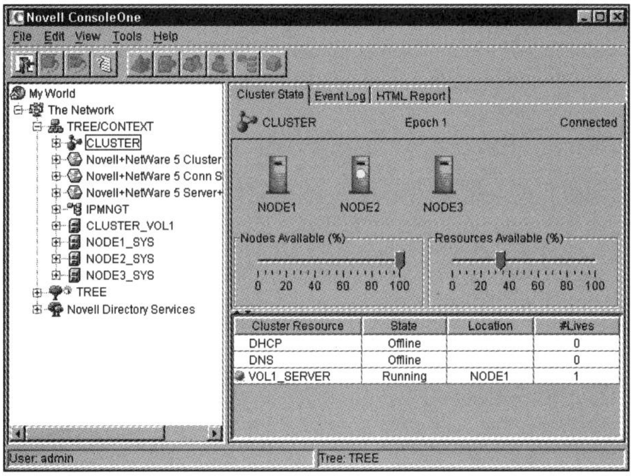

FIGURE 9.28 *Cluster volume resource running on cluster node NODE1*

Figure 9.29 shows Cluster Services executing commands from the load script on cluster node NODE1. The volume is first activated and mounted. Then trustee IDs are migrated. Only when migration is complete is the virtual NCP server instantiated and its IP address bound to the server.

FIGURE 9.29 *Cluster Services executes commands from the load script.*

Use the server console command VMVOLUMES to verify volume identifiers. Cluster-enabled volumes have volume identifiers that start at 254 and descend. You can list volumes (and verify volume identifiers) using three different server console commands:

- ▸ VOLUMES — List all mounted volumes.

- ▸ NSS VOLUMES — List NSS volumes.

- ▸ VMVOLUMES — List all mounted volumes and volume identifiers.

Figure 9.30 compares output from the different volume commands available at the server console. Because VOL1 is the first cluster-enabled volume, it has a volume identifier of 254, shown in the Number column of the volume information displayed by VMVOLUMES. Subsequent cluster-enabled volumes have identifiers 253, 252, and so on.

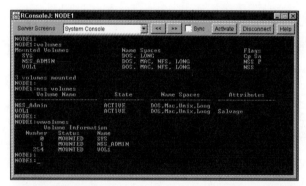

FIGURE 9.30 *Examples of three different console commands to list volumes*

Your cluster-enabled shared disk NSS volume is now ready to be accessed by NetWare clients. Because Cluster Services is now managing your cluster volume resource, access to your cluster-enabled volume is guaranteed. If the cluster node on which the cluster volume resource was started unexpectedly fails or is shut down for maintenance, Cluster Services will restart the cluster volume resource by executing its load script on the next available node in its preferred nodes list. This ensures that the cluster-enabled volume stays available and allows you to access files no matter what happens to individual servers.

Using Cluster-Enabled Volumes

In general, you use cluster-enabled shared disk NSS volumes just like regular NetWare volumes. The standard Novell NetWare clients behave normally. Use the standard NetWare Administrator (NWAdmin) or ConsoleOne tools to grant rights, enable quotas, or perform any other standard volume administration. Configuring services to access files on cluster-enabled volumes offers no surprises either.

The recommended way to access a cluster-enabled volume is through its NDS volume object. You can also map a drive to the volume using the IP address of the NCP virtual server followed by the volume name — for example, \\10.7.5. 101\vol1. Figure 9.31 shows browsing to a cluster-enabled volume via its NDS volume object. Cluster-enabled volumes look no different than regular volumes when browsing the NDS tree. In fact, you're not supposed to be able to tell the difference.

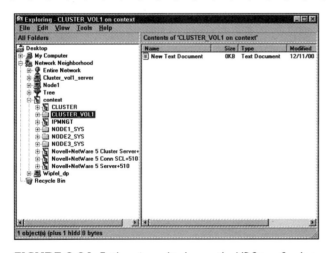

FIGURE 9.31 *Explorer is used to browse the NDS tree for cluster-enabled volumes.*

When you select a cluster-enabled volume in the NDS tree, your NetWare client connects to its host server. The host server for a cluster-enabled volume is a virtual NCP server instantiated on a physical cluster node. You cannot tell from the NetWare client which physical server it is. The standard Windows Explorer screen in Figure 9.31 shows the result of browsing to the cluster-enabled volume CLUSTER_VOL1 in the NDS tree. Note also the presence of what looks like a regular NetWare file server called CLUSTER_VOL1_SERVER. This is the host server for the cluster-enabled volume, CLUSTER_VOL1. It is a virtual NCP server. To you, the user of the NetWare client, it appears just like a regular file server. This is intentional. If the cluster node that currently has VOL1 mounted unexpectedly fails, VOL1 will failover to another node. This does not change the name of the host server. The NetWare client reconnects to what it thinks is the same host server: CLUSTER_VOL1_SERVER, in this example. Thus, volume failover is transparent to users of the NetWare client.

Figure 9.32 shows the NetWare client connection table. To display it, right-click the red Novell "N" on your system tray and select NetWare Connections. Connection number 30 is a connection to the virtual NCP server corresponding to the cluster-enabled volume CLUSTER_VOL1. The resource name is CLUSTER_VOL1_SERVER. As you can see, the name by which the NetWare client knows the cluster-enabled volume's host server is the virtual NCP server.

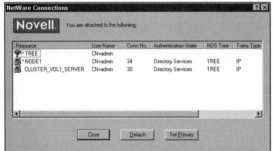

FIGURE 9.32 *NetWare client connections*

NOTE

Connections to cluster-enabled volumes require an IP client. IPX is not supported by Cluster Services.

Mapping by NDS Volume Object

You map drives to cluster-enabled volumes the same way you map them to regular NetWare volumes. Figure 9.33 shows one of the standard ways to do this. Right-click the NDS volume object and select Novell Map Network Drive.

The standard Novell Map Drive dialog box displays, as in Figure 9.34. The path is a Universal Naming Convention (UNC)–formatted fully distinguished NDS name of the cluster-enabled volume object. Drive mapping works the same way for cluster-enabled volumes as it does for regular NetWare volumes. You select the desired map options and then click the Map button.

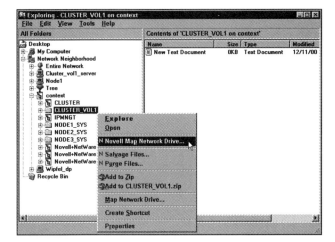

FIGURE 9.33 *Mapping a drive by NDS volume object*

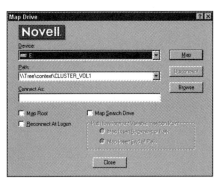

FIGURE 9.34 *The standard Novell Map Drive dialog box*

Figure 9.35 shows the result of the map drive operation, a new E: drive accessible via the standard Windows Explorer.

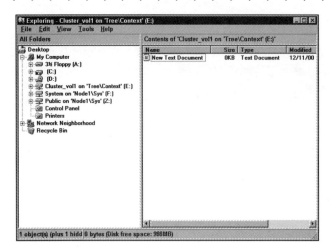

FIGURE 9.35 *Drive E: mapped to the cluster-enabled volume*

Just like regular drives, drives mapped to cluster-enabled volumes are accessible from a DOS command shell, as in Figure 9.36. The Volume Serial Number displayed by the DOS command shell is an encoding of the virtual NCP server's IP address. The serial number in this example is 0A07-0565. The IP address is 0A.07.05.65. Translate the hex fields into decimal to get the dotted decimal IP address of 10.7.5.101.

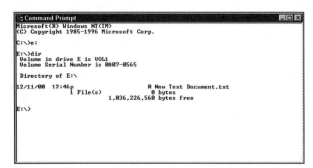

FIGURE 9.36 *DOS command shell accessing a mapped cluster-enabled volume*

Mapping by IP Address

You can map a drive to a cluster-enabled volume via the IP address of the virtual NCP server, as shown in Figure 9.37. Using the standard DOS `map` command or Windows Explorer Novell Map Network Drive, map to the cluster-enabled volume by specifying a UNC pathname using the virtual NCP server's IP address in place of the server name. It's also possible to configure a Domain Name System (DNS) entry for the IP address and use the DNS name instead of the IP address.

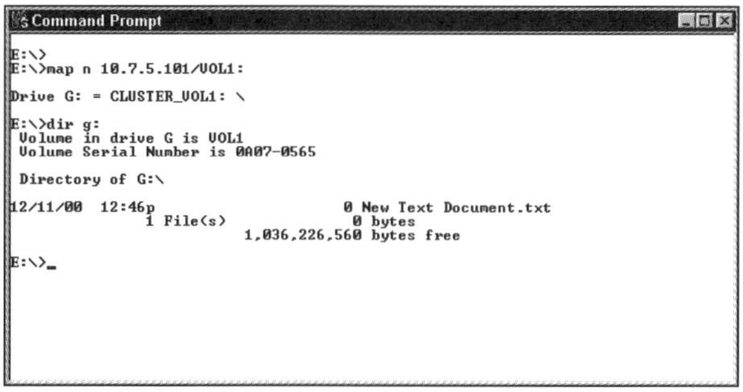

```
Command Prompt                                          _ □ X
E:\>
E:\>map n 10.7.5.101/VOL1:

Drive G: = CLUSTER_VOL1: \

E:\>dir g:
 Volume in drive G is VOL1
 Volume Serial Number is 0A07-0565

 Directory of G:\

12/11/00  12:46p                 0 New Text Document.txt
                1 File(s)          0 bytes
                      1,036,226,560 bytes free

E:\>_
```

FIGURE 9.37 *Mapping a drive by IP address*

Mapping by Virtual Server Name

To map a drive to, or generally access, a cluster-enabled volume by its virtual NCP server name, you must download and install the CVSBIND utility from Novell at `http://support.novell.com/cgi-bin/search/searchtid.cgi?/2957434`. With this utility installed, you map a drive using standard UNC pathname syntax and a virtual NCP server name in place of a regular server name.

CVSBIND is an acronym for Cluster Virtual Server Bindery. CVSBIND advertises virtual servers in the NetWare bindery namespace via Service Location Protocol (SLP) emulation. If you have an application or service that can be configured to access its files only from a classic server name–based UNC pathname and you want to configure your software to use cluster-enabled volumes, you need to use the CVSBIND utility.

If you are running Novell Cluster Services software version 1.01 SP2 or later, CVSBIND is included with your software. You only need to download CVSBIND from Novell's Support Web site if you have an older version of Cluster Services software. For NetWare 5.x clusters, regardless of which version of Cluster Services software you are running, CVSBIND is not installed by default and you must use the steps outlined in the following section.

Installing CVSBIND   If you have downloaded CVSBIND from Novell's Support Web site or you are running Novell Cluster Services 1.01 SP2 or later and already have CVSBIND, follow these steps:

1. Down the cluster. Enter the CLUSTER DOWN command at one node in the cluster. All nodes will leave the cluster.

2. Unload the cluster software on all nodes. Enter ULDNCS at each server in the cluster. The Cluster Services NLMs are unloaded.

3. Copy CVSBIND.NLM to SYS:\SYSTEM on each server in the cluster.

Omit this step if you have Novell Cluster Services version 1.01 SP2 or later.

NOTE

4. On each server in the cluster, edit SYS:\SYSTEM\LDNCS.NCF to load CVSBIND. Add this command — CVSBIND — after this command — CMON — but before this command — CLUSTER JOIN.

5. On each server in the cluster, edit SYS:\SYSTEM\ULDNCS.NCF to unload CVSBIND. Add this command — unload CVSBIND — after this command — CLUSTER LEAVE — but before this command — unload CMON.

6. Restart the cluster. Enter LDNCS at the console prompt of each server in the cluster. This loads Cluster Services software and restarts clustering on all your nodes.

Using CVSBIND   Once loaded, CVSBIND enables the following console commands:

▶ CVSBIND ADD VIRTUAL_SERVER_NAME IP_ADDRESS

The CVSBIND ADD command adds a virtual NCP server name and its corresponding IP address to the SLP bindery namespace on the server that it is executed on.

▶ CVSBIND DEL VIRTUAL_SERVER_NAME IP_ADDRESS

The CVSBIND DEL command deletes the virtual NCP server name and its corresponding IP address from the SLP bindery namespace on the server that it is executed on.

The syntax is similar to the NUDP ADD and DEL commands. CVSBIND commands should be added to cluster volume resource load and unload scripts. The simplest way to do this is to copy and then paste the existing NUDP command and substitute CVSBIND for NUDP. The CVSBIND command is case-insensitive, but the server name must be entered in upper case.

Add the CVSBIND ADD command to the cluster volume resource load script before the NUDP command.

1. Launch ConsoleOne, then browse to the cluster container object. Your cluster resources are displayed in the right-hand pane.

2. Right-click the Cluster Volume Resource, then select Properties to display its property pages.

3. Select the Load tab, then edit the CVSBIND command into the load script. Add the CVSBIND ADD command to the load script before the NUDP command.

```
nss /activate=VOL1

mount VOL1 VOLID=254

trustmig VOL1 watch

CVSBIND ADD CLUSTER_VOL1_SERVER 10.7.5.101

NUDP ADD CLUSTER_VOL1_SERVER 10.7.5.101

add secondary ipaddress 10.7.5.101
```

Add the CVSBIND DEL command to the cluster volume resource unload script after the NUDP command.

1. Launch ConsoleOne, then browse to the cluster container object. Your cluster resources are displayed in the right-hand pane.

2. Right-click the Cluster Volume Resource, then select Properties to display its property pages.

3. Select the Unload tab, then edit the `CVSBIND` command into the unload script. Add the `CVSBIND DEL` command to the unload script after the `NUDP` command.

```
del secondary ipaddress 10.7.5.101

NUDP DEL CLUSTER_VOL1_SERVER 10.7.5.101

CVSBIND DEL CLUSTER_VOL1_SERVER 10.5.7.101

trustmig VOL1 unwatch

dismount VOL1 /force

nss /forcedeactivate=VOL1
```

The `CVSBIND ADD` and `DEL` commands add or delete bindery service entries in the SLP namespace for the supplied virtual NCP server name and its corresponding IP address. NetWare bindery emulation is implemented via the SLP URL `service:bindery.novell`. You can inspect the SLP namespace using the following console commands:

```
display slp services

display slp attributes service:bindery.novell:
```

Adding Virtual Server Names to the HOSTS File

For some server-side applications that cannot resolve the name of a virtual server to an IP address any other way, the virtual server name can be added to the `HOSTS` file on all servers in the cluster. To add a virtual server name and its corresponding IP address to the `HOSTS` file, follow these steps:

I. On each server, enter `EDIT SYS:ETC\HOSTS` at the server console prompt.

2. At the bottom of the file, add a line for the Virtual Server (not Volume) name and its IP address:

```
10.7.5.101    CLUSTER_VOL1_SERVER.CLUSTER.COM
CLUSTER_VOL1_SERVER
```

3. Press Esc and select Yes to save your changes.

Mapping from an NDS Login Script

To map a drive to a cluster-enabled volume from an NDS user or container login script, use any of the three map-by alternatives:

- NDS volume object

- Virtual NCP server IP address

- Virtual NCP server name

Figure 9.38 shows commands in an NDS user login script to map a drive to a cluster-enabled volume. The V: drive is mapped to the cluster-enabled volume by the NDS volume object's fully distinguished name: `.cluster_vol1.context`.

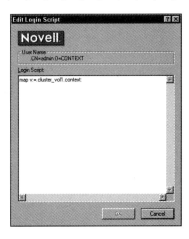

FIGURE 9.38 *Mapping a cluster-enabled volume in an NDS login script*

Failover and Cluster-Enabled Volumes

Cluster-enabled volumes are managed via their corresponding cluster volume resource. Like all cluster resources, Cluster Services ensures high availability by managing the failover process should a cluster node fail. If a cluster node unexpectedly fails, and it is running a cluster volume resource (has a cluster-enabled volume mounted), Cluster Services does the following to achieve a failover: It executes the cluster volume resource load script on the next most preferred node available in the cluster. The load script performs these steps:

1. Activates and mounts the shared disk NSS volume. NSS activates the volume quickly, regardless of the size of the volume or the nature of the previous node's failure.

2. Migrates trustee identifiers and enables trustee watching. The volume is scanned and all embedded trustee IDs are translated into new trustee IDs valid in the local server's NDS context. Trustee ID migration requires an amount of time roughly proportional to the number of unique trustees present on the volume, not to the volume size nor the number of files or directories. Once complete, a trustee watcher is enabled on the volume. This monitors in realtime the creation or modification of trustees on the volume and updates a database held on the volume as changes are made.

3. Instantiates the virtual NCP server and binds its IP address. This establishes a mapping between the IP address and virtual NCP server name. NetWare clients connecting to the virtual server IP address are given the virtual server name in place of the physical server name. Binding the virtual NCP server's IP address is the final step that allows NetWare clients to connect or reconnect to a server.

NetWare Client Reconnect

NetWare clients accessing a cluster-enabled volume on a node that unexpectedly fails lose their connections. The standard Novell NetWare client is designed to handle this situation by automatically reconnecting to the same network address. Because cluster-enabled volumes have a constant host virtual NCP server and IP address regardless of which physical server is running the corresponding cluster volume resource, the NetWare client reconnects to what it believes is the same file server. Depending on the client OS, you will experience different behavior as your client reconnects. Table 9.3 lists the standard NetWare clients and their reconnect behavior.

TABLE 9.3

NetWare Client Reconnect Behavior

CLIENT	RECONNECT BEHAVIOR
Windows 95/98/Me	Drive letters and file handles are reconnected.
	If an application is referencing a file, it will suspend until the reconnect completes. Files opened with an exclusive access mode cannot be reconnected. If your application opens a file deny-all, it will receive an error when reconnected.
	You do not have to relogin nor remap drive letters.
	Client reconnect is transparent in most cases.

TABLE 9.3	
NetWare Client Reconnect Behavior	
CLIENT	**RECONNECT BEHAVIOR**
Windows NT/2000	Drive letters are reconnected.
	If an application is referencing a file, it will receive an error. Some applications open a file only to read or write its contents, then immediately close it.
	You do not have to relogin nor remap drive letters.
	Client reconnect on Windows NT/2000 can be less transparent than it is on Windows 98, depending on the application being used. In some cases, you will need to manually retry the operation if it fails during a reconnect.

Space Restrictions

User space restrictions do not failover with cluster-enabled volumes. If you create user space restrictions on a cluster-enabled volume, they will be lost on failover to another cluster node. Novell intends to support user space restrictions failover in the version of Cluster Services slated for release with NetWare 6.

 Do not create user space restrictions on cluster-enabled volumes. They become invalid if the cluster-enabled volume fails over.

WARNING

Directory space restrictions are supported on cluster-enabled volumes and remain valid after failover. Directory space restrictions are always enforced regardless of what cluster node mounts a volume.

Managing Cluster-Enabled Volume Trustees

Trustee identifiers embedded in a cluster-enabled volume are managed by the Cluster Services TRUSTMIG utility. Trustee migration is automatic for cluster-enabled volumes; the appropriate TRUSTMIG commands are added to cluster volume resource load and unload scripts. For each cluster-enabled volume, TRUSTMIG creates a database of fully distinguished NDS trustee names and corresponding local server NDS identifiers. The database file is held in a hidden directory at the root of the cluster-enabled volume: _NETWARE\trustmig.fil.

Watching for Trustee Changes

When a cluster-enabled volume resource is running on a cluster node, which implies the TRUSTMIG watch command has been executed by its load script, changes to NDS trustee objects are caught and applied to TRUSTMIG's local database of NDS trustee names and identifiers. For example, if you grant a user rights to a directory on the cluster volume and then delete the user object from the NDS tree, TRUSTMIG catches this operation and deletes the corresponding entries in its database. Renaming trustee objects in NDS also translates into events that TRUSTMIG catches. TRUSTMIG continuously watches for events that affect its database.

WARNING

A large percentage of the support calls Novell receives concern trustee assignments and failover. If you perform NDS trustee operations and TRUSTMIG is not watching the corresponding volume, it can lose track of changes that would otherwise be applied to its database. If you manually mount a shared disk NSS volume, TRUSTMIG won't be run, and therefore, changes will not be tracked. Try to avoid renaming or moving NDS trustee objects if they have been granted rights to cluster-enabled volumes and the volume resource is offline. If objects are renamed or moved when TRUSTMIG is not watching the volume, the rights those objects had to the files or directories on the volume are lost if the volume fails over.

TRUSTMIG

TRUSTMIG provides the following server console commands:

- ▶ TRUSTMIG list — Lists the cluster-enabled volumes currently being watched.

- ▶ TRUSTMIG *volumeName* watch — Migrates all trustee IDs and enables trustee watching. This command is automatically added to your cluster volume resource load script when you cluster enable a volume.

- ▶ TRUSTMIG *volumeName* unwatch — Disables trustee watching on the cluster-enabled volume. This command is automatically added to your cluster volume resource unload script when you cluster enable a volume.

- ▶ TRUSTMIG *volumeName* migrate — Migrates all trustee IDs on the cluster-enabled volume.

TRUSTOOL

TRUSTOOL is a trustee ID diagnostic and repair tool. It provides the following server console commands:

► TRUSTOOL *volumeName* DUMP — Lists to the console screen and to SYS:ETC\TRUSTDMP.TXT all NDS distinguished names and the state of trustee ID migration.

► TRUSTOOL *volumeName* FIX — Forces TRUSTMIG to finish a partial migrate back to the previous server.

► TRUSTOOL *volumeName* PURGE — Deletes bad NDS distinguished names in the TRUSTMIG database. You must first manually mount the volume before using TRUSTOOL with the PURGE option. This will rename TRUSTMIG.FIL to TRUSTMIG.BAK and make a new TRUSTMIG.FIL in the _NETWARE directory.

Bad NDS distinguished names occur when a user or group is deleted without trustee rights to files being removed from the cluster-enabled volume, or when NDS doesn't synchronize soon enough after new users with trustee assignments are added. Occasional problems occur if a volume fails over immediately after a user is deleted and the user had trustee rights to files on the volume. If you experience errors when a cluster-enabled volume fails over and its trustee IDs migrate to a new server, you will need to run TRUSTOOL with the PURGE option to delete bad entries from the database. You will then have to manually reassign whatever trustee assignments were lost.

To display the contents of the TRUSTMIG database for a cluster-enabled volume, first ensure that the volume is not being watched. Use TRUSTMIG to unwatch the volume, as shown in Figure 9.39. You run TRUSTOOL by specifying the name of the volume and the DUMP option. Only one trustee exists on volume VOL1 in Figure 9.39. Its NDS fully distinguished name is .CN=user.O=context. T=TREE, and the corresponding trustee identifier is 809B. Old Node is the name of the cluster node where TRUSTMIG was last run against the volume: NODE1. State shows the volume ready to MONITOR. This means it is in a state appropriate to watch for trustee assignment changes. To return the volume to its previous state, run TRUSTMIG with the watch option, also shown in Figure 9.39.

FIGURE 9.39 *Using TRUSTOOL to inspect trustee IDs on a cluster-enabled volume*

Reconfiguring NSS Volumes

You can reconfigure shared disk NSS volumes when you want to do one of the following:

▶ Expand a volume by allocating free space from a storage group.

▶ Rename a volume by changing its physical or corresponding NDS volume object name.

▶ Delete a volume.

WARNING **The instructions in this section assume you are running Novell Cluster Services software version 1.01 SP2 or later. If you are using an earlier version of Cluster Services software, you must perform these reconfiguration steps from a single cluster node with all other cluster nodes shut down. If you do not do this, you risk multiple nodes having an inconsistent view of shared storage and possible volume corruption.**

If a shared disk NSS volume is cluster-enabled, you can change the virtual NCP server's IP address. If a shared disk NSS volume is cluster-enabled, there will be a corresponding NDS cluster volume resource object in the cluster container. If it is not cluster-enabled, a cluster application resource will reference the shared disk NSS volume. A shared disk NSS volume may not need to be cluster-enabled if transparent access from NetWare clients is not required, as is the case for the Netscape Web server or the Oracle database. In the case of either a cluster volume resource or application resource that references a shared disk NSS volume, the current location of a shared disk NSS volume is determined by inspecting the state of its corresponding cluster resource. Shared disk NSS volumes are activated and deactivated from load and unload scripts belonging to a cluster volume or application resource.

Before reconfiguring a shared disk NSS volume, first determine whether your volume is in the ACTIVE state on any one of your cluster nodes. To do this, use ConsoleOne to inspect the current state and location of the corresponding cluster volume or application resource. Select your cluster container object, and click View ⇨ Cluster State View. Figure 9.40 shows the Cluster State view and a cluster volume resource VOL1_SERVER in the Running state on NODE1. The corresponding shared disk NSS volume is therefore currently in the ACTIVE state on NODE1. You can verify this by listing NSS volumes on NODE1 using the NSS VOLUMES command from NODE1's server console.

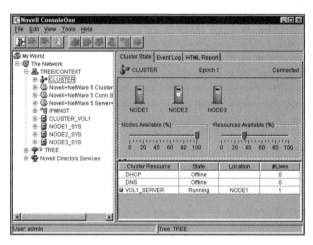

FIGURE 9.40 *Use ConsoleOne to locate your shared-disk NSS volumes.*

If your shared disk NSS volume is in the ACTIVE state on a cluster node different than the one you are working from, NWCONFIG blocks the operation you are attempting, and you receive an error message. Figure 9.41 shows a case in which NWCONFIG is running on NODE2, but the shared disk NSS volume VOL1 is in the ACTIVE state on NODE1. As you can see, NWCONFIG cannot perform the desired operation from NODE1. So to avoid this issue, run NWCONFIG from the node where the shared disk NSS volume is in the ACTIVE state. If your volume is in the DEACTIVE state on all nodes, you can run the NWCONFIG utility on any node.

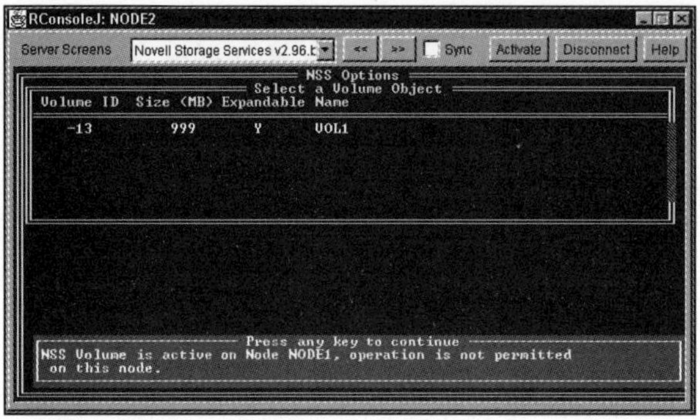

FIGURE 9.41 *If you attempt to reconfigure a shared disk NSS volume that is ACTIVE on a different cluster node, NWCONFIG will block the operation.*

To reconfigure NSS volumes, you use the NWCONFIG utility to:

▶ Expand or rename your volume.

▶ Delete your volume.

Expanding Volumes

To expand an NSS volume, use the NWCONFIG utility on the node where the volume is active or on any node if it is not active anywhere, follow these steps:

1. Select NSS Disk Options ⇨ NSS Volume Options.

2. Select Modify ⇨ Increase NSS Volume Size.

3. Select the volume you wish to expand.

4. Select a storage group and specify how much free space to take from the storage group to add to your volume.

Renaming and Deleting Volumes

To rename or delete a cluster-enabled shared disk NSS volume, you must first offline and delete the corresponding cluster volume resource. If your cluster volume resource is in the Running state, offline it. To do this, use ConsoleOne. From the Cluster State view, click the corresponding cluster volume resource object to launch the Cluster Resource Manager dialog box, shown in Figure 9.42. Your choices are Offline, Migrate, Cancel, and Help. Click the Offline button to offline the resource.

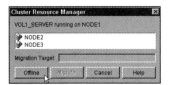

FIGURE 9.42 *Offline the cluster volume resource before reconfiguring the NSS volume.*

Deleting Volumes   To delete a cluster volume resource, use ConsoleOne and select the cluster container in the left-hand Console view and then select the cluster volume resource you wish to delete. Right-click it, and select Delete NDS Object. Figure 9.43 shows the Delete NDS Object option displayed when the VOL1_SERVER cluster volume resource is right-clicked. When a cluster volume resource is deleted, ConsoleOne automatically deletes the corresponding virtual NCP server and cluster volume objects from NDS. This does not delete your shared disk NSS volume, only the NDS objects that describe it.

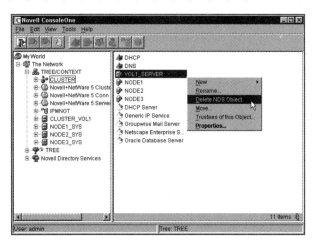

FIGURE 9.43 *Deleting a cluster volume resource from the cluster container*

To delete an NSS volume, use the NWCONFIG utility on the node where the volume is active or on any node if it is not active anywhere and then follow these steps:

1. Select NSS Disk Options ➪ NSS Volume Options.

2. Enter a user name with sufficient rights and the password.

3. Select Delete ➪ NSS Volume.

4. Select the volume you wish to delete.

5. Confirm the action by hitting the Return key.

Renaming Volumes   To rename a volume, use the NWCONFIG utility on the node where the volume is active or on any node if it is not active anywhere and then follow these steps:

1. Select NSS Disk Options ➪ NSS Volume Options.

2. Enter a user name with sufficient rights and the password.

3. Select Modify ➪ Rename NSS Volume.

4. Select the volume you wish to rename.

5. Enter a new name for your volume.

6. Confirm the action by hitting the Return key.

7. If your shared disk NSS volume was cluster-enabled, follow the previously described steps to cluster enable the renamed volume.

Changing a Virtual NCP Server's IP Address

To change a virtual NCP server's IP address, use ConsoleOne, and follow these steps:

1. Offline the cluster volume resource. Changes to cluster resource properties take effect only when the cluster resource is brought online.

2. From the Console view, select the cluster container, then right-click the cluster volume resource object, and choose Properties. Select the IP Address property tab and change the IP address as desired, ensuring that the new IP address is unique and unused. Click the Apply button to save and apply the changes. Figure 9.44 shows the current IP address for a cluster volume resource VOL1_SERVER. The IP address is 10.7.5.101.

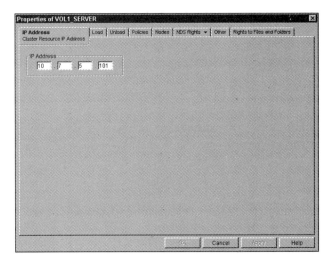

FIGURE 9.44 *Changing a virtual NCP server's IP address*

3. To activate the change you made, you need to online the cluster volume resource. From the Cluster State view in ConsoleOne, click the corresponding cluster volume resource to start the Cluster Resource Manager dialog box. Click the Online button to online the resource.

Tuning Recommendations

Follow the tuning recommendations in this section to ensure that your NSS volumes are operating at peak performance and that the load is evenly distributed across your cluster nodes and shared disk devices.

NSS Parameters

Default NetWare 5.*x* installations are tuned for the Traditional NetWare File System (TFS). NSS requires parameter modifications to obtain enhanced performance. Failure to tune the server for NSS will most likely result in poor performance.

NSS has a set of unique parameters configured when loading NSS modules. Following are some of the parameters that tune NSS performance:

► `CacheBalance`— Sets what percentage of memory to use for the buffer cache.

► `FileFlushTimer`— Sets the flush time for modified open files in seconds.

► `BufferFlushTimer`— Sets the flush time for modified cache buffers in seconds.

► `ClosedFileCacheSize`— Sets the number of closed files that can be cached in memory.

CacheBalance   This is the single most important parameter in tuning NSS. `CacheBalance` controls how much memory is available for NSS to use for cache and therefore directly affects the performance of the NSS file system. The default value for NetWare 5.0 SP2 is 10 percent of server memory. Increasing this to 80 or 90 percent achieves performance close to TFS.

TFS takes 100 percent of memory unless NSS is loaded, in which case TFS receives what is left after NSS takes its share.

NOTE

FileFlushTimer and BufferFlushTimer   Increasing `FileFlushTimer` and `BufferFlushTimer` from their default values helps with caching up to a certain point, but increasing them too much causes a throttling problem when writing back metadata. This effect is dependent on processor and disk speed, so you should experiment with these parameters for your system. If NSS performance is bad, 75 might be too high and you should try 50. If performance is just sub par, try increasing them a little.

ClosedFileCacheSize   `ClosedFileCacheSize` controls how many closed files are kept in cache. With sufficient memory, set this to 50,000, and adjust as necessary.

Setting NSS Parameters   To set NSS parameters, issue the following command when loading NSS:

```
NSS /AUTODEACTIVATEVOLUME=ALL /cachebalance=80 /fileflushtimer=75 /
bufferflushtimer=75 /closedfilecachesize=8192
```

Parameters should be listed on a single command line. Remember to ensure that the `/AUTODEACTIVATEVOLUME=ALL` **option remains in the** `AUTOEXEC.NCF` **file.**

NOTE

Partitioning Data across Volumes

Cluster-enabled NSS volumes are mounted by a single cluster node at a time. In order to effectively utilize all your clustered servers, partition your data into at least kN separate volumes, where N is the number of nodes in your cluster and k is a small constant number like 2 or 3. Configure the preferred nodes list for each cluster volume resource so that corresponding cluster-enabled volumes are distributed over available nodes. Adopting this approach offers the following benefits:

▸ Your data is distributed over many volumes, and the volumes are distributed over many cluster nodes. Thus, all your servers do useful work, and you obtain the maximum use of your hardware.

▸ Because data is distributed over more volumes and cluster nodes, every node will have more volumes mounted concurrently. If a node unexpectedly fails, its volumes are redistributed across surviving nodes. Each volume can be configured to failover to a different cluster node. This allows the resources to fan out during the failover process so each surviving node takes over only a fraction of the load previously handled by the failed node. Failover is faster and more reliable if data is partitioned over more volumes and cluster nodes. You won't overload a single surviving node during failover.

▸ The time to failover a cluster-enabled volume is a function of the number of unique NDS trustee IDs it contains. If you have more volumes, each can failover to a different cluster node, and the trustee ID migration processes can run in parallel.

▸ Managing your data is easier if you create a number of smaller volumes rather than one very large one. You will have problems if you create one very large volume for all your data because only a single cluster node can mount it; other nodes will be left unused and therefore redundant.

RAID-Sets and NSS Storage Groups

RAID-sets and NSS storage groups are useful ways to aggregate a number of physical disks. You create a RAID-set from a configurable number of disks and then assign ownership to NSS. More disks per RAID-set increases the size of virtual disks presented to NetWare. Try to strike a balance between the number of RAID-sets and NSS storage groups. Shared disk arrays typically limit the maximum number of RAID-sets you can create. And once NetWare has partitioned a RAID-set, its size cannot be increased. If you desire future expandability, create a number of RAID-sets. Then create an NSS storage group per RAID-set and create volumes in your storage groups.

TIP

If your configuration is limited by the number of LUNs the storage array can provide, but you desire the flexibility of dynamically assigning a larger number of smaller (than LUN) storage units to individual servers, then use NSS storage groups to create more volumes than you have LUNs and then use Cluster Services to manage the assignment of volumes to servers. Some customers have discovered that this method of storage virtualization is actually one of the most valuable features of the Cluster Services product. Sub-LUN level storage configuration can be performed with all servers and storage online.

Summary

This chapter covered the difference between direct attach and shared disks. You learned how to work with shared disks and how to create NSS storage groups and volumes on shared disks. Cluster-enabled volumes are NSS volumes created on shared disks with a virtualized host file server. The chapter described how to cluster enable a shared disk NSS volume by providing a unique IP address for the virtual NCP server.

Mapping drives to cluster-enabled volumes is no different than mapping drives to regular NetWare volumes, and you examined how to map via NDS volume object, IP address, and UNC server pathname. If a cluster node unexpectedly fails, its cluster-enabled volumes failover to other nodes in the cluster. This chapter explained what happens during cluster volume failover and how the standard NetWare clients reconnect.

You learned how trustee assignments are managed on cluster-enabled volumes. You also learned how to reconfigure shared disk NSS volumes and cluster-enabled shared disk NSS volumes. Finally, to ensure your cluster is operating at peak performance, you learned how to configure NSS tunable parameters and how to manually load balance shared disk NSS volumes across cluster nodes.

After examining this material, you are ready to use cluster-enabled volumes to enable highly available access to NetWare file system services for users running the

NetWare client software. They will experience rapid and transparent client reconnection should a cluster node fail and its cluster-enabled volumes are failed over to surviving nodes.

Armed with the fundamentals of creating shared disk NSS volumes, you are now in an excellent position to build upon this knowledge by creating applications or network services that require the use of cluster-enabled volumes. Many of the other chapters that describe how to configure applications or services with Cluster Services require you to create a cluster-enabled shared disk NSS volume.

The information in this chapter gives you a solid grounding in practical shared storage management using Novell Cluster and Storage Services software that enables you to manage your storage area network disk data even if cluster nodes and storage are online.

## CHAPTER 10

Applying Novell Cluster Services with NDPS

This chapter explores Novell's newest print services, Novell Distributed Print Services (NDPS), examining how to configure NDPS for automatic failover in a cluster environment and how to migrate an existing NDPS implementation to Novell Cluster Services.

To achieve a fault-tolerant printing solution in Novell Cluster Services, you must implement NDPS. NDPS is required if you wish to implement pure TCP/IP printing or create a fault-tolerant printing environment using Novell Cluster Services. Legacy printing to print queues is not supported in a cluster environment. This is due to the legacy-printing tie to physical servers; thus, no easy or automated way to transfer a print queue to another server exists.

If you're already familiar with NDPS, jump ahead to the section titled "Cluster Enabling NDPS," later in the chapter. If you're not, the following sections lead you through the basic components of NDPS.

Introducing NDPS

NDPS is the result of the development efforts of Novell, Hewlett-Packard, and Xerox to upgrade legacy queue–based printing to a feature-rich distributed architecture that fully integrates printing into NDS and removes the single-server ties created by print queues. The result is a highly scalable printing environment that supports bidirectional communications with printers, pure IP implementation, and enhanced TCP/IP features, including support for Line Printer/Line Printer Daemon LPR/LPD and Internet Printing Protocol (IPP).

NDPS offers several major benefits:

▶ Tight integration with NDS allows network administrators the ability to centrally administer NDPS printer configuration, rights assignments, and queue management.

▶ Services legacy queues allow an easy migration path from the legacy-printing environment, making NDPS fully backward compatible with NetWare 3.x and 4.x systems.

▶ Automatically delivers (or removes NDPS-delivered) printer drivers to (or from) the workstations based on NDS assignment at the container, group, or individual user level.

- Bidirectional communication with printer agents gives users and print administrators meaningful "pop-up" status notification.

- Supports major TCP/IP protocols, including LPR, LPD, and IPP, which facilitates the protocol migration to pure IP and the integration with other operating systems such as UNIX.

- Allows for print job scheduling based on time of day, job size, and media availability.

- The protocol independence of NDPS means that it works in Pure IPX, Pure IP, NetWare IP (NWIP), or mixed environments.

NDPS consists of four major components: printer agents, the NDPS Manager, NDPS gateways, and the NDPS Broker. Figure 10.1 illustrates this architecture and the logical location of each of these components.

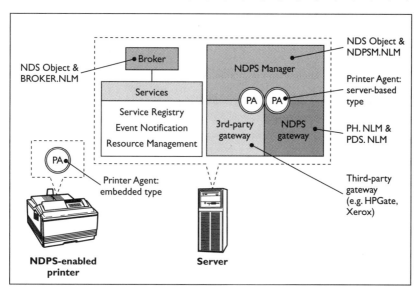

FIGURE 10.1 *NDPS architecture*

The next sections discuss each of these architectural components.

NDPS Printer Agents

NDPS supports two broad categories of printers: *controlled access printers* and *public access printers*. Controlled access printers are represented with NDS objects, which allow administrators to utilize NDS to control who can print and manage the corresponding printer. *Public access printers* do not have a corresponding NDS object—they allow anyone to print to them (with or without an NDS authentication), and they provide no managed control. Either of these models works with NDPS, although the majority of Novell's clients implement controlled access printers for most of their printers to facilitate the NDS management of their printing environment.

NDPS printer agents represent the physical printer on the network. These printers can be attached as shown in Table 10.1.

TABLE 10.1

Printer Agent Attachment Method

ATTACHMENT	DESCRIPTION
Network-direct printers	Directly attach to network using a gateway provided by a third-party printer manufacturer. These include a network card, either internal or external to the printer.
Remote printers	Attach using Remote Printer (RP-IPX), Line Printer (LPR-TCP/IP), or queue-based protocols.
Local printers	Attach directly to a server.

A one-to-one relationship exists between the printer agent and physical printers—each agent can represent one and only one printer. The printer agent combines the functions previously performed by the legacy printer, print queue, printer server, and spooler into one intelligent and simplified entity. Printer agents can be any of the following:

▶ A software entity running on a server that represents a printer attached to a server or workstation

▶ A software entity running on a server that represents a network-attached printer

▶ An entity embedded within a network-attached printer (in firmware)

The printer agent performs the following functions:

▸ Managing print job processing and many operations performed by the printer itself

▸ Answering queries from network clients about a print job printer attributes

▸ Generating notifications of job completion, printing problems, errors, or changes in the status of a print job, document, or printer

NDPS Manager

The *NDPS Manager* provides a platform for printer agents and runs as an NLM on a NetWare server. You must create an NDPS Manager in NDS prior to creating any printer agents. The NDPS Manager object stores all configuration information that is used by the server's NDPS service module.

An NDPS Manager can control multiple printer agents and public access printers. There is no hard-coded or theoretical limit to the number of printer agents a manager can control, but each printer agent uses approximately 50K of memory on the server, making RAM the limiting factor. On servers with adequately provisioned resources, sites have successfully implemented 300 to 500 printer agents on a single nondedicated server.

Only one NDPS Manager can load on a server at a time, so you must plan your cluster to ensure that two managers will not attempt to load on a server at one time.

Printer Gateways

Gateways allow NDPS clients to send jobs to printers that do not have embedded NDPS printer agents. When you create a printer agent for a printer that does not include an embedded agent, you must designate the appropriate gateway to use. When NDPSM.NLM loads on a server, it automatically loads all appropriate third-party gateways based on the printer agents assigned to the manager.

The gateways translate NDPS queries or commands to the printer-specific language used by the physical printer the printer agent represents. The gateway also functions as the intermediary between the printer and NDPS for all supported bidirectional communication.

Third-party gateways are developed by printer manufacturers to support their printers when they are directly attached to the network. These gateways are designed to interact with specific proprietary printer functions.

The Novell Gateway

The *Novell gateway* provides generic support for local and remote printers, including NPRINTER or queue-based technology, as well as Remote Printer (RP)–, Line Printer (LPR)–, and Internet Printing Protocol (IPP)–enabled devices in a TCP/IP environment. The Novell gateway is designed for printers that don't have an embedded printer agent, and don't yet have a proprietary third-party gateway provided by their manufacturer. Whenever a third-party gateway exists, you should use it rather than the Novell gateway since it provides manufacturer-specific functions.

The Novell gateway includes two major subcomponents: the Print Device Subsystem and the Port Handler.

The Novell Print Device Subsystem (PDS) is a component of the Novell gateway that retrieves printer-specific information and stores this information in a database. The PDS automatically loads when a printer agent is created using the Novell gateway.

The NDPS Port Handler is a component of the Novell Gateway that allows NDPS to communicate through hardware ports and legacy methods, including the following:

- ▸ A server's serial and/or parallel ports

- ▸ Queue-based printing

- ▸ Remote printers (RP in IPX environments, LPR in TCP/IP environments)

The Port Handler is an abstraction of the physical connection between the PDS and the physical printer. It ensures that the PDS can communicate with the printer regardless of the type of interface being used.

NDPS Broker

The *NDPS Broker* provides three new print services: Service Registry Service (SRS), Event Notification Service (ENS), and Resource Management Service (RMS). These services are not visible to end users, but they play a critical role in the NDPS environment.

Service Registry Service

SRS allows public access printers to advertise themselves on the network so that users and administrators can find them. Though IPX utilizes Service Advertisement Protocol (SAP) to advertise and find services, in a pure IP environment we need other methods of locating services. The SRS provides this mechanism for public access printers while minimizing network traffic.

When you attach a public access printer to the network, it registers with the SRS. SRS then advertises the public access printers using SAP for IPX and multicast for TCP/IP environments (or both for environments using both IPX and TCP/IP).

If multiple Service Registries exist on the network, they automatically synchronize with each other, thus propagating the public access printers throughout the entire network.

For environments not utilizing public access printers, you may wish to disable this service (this is done by disabling the service in the NDPS Broker object).

Event Notification Service

The Event Notification Service is responsible for notifying users and/or administrators of NDPS-related events. By default, users are notified of events that affect their particular print jobs. By configuring the NDPS Broker object in NDS, administrators can designate events to go to various administrators, such as to the help desk administrator, for notification of printer events in the network. You can deliver these events using the methods described in Table 10.2.

T A B L E   1 0 . 2

NDPS Event Notification Methods

METHOD	DESCRIPTION
Pop-Up Notification	Pop-up messages will be displayed on the workstations of designated personnel when the event occurs, assuming they are currently logged into NDS.
GroupWise Notification	Messages can automatically be sent to the designated personnel using the GroupWise messaging system.
MHS Notification	Messages can automatically be sent to the designated personnel using MHS.
SMTP Notification	Messages can automatically be sent to the designated personnel using any SMTP-compliant system.
Log File	Messages can be written to a file at a designated location on a NetWare server.
Programmatic Notification	Using NDPS APIs, programmatic notification can be delivered using NDPS: SPX and/or RPC.
SNMP	NDPS is SNMP-enabled, allowing notifications to be delivered using SNMP traps.

Resource Management Service

The Resource Management Service (RMS) centralizes NDPS resources on the network for easy distribution to clients. These resources include printer drivers, printer definition files (PDFs), banners, and fonts. RMS allows administrators to utilize NDS to configure drivers, and RMS to deliver these drivers to the appropriate workstations based on NDS containers, groups, or user objects (group and user object functionality is available only with NetWare 5.1 Support Pack 1 or later).

For large distributed environments, RMS should be planned to ensure that the resources are distributed locally to clients — proper NDPS Broker placement will prevent delivering drivers across WAN links. Without proper Broker placement, clients may actually download drivers from a slow or expensive WAN link when a closer or less expensive link is available.

Client Requirements

To utilize NDPS printing, the clients must be configured with NDPS. This service is installed by default during a "typical" installation of a NetWare 5.x–compatible client. When you're doing a custom installation, ensure that the NDPS component is selected during the installation.

If you have not installed the NDPS portion of the Novell client, you must add this before users can print directly to NDPS printers or have print drivers automatically deployed or upgraded. This process can be automated using the Automatic Client Upgrade (ACU) routine of the client installation, or pushed out using ZENworks.

Cluster Enabling NDPS

Cluster enabling NDPS puts the NDPS Broker database and the NDPS Manager database on the shared storage, allowing any node in the cluster to activate the database and provide the print services. NDPS can be clustered as a single resource with the broker and the manager migrating together, or configured as two resources — one for the broker and another for the manager. Large environments may need multiple NDPS Managers for each broker.

If you intend to run multiple NDPS Managers or Brokers in your cluster, you must plan the nodes carefully to guarantee that no two managers or brokers have a common node in their failover path; you can load only one broker or manager on a server at a time (that is, each NLM can be loaded only once).

WARNING

If you try to load two or more Brokers or Managers on the same server, only the first instance will actually load. All subsequent instances will fail, making their services unavailable.

Though cluster enabling NDPS is fairly simple if you follow the prerequisite tasks, users tend to have more questions about configuring NDPS for cluster use than all other services combined. Two key areas cause NDPS to not work in a cluster: failure to put the virtual servers in all nodes' HOSTS file, and failure to upgrade the volume used for NDPS into the directory prior to cluster enabling the volume. Forgetting either of these two steps prevents you from successfully implementing NDPS in a cluster.

To configure NDPS as a cluster resource, you must complete these steps:

1. Install NDPS to each node in the cluster that will be in the Assigned Nodes list for the NDPS resource.

2. Configure the cluster-enabled volume and copy the NDPS directory to it.

3. Configure the HOSTS file on all cluster nodes that will be in the Assigned Nodes list for the NDPS resource for the virtual server.

4. Create the NDPS Broker and the NDPS Manager in NDS.

5. Configure the cluster resource.

Installing NDPS to Each Cluster Node in the Assigned Nodes List

You must install NDPS to each node in the cluster that will be in the failover path for the NDPS resource. You can install NDPS using the NetWare 5.*x* installation utility or the deployment manager with NetWare 5.1. NDPS requires the NDPS Manager and Broker modules to exist on the SYS volume, so you must individually install NDPS to each node.

Once you have installed NDPS to each node, remove any lines in the AUTOEXEC.NCF file that load NDPS resources. Since you will be configuring the cluster load script to handle starting and stopping NDPS, you do not want the server to automatically load these modules upon startup.

Even though you are installing NDPS to each node in the cluster, you will copy the database from only one server to the cluster-enabled volume for NDPS. Each resource will be configured only once, and this configuration will be used by whichever node starts the NDPS resource.

Configuring the Cluster-Enabled Volume

To configure NDPS as a cluster resource, you must designate a volume in the shared storage for use with NDPS. You can either create a single resource on one volume for both the NDPS Broker and the NDPS Manager, or you can configure each of these as individual resources. Novell Cluster Services is generally implemented in conjunction with server consolidation or in a centralized IT environment, and thus a single resource with both a broker and a manager is most often used.

The size of the cluster-enabled volume should be sufficient to hold the broker's resource management database (printer drivers) and for the manager to spool print jobs. Base the size on your existing printing environment.

Creating the NSS Volume and Upgrading It into the Directory

To prepare a volume for NDPS, you must first create the NSS volume on the shared storage. Prior to cluster enabling this volume, you must upgrade the volume into NDS, or NDPS will not recognize the volume as valid.

To create the volume and prepare it for NDPS, do the following:

I. Create the volume on the shared storage.

X-REF

Refer to Chapter 9 for complete instructions on creating a volume on the shared storage.

TIP

At this point, the NDS volume object for the NDPS volume has been created. However, since this volume was not mounted when the volume was created, the NWCONFIG utility was not able to write the volume ID to this newly created volume. The following steps have you mount this volume, then upgrade the mounted volumes into the directory. Since the volume is mounted at this point, this process allows the volume ID to be properly written to the volume. Without the volume ID written on the volume, the NDPS Manager will not see the volume as a valid choice for its database, and you will not be able to create a manager on this volume. You must perform these steps prior to cluster enabling the volume, or you will need to delete the cluster-enabled volume and start over again.

Omitting these steps is the single most common error when configuring NDPS in a cluster.

2. Press Alt+Esc until you return to the system console prompt, then enter the following two commands:

NSS /ACTIVATE=<*VolumeName*>

MOUNT <*VolumeName*>

Be sure to substitute the name of your NDPS volume for <*VolumeName*>.

3. Press Alt+Esc until you return to the NWCONFIG screen, then select Directory Options and press Enter.

4. Select Upgrade Mounted Volumes into the Directory, then press Enter.

5. When prompted, select Yes to Place volume <*VolumeName*> in the Directory, then press Enter.

TIP

You might also be prompted to place other volumes into the directory. You should not place any volume into the directory if that volume has already been cluster-enabled. Cluster enabling a volume renames the old SERVER_VOLUME volume object to CLUSTER_VOLUME. If you later upgrade the volume into the directory, you will add the SERVER_VOLUME object back, and this volume will again be tied to the server on which you create the object and will not offer any fault tolerance if users map drives to it.

6. If prompted, enter the user name and password of a user with the appropriate rights to create the volume in NDS, then press Enter.

7. Press Esc until you exit NWCONFIG.

8. Enter the following commands to dismount and deactivate the NDPS volume:

DISMOUNT <*VolumeName*>

NSS /DEACTIVATE=<*VolumeName*>

Cluster Enabling the Volume

Once you have created the NSS volume, you must cluster enable it for NDPS. To cluster enable the volume, follow these steps:

1. Using ConsoleOne, browse and select the Cluster object, then click the New Cluster Volume button as shown in Figure 10.2.

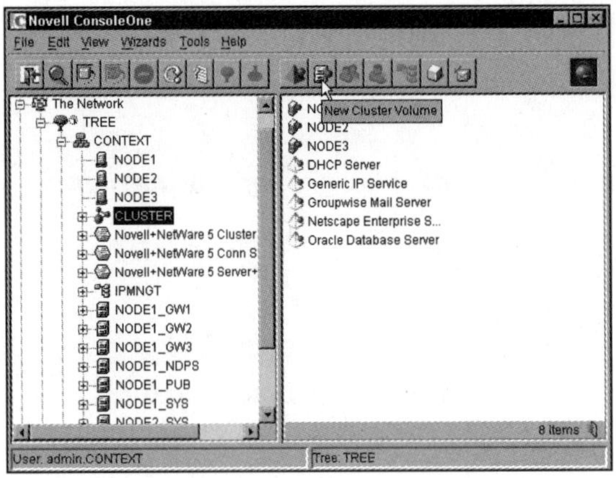

▶ · ◀

FIGURE 10.2 *Creating a new cluster volume*

2. In the New Cluster Volume dialog box that appears (see Figure 10.3), browse to the volume you created for the NDPS resource and enter the IP address to use for this resource. Select Define Additional Properties, then click Create.

▶ · ◀

FIGURE 10.3 *New Cluster Volume dialog box*

3. Using ConsoleOne, select the Cluster object and change to the Cluster State view by selecting View ⇨ Cluster State from the menu, as shown in Figure 10.4.

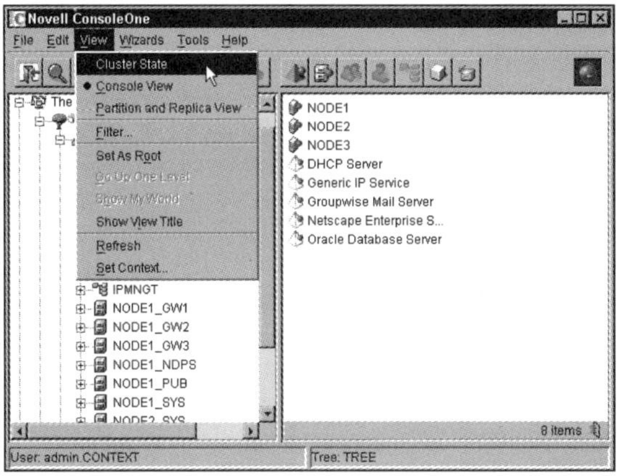

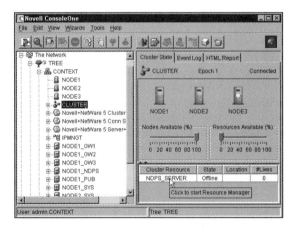

FIGURE 10.4 *Cluster State view*

4. Click once on the NDPS_SERVER cluster resource you created, as shown on the bottom half of the Cluster State screen (see Figure 10.5). This will start the Cluster Resource Manager, which allows you to manage the state of this cluster resource.

FIGURE 10.5 *Start the Resource Manager.*

5. Click the ONLINE button to start the resource.

6. Using Network Neighborhood, browse to the NDS context of your cluster. Find your cluster volume, right-click, and then select Novell Map Network Drive, as shown in Figure 10.6.

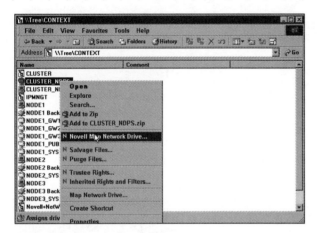

FIGURE 10.6 *Map the drive to your cluster-enabled volume.*

7. Select an available drive letter for this drive mapping, then click OK. This will map a drive to the cluster-enabled volume through the virtual server, and force a TCP/IP-based connection to the virtual server.

8. Copy the SYS:\NDPS directory and its contents from one server's SYS volume to the root of the NDPS volume. It is critical that NDPS be the root directory and that resdir be directly under NDPS. It is also critical that the version of NDPS on the server you choose to copy is the same as the version you will be running in the cluster. We recommend copying the NDPS directory from the SYS volume of the same server that has currently activated the NDPS volume.

Modifying the HOSTS Files for NDPS

For any cluster node to properly load the NDPS Broker and NDPS Manager, it must be able to resolve the name for the virtual server. To ensure proper name resolution, the virtual server should be added to the HOSTS file on all servers in the cluster that can run this service. To configure the HOSTS file, follow these steps:

1. On each server, change to the server console prompt and enter LOAD EDIT SYS:ETC\HOSTS.

2. At the bottom of the file, add a line for the Virtual Server (not Volume) object and its IP address:

```
10.7.5.105    CLUSTER_NDPS_SERVER.CLUSTER.COM CLUSTER_NDPS_SERVER
```

3. Press Esc, and select Yes to save your changes and exit the editor.

Creating the NDPS Broker and NDPS Manager

Once you have cluster enabled the volume, copied the NDPS directory to it, and modified the HOSTS files, you are ready to create the NDPS Broker and NDPS Manager objects. To create these objects, follow these steps:

1. Verify you have a drive mapped to the cluster-enabled volume for NDPS. This ensures that you already have a TCP/IP connection to the virtual server.

2. Launch NetWare Administrator from the SYS:\Public\Win32 directory of the server that is currently running the volume resource.

3. Select the container that you want to create the broker in, then click the Create button.

4. Select NDPS Broker, then click OK to create the NDPS Broker object.

5. In the Create NDPS Broker Object dialog box (see Figure 10.7), do the following:

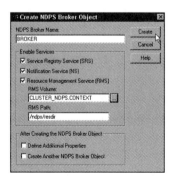

FIGURE 10.7 *Create NDPS Broker Object dialog box*

   a. In the NDPS Broker Name field, enter a name for the broker.

   b. Enable the desired services by selecting the appropriate check boxes.

   c. In the RMS Volume field, click the Browse (...) button.

6. Browse for the cluster-enabled volume configured for NDPS, then click OK, as shown in Figure 10.8. This should bring you back to the Create NDPS Broker Object dialog box, shown previously in Figure 10.7, and allow you to finish configuring the new Broker.

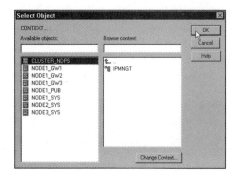

FIGURE 10.8 *Browse for the cluster-enabled volume*

TIP

Errors often occur here. If you encounter an error, make sure that you have completed all the steps and verify that you have an IP connection to both the server running the volume resource and the virtual server for the NDPS volume. If all this is correct and you still have an error, migrate the NDPS volume to another node in the cluster, then try again.

7. Verify that the information has been entered correctly, then click Create, as shown back in Figure 10.7.

8. Select the container in which you wish to create the NDPS Manager, then click the Create New Object button.

9. Select NDPS Manager, then click OK.

10. In the Create NDPS Manager Object dialog box, enter a name for the manager in the NDPS Manager Name field, as shown in Figure 10.9.

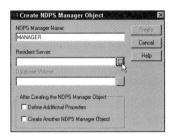

FIGURE 10.9 *Name the manager in the Create NDPS Manager Object dialog box.*

11. For the Resident Server, select the Virtual NCP Server for the NDPS cluster-enabled volume, then click OK.

You must select the virtual server, not the physical NCP server the volume is hosted on. For example, select CLUSTER_NDPS_SERVER.

NOTE

12. For the Database Volume, select the cluster-enabled volume you created for NDPS, as shown in Figure 10.10.

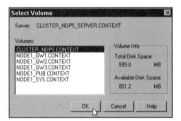

FIGURE 10.10 *Select Volume dialog box*

This is by far the most common place things go wrong. If you do not have an IP connection to the server hosting the volume and the cluster-enabled volume, this step will most likely fail. If you did not upgrade the volume into the directory before cluster enabling it, this step will fail. If you are sure you followed all the steps up to this point but the cluster-enabled volume does not show up as an available volume, try canceling this operation and then migrating the NDPS_SERVER resource to a different node in the cluster. Then repeat these steps.

TIP

13. Confirm the NDPS Manager settings, then click Create, as shown in Figure 10.11.

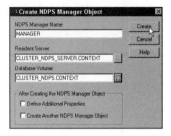

FIGURE 10.11 *Confirm NDPS Manager settings in the Create NDPS Manager Object dialog box*

Configuring the Cluster Resource

The last step in cluster enabling NDPS is to modify the cluster-enabled volume resource object to load and unload NDPS. To configure the resource, follow these steps:

1. Launch ConsoleOne if it isn't already running.

2. Browse to the container that holds your NDPS_SERVER resource object.

3. Select the NDPS_SERVER resource object, then right-click and select Properties.

4. Select the Load tab, as shown in Figure 10.12. In the load script, add the following two lines at the end of the script and click Apply:

```
LOAD BROKER .BROKER.CONTEXT /ALLOWDUP

LOAD NDPSM .MANAGER.CONTEXT /DBVOLUME=NOCHECK
```

Substitute the name and context of your NDPS Broker object for the `.BROKER.CONTEXT` statement in the preceding lines. Substitute the name and context of your NDPS Manager object for the `.MANAGER.CONTEXT` statement in the preceding lines.

5. Click OK to acknowledge the warning that your change will not take effect until you offline the volume.

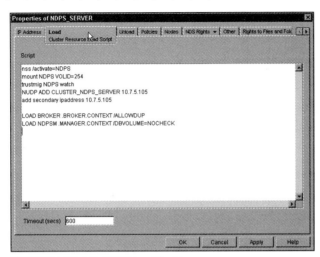

FIGURE 10.12 *NDPS Load Script*

6. Click the Unload tab, as shown in Figure 10.13. Then add the following commands to the beginning of the unload script, and click Apply:

UNLOAD NDPSM

UNLOAD BROKER

7. Click the Nodes tab, modify the assigned node order as desired, and click OK.

8. Change to the Cluster State view by selecting View ➪ Cluster State from the menu.

9. Offline and online the NDPS resource to implement the resource modifications:

a. Click your NDPS_SERVER resource to start the Resource Manager.

b. Click the Offline button.

c. Click your NDPS_SERVER resource to start the Resource Manager.

d. Click the Online button.

Properties of NDPS_SERVER

IP Address | Load | **Unload** | Policies | Nodes | NDS Rights ▼ | Other | Rights to Files and Fold ◄ ►
Cluster Resource Unload Script

Script

```
UNLOAD NDPSM
UNLOAD BROKER

del secondary ipaddress 10.7.5.105
NUDP DEL CLUSTER_NDPS_SERVER 10.7.5.105
trustmig NDPS unwatch
dismount NDPS /force
nss /forcedeactivate=NDPS
```

Timeout (secs) 600

OK | Cancel | Apply | Help

FIGURE 10.13 *NDPS Unload Script*

NOTE

For your changes to take effect, the resource must be taken offline and back online. It is not sufficient to migrate it to another node in the cluster.

10. Launch NetWare Administrator if it isn't already running.

11. Browse to the context you wish to create your NDPS printer agents in, then click the New Object button.

12. Select NDPS Printer, then click OK.

13. In the Create Printer dialog box (not shown), enter the following information:

  a. In the Printer Agent (PA) Name field, enter the name of your NDPS printer agent.

  b. Make sure that the Create a New Printer Agent radio button is selected and then click Create. This will bring up the Create Printer Agent dialog box, shown in Figure 10.14.

14. In the Create Printer Agent dialog box, click the Browse (...) button and browse for the NDPS Manager that you want to assign this printer agent to. Select the appropriate option from the Gateway Types field for your printer, then click OK, as shown in Figure 10.14.

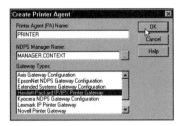

FIGURE 10.14 *Create Printer Agent dialog box*

15. In the Configure Printer Gateway dialog box, select the Printer Type, appropriate protocol, and the network printer, and then click OK.

16. Select the appropriate driver for this printer for each client platform, then click Continue.

17. After the printer agent is created, check the server console screen on the server hosting the NDPS Manager cluster resource, and verify that the printer agent has been bound.

Migration/Failover Characteristics

In the lab, you will find that NDPS migrates very quickly since you will probably have only a handful of printer agents. In practice, the NDPS Manager will be the bottleneck on migration, and the more printer agents you have, the longer the manager will take to migrate. The NDPS Manager also tends to take a long time to show the proper status of printer agents. If you are experiencing excessive startup times on the manager, consider creating a second NDPS Manager to balance the printers across two managers.

TIP

Currently, no method exists for moving a printer agent from one NDPS Manager to a different one. You must delete the printer agent and re-create it to move it, which also requires updating the client workstations.

The client behavior when a migration/failover occurs varies based on the application and operating system.

Windows NT/Windows 2000 Behavior

When printing from Windows NT or Windows 2000, the printing symptoms depend on the state printing is in prior to the migration or failover.

If the current print job has finished spooling to the NDPS Manager, the print job migrates with NDPS, and no error occurs at the workstation. Further print jobs submitted after the migration is complete also process properly.

If the client is actively spooling a job, you receive an error message similar to the one displayed in Figure 10.15.

FIGURE 10.15 *Windows NT/2000 printer error (actively spooling)*

Once NDPS has migrated to the new node, printing resumes, and the current print job completes. However, in many cases, subsequent print jobs are not possible after this error until the workstation is rebooted. When you check Start ⇨ Settings ⇨ Control Panel ⇨ Printers after this error occurs, no printers show up until after the workstation is rebooted.

If a print job is submitted during the time that the NDPS Manager is unloaded on one node but not yet loaded on the new node, the client receives an error message, as shown in Figure 10.16. After acknowledging this message, the user must resubmit the print job, which will successfully complete assuming the NDPS Manager has finished migrating.

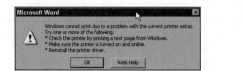

FIGURE 10.16 *Windows NT/2000 printer error (printing while NDPS Manager is migrating)*

Windows 95/98/Me Behavior

As is the case with Windows NT/2000, the printing symptoms when printing from Windows 95, 98, or Me depend on the state printing was in prior to the migration or failover.

If the current print job has finished spooling to the NDPS manager, the print job migrates with NDPS, and no error occurs at the workstation. Further print jobs submitted after the migration is complete also process properly.

If the client is actively spooling a job, you receive an error message stating that there was an error writing to the printer. After acknowledging this message, you can resubmit the print job, which will successfully complete assuming the NDPS Manager has finished migrating.

Active/Active versus Active/Passive

NDPS is an Active/Passive cluster resource. When the migration/failover occurs, all NLMs must be loaded on the target node. The broker and manager can be active on only one cluster node at a time.

Discussing Legacy Queue Support

The following question is frequently asked: "Can I use legacy print queues in a cluster?" Although you can use legacy print queues in a cluster, this will not enable fault tolerance. Legacy print queues are assigned to physical volumes and will not failover. It is theoretically possible to configure a print queue on a cluster-enabled volume. However, the cluster-enabled volume only provides fault tolerance using an IP connection. Most environments configure their legacy printing with the print server running on the printer network card, where the network card (such as HP's JetDirect card or Intel's NetportExpress) functions as the print server. Since most printing vendors currently do not support NetWare Core Protocol (NCP) over TCP/IP, you cannot configure the network card in Print Server mode to connect to the virtual server.

It is possible to create a legacy print queue on a cluster-enabled volume and service this print queue with an NDPS print agent. In this manner, IP clients can capture the print queue and reconnect to this queue after a migration or failover. The migration and failover behavior of this method is similar to NDPS failover in general—if the job is spooling on the workstation during the migration or failover, the client will most likely need to be restarted or the print job restarted.

If the job has finished spooling at the workstation prior to the migration or failover, the job should reconnect and complete normally after the migration/failover.

Whereas the queue methods may failover cleanly, it is very common for this method to lose the print queue when the cluster-enabled volume migrates or fails. When this occurs, the user must either recapture the queue, or log off and then log in again to re-establish the print queue. Since Novell does not support using legacy print queues in a cluster environment, there will likely be no improved behavior in the reconnection of queues.

Migrating from an Existing NDPS Implementation

An NDPS Manager may be moved from one server to another (as described in Novell's TID number 10016871). However, it is currently not possible to combine two managers into a single manager, and it is not possible to move an NDPS printer agent from one NDPS Manager to another manager without deleting and recreating the printer agent. If you currently have a single NDPS Manager, it is easy to migrate this into the cluster. If you have multiple NDPS Managers and wish to combine them into a single resource, such a process requires significantly more work. Whether you are moving an NDPS Broker, NDPS Manager, or both, be sure NDPS is installed to all nodes in the cluster that will be in the Available Nodes path for the resource.

Prior to moving an NDPS resource from an existing nonclustered server to the cluster, you must first create a cluster-enabled volume following the steps outlined previously in the "Configuring the Cluster-Enabled Volume" section of this chapter. As mentioned earlier, you must upgrade the NDPS volume into the directory (NDS) prior to cluster enabling the volume, or the volume ID will not be placed in the volume, and the NDPS Manager will not recognize the volume as valid.

Moving an Existing Broker to a Cluster Node

The NDPS Broker database consists of the print drivers that have been added to the NDPS Broker. Each time you add a resource, subdirectories are created below the \NDPS\RESDIR directory on the resource management volume. To move a broker, simply copy this structure to the new cluster-enabled volume, edit the SYS:ETC\HOSTS file in each of the cluster nodes (as outlined previously in the "Modifying the HOSTS Files for NDPS" section of this chapter), and create the NDPS Broker object. Modify the load and unload scripts of the cluster-enabled volume based on the "Configuring the Cluster Resource" section that appeared earlier in this chapter.

The NDPS Broker also has an NDS tie to the host server. When you move the Broker to the cluster, you must use ConsoleOne to change this host server attribute by following these steps:

1. Launch ConsoleOne and find the NDS Broker object.

2. Select Broker, right-click it, and select Properties.

3. Click the Other tab to see the properties that do not have an available snapin to manage.

4. Find the property "Host Device", and click the + sign to the left of the property to expand it.

5. You should now see the fully distinguished NDS name of the current host server. Double-click this server object, and you will see a Browse button appear to the right of the server name.

6. Browse the NDS tree until you find the virtual server that you wish to associate with the Broker. Select the virtual server, and then click OK. This will bring you back to the Other property page.

7. Click Apply to apply your changes, then close the NDPS Broker object.

Moving an Existing Print Manager to a Cluster Node

Moving an NDPS Manager requires that all NDPS-related NLMs are the same version on the current NDPS server and on all nodes in the cluster that will run NDPS. To move a manager:

1. Verify that NDPS has been installed on each node of the cluster, and that the NDPS NLMs on the cluster are the same version as the ones on the servers from which you are moving the NDPS Manager.

2. Verify that NDS synchronization is performing properly.

3. Run DSREPAIR and choose the Advanced Options menu, which allows you to Repair Local Database on the existing NDPS server and on the cluster node you will move the NDPS Manager to. Run this as many times as is necessary to ensure there are zero errors.

4. Back up the Print Manager database:

   a. Change to the NDPS Manager screen on the server console of the existing NDPS Manager.

   b. From the Available Options menu, select NDPS Manager Status and Control.

   c. Select Database Options.

   d. Select Backup Database Files.

5. Unload the Print Manager (NDPSM.NLM) from the current server.

6. Load the Print Manager on the new server.

7. Accept the warning that the database does not reside on this server, as shown in Figure 10.17.

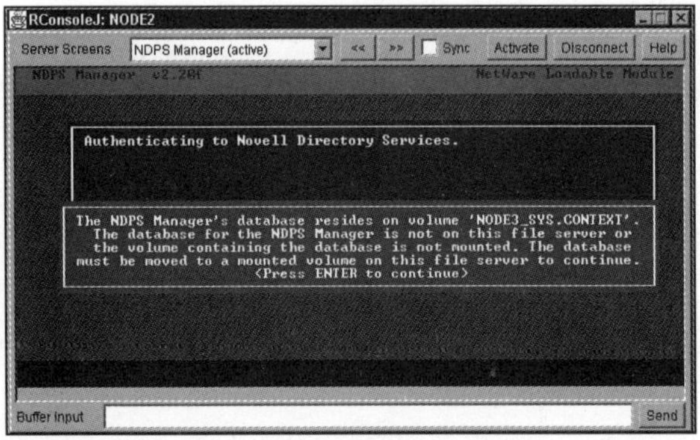

FIGURE 10.17 Database warning

8. Select Yes to move the database to this server.

9. Select the cluster-enabled volume as the destination, as shown in Figure 10.18.

FIGURE 10.18 *Select the NDPS volume*

NOTE

You must select a cluster-enabled volume, not a physical volume on this server. If you do not have an option for a cluster-enabled volume (the volume name would begin with the name of the cluster rather than the name of the server), then do not move the manager. Instead, go back and review your steps and resolve this issue prior to proceeding.

10. Modify the cluster resource load and unload scripts as described in Steps 3 through 6 of the section "Configuring the Cluster Resource," earlier in this chapter.

Moving Existing Printer Agents to a New Manager

As previously mentioned, no facility exists to move an existing printer agent from one NDPS Manager to another. To accomplish this, the agent must be re-created on the new manager. In fact, even if you delete the printer agent and re-create it with the same name and a different NDPS Manager, the printer must be delivered to the workstation again.

If you are consolidating multiple NDPS Managers to a single cluster-enabled NDPS Manager, moving the agents will be much more complicated than moving the first NDPS Manager and its agents. To facilitate this, the agents can be created on the new cluster-enabled NDPS Manager and serve the same printers during a transition phase. During this transition, two agents (on different NDPS Managers) would be configured to serve the exact same printer. If the context needs to remain the same, this second printer agent must be configured with a different name. Put an identifier in the new name that will make it easy for administrators to distinguish the old agents from the new agents, such as appending a –2 to the end of the previous name.

Once all printer agents have been configured on the new NDPS Manager, workstations must be modified to remove the old driver. NDPS allows an administrator to configure a policy to add or remove print drivers. Depending on how the drivers were originally deployed to the workstations, configure the same level policy (at the container, group, or user level) to remove the old drivers and push out the replacement printer agents.

▶ · ◀

Summary

This chapter examined the basics of Novell's NDPS services and explained how to configure these services in a cluster. You walked step by step through the process of enabling NDPS as a cluster resource, using the appropriate load and unload script syntax. The cluster migration and failover characteristics of NDPS were discussed as follows:

CLUSTER FAILOVER CLASSIFICATION INDEX	
Transparency	Moderate
Active/Active or Active/Passive	Active/Passive
Length to failover	Slow depending on number of printer agents

Finally, you were introduced to various migration issues to help you migrate from an existing NDPS implementation to Novell Cluster Services.

Applying Novell Cluster Services with GroupWise 5.5 Domains and Post Offices

This chapter brings the discussion of clustering into the context of Novell's premier messaging service—GroupWise 5.5. It starts by discussing the basic GroupWise components that you must configure in a cluster to achieve a fully fault-tolerant enterprise messaging system, and how these can be configured differently than in a nonclustered system. Whereas it does briefly cover the basics, this book cannot cover everything you need to know about GroupWise—it's assumed that you have a fundamental understanding of GroupWise and that you know how to administer it without clustering before you try to add the complexity of a cluster.

TIP

Novell Press publishes several excellent GroupWise books. You should have an in-depth understanding of GroupWise before you attempt to configure it in a cluster.

After explaining each component, this chapter discusses various topics regarding cluster enabling the GroupWise component. This includes deciding whether or not you should cluster enable your GroupWise volumes, planning your IP addresses and ports, and deciding whether you should configure a single resource with multiple GroupWise components, or split them into their own resource.

Once this foundation is set, the chapter moves on to several configuration options. The first option walks you through creating a new GroupWise system with a single Domain and Post Office configured as one resource. The next scenario adds a Post Office as its own resource to an existing GroupWise system without cluster enabling the volume. The final scenario in this chapter explains how to add a GroupWise Domain and Post Office as a single resource to an existing GroupWise system.

X-REF

In Chapter 12, we discuss the GroupWise gateways, which allow you to connect your GroupWise system to the Internet. To the last scenario discussed in this chapter, we add a GroupWise Internet Agent (GWIA), and the final scenario in Chapter 12 finishes with a Web Access Gateway.

After you have learned how to configure GroupWise in a cluster, you'll examine various migration and failover characteristics of the various components. This discussion will help you know what to expect from both the server and the client perspectives when a clustered system fails and the resource is migrated.

Introducing GroupWise 5.5

GroupWise 5.5 is a seamless cross-platform collaboration and messaging system that is ideal for businesses of all sizes. With GroupWise 5.5, you can communicate across intranets and the Internet simply and easily. GroupWise makes it easy for you to gather, access, and communicate information.

X-REF

This chapter briefly introduces GroupWise 5.5 components and discusses how each of these components affects a Novell Cluster Services configuration. For more in-depth discussion of GroupWise, refer to Novell's Web site at www.novell.com/documentation.

Enabling fault-tolerant GroupWise with Novell Cluster Services requires GroupWise 5.5 with Support Pack 3 or later, or the GroupWise Enhancement Pack with Support Pack 1 or later. The GroupWise Enhancement Pack is recommended for clustering, as most of the Novell Cluster Services testing is done with the Enhancement Pack, and the procedures in this chapter were tested using only the Enhancement Pack version of GroupWise.

GroupWise is one of the key applications to use with Novell Cluster Services (NCS), and perhaps the most common after File and NDPS/print services. Since GroupWise is considered a mission-critical application in many organizations, requests for a higher level of service have been constant. Although GroupWise has an excellent wealth of features, it has always had a single point of failure in each of the agents. With client/server mode, this single point of failure has become even more apparent since all of the clients must communicate directly with the POA. If the POA fails, all functionality ceases. Novell Cluster Services resolves this issue by providing failover not only for the POA, but also for the Message Transfer Agent (MTA) and gateways as well. This ensures continued access for the clients as well as minimal interruption with inter–post office communications.

The most basic GroupWise configuration consists of a single GroupWise Domain and a single Post Office. The Domain functions are handled by the MTA, and Post Office functions are handled by the POA; both can run on various platforms but can be clustered only on NetWare.

Message Transfer Agents

A Domain is the highest-level container object in the GroupWise system and is serviced by the Message Transfer Agent (MTA), which runs on a server. There are two types of Domains: Primary and Secondary. Each GroupWise system has a single Primary Domain, and as many Secondary Domains as needed. The Domain logically groups multiple Post Offices together, with the MTA functioning as the router to get user and administrative messages from one Post Office to another, or to an external system through a gateway.

Normally, MTAs are allowed to communicate with each other using either UNC paths or TCP/IP links. In a clustered environment, all MTA communications must be configured to use TCP/IP. Normally, the MTA can also communicate to the Post Offices using either TCP/IP or UNC paths. Once again, Novell Cluster Services requires that these communication pathways be configured to use TCP/IP. When you create a new GroupWise system, the installation program gives you the choice of using either UNC paths or TCP/IP links. However, any future Domain or Post Office will default to UNC paths, which requires you to go back and modify the links once the agent is created.

Avoiding UNC links is important in a clustered environment for both performance and data integrity reasons. By using TCP/IP links, the agents (and the client) communicate using direct TCP/IP connections, rather than manipulating the remote file system directly. Since using TCP/IP links ensures that only the agent itself opens the database files, shutting down the agent helps guarantee that the database is closed cleanly and no repair operations will be necessary when the resource migrates.

Using Protected Memory

Under nonclustered scenarios, you can run multiple MTAs on the same server without worrying about issues beyond server performance. However, with Novell Cluster Services, you must take additional precautions if there is any chance that two MTAs might reside on the same server at the same time. The issue deals with the UNLOAD command — if you UNLOAD GWMTA, this command will unload all Domain MTAs that are currently running on the server. If you are trying to migrate one Domain to another server but leave your other Domains running, this would be a bad thing, since the command to unload the resource you are migrating would also unload all other agents on the same server. To allow for this, you can load each GroupWise resource into its own protected memory space. This allows you to selectively unload a module without unloading all instances of that module, and allows you to migrate one MTA without unloading another one.

Protected memory also helps in another way — by preventing GroupWise corruption. Novell has found that the leading cause of GroupWise corruption has to do with server ABENDS that do not allow the cache to properly flush before the server shuts down. Novell Cluster Services requires that the Auto Restart After ABEND parameter be set to zero (0), which does not flush the cache and may contribute to GroupWise database problems, which will require the agent to repair the database the next time it starts. By using protected memory, you can set the address space to automatically restart if a module in that space ABENDS; such a setting also prevents the database errors that would occur if the system halted. Of course, that doesn't help you if the module that ABENDS isn't running in the protected memory space (for example, some third-party backup software).

There are currently two exceptions to using protected memory — one is the NDS User Synchronization event, and the other is with the gateways (such as the GWIA and Web Access gateway). Since you will most likely not have any node in the cluster with the possibility of running two instances of the same gateway, it should not be necessary to run the gateway in protected memory. Since running the gateway in protected memory will cause a performance hit, the best solution is to keep them in the OS memory space.

X-REF

Protected memory is addressed in more detail later in this chapter in the section, "Discussing Protected Memory."

TIP

While GroupWise 5.x does not require the gateways to run in Protected Memory, GroupWise 6 does. If you are implementing GroupWise 6, be sure that the gateways are loaded in the same protected memory space as the MTA for the gateway.

NDS User Synchronization

One of the functions of the MTA is to perform NDS user synchronization. This process replicates changes to the user objects into the GroupWise Domain database (if you modify the user with the GroupWise snapins loaded, the snapins automatically update both, so user synchronization is not required by the MTA). Situations in which MTA NDS synchronization is required include the following:

▸ A user was modified using a version of NetWare Administrator run on a server without the GroupWise snapins.

▸ A user was modified using NETADMIN, the DOS-based administration program.

▸ A user was modified using the NetWare NDS API (NWDS API).

Currently, the NDS user synchronization event does not function properly if the MTA is running in protected memory and DSAPI.NLM is in conventional memory. The Enhancement Pack (SP1 or SP2) has a problem authenticating to NDS when run in protected memory that causes the user synchronization event to fail. This can be avoided by loading the DSAPI.NLM into the same protected memory space as the MTA is running in.

If your MTA is performing the NDS User Synchronization scheduled service, add the DSAPI load command to the cluster resource Load Script. Be sure to load this into the same memory space as the MTA.

TIP

MTA Startup Files

MTA configuration information is stored in NDS, but can be overridden by either command-line switches at load time, or by configuration parameters stored in the MTA startup file. By default, the startup files are placed in the same directory in which the agents are installed, which is normally the SYS volume in the SYSTEM directory.

The startup file includes a /HOME switch, which tells the MTA where the Domain database is stored. Depending on how you installed GroupWise, this will be populated with either a UNC path or legacy file system syntax (SERVER/VOLUME:\PATH).

The recommended approach is that you change the /HOME switch to legacy file system syntax, but remove the server name reference. Thus, the /HOME switch becomes VOLUME:\PATH, which is generic enough to be used by any node that loads it. Using this syntax minimizes the GroupWise agent startup time, since the server does not need to do any name resolution process to determine if the path is local or remote.

As discussed later in the chapter, you have the option of installing the agent files multiple times to each server that can run the MTA or installing the agents once per MTA by creating a SYSTEM directory on the shared volume used by the Domain database. In either case, removing the startup files from the SYS volumes and placing them on the shared volume so you need to maintain only a single copy of the startup file for each resource is a good idea. Alternatively, you can omit the startup file altogether, and put all of the startup switches in the cluster resource Load Script. Either moving the startup files to the shared volume, or omitting them altogether and using the command line switches in the Load Script is much easier to administer than trying to maintain individual startup files on every node in the cluster. If you consolidate to one location and then need to make a change, you only need to make the change once.

You should use a cluster-enabled volume for the Domain directory, and install the agents through a drive mapping using the virtual server created when you cluster enable the volume. When installed in this manner, the UNC path properties in NDS and in the startup files will reflect the proper UNC path using the virtual server. This proper UNC path is critical if you are installing a GroupWise gateway into this Domain.

TIP

Even though using a cluster-enabled volume causes the correct UNC path to be used in the startup files, you should modify the startup files to the legacy file system syntax (volume:\path). Using the legacy syntax bypasses the need for extra name resolution processes and dramatically decreases the time it takes for the agents to initialize.

Post Office Agents

GroupWise clients connect to Post Office Agents (POAs) running on a server that communicates with the actual Post Office directory structure stored in the file system. How these agents are configured within your cluster can have significant impact on how your network continues to perform, as well as on the end-user's perception of the messaging system performance.

Novell recommends no more than 750 active users in any given GroupWise 5.x Post Office. This recommendation does not change with Novell Cluster Services, as the limiting factors are the I/O to the server and the current TCP/IP stack. You must keep this limitation in mind with a cluster, and understand that there will be a significant performance impact if a node running 1,500 active connections suddenly fails, and the Post Office migrates to another server running 1,500 GroupWise users.

As stated earlier, a Post Office can typically communicate with the Domain it belongs to either by the UNC path to the Domain directory or by a TCP/IP link. However, when using Novell Cluster Services, you must ensure that the communication links are configured TCP/IP rather than UNC. Using direct TCP/IP links prevents the Domain MTA from directly accessing the remote POA file structure, which both improves performance and helps to ensure a clean database shutdown when the resource is brought offline or migrated to another node.

It is also possible to configure a Post Office agent on one server, which accesses a Post Office on a remote server. This, too, is not recommended for Novell Cluster Services — configure the cluster resource to run the POA on the same node as the server that mounts the Post Office volume. Again, you don't want a remote application directly accessing the file system—instead, the application should interact with the agent, and the agent directly accesses the file system for enhanced performance and data integrity.

The POA is normally configured with several scheduled events, including the Disk Check Event and the Structure, Index, and Contents checks. When planning your cluster, you should try to plan these events to ensure that each Post Office runs the events at a different time. Otherwise, if a Post Office migrates to a node that is running another Post Office, you will have two resource-intensive events running on the same node at the same time, which affects performance.

Another event that can impact performance is the QuickFinder indexing. By default, this is scheduled to run at midnight each night and can be configured as an offset in hours from midnight (it is configured on the POA on the Agent Settings tab). If you configure this to run at a different offset for each Post Office, you can ensure that no two Post Offices run this at the same time on the same node. Table 11.1 demonstrates how you might configure cluster QuickFinder indexing.

TABLE 11.1

GroupWise QuickFinder Indexing

CLUSTER RESOURCE	PO NAME	QUICKFINDER INTERVAL	QUICKFINDER OFFSET
GW1	GWPO1	24 hours	0
GW2	GWPO2	24 hours	1
GW3	GWPO3	24 hours	2
GW4	GWPO4	24 hours	3
GW5	GWPO5	24 hours	4
GW6	GWPO6	24 hours	5

The GroupWise Enhancement (with Support Pack 1 or later) has added some additional Post Office Agent switches to improve GroupWise performance. These switches allow you to specify specific IP addresses and ports for the POA to use when communicating. Without the switches, the agent will listen on all IP addresses and ports, but send communications using the primary server address. The new switches are displayed in Table 11.2.

TABLE 11.2

New GroupWise POA Switches

SWITCH	VALUE	FUNCTION
/mtpinip	Secondary IP address used by this PO	This switch tells the agent what TCP/IP address to use for Message Transfer communications.
/mtpinport	Cluster-unique port that is used by this PO	This switch tells the agent what TCP/IP port to use for inbound Message Transfer communications.
/cluster	None	This switch tells the agent that the POA is running on a cluster. Available in the Enhancement Pack with Support Pack 2 or later (when the POA knows it is running on a cluster), it also informs the GroupWise client that it is connected to a cluster, and the client will be more forgiving of TCP/IP timeouts (that is, the client will wait longer to report an error).

In addition to these new POA switches, you can also use the /port switch, which tells the agent which port to use for client/server communications, and the /ip switch, which tells the agent which IP address to use for client/server communications. All of these settings, except /ip and /cluster, are configurable using NetWare Administrator. However, you may find that setting the parameters in NetWare Administrator doesn't always get the settings to the agent. This typically occurs when the configuration is incorrect when you make the changes (for example, the Domain link to the POA in UNC using an incorrect path). When this occurs, you can either rebuild the Post Office, or you can load the POA with the startup switches to override NDS.

TIP

The /ip switch should be considered mandatory in a cluster, and refers to the resource's secondary IP address. If you don't use it, the POA binds to the server's primary IP address, even if NDS is properly configured with the secondary IP address. This binding with the wrong (primary) IP address will cause MTA-to-POA communications to fail, and may or may not cause the MTA to report the POA as closed. (Secondary IP addresses are discussed in more detail in Chapter 4.)

Using Protected Memory

As mentioned earlier in the chapter, the GroupWise modules should be run in protected memory to prevent one resource migration from bringing down other resources. Protected memory is available with NetWare 5.0 and later and allows you to load various modules into their own memory space so problems with one module will not affect the server memory space (ring 0) or other address spaces in the system. Not all modules can be loaded in protected memory. (For example, system modules, such as LAN or disk drivers, or modules such as MONITOR.NLM cannot be loaded in protected memory.)

You can load the same module into multiple protected memory spaces, and you can load multiple modules into the same protected memory space. If a module autoloads another NLM, it, too, is added to the protected memory space.

However, for all its gains, using protected memory spaces can have costs. It does affect system performance and can also significantly add to the memory requirements of the system. Novell estimates that using protected memory results in a 5 to 10 percent performance hit.

To load a module in protected memory, issue the following command:

```
LOAD ADDRESS SPACE = <NAME> <MODULE> <PARAMETERS>
```

For example:

```
LOAD ADDRESS SPACE=GW1 GWMTA @GWDOM1.MTA

LOAD ADDRESS SPACE=GW1 GWPOA @GWPO1.POA
```

To unload a module in protected memory, issue the following command:

```
UNLOAD ADDRESS SPACE = <NAME> <MODULE>
```

For example:

```
UNLOAD ADDRESS SPACE=GW1 GWMTA
```

You can also flag a memory space to restart. Then, when the address space faults and dies (for example, a module in the address space ABENDS), a new address space is created and the same exact modules are loaded into the new one. The address space isn't literally reused, but the new one has the same name and has the identical modules (with the same command-line options and the same load order) and everything in place. You do this by loading all of the modules in the address space and then issuing this command:

```
PROTECTION RESTART <NAME>
```

For example:

```
PROTECTION RESTART GW1
```

If you want to remove an address space and everything in it, you can issue the following command:

```
UNLOAD KILL ADDRESS SPACE= <NAME>
```

For example:

```
UNLOAD KILL ADDRESS SPACE=GW1
```

To see all of the modules, and which address space they are loaded in, issue the following command:

```
PROTECTION
```

Now that you know all the protected memory commands that you will need to use for GroupWise, you should also understand the process of loading and unloading GroupWise modules in the cluster resource. This section will give you an idea of how to approach these important tasks.

Each set of GroupWise modules that will be configured as the same cluster resource should be loaded in the same address space. For example, if you will run a GroupWise Domain and Post Office in the same resource, use one memory space for both of them. This saves system resources, since separating these into two address spaces is not required to safely migrate them without losing any other GroupWise component.

NOTE **You might prefer to use separate memory spaces for the MTA and POA even if they are configured as the same cluster resource. The advantage of using different memory spaces is that if the POA fails, it will not affect the MTA or vice versa. The drawback is the extra memory requirement and performance penalty for the extra memory space. You must weigh the pros and cons in your own environment and decide which option is best for you. All the examples in this book assume that you will use one memory space for both agents when they are configured as a single resource.**

The cluster Unload Script should unload the modules from their protected memory spaces. However, it is possible that the modules may hang when unloading from the memory space, which causes the resource to fail to migrate (it just sits in the unloading stage forever). To prevent this, kill the address space. But remember, killing the address space does not unload the modules first, which could lead to database corruption. So, what's the compromise? Unload the modules from the protected memory space first, then delay for an appropriate time (use trial and error with your system once you determine normal unload times), then kill the address space. By trying to unload the modules first, the modules will unload normally under most circumstances, and you will avoid potential database integrity issues that will require the agent to rebuild the database.

Document Management

GroupWise offers sophisticated Document Management features that enhance document access, conversion, integration, and security. GroupWise can copy documents to your local disk so you can find them easily and retain access to them even if the network goes down. Default folders hold newly created and recently stored documents so they are readily accessible as you work. Using the librarian function, an administrator can manage all the documents in a library without requiring users to give the administrator access to the contents of sensitive documents.

With Document Management, GroupWise offers the option of storing the document library in the Post Office itself or in a file system structure outside of the Post Office. Most clients using Document Management store the documents outside of the Post Office for enhanced scalability.

However, to cluster enable Document Management, Novell only supports DMS if the document library is stored within the Post Office. Since this configuration does not scale nearly as efficiently as storing the library outside of the Post Office, this is not a viable solution for most clients desiring Document Management. Though you can still use Document Management external to the Post Office when implementing clustering, you will not receive the benefit of reconnection if the document library server fails.

Client

The GroupWise client provides the user interface to messages and connects directly to the user's Post Office. The client provides two main connection methods, including direct UNC connection to the file system or TCP/IP (client/server) connection to the POA. For Novell Cluster Services, the client must communicate via client/server, which uses a TCP/IP connection to the secondary IP address used by the Post Office resource.

When a new client starts up for the first time, the client checks NDS to see if it can determine the correct Post Office the user belongs to. If the NDS rights have been set for the GroupWise system, the client should automatically find the correct Post Office and make the connection.

If the client cannot read NDS, then it checks the workstation's DNS zone for an ngwnameserver or an ngwnameserver2 entry. If it finds one of these entries, it attempts to connect to that IP address on Port 1677. If the client can connect to a Post Office using these entries, that Post Office will direct the client to the proper Post Office if it can resolve the name in the address book.

Since you will be using different ports for each of the GroupWise Post Offices, it is important to make sure that the IP address you use for the ngwnameserver entry corresponds to a Post Office that is running on Port 1677.

Starting with Support Pack 1 to the Enhancement Pack, the GroupWise client has been enhanced to detect whether its Post Office is running in a cluster. If a cluster is detected, the client will be more patient when the Post Office does not respond, which adds to the transparency of GroupWise migration.

TIP

With the current GroupWise code, the client cannot detect whether the POA is running on a cluster if the agent is running in protected memory. To compensate for this, use the /CLUSTER **switch in the POA startup file. The** /CLUSTER **switch enables the GroupWise client to try more persistently to reconnect during a failover, failback, or migration situation.**

Cluster Enabling GroupWise 5.5

GroupWise offers a wealth of services and configuration options, and several books on the market deal exclusively with GroupWise. This chapter cannot possibly cover all possible configurations of GroupWise in a cluster. Therefore, the information provided in this chapter is limited to the most common configurations.

Cluster Enabling the Volume

To administer GroupWise, you must first connect to the GroupWise Domain database. Without clustering, all administrators will know where the Domain database is, since it never moves. Once you implement GroupWise in a cluster, unless you cluster enable the database volume, you must figure out which node has the Domain volume activated before you can administer it. By cluster enabling the volume, you can use the UNC path provided with the virtual server and always establish a connection to the Domain. Since the personnel that creates GroupWise accounts may not administer the servers, this provides a significant benefit.

Depending on which components you are configuring in the cluster, you may or may not need to cluster enable the GroupWise volume. If you are configuring a cluster resource that includes only a GroupWise Post Office, you should not cluster enable the volume. For almost all other configurations, you should cluster enable the GroupWise volume.

GroupWise gateways currently cannot be configured to communicate with the Domain using TCP/IP — they are configured as UNC paths relative to the Domain database. This communication requirement means that cluster enabling the Domain database for any Domain that includes gateway agents should be required.

NOTE

With GroupWise 5.5 SP3 and the Enhancement Pack SP1, Novell has modified the way the MTA finds the gateway. If the MTA cannot find the gateway using the configuration in the Domain database/NDS, it will automatically search for the gateway on whatever server has loaded the MTA. This MTA modification means that the gateway will actually work without a cluster-enabled volume, even though you cannot configure the MTA-to-gateway link. However, cluster enabling the Domain volume is still recommended for all of the other reasons listed in this chapter.

When using a cluster-enabled volume for the GroupWise resource, it is important that you don't create two resources for the same GroupWise component. Create the cluster-enabled volume and then modify its load and Unload Script to include the commands to load GroupWise. Don't create a second resource for GroupWise that depends on the cluster-enabled volume resource.

Modifying the HOSTS Files and DNS for GroupWise

When using cluster-enabled volumes, modify the HOSTS files for the virtual server names. This allows the server to resolve the virtual server name to the secondary IP address used for the resource. To configure the HOSTS file, follow these steps:

1. On each server, change to the server console prompt and enter **LOAD EDIT SYS:ETC\HOSTS**.

2. At the bottom of the file, add a line for each Virtual Server (not Volume) object and its IP address:

```
10.7.5.106    CLUSTER_GW1_SERVER.CLUSTER.COM      CLUSTER_GW1_SERVER

10.7.5.108    CLUSTER_GW3_SERVER.CLUSTER.COM      CLUSTER_GW3_SERVER

10.7.5.109    CLUSTER_GW4_SERVER.CLUSTER.COM      CLUSTER_GW4_SERVER

10.7.5.110    CLUSTER_GW5_SERVER.CLUSTER.COM      CLUSTER_GW5_SERVER

10.7.5.111    CLUSTER_GW6_SERVER.CLUSTER.COM      CLUSTER_GW6_SERVER

10.7.5.112    CLUSTER_GWGWIA_SERVER.CLUSTER.COM   CLUSTER_GWGWIA_SERVER

10.7.5.113    CLUSTER_GWWEB_SERVER.CLUSTER.COM    CLUSTER_GWWEB_SERVER
```

You can see in the code listing that we did not cluster enable the GW2 volume for a single Post Office, so it does not need an entry in the HOSTS file.

NOTE

3. Press Esc, and select Yes to save your changes.

If your DNS server supports the underscore (_) character, you should also create DNS entries for each virtual server, which allows both clients and servers to utilize DNS for name resolution.

Using CVSBIND

Novell Cluster Services version 1 and 1.01 do not participate with Service Location Protocol (SLP). Thus, resolving short names (for example, server names) for the virtual servers must be done using NDS, DNS, HOSTS files, or NWHOSTS files.

DNS and the Underscore

The underscore (_) character is not supported by the DNS RFC, and many vendors' DNS servers do not support this character. Novell's DNS server with NetWare 5.x does not officially support this character either, although testing has shown that it works (though there have been cases where it didn't).

The next version of Novell Cluster Services will no longer force the virtual server name to CLUSTER_VOLUME_SERVER and will instead allow you to specify the virtual server name. This will allow you to dodge the underscore issue altogether by avoiding this character in your server names.

Short name resolution using NDS will produce only the desired results (that is, successful name resolution) if the user's current context happens to be the same context as the virtual server. In most environments, this will not be the case, so NDS short name resolution will not provide the desired results for the virtual servers.

DNS would be the next logical choice for short name resolution. However, this, too, can be problematic if the DNS server you are using does not support the underscore character. That leaves HOSTS files or NWHOSTS files for short name resolution, which would be tedious at best (of course, ZENworks can help here).

If none of these methods provides you the desired short name resolution, Novell has a utility called CVSBIND.NLM (you can find this by searching Novell's knowledge base for TID 2957434). This NLM allows you to modify the load and Unload Scripts for your cluster resources and force the SLP propagation of the virtual server names. The README.TXT file that comes with this module includes installation and configuration instructions.

With the next version of Novell Cluster Services, this extra NLM will no longer be required, as the Novell Cluster Services software itself will automatically propagate the virtual server information in SLP.

Deciding Where to Install the NLMs

When installing GroupWise NLMs, the installation process assumes that you wish to install the agents to the server's SYS volume. Depending on how you are configuring your system, you may wish to accept this default and install all agents to the SYS volume of each cluster node. Choosing this option requires that each node in the cluster that can run GroupWise must have the agents installed individually to that server. Thus, if you have a 12-node GroupWise cluster, you will install the agents 12 times. This also adds complexity to patching the GroupWise system. If you have multiple Domains, you must patch all the Domains at the same time, or you may end up with a situation in which the MTA migrates to a nonpatched server and possibly corrupts the Domain database.

An alternative is to create a SYSTEM directory on the shared storage volume you are using for the resource. Then, when you install the GroupWise agents, you install the agents into the resource volume's SYSTEM directory. Using this method, all nodes in your cluster will immediately be able to use this cluster resource, since there will not be any SYS volume dependencies. Additionally, since each

GroupWise resource will have the NLMs on the resource volume, when you patch one node, you are actually patching all nodes that will use that resource. However, in a cluster that has 12 GroupWise Domains but only six nodes, you actually end up installing the agents more times using this method than by installing the agents once to each server's SYS volume.

While not required, we recommend using a directory named "SYSTEM" so that its purpose will be apparent to all administrators.

TIP

Whichever method you choose, remain consistent throughout your cluster. You must ensure that each GroupWise resource is accessed using only NLMs that are the appropriate version for that resource. Do not have non-Enhancement Pack Support Pack 1 NLMs loaded on a database that is running the Enhancement Pack Support Pack 1 version of GroupWise. Running the wrong agents (older) against a newer version of the database would have sporadic results at best, and database corruption at worst. In the examples throughout this chapter, the SYSTEM directory is created on the resource volume.

Configuring IP Addresses and Ports

When configuring GroupWise in a cluster, each GroupWise resource must have its own dedicated TCP/IP address. Additionally, each agent must have a unique port address if there is any possibility that two of the same agents will reside on the same server. For example, if NODE1 normally has GWPO1, and NODE2 normally has GWPO2, and NODE2 was to fail and migrate the GWPO2 to NODE1, if both POAs were configured to use the default port 1677, client/server communications would be sporadic at best.

To avoid this issue, configure all agents with unique ports throughout the entire cluster. To assist with the planning of your resources, use a table similar to Table 11.3. You should complete this planning before installing the first component, as ad hoc planning will most likely lead to duplication that may not be discovered until the right combination of migrations doubles up the wrong resources.

Table 11.3 shows all of the GroupWise resources used in this chapter and Chapter 12, with the resource name, ports, Domain names, Post Office names, and TCP/IP addresses.

TABLE 11.3

GroupWise Port Planning

CLUSTER RESOURCE	POA C/S PORT	POA MTP PORT	POA HTTP PORT	MTA PORT	MTA HTTP PORT	AGENT PORT	DOMAIN NAME	PO NAME	TCP/IP
GW1	1677	7300	2800	7100	3800	N/A	GWDOM1	GWPO1	10.7.5.106
GW2	1678	7302	2802	N/A	N/A	N/A	N/A	GWPO2	10.7.5.107
GW3	1679	7303	2803	7103	3803	N/A	GWDOM3	GWPO3	10.7.5.108
GW4	1680	7304	2804	7104	3804	N/A	GWDOM4	GWPO4	10.7.5.109
GW5	1681	7305	2805	7105	3805	N/A	GWDOM5	GWPO5	10.7.5.110
GWGWIA	N/A	N/A	N/A	7101	3801	4800	GWGWIA	N/A	10.7.5.112
GWWEB	N/A	N/A	N/A	7102	3802	7205	GWWEB	N/A	10.7.5.113

Note that for resource GW2, we configured a Post Office as a resource without a Domain (see the Domain Name column of Table 11.3). This Post Office actually belongs to Domain GWDOM1, but is listed as N/A because the cluster resource does not include a Domain MTA.

Creating an MTA and POA as One Resource

This chapter includes several sections on configuring various components of GroupWise in a cluster. This first section walks you through the process of creating a new GroupWise system with an MTA and POA configured as a single GroupWise resource. The remaining sections assume that this task is already complete or that you are following the procedures in an environment that already has a Primary Domain configured. The examples in Chapter 12 also assume that you already have a Primary Domain configured before adding additional components.

In this example, we are configuring a Domain (MTA) and a Post Office as a single cluster resource. These two components will migrate or failover together, and will both reside on the same shared storage volume.

This example also follows the general recommendation of cluster enabling the volume used for the Domain database, which makes it easy for administrators to connect to the Domain and administer it.

The major tasks in creating an MTA and POA as a single resource are as follows:

- ▸ Cluster enabling the volume

- ▸ Creating the GroupWise system

- ▸ Running the NetWare Administrator utility to configure GroupWise

- ▸ Installing the GroupWise agents

- ▸ Installing the client software

- ▸ Modifying the startup files

- ▸ Configuring the cluster resource

Creating the GroupWise System

This section assumes that you are creating a brand new system (perhaps in your test lab), and walks you through the complete installation process. If you already have a GroupWise system and just wish to add another Domain and PO to it in a cluster, jump ahead to the section "Creating a Secondary Domain and Post Office Resource."

NOTE

Before you begin working in a production environment, you should first perform these steps in a lab. This will help you get a feel for how the process and configuration works, without potentially jeopardizing your production environment. Sometimes production systems are used as labs, but this has never been a successful long-term solution.

1. Create a cluster-enabled volume for the GroupWise MTA/POA (for this example, GW1 is used as the volume name).

X-REF

Refer to Chapter 9 to learn how to cluster enable a volume.

2. Modify each server's SYS:ETC\HOSTS file by adding an entry for the newly created virtual server. In our example, our HOSTS file is as follows:

```
10.7.5.51    NODE1.CLUSTER.COM   NODE1

10.7.5.52    NODE2.CLUSTER.COM   NODE2

10.7.5.53    NODE3.CLUSTER.COM   NODE3

10.7.5.101   CLUSTER_PUB_SERVER.CLUSTER.COM   CLUSTER_PUB_SERVER

10.7.5.102   CLUSTER_APPS_SERVER.CLUSTER.COM   CLUSTER_APPS_SERVER

10.7.5.105   CLUSTER_NDPS_SERVER.CLUSTER.COM   CLUSTER_NDPS_SERVER

10.7.5.106   CLUSTER_GW1_SERVER.CLUSTER.COM   CLUSTER_GW1_SERVER
```

3. Online the GroupWise cluster-enabled volume (GW1_SERVER) resource and then map a drive to it (we used M).

4. Create a directory named SYSTEM on the (M drive) cluster-enabled volume.

5. Map a drive to the PUBLIC directory of the server that you will use to install the GroupWise snapins.

6. Insert the GroupWise Enhancement Pack CD in the CD-ROM drive of your workstation.

7. The GroupWise Installation dialog box should display on your screen (auto run).

8. Click the Install Products button.

9. Click the GroupWise Administration button.

10. Select the Install GroupWise Administration button. This will spawn a new process that begins a wizard to install the GroupWise system.

11. In the Welcome to GroupWise Install dialog box, click Next.

12. Click Accept to accept the license agreement. A list of NDS trees seen by the installation program will appear.

13. Select your tree and then click Next. The schema will be read to see if the GroupWise extensions already exist. If they do, no schema extension will be necessary, and you will skip step 14.

14. Click Next to extend the schema.

15. Click Next to acknowledge that the tree has been extended.

16. If desired, select any additional languages. Then click Next to accept English and your additional language selection. Depending on the particular software version you are using, you may or may not have a choice other than English.

17. In the NetWare Administrator Path dialog box (see Figure 11.1), select the drive mapped to the PUBLIC directory where you want the GroupWise Administration tools (snapins) installed. Then click Next.

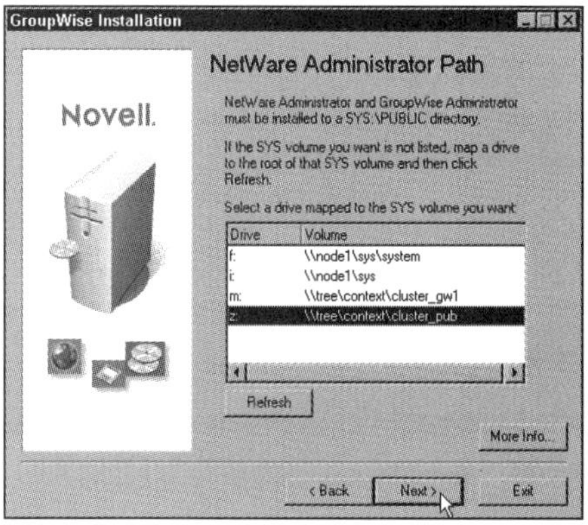

FIGURE 11.1 *NetWare Administrator Path dialog box*

It's recommended that you create a cluster-enabled volume for the PUBLIC utilities. After you create the cluster-enabled volume (in our cluster, this is named PUB), copy the SYS:PUBLIC directory and its contents from the server you installed the GroupWise snapins to. Any time you patch your servers, don't forget to recopy the SYS:PUBLIC directory, so you can keep the shared storage PUBLIC directory up to date.

TIP

18. In the Software Distribution dialog box, enter the desired location for the Software Distribution Directory and then click Next. The Software Distribution Directory needs to be in a location that users will have rights to read so they can install the GroupWise client software.

Alternatively, you can use ZENworks to deploy the GroupWise client, in which case only administrators would need access to the software distribution directory.

TIP

19. At a minimum, select the following software to install:

- GroupWise Administrator

- GroupWise Monitor (optional)

- NLM Agents

- NT Agents (optional)

- GroupWise WebAccess (optional)

- Windows 95/98/NT Client

- GroupWise Internet Agent (optional)

Installing the optional components places the installation files into the software distribution directory for installation later.

NOTE

20. Click Next to continue.

21. Click Next to accept the default ConsoleOne path.

22. After the file check is completed, make sure that the "Do not replace newer files" option is selected, and then click Next.

23. Click Install to begin the installation.

24. When the installation is complete, click Finish.

Running the NetWare Administrator Utility to Configure GroupWise

Once you have installed the GroupWise snapins, you must actually create the new GroupWise system. You will use NetWare Administrator to create the new GroupWise system. The first time you run NetWare Administrator after installing the snapins, it should automatically start the new system installation (in which case, you start this procedure at step 5).

To create the new GroupWise system, perform the following steps:

1. Launch NetWare Administrator from the location that you installed the snapins.

2. Click Cancel when asked for the GroupWise Domain path. This dialog box will appear if you have previously used your workstation to administer a GroupWise system.

3. Click OK to acknowledge the message that there is no GroupWise Domain to administer.

4. From the NetWare Administrator utility, select Tools ⇨ GroupWise Utilities ⇨ New GroupWise system. This will launch the wizard to create a new GroupWise system.

5. Click Next to begin the system installation.

6. In the Software Distribution dialog box, either enter or browse to your Software Distribution Directory, and then click Next.

7. In the NDS Tree Name dialog box, verify or enter your tree name, and then click Next.

8. In the System Name dialog box, enter a name for the GroupWise system (this cannot be changed later), and then click Next.

9. In the Primary Domain Name dialog box, enter the name for the Primary Domain, and then click Next.

10. In the Domain Directory dialog box, enter a path to the location you wish to use for the domain, for example, M:\grpwise\GWDOM1, and then click Next.

Be sure that you enter this path via the cluster-enabled volume, such as the M drive you mapped in step 3 of "Creating the GroupWise System." By using a path through the cluster-enabled volume, the Domain's UNC path will automatically be set to `\\virtual-server-name\volume\path`, which is required for any gateways that you later install.

The directory names in the path to the Domain database must comply with the 8.3 naming convention — GroupWise does not support long filenames in the Domain path, even though it will let you enter long names here.

TIP

11. When prompted, click Yes to confirm the creation of the Domain subdirectory, and then click Next.

12. Enter the NDS context for the domain, for example, Context, and then click Next.

13. Select the Domain's language, for example, English-US, and then click Next.

14. Select the Domain's time zone, and then click Next.

15. Enter a name for the Post Office, for example, GWPO1, and then click Next.

16. In the Post Office Directory dialog box, enter a path to the location you wish to use for the Post Office, for example, `M:\grpwise\GWPO1`, and then click Next.

Once again, select this directory using the cluster-enabled volume, either by drive letter mapped to the cluster-enabled volume or by UNC path using the virtual server. Be sure to place the Post Office in a different directory than the Domain, but on the same volume if you plan on having the Domain and Post Office configured as a single cluster resource.

TIP

The directory names in the path to the Post Office database must comply with the 8.3 naming convention — GroupWise does not support long filenames in the PO path, even though it will let you enter long names here.

17. When prompted, click Yes to confirm the creation of the Post Office subdirectory, and then click Next.

18. Enter the context for the Post Office, for example, Context, and then click Next.

19. Enter the Post Office language, for example, English-US, and then click Next.

20. Enter the Post Office time zone, and then click Next.

21. In the Post Office Access Mode dialog box, select Client/Server Access only, and then click Next.

You must use Client/Server access when clustering the Post Office. Do not use Direct or Client/Server and Direct. Refer back to the "Post Office Agents" section for more details.

TIP

22. In the Post Office Link dialog box, select TCP/IP Link, and then click Next.

You must use a TCP/IP link when clustering the Post Office. Do not use a direct link. Refer back to the "Post Office Agents" section for more details.

TIP

23. In the POA Network Address dialog box (see Figure 11.2), do the following:

   a. TCP/IP Address — Enter the secondary IP address that the Post Office will use.

   b. C/S Port — Enter the clusterwide unique port (from Table 11.3) that the Post Office will use for client/server connections.

   c. Message Transfer Port — Enter the clusterwide unique port (from Table 11.3) that the Post Office will use for message transfers.

   d. HTTP Port — Enter the clusterwide unique port (from Table 11.3) that the Post Office will use for HTTP monitoring.

   e. Click Next to continue.

If there is any possibility that more than one Post Office will reside on the same node in the cluster, it is critical that the C/S Port, Message Transfer Port, and HTTP Port be unique throughout the entire cluster. The HTTP Port must be unique for all agents — you cannot use the same HTTP Port for both the Post Office and an MTA that could possibly exist on the same node together.

TIP

▶ • ◀

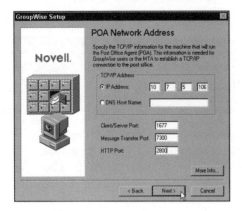

FIGURE 11.2 *POA Network Address dialog box*

24. In the MTA Network Address dialog box (see Figure 11.3), do the following:

    a. TCP/IP Address — Enter the secondary IP address you will use for the Domain MTA (if you are creating a single cluster resource for the MTA and the POA, this can be the same address you used for the POA).

    b. Message Transfer Port — Enter the clusterwide unique MTA Message Transfer Port.

    c. HTTP Port — Enter the clusterwide unique port that the MTA will use for HTTP monitoring.

    d. Click Next to continue.

TIP

If there is any possibility that more than one MTA will reside on the same node in the cluster, it is critical that the Message Transfer Port and HTTP Port be unique throughout the entire cluster. The HTTP Port must be unique for all agents — you cannot use the same HTTP Port for both the Post Office and an MTA that could possibly exist on the same node together.

25. In the Post Office Users dialog box, browse and select all NDS users that you would like to add to this Post Office, and then click Next. You can always add users later.

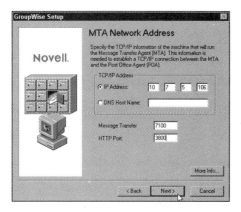

FIGURE I I.3 *MTA Network Address dialog box*

26. Click Next to create the system.

27. At the Summary dialog box (see Figure 11.4), verify all of the system information. At this point, the installation program will convert the paths you used with drive mappings to UNC paths. These must be UNC paths using the virtual server for the cluster-enabled volume. Once you have verified all the information, click the Create button.

FIGURE I I.4 *Summary dialog box*

28. In the GroupWise Administrator — User Access Control dialog box, click the Yes button to set the appropriate NDS rights for users to read their Post Office information from NDS.

29. Click the Next button to begin installing the GroupWise agents.

Installing the GroupWise Agents

Once the NDS objects and Domain/Post Office directory structure has been created, you must install the NLM agents and create the agent startup files. The wizard that you launched in the previous step continues to walk you through this process, so you can continue to run the wizard. If you need to repeat this process, you can also run the INSTALL.EXE program from the software distribution \agents directory.

To install the agents, perform the following steps:

1. In the Agent Information dialog box continued from the preceding steps, click Next to continue.

2. In the GroupWise Agent Platform dialog box, select NetWare NLM and then click Next.

3. Click the Install Agents button.

4. In the Installation Path dialog box, either enter or browse to the directory that you wish to install the agents to and then click Next. You can create a SYSTEM directory on the resource volume to use for the agents as discussed in the "Deciding Where to Install the NLMs" section earlier in this chapter, or you can install them to each node in the cluster that will be in the failover path.

5. In the Web Console Information dialog box (see Figure 11.5), do the following:

   a. Enable web console — Check this box if you wish to use the HTTP Web Console tool. You should enable this tool for enhanced monitoring of the GroupWise agents.

   b. Specify user name — Enter a user name to use for Web Console authentication purposes. This should not correlate to an NDS user account since the account will be used via clear-text HTTP.

   c. Specify password — Enter the password to use to access the Web Console.

d. Verify password — Reenter the password to use to access the Web Console.

e. Click the Next button to continue.

6. In the Language dialog box, confirm your language selection, and then click Next.

7. In the Summary dialog box, confirm your selections, and then click the Install button.

8. In the Installation Complete dialog box, do the following:

a. Deselect the Update AUTOEXEC.NCF file button.

b. Deselect the Launch GroupWise Agents Now button.

c. Click the Finish button.

9. In the NLM Agent Setup dialog box, click the Next button, which concludes the agent setup and begins the client installation process.

If you did not install the agents to the shared volume, do not click Next here. Instead, click Install Agents and repeat steps 4 through 8 for each node that will run the GroupWise agents. If you did not install the agents to the shared volume, then they must be installed to the SYS:SYSTEM volume of every server that may run the cluster resource; otherwise, the resource will not have the necessary support files to activate.

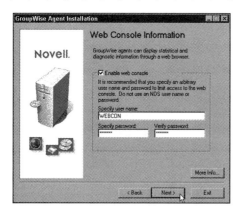

FIGURE 11.5 *GroupWise Agent Installation — Web Console Information dialog box*

Installing the Client Software

While not a necessary step in clustering GroupWise, the wizard that you started in the first section also walks you through the client installation procedure. GroupWise allows you to run older clients against newer database systems, so if you have an existing GroupWise client, you may skip this step and come back to it later. Not all of the enhanced GroupWise features will be available without running the newest version of the client. For example, the new client feature that allows the client to detect that it is running against a cluster doesn't do you any good if you don't upgrade your client!

To install the client, perform the following:

1. Click the Setup Client button. If you are not still running the New System Wizard, start the client installation program by running SETUP.EXE from the software distribution directory \clients\win32 directory.

2. Click the Next button.

3. Select Standard Install, and then click Next. Optionally, you may choose the workstation installation, which will run the GroupWise client across the network. In this case, the GroupWise client would only be available when logged into the network.

4. Either accept or modify the default path, and then click Next.

5. Accept or modify the default components, and click Next.

6. Accept or modify the default folder location, and click Next.

7. Select or deselect to have Notify run at Startup, and click Next.

8. Accept English or modify your language, and then click Next.

9. If asked, choose which components you wish to integrate with GroupWise, or select do not integrate GroupWise with applications, and then click Next.

10. Click Next to start copying client software files.

11. When the copying is complete, choose to view (or not view) the README file, and choose to launch (or not launch) the client now.

12. Complete and close the wizard.

Modifying the Startup Files

Before you start the agents, you must modify the agent startup files. If you don't modify the startup files, the agent's parameters will only be valid for the servers that you actually ran the installation from. Additionally, if you used a cluster-enabled volume, the startup files will have the UNC path using the virtual server syntax. While the virtual server syntax is beneficial from a client workstation, it currently causes a performance penalty for the agent files as the name resolution process occurs — performance is significantly enhanced by stripping of the server names from the /home switches. In addition, the POA should be modified with the /IP switch at a minimum to guarantee proper binding to the secondary IP address.

If you installed the agents to the shared volume, you need to do this only once by modifying the agent startup files on the shared volume.

If you installed the agents to the SYS volume of each node in the cluster, you have three options. First, you can modify the startup files on all nodes that you installed the agents to. Second, you could modify the startup files on one node, and then copy it to all the nodes that you installed the agents to. Alternatively, you can move the startup files to the shared volume to modify them, and use the startup files off the SAN even though you are running the agents on each server's SYS volume.

It's recommended that you put the agent files on the shared volume so you have only one location at which to make changes. If you keep individual agent startup files on each server, any time you decide to modify the startup files, you must manually modify the files on every node that might run GroupWise.

The installation program will create the agent files using UNC syntax for the /HOME switch, for example, \\NODE1\GW1\GWDOM1 or \\CLUSTER_GW1_SERVER\ GWDOM1. For best results, change the startup file to the traditional NetWare syntax, GW1:\GWDOM1. By removing the server name from the path, you can use the same agent file on all servers, and name resolution will be avoided, thus significantly speeding the agent load time.

To modify the startup files, edit the <Domain>.MTA and <PO>.POA files (in our example, these are M:\SYSTEM\GWDOM1.MTA and M:\SYSTEM\GWPO1.POA).

> In the .MTA file, change the /HOME switch to:

/HOME-<VOLUME>:\<path to Domain>

For example:

/HOME-GW1:\GWDOM1

▶ In the `.POA` file, change the `/HOME` switch to:

`/HOME-<VOLUME>:\<path to PO>`

For example:

`/HOME-GW1:\GWPO1`

▶ In the `.POA` file, add the `/IP`, `/port`, `/mtpinip`, and `/mtpinport` parameters:

- /ip-*<client/server TCP/IP secondary IP address>* (required)

- /port-*<client/server port>* (optional)

- /mtpinip-*<secondary IP address of POA>* (optional)

- /mtpinport-*<MTP port of POA>* (optional)

For example:

`/ip-10.7.5.106`

`/port-1677`

`/mtpinip-10.7.5.106`

`/mtpinport-7300`

Creating and Starting the GroupWise Cluster Resource

Now that you have performed all of the required GroupWise configuration, including creating the new system, installing the agents, and modifying the startup files, you are ready to create the cluster resource for GroupWise. Since you are using a cluster-enabled volume for the Domain and Post Office, you already have a resource object for GroupWise — the cluster-enabled volume resource object. You will need to modify this existing object with all of the commands to load and unload GroupWise.

To modify the cluster resource object, perform the following:

1. Using ConsoleOne, change to the Console View, and select your cluster-enabled volume resource object, for example, the `GW1_SERVER` object.

2. Right-click the resource object, then select Properties.

3. Click the Load tab, then check to make sure the following commands are included in the Load Script:

```
NSS /ACTIVATE=<volume>

MOUNT <volume>

TRUSTMIG <volume> watch

NUDP ADD <cluster name>_<volume>_SERVER <IP Address of resource>

ADD SECONDARY IPADDRESS <IP Address of resource>
```

You can also remove the TRUSTMIG watch **command here—since you are using only client/server connections, you do not need file system trustees for GroupWise, and therefore you don't need to migrate them.**

TIP

4. Add the following commands to the Load Script at the bottom of the script:

```
LOAD ADDRESS SPACE=<name> <volume>:\SYSTEM\GWMTA @GWDOM1.MTA

LOAD ADDRESS SPACE=<name> <volume>:\SYSTEM\GWPOA @GWPO1.POA

PROTECTION RESTART <name>
```

You can see an example of a Cluster Resource Load Script in Figure 11.6.

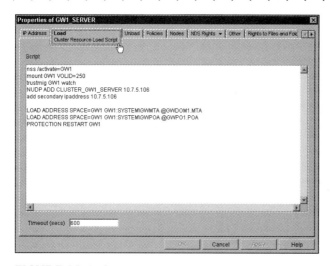

FIGURE 11.6 *GroupWise Cluster Resource Load Script*

If this Domain will run the NDS User Synchronization event, be sure to load DSAPI.NLM in the same protected memory space as the MTA. Also remember to unload it in the Unload Script.

TIP

5. Click the Unload tab, then add the following commands at the top of the Unload Script:

```
UNLOAD ADDRESS SPACE=<name> GWMTA

UNLOAD ADDRESS SPACE=<name> GWPOA

UNLOAD ADDRESS SPACE=<name> GWENN2

LOAD DELAY.NLM

DELAY 10

UNLOAD KILL ADDRESS SPACE=<name>
```

6. Check to make sure the following commands are at the bottom of the Unload Script:

```
DEL SECONDARY IPADDRESS <IP Address of resource>

NUDP DEL CLUSTER1_GW1_SERVER <IP Address of resource>

TRUSTMIG <volume> unwatch

DISMOUNT <volume> /FORCE

NSS /FORCEDEACTIVATE=<volume>
```

You can see an example of a Cluster Resource Unload Script in Figure 11.7.

If you removed the TRUSTMIG watch **command from the Load Script, also remove the** TRUSTMIG unwatch **command from the Unload Script.**

TIP

7. Select the Nodes tab, and edit the assigned cluster nodes as required.

8. Click OK to add the GroupWise cluster resource object.

9. Change the ConsoleOne View to Cluster State View.

10. Offline the resource.

11. Online the resource and verify that GroupWise is functioning properly.

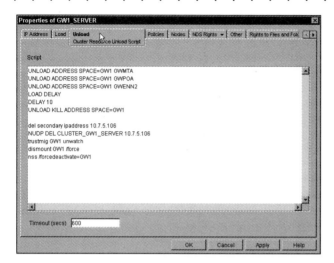

FIGURE 11.7 *GroupWise Cluster Resource Unload Script*

Creating a POA-Only Resource

Once you have your GroupWise system up and clustered, you may wish to add a second Domain or Post Office to the cluster. As we mentioned earlier in the "Discussing Cluster Enabling the Volume" section, in some cases it makes sense not to cluster enable the volume for a particular GroupWise resource, and a POA as a single resource is one of these cases. Since the NetWare Administrator Snapins only require a path to the Post Office when you are performing tasks such as rebuilding the Post Office, not having the correct path to the Post Office in NDS is not as big of an issue as not having the correct path to a Domain database. Recall that the only way the UNC path can be correct no matter where the resource is running is if you have a cluster-enabled volume, and the path is configured using the virtual NCP server.

TIP **While it is not of great benefit to cluster enable the volume for a single POA resource, creating a single MTA as a resource by itself may still benefit by cluster enabling the volume. This is so that administrators can have a consistent drive mapping to the Domain directory, which eases Domain administration.**

This section walks you through creating a new cluster resource for a single Post Office (PO2), assuming that you already have a GroupWise system up and running in the cluster. This Post Office is attached to the GWDOM1 Domain, and the links are configured as TCP/IP. This example uses a new volume GW2, but does not cluster enable it.

If you choose not to create a cluster-enabled volume for the Post Office (or Domain), you must select any node in the cluster to perform the initial configuration. This node will be used to configure the Post Office, and then all of the references to this node will later be removed to make the file locations relative to the server that is using it. Note that it is best to choose the most preferred cluster node to do the initial installation if you are not cluster enabling the volume. The node you choose (when not cluster enabling the volume) will be used in NDS for the Post Office UNC path. This path will only be correct when the Post Office resides on that cluster node. While most administrative functions don't use this path, if you rebuild the Post Office, NetWare Administrator will default to the UNC path that is configured in NDS.

The next few sections walk you through creating a new Post Office resource.

Creating and Mounting the Volume

The first step to creating the Post Office is to create the NSS volume on the shared storage for the Post Office database. This volume may be cluster-enabled if desired, although this example assumes that it is not.

To create the NSS volume, perform the following:

1. From any node in the cluster, create an NSS volume for this resource.

Remember, each GroupWise resource needs its own volume.

TIP

Refer to Chapter 9 for the procedure to create a NSS volume.

X-REF

2. From the node you chose for step one, enter the following commands at the server console:

```
NSS /ACTIVATE=<VOLUME>

MOUNT <VOLUME>
```

3. From your workstation, map a drive to this volume (for example, to \\NODE2\GW2).

4. Create a directory named SYSTEM on this new volume (optional). As with the new system, you have a choice of installing the agents to each server's SYS volume, or to the shared volume for the cluster resource.

Creating the Post Office Object

Once you have the volume ready, you must create a Post Office object in NDS. Before creating the PO, make your GroupWise connection to the Domain that you wish to assign this PO to.

To create the Post Office, perform the following:

1. Launch NetWare Administrator.

2. Connect to the GroupWise Domain you wish to create the Post Office in by browsing to the Domain, right-clicking it, and selecting Connect.

3. Browse to the context you wish to create the Post Office object in.

4. Select Object ⇨ Create from the menu.

5. Select GroupWise Post Office, and then click OK.

6. In the Create GroupWise Post Office dialog box (shown in Figure 11.8), do the following:

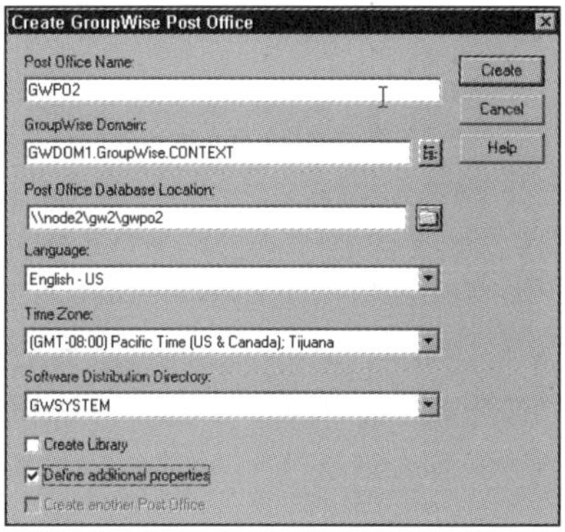

FIGURE 11.8 *Create GroupWise Post Office dialog box*

a. In the Post Office Name field, enter the name for the Post Office (for example, GWPO2).

b. In the GroupWise Domain field, browse and select the Domain this Post Office will belong to (for example, GWDOM1).

c. In the Post Office Database Location field, enter the UNC path to the Post Office directory, using the server you mounted the volume on (for example, \\NODE2\GW2\GWPO2).

TIP

The directory names in the path to the Post Office database must comply with the 8.3 naming convention — GroupWise does not support long filenames in the PO path, even though it will let you enter long names here.

d. In the Language field, select the appropriate Post Office language.

e. In the Time Zone field, select the time zone for the Post Office.

f. In the Software Distribution Directory, select the system name you wish to use for the software distribution.

g. If you wish to create a library for this Post Office, check the Create Library option box.

h. Check the Define additional properties option box.

i. Click the Create button. This will bring you to the properties pages of the Post Office object. By default, this should show you the Information tab of the Post Office.

7. In the Post Office Information tab (see Figure 11.9), do the following:

a. In the Description field, enter a description for the Post Office.

b. For security reasons, Novell recommends setting the Default Security Level to High. Although it is not required for Novell Cluster Services, increasing the security level helps prevent unauthorized users from viewing other mailboxes.

c. Change the Delivery Mode to Client/Server only.

d. Click OK.

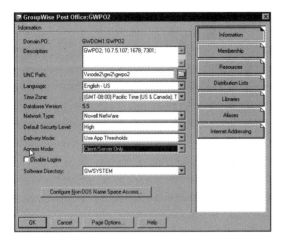

FIGURE 11.9 *GroupWise Post Office Information tab*

8. Double-click the Post Office object, and then double-click the POA object for this Post Office to modify its properties.

TIP If you are in **GroupWise** view, instead of double-clicking the **Post Office** object, click the plus sign (+) to the left of the **Post Office** to expand it.

9. In the Description field, enter a description for the Post Office.

TIP Including the IP address and ports you will use for the cluster resource in the description is generally a good idea because this information will be displayed on the agent NLM screen on the server console. With the added complexity of configuring GroupWise in a cluster and using different IP addresses and ports for your configuration, it is very handy to have this information appear on the NLM screen if you ever need to troubleshoot an individual agent.

10. Click the Network Address tab.

11. Select the TCP/IP radio button, then click Add.

12. In the Add Network Address dialog box (see Figure 11.10), do the following:

a. In the IP Address field, enter the secondary IP address you will use for this cluster resource (for example, 10.7.5.107).

b. In the Message Transfer Port field, enter the cluster-unique port this Post Office will use for message transfer (for example, 7302).

c. In the HTTP Port field, enter the cluster-unique port this Post Office will use for the HTTP monitor, if you plan on using this function (for example, 2802).

d. Click OK.

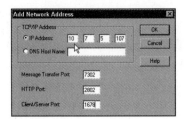

FIGURE 11.10 *Add Network Address dialog box*

13. Click OK to close the Network Address dialog box.

14. Next, you must rebuild the GroupWise Post Office. This is required because the Post Office was not running when you modified the Network Address information in step 12. Since the POA wasn't running, it was not able to receive the administrative messages required to change this configuration. To rebuild the Post Office, follow these steps:

a. From the GroupWise view, right-click the Post Office object (not the POA), and select Systems Maintenance.

b. Verify that the correct Post Office is selected, then click the Rebuild Database radio button.

c. Click the Run button.

d. In the Database Path dialog box, verify that the path reflects the node that currently has the volume mounted, then click OK.

e. Click OK.

f. Click Close.

Where Has the Database Gone?

In step 14 of "Creating the Post Office Object," you rebuild the Post Office database. You do this because the Post Office configuration was modified while the Post Office was not running, which means the administrative messages may not reach the Post Office to tell it of the new configuration. You will also encounter this if you are creating multiple Domains. When you create a new Domain, the default link to the Domain will be a UNC path, but you shouldn't use a UNC path in a cluster, you should always use TCP/IP. If you change the link before the Domain is up, the administrative message will never reach the Domain to tell it about its new information.

This also leads to a discussion about the database path when rebuilding a Post Office or Domain. If you are using a cluster-enabled volume, you may notice that the path to the database is incomplete using the UNC path through the virtual server (because the path is too long). This means that you must either manually browse to this path any time you are rebuilding a Domain, or rebuild the Domain to a temporary path and copy the database back once complete (rebuilding to a temporary path is the recommended procedure for Domains that are large enough to take a significant time to rebuild, or across slow WAN links).

If you are not cluster enabling the volume, this brings up yet another issue. The agents function correctly in a cluster because you modify the startup files. If the startup file parameters differ from the properties in NDS, the agent uses the startup file. Since the modified /HOME switch in the startup file is modified to remove the server name, this switch is valid on any node in the cluster, even though the UNC path in NDS may be wrong. However, the UNC path stored in NDS will be the original UNC path from the node the agent was originally configured on. This may not be the node GroupWise is running on when you rebuild the database, so you must know where the agent is running any time you wish to rebuild the database, and modify the destination path prior to completing the rebuild. This is yet another reason why cluster enabling the volume is helpful when you're configuring GroupWise in a cluster.

Modifying the Domain Link to the Post Office

After you modify the network address of the Post Office, you must also modify the Domain link to the Post Office. Recall that the Domain link always defaults to UNC, which would have the Domain directly access the Post Office database. This direct access can prevent clean shutdowns of the POA when you offline or migrate the resource, so the link should be changed to TCP/IP.

To modify the Domain link, perform the following:

1. Select the GroupWise Domain object that contains the new Post Office.

2. From the menu, select Tools ➪ GroupWise Utilities ➪ Link Configuration.

3. Click the Post Office Links button (or use the menu and select View ➪ Post Office Links).

4. Double-click the link to your newly created Post Office.

5. In the Edit Post Office Link dialog box (see Figure 11.11), do the following:

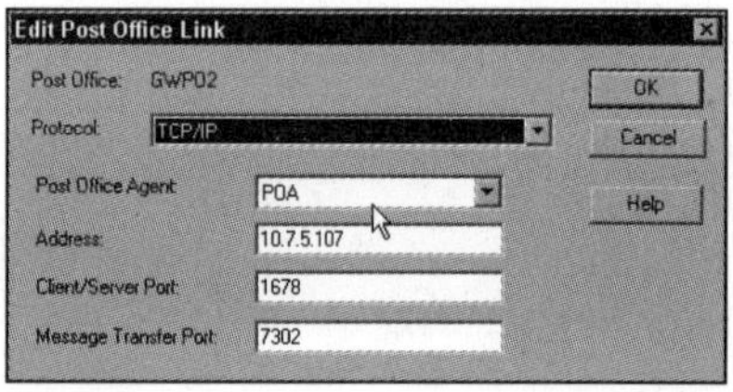

FIGURE 11.11 *Edit Post Office Link dialog box*

    a. In the Protocol field, select TCP/IP.

    b. In the Post Office Agent field, accept the default of POA.

    c. In the Address field, confirm that the address matches the secondary IP address you are using for the Post Office Agent.

    d. In the Client/Server Port field, confirm that the port matches the C/S port you are using for this PO.

    e. In the Message Transfer Port field, confirm that the port matches the C/S port you are using for the PO MTP.

    f. Click OK.

6. Exit the Link Configuration tool and make sure you click Yes when asked to save the link changes for the Post Office.

Installing the Post Office Agents

The next step in the process is to install the Post Office Agents. If you are installing the agents to the cluster resource volume, then you install the agents once to the cluster volume. If you install the agents to the SYS volume, and you have already installed POA agents to the SYS volume of all the servers in the resource path, then all you need to do is create the startup files for each server. You can simply copy another .POA file and customize it for this resource if you already have the agents on all the servers.

If you are installing to the SYS volume and you don't already have POA agents installed, you must install the agents to all servers in the resource failover path.

To install the agents, perform the following:

1. Use Windows Explorer and browse to your GroupWise software distribution directory.

2. From the Agents subdirectory, run INSTALL.EXE.

3. From the Overview dialog box, click Next.

4. From the License Agreement dialog box, click Accept to accept the license agreement.

5. In the Install/Uninstall dialog box, make sure the Install radio button is selected, then click Next.

6. In the Select Platform dialog box, make sure NetWare is selected, then click Next.

7. From the Installation Path dialog box, either browse or enter the path to the location you wish to install the GroupWise agents. If you choose to install the agents to the SYS volume, you must make sure the Post Office agents are installed to all cluster nodes that might run GroupWise. Optionally, you can install the agents to the shared volume.

TIP

If you have already installed other Post Office Agents, you do not need to install them again to all nodes. However, you must have unique agent startup files for each Post Office; you should place these startup files on the shared volume even if you are running the NLMs from the SYS volume.

8. In the Web Console Information dialog box, do the following:

   a. To enable Web Console, make sure the Enable web console check box is selected.

b. If you are enabling Web Console, specify a user name in the Specify user name field. Do not use an NDS user name here for security reasons. Since the Web Console username and password will be transmitted in the clear over the designated port, you do not want this to match an NDS administrator account, since it would be easy to capture on the wire. Compromising the Web Console password only gives the hacker the ability to monitor your agents.

c. If you are enabling Web Console, specify a password in the Specify password field. Confirm this password in the Verify password field.

d. Click Next to continue.

9. In the Language dialog box, confirm your language, and then click Next.

10. In the Domains/Post Offices dialog box, do the following:

a. Click the Add button.

b. In the Facility type field, select Post Office.

TIP

These instructions were written to create a single Post Office resource. If you wish to create a Domain resource instead, you would substitute the Domain facility type. If you are creating a Domain and a Post Office, you would click Add to add and configure the Domain, then click Add again to add and configure the Post Office prior to continuing.

c. In the Name field, enter the name for the Post Office (for example, GWPO2).

d. In the Path to database field, enter or browse to the Post Office database path. This should still reference the node that has the Post Office volume mounted, and you will change the startup file to remove the node-specific information later.

e. In the HTTP port field, enter the Cluster-unique HTTP port this Post Office uses for Web Console, or delete the default port if desired.

f. Click the OK button.

g. Click the Next button.

11. In the Summary dialog box, click Install.

12. In the Installation Complete dialog box, do the following:

   a. Deselect the Update AUTOEXEC file option.

   b. Deselect the Launch GroupWise agents now option.

   c. Click the Finish button.

Modifying the Post Office Startup Files

After you install the agents, you need to modify the startup files. In this example, we use all of the switches presented earlier in the text. However, recall that /HOME, /IP, and /CLUSTER are the only required switches — the other information is obtained straight from NDS, and only required in the startup files as a primer in case of configuration issues with NDS.

To modify the startup files, perform the following:

1. Use Windows Explorer and browse to the location you installed the GroupWise agents to (for example, `SYS:SYSTEM` or `GW2:\SYSTEM`).

TIP

If you installed the agents to the SYS volume, you should consider copying the startup files to the shared volume and then deleting them from the SYS volume. Keeping up with multiple startup files for the same agents is tedious and prone to errors.

2. Find the `.POA` startup file (for example, `GW2.POA`), and open it with Notepad.

3. Find the `/HOME` switch and modify it to the *volume*:*path* syntax. For example, if the switch were:

```
/home-\\node2\gw2\gwpo2
```

then change it to:

```
/home-gw2:\gwpo2
```

4. Anywhere in the file, add the following switches (recall that you should have a table similar to Table 11.3 — GroupWise Port Planning. This table is invaluable when configuring the agents):

```
/ip-<Client/Server TCP/IP Address>
/port-<Client/Server port>
/mtpinip-<IP Address of resource>
```

```
/mtpinport-<MTP Port for Post Office>
/cluster
```

For example:

```
/ip-10.7.5.107
/port-1678
/mtpinip-10.7.5.107
/mtpinport-7302
/cluster
```

NOTE Substitute the appropriate **PO** information for the examples given. These switches were explained in the **POA** section of this chapter.

5. Exit Notepad, saving your changes.

Creating the Cluster Resource

Now that you have created the Post Office, installed the agents, and modified the startup files, you are ready to create the cluster resource object. If you cluster enabled a volume for the resource, you will modify the existing cluster-enabled volume resource object. If not, you will create a new cluster resource object.

You may use the GroupWise template if desired, or simply use this procedure as a guide for the commands to use. Since the template object does not fully implement many of the GroupWise recommendations, you may wish to simply create the resource without using it.

To create the cluster resource object, perform the following:

1. Launch ConsoleOne and browse to your cluster object (and select it).

2. Click the New Cluster Resource Button (or from the menu, select File ➪ New ➪ Cluster ➪ Cluster Resource).

3. In the New Cluster Resource dialog box, do the following:

    a. In the Cluster Resource Name, enter the name for your resource (for example, GW2).

    b. In the Inherit From Template field, browse to the GroupWise Mail Server Template, and then click OK. (This is optional.)

c. Select the Define Additional Properties option.

d. Click the Create button.

TIP

Because the templates were created before all the GroupWise nuances were known, the templates do not adequately support GroupWise. So be careful to properly modify the resource Load Script and Unload Script to reflect what is shown below.

4. Modify the Load Script as follows (see Figure 11.12 for an example of a Cluster Resource Load Script):

NSS /activate=<*Volume*>

Mount <*Volume*>

Add secondary ipaddress <*IP Address*>

Load address space=<*Name*> <*Volume*>:\system\gwpoa @<*Volume*>:\system\<*PO Name*>.POA

Protection restart <*Name*>

NOTE

In both this load script and the unload script that follows, substitute your volume, IP address, name of the address space, and startup files from the preceding example.

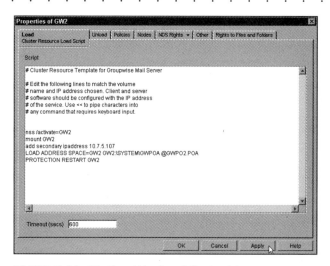

FIGURE 11.12 *GroupWise Post Office Load Script*

5. Modify the unload script as follows (see Figure 11.13 for an example of a Cluster Resource Unload Script):

```
UNLOAD ADDRESS SPACE=<Name> GWPOA

UNLOAD ADDRESS SPACE=<Name> GWENN2

LOAD DELAY

DELAY 10

UNLOAD KILL ADDRESS SPACE=<Name>


DISMOUNT <Volume> /force

NSS /FORCEDEACTIVATE=<Volume>

Del secondary ipaddress <IP Address>
```

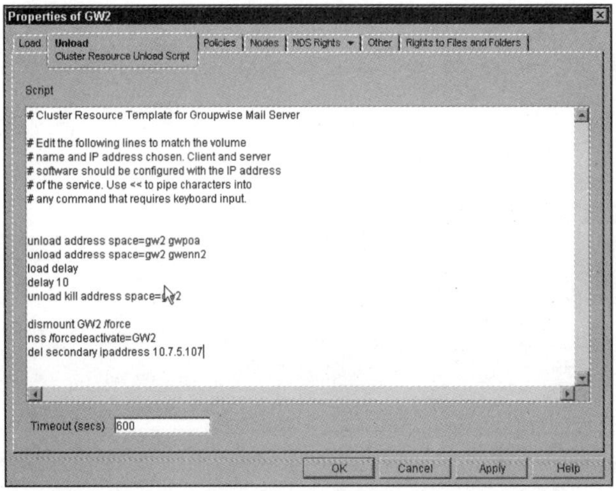

FIGURE 11.13 *GroupWise Post Office Unload Script*

6. Modify the Policies and Nodes tabs as desired.

7. Click OK.

8. On the server console that has the GroupWise volume mounted, issue the following commands:

```
DISMOUNT GW2
NSS /DEACTIVATE=GW2
```

9. In ConsoleOne, select View ⇨ Cluster State from the menu to change to the Cluster State View.

10. Click on your GroupWise resource to start the Cluster Resource Manager.

11. Click the Online button.

12. Verify that the GroupWise resource starts and functions properly.

Creating a Secondary Domain and Post Office Resource

This section walks you through the process of creating a Secondary Domain and Post Office as one cluster resource. The advantage of configuring Post Offices in a cluster this way is that each Post Office has its own MTA for message routing, so you do not burden a single MTA for routing multiple PO messages. You must weigh this against the disadvantages of extra routing, administrative messages, and administrative overhead caused by having excessive Domains. In large GroupWise systems, you will probably want to configure multiple Post Offices for each GroupWise Domain to avoid overcomplicating the system. This procedure can easily be modified to create just a Secondary Domain resource by omitting the Post Office installation and configuration steps.

Use a cluster-enabled volume for this resource so that the GroupWise snapins function properly, and so that if you later decide to add a gateway to the Domain, it will also function properly (although each gateway should also have its own dedicated MTA in a cluster).

Creating and Configuring the GroupWise Domain Object

The first step in creating the Secondary Domain resource is to create the Secondary Domain. Your GroupWise connection should be to the Primary Domain before creating a Secondary Domain, so if you haven't already set this, set your connection to the Primary Domain before proceeding.

The following steps detail the process of creating a Secondary Domain with a Post Office, and cluster enabling this as a single resource.

1. Create a cluster-enabled volume for the GroupWise Domain.

   Refer to Chapter 9 to learn how to cluster enable a volume.

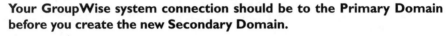

X-REF

2. Map a drive to the cluster-enabled volume (for these instructions, we assume drive N), and create a directory named SYSTEM at the root of this volume.

   Your GroupWise system connection should be to the Primary Domain before you create the new Secondary Domain.

TIP

3. Launch NetWare Administrator, and browse to the context you wish to create the domain in.

4. Click the Create button on the toolbar, or select Object ➪ Create from the menu.

5. Select GroupWise Domain, then click OK.

6. In the Create GroupWise Domain dialog box (see Figure 11.14), do the following:

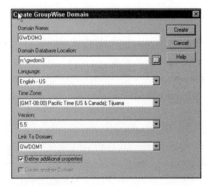

FIGURE 11.14 *Create GroupWise Domain dialog box*

   a. In the Domain Name field, enter the name of the domain (for example, GWDOM3).

   b. In the Domain Database Location field, use the drive letter you mapped to the cluster-enabled volume (N), then add any sublocation information you desire.

TIP

If you use the path through the virtual server or cluster-enabled drive mapping, this greatly simplifies configuration later, especially if you are going to add a gateway. In our example, we use GWDOM3 **even though there is not a** GWDOM2**, so that the volume names match up with the Domain names. This makes the system more logical, even though it jumps numbers.**

   c. In the Language field, enter the primary language for the Domain.

   d. In the Time Zone field, select the proper time zone for the Domain.

   e. In the Version field, accept the default of 5.5.

   f. In the Link To Domain field, select your primary domain.

   g. Check the Define additional properties box.

   h. Click the Create button. When the Domain is created, you will be switched to the properties of the Domain. By default, you will already be on the Information tab.

7. In the Information tab of the Secondary Domain, do the following:

   a. Enter an appropriate description in the Description property field.

   b. Verify that the UNC path contains the path using the virtual server. For example, our path reads \\cluster_gw3_server\gw3\gwcdom3.

   c. In the Administrator field, browse to the NDS user account you wish to have administer this Domain.

   d. Click OK.

8. Double-click the GroupWise Domain to expand it, then right-click the MTA and select Details. If you are in GroupWise view, instead of double-clicking the Domain, click the plus sign (+) to the left of the Domain to expand it.

9. In the Information tab, enter an appropriate description in the Description property. We recommend including the Domain name, IP address, and all ports used by the Domain. You may also wish to include the associated Post Office and its configuration information.

TIP

You should include the IP address and ports you will use for the cluster resource in the description. The information in this field will be displayed on the MTA status screen on the server console. For complex GroupWise systems, displaying this information on the agent screen is very useful in troubleshooting a complex system. By having this information displayed on the agent screen, you can more easily troubleshoot the specific agent should you encounter problems.

10. Click the Network Address tab.

11. Click the TCP/IP radio button, then click Add.

12. In the Add Network Address dialog box (refer back to Figure 11.10 for an example of what this dialog box looks like), do the following:

    a. In the TCP/IP Address field, enter the secondary IP address you will use for this resource.

    b. In the Message Transfer Port field, enter the cluster-unique port this MTA will use for message transfer.

    c. In the HTTP Port field, enter the cluster-unique port this MTA will use for the Web Console function (if you use it).

    d. Click OK.

13. Click OK to finish the MTA.

14. Select the new Domain object, then select Tools ➪ GroupWise Utilities ➪ Link Configuration.

15. Double-click the outbound link to the primary Domain. The Edit Domain Link dialog box appears (see Figure 11.15).

16. In this dialog box, select the Protocol drop-down list, and change the link to TCP/IP.

17. Verify that the Address and Port information are correct for the link to the primary Domain, and then click OK.

18. Double-click the inbound link from the primary Domain. The Edit Domain Link dialog box appears.

19. Select the Protocol drop-down list, and change the link to TCP/IP.

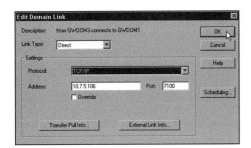

FIGURE 11.15 *Edit Domain Link dialog box*

20. Verify that the Address and Port information are correct for the link to the newly created Domain, and then click OK. If the network addresses are entered correctly and synchronized, this information should already be correct.

21. Repeat steps 15 through 20 for each domain if you have multiple Domains in the system. If you have any indirect links to other clustered Domains, drag the link from the Indirect box to the Direct box, and configure it for TCP/IP instead of UNC.

TIP

Use Direct TCP/IP links between all GroupWise Domains within the cluster so that each MTA can communicate directly with each of the other MTAs without needing a routing Domain between them.

22. Close the link configuration window, and select Yes to save the link changes for the Domain.

23. Next, rebuild the GroupWise Domain. To do this, follow these steps:

    a. Change your GroupWise connection to the Primary GroupWise Domain for this system by right-clicking it in the GroupWise view and selecting Connect.

    b. From the GroupWise view, right-click the Domain object (not the MTA), and select Systems Maintenance, or from the menu select Tools ⇨ GroupWise Utilities ⇨ System Maintenance.

    c. Verify that the correct Domain is selected, and then click the Rebuild Database radio button.

d. Click the Run button.

e. In the Database Path dialog box, verify that the path reflects the complete path to the Domain, and then click OK.

If you have too many characters in the UNC path using the cluster-enabled volume, you will find that this path gets cut off. Use the browse button to correct the path, or type it in manually.

You may also want to rebuild the database to a temporary location and then copy it back over to the current database. In large systems, rebuilding the database to a local drive will be much faster.

f. Click OK.

g. Click Close.

See the sidebar "Where Has the Database Gone?" earlier in this chapter for more information about why rebuilding the database is an important step in this process.

Creating and Configuring the GroupWise Post Office Object

1. Connect to the GroupWise Domain you wish to create the Post Office in by browsing to the Domain, right-clicking it, and selecting Connect.

2. Browse to the context you wish to create the Post Office object in.

3. Select Object ⇨ Create from the menu, or right-click the container and select Create.

4. Select GroupWise Post Office, and then click OK. The Create GroupWise Post Office dialog box appears.

5. In the Create GroupWise Post Office dialog box, do the following:

a. In the Post Office Name field, enter the name for the Post Office (for example, GWPO3).

b. In the GroupWise Domain field, browse and select the Domain this Post Office will belong to (for example, GWDOM3).

c. In the Post Office Database location field, enter the UNC path to the Post Office directory and any directory path you wish to use for the Post Office. Be sure to use the virtual server or the drive mapping that you already have to the volume (`N:\gwpo3` in our example).

TIP **The directory names in the path to the Post Office database must comply with the 8.3 naming convention — GroupWise does not support long filenames in the PO path, even though it will let you enter long names here.**

d. In the Language field, select the appropriate Post Office language.

e. In the Time Zone field, select the time zone for the Post Office.

f. In the Software Distribution Directory, select the Software Distribution Directory you wish to use for the software distribution source for this Post Office.

g. If you wish to create a library for this Post Office, check the Create Library option box.

h. Check the Define additional properties option box.

i. Click Create. The Post Office will be created, and then you will be placed in the properties of the PO object, on the Information tab (by default).

6. In the Information tab, do the following:

a. In the Description field, enter a description for the Post Office.

b. Novell recommends setting the Default Security Level to High to prevent unauthorized access of users' mailboxes, although it is not required for Novell Cluster Services.

c. In the Access Mode property, change the mode to Client/Server only.

d. Click OK.

7. Double-click the Post Office object, and then double-click the POA object for this Post Office to modify its properties. If you are in GroupWise view, instead of double-clicking the Post Office object, click the plus sign (+) to the left of the Post Office to expand it.

8. In the Description field, enter a description for the Post Office Agent.

TIP **Include the IP address and ports you will use for the cluster resource in the description. The information in this field will be displayed on the POA status screen on the server console. For complex GroupWise systems, displaying this information on the agent screen is very useful when troubleshooting the agent.**

9. Click the Network Address tab.

10. Select the TCP/IP radio button, then click Add. The Add Network Address dialog box appears.

11. In the Add Network Address dialog box, do the following:

    a. In the IP Address field, enter the secondary IP address you will use for this cluster resource (for example, 10.7.5.108).

    b. In the Message Transfer Port field, enter the cluster-unique port this Post Office will use for message transfer (for example, 7303).

    c. In the HTTP Port field, enter the cluster-unique port this Post Office will use for the HTTP monitor, if you plan on using this function (for example, 2803).

    d. Click OK.

12. Click OK to close the POA object.

13. Next, rebuild the GroupWise Post Office. To do this:

    a. From the GroupWise view, right-click the Post Office object (not the POA), and select Systems Maintenance. The Systems Maintenance dialog box appears.

    b. Verify that the correct Post Office is selected, then click the Rebuild Database radio button.

    c. Click the Run button. The Database Path dialog box appears, with the path configured based on the UNC path property of the Post Office object in NDS.

    d. In the Database Path dialog box, verify that the path reflects the proper path to the Post Office, and then click OK.

e. Click OK. The database rebuild process will now run. This may take several minutes or longer if the Post Office is large and across a slow WAN link. (We assume this is local for a Novell Cluster Services configuration — if this is remote across a WAN link, it is better to rebuild the Post Office to your local hard drive, then copy the file over the WAN link).

f. Click Close once the rebuild successfully finishes.

14. Click the domain object this post office belongs to, then select Tools ⇨ GroupWise Utilities ⇨ Link Configuration.

15. Click the Post Office Links button, or select View ⇨ Post Office Links from the menu.

16. Double-click the Post Office Link for this Post Office. The Edit Post Office Link dialog box appears (refer back to Figure 11.11 to see what this dialog box looks like).

17. Select the Protocol drop-down list, and change it to TCP/IP.

18. Verify that the TCP/IP address and ports to the Post Office are correct, and then click OK.

19. Click OK, and then close the Link Configuration utility, making sure that you save the link changes.

Installing the Agents

Once you have the GroupWise Domain and Post Office objects installed and configured, you must install the GroupWise agents. To install the agents:

1. Create a directory called SYSTEM on your cluster-enabled volume. As with the preceding steps, the N drive is used in this example.

TIP

You can also install the agents to the server's SYS volume instead, in which case you must repeat this procedure for each node in the cluster that might run GroupWise.

If you have already installed GroupWise agents on each server for another Domain and Post Office, you do not need to install the agents again. However, you do need to create the startup files by copying and modifying them as appropriate for this system.

2. Browse to the Software Distribution Directory, then to the \agents subdirectory, and run INSTALL.EXE. The Overview dialog box appears.

3. In the Overview dialog box, click Next to begin the installation. The license agreement appears.

4. Click Accept to accept the license agreement. The Install/Uninstall dialog box appears.

5. In the Install/Uninstall dialog box, click Next to install the agents.

6. Click Next to accept the NetWare agent platform. The Installation Path dialog box appears.

7. In the Installation Path dialog box, enter or browse to the path on the cluster-enabled volume to install the agents (for example, N:\SYTEM).

8. If you're enabling the Web Console, enter the user name and password for Web Console access, and then click Next.

9. Accept or modify the agent language, and then click Next to continue.

10. In the Domains/Post Offices dialog box, click Add to configure the domain. The Domain/Post Office Information dialog box will appear, allowing you to enter the path to the database and the TCP/IP configuration..

11. In the Domain/Post Office Information dialog box (see Figure 11.16), do the following:

FIGURE 11.16 *Domain/Post Office Information dialog box*

a. Select the Domain radio button.

b. In the Name field, enter the name of the Domain.

c. In the Path to database field, enter or browse to the Domain database, using the drive mapping you have to the cluster-enabled volume.

d. In the HTTP port field, enter the cluster-unique port to use for Web Console, or delete the default port if you don't use this feature.

e. Click the OK button, which returns you to the Domain/Post Offices dialog box and shows you a summary of the information you just entered.

12. Click the Add button again to add the Post Office information to the agent. The Domain/Post Office Information dialog box will once again appear.

13. In the Domain/Post Office Information dialog box, do the following:

a. Select the Post Office radio button.

b. In the Name field, enter the name of the Post Office.

c. In the Path to database field, enter or browse to the Post Office database, using the drive mapping you have to the cluster-enabled volume.

d. In the HTTP port field, enter the cluster-unique port to use for Web Console, or delete the default port if you don't use this feature.

e. Click the OK button, which returns you to the Domain/Post Offices dialog box and shows you a summary of the information you just entered.

14. Verify the domain and post office configuration in the Domain/Post Offices dialog box (see Figure 11.17), then click Next to install.

15. From the Summary screen, click Install to proceed.

16. Deselect the Update AUTOEXEC file and the Launch GroupWise agents now options; then click Finish.

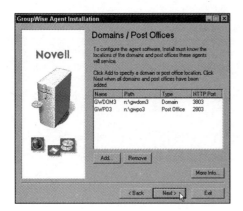

FIGURE 11.17 *Domains/Post Offices dialog box*

Modifying the Startup Files

Before you start the agents, you must modify the agent startup files. If you installed the agents to the shared volume, you need to do this only once by modifying the agent startup files on the shared volume.

If you installed the agents to the SYS volume of each node in the cluster, you have two options. First, you could modify the startup files on all nodes that you installed the agents to. Alternatively, you could move the startup files to the shared volume and use the startup files off the shared storage even though you are running the agents on each server's SYS volume.

Putting the agent files on the shared volume allows you to have only one location where you must make changes. If you keep individual agent startup files on each server, any time you decide to modify the startup files, you must manually modify the files on every node that might run GroupWise.

The installation program will create the agent files using UNC syntax for the /HOME switch — for example, \\CLUSTER_GW3_SERVER\ GWDOM3. For best results, change the startup file to the traditional NetWare syntax, GW3:\ GWDOM3. By removing the server name from the path, you can use the same agent file on all servers.

To modify the startup files, edit the <Domain>.MTA and <PO>.POA files (in our example, these are GWDOM3.MTA and GWPO3.POA).

▶ In the .MTA file, change the /HOME switch to:

```
/HOME-<VOLUME>:\<path to Domain>
```

For example:

```
/HOME-GW3:\GWDOM3
```

▶ In the .POA file, change the /HOME switch to:

```
/HOME-<VOLUME>:\<path to PO>
```

For example:

```
/HOME-GW3:\GWPO3
```

▶ In the .POA file, add the /cluster, /IP, /port, /mtpinip, and /mtpinport parameters:

- /ip-<*client/server TCP/IP address*> (required)

- /port-<*client/server port*> (optional)

- /mtpinip-<*IP address of POA*> (optional)

- /mtpinport-<*MTP port of POA*> (optional)

- /cluster

▶ For example:

```
/ip-10.7.5.108
/port-1679
/mtpinip-10.7.5.108
/mtpinport-7303
/cluster
```

Creating and Starting the GroupWise Cluster Resource

Now that you have created the Domain and Post Office, installed the agents, and configured the startup files, you are ready to create the cluster resource. Since you created the Domain on a cluster-enabled volume, you already have a cluster resource object for the cluster-enabled volume. You will modify this resource object by adding the necessary commands to load and unload GroupWise.

TIP

Never have more than one cluster resource object for the same logical resource. If you have multiple objects such as a cluster-enabled volume and a cluster resource object for the application, the two objects will conflict with each other, and migrating one resource will break the other one, making your resource unavailable.

To configure the cluster resource, perform the following:

I. Using ConsoleOne, change to the Console View, and select your cluster-enabled volume resource object, for example, the GW3_SERVER object.

2. Right-click the resource object, then select Properties.

3. Click the Load tab, then check to make sure the following commands are included in the Load Script:

```
NSS /ACTIVATE=<volume>

MOUNT <volume>

TRUSTMIG <volume> WATCH

NUDP ADD <cluster name>_<volume>_SERVER <IP Address of resource>

ADD SECONDARY IPADDRESS <IP Address of resource>
```

TIP

You can also remove the TRUSTMIG WATCH **command here; since you are using only client/server connections, you do not need file system trustees for GroupWise, and therefore, you don't need to migrate them.**

4. Add the following commands to the Load Script at the bottom of the script:

```
LOAD ADDRESS SPACE=<name> <volume>:\SYSTEM\GWMTA
@<volume>\<path>\GWDOM3.MTA

LOAD ADDRESS SPACE=<name> <volume>:\SYSTEM\GWPOA
@<volume>\<path>\GWPO3.POA

PROTECTION RESTART <name>
```

TIP

If this MTA will be performing the NDS User Synchronization scheduled event, be sure to load the DSAPI.NLM in the same protected memory space as the MTA. Also make sure you unload it in the Unload Script.

5. Click the Unload tab, then add the following commands at the top of the Unload Script:

```
UNLOAD ADDRESS SPACE=<name> GWMTA

UNLOAD ADDRESS SPACE=<name> GWPOA

UNLOAD ADDRESS SPACE=<name> GWENN2

LOAD DELAY.NLM

DELAY 10

UNLOAD KILL ADDRESS SPACE=<name>
```

6. Check to make sure the following commands are at the bottom of the Unload Script:

```
DEL SECONDARY IPADDRESS <IP Address of resource>

NUDP DEL CLUSTER1_GW1_SERVER <IP Address of resource>

TRUSTMIG <volume> UNWATCH

DISMOUNT <volume> /FORCE

NSS /FORCEDEACTIVATE=<volume>
```

TIP

If you removed the TRUSTMIG WATCH **command in the Load Script, you must also remove the** TRUSTMIG UNWATCH **command in the Unload Script.**

X-REF

To see what a Cluster Resource Load Script and Unload Script might look like in the resource object's Properties screen, see Figures 11.6 and 11.7 earlier in the chapter.

7. Select the Policies and Nodes tabs, and edit the settings as required.

8. Click OK to add the GroupWise cluster resource object.

9. Change the ConsoleOne view to Cluster State.

10. Offline the resource.

11. Online the resource and verify that GroupWise is functioning properly.

Migration/Failover Characteristics

This section discusses what you should expect to occur in your GroupWise system if you migrate a resource from one node to another, or if a node servicing a GroupWise resource were to fail.

In our explanation, we refer to a migration as an administrative function that voluntarily moves a resource from one node in the cluster to another — either for load balancing purposes, or because you are taking a node down for maintenance. In a migration, the Unload Script executes on the current node, then the Load Script executes on the target node. This causes a clean shutdown and easy startup of the database.

In the case of a failover, a node has failed and the resource is moving to another node. This could be a software fault (ABEND) or a hardware fault. In either case, the database does not shut down cleanly, so some database integrity checking and possible rebuilding will need to occur. In addition to the database rebuilding, since NSS did not shut down clean, it is also possible to have NSS recovery processes performed on the target node.

The section breaks the GroupWise system down into logical components, and discusses migration and failover behavior of each component.

MTA Behavior

The GroupWise MTAs failover and migrate relatively rapidly, but your time will vary according to the size of your system and the Domain database. In a failure scenario, the MTA may need to repair the database prior to starting message flow, which can significantly add to the startup time. The good news here is that the primary noticeable functions of GroupWise will still function during this time — the user will be able to make the client/server connection to the Post Office, but mail entering or leaving the Post Office will be queued until the MTA fully starts.

Administrative migrations of resources will take significantly longer than a server failure, as closing the Domain database can take some time to process.

Once the MTA comes up on the new node, it is common for the initial startup to leave many of the other Domains and possibly Post Offices and Gateways in a closed state. This is normal and expected behavior, and in a properly configured system it will be resolved in 10 minutes when the MTA does its automatic restart. This means that the first 10 minutes after a migration or failure, you may not have

MTA-to-MTA message flow, even though users are accessing their mailboxes normally. If you cannot wait the 10 minutes, manually restart the MTA by using the F6 key at the server console.

POA Behavior

Post Office behavior is very similar to MTA behavior — failures are relatively quick, whereas a manual migration may take some time for the Post Office to unload. Again, the larger the Post Office, the more significant delay you will see in the startup and shutdown times.

Like the MTA, if the POA database goes down dirty, it may need to perform some repairs when restarted. This is the primary reason to insist on client/server connections only — if you have users connecting directly to the Post Office, your risk of data corruption is significantly increased.

The Post Office will generally be up and ready to go long before the MTA is fully communicating. From the users' perspective, they will be able to connect (or reconnect) to the Post Office and send mail very quickly once the POA starts backup, and unless they are on the phone talking to the person sending them a message, they probably won't even realize that the MTA is not fully communicating.

Client Behavior

The GroupWise Enhancement Pack client can now detect when it is connected to a cluster, and it modifies its behavior in that case. If the user is not actively sending messages during a Post Office migration, they will never know anything happened. The only time the client will produce an error is if the client is in the process of sending a message when the POA is not up, and the client needs to do an address book search. In this case, the client will receive an error and force the user to shut down the GroupWise client (not the workstation) and restart it.

The Notify program is not quite as nice; it will most likely lose the connection to the Post Office during a migration or failure and will then need to be restarted.

Active/Active versus Active/Passive

All GroupWise components function in an Active/Passive manner. Only one server can have the database volume mounted and the agent loaded, so migrating a resource will require starting all of the appropriate NLMs on the destination node.

▶ · ◀

Summary

In this chapter, you learned the basic components of a GroupWise system, and the factors you must consider when clustering these components. The importance of cluster enabling the GroupWise Domain volumes was discussed, as was how to install and configure a GroupWise Domain in a cluster.

Planning your TCP/IP environment, including the resource IP addresses and GroupWise ports within the cluster, is another important step toward clustering.

You learned how to install and configure a GroupWise Post Office in a cluster, as well as how to install and configure a cluster resource consisting of a GroupWise Domain and Post Office.

Finally, you learned the basic failover and migration characteristics of the various GroupWise components:

CLUSTER FAILOVER CLASSIFICATION INDEX	
Transparency	Client is very transparent unless doing an address book search.
Active/Active or Active/Passive	Active/Passive
Length to failover	Each component is different. Post Office is quick, while MTA can be slow. Migrations are much slower than failovers.

The material presented in this chapter gives you good flexibility when configuring a highly available messaging system using the LAN-based components. It provides the messaging foundation that can be built upon to provide 7x24x365 availability for the mission-critical collaboration system that your organization depends on.

This chapter laid the foundation for building your messaging system. The next chapter builds on this foundation, and walks you through connecting this highly available messaging system to the Internet, providing a well-rounded, highly available collaboration system anytime, anywhere.

Applying Novell Cluster Services with GroupWise 5.5 Gateways

This chapter continues the GroupWise discussion where Chapter 11 left off—connecting your GroupWise system to the Internet. Various GroupWise gateways, specifically the gateways that have been tested and supported on Novell Cluster Services, are discussed.

The chapter begins by examining the GroupWise Internet Agent (GWIA) gateway and how to successfully configure it in a cluster. Next, the chapter turns to the WebAccess Gateway and how to enable high availability for both the WebAccess Gateway as well as the WebAccess Servlet. Finally, after you've had a chance to look at how to configure GroupWise gateways in a cluster, the chapter reviews various migration and failover characteristics of the gateways.

► . . . . ◄

Introducing GroupWise 5.5 Gateways

GroupWise gateways provide the mechanism to communicate with systems foreign to the GroupWise system. These gateways include the GWIA, the WebAccess Gateway, the API Gateway, and the Asynchronous Gateway. This chapter addresses the two most common gateways: the GWIA and the WebAccess Gateway.

Though the remaining gateways have not been tested, the same approach should work with these gateways as well.

NOTE

GWIA

The GroupWise Internet Agent (GWIA) adds complete Internet messaging services to your GroupWise system. It allows access via Simple Mail Transfer Protocol (SMTP), Internet Messaging Access Protocol version 4 (IMAP4), Post Office Protocol version 3 (POP3), and Lightweight Directory Access Protocol (LDAP) communications from internal sources or the Internet. It also supports connecting GroupWise systems together through the Internet via pass-through addressing.

To configure the GWIA in a cluster, you should be sure that the Domain directory resides on a cluster-enabled volume. This allows for a correct UNC path to the Domain, which in turn allows the GroupWise snapins, third-party applications, and the gateways to properly find the Domain no matter which node it is running on.

If you cluster enable the Domain volume, and install the GroupWise Domain either with the UNC path through the virtual server (\\cluster_gwgwia_server\ gwgwia) or with a drive mapped to the cluster-enabled volume, then all of the NDS properties for the Domain will automatically be configured with the correct values for cluster operation. This is critical to successful failover behavior and the ability to manage the gateways in the cluster, no matter where they may be running.

You should create one cluster resource, which includes a secondary Domain dedicated to the GWIA, and the gateway itself. You should not create two resource objects. Instead, put all of the commands to load the Domain MTA and the GWIA in the load and unload scripts for the cluster-enabled volume.

WARNING

Never have two NDS cluster resource objects for the same resource. If you create one object for the volume and another object for the GWIA, migrating one without the other will break both!

Firewall Issues

The GWIA cluster resource will use the secondary IP address of the cluster-enabled volume. This is the IP address to use for incoming messages to the GWIA (assuming there is not a relay between the GWIA and the Internet). Your firewall should be configured to allow TCP/IP traffic inbound from the Internet to this address (the secondary IP address of the cluster-enabled volume) on the proper ports for the services you are using (see Table 12.1).

TABLE 12.1

GroupWise Ports

SERVICE	PORT
SMTP	25
POP3	110
IMAP4	143
LDAP	389

Currently (Enhancement Pack with Support Pack 2 and earlier), the GWIA will send outgoing messages using the server's primary TCP/IP address. This means that your firewall must also be configured to allow outgoing messages from each node in the cluster in the failover path, using the primary interface in addition to the incoming filter on the secondary IP address.

TIP

Configure your firewall to allow incoming traffic on the GWIA's *secondary* IP address, and outgoing traffic using each node's *primary* IP address.

One way to minimize this firewall configuration issue is to use an SMTP relay, and configure the GWIA to forward to a relay. In the event the relay is down, outgoing SMTP messages would queue until the relay is backed up. This would allow simplified firewall configuration, and still allow high availability to incoming SMTP messages.

Agent and Configuration Files

Chapter 11 discusses modifying MTA and POA startup files. Just as you modify those startup files, you also modify the GWIA startup files in the cluster. You can install the gateway and startup files to each node in the cluster, or you can install them once to a cluster-enabled volume. Certainly, maintaining a single startup file on the cluster-enabled volume simplifies management.

If you install the gateway through a UNC path through the virtual server, or to a drive mapped to the cluster-enabled volume, then the startup files for the GWIA should include a UNC path using the virtual server. However, you will have better luck with the GWIA if you modify the GWIA.CFG file to the legacy file system syntax. Modify the /HOME- and /DHOME- switches from:

```
/Home-\\cluster_gwgwia_server\gwgwia\WPGATE\GWIA
```

```
/DHome-\\cluster_gwgwia_server\gwgwia\WPGATE\GWIA
```

to:

```
/Home-GWGWIA:\gwgwia\WPGATE\GWIA
```

```
/DHome-GWGWIA:\gwgwia\WPGATE\GWIA
```

By modifying these paths to remove the server names, you avoid the extra overhead on the server of processing TCP/IP name resolution — a local path does not need to be resolved for an IP address.

You should also check the EXEPATH.CFG file, which is located in the GroupWise Domain directory under the WPGATE\GWIA subdirectory. This file is used by the GroupWise snapins, and if it is incorrect, you will not be able to fully configure the GWIA using NetWare Administrator. Verify that the path listed in EXEPATH.CFG is the UNC path to the SYSTEM directory where the GroupWise startup files are located. It should be configured using the virtual server, as shown here:

```
\\CLUSTER_GWGWIA_SERVER\GWGWIA\system
```

The Domain's UNC path property must also reflect the UNC path through the virtual server for proper cluster communications. (NetWare Administrator uses the Domain Path property in NDS to determine where it should look for the EXEPATH.CFG file.)

Once you have configured the GWIA in the cluster, modify all of the Post Office links to utilize TCP/IP and configure the appropriate TCP/IP addresses and ports in the link configuration.

Refer to Chapter 11 for more information on the TCP/IP configuration of the Domain and Post Office.

X-REF

WebAccess

The WebAccess Gateway allows users to access their mailbox and calendar using a Web browser. Though this does not provide all of the same functionality as the 32-bit client, the vast majority of the client features have been enabled, and each new version of WebAccess has added more features, which brings the functionality fairly close.

The WebAccess Gateway consists of the following components:

▸ WebAccess Gateway (GWINTER.NLM)

▸ WebAccess CGI extension

▸ Java-based spell checker servlet (optional)

The WebAccess Gateway requires a Web server, which can be Novell's Enterprise Web Server or one of many third-party Web servers. This chapter's examples for clustering WebAccess concentrate on the Novell Enterprise Web Server, which can also be clustered.

Chapter 13 discusses clustering the Enterprise Web Server (EWS).

X-REF

With the WebAccess Gateway, you can run the Web server component separately from the gateway NLM. This enables you to balance the load of these services across multiple servers. The servlet component requires installing the Web server component on each node that runs the Enterprise Web Server, as the servlet component resides on the SYS volume of the Web server (see Figure 12.1).

Clustering the Web server component has one side effect: you will no longer be able to manage the `COMMGR.CFG` file through NetWare Administrator. The snap-ins will point to a single server (`SYS:NOVELL\WebAccess` and `SYS:NOVELL\WebPublisher`). If you make changes through NetWare Administrator, you must copy the `COMMGR.CFG` file to each Enterprise Web Server in the cluster.

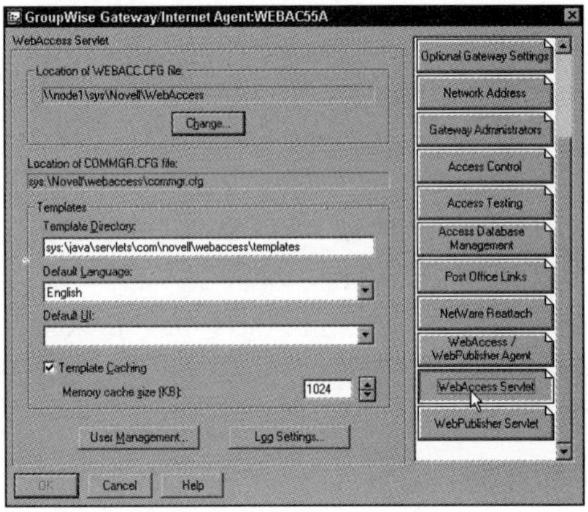

FIGURE 12.1 *WebAccess Servlet page*

The loss of centralized administration for the `COMMGR.CFG` file is a small price to pay for the increased availability of the Servlet. Since this file only needs to be modified if you change the IP address or encryption information, you typically do not need to worry about this issue. Clustering the WebAccess Gateway has many of the same caveats as clustering the GWIA Gateway. Configure the Domain on a cluster-enabled volume, and configure the Domain UNC path using the path through the virtual server or a drive mapped to the cluster-enabled volume.

Once you have configured the WebAccess Gateway in the cluster, modify all of the Post Office links to utilize TCP/IP and configure the appropriate TCP/IP addresses and ports in the link configuration.

See Chapter 11 for more information on TCP/IP link configuration.

X-REF

Cluster Enabling the Volume

Depending on which components you are configuring in the cluster, you may or may not need to cluster enable the GroupWise volume. If you are configuring a cluster resource that includes only a GroupWise Post Office, consider not cluster enabling the volume. For almost all other configurations, cluster enabling the GroupWise volume makes administering GroupWise much simpler.

To administer GroupWise, you must first connect to the GroupWise Domain database. Without clustering, all administrators will know where the Domain database is, since it never moves. Once you implement GroupWise in a cluster, unless you cluster enable the database volume, you must figure out which node has the Domain volume activated before you can administer it. By cluster enabling the volume, you can use the UNC path through the virtual server and always establish a connection to the Domain. Since the personnel that created GroupWise accounts may not administer the servers, this configuration provides a significant benefit.

GroupWise agents currently cannot be configured to communicate with the Domain using TCP/IP; they are configured as UNC paths relative to the Domain database. This requires cluster enabling the Domain database for any Domain that includes agents so that those agents have UNC paths properly configured.

NOTE

With GroupWise 5.5 SP3 and the Enhancement Pack SP1, Novell has modified the way the MTA finds the gateway. If the MTA cannot find the gateway using the configuration in the Domain database/NDS, it will automatically search for the gateway on whatever server has loaded the MTA. This MTA modification means that the gateway will actually work without a cluster-enabled volume, even though you cannot configure the MTA-to-gateway link. However, you should still cluster enable the Domain volume, for all of the other reasons listed in this chapter.

When you use a cluster-enabled volume for the GroupWise resource, be sure that you don't create two resources for the same GroupWise component. Create the cluster-enabled volume and then modify its load and unload script to include the commands to load GroupWise. Don't create a second resource for GroupWise that depends on the cluster-enabled volume resource. Since Novell Cluster Services does not provide the ability to make one resource dependent on another, configuring two resource objects for the same application causes a conflict between the two resources. The result of this conflict is that if you migrate one resource, the other loses its dependent resources (such as the TCP/IP address, volume, or supporting NLMs) and stops functioning.

Modifying the HOSTS Files and DNS for GroupWise

When you use cluster-enabled volumes, modify the HOSTS files to include the virtual server names. This allows the server to resolve the virtual server name to the secondary IP address used for the resource. To modify the HOSTS file, follow these steps:

1. On each server, change to the server console prompt and enter **LOAD EDIT SYS:ETC\HOSTS**.

2. At the bottom of the file, add a line for each Virtual SERVER (not Volume) object and its IP address:

```
10.7.5.106     CLUSTER_GW1_SERVER.CLUSTER.COM      CLUSTER_GW1_SERVER

10.7.5.108     CLUSTER_GW3_SERVER.CLUSTER.COM      CLUSTER_GW3_SERVER

10.7.5.109     CLUSTER_GW4_SERVER.CLUSTER.COM      CLUSTER_GW4_SERVER

10.7.5.110     CLUSTER_GW5_SERVER.CLUSTER.COM      CLUSTER_GW5_SERVER

10.7.5.111     CLUSTER_GW6_SERVER.CLUSTER.COM      CLUSTER_GW6_SERVER

10.7.5.112     CLUSTER_GWGWIA_SERVER.CLUSTER.COM   CLUSTER_GWGWIA_SERVER

10.7.5.113     CLUSTER_GWWEB_SERVER.CLUSTER.COM    CLUSTER_GWWEB_SERVER
```

NOTE

In this example, the GW2 volume is used only for a single Post Office, so it is not cluster enabled. Thus, it does not need an entry in the HOSTS **file.**

3. Press Esc, and select Yes to save your changes.

If your DNS server supports the underscore (_) character, you should also create DNS entries for each virtual server, which allows both clients and servers to utilize DNS for name resolution.

Using CVSBIND

Novell Cluster Services version 1 and 1.01 do not advertise their services through Service Location Protocol (SLP). Thus, resolving short names (for example, server names) for the virtual servers must be done using NDS, DNS, HOSTS files, or NWHOSTS files.

Short name resolution using NDS produces the desired results (that is, successful name resolution) only if the user's current context happens to be the same context as the virtual server. In most environments, this situation will not be the case, so NDS short name resolution does not provide the desired results for the virtual servers.

DNS is the next logical choice for short name resolution. However, this, too, is problematic if the DNS server you are using does not support the underscore character. That leaves HOSTS files or NWHOSTS files for short name resolution, which would be tedious at best (of course, ZENworks would help here).

If none of these methods provides you with the desired short name resolution, Novell has a utility called CVSBIND.NLM (you can find it by searching Novell's knowledge base for TID 2957434). This NLM allows you to modify the load and unload scripts for your cluster resources and force the SLP propagation of the virtual server names. The README.TXT file that comes with this module includes installation and configuration instructions.

With the next version of Novell Cluster Services, this extra NLM will no longer be required, as the Novell Cluster Services software itself will propagate the virtual server information in SLP.

Deciding Where to Install the NLMs

When installing GroupWise NLMs, the installation process assumes that you wish to install the agents to the server's SYS volume. Depending on how you are configuring your system, you may wish to accept this default and install all agents to the SYS volume of each cluster node. Choosing this option requires that each node in the cluster that might run GroupWise must have the agents installed individually to that server. Thus, if you have a 12-node GroupWise cluster, you will install the agents 12 times. This also adds complexity to patching the GroupWise system. If you have multiple Domains, you must patch all the Domains at the same time, or you might end up with a case where the MTA migrates to a nonpatched server and possibly corrupts the Domain database.

TIP

Currently, GroupWise agents will install only into a directory called SYSTEM**. This does not need to be the SYS volume.**

An alternative is to create a SYSTEM directory on the volume you are using for the resource. Then, when you install the GroupWise agents, you install the agents into the resource volume's SYSTEM directory. Using this method, all nodes in your cluster are immediately able to use this cluster resource, since no SYS volume dependencies exist. Additionally, since each GroupWise resource has the NLMs on the resource volume, when you patch one node, you are actually patching all nodes that use that resource. However, in a cluster that will have 12 GroupWise Domains but only 6 nodes, you end up installing the agents more times using this method than by installing the agents once to each server's SYS volume. In the examples throughout this chapter, the SYSTEM directory is on the resource volume.

Whichever method you choose, remain consistent throughout your cluster. You must ensure that each GroupWise resource is accessed only using NLMs that are the appropriate version for that resource; do not have Enhancement Pack Support Pack One NLMs loaded on a database that was patched with Enhancement Pack Support Pack Two.

Creating an MTA and GWIA Agent Resource

As discussed earlier, if you want to cluster the GWIA, you should install the GWIA into a Domain that is residing on a cluster-enabled volume. The Domain should have been installed using a drive mapped to the cluster-enabled volume, so the NDS Domain object lists its path property through the virtual server, such as \\cluster_gwgwia_server\gwgwia\gwiadom. This is key to having a successful GWIA installation.

Additionally, you should meet all of the normal GWIA requirements before you try to create the GWIA in a cluster. For example, DNS should be functioning, the server you are installing on should be in DNS, and the MX record should be created for the virtual server you will use to receive mail.

Creating the Secondary Domain Resource

The first step to creating the GWIA in the cluster is to create the secondary Domain that it will be configured with and cluster enable it. Follow the steps in Chapter 11 under the section "Creating a Secondary Domain and Post Office Resource," omitting the steps that create or configure a Post Office. Before you install the GWIA, fully test your Domain and verify that it works on all nodes that you desire in the cluster.

Installing the GWIA

To install the GWIA to a cluster-enabled Domain:

1. Map a drive to the cluster-enabled volume you are using for the Domain database.

2. Map a drive to either the SYS volume of the first node you plan on installing the GWIA to, or the root of the cluster-enabled volume that has the directory named SYSTEM.

3. Browse to the Software Distribution Directory, then the \INTERNET\GWIA subdirectory and run INSTALL.EXE. The Welcome dialog box appears.

4. In the Welcome dialog box, click Next. The license agreement appears.

5. After reading the license agreement and accepting the terms, click Accept.

6. Accept the default software platform of NetWare by clicking Next.

7. In the NLM Installation Paths dialog box, enter or browse to the path you wish to install the NLMs and load script files to, and then click Next. The Web Console dialog box appears.

8. If desired, enable Web Console by checking the Enable Web Console check box and entering a user name and password for Web Console. Click Next to continue.

9. In the Relay Host dialog box, select your preferred method for outbound mail delivery, and then click Next. If you use an outbound mail relay host, you must enter the IP address of the relay. One reason to use an outbound mail relay host was discussed earlier in the "Firewall Issues" section of this chapter.

10. In the GroupWise Domain dialog box, enter the path to the GroupWise Domain, or browse to a drive mapped to the cluster-enabled volume. Enter the name you wish to use for the gateway subdirectory, and then click Next.

TIP

If you use either a UNC path through the virtual server or a drive mapped to the cluster-enabled volume in the GroupWise Domain dialog box, the GWIA will be properly configured to work with Novell Cluster Services. If, however, you enter the server node where the volume is currently mounted, you will have a much more difficult time making the GWIA work on any other node in the cluster.

11. If prompted, click Yes to have the installation program create the GWIA directory for you.

12. Enter the name you wish to use for the GroupWise Internet Agent, and then click Next. In most cases, simply accept the default name of GWIA.

13. In the Internet Mail Domain Name dialog box, enter the Domain Name that external users will use to send mail to your GroupWise system, and then click Next to continue. The Ready to Install dialog box will appear.

14. From the Ready to Install dialog box, click the Install button. This will begin the actual file copy process, which can take several minutes.

15. In the Post Installation Task List dialog box, note any discrepancies that you may need to resolve, and then click Finish. Discrepancies may include failed Internet access, failed DNS access, or the inability to resolve the server's host name. The installation program will provide tips on resolving any errors that it encounters. Additionally, you will be reminded that the RFC for SMTP requires that you designate a Postmaster for your system.

16. Use Windows Explorer to open the GWIA.CFG file. This file was installed to the location that you chose to copy the startup files to, in this example the SYSTEM directory on the cluster-enabled volume.

17. Modify the /HOME- and /DHOME- switches to use the legacy file system syntax without any server names. For example, if the switch is:

```
/Home-\\CLUSTER_GWGWIA_SERVER\GWGWIA\GWGWIA\WPGATE\GWIA
```

Change it to:

```
/Home-GWGWIA:\GWGWIA\WPGATE\GWIA
```

This allows all nodes in the cluster to utilize the same GWIA.CFG file on all nodes in the cluster, thus simplifying administration.

If you installed the GWIA NLMs to the shared storage (cluster-enabled volume), then you can proceed to modify the cluster load and unload scripts. If you installed the NLMs to the SYS: volume, you must install the agents again to each node in the cluster that will be in the failover path of the GWIA. In this case, move the GWIA.NCF and GWIA.CFG files to the cluster-enabled volume so that you have a single location to modify these files when making changes.

WARNING

If you install the GWIA NLMs to the SYS: volume, remember that the NetWare Administrator snapins will have no way to know about this configuration. If you change any GWIA parameters that are stored in the GWIA.CFG file, you must make sure all of these files are updated if you leave them on the SYS: volume.

Modifying the Cluster Load and Unload Scripts

Next, you need to modify the load and unload scripts for the cluster-enabled volume to load the GWIA. The scripts, nodes, and policies should already be configured to load the Domain, so the modification simply adds the line to load or unload the GWIA.

1. Launch ConsoleOne, and browse to your cluster-enabled volume resource object (for example, GWGWIA_SERVER).

2. Right-click the resource object, and then select Properties.

3. Click the Load Script tab, and add a line to the end of the load script (see Figure 12.2) to start the GWIA:

```
<VOLUME>:\SYSTEM\GWIA.NCF
```

For example:

```
GWGWIA:\SYSTEM\GWIA.NCF
```

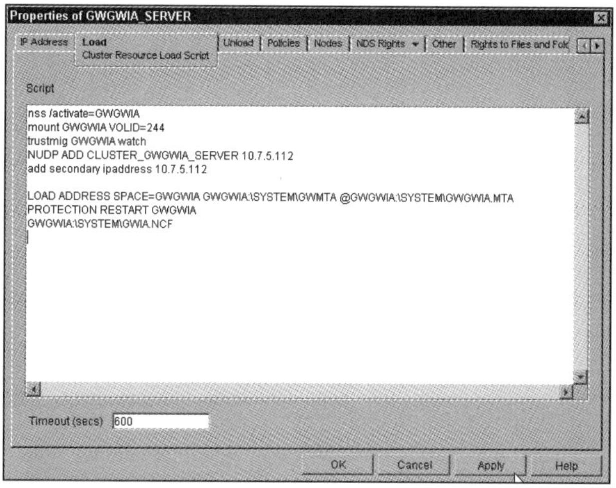

FIGURE 12.2 *GWIA load script*

> You may also wish to remove the TRUSTMIG command from the load script, since you do not need to migrate trustees on a GroupWise volume.
>
> **TIP**

4. Click the Unload Script tab, and add the following line at the beginning of the unload script (see Figure 12.3):

```
UNLOAD GWIA
```

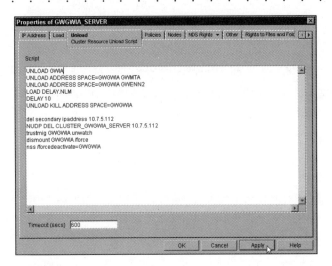

FIGURE 12.3 *GWIA unload script*

5. Change to the Cluster State View, and offline the cluster-enabled volume resource.

6. Online the cluster-enabled volume resource.

You must offline and online the resource for your changes to take effect. Migrating the resource to another node will not be sufficient.

NOTE

Modifying the Internet Addressing for Your GroupWise System

The next step to configuring the GWIA is to modify system-wide Internet Addressing for your GroupWise system. To do this, follow these steps:

1. Launch NetWare Administrator.

2. From the menu, select Tools ➪ GroupWise System Operations to open the GroupWise System Operations window.

3. Double-click the Internet Addressing icon. The Internet Addressing dialog box appears (see Figure 12.4).

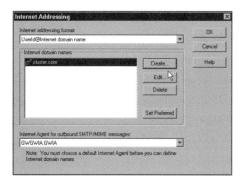

FIGURE 12.4 *Internet Addressing dialog box*

4. In the "Internet Agent for outbound SMTP/MIME messages" drop-down list, select the GWIA you just configured.

5. In the "Internet addressing format" drop-down list, select the preferred Internet addressing method for your Domain.

6. Click the Create button.

7. Enter your Internet Domain Name, for example, `cluster.com`, and then click OK.

8. Click OK, and then click Close to close the GroupWise System Operations window.

Modifying the GWIA Configuration

Several configuration options in the GWIA also need to be configured, both for the GWIA operations itself, and to support clustering. The modifications include assigning a Postmaster for RFC compliance, configuring a hostname for the GWIA to support sending and receiving messages to and from systems that verify hostnames, and modifying the links to TCP/IP, which is required for clustering.

The following steps don't go through every configuration option, but you should, at least, complete these:

1. Launch NetWare Administrator, browse to your GWIA object, and double-click it to modify the details.

2. Click the Gateway Administrators tab.

3. Click the Add button to select the GroupWise user you wish to assign the Postmaster role to.

4. Browse to and select the appropriate NDS user, and then click OK. Next, assign the Postmaster role by clicking the Postmaster checkbox. This assignment is required for RFC compliance.

5. Click the SMTP/MIME Settings tab to configure the hostname of the GWIA, which is used for systems that require DNS verification to receive incoming e-mail.

6. Verify that the Hostname/DNS "A record" name contains the hostname that you configured as your MX record. This should correspond with the secondary IP address used by the cluster resource, not any particular node in the cluster.

7. Click the Server Directories tab to verify the UNC paths used by the GWIA.

8. Verify that the directories reflect UNC paths through the virtual server, not a path to an individual cluster node.

9. Click the Post Office Links tab (see Figure 12.5) to change the links to TCP/IP only.

10. Modify each Post Office link by doing the following:

   a. Double-click the link you wish to modify.

   b. In the Access Mode dialog drop-down box, select Client/Server only.

   c. In the Host name or IP Address field, enter the IP address of that Post Office. Refer to your version of Table 11.4 for this information.

   d. In the TCP Port field, enter the port that Post Office uses. Refer to your version of Table 11.4 for this information.

   e. Click OK.

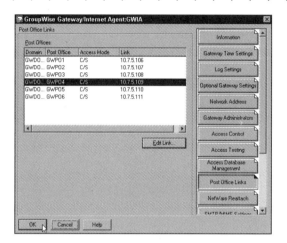

FIGURE 12.5 *Post Office Links dialog box*

Once you complete these final configuration steps, you have met all of the minimum required configurations necessary to cluster the GWIA. Your next step is to modify any other GWIA parameters to suit your organization's policies. Finally, you should test the GWIA on every node in the failover path, and then test it again. Be sure to test all functionality of the GWIA — if you use IMAP, test IMAP while the resource is on each of the nodes in the failover path.

Creating an MTA and WebAccess Resource

The WebAccess Gateway is the most complicated GroupWise resource to cluster, as this involves clustering both a GroupWise Domain (with gateway) and a Novell Enterprise Web Server (EWS). Configuring the GroupWise Domain in the cluster is discussed in Chapter 11, and clustering EWS is discussed in Chapter 13. Before you begin configuring this resource, you should read Chapter 13, and configure the EWS in your cluster.

To configure the Enterprise Web Server for Active/Active failover, see Chapter 13.

X-REF

NOTE You do not need to cluster the Web server together with the GroupWise WebAccess Gateway. These can be completely separate resources, or configured in the same cluster resource, whichever you prefer.

Installing the WebAccess Gateway

To configure cluster-enabled WebAccess, you must first install the WebAccess Gateway. To do so, follow these steps:

1. Using NetWare Administrator GroupWise View, change your Domain connection to the Domain to which you wish to install the WebAccess Gateway.

2. Configure the Domain in the cluster using the UNC path through a virtual server on a cluster-enabled volume. Verify that all links and failover occur properly. Chapter 11 covers this process in detail.

3. Configure the Web server on all nodes that will run the WebAccess Gateway. See Chapter 13 for the steps to configure your Web server.

4. Map a drive to the cluster-enabled volume and to the SYS volume of the server you wish to configure (you will repeat these steps for each server).

5. Using Windows Explorer, browse to the Software Distribution Directory, then to the \internet\WebAccess subdirectory, and run SETUP.EXE.

6. Choose your language from the drop-down list box. Click OK, then click Yes to accept the license agreement.

7. In the Select Components dialog box, select the components you wish to install. At a minimum, select the following, and click Next:

- GroupWise WebAccess Servlet

- GroupWise WebAccess/WebPublisher Agent

- GroupWise Administrator Files

8. In the GroupWise WebAccess Agent: Update Administration Files dialog box, enter or browse to the Public directory where you want the updated snapins placed. In this example, a cluster-enabled Public volume is used for this purpose. By using a cluster-enabled volume for the NetWare Administrator snapins, you can set up a shortcut to run NetWare

Administrator from the cluster-enabled volume, and you will have high availability for NetWare Administrator using Novell Cluster Services.

9. In the GroupWise WebAccess Agent: Gateway Directory dialog box (see Figure 12.6), browse to the GroupWise domain you wish to use for WebAccess, and enter a name for the Agent directory. Then click Next.

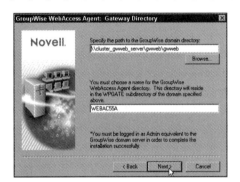

FIGURE 12.6 *GroupWise WebAccess Agent: Gateway Directory dialog box*

TIP

Make sure you use a UNC path through the virtual server or a drive mapped to the cluster-enabled volume for this step! If your GroupWise connection was correct, this should already be entered for you.

10. Enter the unique name for the WebAccess NDS object, and then click Next.

11. In the GroupWise WebAccess Agent: Destination dialog box (see Figure 12.7), do the following:

   a. Verify the NetWare radio button is selected

   b. In the "Specify the installation path for the GroupWise WebAccess Agent module" field, enter or browse to the SYSTEM directory you wish to install the agent to. You should probably use a SYSTEM directory on the cluster-enabled Domain volume, as this is also where the startup files will be placed.

   c. Enter the secondary IP address you will use for the WebAccess Gateway.

   d. Enter the cluster-unique port to use for the WebAccess Gateway.

   e. Click the Next button.

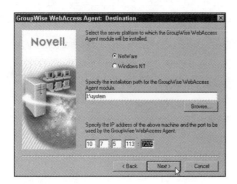

FIGURE 12.7 *GroupWise WebAccess Agent: Destination dialog box*

12. If you wish to use Web Console, check the Enable Web console box and enter a user name and password for Web Console, then Click Next.

13. In the GroupWise WebAccess Agent: Authentication dialog box, specify the distinguished name of an NDS user object to use by the GroupWise agent, along with this user's password, then click Next. This user must have rights to all post offices that this WebAccess Agent will service.

14. In the GroupWise WebAccess/WebPublisher Servlet: Destination dialog box, select the platform you will use for the Web server. For the Enterprise Web Server, accept the default Netscape FastTrack/Enterprise Server for NetWare. You must also select the path to the root of this server. Select the first node you are installing on. You will need to install this agent again for each node that will be in the failover path. When satisfied, click Next to continue.

The root of the HTTP server refers to the system root, not the document root. Do not enter the shared volume in this path; you must enter the SYS:novonyx\suitespot **path.**

TIP

15. In the GroupWise WebAccess/WebPublisher Servlet: Default HTML file dialog box, choose whether to keep your existing default HTML file or replace it with the WebAccess Servlet, then click Next.

16. Enter the location in which to place the WebAccess/WebPublisher Servlet configuration files, and then click Next. You should accept the default, which should be SYS:\NOVELL on the server you chose in step 14. You will need to repeat this installation for each Web server in your cluster if you chose to cluster the servlet.

17. When prompted to have the installation program create the directory for you, click Yes.

18. Select the available languages you wish installed, then click Next.

19. In the GroupWise WebAccess Agent: Authentication dialog box, specify the distinguished name of an NDS user object to use by the WebPublisher, along with this user's password, then click Next. This user is used to publish and share documents if you are using WebPublisher. If you wish to change the agent cache directory, you can also change that at this point.

20. When you are prompted to have the installation program create the cache directory for you, click Yes.

21. If you are using WebPublisher, select the library or libraries you wish to make available for WebPublisher, then click Next.

22. In the GroupWise WebPublisher: Publish General User Access Documents dialog box, specify whether you want to enable general user access of view to all users, then click Next.

23. In the Java Servlet Enabling dialog box, specify the Java Servlet Gateway to use, then click Next. If you are not already using a different servlet gateway, accept the default Novell Servlet Gateway.

24. In the Start Copying Files dialog box, confirm the Current Settings, and then click Next.

25. If prompted to replace an existing servlet gateway, select Yes if you wish to replace the existing gateway, or No if you do not. The installation program will show you the dates of each gateway to help in your decision.

26. If prompted, click Yes to have the installation program unload the Web server for you.

27. If prompted to replace an existing Java Virtual Machine (JVM), select Yes if you wish to replace the existing JVM, or No if you do not. The installation program will show you the dates of each JVM to help in your decision.

28. At the Installation Complete dialog box, click Finish.

29. Modify the `AUTOEXEC.NCF` of this server to add the `SPELLSRV.NCF` command.

30. Next, you will unload and then reload the Web Server, which will enable the Servlet. At the server console of the node you just installed, enter the following commands:

NSWEBDN

NSWEB

SPELLSRV

31. If you have already configured the WebAccess Gateway, you can test the WebAccess functionality at this point. If you haven't done the Gateway yet, continue installing the Servlet to the other cluster nodes, and do all of your testing at the end, or install the Gateway now and test the Servlet before proceeding to the other nodes.

32. Repeat this procedure for each node that will be in the failover path.

Once you have installed the WebAccess Gateway and the WebAccess Servlet, you are ready to modify the cluster resource. Since you already created a cluster-enabled volume for the GroupWise domain, all you need to do is modify the existing resource with the commands to load and unload the WebAccess Gateway.

For an Active/Active Web Server cluster resource, no modification is necessary for the Web Server cluster resource, since the Servlet automatically starts each time the Web Server starts.

Configuring the Cluster Resource

Once you have installed the WebAccess Gateway, you need to modify the load and unload scripts for the cluster-enabled volume resource. The scripts, nodes, and policies should already be configured to load the Domain, so the modification simply adds the line to load or unload the WebAccess Gateway. To modify the scripts, follow these steps:

1. Launch ConsoleOne, browse to your cluster resource, right-click it, and select Properties.

2. Click the Load Script tab. At the end of the load script, add the following line (see Figure 12.8):

<volume>:SYSTEM\STRTWEB5.NCF

For example:

```
GWWEB:SYSTEM\STRTWEB5.NCF
```

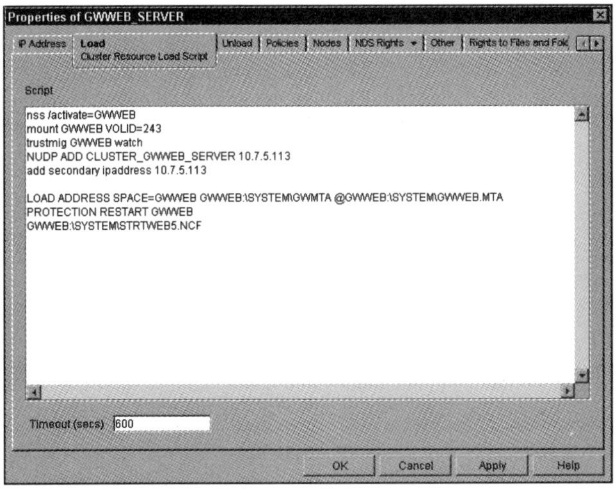

FIGURE 12.8 *WebAccess load script*

3. Click the Unload Script tab, and add the following line at the beginning of the script (see Figure 12.9):

```
UNLOAD GWINTER.NLM
```

4. Modify the WebAccess Gateway startup file (STRTWEB5.NCF) by finding the /ph (path) switch and removing the server name from the syntax. For example, change:

```
/ph-cluster_gwweb_server\gwweb:gwweb\WPGATE\WEBAC55A
```

to:

```
/ph-gwweb:gwweb\WPGATE\WEBAC55A
```

By removing the virtual server from the UNC path, the node starting this resource does not need to perform any TCP/IP name resolution to find the gateway directory. This greatly improves the gateway startup performance.

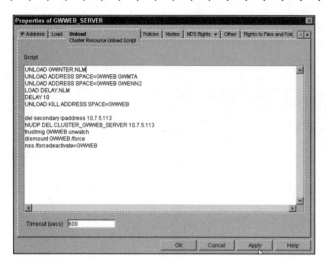

FIGURE 12.9 *WebAccess unload script*

Once you finish modifying the cluster resource, you are almost ready to test the gateway. After you put a few finishing touches on the WebAccess configuration, you're ready to go.

Modifying the WebAccess NDS Configuration

Several configuration options in the WebAccess Gateway need to be configured, both for the gateway operation itself and to support clustering. These tasks include assigning a WebAccess Postmaster (optional), and changing the Post Office links to TCP/IP, which is required for clustering the WebAccess Gateway.

The following steps don't go through every configuration option, but you should, at least, complete those listed here:

1. Launch NetWare Administrator, browse to your WebAccess object, and double-click it to modify the details.

2. Click the Gateway Administrators tab.

3. Click the Add button.

4. Browse to the appropriate NDS user, and assign a Postmaster.

5. Click the Post Office Links tab.

6. Modify each Post Office link by doing the following:

    a. Double-click the link you wish to modify.

    b. In the Access Mode drop-down box, select Client/Server only.

    c. In the Host name or IP Address field, enter the IP address of that Post Office. Refer to your version of Table 11.4 for this information.

    d. In the TCP port field, enter the port that Post Office uses. Refer to your version of Table 11.4 for this information.

    e. Click OK.

7. Click the WebAccess/WebPublisher Agent tab to modify the disk cache path.

8. Change the disk cache path by removing the UNC path and specifying only the volume name and subdirectory, for example:

```
GWWEB:\SYSTEM\CACHE
```

9. If you are using a hardware virtual server to access the WebAccess Gateway, copy the WebAccess images to the shared volume that you are serving the page from. Copy the `SYS:NOVONYX\SUITESPOT\DOCS\COM` subdirectory and all of its contents to the document root on the shared volume. For example, we copied this to `WEB:\Docs` (the COM directory must be just below the document root set for the hardware virtual server).

TIP

If you did not replace the default home page, then you can reference the WebAccess Gateway through the URL `IPADDRESS`/`servlet/webacc`. **For example,** `http://10.7.5.115/servlet/webacc`.

10. Copy the `COMMGR.CFG` file from the Domain `\WPGATE\WEBAC55A` directory to each Web server's `SYS:NOVELL` directory.

TIP

There is currently no way to automatically keep the `COMMGR.CFG` **files correct for all Web servers. If you make any changes that would affect the** `COMMGR.CFG` **(such as the IP address and/or port), you must manually redistribute the** `COMMGR.CFG` **file to each Web server.**

Migration/Failover Characteristics

This section discusses how the various GroupWise components discussed in this chapter normally behave when they are migrated to another node, or the node they are running on fails. Recall that a migration involves a voluntary process by the administrator to move a resource from one node to another, while a failover involves a hardware or software fault that causes a node to fail.

The section gives you a baseline of what to expect from each of the components, including the gateways and the clients, for both the migration or failover event. Actual time taken for these events will naturally vary from system to system based on configuration and usage.

Gateway Behavior

Just as with the MTA and POA, discussed in Chapter 11, resource migrations on the gateways are much slower than the recovery time should a server actually fail. This is especially true and painful with the GWIA, which can be extremely slow to shut down as it finishes processing all of its threads (heavily used GWIAs can take more than 10 minutes to shut down).

During the GWIA migration or failover, POP3, IMAP4, and LDAP clients receive a TCP/IP error message saying that the server is not available. (The actual errors vary depending on the client software used.) Most of these clients do not automatically reconnect, which requires the user to close down the client and reopen it.

The WebAccess symptoms depend on whether it is the Web server (servlet) that fails/migrates, or the WebAccess Gateway itself. The servlet caches the user's credentials, so if the WebAccess Gateway server (GWINTER.NLM) fails or migrates, the user will get an error message stating that the agent is not available. Once the agent has started again, the user will be able to reconnect, as the servlet will pass the user credentials back to the agent. If it is the servlet that fails or migrates, the user will need to reauthenticate, as the cached credentials do not survive a servlet failure.

Both the GWIA and the WebAccess agent are pretty quick to start up, so in the event of a server failure, resources are quickly reestablished.

Client Behavior

Another behavior to be aware of is that of NetWare Administrator. If you open NetWare Administrator (most notably on Windows NT or Windows 2000) and the snapin cannot connect to the path specified by the EXEPATH.CFG file, then when you try to administer the GWIA object, you will receive an error message stating that there is a problem with the snapins. In this case, close NetWare Administrator, restore your connection with the virtual server, and then restart NetWare Administrator.

Active/Active versus Active/Passive

All GroupWise components function in an Active/Passive manner. Only one server can have the database volume mounted and the agent loaded, so migrating a resource will require starting all of the appropriate NLMs on the destination node.

Summary

This chapter examined how to install and configure a cluster resource consisting of a GroupWise Domain and GWIA Gateway and one consisting of a GroupWise Domain and WebAccess Gateway.

Additionally, the chapter ended with a discussion of the basic failover and migration characteristics of these two GroupWise gateways.

CLUSTER FAILOVER CLASSIFICATION INDEX	
Transparency	GWIA — Very transparent during failure, not transparent during a migration
	Web Access — Not transparent; users will not automatically reconnect
Active/Active or Active/Passive	Active/Passive
Length to failover	Web Access is very quick.
	GWIA is fast on failure, but slow to migrate as it closes existing processes.

This chapter built on the GroupWise foundation set in Chapter 11, and helped guide you through the steps necessary for connecting your highly available GroupWise system to the Internet.

This chapter also builds the foundation for Chapter 23, which builds on the first two GroupWise chapters and leads you into configuring GroupWise 6 in a cluster. Much of the information in Chapter 23 relies on the foundation you built with Chapters 11 and 12, while configuration differences in GroupWise 6 are also explained.

Applying Novell Cluster Services with Enterprise Web Server

This chapter delves into the Enterprise Web Server (EWS) for NetWare, Novell's latest installment of their Web server offerings. You learn how to cluster enable the EWS in both an Active/Passive and an Active/Active configuration, the advantages and disadvantages of each, as well as the expected failover and migration behaviors for each of the EWS configurations. Finally, you learn how to migrate an existing EWS installation to a highly available clustered configuration.

Introducing the Enterprise Web Server

The Novell Enterprise Web Server (EWS) — formerly the Netscape Enterprise Web Server — was created as a joint venture between Netscape and Novell to port Netscape's FastTrack and Enterprise Web Servers to the NetWare platform. This chapter focuses on version 5.10a, which is the NetWare 5.1 version with Support Pack 2A applied. Whereas the NetWare 5.0 version of EWS clusters in the same manner, the NetWare 5.1 version has tighter NDS integration.

The Enterprise Web Server for NetWare offers a variety of tools and features that allow companies to connect their users, other businesses, and their customers together through the Internet.

Table 13.1 summarizes some of Enterprise Web Server for NetWare's key features and benefits.

TABLE 13.1	
EWS Benefits	
BENEFIT	**EXPLANATION**
Web publishing	Allows end users to organize and publish their own documents and allows them to use text search and revision control to manage content.
Agents	Allows an administrator to create predefined agents that run on the server and notify you through e-mail if a specific document has been changed.

BENEFIT	EXPLANATION
Lightweight Directory Access Protocol (LDAP) support	Enables you to store users and groups in a centralized directory.
Encryption	Enables you to establish encrypted and authenticated transactions between clients and the server through Secure Sockets Layer (SSL) 3.0 protocol.
Access control	Helps you protect confidential files and directories by implementing access control with user names, passwords, domain names, or IP addresses.
Native Novell Directory Services (NDS)	Enables control of user and group information access to NetWare server resources. NDS allows protected access to Web resources for users to login from HTTP clients using their normal NDS user name and passwords, which enables access control without the need to manage yet another user database.
Multiple Web site management with a single server	EWS allows for both hardware and software virtual servers, which enables a single server to serve multiple Internet or intranet Domains. Each virtual server has its own document root and administration policies.

The EWS is implemented as a series of NLM modules on your server and is administered through an HTML-based Server Manager. The primary Web server functionality is implemented through the NSHTTP.NLM, whereas the Server Manager (also known as the Administration Server) is implemented through ADMSERV.NLM.

These NLMs are originally loaded using the NSWEB.NCF file, which actually calls two other NCF files, NVXALLUP.NCF and NVXADMUP.NCF. The NVXALLUP.NCF loads the NSSHTTP.NLM with the appropriate parameters, and the NVXADMUP.NCF loads the ADMSERV.NLM for the server.

The server is administered through the Server Manager, which in turn is accessed through a Java-compliant Web browser (see Figure 13.1). You may have multiple hardware and software virtual servers, but the Server Manager is always accessed using the primary IP address of the Web server and the port you chose when you installed the Web server component (this is port 2200 by default with NetWare 5.1).

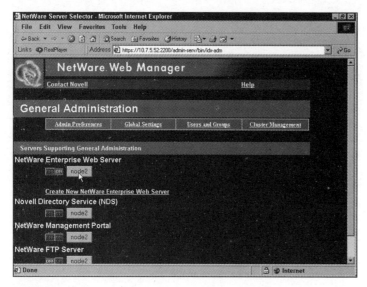

FIGURE 13.1 *NetWare Enterprise Web Manager*

Cluster Enabling the Enterprise Web Server

To support failover, NetWare Enterprise Web Server must be installed separately on each cluster node that will potentially run the application. To simplify administration, keep the admin port number the same for all cluster nodes.

When installing the NetWare Enterprise Web Server, accept the default IP address (the server's primary address) for each server. You add the cluster IP address later when you configure the cluster resource. If static HTML and image files are the only type of files to be accessed by the Web server, then the files can be installed on each server's local storage rather than on the shared volume, although this adds to the management overhead since each server then needs to be updated when the content changes.

Cluster enabling the shared volume is not required, as clients do not directly access data files. This holds true even in a CGI interface application such as GroupWise Web Access.

TIP

The only reason we can think of to cluster enable the volume is to support developers placing the Web content on the server. However, a better option for this eventuality is to configure FTP services and have the developers FTP the content to the Web server. FTP services are discussed in Chapter 14.

After the Web server is installed, you must add the cluster IP address by connecting to the Admin server of NetWare Enterprise Web Server and adding a hardware virtual server. For an Active/Active configuration, you add the secondary IP address for the Web server cluster resource to the hardware virtual server IP address field using the Content Management button's Hardware Virtual Server link.

If shared storage is used, you must point to the shared storage for the document root by using the shared volume name, not the NDS volume object name. For example, you could use WEB:/docs as the hardware virtual server document root. You repeat this configuration for all nodes that will be in the failover path.

TIP

You must use the forward slash (/) to configure the document root directory, not the backslash (\).

When clustering the Enterprise Web Server, you install and fully configure the service on all nodes in the cluster that will be in the failover path. Any future administration to the Web server must be repeated on all nodes in the cluster that are in the failover path. Although you can place the Web content on shared storage, the configuration files reside on each server's SYS volume and must be administered individually.

Active/Active Configuration

With the EWS, you have two choices on how to configure the server in the cluster. You can choose to configure it in an Active/Active configuration, which has the Web server up and running on all nodes in the failover path, or in an Active/Passive configuration, in which case it is running only on the active node.

In an Active/Active configuration, EWS is loaded from the AUTOEXEC.NCF, and you use hardware virtual servers for any site you wish to cluster. In this case, you connect to each server's primary address and use the Server Manager program to configure the hardware virtual server.

For hardware virtual servers to function properly, the secondary IP address must be bound when the Web server starts up, or it will not initialize properly, and that virtual server will not be supported. This requires modification to the

NSWEB.NCF file to allow duplicate IP addresses (in case you start a server when the resource is already active on another node). Then bind the IP address and start the Web server. At the end of the NSWEB.NCF file, you unbind the IP address and disallow secondary IP addresses. Then the server is ready to go.

The modified NSWEB.NCF would be similar to this:

```
# Added for Active/Active Web Server
SET ALLOW IP ADDRESS DUPLICATES=ON
ADD SECONDARY IPADDRESS 10.7.5.115


# Startup for the Netscape Enterprise Server for Netware by
Novonyx


# Load cron for automatic updates of indexes, index
optimization, and log rotation
load cron


# Load SNMP agent for network management
load sys:\novonyx\suitespo\plugins\snmp\nssnmp -d
/novonyx/suitespot/https-NODE1/config


# Load web server(s)
nvxallup.ncf


# Load administration server
nvxadmup


# Added for Active/Active Web Server
LOAD DELAY.NLM
DELAY 10
DEL SECONDARY IPADDRESS 10.7.5.115
SET ALLOW IP ADDRESS DUPLICATES=OFF
```

The `DELAY.NLM` **and** `DELAY 10` **lines are added to make sure the Web server has sufficient time to start up before deleting the secondary IP address. If it is deleted too soon, it will not activate properly.**

You may wish to load `DELAY.NLM` **in the** `AUTOEXEC.NCF` **file, in which case you can omit this line in the** `NCF` **file. Since you may also be using the** `DELAY.NLM` **for other cluster resources, adding this line in the** `AUTOEXEC.NCF` **ensures that it is always loaded.**

The cluster load and unload script for the Active/Active configuration is simple — just mount the shared volume and add the secondary IP address, and the Web server is running. Since you never load or unload the NLMs, this is an extremely fast startup and shutdown application.

Thus, the load script looks like this example:

```
nss /activate=WEB

mount WEB

add secondary ipaddress 10.7.5.115
```

If you are using a secure site with Access Control Lists (ACLs), you should also add a line, `trustmig <volume> /watch`.

Table 13.2 lists the pros and cons of an Active/Active configuration.

TABLE 13.2
Active/Active Pros and Cons

PRO	CON
Very fast failover.	If you need to reload the Web server, all currently running Web server resources must be restarted manually.
Supports multiple Web server resources that run independently.	If you restart another Web server, the current services will temporarily be disabled while the IP address is bound on two servers.
	Requires configuring hardware virtual servers, which requires additional configuration.

The Hidden Problem with Active/Active

At face value, it may not be apparent why needing the secondary IP address bound is a problem with the Active/Active configuration. You can easily work around it by modifying the NSWEB.NCF file to allow the IP address duplicates, binding the address, starting the server, unbinding the address, and then disallowing duplicates.

The problems arise in two major areas. The first is when you make a change to the Web server that requires you to run NSWEBDN.NCF followed by NSWEB.NCF (such as installing the GroupWise Web Access Servlet). If you have eight hardware virtual servers configured in your cluster, and then do an NSWEBDN.NCF followed by NSWEB.NCF, any of the resources that were running on this node will no longer be active! Why? Well, the cluster load script mounted the volume and added the secondary IP address, but the NSWEB.NCF was run later, and it added and deleted all of the IP addresses for all virtual servers. You must now remember which Web servers were running on this node and rebind their secondary IP addresses.

The second problem occurs when one of the servers in the failover path is restarted. The server that is currently running the resources, which depend on the secondary IP addresses, detects the IP address conflict when NSWEB.NCF is run on the restarted server. This results in a temporary period of time when the resource is not available because the server stops responding to the duplicated address. This automatically corrects itself, but it causes the service to be unavailable for a while, when it really should be available.

Active/Passive Configuration

The Netscape Enterprise Server template for Novell Cluster Services assumes an Active/Passive configuration. In this configuration, the Web server NLMs are loaded on only one server at a time and are unloaded during a migration.

This configuration is easier to set up, as the NSWEB.NCF changes, and changes to the hardware virtual server configuration are not required. The drawbacks to this configuration are the load and unload times for both the EWS and the supporting NLMs.

The load script and Active/Passive configuration looks like this example:

```
nss /activate=WEB

mount WEB
```

```
add secondary ipaddress 10.7.5.115
nsweb
```

Table 13.3 lists the pros and cons of an Active/Passive configuration.

TABLE 13.3

Active/Passive Pros and Cons

PRO	CON
No issues with duplicate IP addresses.	Slower to start up and migrate.
Easier to configure.	If you are configuring multiple Web servers, the servers must be configured as a single resource since running NSWEBDN will stop all Web servers running on that particular node.

Configuring the Active/Active NetWare Enterprise Web Server for Novell Cluster Services

The following sections take you through the process of installing and configuring Enterprise Web Server for Novell Cluster Services in an Active/Active configuration.

Installing the EWS

Before you can configure the Enterprise Web Server, it must be installed on all nodes that will be in the failover path. The Web server is installed by default during the NetWare 5.1 installation, or is installed later using the NetWare 5.1 CD. To install the EWS, follow these steps:

1. Place the NetWare 5.x installation CD in the server.

2. If the CD does not automatically activate and mount, type **LOAD CDROM**

3. Enter **LOAD NWCONFIG** at the server console prompt.

4. From the Configuration Options menu, select Product Options, then press Enter to reach the Other Installation Actions menu.

5. Select Install a product not listed, then press Enter, which brings you to the Previously Specified Paths menu option.

6. If the NetWare 5.x CD path is listed in the Previously Specified Paths list, select it and then press Enter. Otherwise:

a. Press Esc to leave the Previously Specified Paths list.

b. Press F3 to specify a different path.

c. Enter the path to the root of the CD (that is, **NW51:**).

7. The GUI installation screen appears. From this screen, select the following components, then press the Next button:

a. NetWare Enterprise Web Server

b. NetWare Web Manager (This is automatically selected when you select NetWare Enterprise Web Server.)

8. If prompted, authenticate as a user with Supervisor rights to the [Root] of the tree.

9. In the NetWare Enterprise Web Server Settings dialog box, do the following:

a. Accept the default Regular port of 80.

b. Accept the default Secure port of 443.

c. Do not select the Optional Settings check box.

d. Click Next to continue.

10. In the NetWare Web Manager Port dialog box, accept the default admin port of 2200, then click Next to continue.

11. Click Finish.

12. From the Installation Complete dialog box, click Close.

13. Reapply the current NetWare support pack after installing any new components.

Creating the Volume for Web Content

Create an NSS volume on the shared storage to hold your Web content. This step is optional depending on the content, as you can store the content on the local servers. However, if you store content on local servers, you have to update all servers any time the content changes.

X-REF

Chapter 9 discusses working with storage and volumes and includes the steps necessary to create an NSS volume on the shared storage.

This volume does not need to be cluster enabled, as clients will not map drives to the content volume.

TIP

The only reason you might have to cluster enable the volume is to support developers placing the Web content on the server. However, a better option for your developers is to configure FTP services and have the developers FTP the content to the Web server. FTP services are discussed in Chapter 14.

Configuring the Administration Server with the Hardware Virtual Server

To configure an Active/Active Web Server with Enterprise Web Server, you must configure a hardware virtual server for each Web Resource that will be in each node's failover path. The hardware virtual server is assigned to the secondary IP address that you are using for each Web Server cluster resource.

The Enterprise Web Server will only activate hardware virtual servers if the secondary IP address is available when the Web server loads. Prior to configuring the hardware virtual server, you should bind the secondary IP address to the node you are configuring. You must also ensure that any time the Web server is restarted on this node, all possible hardware virtual server IP addresses are bound.

To configure a hardware virtual server, do the following:

I. At the server console prompt at one server in the cluster, bind the secondary IP address to be used for the Web server by entering the following command:

```
ADD SECONDARY IPADDRESS <IP Address>
```

2. At the server console prompt on the same server, activate and mount the volume to use for your Web server.

3. Launch your Web browser, and connect to the server's primary address on your administration port. For example, enter:

```
https://10.7.5.51:2200
```

4. Using the appropriate procedures for the Web browser you are using, accept and import the SSL certificate from the Web server.

5. Authenticate to the Web Manager using your admin credentials.

6. Click the button corresponding to your NetWare Enterprise Web Server for the server you are configuring, as shown in Figure 13.2 (for example, node2). This will bring up the server-specific NetWare Enterprise Web Server administration Web page.

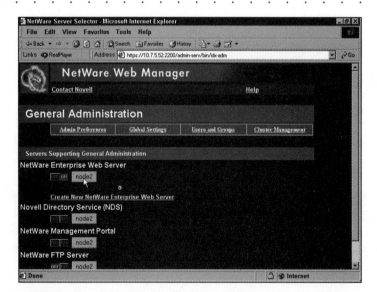

FIGURE 13.2 *NetWare Enterprise Web Manager — Select your Web Server html page*

7. Click the Content Management link, shown in Figure 13.3, along the top toolbar. This will bring up the Web page that allows you to configure the Web content directories, including the hardware virtual server directory.

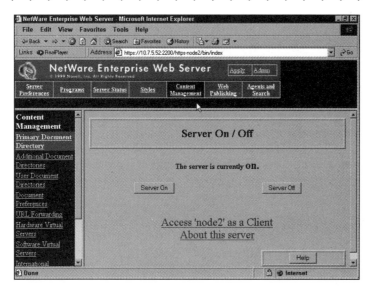

FIGURE 13.3 *Content Management link*

8. Click the Hardware Virtual Servers link along the left side of the screen to configure a new hardware virtual server for your cluster resource.

9. To configure the hardware virtual server, do the following:

a. In the IP Address field, enter the secondary IP address you are using for this cluster resource.

b. In the Port Number field, enter the port to use for this Web server.

c. In the Document Root field, enter the path you wish to use for your document root. For example, to have the document root the `docs` directory on the Web volume, you enter `web:/docs` (as shown in Figure 13.4).

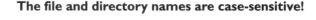

The file and directory names are case-sensitive!

TIP

10. Click OK to save your changes.

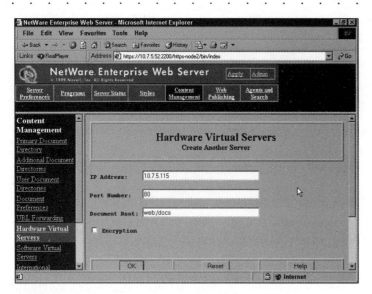

FIGURE 13.4 *Placing a path in the Document Root field*

11. Click the Save and Apply button near the bottom of the screen. Expect a brief delay for the administration program to process your changes before displaying a success (or failure) dialog box.

12. At the Success dialog box, click OK. (This process can take up to a minute to complete — be patient!)

13. Click the Server Preference link along the top toolbar.

14. Click the Restrict Access link along the left side of the screen.

15. Scroll down to the Public Directory Designations section (shown in Figure 13.5) and click the Insert Directory button.

16. In the New Public Directory dialog box (shown in Figure 13.6), enter the path you listed in step 9. Configuring a public directory enables users to use this hardware virtual server without first authenticating to the site. If your cluster resource is for a public site that doesn't require pre-authentication, you need to configure the document root as a public directory.

17. Click the Save Changes button.

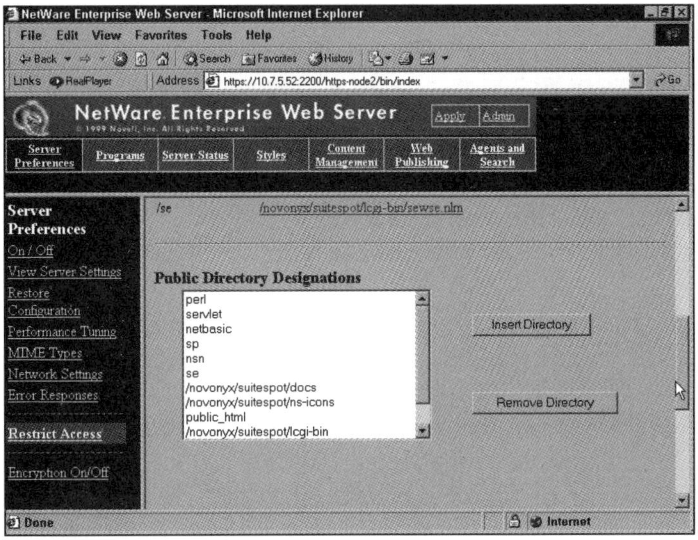

▶ • ◀

NetWare Enterprise Web Server - Microsoft Internet Explorer

File   Edit   View   Favorites   Tools   Help

Back ▼ ⇒ ▼ ⊗ ⓐ ⚹ | ⓠSearch ⚐Favorites ⚽History | ⚘▼ ⚘ ⚘ ▼

Links ⓪ RealPlayer   Address ⚐ https://10.7.5.52:2200/https-node2/bin/index   ▼ ⚘Go

NetWare. Enterprise Web Server

© 1999 Novell, Inc. All Rights Reserved   Apply   Admin

| Server Preferences | Programs | Server Status | Styles | Content Management | Web Publishing | Agents and Search |

Server Preferences

On / Off

View Server Settings

Restore Configuration

Performance Tuning

MIME Types

Network Settings

Error Responses

Restrict Access

Encryption On/Off

/se   /novonyx/suitespot/lcgi-bin/sewse.nlm

Public Directory Designations

```
perl
servlet
netbasic
sp
nsn
se
/novonyx/suitespot/docs
/novonyx/suitespot/ns-icons
public_html
/novonyx/suitespot/lcgi-bin
```

Insert Directory

Remove Directory

⚐ Done   🔒 🌐 Internet

FIGURE 13.5 *Inserting a new public directory*

▶ • ◀

Explorer User Prompt   ☒

JavaScript Prompt: OK

New Public Directory: Cancel

web:/docs

FIGURE 13.6 *New Public Directory dialog box*

18. Click OK to acknowledge the message informing you that you must restart your Web server.

19. To shut down the Web server, enter **NSWEBDN** at the server console prompt.

20. To restart the Web server, enter **NSWEB** at the server console prompt.

21. To delete your secondary IP address, enter the following command at the server console prompt:

```
DELETE SECONDARY IPADDRESS <IP Address>
```

22. Dismount and deactivate the volume you are using for the Web content.

• • • • •

Repeat steps 1 through 22 on each node that you wish to be in the failover path for the Web server.

To configure a hardware virtual server, the secondary IP address must be bound on the server.

TIP

Modifying the Startup Files for EWS

After installing NetWare Enterprise Web Server on the specified servers in the cluster and configuring it to work with a shared disk system, you must add command lines to the beginning and the end of the NSWEB.NCF file of each NetWare Enterprise Web Server in the cluster. These commands provide a workaround for a known NetWare Enterprise Web Server issue that requires all hardware virtual server addresses be bound when the server initializes or it will not activate them. Using hardware virtual servers allows for the Active/Active configuration. Follow these steps for all servers that will be running the Web server:

1. Edit the NSWEB.NCF file as follows (and as shown in Figure 13.7):

   a. At the beginning of the file, add the following commands:

   ```
   # ADDED FOR ACTIVE/ACTIVE WEB SERVER

   SET ALLOW IP ADDRESS DUPLICATES=ON

   ADD SECONDARY IPADDRESS <IP Address>
   ```

   b. At the end of the file (after all other lines), add the following commands:

   ```
   # Added for Active/Active Web Server

   LOAD DELAY.NLM

   DELAY 10

   DEL SECONDARY IPADDRESS <IP Address>

   SET ALLOW IP ADDRESS DUPLICATES=OFF
   ```

2. Verify that each server loads NSWEB in the AUTOEXEC.NCF file.

```
NSWeb.ncf - Notepad
File  Edit  Format  Help
# Added for Active/Active Web Server
SET ALLOW IP ADDRESS DUPLICATES=ON
ADD SECONDARY IPADDRESS 10.7.5.115

# Startup for the Netscape Enterprise Server for Netware by Novonyx

# Load cron for automatic updates of indexes, index optimization, and log rotation
load cron

# Load SNMP agent for network management
load sys:\novonyx\suitespo\plugins\snmp\nssnmp -d /novonyx/suitespot/https-NODE1/config

# Load web server(s)
nvxallup.ncf

# Load administration server
nvxadmup
# Added for Active/Active Web Server
LOAD DELAY.NLM
DELAY 10
DEL SECONDARY IPADDRESS 10.7.5.115
SET ALLOW IP ADDRESS DUPLICATES=OFF
```

FIGURE 13.7 *NSWEB.NCF file, edited for Active/Active configuration*

WARNING

One side effect of this configuration occurs when a server is restarted. When the node runs the `NSWEB.NCF` **file, it binds an IP address that is most likely already in use somewhere else. When that server detects the IP address duplicate, it will stop communicating on that address for a period of time. This normally self-corrects after the duplicate is removed, but it does cause an interruption of service for a short period of time. Keep this in mind before starting the server.**

Creating the Cluster Resource Object

Once you have configured the hardware virtual server and modified the NSWEB file to support the Active/Active Web Server, you must create a new cluster resource for your Web Server. To create the resource object, do the following:

1. Launch ConsoleOne, and browse to the cluster container object.

2. Select File ➪ New ➪ Cluster Resource from the menu.

3. In the New Cluster Resource dialog box, do the following:

   a. In the Cluster Resource Name field, enter a name for the resource.

   b. In the Inherit From Template field, browse, select the Netscape Enterprise Server, and then click OK.

c. Check the Define Additional Properties box.

d. Click Create.

The Load Script tab appears by default.

4. Edit the load script by doing the following (see Figure 13.8):

▸ Modify the following commands based on your volume name and TCP/IP address:

```
NSS /ACTIVATE=<volume>

MOUNT <volume>

ADD SECONDARY IPADDRESS <IP Address>
```

▸ Delete the following command from the load script:

```
NSWEB
```

Because you are configuring this server in Active/Active mode, delete the NSWEB **line from the load script.**

TIP

Note that this load script does not use TRUSTMIG.NLM. **In most cases, this will be fine for the Web server, as you configure public document directories using the Administration program. However, if you are using a Web site that needs NDS access control via file system rights, you need to add the** TRUSTMIG <volume> /watch **command to migrate trustees.**

TIP

5. Select the Unload tab.

6. Edit the unload script by doing the following:

▸ Modify the following commands based on your volume name and IP address:

```
DISMOUNT <volume> /FORCE

NSS /FORCEDEACTIVATE=<volume>

DEL SECONDARY IPADDRESS <IP Address>
```

▶ Delete the following line from the unload script:

NSWEBDN

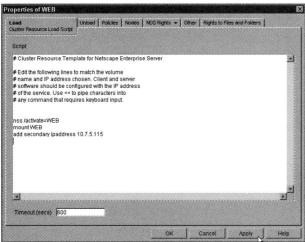

FIGURE 13.8 *Active/Active Web server load script*

Because you are configuring this server in Active/Active mode, you should delete the NSWEBDN **line.**

TIP

7. Modify the Policies and Nodes configurations as desired, and then click Close.

8. Switch to the Cluster State View in ConsoleOne.

9. Click the Web server cluster resource, and then click the Online button.

At this point, you have installed and configured the Web Server as an Active/Active cluster resource. The resource is considered Active/Active because the Web Server is already running on any cluster node that the resource may migrate to — all the resource needs to do is mount the volume and add the secondary IP Address used for the hardware virtual server, and the new node will service this resource. All the Web Content is placed in one location — on the shared storage — so there is only one place to update the content.

Content, Anyone?

Okay, now you have the Web server all configured and clustered, right? Well, you haven't dealt with content yet. One way to validate the configuration is to copy the sample Web site from the server's SYS volume to the document root you specified earlier (or, simply put, your desired content in the hardware virtual server's document root). To do this, do the following (if you have performed step 9 in the preceding "Creating the Cluster Resource Object" section, skip steps 1 and 6 in the following list):

1. At the NetWare cluster server, mount the WEB volume using the following commands:

```
NSS /ACTIVATE=<volume>

MOUNT <volume>
```

2. At the workstation, map a drive to the Web content volume, and create a subdirectory that corresponds with the name you used for the document root.

3. At the workstation, map a drive to the SYS volume of any server that you installed the Web server on (this was specified in step 9 of the procedure outlined in the "Configuring the Administration Server with the Hardware Virtual Server" section earlier in this chapter).

4. Copy the `SYS:\Novonyx\suitespot\Docs` directory to the hardware virtual server document root.

5. Launch your Web browser and enter the IP address of the hardware virtual server you just configured. You should see the content you copied to the hardware virtual server document root.

6. To dismount the volume from your server, enter the following commands at the server console:

```
DISMOUNT <volume>

NSS /DEACTIVATE=<volume>
```

Configuring the Active/Passive NetWare Enterprise Web Server for Novell Cluster Services

If you decide that the hardware virtual server and duplicate IP address configuration will not work for your environment, you must use an Active/Passive configuration. This resource will start and migrate slightly slower than the Active/Active configuration, but you will avoid the duplicate IP address problem. Keep in mind that you must configure all Web sites that will be hosted by any given node as a single cluster resource when using the Active/Passive configuration, so you also lose some granularity with this option.

The following sections take you through the process of installing and configuring Enterprise Web Server for Novell Cluster Services in an Active/Passive configuration.

Installing the EWS

Before you can configure the Enterprise Web Server, it must be installed on all nodes that will be in the failover path. The Web server is installed by default during the NetWare 5.1 installation, and/or later using the NetWare CD. To install the EWS:

1. Place the NetWare 5.x installation CD in the server.

2. If the CD does not automatically activate and mount, type **LOAD CDROM**

3. Enter **LOAD NWCONFIG** at the server console prompt.

4. Select Product Options, and then press Enter.

5. Select Install a product not listed, and then press Enter.

6. If the NetWare 5.x CD path is listed in the Previously Specified Paths list, select it and then press Enter. Otherwise:

    a. Press Esc.

    b. Press F3.

    c. Enter the path to the root of the CD (that is, **NW51:**). The GUI installation screen appears.

7. From the GUI installation screen, select the following components, then press the Next button:

- NetWare Enterprise Web Server

- NetWare Web Manager (This is automatically selected when you select NetWare Enterprise Web Server.)

8. If prompted, authenticate as a user with Supervisor rights to the [Root] of the tree.

9. In the NetWare Enterprise Web Server Settings dialog box, do the following:

  a. Accept the default Regular port of 80.

  b. Accept the default Secure port of 443.

  c. Do not select the Optional Settings check box.

  d. Click Next to continue.

10. In the NetWare Web Manager Port dialog box, accept the default admin port of 2200, and then click Next to continue.

11. Click Finish.

12. From the Installation Complete dialog box, click Close.

13. Reapply the current NetWare support pack after installing any new components.

Creating the Volume for Web Content

Create an NSS volume on the shared storage to hold your Web content. This step is optional depending on the content, as you can store the content on the local servers. However, if you store content on local servers, you have to update all servers any time the content changes. And as always, Novell does not recommend storing production data on a server's SYS volume.

X-REF

Chapter 9 discusses working with storage and volumes and includes the steps necessary to create an NSS volume on the shared storage.

This volume does not need to be cluster enabled, as clients will not map drives to the content volume.

TIP

The only reason you might cluster enable the volume is to support developers placing the Web content on the server. However, a better option for your developers is to configure FTP services and have the developers FTP the content to the Web server. FTP services are discussed in Chapter 14.

Modifying the Document Root Directory

1. Launch your Web browser, and connect to the server's primary address on your administration port. For example, enter:

   ```
   https://10.7.5.51:2200
   ```

2. Using the appropriate procedures for the Web browser you are using, accept and import the SSL certificate from the Web server.

3. Authenticate to the Web Manager using your admin credentials.

4. Click the button corresponding to your NetWare Enterprise Web Server for the server you are configuring, as shown in Figure 13.9 (for example, node2).

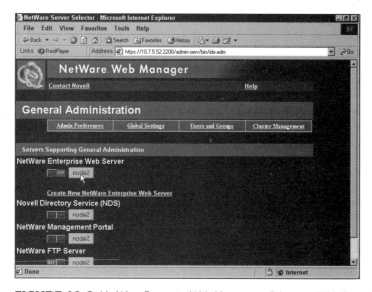

FIGURE 13.9 *NetWare Enterprise Web Manager — Select your Web Server html page*

5. Click the Content Management link along the top toolbar (see Figure 13.10).

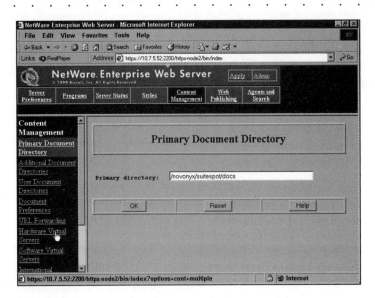

FIGURE 13.10 *Content Management*

6. In the Primary Directory field, enter the path to the primary document directory. For example, enter:

```
web:/docs
```

The file and directory names are case sensitive!

7. Click OK.

TIP

8. Click the Save and Apply button near the bottom of the screen.

9. At the Success dialog box, click OK. (This process can take up to a minute to complete — be patient!)

Creating the Cluster Resource Object

1. Launch ConsoleOne, and browse to the cluster container object.

2. Select File ➪ New ➪ Cluster Resource from the menu.

3. In the New Cluster Resource dialog box, do the following:

    a. In the Cluster Resource Name field, enter a name for the resource.

    b. In the Inherit From Template field, browse and select the Netscape Enterprise Server, and then click OK.

    c. Check the Define Additional Properties box.

    d. Click Create.

4. Edit the load script to include the following commands:

```
NSS /ACTIVATE=<volume>

MOUNT <volume>

ADD SECONDARY IPADDRESS <IP Address>

NSWEB
```

TIP

Note that this load script does not use `TRUSTMIG.NLM`. **In most cases, this will be fine for the Web server, as you configure public document directories using the Administration program. However, if you are using a Web site that needs NDS access control via file system rights, you need to add the** `TRUSTMIG <volume> /watch` **command to migrate trustees.**

5. Select the Unload tab.

6. Edit the unload script to include the following commands:

```
NSWEBDN

DISMOUNT <volume> /FORCE

NSS /FORCEDEACTIVATE=<volume>

DEL SECONDARY IPADDRESS <IP Address>
```

7. Modify the Policies and Nodes configuration as desired, and then click Close.

8. Switch to the Cluster State View in ConsoleOne.

9. Click the Web Server cluster resource, and then click the Online button.

Content, Anyone?

Okay, so now you have the Web server all configured and clustered, right? Well, you haven't dealt with content yet. One way to validate the configuration is to copy the sample Web site from the server's SYS volume to the document root you specified earlier. To do this, follow these steps (if you performed step 9 in the "Creating the Cluster Resource Object" section that precedes this section, skip steps 1 and 6 in the following list):

1. At the NetWare cluster server, mount the WEB volume using the following commands:

```
NSS /ACTIVATE=<volume>

MOUNT <volume>
```

2. At the workstation, map a drive to the Web content volume, and create a subdirectory that corresponds with the name you used for the document root.

3. At the workstation, map a drive to the SYS volume of any server that you installed the Web server on (this is specified in step 6 of the procedure outlined in the section "Modifying the Document Root Directory" earlier in this chapter).

4. Copy the `SYS:\Novonyx\suitespot\Docs` directory to the new document root.

5. Launch your Web browser and enter the IP address of the hardware virtual server you just configured. You should see the content you copied to the hardware virtual server document root.

6. To dismount the volume from your server, enter the following commands at the server console:

```
DISMOUNT <volume>

NSS /DEACTIVATE=<volume>
```

Migration/Failover Characteristics

The Active/Active Web Server has an extremely fast and transparent migration — all you need to wait for is for the volume to mount and IP address to bind! If users happen to hit the site during the migration, they will get an HTTP error indicating that the site is down. By the time they retry the site, it will most likely be up and running again, with very little impact. Of course, if the site requires authentication, users will need to reauthenticate to the Web server since the service is now running on a different node.

The Active/Passive Web Server is also very fast, since the NSWEB.NCF file does not take very long to execute. This configuration also affects users more in a secure configuration, as reauthentication is required if the user happens to hit a site during a migration.

Migrating from an Existing NES Implementation

Migrating from an existing Web Server implementation is very simple, most notably if you are in control of your DNS configuration. To migrate, follow these steps:

1. Configure the new Web server using either the Active/Active or Active/Passive configuration.

2. Install all required Web components, including any necessary Java Virtual Machine updates, CGI, Servlets, and so on. This installation must be done to each node that will be in the failover path.

3. Configure the cluster resource.

4. Copy the content from your existing Web site to the new document root.

5. Modify your DNS entries to reflect the new IP address (unless you are reusing the same address).

By following these simple steps, you can easily convert your existing Web sites into a highly available, fault-tolerant site that will quickly recover from any hardware or software failure on its host server.

Summary

This chapter explored the Enterprise Web Server for NetWare, Novell's latest installment of their Web server offerings. You examined how to cluster enable the EWS in both an Active/Passive and an Active/Active configuration, and the advantages and disadvantages of each. The failover characteristics of the cluster-enabled Enterprise Web Server are as follows:

CLUSTER FAILOVER CLASSIFICATION INDEX	
Transparency	Very transparent
Active/Active or Active/Passive	Can be either
Length to failover	Both configurations are very fast, with Active/Active the quickest

You also learned how to migrate an existing EWS installation to a highly available clustered configuration.

## CHAPTER 14

Applying Novell Cluster Services with FTP Services

FTP services aren't terribly exciting and it might not be immediately apparent why clustering them is important. But in many cases, FTP-based file transfer is a component of an automated business process or Web site's backend functionality. If the FTP Server is unavailable, impact is experienced in other areas. Remember, high availability converges on the least common denominator. This chapter will help you eliminate FTP services as a potential single point of failure in a distributed application that depends on the availability of FTP services.

In this chapter, you learn about the NetWare FTP Server and how to configure FTP services on a cluster. You explore how the FTP Server enables access to files on NetWare volumes in LAN and SAN environments.

In addition, this chapter discusses the difference between Active/Passive and Active/Active clustering of FTP services. After reading this chapter, you will know how to create Active/Passive and Active/Active FTP Server configurations, and the advantages and disadvantages of each.

The chapter also includes steps to verify FTP Server failover, enabling you to test your configuration in a simulated server failure scenario. Finally, you learn about the expected failover behavior of clustered FTP services and what you can expect from different FTP clients.

Introducing the FTP Server

The NetWare FTP Server provides File Transfer Protocol (FTP) services for NetWare servers. FTP clients can transfer files to and from NetWare volumes. The NetWare FTP Server is based on the standard ARPANET File Transfer Protocol that runs over TCP/IP. Novell's FTP implementation conforms to RFC 959. You can perform file transfers using any FTP client by connecting to the FTP Server, running on NetWare.

The FTP Server is integrated with Novell Directory Services. Clients log in to the FTP Server using NDS-based user identity and login/password security. If a user has a default home directory, the FTP Server will automatically change to that directory. The home directory need not be located on the same NetWare server that runs the FTP Server. You can access other NetWare servers in the NDS tree whether or not they are also running FTP Servers.

Exploring the Major Features of the FTP Server

The FTP Server is implemented as an NLM: NWFTPD.NLM. It is selected by default during the NetWare 5.1 installation and might already be installed and running from the SYS volume of all your cluster nodes. A default configuration file named FTPSERV.CFG is created during the FTP Server installation and placed in the SYS:\ETC directory. If you installed NetWare the same way on all your cluster nodes, then your cluster will already have the necessary files installed to run the FTP Server on any cluster node.

Multiple Instances

You can load multiple instances of the FTP Server on the same NetWare server. Each instance can be configured either to bind to a different IP address or to different ports on a single IP address. Each instance can be used to provide FTP service to different sets of users. And each instance can be loaded with different configuration parameters such as IP addresses, port numbers or different access restrictions files, and so forth. However, the combination of IP address and port number should be unique for each instance. If the combination is not unique, then the FTP Servers with a clashing configuration will be unable to bind to their service addresses. The first FTP Server to bind its IP address and port will succeed and other FTP Servers with clashing configuration will fail. On any given node, only one FTP Server can bind to an IP address and port.

FTP Server instances directly support individual failover management via multiple cluster resources. You configure multiple FTP Server cluster resources with each one controlling a different FTP Server instance. By configuring a unique secondary IP address and cluster-enabled volume for each FTP Server cluster resource, you enable multiple FTP Servers to run and failover to any cluster node. It is possible to configure two or more FTP Servers to share the same IP address but have different ports, but this would prevent them from failing over to different nodes. An IP address can only be bound on one node at a time. This means that all FTP Servers that use the same IP address, but with different ports, must run on the same node. This restricts your failover options by forcing every FTP Server to run on the same node where the IP address is bound. It's a better idea to allocate a unique IP address for each individual FTP Server, which enables them to failover to any node independent of one another.

Remote Server Access

Using the remote server access feature, FTP users can navigate and access files from other NetWare servers in the same NDS tree. The remote servers need not be running the NetWare FTP Server and need not be a part of the cluster. You can use the FTP Server as a protocol gateway between FTP clients and volumes hosted by any NetWare server. The FTP Server converts FTP file transfer operations into NetWare Core Protocol (NCP) requests directed at the appropriate (remote) NetWare server.

Figure 14.1 shows how the NetWare FTP Server accesses remote NetWare servers.

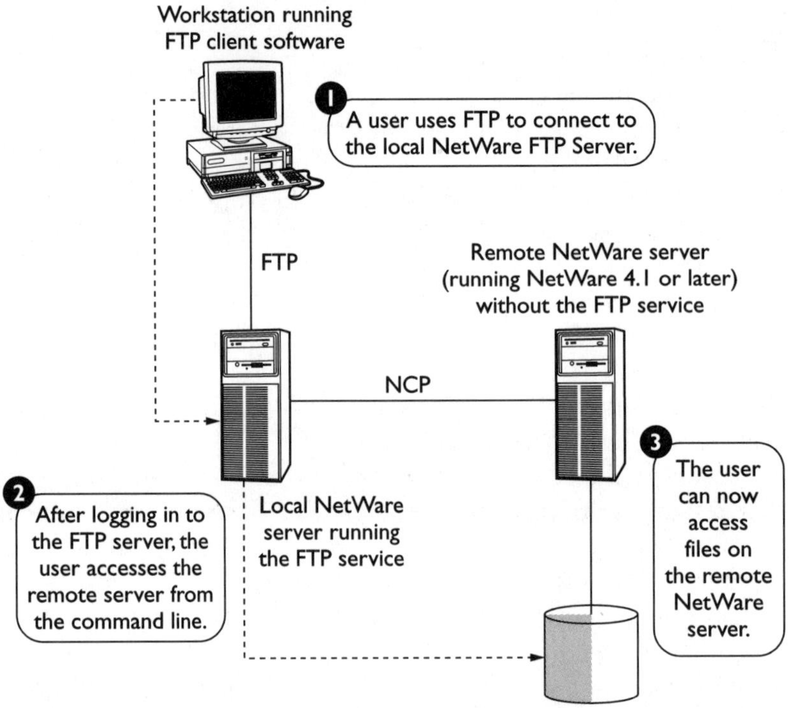

FIGURE 14.1 *Using the FTP Server as a gateway to access files on any NetWare server*

Understanding File Access

When you log in to the FTP Server with your NDS user name, the FTP Server attempts to provide access to your home directory regardless of which server has the corresponding NetWare volume mounted. The FTP Server and your home directory might be located on different NetWare servers. If either server is unavailable, you won't be able to access your files via FTP. If the FTP Server and your home directory are located on the same server, the FTP Server software provides access to your files by accessing the volume directly. Again, if this server is down, you won't be able to access your files.

In a clustered-SAN environment, any shared-disk volume can be mounted by any node in the cluster. If that node also runs the FTP Server, files on the shared-disk volume are accessible to FTP clients. If the node running the FTP Server should fail, any other node can take over by remounting the volume and restarting the FTP Server software. In this scenario, both the FTP Server and your home directory remain available — they failover to another node together.

The difference between remote server access and shared-disk volumes can be confusing at first. Both provide access to files on NetWare volumes from any server. When the FTP Server accesses a file on a remote server, it uses the native NetWare core protocol over the LAN to contact the host server of the volume containing the file. Only this server can do the necessary disk I/O to retrieve the file's contents and return it to the requesting FTP Server. When the FTP Server software accesses a file on a shared-disk volume mounted by the same server that is running the FTP Server software, the file is accessed over the SAN as though it were on a local disk. Performance is better in this scenario. Because any cluster node can mount a volume on the SAN, it is usually better to run the FTP Server on the node that has it mounted. But all this doesn't preclude remote server access to NetWare servers not attached to the SAN. Nor does it preclude an FTP Server running on one cluster node from accessing files on a volume hosted by a different cluster node. It just means that there are tradeoffs to be made. You might not want every cluster node to run an FTP Server, especially if your clients are configured to contact only a single IP address and, therefore, only a single FTP Server instance. For example, to simplify client access, you can configure a single FTP Server instance, IP address and shared disk volume so that all clients need only know one IP address. Alternatively, if you configure an FTP Server and IP address for every shared-disk volume, then clients will need to know which IP address to use in order to reach files on a given volume. Or you can have a single FTP Server and IP address function as a gateway for all shared disk volumes (even those located on other nodes) and simplify client access at the expense of performance. The main consideration is how many shared disk volumes you want to provide FTP access to. If the answer is one, then create a single FTP Server instance. If the answer is more than one, then you have the choice of creating one FTP Server instance per shared disk volume or one FTP Server for all volumes and using that FTP Server to access the other volumes regardless of the node they might be located on but at the expense of remote LAN access.

Figure 14.2 shows how the FTP Server accesses files on cluster-enabled volumes. Any cluster node can run the FTP Server and access files on cluster-enabled volumes over the SAN.

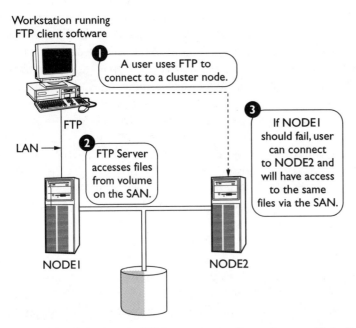

Workstation running
FTP client software

① A user uses FTP to
connect to a cluster node.

② FTP Server
accesses files
from volume
on the SAN.

③ If NODE1
should fail, user
can connect
to NODE2 and
will have access
to the same
files via the SAN.

FTP

LAN →

NODE1   NODE2

FIGURE 14.2 *Using the FTP Server to access files on cluster-enabled volumes*

The FTP Server provides access to files located in individual user home directories. To log in to the FTP Server, you must specify your NDS user name and password. The current working directory of the FTP session will be set to your home directory. If the FTP Server cannot locate your home directory, it will set the current working directory to the SYS:PUBLIC directory of the server running the FTP Server. You can configure the FTP Server to change to a different default home directory if desired.

TIP

The location of user home directories is an important factor when you're designing a clustered FTP Server configuration. The FTP Server and volumes containing user home directories need not be located on the same NetWare server. But as has been discussed, *co-locating* the FTP Server with a NetWare volume offers the best performance in a SAN environment.

Anonymous user login is also supported by the FTP Server. The anonymous user must have a corresponding NDS user object. The current working directory is set to either the anonymous user's home directory, to SYS:PUBLIC if the home directory cannot be located, or to a configured default directory. You might, for example, use the anonymous user's home directory to provide public access to a shared download or file transfer area.

NOTE **Because the FTP Server uses NDS-based rights to enable FTP client users to access NetWare files, Novell recommends using cluster-enabled volumes with the FTP Server. Cluster-enabled volumes provide the necessary trustee management, ensuring that rights remain intact after volume failover. Even if you configure only an anonymous user, the FTP Server requires creation of a corresponding NDS user object and grants rights to the anonymous user's home directory.**

Why Cluster the FTP Server?

Depending on your application, the FTP Server might represent an important potential single point of failure. Suppose your FTP Server is not available because the server it was running on has failed and is being repaired or replaced. How long might this take? Do you have users that can't work while the FTP Server is unavailable? Do you have customers that can't interact with your business while the FTP Server is unavailable?

Some key applications of the FTP Server that you might not want to have unavailable include the following:

▸ Web content publishing to a Web server

▸ Access to software patch downloads

▸ Automated file transfer between applications

By configuring the FTP Server to run on a cluster, you ensure that the FTP service is highly available. Clients can access files via an FTP Server cluster resource no matter what node it is running on. By also configuring the FTP Server to access files on a cluster-enabled volume, you ensure access to files no matter which node mounts the volume. By collocating the FTP Server with a cluster-enabled volume so the same node runs the FTP Server and mounts the volume, you ensure that both the FTP service and file access remain available in the event of node failure. Automatic cluster failover ensures that the FTP Server continues to run and continues to have access to user files, without manual administrative intervention.

FTP Server Cluster Resource

The NetWare FTP Server can be configured to use secondary IP addresses and cluster-enabled volumes. This satisfies the requirements necessary to make FTP services location transparent in a cluster: The same FTP Server instance can run on any cluster node. FTP clients will access the FTP Server via its secondary IP address, and the FTP Server will access files on a cluster-enabled volume. The following three elements comprise an FTP Server cluster resource:

▶ Unique secondary IP address — Configuring a DNS entry for this secondary IP address enables FTP clients to access the FTP Server by name.

▶ Cluster-enabled volume (which requires a unique secondary IP address) — A cluster-enabled volume isn't absolutely necessary if your FTP Server functions only as a gateway to files on remote NetWare servers. However, even if you achieve a highly available FTP gateway service, you still lose access to files if the remote NetWare server is not clustered and becomes unavailable. By combining the FTP Server with a cluster-enabled volume, you achieve highly available FTP services and access to user files via any node running the FTP Server cluster resource. Therefore, we recommend you also configure user home directories on cluster-enabled volumes.

▶ An instance of the FTP Server with configuration parameters set to use the secondary IP address and cluster-enabled volume — It is possible that you might want to provide FTP access to all cluster-enabled volumes in your cluster. Each cluster-enabled volume would then also run a separate FTP Server instance. This is considered an Active/Active FTP Server configuration — any number of nodes will be running different instances of the FTP Server. If you have a single cluster-enabled volume you want to provide FTP access to, then you create an Active/Passive FTP Server — a single instance of the FTP Server runs on one node at a time and fails over to any other node.

Installing the FTP Server

To verify that you already have the FTP Server installed on your cluster nodes, follow these steps:

1. Type **NWCONFIG** at the server console prompt.

2. Select Product Options, and then press Enter.

3. Select View ⇨ Configure ⇨ Remove installed products, then press Enter.

4. Press the down arrow to scroll through the Currently Installed Products. Search for a line that contains "NWFTP" or "NetWare FTP Server."

If you don't have the FTP Server software installed on all the nodes you want to failover FTP services to, install the software from your NetWare 5.*x* installation CD, following these steps:

1. Place the NetWare 5.*x* installation CD in the server.

2. If the CD does not automatically activate and mount, type LOAD CDROM.

3. Type NWCONFIG at the server console prompt. The main menu of the NetWare Configuration utility appears.

4. Select Product Options, and then press Enter.

5. From the Product Options menu, select Install a product not listed, then press Enter.

6. If the NetWare 5.*x* CD path is listed in the Previously Specified Paths list, select it and then press Enter. Otherwise:

  a. Press Esc.

  b. Press F3.

  c. Type the path to the root of the CD (for instance, NW51:), then press Enter.

7. From the GUI installation screen, select the NetWare FTP Server component, and then click Next.

8. Click Finish.

9. Reapply the current NetWare support pack after installing any new components.

With the FTP Server software installed onto the SYS volume of each of your cluster nodes, it's time to examine the tradeoffs of configuring FTP services for Active/Passive or Active/Active failover before you create your first FTP Server cluster resource.

▶ · ◀

Clustering the FTP Server

You have a choice when deciding how to configure FTP services for your cluster:

▶ *Active/Passive FTP Server* — Do you want to run a single instance of the FTP Server on one node of the cluster and have it failover to any other node?

▶ *Active/Active FTP Servers* — Do you want to run multiple instances of the FTP Server on different cluster nodes and allow any instance to failover to any other node whether or not that node is already running a different instance of the FTP Server?

If you have users with home directories located on different cluster-enabled volumes, then you might decide to enable FTP services for each volume. Create an Active/Active configuration in this case. Alternatively, if you intend to provide FTP services to a common public access file area, for example, then create a single Active/Passive FTP Server.

Whether you decide to set up a single Active/Passive or multiple Active/Active FTP Server cluster resources, you need to edit the FTP Server configuration file parameters to specify secondary IP addresses and the names of cluster-enabled volumes. Table 14.1 lists the FTPSERV.CFG parameters that relate to configuring FTP services on a cluster.

TABLE 14.1

FTPSERV.CFG Parameters Relating to Cluster Configuration

PARAMETER	DEFAULT VALUE	DESCRIPTION
HOST_IP_ADDR	All IP addresses bound to all network interfaces.	IP address to accept client FTP requests.
FTP_PORT	Standard FTP port: 21	The port number to which the FTP Server should bind and listen for connection requests.
ANONYMOUS_HOME	SYS:/PUBLIC	The anonymous user's home directory.
DEFAULT_USER_HOME	SYS:/PUBLIC	The default home directory for NDS users.

You must use the forward slash "/" to configure a home directory, not backslash "\". Also, ensure that the necessary trustee assignments are applied to the default or anonymous user home directories if you're not using the FTP Server's default (SYS:/PUBLIC**) location.**

TIP

A default FTPSERV.CFG is copied to SYS:\ETC when the FTP Server is installed. The FTP Server reads its configuration only from a file located in the SYS:ETC directory. However, you can create and then specify different configuration files when you load the FTP Server. To load the FTP Server with an alternative configuration, use the following syntax: NWFTPD -c <configuration file>. Each FTP Server instance requires its own configuration file and that file must be located in the SYS:ETC directory.

Creating an Active/Passive FTP Server

An Active/Passive FTP Server is a single instance of the FTP Server configured to run on any single cluster node. You create only one FTP Server instance for the entire cluster. In this configuration, only one cluster node is active and providing FTP services to clients. Other nodes are passive with respect to FTP services. An Active/Passive FTP Server runs on a single node at a time but may failover to any other node. The failover node starts running FTP Server software as a result of an Active/Passive FTP Server failing over to it.

Follow these steps to create an Active/Passive FTP Server:

1. Create or use an existing cluster volume resource.

Chapter 9 discusses working with storage and volumes. Create an NSS volume on shared disks and then cluster enable it by allocating a unique IP address. The steps provided in Chapter 9 detail this procedure.

X-REF

2. Create an FTP Server configuration file.

3. Extend the cluster volume resource by adding FTP Server startup and shutdown commands to its load and unload scripts.

Creating the FTP Server Configuration File

Using the default FTP Server configuration file found in SYS:\ETC\FTPSERV. CFG as a starting point, make the following edits:

1. Set HOST_IP_ADDR to the IP address of your cluster-enabled volume.

2. If you desire a different default anonymous home directory, set `ANONYMOUS_HOME` to a directory on your cluster-enabled volume.

3. If you desire a different default user home directory, set `DEFAULT_USER_HOME` to a directory on your cluster-enabled volume.

4. Save your changes to a new configuration file dedicated to this instance of the FTP Server.

5. Ensure that the new FTP Server configuration file is copied to the `SYS:\ETC` directory of every cluster node that can run the FTP Server cluster resource.

Figure 14.3 shows the result of editing `FTPSERV.CFG` and saving the changes to a new file called `HA_FTP.CFG`. Note the IP address (10.7.5.101) and name of the cluster-enabled volume (VOL1) in the figure. The anonymous and default user home directories are set to a top-level directory on the cluster-enabled volume named `VOL1:/PUBLIC`.

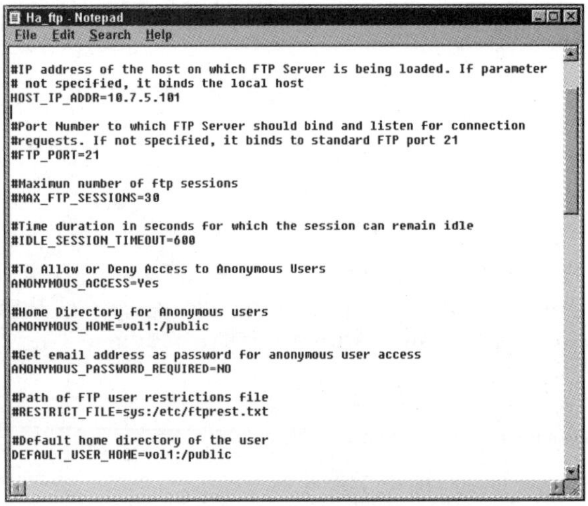


```
#IP address of the host on which FTP Server is being loaded. If parameter
# not specified, it binds the local host
HOST_IP_ADDR=10.7.5.101

#Port Number to which FTP Server should bind and listen for connection
#requests. If not specified, it binds to standard FTP port 21
#FTP_PORT=21

#Maximun number of ftp sessions
#MAX_FTP_SESSIONS=30

#Time duration in seconds for which the session can remain idle
#IDLE_SESSION_TIMEOUT=600

#To Allow or Deny Access to Anonymous Users
ANONYMOUS_ACCESS=Yes

#Home Directory for Anonymous users
ANONYMOUS_HOME=vol1:/public

#Get email address as password for anonymous user access
ANONYMOUS_PASSWORD_REQUIRED=NO

#Path of FTP user restrictions file
#RESTRICT_FILE=sys:/etc/ftprest.txt

#Default home directory of the user
DEFAULT_USER_HOME=vol1:/public
```

FIGURE 14.3 *FTP Server configuration file for an Active/Passive FTP Server*

Extending the Cluster Volume Resource

Add commands to your cluster volume resource's load and unload scripts to start up and shut down the FTP Server software:

TIP

To avoid potential problems, ensure that the proper ordering of load and unload commands is strictly adhered to. It is important that the secondary IP address is bound before the FTP Server software is started, for example. The FTP Server software will fail to start if its IP address isn't bound.

1. Launch ConsoleOne, then browse to the cluster container object. Your cluster resources are displayed in the right-hand pane.

2. Right-click the Cluster Volume Resource, and then select Properties to display its property tabs.

3. Select the Load tab, and then add the following command to the *end* of the load script:

```
nwftpd -c ha_ftp.cfg
```

Figure 14.4 shows the result of editing the load script. VOL1_SERVER is an existing cluster volume resource. The command to start up the FTP Server is added to the end of the existing load script.

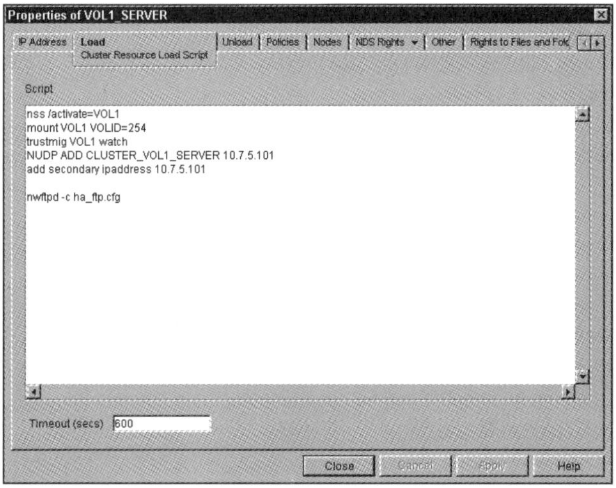

FIGURE 14.4 *Command to start up the FTP Server added to the end of the load script*

4. Select the Unload tab, then add the following command to the *start* of the unload script:

```
unload nwftpd
```

Figure 14.5 shows the result of editing the unload script. VOL1_SERVER is an existing cluster volume resource. The command to shut down the FTP Server is added to the *start* of the existing unload script.

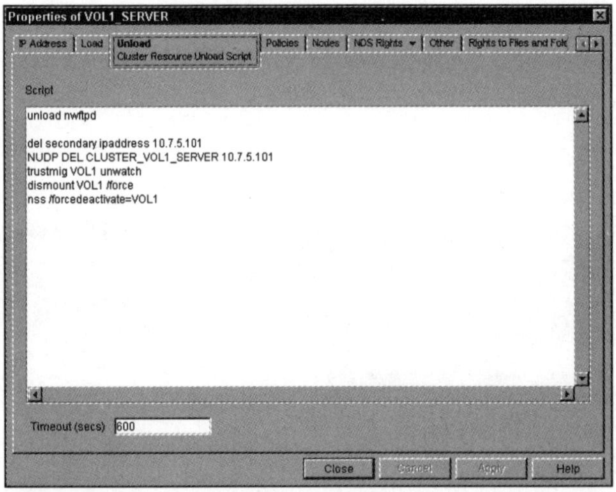

Properties of VOL1_SERVER

| IP Address | Load | **Unload** | | Policies | Nodes | NDS Rights ▾ | Other | Rights to Files and Fold | ◀ ▶ |

Cluster Resource Unload Script

Script

```
unload nwftpd

del secondary ipaddress 10.7.5.101
NUDP DEL CLUSTER_VOL1_SERVER 10.7.5.101
trustmig VOL1 unwatch
dismount VOL1 /force
nss /forcedeactivate=VOL1
```

Timeout (secs) 600

Close   Cancel   Apply   Help

FIGURE 14.5 *Command to shut down the FTP Server added to the start of the unload script*

5. Modify the Policies and Nodes configurations as desired, then click OK.

NOTE

> **If the cluster volume resource is in the Running state when you make these changes, an informational dialog box is displayed to remind you to offline and then online the resource for property changes to take effect.**

Running the FTP Server Cluster Resource

If your cluster volume resource was in the Running state when you edited its load and unload scripts, you will need to offline and then online the resource again before your changes take effect. When you online the cluster resource, it will execute the commands in the load script, including the newly added command to start the FTP Server.

To offline a running cluster resource, follow these steps:

1. Launch ConsoleOne, then browse to the cluster container object.

2. Select View ⇨ Cluster State.

3. Select your resource in the Cluster Resource table. This opens the Cluster Resource Manager dialog box.

4. Click Offline.

To online a cluster resource, follow the preceding steps, but click Online instead.

Verify that the FTP Server cluster resource successfully enters the Running state by inspecting the Cluster Resource table. Figure 14.6 shows VOL1_SERVER running on NODE1 — the result of selecting VOL1_SERVER and clicking Online.

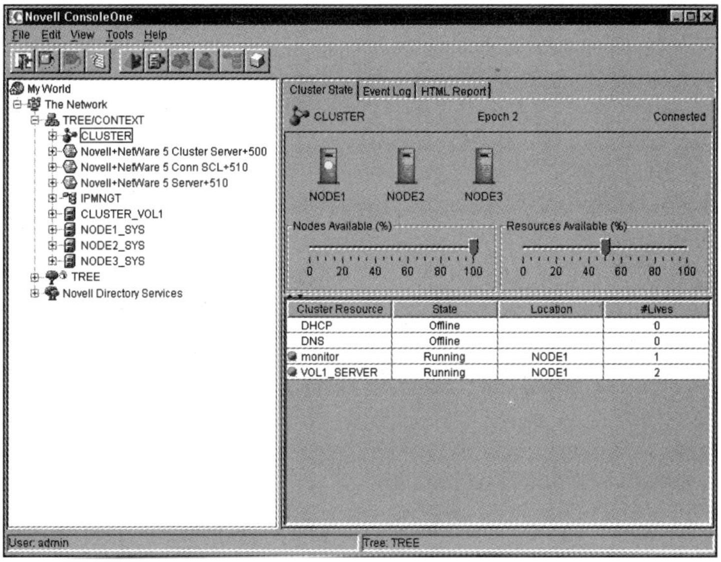

FIGURE 14.6 *VOL1_SERVER running on NODE1*

Creating Multiple Active/Active FTP Servers

An Active/Active FTP Server is a single instance of the FTP Server configured to run on any single cluster node. You can create multiple FTP Server instances for the entire cluster. Multiple cluster nodes are active and provide FTP services to clients. Multiple Active/Active FTP Servers run on multiple nodes and may failover to any other node. All failover nodes run the FTP Server software by default. When an Active/Active FTP Server fails over, the FTP Server software is already running on the failover node and dynamically enables a new FTP Server instance corresponding to the Active/Active FTP Server cluster resource.

An Active/Active FTP Server corresponds to a uniquely configured FTP Server instance. This means each Active/Active FTP Server requires a unique IP address and default home directory configured via a separate FTP Server configuration file. Each Active/Active FTP Server has its own configuration file, secondary IP address, and cluster-enabled volume.

One of the differences between Active/Active and Active/Passive FTP Server configurations is the method used to start the FTP Server software. The FTP Server software is started and shut down from an Active/Passive FTP Server cluster resource's load and unload scripts. In Active/Active FTP Server configurations, your cluster nodes start the FTP Server software from the AUTOEXEC.NCF file. Every cluster node runs the FTP Server software by default, before Cluster Services starts any cluster resources.

To enable any FTP Server instance to migrate from one node to another node (without affecting other FTP Server instances running on either the node the instance is leaving or the node it is joining) the FTP Server software is run on all nodes with all FTP Server instances initially disabled. This initially disabled state for FTP Server instances means the FTP Server software is primed, but it remains dormant until specific FTP Server instances are activated. When an instance is activated, the FTP Server provides FTP service using that instance's configuration parameters. You can activate an FTP Server instance by binding its IP address and mounting the volume containing its default user home directory.

Outlined here are the steps to create an Active/Active FTP Server:

I. Create or use an existing cluster volume resource.

X-REF

Chapter 9 discusses working with storage and volumes. Create an NSS volume on shared disks and then cluster enable it by allocating a unique IP address. The steps provided in Chapter 9 detail this procedure.

2. Create an FTP Server configuration file.

3. Load a disabled instance of the FTP Server on all cluster nodes.

For each Active/Active FTP Server you create, take note of the unique IP address and FTP Server configuration filename. You will need this when adding commands to AUTOEXEC.NCF **to run a disabled instance of the FTP Server on all cluster nodes.**

TIP

Creating the FTP Server Configuration File

Using the default FTP Server configuration file found in SYS:\ETC\FTPSERV. CFG as a starting point, make the following edits:

1. Set HOST_IP_ADDR to the IP address of your cluster-enabled volume.

2. If you desire a different default anonymous home directory, set ANONYMOUS_HOME to a directory on your cluster-enabled volume.

3. If you desire a different default user home directory, set DEFAULT_USER_HOME to a directory on your cluster-enabled volume.

4. Save your changes to a new configuration file dedicated to this instance of the FTP Server.

5. Ensure that the new FTP Server configuration file is copied to the SYS:\ETC directory of every cluster node that will run the FTP Server cluster resource.

The steps to create the FTP Server configuration file are identical whether you are creating an Active/Passive or Active/Active FTP Server.

NOTE

Figure 14.7 shows the result of editing FTPSERV.CFG and saving the changes to a new file called FTP_2.CFG. Note the IP address (10.7.5.102) and name of the cluster-enabled volume (VOL2) in the figure. The anonymous and default user home directories are set to a top-level directory on the cluster-enabled volume named VOL2:/PUBLIC.

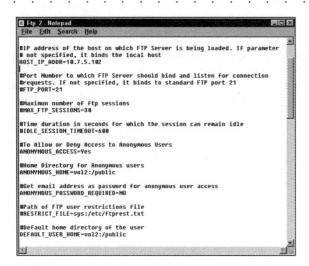

FIGURE 14.7 *FTP Server configuration file for an Active/Active FTP Server.*

Loading the FTP Server Software on all Nodes

On all cluster nodes that could potentially run your Active/Active FTP Server, add the following commands to the server's `AUTOEXEC.NCF` startup file. Ensure you add these commands before the `LDNCS` command used to start Cluster Services:

```
SET ALLOW IP ADDRESS DUPLICATES=ON

#

ADD SECONDARY IPADDRESS <ipaddress>


# Load FTP Server instance(s)

nwftpd -c <instance.cfg>


LOAD DELAY.NLM

DELAY 10
```

```
DEL SECONDARY IPADDRESS <ipaddress>
```

```
SET ALLOW IP ADDRESS DUPLICATES=OFF
```

The `DELAY.NLM` and `DELAY 10` lines are added to make sure the FTP Server software has sufficient time to start up before deleting secondary IP addresses. If they are deleted too soon, the FTP Server may not start up properly. Ten seconds is a good default time for most configurations.

Change `<ipaddress>` and `<instance.cfg>` to match the secondary IP address and FTP Server configuration filename of your Active/Active FTP Server. For each additional Active/Active FTP Server you create, add additional commands to add the secondary IP address, start nwftpd with the configuration file, and delete the secondary IP address.

Figure 14.8 shows the changes made to `AUTOEXEC.NCF` for two Active/Active FTP Servers. The first FTP Server has a secondary IP address of 10.7.5.102 and its configuration filename is FTP_2.CFG. The second FTP Server has a secondary IP address of 10.7.5.103 and its configuration filename is FTP_3.CFG. Note that the FTP Server commands are added before the `LDNCS.NCF` command used to start Cluster Services.

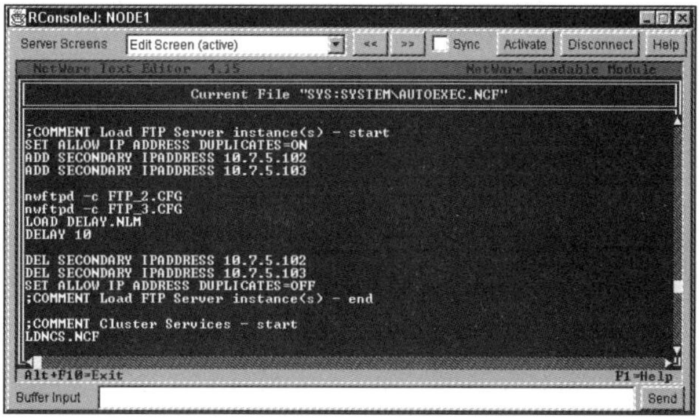

FIGURE 14.8 *AUTOEXEC.NCF changes for two Active/Active FTP Servers*

Once you complete all this, reboot your nodes in the FTP Server failover path and verify that the FTP Server software loads correctly on all nodes.

Running the FTP Server Cluster Resource

Your Active/Active FTP Server is enabled when you online the corresponding cluster volume resource. The cluster volume resource binds its secondary IP address and mounts its volume. The FTP Server software then enables the corresponding FTP Server instance and provides FTP service to clients connecting via the secondary IP address.

To online a cluster resource, follow these steps:

1. Launch ConsoleOne, then browse to the cluster container object.

2. Select View ⇨ Cluster State.

3. Select your resource in the Cluster Resource table. This opens the Cluster Resource Manager dialog box.

4. Click Online.

Verify that the FTP Server cluster resource successfully enters the Running state by inspecting the Cluster Resource table. Figure 14.9 shows two Active/Active FTP Server cluster resources. VOL2_SERVER is running on NODE2, and VOL3_SERVER is running on NODE3.

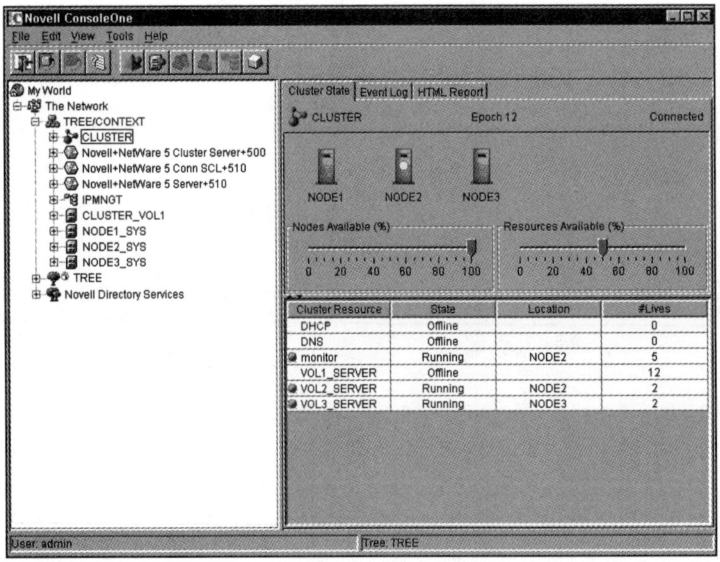

FIGURE 14.9 VOL2_SERVER running on NODE2, and VOL3_SERVER running on NODE3

▶ • ◀

Testing FTP Server Failover

Whether you configure an Active/Passive FTP Server or multiple Active/Active FTP Servers, you should test FTP services in normal and simulated failure scenarios.

With your FTP Server cluster resource running on its most preferred cluster node, if available, or some other node if not, test the FTP Server by connecting to its secondary IP address. For example, on a PC, use the FTP client software that comes with Windows. From a DOS command prompt, type `ftp 10.7.5.101`.

The FTP client responds with a "Connected to" message, then prompts for a user name. Log in by typing your NDS user name and your password. You can also log in as an anonymous user by typing **anonymous** at the prompt. Figure 14.10 shows an anonymous user logged into the FTP Server at 10.7.5.101. The anonymous user's default home directory contains a single subdirectory, named Folder.

NOTE

By default, anonymous access is disabled. To enable it, load `NWFTPD -a`**. This will prompt you for a user name and password of a user with sufficient rights to create a user object in the default context of the server. This will also modify the default configuration file to allow anonymous access. After doing this, you should review the changes and duplicate the appropriate changes to your configuration files.**

▶ • ◀

```
Command Prompt - ftp 10.7.5.101                         _ [] x
C:\>
C:\>ftp 10.7.5.101
Connected to 10.7.5.101.
220 Service Ready for new User
User (10.7.5.101:(none)): anonymous
230 User anonymous Logged in Successfully
ftp>
ftp> dir
200 PORT Command OK
150 Opening data connection
total 0
d [RWCEAFMS] admin                        512 Jun 10 14:46 Folder
226 Transfer Complete
81 bytes received in 0.00 seconds (81000.00 Kbytes/sec)
ftp>
ftp>
```

FIGURE 14.10 *Using the Windows FTP client to log in to an Active/Passive FTP Server*

Simulating Node Failure

You should simulate a node failure to test that your FTP Server cluster resource properly fails over. Consider and test a worst-case failure scenario.

The following test should be performed on a development cluster, as it will force all cluster resources running on your FTP Server node to failover.

WARNING

For example, while still connected to the FTP Server, simulate an unexpected node failure by power cycling NODE1. Your client FTP session is disconnected. Wait for the FTP Server cluster resource to automatically restart on another node, then manually reopen the FTP session to 10.7.5.101. Also try logging into the FTP Server before it has completely failed over. The FTP client will return an error until the FTP Server is available.

Figure 14.11 shows the result of a simulated node failure. The client FTP session is broken but easily repaired by opening a new connection to the same IP address. Access to files is reestablished as soon as the client connection is reopened. The failover process typically takes less than 30 seconds.

```
Command Prompt - ftp 10.7.5.101                          _ □ X
C:\>ftp 10.7.5.101
Connected to 10.7.5.101.
220 Service Ready for new User
User (10.7.5.101:(none)): anonymous
230 User anonymous Logged in Successfully
ftp> dir
200 PORT Command OK
150 Opening data connection
total 0
d [RWCEAFMS]     32800              512 Jun 10 14:46 Folder
226 Transfer Complete
81 bytes received in 0.00 seconds (81000.00 Kbytes/sec)
ftp>
ftp> dir
Connection closed by remote host.
ftp> open 10.7.5.101
Connected to 10.7.5.101.
220 Service Ready for new User
User (10.7.5.101:(none)): anonymous
230 User anonymous Logged in Successfully
ftp>
ftp> _
```

FIGURE 14.11 *Behavior of the Windows FTP client when the FTP Server fails over*

Client Reconnect Behavior

FTP clients react differently to abrupt termination of an FTP connection. The default Windows FTP client is the least sophisticated. You have to manually reconnect to the FTP Server. Other FTP clients offer additional features and increased sophistication. For example, some clients enable you to configure your user name and password and automatically reconnect to the FTP Server with no human intervention whatsoever. Some clients are able to resubmit an interrupted file transfer operation, enabling completely transparent failover from the user's perspective.

Summary

Even though most people take FTP services for granted, if the FTP Server is down, the result can have a negative impact for people or business processes. Clustering the FTP Server is an important part of enabling overall high availability. A holistic approach to high availability should include consideration of every application component no matter how insignificant they might seem. Chances are that if everything else is operating normally, the component you overlooked is the one that resulted in unavailability. This chapter has demonstrated how to prevent the FTP Server from becoming your single point of failure.

In this chapter, you learned about the NetWare FTP Server and how to configure FTP services on a cluster. You examined how the FTP Server enables access to files on NetWare volumes in LAN and SAN environments.

You also learned how to create Active/Passive and Active/Active FTP Server configurations, and the advantages and disadvantages of each.

Finally, the chapter discussed the expected failover behavior of clustered FTP services and what you can expect from different FTP clients. The failover characteristics of clustered FTP services are as follows:

CLUSTER FAILOVER CLASSIFICATION INDEX	
Transparency	Very transparent
Active/Active or Active/Passive	Either
Time to failover	Both configurations are very fast, typically taking a few tens of seconds to failover

Applying Novell Cluster Services with DNS and DHCP Services

In this chapter, you learn about Novell's NetWare 5.*x* implementation of Domain Name System (DNS) and Dynamic Host Configuration Protocol (DHCP) services and the DNS-DHCP Management Console and explore how to configure DNS and DHCP services in a cluster environment for automatic failover of these services.

Novell's newest approach to both DNS and DHCP services is unique in the industry — by storing the databases in Novell Directory Services (NDS) instead of a flat text file, you now have the ability to easily move these services from one machine to another without worrying about copying files around or backing up and restoring the database. This flexibility in administration makes clustering these services very easy — the data is already in NDS.

If you're already familiar with the NetWare 5.*x* implementation of DNS and DHCP, jump ahead to the section "Cluster Enabling DNS and DHCP Services" later in the chapter. If not, the following sections lead you through Novell's implementation of DNS, DHCP, and the Java-based DNS/DHCP Management Console.

Introducing Domain Name System and Dynamic Host Configuration Protocol Services

Novell's DNS/DHCP Services integrates the Domain Name System (DNS) and Dynamic Host Configuration Protocol (DHCP) into the NDS database. This provides centralized administration, configuration, and enterprise-wide management of IP addresses and hostnames, utilizing NDS replication to distribute and back up this information.

The DNS/DHCP Management Console is a Java application that provides a graphical user interface to manage the objects created to support DNS and DHCP. The DNS/DHCP Management Console can function as a standalone application, or it can be accessed from the Tools menu of the NetWare Administrator utility.

DNS Services

The DNS software in Novell DNS/DHCP Services integrates DNS information into the NDS database. You can use the DNS/DHCP Management Console to configure DNS from the desktop of a client where it is installed, or it can be launched from the NetWare Administrator utility.

Integrating DNS with NDS also enables an update interaction between DNS and DHCP through the Dynamic DNS (DDNS) feature. When the DDNS feature is active, whenever a host is assigned an IP address by DHCP, the DNS information is automatically updated to associate the hostname with the new address.

By implementing DNS in this manner, Novell has shifted the concept of a primary or secondary zone away from the server to the zone itself. Once you use the configuration utility to configure the zone, the data is available to any Novell DNS servers you choose to make authoritative for the zone. Thus, it is possible to have multiple servers throughout the organization configured for the same "primary" zone, all with the ability to update the zone information directly. The Novell DNS server takes advantage of NDS replication to distribute and protect the DNS data.

Novell DNS/DHCP Services can fully interoperate with non-Novell DNS servers. The DNS software in Novell DNS/DHCP Services conforms to BIND 4.9.5 and can process zone transfers with BIND 8.*x*-compliant DNS servers. The Novell DNS server can act as either a master DNS server or a secondary DNS server in relation to non-Novell DNS servers. Thus the Novell DNS server can act as the master DNS server and transfer data to non-Novell secondary servers. Or alternatively, one Novell DNS server can act as a secondary DNS server and transfer data in from a non-Novell master server. All Novell DNS servers can then access the data through NDS replication.

Novell DNS/DHCP Services provide the following DNS features:

▸ All DNS configuration is stored in NDS, facilitating enterprise-wide management and the ability to quickly replace a failed DNS server.

▸ A Novell DNS server can be a secondary name server to another zone (DNS data loaded into NDS through a zone transfer), or it can be a primary name server (on which you configure DNS data using the DNS/DHCP Management Console), allowing you to mix NetWare DNS servers in your existing environment without the need to replace all current DNS servers.

▸ DNS data can be read in from a BIND master file to populate NDS for convenient upgrades from BIND implementations of DNS. This allows you to take your existing DNS database from UNIX, Linux, Windows NT, or previous versions of NetWare, and import the data into NDS without the need to reenter any data.

▸ DNS data can be exported from NDS into BIND master file format, enabling you to export a NetWare 5.*x* DNS database to an industry standard format should you decide to migrate from NetWare's DNS to another vendor's DNS.

▸ Root server information is stored in NDS and shared by all NDS-based DNS servers, allowing a single root server update to be used by all NetWare DNS servers without your having to manually update each server's database.

▸ Zone transfers can be made to and from NDS through NetWare servers and include interoperability with non-NDS–based DNS, allowing NetWare's DNS server to coexist with your ISP or other corporate (non-NetWare) DNS servers.

▸ A Novell DNS server can be authoritative for multiple domains.

▸ Novell DNS servers maintain a cache of data from NDS so they can respond to queries quickly, even if NDS is not currently available. This cache also allows a Novell DNS server to act as a caching or forwarding server instead of an authoritative server for zones.

▸ Novell DNS Services supports multihoming and will respond to DNS queries on all interfaces bound to the server.

▸ Novell DNS Services supports a round-robin process of responses to queries with multiple Address records (A records) for a domain name, which allows multiple hosts to share the same DNS name for load balancing.

Novell DNS Services supports the standards of the Internet Request For Comments (RFCs) in Table 15.1.

T A B L E   15.1

Novell DNS Service Support for RFCs

INTERNET RFC NUMBER	RFC DESCRIPTION
RFC 819	Domain Naming Convention for Internet User Applications
RFC 920	Domain Requirements
RFC 974	Mail Routing and Domain System

INTERNET RFC NUMBER	RFC DESCRIPTION
RFC 1032	Domain Administrator's Guide
RFC 1033	Domain Administrator's Operations Guide
RFC 1034	Domain Names, Concepts, and Facilities
RFC 1035	Domain Names, Implementation, and Specification
RFC 1036	Standard Interchange of USENET Messages
RFC 1101	DNS Encoding of Network, Names, and other Types
RFC 1122	Requirements for Internet Hosts, Communications Layers
RFC 1123	Requirements for Internet Hosts, Application, and Support

DHCP Services

A NetWare 5.x DHCP server automatically provides IP addresses and configuration information to DHCP clients upon request. This automatic assignment of IP address and configuration information greatly reduces the amount of work required to configure and maintain large IP networks.

DHCP provides for both static and dynamic configuration of IP clients. Static configuration enables you to assign a specific IP address and configuration to a client with a specific MAC address. When DHCP assigns IP addresses dynamically, DHCP clients are assigned an IP address that is chosen from a range of available addresses that are valid for that client's physical network. You can use dynamic address assignment when you are not concerned about which IP address a particular client uses. Each DHCP client that requests an address assignment can also use the other DHCP configuration parameters, such as default gateway, DNS Name Server address, WINS server address, Service Location Protocol (SLP) configuration, and NetWare IP (NWIP) configuration, among many others.

DHCP can limit the amount of time a DHCP client can use an IP address. This is known as the *lease time*. You can use the lease time to allow a large number of clients to use a limited number of IP addresses. DHCP is based on BOOTP and maintains backward compatibility, allowing clients to make either BOOTP or DHCP requests to obtain an IP address.

Key Features of Novell's DHCP Service

Novell's DHCP Service differs from most other vendors' implementations by storing all configuration and lease information in the NDS database. Such an arrangement allows for enterprise-wide management from any location, as well as NDS access controls to determine which users have the rights to modify DHCP configuration. Storing the configuration and lease information in NDS also gives administrators the ability to quickly recover from a server failure — if a DHCP server fails, another server can be configured to handle the subnets of the failed server. The service is then started on that server, and all configuration and lease information is maintained.

Novell's DHCP service allows DHCP option configurations, such as default gateway, DNS server address, SLP information, NetWare IP information, and so on, to be set at three levels:

- ▶ The enterprise level for DHCP options such as DNS servers that do not vary from subnet to subnet

- ▶ The subnet level for DHCP options such as default gateway that will be different for each subnet

- ▶ The specific client level for any option that should be unique to a single client

Novell's DHCP Service is implemented as a single NLM (DHCPSRVR.NLM) that works for both LAN-based clients and remote access (RAS) clients. This allows a single point of administration and configuration for all clients needing IP configuration whether they are local, across the WAN, or dialing in.

The DHCP server includes a "Ping Ahead" function, which, if enabled, causes the server to attempt to ping an address before it leases the address to a client. If the server receives a response, it knows that this address is already in use, and it will skip this address and go to the next address in the range (and attempt to ping it). This function prevents a common problem that occurs when a user configures his or her workstation with a static IP address that happens to be in the DHCP server's range.

Novell DNS/DHCP Services supports the features that were previously provided by Novell DHCP Server 2.0 and supports the standards of the RFCs in Table 15.2.

TABLE 15.2

Novell DNS/DHCP-Supported RFC Standards

RFC NUMBER	RFC DESCRIPTION
RFC 2131	Dynamic Host Configuration Protocol
RFC 2132	DHCP Options and BOOTP Vendor Extensions
RFC 2241	DHCP Options and Novell Directory Services
RFC 2242	NetWare/IP Domain Name and Information

Novell DNS/DHCP Services also supports the BOOTP standards of the RFCs in Table 15.3.

TABLE 15.3

Novell's BOOTP-Supported RFC Standards

RFC NUMBER	RFC DESCRIPTION
RFC 1497	BOOTP Vendor Information Extensions
RFC 1534	Interoperation between DHCP and BOOTP
RFC 1542	Clarifications and Extensions for the Bootstrap Protocol

Identifying DNS and DHCP Objects in NDS

By default, DNS and DHCP services are installed to every NetWare 5.*x* server. However, the extensions to the NDS schema to support these services along with the required NDS objects are not created. When performing the NetWare 5.*x* installation, checking the box to include DNS/DHCP services does not install any extra software, but does extend the schema and create the required NDS objects.

Global DNS/DHCP Objects

When you install the DNS and DHCP services, the schema is extended to support DNS/DHCP functions. The installation program creates three global

DNS/DHCP objects, which are used by all DNS and DHCP servers in the tree. Only one copy of these objects can exist in the tree. These objects are as follows:

- ► DNS/DHCP Locator object
- ► DNSDHCP-GROUP Group object
- ► RootSrvrInfo zone

DNS/DHCP Locator Object

The DNS/DHCP Locator object is an NDS object that contains a list of all DHCP and DNS server objects, subnet objects, zone objects, DHCP global defaults, and excluded MAC addresses. This object is used by the DNS/DHCP Management Console to build the list of all DNS/DHCP-related objects without regard to their context. The DHCP and DNS servers also use it for reading their configuration information.

The first time the DHCP server loads, it requires access to the DNS/DHCP Locator object to obtain a copy of any global configuration from the object. The DHCP server then saves a copy of the global configuration in SYS:\ETC\DHCP\DHCPLOC.TAB. Any time the DHCP server starts again, it will look for the DNS/DHCP Locater object and attempt to read its configuration. Should the DNS/DHCP Locator object be unavailable, the DHCP server uses the configuration stored in the DHCPLOC.TAB file.

The DNS server does not require access to the DNS/DHCP Locator object in most cases. It only requires access to the DNS/DHCP Locator object if the NAMED command line arguments are specified to create zones in NDS.

DNSDHCP-GROUP Group Object

The DNSDHCP-GROUP Group object is a modified group object that allows the membership attribute to contain NetWare Core Protocol (NCP)/NetWare Server objects. When you use the DNS/DHCP Management Console to create a DNS or DHCP Server object, the corresponding NCP Server object is automatically placed in this group, which is used to give that server the appropriate NDS rights necessary to read and modify the DNS and DHCP objects in NDS.

TIP

The only way to add the servers to the DNSDHCP-GROUP object is by using the DNS/DHCP Management Console — you cannot use NetWare Administrator to accomplish this.

RootSrvrInfo Zone

The RootSrvrInfo zone contains the host records for the servers responsible for the Root domain. When the DNS server receives a request for a name that it is neither responsible for nor has cached, the DNS server begins its query with one of the Root name servers.

The DNS server only requires access to the RootSrvrInfo zone stored in NDS the first time it loads, at which time it caches this information to the `SYS:ETC\DNS\ROOTSRVR.DAT` file. On subsequent loads, it first tries to find the RootSrvrInfo zone in NDS, but if it is not available, the DNS server uses the copy of the information found in the `ROOTSRVR.DAT` file.

DNS Services Objects

DNS services extend the schema with new classes for the DNS zones, resource records, and DNS servers required by DNS. Like DHCP services, these objects can be administered only with the DNS/DHCP Management Console.

DNS Zone Object

The DNS Zone object is a container object that contains all the data for a single DNS zone. A Zone object is the first level of the DNS zone description. Examples of zones include `Novell.Com`, `Consulting.Novell.Com`, and `Support.Novell.Com`. Each zone includes a "start of authority" record that designates the specific servers that are responsible for this specific zone.

DNS Resource Record Set Object

The DNS Resource Record Set (RRSet) object is an NDS leaf object contained within a DNS Zone object. An RRSet object represents an individual domain resource within a DNS zone. There are several types of resource records, including:

- *A Record* — These are records you create for specific hosts on your network (Host records). Dynamic DNS also creates A records for each host assigned an IP address through Novell's DHCP.

- *CNAME Record* — These are "alias" records used when a host has multiple names. For example, should you decide to host a Web server, a CNAME record can be created for host "WWW," allowing external entities to access the Web server without knowing the true hostname of the device.

> ▸ *MX Record* — These are Mail Exchanger records used to designate an SMTP mail server.

> ▸ *NS Record* — These are Name Server records, which report authoritative name servers. By default, an NS record is created for the DNS server responsible for the zone.

DNS Server Object

The DNS Server object represents the DNS server and contains a multivalued attribute listing of the zones the DNS server is servicing. The DNS Server object also contains all server-specific DNS configurations for this server.

DHCP Services Objects

DHCP services extend the schema with five new object classes. You must use the DNS/DHCP Management Console to manage these objects.

DHCP Server Object

The DHCP Server object represents the DHCP server and contains a multivalued attribute listing of the subnet ranges the DHCP server is servicing. The DHCP server also contains all server-specific configuration and policy information.

Subnet Object

The Subnet object represents a subnet and is the most fundamental DHCP object. The Subnet object acts as a container object for the IP Address and Address Range objects. To serve an address, it must be included in the Address Range object, which must exist within a Subnet object.

Subnet Address Range Object

The Subnet Address Range object is primarily used to denote a range of addresses to create a pool of addresses for dynamic address assignment, or to identify a range of addresses to be excluded from address assignment. Optionally, the Address Range object stores the start of hostnames that can be assigned to clients when addresses are assigned.

IP Address Object

The IP Address object represents a single IP address. The IP Address object must include an address number and an assignment type. The address assignment type can be manual, automatic, or exclusion. *Manual* assignment ties an IP address to a MAC address so that only a specific client can receive a specific address. *Automatic* configuration allows the DHCP server to assign this address to any available client. *Exclusions* are automatically created for the first and last address of every subnet created, and can be explicitly set by an administrator to exclude specific desired addresses.

Subnet Pool Object

The Subnet Pool object provides support for multiple subnets through a DHCP or BOOTP forwarder by identifying a pool of subnets for remote LAN address assignments.

Installing and Configuring DNS and DHCP Services

Installing and configuring DNS and DHCP services involves three main areas:

- ▶ Extending the schema and creating the global objects

- ▶ Installing the management console

- ▶ Configuring the services

By default, every NetWare 5.*x* server has all of the necessary NLMs to run DNS and DHCP services. However, the schema extensions are not added by default, and the management console must be installed onto a client workstation so that you can administer the new DNS and DHCP objects.

Extending the Schema and Creating the Global Objects

During the NetWare 5.*x* installation, one of the optional products to install is DNS/DHCP services. If you choose this option during the installation, the schema is extended and a dialog box will ask you where to place the global objects in the tree. You need to do this only once per tree, so if you selected this option on one of your servers, you do not need to select this option again during any future server installations.

TIP

Even if you do not select to install DNS/DHCP services, all of the NLMs are installed, and the SYS:PUBLIC\DNSDHCP **directory is created. Selecting the install option affects only the schema extension and global object creation.**

If you did not choose to install DNS/DHCP services on any of your NetWare 5.*x*
servers, you can easily create them without reinstalling. To do so, follow these steps:

1. At a NetWare 5.*x* server console prompt, enter **DNIPINST**.

2. When prompted, authenticate to NDS as a user with Supervisor object
rights to [Root] to extend the schema. In the Username field, enter the full
distinguished name of a user with Supervisor object rights to [Root]. In the
Password field, enter the password for that user object. Select "Press Enter
to log in to NDS" and press Enter, as shown in Figure 15.1.

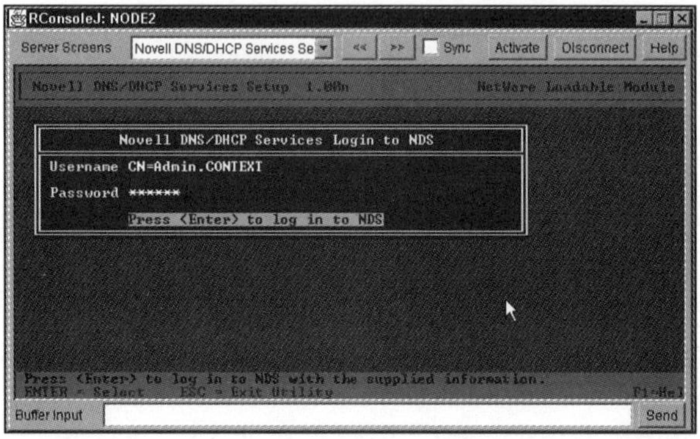

FIGURE 15.1 *Novell DNS/DHCP Services Login to NDS dialog box*

3. Enter the NDS context where you want to create the DNS/DHCP Locator,
DNSDHCP-GROUP Group, and RootServerInfo Zone objects. To change
the default NDS context for these objects, select the Context field and enter
the new context for these objects — for example, **IPMNGT.CONTEXT**. After
the desired context is set, select "Press Enter to create the objects" and then
press Enter, as shown in Figure 15.2.

4. After the DNS/DHCP schema extensions are added, press Enter to finish
the installation.

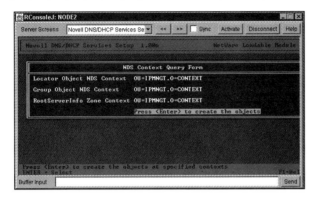

FIGURE 15.2 *NDS Context Query Form dialog box*

Installing the Management Console

The DNS/DHCP Management Console is a Java-based user interface used to configure and manage NDS-based DNS and DHCP objects. NDS is used as the database to store the administered IP address and name service objects. The DNS/DHCP Management Console is an independent executable Java application that can be launched from a Windows 95/98/Me, Windows NT, or Windows 2000 workstation that is running current Novell Client software.

By default, NetWare 5.x places the installation files for the management console in SYS:\PUBLIC\DNSDHCP. To install the management console, follow these steps:

1. Exit any Windows applications that you might have running.

2. Click Start and then click Run.

3. Browse to SYS:\PUBLIC\DNSDHCP, and double-click SETUP.EXE.

4. Click Next to begin the installation, as shown in Figure 15.3.

5. You will be prompted to select the installation directory. Either accept the default directory or browse to the desired location, then click Next to continue.

FIGURE 15.3 *DNS/DHCP Console Installation Welcome dialog box*

6. After the files are copied, you will be prompted to copy the snapin files. The snapin files should be copied to all NetWare servers that you will run NetWare Administrator from so the DNS/DHCP objects do not show up as "unknown" objects. Although you copy the snapin files for NetWare Administrator, all DNS and DHCP administration must be done with the DNS/DHCP Management Console — you cannot use NetWare Administrator or ConsoleOne to administer these services. To copy the snapins, browse to the SYS:PUBLIC\WIN32 location on the server you use to administer NDS and click Next to continue.

7. If prompted to replace any read-only files, select the check box Don't display this message again, and click Yes to replace the files and continue.

8. If desired, read the "readme" file by clicking Yes; otherwise, click No to continue.

9. Click OK to complete the installation.

10. You should now have a DNSDHCP icon on your desktop, which you can use to run the console. Alternatively, when you run NetWare Administrator from the server on which you installed the snapins, you can select DNS-DHCP Management Console from the Tools menu, as shown in Figure 15.4.

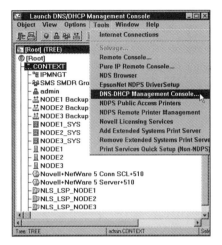

FIGURE 15.4 *DNS-DHCP NetWare Administrator snapin*

Configuring DNS Services

Once installed, the DNS/DHCP Management Console is used to create and manage all DNS information. You use this console to create and manage the following DNS items:

- ▶ DNS servers

- ▶ DNS zones

- ▶ DNS resource records

You can find detailed instructions on all available DNS options at www.novell.com/documentation.

Creating a DNS Server

To create a DNS server, follow these steps:

1. Launch the DNS/DHCP Management Console.

2. Click the DNS Service tab, as shown in Figure 15.5.

FIGURE 15.5 *DNS Server Create button*

3. Click the Create button, the second button from the left on the toolbar. The Create New DNS Record dialog box will appear.

4. Select DNS Server and click OK. The Create DNS Server dialog box will appear.

5. In the Create DNS Server dialog box, as shown in Figure 15.6, browse to select the NetWare server you are using for your DNS server in the Select Server Object field. Enter the Host Name and Domain of the server, and then click the Create button.

FIGURE 15.6 *Create DNS Server dialog box*

6. The DNS server will appear at the bottom of the DNS/DHCP Management Console window, as illustrated in Figure 15.7. A Red X indicates that the DNS service (NAMED.NLM) is not currently loaded on this server.

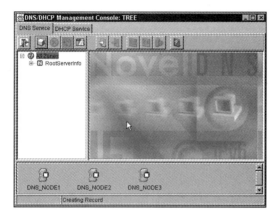

FIGURE 15.7 *The DNS/DHCP Management Console*

Creating a DNS Zone

To create a DNS Zone, follow these steps:

1. Launch the DNS/DHCP Management Console if it isn't already loaded.

2. Click the DNS Service tab and then click the Create button, as shown in Figure 15.8.

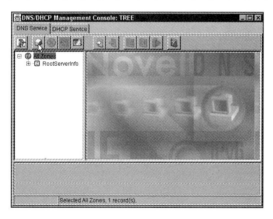

FIGURE 15.8 *Creating a new DNS Zone*

3. In the Create New DNS Record dialog box, select Zone, and click OK.

4. In the Create Zone dialog box shown in Figure 15.9, do the following:

    a. Click Create New Zone.

    b. Browse to the context you wish to create the zone objects in and enter the domain name for the zone (or subdomain name if this is a child domain).

    c. Enter the zone type — Primary or Secondary.

    d. Select the server to be authoritative for this zone from the drop-down list (this can be modified later).

5. Click the Create button.

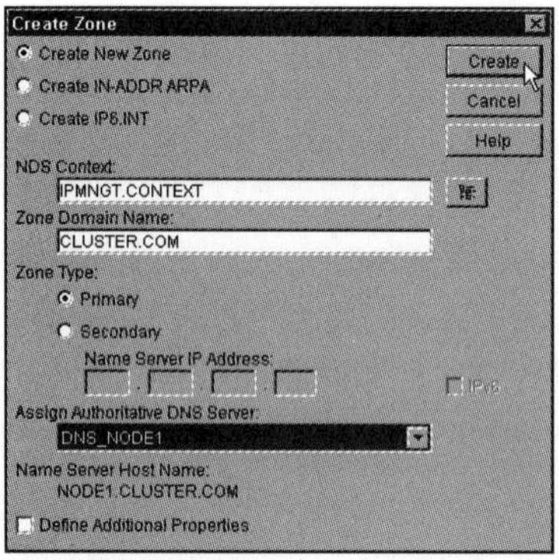

FIGURE 15.9 *Create Zone dialog box*

6. You will receive the warning, shown in Figure 15.10, that you must create an A record for this zone to properly configure the zone for DNS. You must also create the inverse lookup zone (also known as the *reverse DNS zone*) so that the DNS/DHCP Management Console can automatically create the inverse-lookup records (also known as *pointer records*) for every host record you create. Click the OK button to acknowledge this warning.

7. To create the Inverse-Address lookup (IN-ADDR ARPA) zone, click the Create button as shown in Figure 15.5, and then select Zone in the Select New DNS Record dialog box. Click OK to confirm your selection.

Create Resource Record ▬▬▬▬▬▬▬▬▬ ☒

The zone "CLUSTER.COM" is successfully created. Please be sure to create the A resource record for the host server domain name and the corresponding PTR record in the IN-ADDR.ARPA zone if you have not done so.

OK

FIGURE 15.10 *Create Resource Record warning*

8. In the Create Zone dialog box (see Figure 15.9), do the following:

a. Select Create IN-ADDR.ARPA.

b. Browse to the context you wish to create the zone objects in, and enter the network/subnet address for the reverse-lookup zone.

c. Enter the zone type — Primary or Secondary. If Secondary, enter the Primary Name server's IP address.

d. Select the server to be authoritative for this zone from the drop-down list (this can be modified later).

9. Click Create.

TIP

Some other vendors' implementations require you to enter the subnet in reverse octet order. Novell's implementation automatically reverses this for you, so you can enter the actual network/subnet address here.

10. Each zone will have a Start of Authority (SOA) record, which NetWare indicates with an at (@) symbol, as shown in Figure 15.11. Under this SOA entry, you must create an A record for the domain itself (many e-mail systems refuse e-mail from your domain if there is no A record for the domain), Name Server (NS) records for each authoritative DNS server, and Mail Exchange (MX) records for your e-mail servers. To enter these records, select the @ record and click the Create button.

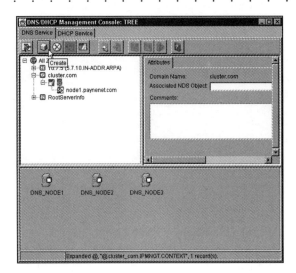

FIGURE 15.11 SOA record

II. Select Resource Record, and click OK.

12. Leave the Host Name field blank, and enter the IP address of your Name Server (this becomes the A record for the domain), then click Create as shown in Figure 15.12.

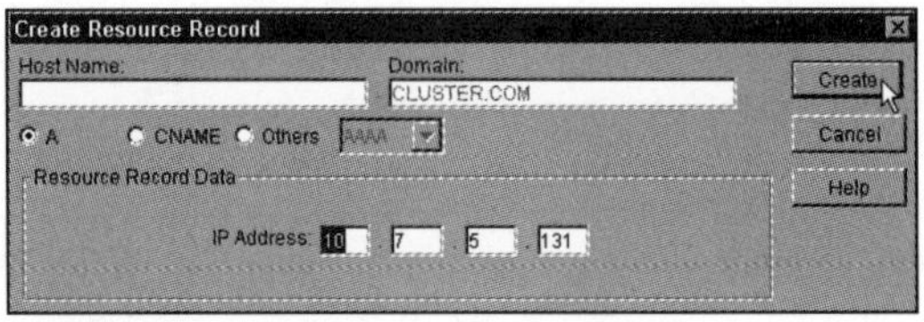

FIGURE 15.12 Domain Host record

13. To enter an additional Name Server record, repeat steps 11 and 12 for each additional record you wish to create. For example, to create a Name Server record for a non-NetWare 5.x DNS server, leave the Host Name field blank, click Others, and then select NS from the drop-down box. Enter the fully qualified domain name (FQDN) of any other Name Servers that are authoritative for this zone, then click Create.

NOTE

When you add a NetWare server to a zone, the NS record is automatically created for you. You need to follow this procedure only for non-NetWare 5.x Name Servers that will be authoritative for this zone.

14. To configure your Authoritative NetWare Servers for the zone, select the zone object, then select any "available" DNS server and click the Add button as shown in Figure 15.13. Authoritative servers appear on the right side of the window, and available (nonauthoritative) servers appear on the left. Only one DNS server can be selected for the Dynamic DNS role for each zone.

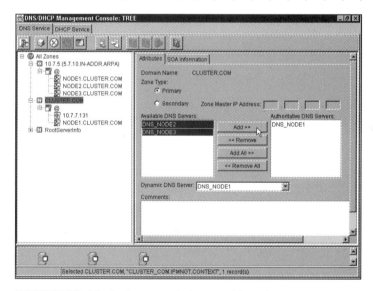

FIGURE 15.13 *Configuring an Authoritative Name Server*

Configuring DHCP Services

Configuring DHCP services includes creating a DHCP server, defining a subnet, defining a subnet address range, and defining global/subnet options. You can find detailed instructions on all available DHCP options at www.novell.com/documentation.

This section walks you through the basics of creating the DHCP server, the subnet, the subnet address range, and simple subnet options.

Creating the DHCP Server

As described later in this chapter, each node that you wish to be in the failover path for DHCP services must have a corresponding DHCP Server object in the tree. The following steps walk you through creating a DHCP server:

1. Launch the DNS/DHCP Management Console if it isn't already running.

2. Select the DHCP Services tab.

3. Click the Create button, as shown in Figure 15.14. The Create New DHCP Record dialog box will appear.

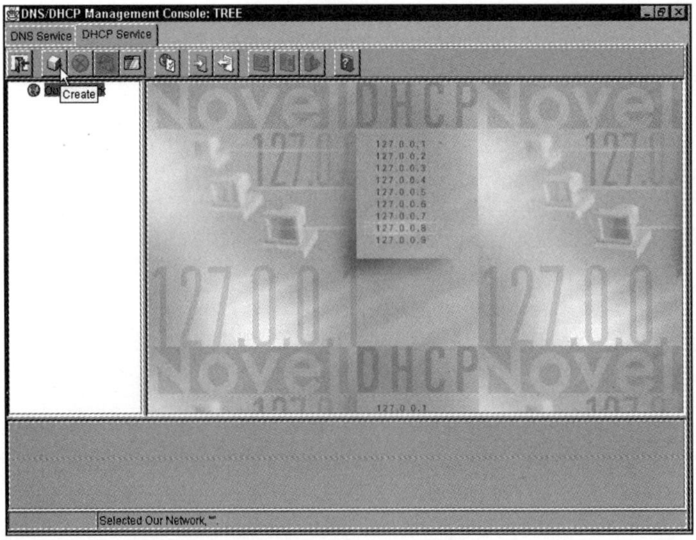

FIGURE 15.14 Creating a DHCP server

4. Select DHCP Server, then click OK.

5. In the Create DHCP Server dialog box, browse for the server object to which you wish to add DHCP services, as shown in Figure 15.15, then click Create.

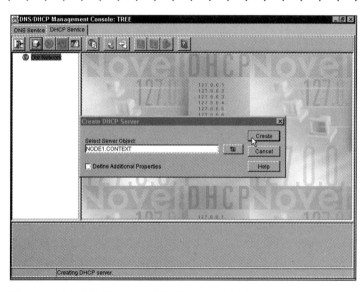

FIGURE 15.15 *The Create DHCP Server dialog box*

6. Repeat steps 1 through 5 for any additional DHCP servers you wish to create. As discussed later in this chapter, all cluster nodes that will be in the failover path for DHCP services should have corresponding DHCP server objects. Once you've created the DHCP servers, they will appear in the bottom of the DNS/DHCP Management Console window, as shown in Figure 15.16. A Red X will appear on the server object until DHCPSRVR.NLM is actually loaded on that server.

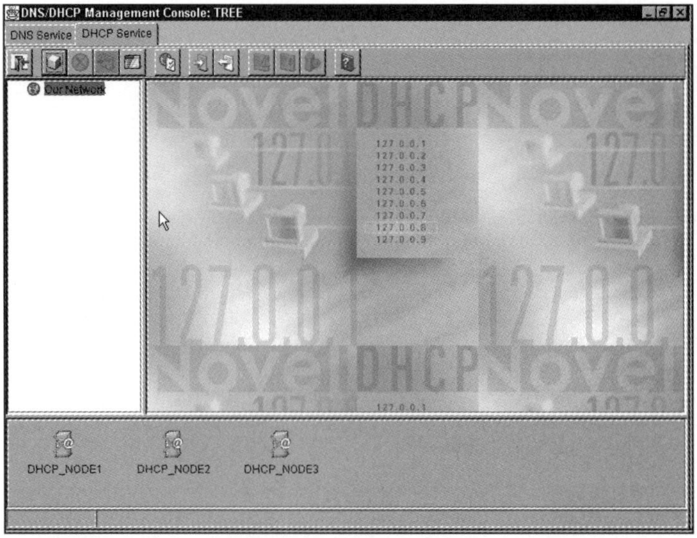

FIGURE 15.16 *DNS/DHCP Management Console—DHCP server*

Creating a DHCP Subnet

After you have created the DHCP server(s), you must create the subnets that this DHCP server will service. You should create a subnet object for every subnet in your network that this server will service. To configure the subnet:

1. Launch the DNS/DHCP Management Console if it isn't already running.

2. Select the DHCP Services tab.

3. Click the Create button. The Create New DHCP Record dialog box will appear.

4. Select Subnet, then click OK.

5. Enter the following subnet information in the Create Subnet dialog box, as shown in Figure 15.17:

   • Subnet Name—Enter a name for the subnet.

   • Select NDS Context—Browse to the context to create the NDS subnet object.

   • Subnet Address—Enter the subnet address.

- Subnet Mask — Enter the subnet mask for the subnet.

- Default DHCP Server — Enter the DHCP server to use for this subnet.

6. Click Create to complete the subnet object.

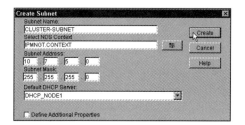

FIGURE 15.17 *The Create Subnet dialog box*

Just because you assign a subnet does not mean that these addresses will actually be given out. You must define an entire subnet, then use a Subnet Address Range to define the addresses to be delivered, which is the topic of the next section.

Creating the Subnet Address Range
Once you create a subnet, you must create a subnet address range (SAR) within the subnet object. To create the SAR object, follow these steps:

1. Launch the DNS/DHCP Management Console if it isn't already running.

2. Select the DHCP Services tab.

3. Select your subnet object, then click the Create button. The Create New DHCP Record dialog box will appear.

4. Select Subnet Address Range, then click OK.

5. Enter the following information in the Create Subnet Address Range dialog box, as shown in Figure 15.18:

- Subnet Address Range Name — Enter the name for the NDS SAR object.

- Enter the start and end address for the Subnet Address Range.

6. Click Create to finish the SAR.

NOVELL'S GUIDE TO STORAGE AREA NETWORKS AND NOVELL CLUSTER SERVICES

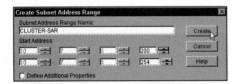

FIGURE 15.18 *The Create Subnet Address Range dialog box*

Configuring DHCP Options

After you have created the subnet and subnet address range, you need to configure the DHCP options such as default gateway, DNS servers, and so on. These options can be configured globally, at the subnet level, at the SAR level, or even at the individual IP address level. You should configure the options at the highest level to which they apply. This might mean different options at different levels — in other words, the DNS servers might be valid for your entire organization (global), whereas default gateways will be different for each subnet.

To configure the DHCP options:

1. Launch the DNS/DHCP Management Console if it isn't already running.

2. Select the DHCP Services tab.

3. Select the level you wish to configure:

- For global options, click the Global Preferences button, as shown in Figure 15.19.

- For subnet options, select the Subnet object, then click the Other DHCP Options tab, as shown in Figure 15.20.

- For individual IP address options, select the IP Address object, then click the Other DHCP Options tab.

4. Click the Modify button.

5. Select the option you wish to configure, then click the Add button.

FIGURE 15.19 *Global Preferences button*

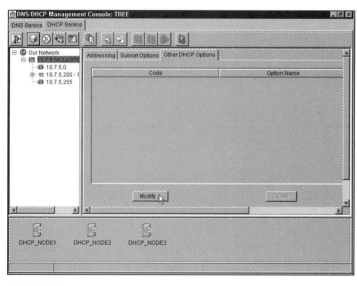

FIGURE 15.20 *Other DHCP Options tab*

6. In the Modify DHCP Options dialog box, as shown in Figure 15.21, select the Selected DHCP Options parameter that you wish to configure, such as Router (default gateway), then click the lower Add button.

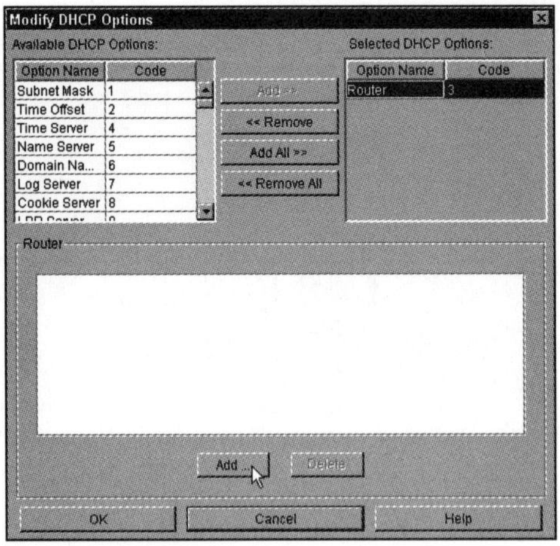

FIGURE 15.21 *Modify DHCP Options dialog box*

7. Enter the configuration information, as shown in Figure 15.22, then click OK.

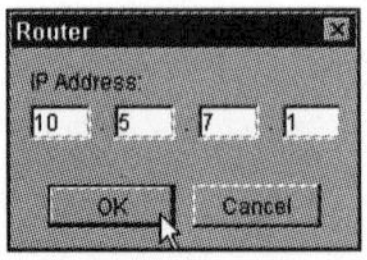

FIGURE 15.22 *Default Router details*

8. Repeat steps 5 through 7 for all the options you wish to configure.

9. When your options are complete, click OK.

Where you configure the DHCP options will depend on your environment. You may want to create options such as DNS servers in the global DHCP options, since they will probably be the same for all of your subnets. You may want to create options such as default gateway as subnet options, since each subnet will have a different default gateway.

The options you wish to enable will also depend on your environment. The most basic required options are default gateway and DNS servers. If you have configured SLP, you will also want to include the SLP DA option, and possibly the SLP Scope option. Configuring these as options to DHCP greatly simplifies the task of assigning this information to all of your TCP/IP clients.

Cluster Enabling DNS and DHCP Services

Both DNS and DHCP services store their respective databases in NDS, making these services relatively easy to configure in a cluster.

Configuring DNS as a Cluster Resource

DNS implementations are already fault tolerant without your having to implement Novell Cluster Services—the clients can be configured to use up to three DNS servers, so if the primary DNS server fails, a secondary DNS server is utilized. Novell's implementation of DNS is even further fault tolerant since it stores the DNS database in NDS, and NDS replication provides fault tolerance for the DNS information. If a DNS server fails, any other NetWare 5.*x* server can easily be configured to serve the proper DNS zones, and the NAMED.NLM loaded to make an additional DNS server.

Even with this level of fault tolerance, many clients desire the ability to cluster enable DNS services. In this manner, fewer servers need to actively service DNS— if the primary DNS server fails, another node in the cluster takes on that role, and the client doesn't realize that it has moved to a different DNS server.

Novell's implementation of DNS makes clustering this service very easy. However, due to the fault tolerant nature of DNS, Novell does not actively support this configuration. Though this configuration is generally successful, you must be willing to assume some risk in utilizing this "nonsupported" configuration.

WARNING

Dynamic DNS (DDNS) is not currently functional in a failover capacity, so if the primary DDNS server fails, the Dynamic DNS functionality will not function.

With NetWare's DNS, the concept of a primary server and secondary server is modified. Instead, the zone itself becomes either primary or secondary, thus allowing multiple DNS servers to service the same "primary" zone. Thus, to cluster DNS, all servers that are in the failover path should be configured to service the appropriate zones desired.

To configure DNS for fault tolerance:

1. Configure your DNS services as usual for the primary server. Assign the server to the zones as usual.

2. Configure all other servers in the cluster that will be in the failover path to service the same zones. Since it is the zone that is primary or secondary, you will not need to designate a role for the servers.

3. Launch ConsoleOne, and browse to the Cluster container object.

4. Click the New Cluster Resource button, as shown in Figure 15.23. This button is the tenth button (sixth active button) from the left on the taskbar, and looks like a pyramid with a red dot on it.

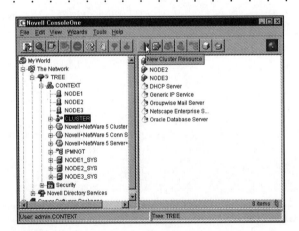

FIGURE 15.23 *New Cluster Resource button*

5. Enter the Resource Name for the DNS server, check the Define Additional Properties option, and click Create.

TIP

When you use ConsoleOne from a server, you may find that selecting Define Additional Properties often results in a 601 error, as the server hasn't realized the object was created yet. If this occurs, simply reopen the object and continue. You may find it less troublesome not to select Define Additional Properties when you are using a server to run ConsoleOne.

6. Select the Load Script tab, as shown in Figure 15.24, and enter the following commands:

```
ADD SECONDARY IPADDRESS <IPADDRESS>

LOAD NAMED
```

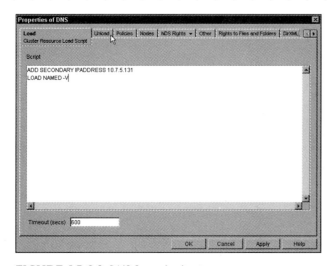

FIGURE 15.24 *DNS Server load script*

TIP

`NAMED` **has many options available, including the –V option for Verbose — this creates an extra screen on the server console and displays DNS request information that is very helpful in debugging problems with the DNS server. Load** `NAMED` **with the -? parameter to get a list of all available options.**

7. Select the Unload Script tab as shown in Figure 15.25, and enter the following commands:

```
UNLOAD NAMED
DEL SECONDARY IPADDRESS <IPADDRESS>
```

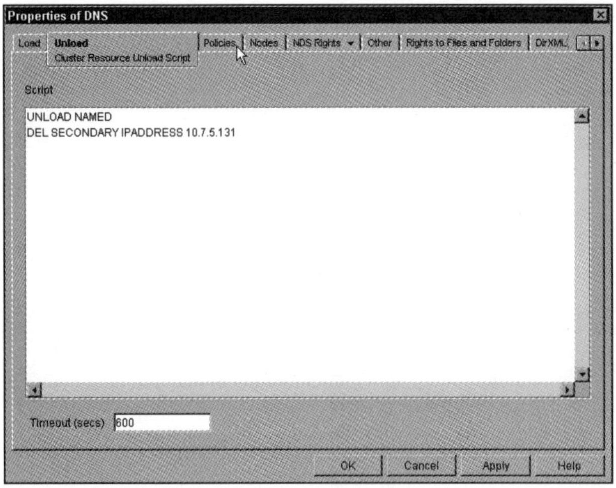

FIGURE 15.25 *DNS Server unload script*

8. Select the Policies tab, and enter the desired startup, failover, and failback policies.

9. Select the Nodes tab, and enter the desired available nodes and node preference order.

10. Click OK to finish the configuration.

11. Change to the Cluster State view by selecting View ⇨ Cluster State from the menu, as shown in Figure 15.26.

12. Click the DNS Cluster Resource to start the Resource Manager, as shown in Figure 15.27.

13. Click the Online button to online the resource.

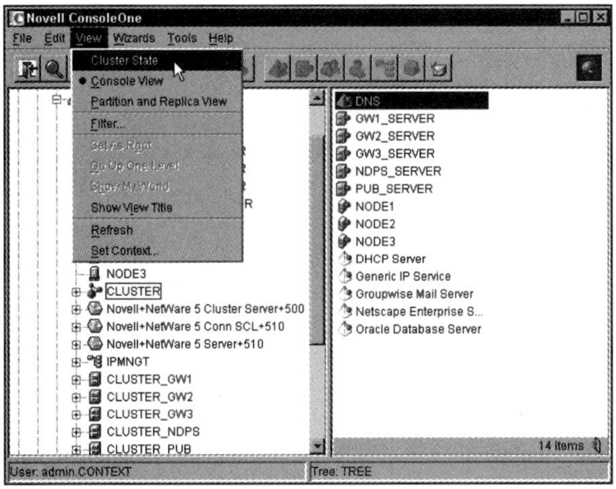

FIGURE 15.26 *Cluster State view*

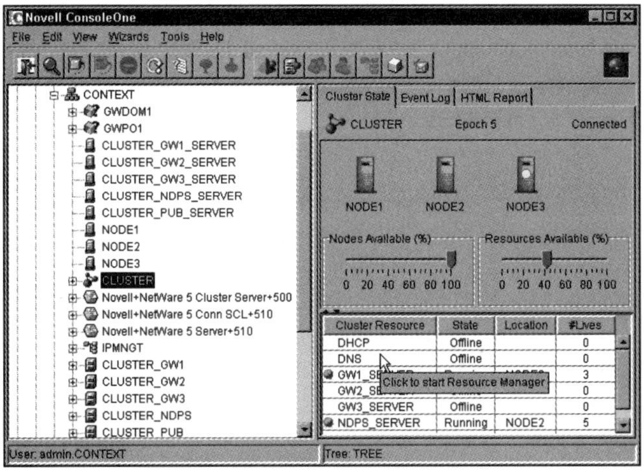

FIGURE 15.27 *Starting the Resource Manager*

14. Configure your clients to use this new resource as their primary DNS server. Better yet, configure your DHCP server to pass this Name Server address to your clients using DHCP.

Configuring DHCP as a Cluster Resource

Since NetWare 5.x stores the DHCP database in NDS, Novell's DHCP solution already provides rapid recovery if a server fails — simply configure another server to serve the subnets, then load the DHCPSRVR.NLM on that server, and you're up and running again. Storing the lease information in NDS makes this possible. Even with this level of fault tolerance, many clients wish to cluster enable DHCP to provide automatic failover of services in the event of a server failure.

While the DHCP database is stored in NDS, the DHCP server is not overly aggressive at updating NDS with lease information. The server will give out or renew leases and cache this information locally, and later update NDS with this updated information. Since this makes it possible for NDS to be out of date when the DHCP server fails, you should enable "ping ahead" on the DHCP servers used in the cluster. In this manner, if the NDS database does not know about a leased address due to a server failure, the new server will try to ping the address before leasing it. If the server successfully pings the address, it will skip that address and lease the next address in the range, assuming it passes the ping test. The next time the client workstation tries to renew that lease, the database will be updated and that IP address will be renewed for the workstation.

Secondary IP Address

The DHCP server template included with Novell Cluster Services 1.01 does not bind a secondary IP address. However, if your network has routers, then you will most likely need to bind a secondary IP address for the "IP Helper" or "BOOTP forwarder" function on your routers, or you must put a DHCP server on every network segment in your environment.

For DHCP to work in a routed environment, the routers must know the IP address of the DHCP server in the network. When a client needs an IP address, it sends a DHCP or BOOTP broadcast on its local segment. If there is no DHCP server on this segment, the router must be manually configured with an "IP Helper" or "BOOTP forwarder" IP address. When configured, the router sends a unicast packet to the DHCP server on behalf of the client, and then passes the returning IP address to the client, assuming the DHCP server was configured with IP addresses valid for this subnet.

Figure 15.28 illustrates a DCHP server on subnet 10.1.1.0, configured with addresses (subnets and subnet address ranges) for the 10.1.1.0, 10.1.2.0, and 10.1.3.0 subnets. When the client on the 10.1.3.0 subnet starts up, it sends out a broadcast requesting an IP address. If the router on this subnet knows about the DHCP server at 10.1.1.187, it will forward this request to the DHCP server, and pass the lease information on to the client.

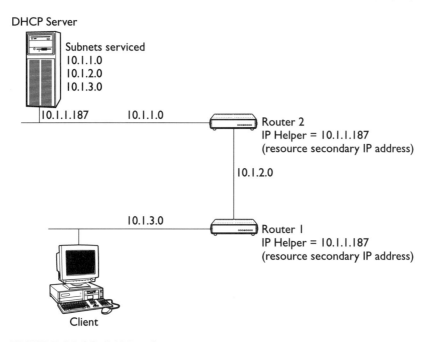

FIGURE 15.28 *IP Helper illustration*

With Novell Cluster Services, the DHCP resource should be configured with a secondary IP address for use in configuring the routers. This secondary IP address is then used in the router's IP Helper configuration for proper forwarding of DHCP requests.

Clustering DHCP

Clustering DHCP requires Novell Cluster Services version 1.01, or Novell Cluster Services version 1.0 with Support Pack 1. These versions add a special command—`CLUSTER_START DHCP`—that allows you to configure a single DHCP server and use this configuration for the entire cluster.

To cluster DHCP, follow these steps:

1. Install DHCP services to one node in the cluster.

2. Configure DHCP services for any *one* node in the cluster. Create the subnets, scopes, and all required configuration based on this one node.

3. Create a DHCP Server object for each node that you wish to run DHCP services on. You need to configure only one server, but all servers must have the DHCP Server object created so that these servers are in the DNSDHCP-GROUP group. This is what grants the servers the appropriate rights to read the Locator and DHCP objects.

4. Launch ConsoleOne, select the Cluster container, and click the New Cluster Resource button, as shown in Figure 15.29.

FIGURE 15.29 *New Cluster Resource button*

5. Name the Resource in the Cluster Resource Name field of the New Cluster Resource dialog box, as shown in Figure 15.30. Browse for the DHCP Server template. If this template doesn't exist, it means that you installed Novell Cluster Services version 1.0 and applied the 1.01 patch. This is fine; you will just need to manually type in all the Load and Unload script commands. Select the Define Additional Properties button, and click Create.

6. Select the Load Script tab, as shown in Figure 15.31, and enter the following load script:

```
CLUSTER_START DHCP CN=<Distinguished name including tree of the
NDS Server Object of the node you configured in step 2>

LOAD DHCPSRVR

ADD SECONDARY IPADDRESS <IP ADDRESS>
```

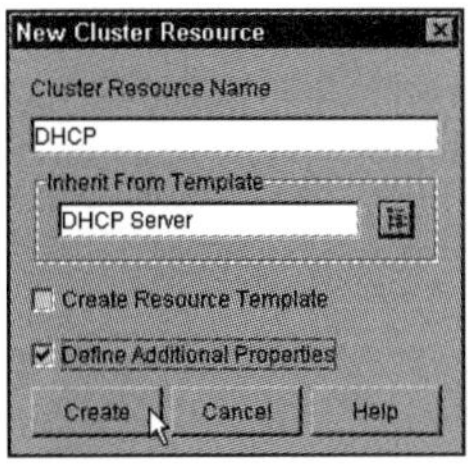

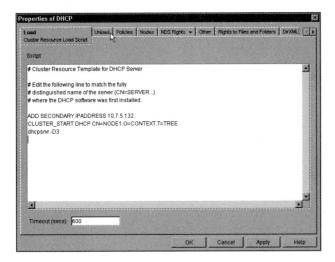

FIGURE 15.30 *Creating a DHCP Cluster Resource*

FIGURE 15.31 *The DHCP Server Load Script tab*

It is critical that you use the NDS object of the server you configured, not the DHCP Server object:

NOTE

Right:

```
CLUSTER_START DHCP CN=NODE1.O=CONTEXT.T=TREE
```

Wrong:

```
CLUSTER_START DHCP CN=DHCP_NODE1.O=CONTEXT.T=TREE
```

TIP

DHCPSRVR.NLM **has many command-line switches, including the –D3 for Debug level 3. This option adds an additional server console screen and writes a log to the server's** SYS:\ETC\DHCP\DHCPSRVR.LOG **file. Both the screen and log file show DHCP requests and responses for aid in troubleshooting DHCP services.**

7. Select the Unload Script tab as shown in Figure 15.32, and enter the following unload script:

UNLOAD DHCPSRVR

DEL SECONDARY IPADDRESS <IP ADDRESS>

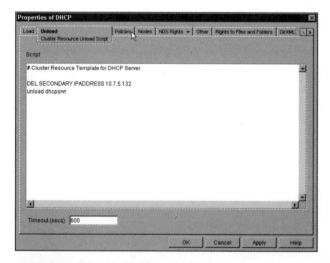

FIGURE 15.32 *The DHCP Server Unload Script tab*

8. Select the Policies tab, and enter the desired Policy information for start mode, failover mode, and failback mode.

9. Select the Nodes tab, and enter the assigned nodes as desired.

10. Click OK to finish the configuration.

11. Change to Cluster State view by selecting View ⇨ Cluster State from the menu.

12. Click the DHCP Resource button to start the Resource Manager.

13. Click the Online button.

Cluster Migration and Failover Characteristics

Both DHCP and DNS services store their configuration and data in NDS, and each rely on a single NLM module to run their service. This makes the migration of these services from one node to the next a very quick and simple task—unload the NLM, unbind the IP address, then rebind the IP address, and reload the NLM on the new server. Neither of these resources requires a dedicated volume to function, so there are no data and trustee issues to deal with. Thus, migrating these resources should take less than 10 seconds in most environments.

Deciding between Active/Active or Active/Passive Configurations

The DHCP server falls in the Active/Passive category of services, since the NLM can only be active on one node at a time in the cluster. Though Active/Passive normally indicates longer failover or migration times, this service actually starts and stops very quickly.

Earlier in this chapter, DNS services were demonstrated in an Active/Passive mode as well. However, based on the fact that each node is being configured as a DNS server for the same zones, this service could also be configured in an Active/Active mode. In this configuration, you would remove the LOAD NAMED.NLM from the load scripts, remove the UNLOAD NAMED.NLM from the unload scripts, and load NAMED.NLM in the AUTOEXEC.NCF file instead. Thus, the migration and failover time is as quick as moving the secondary IP address from one node to another.

Connecting the Client to the Service

For the DNS server, the clients should be using the secondary IP address assigned to this resource as their primary DNS server. Since adding clustering adds fault tolerance to DNS without permanently tying up another server, you might choose to simply configure one DNS server at the client workstation for DNS resolution. If the client makes a DNS request during the short migration time for this resource, the client request may time out, which would produce an error in the Web browser or other application in use. However, by the time the client retries the operation, the new cluster node has most likely started this resource and the subsequent attempt will succeed.

For the DHCP server, the client handles the vast majority of DHCP lease requests in the background automatically. Once the client has leased an IP address, the client will periodically try to renew that lease. If the DHCP server is not responding when the client tries to renew the lease, the client will try again at the next predetermined interval. As long as one of the cluster nodes is running the DHCP server the next time, the user will never know that the DHCP server was ever unavailable.

The DHCP server will answer to the secondary IP address, but will always respond with the server's primary IP address. When using WINIPCFG on a Windows 95/98/Me workstation or IPCONFIG on a Windows NT/2000 workstation, you will see the primary IP address of the cluster node that issued that particular lease. This can be a problem if the DHCP server has moved to a different node, and the client manually forces a lease renewal. When this happens, the client produces an error because the DHCP server is no longer running on that particular server. If you manually release the IP address, then renew it, it will function properly because the new request will once again be broadcast. This problem occurs only when forcing a renewal — the automatic renewal will hide the error from the user.

Data Integrity in Migration/Failover

Both the DNS and DHCP services store all configuration information in NDS, which means the chance of data corruption during a failover is very low. As long as NDS does not incur corruption, the data will be maintained, and there is no special database that needs to have any integrity check with the services start.

While the configuration is stored in NDS, the DHCP server is somewhat lazy in updating NDS with lease information to improve performance (clustering does not change this behavior). This leaves the possibility that when a server fails and the service moves to the next node, some lease information might be missing (this is the same problem without clustering if a server fails). To account for this, you should enable "Ping Ahead" on the DHCP server so the server will verify that no client is using an IP address before it leases it.

Migrating Existing Services to the Cluster

If you have an existing DNS or DHCP server, you will probably want to migrate your existing configuration into the cluster. The exact steps on how you do this depend on what your current system is — NetWare 4.x DNS/DHCP services, already running NetWare 5.x services, or migrating another vendor's implementation to NetWare 5.x.

Whichever route you choose, you are strongly encouraged to test the procedures in a lab environment prior to migrating in production. This section provides a high-level overview of the steps to migrating an existing DNS server to the cluster, or an existing NetWare DHCP server to the cluster. Migrating another vendor's DHCP implementation to Novell Cluster Services is not covered here, because re-creating your existing configuration in the cluster is best in this case.

Always test your migration procedures in a lab before performing them in production!

WARNING

Migrating an Existing NetWare 3.12, 3.2, or 4.x DNS System to Novell Cluster Services

To upgrade a NetWare 4.x DNS system to the Novell Cluster Services resource, follow these steps:

1. Create the cluster-enabled DNS resource as described in the "Configuring DNS as a Cluster Resource" section earlier in this chapter. Be sure to online the resource so the DNS server is running.

2. From the NetWare 4.x DNS server, unload NAMED.NLM to disable the DNS service.

3. Copy the SYS:ETC\DNS\HOST.DB and SYS:\ETC\DNS\HOSTSREV.DB files from the NetWare 4.x DNS server to the cluster node that is currently running the DNS server.

4. On the NetWare 5.x server console on the server running DNS, type LOAD DNSCNVRT.NLM.

5. The DNSCNVRT.NLM will convert the Btrieve DNS database into a BIND formatted database and save the files as SYS:ETC\DNS\H.DAT and SYS:ETC\DNS\HR.DAT.

6. Launch the DNS/DHCP Management Console, and click the DNS Service tab.

7. From the toolbar, click the Import DNS Database button, as shown in Figure 15.33.

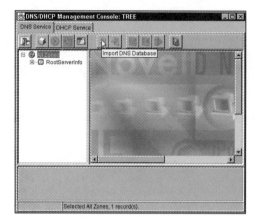

FIGURE 15.33 *The Import DNS Database button*

8. Select Import DNS Database.

9. You will be prompted for the file to import. Browse to the SYS:ETC\DNS\ H.DAT file.

10. You will be prompted for the NDS context to create the DNS object. Browse for the desired context and click OK.

11. Repeat steps 8 through 10 for the SYS:ETC\DNS\HR.DAT file.

12. Assign your DNS servers to be authoritative for the imported zones.

13. Verify that the DNS information came across correctly.

Migrating from an Existing NetWare 5.x DNS Implementation

Migrating from an existing NetWare 5.x implementation to Novell Cluster Services is a snap since all the zone information is already stored in NDS. All you need to do is follow the steps to create the cluster-enabled DNS resource as described in the "Configuring DNS as a Cluster Resource" section earlier in this chapter. Next, add the cluster-enabled DNS servers to the zones, and remove the old DNS server from the zone. Online the resource, and you're set!

Migrating from Another Vendor's DNS Implementation

As long as the other vendor's DNS implementation has the ability to export to a BIND format, upgrading from another vendor's version is also easy. Follow the other vendor's directions to export the zone information to a BIND file, then follow steps 6 through 13 in the "Migrating an Existing NetWare 3.12, 3.20, or 4.*x* DNS system to Novell Cluster Services" section of this chapter.

Migrating from a NetWare 4.*x* Version of DHCP

NetWare 5.*x* provides the ability to import a NetWare DHCP version 2.0 or 3.0 file format into the NetWare 5.*x* DHCP configuration. This makes it easy to move your existing DHCP database (including lease information) from an existing NetWare 4.*x* server to the new cluster resource. To migrate, follow these steps:

1. Configure a DHCP resource as described in the "Configuring DHCP as a Cluster Resource" section earlier in this chapter and online the DHCP server (without configuring any subnets).

2. Launch the DNS/DHCP Management Console.

3. Click the DHCP Service tab.

4. Click the Import DHCP Database button on the toolbar, as shown in Figure 15.34.

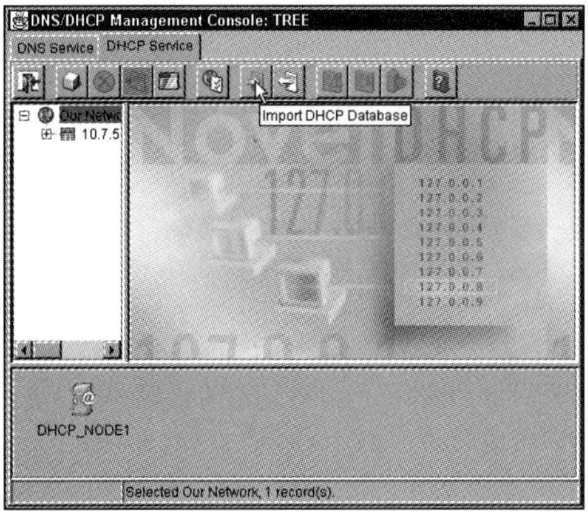

FIGURE 15.34 *The Import DHCP Database button*

5. Enter the drive and path to the DHCP database file (DHCPTAB) on the existing NetWare 4.*x* server, then click Next.

6. Select the desired subnet(s) to import, then click Add (or click Add All to add all subnets from the DHCPTAB file).

7. Select the context to create the NDS objects for the subnets, subnet address ranges, and IP addresses, then click OK.

8. Click Import.

9. You will be prompted for the DHCP server to service these subnets. Select the DHCP server that you choose to configure for the cluster resource, then click OK.

10. Verify that the information imported properly.

11. Online the DHCP resource.

Migrating from an Existing NetWare 5.x DHCP Implementation

Migrating from an existing NetWare 5.x implementation to Novell Cluster Services is a snap since all DHCP information is already stored in NDS. Simply follow the steps to create the cluster-enabled DHCP resource as described in the "Configuring DHCP as a Cluster Resource" section earlier in this chapter. Next, add the node that you choose to configure for DHCP to the subnets in your existing system, and remove the existing DHCP server. Online the resource, and you're set!

▶ . . . . ◀

Summary

This chapter discussed the basics of Novell's DNS and DHCP services, and how to configure these services in a cluster. It covered Novell's implementation of DNS/DHCP services by storing all information in NDS, and how to manage these services using the DNS/DHCP Management Console. You learned how to install the DNS/DHCP services into your NDS tree, and how to install the Java-based Management Console. Next, you learned how to enable DNS and DHCP as cluster resources, using the appropriate load and unload script syntax.

The chapter examined the following cluster failover/migration characteristics for DNS/DHCP services:

CLUSTER FAILOVER CLASSIFICATION INDEX	
Transparency	Very High
Active/Active or Active/Passive	Active/Passive (DNS can be Active/Active)
Length to failover	Less than 10 seconds

Finally, the chapter explained various migration issues to help you migrate from the following:

- NetWare 3.12 or NetWare 4.*x* DNS Services

- NetWare 5.*x* DNS Services

- Other vendors' DNS services

- NetWare 4.*x* DHCP Services

- NetWare 5.*x* DHCP Services

Since both DNS and DHCP use the NDS database for their data store, you can easily set up a fault-tolerant, highly available DNS or DHCP resource without even using shared storage. This makes a very cost-effective way to add fault tolerance to your mission-critical name resolution services using your existing hardware and very little added configuration. Since few vendors provide a good way to provide fault-tolerant DHCP, clustering DHCP provides an excellent value proposition.

## CHAPTER 16

Applying Novell Cluster Services with BorderManager

So, you want a firewall solution to control users' access to the Internet and protect private resources, and you want this solution to be highly available? In addition, you want to control access using your existing NDS database, and log activity based on NDS accounts? If so, Clustering Novell's BorderManager may be the solution for you.

In this chapter, you learn about the components of Novell BorderManager Enterprise Edition (BMEE) 3.6 that can be configured as fault-tolerant services in a cluster. The chapter begins by briefly discussing the components of BMEE and examining which components are clusterable. Next, the chapter discusses the general guidelines for clustering BMEE and the caveats that you must understand when deploying this solution. The chapter concludes with a detailed process for setting up BMEE in a fault-tolerant cluster configuration, and discusses the failover characteristics of BorderManager.

Introducing BorderManager Services

BorderManager Enterprise Edition is a suite of software that provides various Internet services, including firewall services, content caching services, Virtual Private Network (VPN) services, and authentication services (Remote Dial-In User Services or RADIUS services). Of the services provided by BMEE, only the HTTP proxy services currently support a fault-tolerant configuration with Novell Cluster Services. If you need a fault-tolerant solution for the other (non-Proxy) services, you must consider alternatives such as Novell Standby Server.

TIP

This book was written using BMEE version 3.6, although version 3.5 is also supported in a cluster (with Support Pack 1). Due to many functionality and stability improvements in version 3.6, you should utilize 3.6 if possible.

Although many people also think of Network Address Translation (NAT) and packet filtering as components of BorderManager, these components are included in the NetWare operating system. Even so, this chapter briefly discusses these components since they typically go hand in hand with a BorderManager installation.

Firewall/Caching Services

BorderManager offers comprehensive firewall services, as illustrated in Table 16.1.

T A B L E 16.1	
BorderManager Firewall Services	
SERVICE	DESCRIPTION
Packet Filtering*	Provides network and transport-layer security to control the type of information allowed to be routed between hosts.
Proxy Services	Uses caching to accelerate Internet access and maximize performance. Also provides protocol filtering and improves network security by hiding the private network names and addresses from the public by sending all requests with the Border address.
Access Control	Enables administrators to control which users are allowed access to which Internet or intranet services.
Novell IP Gateway	Consists of a circuit-level gateway, which allows clients to access the Internet using nonregistered IP addresses, or IPX. Also supports SOCKS clients.
NAT*	Allows IP clients on your private network to access Internet resources without registered IP addresses, or with registered IP addresses that are not transmitted to the Internet.
BorderManager Alert	Monitors server performance and security and reports potential or existing server problems to administrators.

* Indicates services that are included with the operating system but typically considered to be BorderManager firewall services.

As previously stated, proxy services is the only service that can be configured as a fault-tolerant service with Novell Cluster Services. This service enables application-level security by providing application proxies that forward and filter connections to Internet services such as HTTP, Gopher, FTP, SMTP, RealAudio, DNS, and user-definable services. Typically, a proxy service functions only for TCP/IP applications that the proxy server specifically understands and for which the proxy server has been configured. So, although the proxy server supports FTP, if the administrator has not enabled this proxy service, the BorderManager server will not allow hosts to utilize this service on the Internet.

HTTP proxy accelerates performance to the Internet by caching frequently used Web sites. This cache can be in RAM on the server, or for less frequently accessed sites, it can be stored on the hard drive of the server (which is still significantly faster than hitting the site directly).

BorderManager allows NDS-based access control, which enables the administrator to determine who can access what services on the Internet based on their NDS authentication.

Virtual Private Network Services

Virtual Private Networking (VPN) services allow users to transfer sensitive company information across the Internet or through other untrusted networks in a safe, secure manner. The services rely on encryption and encapsulation, and support both site-to-site (server-based) and client-to-site (client/server) services.

Because of the methods utilized for the encryption tunnel, key management, and the Master server/Slave server concepts of BorderManager's VPN services, these services cannot be made fault tolerant using Novell Cluster Services. If you need fault tolerance of the VPN services beyond BorderManager's own capabilities, consider Novell's Standby Server as a viable alternative.

BorderManager Authentication Services

BorderManager Authentication Services (BMAS) allows BorderManager to utilize the NDS database and provide authentication to RADIUS (Remote Authentication Dial-In User Service) capable devices. BMAS uses the RADIUS protocol, and supports RADIUS logging of user access.

BMAS is currently not clusterable, although Novell product management is reviewing this as a potential future enhancement.

Cluster Enabling BorderManager Services

As we mentioned earlier, the only BorderManager service that can be clustered is the proxy cache service. These proxy services include forward proxy for various Internet services including HTTP, HTTPS, FTP, SMTP, NNTP, and Gopher services, and reverse proxy services (also known as accelerators or backward proxy) for HTTP/HTTPS Web servers.

All BorderManager configuration information is stored in NDS as attributes of the NCP (NetWare Core Protocol) server object. Because all configuration information is stored in the server object, you must manually configure each cluster node hosting BorderManager services separately. It is vitally important that you configure them in an identical manner, and test all functionality with each node active to verify that performance is the same no matter which node is hosting your services.

WARNING **If you do not configure your BorderManager servers in an identical manner, you may have security holes using one server that don't exist when using another. Be sure to test your security with the service running on each potential cluster node.**

You use a secondary IP address for the BorderManager services — the clients connect to this secondary IP address, which is configured in the resource load and unload script to move with the BorderManager service. If you are manually configuring the browsers for their proxy server, you use this address as the proxy server. If you are using transparent proxy services, you will want this address to be configured as the gateway route to the Internet.

Planning the Proxy Cache Volume

BorderManager defaults to using the SYS volume for caching Web content. Obviously, you will want to change this to a different volume, preferably on the shared storage. Note, however, that BorderManager is one of the few applications that can be configured as a fault-tolerant service in a cluster without actually requiring shared storage. You could configure a local volume for each server's cache and configure BorderManager without any shared storage at all. In this case, if one server fails, the next server takes over, although it must start building the cache from scratch.

The preferred configuration uses shared storage for the cache, so that the next server taking over the BorderManager resource has the benefit of initializing the previously cached content. Be sure to configure each BorderManager server with the same number of cache directories as shown in Figure 16.1.

TIP

Novell recommends setting the number of cache directories to 128. For this and other BorderManager tuning tips, see Novell TID 10018669.

BMEE Licensing in a Cluster

BorderManager requires a BorderManager server license for each service in the suite you plan on utilizing. Although Novell Cluster Services does modify NetWare's user-based licensing for file access, which allows Client Access Licenses (CALs) to failover from one node in the cluster to the next, it does not provide this same functionality for services such as BorderManager. This means that you must have BorderManager licenses for each BorderManager server in your cluster (unless you are using MLA licenses). If you don't have a BorderManager license assigned to the cluster node that will run BorderManager, the service will not start on that node, and you will not achieve fault tolerance for this service.

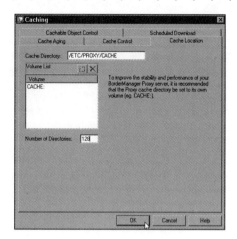

FIGURE 16.1 *Caching dialog box*

Authentication

BorderManager allows two different schemes for allowing incoming and outgoing access through the server, Single Sign On authentication and proxy authentication using SSL.

Single Sign On authentication is accomplished using two different executables found in SYS:PUBLIC of the BorderManager server:

- ▶ CLNTRUST.EXE — This application runs in the system tray of Windows 32-bit desktops (Windows 9x, NT, 2000) and automatically sends the user's credentials over port 3024 to the BorderManager server when required and if enabled on the server.

- ▶ DWNTRUST.EXE — This application forces CLNTRUST to unload on the workstation and should be scheduled to run whenever a user logs off so that their credentials are not left running for the next user to log in.

TIP

In your login scripts, consider running DWNTRUST and immediately following it with CLNTRUST. This way, any existing CLNTRUST session is ended immediately before logging in to NDS. Another alternative is to use a ZENworks policy to run DWNTRUST on logoff and CLNTRUST upon login.

Technically speaking, CLNTRUST does not "failover" if the BorderManager resource is migrated to another node in the cluster. However, functionally this is accomplished because CLNTRUST automatically makes a new background authentication request any time the client tries to access a secure resource, so the client is not prompted with an SSL authentication request even if the BorderManager service is running from a machine other than the one the client first used to make the connection.

NOTE **Previous versions of** CLNTRUST **required that the module be run from the BorderManager server that the client was using. This is no longer required; you can run** CLNTRUST **from any server, and it will function properly for all your BorderManager nodes.**

For non-Windows based clients, or when using reverse proxy, BorderManager provides a Web-based SSL authentication screen that is automatically presented any time a user tries to access a protected resource and does not have CLNTRUST to authenticate them in the background.

This SSL-enabled authentication provides a secure mechanism for users to authenticate using their NDS account to the server. This means that you don't have to manage another database for proxy users; you manage who has access to the Internet using the existing NDS database.

SSL authentication requires that each node in the cluster have a valid SSL certificate and the proper Secure Authentication Service (SAS) enabled and functioning. SSL authentication is server based, so if the BorderManager server that authenticated your access fails or is migrated to a new server, the new server prompts the user to authenticate again.

Rules

BorderManager controls access to content based on rules configured in NDS. These rules can be configured at the BorderManager Server level, Organizational Unit level, the Country level, or at the Organization level. The rules allow administrators the ability to control access to Internet content based on protocol, URL, NDS (such as user name, group membership, and container membership), and domain names. Third-party products such as Cyber Patrol allow additional rules based on classification of content, such as pornography, leisure, and so on.

When BorderManager reads the rules to determine whether access is to be granted or denied, it starts with rules that are configured on the server object, then moves up the NDS tree reading the rules of its parent container, then that container's parent, and so on, until it reaches the Organization object. Once it finds a rule that pertains to the type of access requested, it executes that rule and then discontinues processing any further rules. There is also a default Deny All rule (not shown in the interface unless viewing "effective rules") that executes last (if access control is enabled), so if there is no Allow rule allowing access, access will eventually be denied as all the rules process.

For example, if user SPAYNE tries to go to www.novell.com, BorderManager begins by reading the rules assigned to its NDS server object. If it finds a rule that says "allow the NDS Group 'INTERNET' access to any HTTP site" and SPAYNE is a member of 'INTERNET,' the server stops processing the rules and allows SPAYNE access to the site.

Administrators can manually reorder the rules, which will affect the rule execution scheme.

NOTE

To simplify administration of the BorderManager cluster, configure all of your rules at the container level, rather than the server level. This way, you can enter the rules once at the server's container, and you don't need to worry about having one server allow a user access to a specific site while the next server denies it. For improved performance, place these rules close (in the same NDS partition) to the BorderManager servers in the NDS tree, and add your own Deny All rule at the same level so that the servers do not have to walk farther up the tree than where you have configured all your rules.

Currently, Cyber Patrol allows you to create content access rules only on the NDS server objects. This means that if you are using Cyber Patrol, you must configure the rules on *all* BorderManager servers in the cluster and make sure that they are all configured identically. If you make a change to one server, be sure to change them all, otherwise users may be able to access unauthorized content when BorderManager is active on certain nodes in the cluster.

Network Address Translation and Novell Cluster Services

NetWare 5.x supports Network Address Translation (NAT) as a function of the server operating system. Although NAT is not a component of BorderManager, it is commonly configured in conjunction with a BorderManager installation.

NAT itself is not a service that can be configured as a cluster resource for fault tolerance. However, you can configure each of the nodes in the cluster with the NAT configuration you desire based on the secondary IP addresses that you use in your cluster resource. Though each server will have a unique public IP address (or possibly use a secondary IP address on the public interface if using reverse proxy), you can configure the NAT translation on each server based on the secondary IP address being present. To do so, bind the secondary IP address to the server, and then configure your NAT translations as you normally would. NAT then functions on the server if the secondary IP address is bound, and is ignored if it is not.

The actual connection table for existing NAT connections using dynamic NAT is stored in RAM on the server. This means that if a NAT server fails and the secondary IP address used for NAT moves to another server, all of the sessions in progress on the first server will no longer be valid. The significance of this invalidity depends on the application involved. The results of the invalidity may be as simple as a behind-the-scenes retry or may involve a new authentication to the application. Be sure to test the applications you are concerned with so that you know "normal" behavior of these applications in the event of a resource migration or server failure.

Packet Filtering and Novell Cluster Services

Just like NAT, packet filtering is a function of the NetWare operating system and cannot be failed over in a cluster. However, each BorderManager server can be configured with packet filters based on its view of the world. Configure the filters using the interfaces installed on each node and assume the cluster resource secondary IP address is on the server.

Make sure that you configure the packet filters in the same manner on all BorderManager servers; any time you change one, you need to change them all. Otherwise, you may end up with one server blocked exactly as desired, but other servers leaving a gaping hole in your security!

Installing BorderManager Enterprise Edition to the Cluster

To cluster BorderManager, you first install and configure BorderManager on each node in the cluster that will be in the failover path. The following procedure walks you through installing and configuring BorderManager on each cluster node:

1. Create an NSS partition and storage group on the shared storage for the BorderManager cache.

You can cluster BorderManager without using shared storage if you don't care about losing the file cache in the event of a failure.

TIP

2. Install BorderManager on the first node by following these steps:

a. Bind the secondary IP address you plan to use for the resource to the server by issuing the following command:

```
ADD SECONDARY IPADDRESS <IPADDRESS>
```

This example uses 10.7.5.133 for the BorderManager IP address.

b. Insert the BorderManager CD into the server and mount it.

c. Load NWCONFIG.NLM.

d. Select the Product Options menu item.

e. Select Install a product not listed.

f. Enter the path to the BorderManager installation (that is, BMEE36:\). After a brief delay of several seconds to a couple minutes, the Graphic User Interface (GUI) screen should appear and allow you to continue the installation on the server GUI.

g. Wait for the GUI installation to begin, then click Next to begin the installation.

h. Click Accept to confirm that you already have the latest NetWare OS support pack installed.

If you do not already have the current NetWare Support Pack installed, exit the installation and install the latest Support Pack first.

i. Click Accept to accept the license agreement.

j. In the BorderManager Services Installation dialog box, shown in Figure 16.2, select the products you wish to install, and enter the path to the BorderManager license.

Recall that only the BorderManager firewall/caching services are clusterable. If you select BorderManager VPN services and/or BorderManager Authentication Services, you can install these services but cannot cluster them.

FIGURE 16.2 *BorderManager Services Installation dialog box*

k. Authenticate as a user with rights to extend the NDS schema. The schema will then be extended, and you will either receive confirmation of the success, or an error message if there was a problem.

l. Specify the private and public interfaces, and if desired enable Filters on the public interface and HTTP Proxy on all private interfaces, as shown in Figure 16.3. Note that the private IP address should be the secondary IP address that you used in Step A of this procedure.

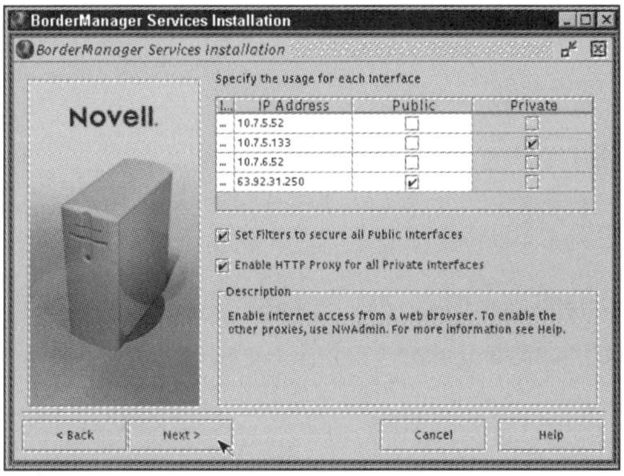

FIGURE 16.3 *Specifying private and public interfaces*

m. If you selected to enable HTTP Proxy on all private interfaces, select whether or not you wish to enable access control on the private interfaces to control outbound Internet access. You can always reconfigure this later if you aren't sure how you want it configured during the installation. If you do not enable access control, then all users can access all Internet sites through the BorderManager server.

n. Verify (or modify) the DNS Domain name for the server.

o. Verify (or modify) the DNS servers for your network. Novell recommends specifying three DNS servers on each of your BorderManager nodes.

p. From the Products to be installed dialog box, click the Finish button to finish the installation. The server will then copy files for several minutes, after which you will be prompted to reboot the server. Each node must be restarted after you install BorderManager.

TIP

You may find that the Java progress bar disappears periodically, most annoyingly at the end of the installation. Be patient, as it will come back. The installation is not complete until you see the Installation complete dialog box shown in Figure 16.4.

FIGURE 16.4 *Installation complete dialog box*

q. Edit the AUTOEXEC.NCF file and remove the LOAD BRDSRV.NLM command. You will be adding this command into the cluster load script, so you do not need it to start automatically any time the server reboots.

3. Repeat the procedure outlined in step 2 on each node in the cluster that you wish to have in the BorderManager resource failover path.

Once you've installed BorderManager to each of the cluster nodes, you must individually configure each server. The server configurations should be identical (with the exception of the public IP addresses, which must be correct for each server), so any configuration you make to one node, you must also make to any other nodes that will be in the failover path for the resource.

Setting Up Login Policies

To access services through BorderManager when using NDS authentication, users must be authenticated to the BorderManager server if you enabled access control. The types of authentication allowed are configured in NDS using a single tree-wide policy that is contained in a Login Policy object located in the security container for the tree.

NOTE

The Login Policy object is new for BorderManager versions 3.5 and later.

If you are only using NDS authentication, you do not need to configure a Login Policy. The Login Policy Object only needs to be implemented when you have more than one form of authentication, such as ActiveCard.

If you already have a login policy in your NDS tree, you do not need to modify it for Novell Cluster Services. If you don't have a login policy, create one using the following procedure:

1. Using NetWare Administrator, select the Security container object for your tree.

2. Right-click the Security container and then click Create. The New Object dialog box appears.

3. From the New Object dialog box, select Login Policy and then click OK. The Create Login Policy dialog box appears.

TIP

If Login Policy is not an option, you are not running NetWare Administrator from a server with the BorderManager snapins installed.

4. From the Create Login Policy dialog box, click Create. A dialog box appears, warning you that you must create at least one rule or all authentications to BorderManager will fail.

5. Click OK to acknowledge this warning.

6. Click the Rules tab of the Login Policy object.

7. Click the Add button to create a new rule. This will bring up the Login Rule Configuration dialog box (see Figure 16.5).

FIGURE 16.5 *Login Rule Configuration dialog box*

8. Verify that the Rule is enabled, then select PROXY from the Service Type drop-down box. Click Add, then browse to the NDS user, group, or container object that you wish this rule to apply to, and then click OK.

9. Click the Methods tab to configure a Login method for the previously selected NDS object.

10. Click the Add button to add a new method, select the authentication method desired, and then click OK three times to close the Login Policy object.

Configuring the BorderManager Nodes

Once you have BorderManager installed on each of the desired nodes, and you have your login policy set, you are ready to configure your BorderManager servers. You must configure each server in an identical manner, or you will get sporadic results depending on where the resource is residing in your cluster. Detailed documentation on all of the BorderManager configuration options can be found on Novell's Web site at www.novell.com/documentation/lg/bmee36/index.html.

The following steps walk you through the minimum required configuration to enable BorderManager Proxy Cache services on one node of the cluster. You must repeat these steps for each node that will be in the failover path:

1. Bind the secondary IP address used for the BorderManager cluster resource to the server you are about to configure, and mount the NSS volume that you will use for the Proxy cache volume.

2. Load BRDSRV.NLM on the server you are about to configure. If BorderManager is not loaded, you will not be able to configure the server using NetWare Administrator. When you load BRDSRV, the BorderManager modules will load, which may take several seconds. Wait for the PROXY.NLM module to fully load before proceeding to step 3.

3. Launch NetWare Administrator and select the NCP object for the server you wish to configure.

4. Right-click the Server object, then select Details.

5. Select the BorderManager Setup page.

6. Verify that the HTTP Proxy service is enabled, then click the Caching button, as shown in Figure 16.6.

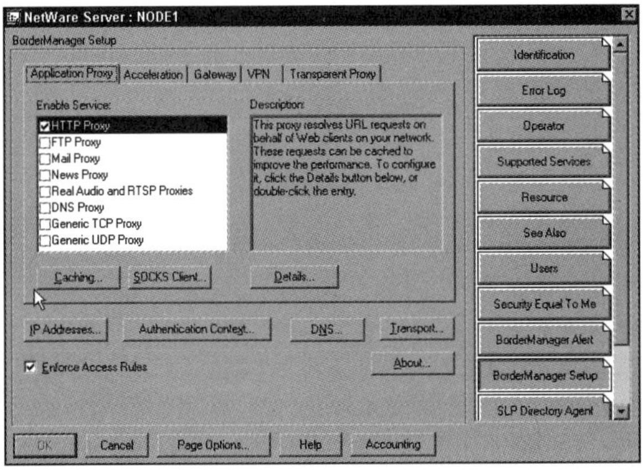

FIGURE 16.6 *BorderManager Setup dialog box*

7. Click the Cache Location tab to configure the cache. (This tab is shown back in Figure 16.1.)

8. Click the SYS volume listed in the Volume List, then click the red X to remove SYS as a cache location.

9. Click the "Add a volume to the list" button (just to the left of the red X), then enter the name of the volume on the shared storage you wish to utilize for caching.

10. If desired, increase the number of cache directories to 128, as recommended by Novell.

Be sure to use the same volume name and cache directories on all nodes that service the BorderManager resource.

TIP

11. Click OK to finish the Cache setup. This will return you to the BorderManager Setup page.

12. Back in the BorderManager Setup page, click the IP Addresses button. In the dialog box that appears, verify that the private IP address corresponds to the cluster resource address and that the public address is the public IP address for this BorderManager server, as shown in Figure 16.7. This will return you to the BorderManager Setup Page once again.

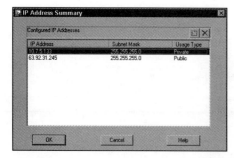

FIGURE 16.7 *Configured IP Addresses dialog box*

13. To enable NDS authentication, click the Authentication Context button (shown in Figure 16.6), and then complete the following in the dialog box shown in Figure 16.8:

a. Select the Enable HTTP Proxy Authentication check box.

b. Select the authentication schemes you wish to use, such as Single Sign On and/or SSL.

c. Configure the time to wait for a Single Sign On reply prior to sending the SSL page, and the maximum idle time prior to forcing a new authentication.

d. Using the Key ID drop-down box, select the appropriate SSL Certificate this BorderManager server should use if using SSL authentication.

e. If desired, check the box to force authentication only when users try to access a restricted page.

f. If desired, enable Transparent Telnet Proxy Authentication.

14. Click the Context tab, click the Add a default NDS context to the list button, and then enter a default NDS tree and NDS context for user authentication. By adding all the contexts that contain users, your users can simply enter their common name on the SSL authentication screen to authenticate to BorderManager. However, the more contexts you enter, the slower the authentication performance will be.

15. If desired, change the logging location from the SYS volume to the shared volume.

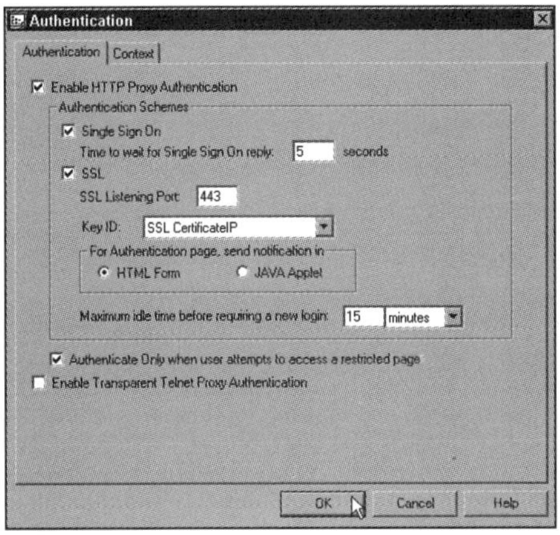

FIGURE 16.8 *Authentication dialog box*

Once you have configured the first node, you must configure all other nodes in the BorderManager failover path with the identical configuration.

Creating the Cluster Resource

Now that you have installed and configured BorderManager on all the nodes in the resource path, you are ready to create the new cluster resource. To create the resource, complete the following steps:

1. Launch ConsoleOne, and select the cluster container object.

2. Click the New Cluster Resource button.

3. Enter the name for the resource, select Define additional properties, and then click Create.

4. Enter the following load script commands, as shown in Figure 16.9:

```
NSS /ACTIVATE = <Volume Name>

MOUNT <Volume Name>

ADD SECONDARY IPADDRESS <IP Address>

LOAD BRDSRV
```

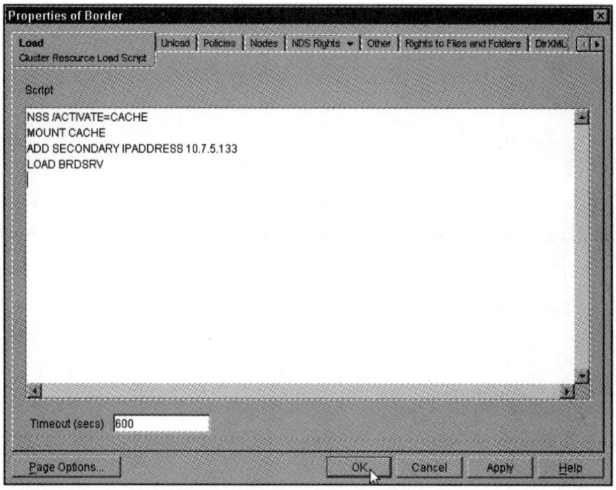

FIGURE 16.9 *BorderManager load script*

TIP

It is not necessary or beneficial to use a cluster-enabled volume for BorderManager since clients do not need to map drives to the cache volume.

5. Click the Unload Script tab, and enter the following commands in the unload script, as shown in Figure 16.10:

```
UNLOAD PROXY

UNLOAD IPXIPGW

UNLOAD BRDMON

UNLOAD PROXYCFG

UNLOAD ACLCHECK

UNLOAD NBMALERT

UNLOAD BRDSRV

DEL SECONDARY IPADDRESS <IP Address>

DISMOUNT <Volume Name> /FORCE

NSS /DEACTIVATE = <Volume Name>
```

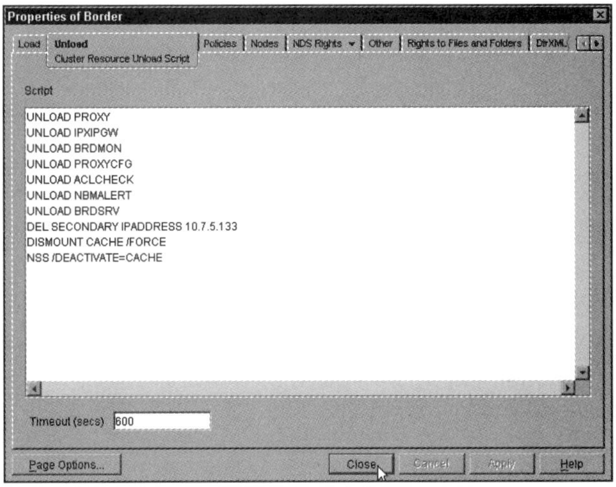

FIGURE 16.10 *BorderManager unload script*

6. Configure the policies and preferred nodes as desired.

7. Prior to setting the resource online, execute all of the "unload" commands listed in step 5 on each of your BorderManager servers and make sure that none of them have the resource volume or secondary IP address activated.

8. Online the resource, and test the configuration.

9. Migrate the resource to each server in the failover path and test the configuration.

Migration/Failover Characteristics

The time it takes BorderManager to migrate or failover is very dependent on the actual configuration and cache size, and varies widely according to the usage. In a lab environment, it will migrate very quickly, whereas a heavily used production server may take a few minutes to initialize.

Authentication Characteristics

BorderManager allows either Single Sign On or SSL authentication. Single Sign On authentication is accomplished with CLNTRUST.EXE, which will automatically authenticate the user to the BorderManager server any time an authentication request is needed. Because this is done in the background, the user is not aware that a failure or migration has occurred, making it very transparent to the user. In the event the user tries to access a site during the short time it takes the BorderManager service to start on the new node, the client experiences either a timeout or very slow access to the page. Since users are used to timeouts on the Web, they will most likely retry the page anyway and never know the service was unavailable.

If the users are using SSL authentication, the authentication is server-centric and cannot transparently reconnect to the new server. If the BorderManager resource is migrated to a new server, the next time an authentication is required a new authentication page will be sent to the user, and the user must relogin. This is somewhat inconvenient, but it does hide the server failure from the user and allows the user to continue working after a server failure with very little disruption.

Active/Active versus Active/Passive

BorderManager is an Active/Passive resource, which can only be active on one node at a time since it must initialize the cache volume when loading.

Summary

In this chapter, you learned about the components of Novell BorderManager Enterprise Edition (BMEE) 3.6 and examined which of those can be configured as fault-tolerant services in a cluster. You also learned the general guidelines for clustering BMEE and the caveats that you must understand when deploying this solution. Finally, you learned the process for setting up BMEE in a fault-tolerant cluster configuration, and the failover characteristics of BorderManager, which are as follows:

CLUSTER FAILOVER CLASSIFICATION INDEX	
Transparency	Very transparent when using `CLNTRUST`; requires new authentication when using SSL
Active/Active or Active/Passive	Active/Passive
Length to failover	Varies according to configuration

With the knowledge gained from this chapter, you can now set up a fault-tolerant, highly available firewall with NDS-based logging and access rules. This allows you to set up a fault-tolerant border to the Internet without purchasing the high-end hardware switching solutions at significantly more cost.

## CHAPTER 17

Backing Up Cluster Volumes on Storage Area Networks

One of the reasons to deploy a Storage Area Network is to enable flexible storage management, such as online allocation and reconfiguration of storage. However, another critical part of managing storage remains your backup and restore strategy. (When this chapter discusses backup, it's referring to both backup and restore.) In this chapter, you learn how to back up a Novell Cluster Services Storage Area Network.

Before the chapter moves into SAN backup concepts, it reviews the traditional server backup architecture of current production local area networks and analyzes some of the problems faced by organizations when they try to protect data via backup. It will then discuss the relative merits of file- versus volume-level backup. Traditional backup is file-oriented, whereas SANs are block-oriented and enable some new backup possibilities.

Next, backup concepts for SANs are introduced. Here you learn about LAN-free backup and volume snapshots, for example. The chapter offers some tips for designing a successful backup strategy and gives detailed steps for backing up Novell Custer Services SANs. It focuses on backup strategies for clusters and explores how single system image cluster management simplifies backup procedures compared to those required for a number of individual non-clustered SAN attached servers.

Reviewing Traditional Backup Architectures

In the client/server storage management era as it existed prior to the advent of storage area networking, direct attached file server data was backed up in one of two ways:

► *Direct attached tape device* — To back up the data owned by a file server, you attach a tape drive to the file server and copy data from its disks to tape using the file server as an intermediary for managing the data copy process. In this direct attached disk and tape type of file server configuration, data flows from disks, through the file server's memory, and onto tape. Backing up a file server is an I/O intensive activity; file servers are busy while being backed up.

▸ *Shared local area network tape device* — Because it's typically not feasible from a cost or operational perspective to equip every file server with a dedicated tape device, a single tape device is instead attached to a special-purpose backup server. A backup server accesses other target file servers to retrieve file data to be backed up to the tape device to which only the backup server has physical access. The backup server requests data, and target file servers return the data to be backed up, using local area network–based protocols. To be written to tape by the special backup server, file server data travels over the local area network. Backing up many remote file servers over a local area network is also an I/O intensive activity; file servers and the local area network are both busy while being backed up. Consider also the amount of data that flows during a network backup; during a full weekly dump, for example, all the data held by all file servers flows across the network.

Novell Storage Management Services (SMS) is an excellent example of the traditional local area network–based client/server backup architecture. SMS architecture demonstrates the implicit assumption made by most traditional client/server backup systems: File system (or other) data to be backed up is physically located on disk drives directly attached to "owner" file servers.

Figure 17.1 illustrates the SMS architecture. There are three NetWare file servers in the diagram. Only one of them, called the Storage Management Engine (SME), has direct access to a tape device. All three servers are attached to a local area network. Target servers are regular NetWare 5 file servers with direct attached disks. To back up the target file servers, the Storage Management Engine runs software called the Storage Management Data Requester (SMDR). The Storage Management Engine uses SMDR to send requests for data to target servers over the local area network. Every target server runs SMS software called a Target Service Agent (TSA). TSAs respond to SMDR requests by reading data from local disks and returning that data over the local area network. When SMDR receives the target server's reply, it returns it to the Storage Management Engine, which writes the data to the local tape device. SMDR is loaded on the local and remote servers and provides communication services between the SME and TSAs.

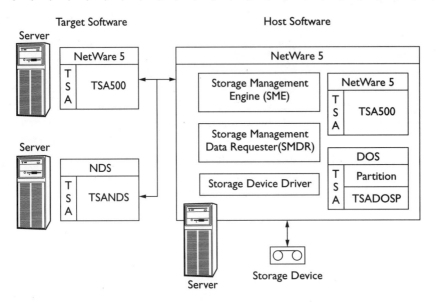

FIGURE 17.1 *Novell's Storage Management Services demonstrates the classic local area network–based client/server backup architecture—file server data is accessible only to the owning file server.*

Storage Management Services comprises the following components:

- *Storage Management Engine (SME)* — Generic backup and restore software. Novell provides the `SBACKUP` utility as a basic SME for NetWare. `SBCON.NLM` is the server-based interface and `NWBACK32.EXE` is the Windows interface for `SBACKUP`. Many third-party vendors provide SMEs for NetWare, such as Veritas's Backup Exec and Computer Associates' ARCserve.

- *Storage Management Data Requester (SMDR)* — The communication layer between SMEs and Target Service Agents. It provides transparent access to SMS services by exposing a set of SMS APIs, which can be used to access local or remote SMS services. These APIs are used by `SBACKUP` and many other third-party backup applications.

- *Storage Device Driver* — Passes data between the SME/SMDR and direct attached storage device hardware such as a tape drive or optical disk. The Storage Device Driver is typically a regular NetWare SCSI driver, such as `NWTAPE.CDM`.

▸ *Target Service Agents (TSAs)* — Receives requests and commands from the SME (via SMDR) and retrieves and returns formatted data in response. TSAs package data in a generic format. This allows a single SME to interact with many types of TSAs.

Storage Management Services enables generic backup via application-specific Target Service Agents. There are TSAs for the NetWare file system, for GroupWise post offices, and for Novell Directory Services databases. Each TSA understands its application-specific data format. It translates backup requests into application-specific data retrieval, then returns that data to be backed up.

For example, when backing up a GroupWise post office, the GroupWise TSA (GWTSA), new with GroupWise 6, retrieves data from its post office and domain databases in a GroupWise-specific manner but returns that data to the backup engine in a generic format suitable for backup.

NetWare file system volumes are backed up using a file system–specific TSA; for NetWare 5, it is called TSA500. TSA500 accesses file and trustee information from disk and returns it to the backup engine. A NetWare 5 server can run a number of Target Service Agents depending on the applications and services it provides. NetWare volumes that are physically mounted by a remote file server are backed up by communicating with that file server's corresponding Target Service Agent (TSA500) via local SMDR to remote SMDR communication. Volumes that are physically mounted on the same server that is running the backup engine are backed up by interacting with a local TSA.

If you review the way data is accessed and flows in the traditional client/server backup architecture, some interesting operational factors are revealed:

▸ To back up the data on a file server's locally attached disks, it has to be running a TSA. If the file server is unavailable because the TSA isn't running or the file server is down, its data cannot be backed up. Typical scheduled backup windows are open only during certain times of the day. If a file server isn't available during the backup window, its data won't be backed up until the next time the backup window is open.

▸ Backing up a file server is an expensive operation. Volumes are scanned for incremental changes, and data has to travel across the local area network. One of the reasons backup windows exist is to avoid unnecessarily loading production servers and networks during peak hours. The impact of running a backup during the middle of the day can reduce the availability of servers for users accessing them because they become less responsive to client requests when busy.

▸ The rate at which data can be backed up is limited to the slowest data path in the system. If data travels over a 100 megabits-per-second Ethernet link between target server and backup server, it doesn't matter how much faster either server can access disk or write to tape — backups proceed at a rate no faster than the rate of the Ethernet, around 10 megabits per second. If the same Ethernet segment is also shared by clients that are accessing file servers, the sustainable bandwidth is typically much less.

NOTE

In practice, actual backup performance is much less than the theoretical maximum bandwidth of a hardware channel. Many factors contribute to reduce the application-level bandwidth compared to the hardware-level bandwidth. The theoretical maximum numbers are used only to demonstrate the kind of calculations necessary to capacity plan for backup. Results at least indicate the ceiling, the maximum theoretical bandwidth attainable.

▸ The elapsed time to complete a backup is a function of the backup rate and amount of data to be processed. Processing includes the time needed to scan data for changes that satisfy the backup selection criteria and to format the data ready for backup. For example, suppose you are backing up the data attached to 10 file servers and each file server has volumes containing 100GB of data. If you have a single backup engine (SME), it has to contact each of the 10 file servers to back up that server's 100GB. A simple calculation that ignores the time to process data on each file server results in a total elapsed time of approximately 28 hours: (10 × 100GB) / 10 megabytes per second = 100,000 seconds.

▸ In the previous example, one SME and its attached tape device processes every target file server in sequential order. The ratio of target file servers to SME is 10 to 1. By installing a second SME, the ratio is halved to 5 to 1. Assuming that the local area network bandwidth also scales to support both SMEs, the total elapsed time is reduced to approximately 14 hours. This illustrates how I/O parallelism applied at the right place has a dramatic effect. Taking this example to its logical extreme, suppose every target file server has its own direct attached tape drive. The backup rate is now independent of Ethernet bandwidth or utilization. Each file server can transfer data between its locally attached disks and tape device at a rate limited only by the server's I/O channel. For a standard enterprise server equipped with a Wide Ultra2 SCSI I/O subsystem, this is around 80MB per second. Each file server enjoys eight times the LAN bandwidth, and all file servers can back up in parallel, for an aggregate 80 times Ethernet bandwidth. Note, however, as with the previous calculation, that this also assumes an otherwise unused data transfer channel and ignores many other practical considerations.

These simplistic calculations ignore some important factors, but the point is that successful client/server backup is all about speeds, feeds, and availability. Backup is both bandwidth and I/O intensive. System availability is partly a function of server and network load. Systems are heavily loaded when backed up, so they are effectively less available to end users. Backup availability is a function of matching access to disks with access to tape devices. Because the ratio of file servers to tape devices is usually high, a majority of data has to travel across a local area network from target file servers to a backup server to be backed up.

The preceding issues are real and faced by many organizations. They are compounded by the following factors:

▶ Much more data must be protected than ever before. Data growth is exploding.

▶ Local area networks aren't getting substantially faster. As soon as you add capacity, client workstations find a way to use it. For example, with extra local area network bandwidth, employees usually discover the novelty of watching Internet videos or listening to their favorite radio shows from their desktops.

▶ Backup windows are being closed by the demand for system availability. Dark periods no longer exist; systems are required to be available 24 hours a day, 7 days a week. How is data to be protected when it also has to be available all the time?

These issues present a common theme discussed throughout this book. It's no coincidence that effective storage management and high availability are enabled by the combination of Cluster Services and Storage Area Networks. Consider these backup possibilities:

▶ A backup server that is attached to a Storage Area Network has access to all disks regardless of individual target servers. With the right kind of software, the backup server doesn't even need to contact the target server to back up its volumes. It can simply mount the volumes directly and back them up to its locally attached tape drive as though the disks were also locally attached. This has the effect of dynamically collocating target volumes with the backup server for the purpose of backup. Target volumes move to the tape device to back up each volume's data. No local area network communication exists.

▶ Instead of attaching a tape device to a backup server's local I/O channel, if you attach it directly to a Storage Area Network port, any file server can temporarily acquire use of the tape device to back up data it has access to at that time. This shifts the responsibility of the special backup server to any server capable of doing I/O to shared disks and a commonly accessible tape device. Any server on the Storage Area Network can function as a backup engine, and this responsibility can shift from server to server. This has the effect of dynamically collocating the tape device with target volumes for the purpose of backup. The tape device can move from server to server to back up each server's volumes. Again, no local area network communication exists.

▶ When a Storage Area Network attached file server reads from disks and writes to tape, it does so at full fibre channel bandwidth of 100MB per second. Data doesn't go anywhere near the already busy local area network; instead, it travels the Storage Area Network at a rate approximately 10 times faster that of the LAN. Furthermore, data transfers benefit from block-oriented streaming performance on the Storage Area Network in contrast to the remote procedure call (request/respond) kind of traffic, characterized by long round-trip delays, on local area networks.

The remainder of this chapter discusses how to use Novell NetWare Clusters and Storage Area Networks to virtually eliminate traditional backup issues.

Exploring File- versus Block-Level Backup

File servers translate file operations into block-level device I/O. They access disk and tape devices using SCSI block-level protocols. Traditional backup and restore software is a file server application that accesses files on volumes owned by a file server. However, there are two fundamental ways to access or back up data owned by a file server:

▶ File-level backup

▶ Block-level backup

File-Level Backup

File-level backup software uses file system APIs to access files. Whole files are opened, read, and backed up by having their entire contents written to tape. Catalog and file metadata is also written to tape. SMS is a file-level backup architecture. Files are accessed by a TSA when running on a file server as a file server application. Even when files are backed up remotely over the local area network, they are nonetheless accessed using file system APIs.

When the backup software opens a file to read and back up its contents, the file might already be in the open state on behalf of a different server application or a client. The possibility of open files complicates the file-level backup process because backup software cannot guarantee consistent access to the file's contents while it is open. The other party may not have flushed updated buffers back to the file and so the image of the file from the file system's perspective is potentially corrupt from the application's point of view. Novell solutions to this inconsistent open file issue are discussed in the section "Backing Up Open Files on Cluster Volumes".

Block-Level Backup

To perform a block-level backup, all of the disk blocks that compose an entire file system are read directly from disk and written to tape. This process is also called *image* backup because an image of a file system is captured via its underlying disk blocks. Block-level backup is usually faster than scanning and reading individual files, but suffers from a lack of knowledge of file system data structures and layout. Though it's physically possible to back up a file system block by block if the file system is also active, it is extremely likely that the backup process will capture an inconsistent snapshot of the file system image.

For example, suppose you back up an entire file system by reading all of its disk blocks and writing them to tape. If an application updates files or file system organization midway through the backup, it's possible for the blocks that are written to tape to include data from before and after the update. The image of the file system thus captured to tape is inconsistent. If you restore the file system by writing all of the blocks from tape back to disk, the file system may or may not be corrupt depending on the nature of the block-level conflict.

Block-level backup works only when the backup software and the file system coordinate their access to disk blocks. In practice, one of the easiest ways to ensure a consistent block-level backup is to deactivate the file system so that disk blocks cannot be changed while the backup software is running. The disadvantage with this approach is that the file system is necessarily offline for as long as it takes to copy all of its disk blocks to other media (usually tape).

The other problem with block-level backup is that the snapshot image of a file system isn't very portable. Blocks are a low-level representation of a file system and lack the higher-level meaning that makes files portable in a network. For example, the data blocks comprising a NetWare file system contain server-specific encoding of file-level trustee assignments. If file system blocks are backed up from one server, then restored to a different server, file-level trustee assignments become invalid. When the second file server accesses restored data blocks, it finds trustee data it has no way to decode. Novell solutions to these issues are discussed in the section "Implementing Cluster Volume Snapshot".

Introducing Backup Concepts for Clustered SANs

In a Novell Cluster Services Storage Area Network, only one node is allowed to activate a volume for disk I/O at any given time. That node acquires an exclusive distributed lock on the volume. No other node is allowed to acquire the same lock while the volume remains active on the first node. This guarantees mutual exclusion of block-level access between cluster nodes. This mechanism creates the notion of temporary ownership of volumes. Just because a volume is owned by one node on one day, it doesn't necessarily follow that the volume is owned by that node for all time. Volumes migrate between cluster nodes as a function of node availability.

File-level backup of cluster volumes is enabled in one of two ways:

- ▸ If the cluster node that happens to have the volume mounted also has access to a tape device, it reads files from the volume and writes them directly to tape. There is no local area network traffic. By running backup software, the node functions as an SME for the duration of the backup.

- ▸ If the cluster node that has the volume mounted doesn't have access to a tape device, it can instead run a TSA and enable a backup server that does have access to a tape device to run the SME and back up its data over the local area network. Suppose the backup server is actually a cluster node attached to the same SAN. Even though it also has access to the volume's disk blocks via the SAN, it cannot access them directly because it can't activate the volume while the first node owns it. The backup server must send requests to the TSA running on the node that has the volume mounted to gain file level access, thereby forcing unnecessary remote LAN access. Instead of requiring the backup server to remotely access the volume over the local area network, you can have the cluster volume migrate to the backup server. This is essentially the same idea as moving the volume to the tape drive and enables the equivalent of direct disk to tape backup. The backup engine accesses the volume as though it were located on direct attached disks and writes data directly to the tape device.

Consider the diagram in Figure 17.2. It depicts a cluster of four NetWare servers attached to a Storage Area Network. Cluster nodes are named Node0, Node1, Node2, and Node3. They all share access to an external storage array. Twelve cluster-enabled volumes are located on storage array disks named V1–V12. The preferred node lists are configured so that each node has access to three volumes by default, and access to other volumes in failover situations. For example, Node0 has access to three volumes: V1, V2, and V3. Other nodes have access to different volumes. Figure 17.2 also shows three possible places to attach a tape device relative to servers and volumes. The first option is to attach the tape device directly to the SAN. The second option has a tape device directly attached to one of the servers — Node3 in the figure. The third option is similar to the first; the tape unit is attached to the SAN via an integrated storage array that contains disks and the tape unit. Not shown in the diagram is the local area network, but assume that all cluster nodes are also attached to at least a common IP subnet. There is, therefore, a fourth place a tape drive might be located: directly attached to the local I/O bus of a traditional backup server that is connected to the local area network external to the cluster.

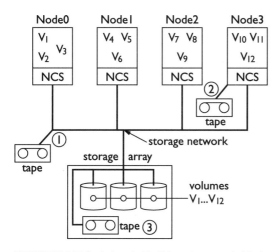

FIGURE 17.2 *A 4-node NetWare cluster with 12 cluster volumes located in an external SAN storage array*

From a backup configuration perspective, Storage Area Networks enable new options for managing tape access and the transfer of data between volumes and tapes. To review, the four possible places to attach a tape device are as follows:

▶ The tape device is directly attached to the Storage Area Network and is accessible to all servers in a manner that emulates the kind of access a server would have if the tape were attached to its local I/O channel. To enable this kind of direct access, the tape device requires a fibre channel port. Alternatively, any existing SCSI tape device or library can be attached to a Storage Area Network using a SCSI–to–Fibre Channel router/bridge product. You plug the router into a fibre channel port and the tape device into the SCSI connector on the router. For example, if you already own a large expensive tape library and it is connected to one of your servers via a local SCSI bus, unplug it from the server and attach it to the SAN via a SAN router. To transfer data from a file system volume to tape, any server reads the corresponding disks and writes to the tape via the SAN. The need for a special backup server disappears. This is called the *floating tape* backup method because access to the tape device floats to the server that needs to back up its volumes.

▶ The tape device is attached to the local I/O channel of one of the servers in the cluster. Only that server can access the tape device, but that server nonetheless has access to all the disks on the SAN. This at least enables volumes to migrate from other nodes to the backup server to be backed up at the equivalent of local SCSI I/O channel bandwidth. The backup server mounts each volume, and its backup software uses file-level access to read files from the file system and write their contents to the local tape. This is called the *floating volume* backup method because access to a volume floats to the backup server so the backup server can back the volume up. The floating volume backup method is also used when ownership of a SAN attached tape device is assigned to a dedicated backup server. You might dedicate a shared tape device to a fixed server if that server is the only one that has the backup software installed on it, for example. If that server fails, a shared tape device can quickly be assigned to any other server, however.

▶ The tape device is directly attached to the SAN via an integrated storage array. The tape and disks are located inside the storage array. Servers have access to any disk and the tape unit over the SAN at the equivalent of SCSI I/O channel bandwidth. This is the same kind of access as mentioned in the first bullet point in this list. Some storage array products enable block-level backup using firmware that runs on an embedded processor located inside the storage array cabinet. Because block-level backup doesn't require file system knowledge, the storage array firmware copies blocks from its disks to tape independent of the file servers. To avoid the potential for capturing an inconsistent image, some interaction between backup software and file server is required to suspend file system I/O while the backup is running.

▶ When the tape device is attached to a remote backup server, the only way to perform backup is via the traditional client/server local area network method. The backup server runs the backup software. Each cluster node runs a TSA that enables the backup server to reach its volumes. Data has to travel across the local area network, from cluster nodes to the backup server, for the backup software to write that data to tape. The only advantage offered by the cluster and SAN in this scenario is high availability. If one of the nodes should fail, its volumes are mounted by surviving nodes. Access to volumes is restored via TSAs running on failover nodes. To make this work in practice, the backup software has to switch to a different server-volume-centric backup job for the failover server and volume. This is called a *failover backup job*. Creating failover backup jobs for Novell Cluster Services is discussed later in this chapter.

Many of the previously discussed ideas relative to shifting the transfer of backup data from local area networks to SANs has corresponding industry standard terminology. The next several sections describe the standard SAN terminology for these ideas.

LAN-Free Backup

LAN-free backup describes the idea that backup data need not flow across local area networks in order to move from disk to tape. The backup process is "LAN free." Your poor old local area network isn't burdened every night with having to transfer every single file from every single file server to the backup engine's tape device.

Serverless Backup

Once you realize that individual servers have become less important in the overall Storage Area Network, the flow of backup data from disk to tape need not even pass through a traditional file server. File servers are merely processing elements that run file system software. The actual data is held on SAN disks. To back up a file system, it's possible to copy data from disks directly to tape without that data passing through a file server.

The idea of *serverless backup* is to shift the actual processing of backup-related file level operations from busy production file servers to special embedded devices attached to the SAN. For this to work in practice, the embedded device must understand the file system format and cooperate with the file server that is accessing shared disk blocks.

Serverless file-level backup hasn't really caught on because of the difficulties of negotiating file-level access to shared file system data blocks. Block-level serverless backup is more commonplace.

Third-Party Copy

Third-party copy is the terminology given to the actual process of serverless backup. A third-party copy engine, also sometimes called a *Data Mover*, is a device separate from file servers, disks, or tapes. It is special hardware comprising an embedded CPU and memory and is responsible for independently moving data from disk to tape for backup and from tape to disk for restore. For file-level backup, third-party copy engines necessarily have to negotiate access to shared devices with file servers. Third-party copy engines are often integrated with existing SAN infrastructure devices via fibre channel switch-based option blades or embedded within tape device electronics.

Volume Snapshot

When a file system's data blocks are duplicated across mirrored disks by an intelligent storage array, it is possible to take a very fast block-level *volume snapshot* of the corresponding file system by separating the logical connection between the two sides of the mirror. This is called *breaking the mirror*. The result is two identical copies of the same file system (volume) image. Volume snapshot is much faster than copying all of the data blocks to secondary media. Breaking a mirror simply involves toggling an internal storage array flag. This can be accomplished in a matter of seconds.

Once there are two identical block-level copies of the same file system, one copy stays online while the other copy is taken offline for backup. The online copy of the file system continues to be accessed by the original file server.

WARNING Unless there is file system involvement in the volume snapshot process, the offline copy of the volume will lack any file system changes that remain in cache. The blocks of the offline copy are essentially equivalent to what would be on disk had the file server failed or been abruptly powered down. This is called a *crash-consistent* image. It's not considered harmful since Novell Storage Services is designed to recover from this state. But unless you take steps to sync (flush) the file system cache before taking the snapshot, the offline copy of the volume will not contain recent changes.

Volume snapshot enables two main benefits:

▶ Because the file system stays online, access is virtually uninterrupted during the actual snapshot process. What the file server had access to before the mirror was broken, it continues to have access to afterward.

▶ The offline copy of the file system is backed up by mounting it on a different backup server. Backup happens while the original file server continues to provide uninterrupted access to the online copy.

Volume snapshot enables online backup. Regular access to a file system isn't affected during online backup because the processing overhead to back up the offline copy of the file system is shifted away from the original file server to a backup server with capacity dedicated to this purpose. You use the backup server to perform traditional incremental or full file level backup of the offline copy of the file system absent open file issues.

X-REF Using volume snapshot with Novell Cluster Services is described later in this chapter in the section "Implementing Cluster Volume Snapshot."

Designing Clustered SANs to Enable Backup

Implementing a successful clustered-SAN backup strategy requires analysis and design no different than implementing a successful client/server local area network backup strategy. As mentioned earlier, a successful backup strategy is all about speeds, feeds, and availability. Storage Area Networks enable more options and much better performance, but the basic backup design analysis remains essentially unchanged. Phrased as a question: How do you implement a Storage Area

Network–based backup strategy capable of backing up the required amount of data in the required amount of time?

Here are the factors you need to consider in your backup analysis and design:

▶ *How much data is there?* For example, perhaps you have 50GB per file server and 100 file servers. Total data size is therefore 5000GB.

▶ *How long is the backup window?* Typical backup windows start at the end of the business day and end the following day. Perhaps you have an eight-hour window.

▶ *Where will the data flow?* The answer to this question depends on the location of the tape device relative to data to be backed up. Will data travel over the LAN or the SAN?

▶ *How many tape devices?* What is the ratio of number of file servers to number of tape devices? Perhaps you own a multicartridge tape robot.

▶ *How much parallelism is possible?* Analyze the backup data flow. Where is the data coming from and where is it going? Is it possible to run multiple data flows in parallel? Can your infrastructure sustain this?

▶ *Where is the bottleneck?* There is always a bottleneck — the point where bandwidth is limited by the slowest element. Identifying the bottleneck will help you design around it.

TIP

Don't design your Storage Area Network without considering backup and restore. Think about backup data flows and data size during the initial design stages. Don't build a system that's impossible to back up!

Table 17.1 lists some ballpark numbers you can use as a baseline for analyzing backup performance. Backup performance is typically measured in megabytes per second. The numbers in Table 17.1 are typical real-world numbers reported by Novell customers or engineers.

T A B L E 17.1	
Baseline LAN and SAN Backup Performance Data	
100 MBPS LAN	**1 GBPS SAN**
1- to 3MB per second per channel	40- to 60MB per second per channel

When you plan a backup, use the following calculation:

(Number of volumes × Size of each volume) / (Backup rate × Parallelism)

The result is an amount of time. Is this amount of time larger than your backup window? If so, then the system is impossible to back up. To fix the problem, you need to work on the right-hand side of the equation. Can you increase the backup rate by moving data off the local area network and onto the SAN? Can you increase parallelism by deploying more tape devices and I/O channels? For example, perhaps you can install a redundant fibre channel switch for high availability purposes, but use the switch to enable a second I/O path for parallel backup.

TIP

One design strategy to help your backup capabilities is to limit your volumes to no more than 100GB. A larger number of smaller volumes is better than a small number of large ones. In addition to optimizing cluster fan-out failover, a design with more small volumes is easier to back up, especially if you have SAN-attached shared tape devices and multiple cluster nodes that can run backup in parallel across the SAN.

Backing Up Novell Cluster Services SANs

By taking into account the results of your backup analysis and resulting design, follow the following cross-references to the information concerning the backup strategies you have chosen to use:

- ▶ If you need to back up open files, then first read the upcoming section "Backing up Open Files on Cluster Volumes" for more information.

- ▶ If you have decided to use the volume snapshot backup strategy, read the section "Implementing Cluster Volume Snapshot" later in this chapter for more information.

- ▶ If your tape device is connected to a backup server that is external to your cluster, read the proceeding section "Working with Failover Backup Jobs" for more information.

If none of those three scenarios apply in your case, you have probably decided to use either the floating tape method or the floating volume method to back up your cluster.

▸ *Floating tape* — Your tape device is attached to the SAN and is shared by all the nodes in the cluster. The tape device is reserved by an individual node when it starts running a backup job. *Reserve* and *release* is a hardware mechanism that grants a server exclusive access to the tape device for the duration of the backup job. Since any node can run a backup job, install backup software on all your cluster nodes. Create duplicate cluster-enabled volume backup jobs on each node that is identified by the corresponding cluster volume resource's preferred node list. First read the section "Working with Failover Backup Jobs" and then read the section "Implementing Floating Tape Backups" for more information.

▸ *Floating volume* — Your tape device is directly attached to one of the nodes in the cluster or is attached to the SAN but is dedicated to a single node in the cluster. This node is the designated "backup server" and is the only node that runs backup software. Install backup software to the backup server node. Create backup jobs on the backup server node for every cluster-enabled volume. Read the section "Implementing Floating Volume Backups" for more information.

NOTE

Neither the floating tape nor the floating volume backup method is terribly well field proven. No one has very much experience with using these methods in production clusters. Therefore, you should work with Novell and your backup vendor to fine-tune these methods to your configuration. The floating volume method is simply a combination of designating one cluster node as the backup server and using Cluster Services software to migrate volumes to that server for backup. The floating tape method requires third-party support for shared SAN tape reserve and release and, therefore, is backup software vendor dependent. For example, Veritas's Shared Storage Option (SSO) supports shared SAN tape devices and libraries with Novell Cluster Services.

Working with Failover Backup Jobs

All currently available backup and restore software for NetWare is of the traditional client/server variety and explicitly assumes that volumes are accessible only to fixed "owner" file servers. This has a direct effect on the way you create and schedule backup jobs for clusters.

Backup jobs are server-volume centric, meaning the backup software presents a user interface that forces you to first identify a file server, then volumes on that file server to configure in a backup job. Because cluster volumes can failover from one node to another, there is no guarantee that a backup job created for one node will actually back up the volume if it happened to have failed over to another node. To protect all volumes in the cluster, you must create duplicate backup jobs for each node in the cluster.

NOTE

For NetWare 6 clusters, Novell has enhanced SMS to enable *server independent* backup jobs. Instead of creating multiple failover backup jobs (one per physical server), you create a single backup job corresponding to the virtual NCP server that hosts the cluster volume. This greatly simplifies file level backup job management for clusters. You only need create one backup job per cluster volume regardless of which physical server it is mounted on at the time it is backed up. This is another place that Novell Cluster Services provides single-system image — the illusion of working with and managing a single system that is presented by clustering software. The procedure described in the following text is for NetWare 5 clusters.

For every cluster-enabled volume, create a backup job for that volume on each node listed in the corresponding cluster volume resource's preferred nodes list. The preferred nodes list identifies all the nodes a cluster volume could possibly failover to. To catch a volume on a node to back it up, backup jobs are created on all of the volume's preferred nodes.

TIP

You don't need to create backup jobs on all of a volume's preferred nodes unless you require total protection. For example, suppose a volume has preferred nodes: Node0, Node1, Node2, and Node3. You might decide to create a backup job for the volume only when on Node0 or Node1. This assumes that the volume will be located on those nodes in all but the most extreme failure scenarios.

You have two ways to create duplicate backup jobs for volumes located on one of many potential cluster nodes:

▶ Use the backup software to create a backup job on the first cluster node. By default, when you create a backup job on a node, it enables backup for all volumes currently mounted on that node. As we've discussed, this will probably exclude volumes mounted on other nodes. Next, use a backup job editor to edit the job to include the missing volumes. Repeat this process for all nodes and all volumes in the cluster.

> ▸ Use ConsoleOne to migrate cluster volumes to each node, and then create a backup job for each node that includes the volumes. Repeat this process for all nodes and all volumes in the cluster.

TIP

It is highly recommended that you name the failover jobs so that they can quickly be distinguished from normal backup jobs. The only backup job that will succeed is the job that is run on the node that has the volume mounted at the time. Jobs on other nodes that list the same volume will fail when they run because the volume isn't mounted on those nodes at that time.

For example, consider the cluster in Figure 17.3. It has 12 volumes and 4 nodes.

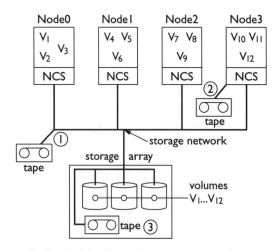

FIGURE 17.3 *A NetWare cluster comprising 4 nodes and 12 cluster volumes*

A relatively easy method to manage multiple duplicate backup jobs for cluster volumes and nodes is by using a spreadsheet. Create a spreadsheet as shown in Table 17.2. Because you typically have fewer nodes than volumes, organize the spreadsheet so node names are the column headings and cluster volume names are listed in the rows. Table cells are the names of backup jobs for each volume on each node. In the interest of saving space, Table 17.2 doesn't show all 12 volumes from Figure 17.3. The idea is to name backup jobs corresponding to the most preferred node for each volume because that's where it will be backed up a majority of the time. For example, V1_Primary is the name of the backup job for volume V1 when on its primary node. V1_Failover1, V1_Failover2, and V1_Failover3 are the names of backup jobs for V1 when on any of its three failover nodes.

The backup job run on the most preferred node for a volume is considered the primary job. If a volume is located on another node, its failover backup job succeeds, and the primary job fails. For each volume, only one job succeeds. By adopting this kind of job-naming scheme, you can quickly identify successful backups and the nodes they occurred on.

TABLE 17.2

Using a Spreadsheet to Manage Cluster Volume/Node Backup Jobs

VOLUME	NODE0	NODE1	NODE2	NODE3
V1	V1_Primary	V1_Failover1	V1_Failover2	V1_Failover3
V2	V2_Failover0	V2_Primary	V2_Failover2	V2_Failover3
V3	V3_Failover0	V3_Failover1	V3_Primary	V3_Failover3
V4	V3_Failover0	V3_Failover1	V3_Failover2	V4_Primary

NOTE

NetWare 6 alleviates many of the difficulties created by the traditional server-volume-centric backup architecture by introducing the concept of cluster-volume backup jobs. This enables the creation of a single job per cluster volume regardless of the node it's mounted on.

Implementing Floating Tape Backups

The floating tape backup method is enabled with both hardware and backup software support. Your backup software must support shared SAN tape reserve and release. This functionality is provided a number of ways:

▶ The tape device supports reserve and release, and the backup software has the necessary intelligence to coordinate multiple backup jobs attempting to reserve the tape at the same time. If the tape device itself doesn't support reserve and release, some SAN router products can be used instead. The reserve and release logic is enabled by the router hardware on behalf of an attached tape device.

▶ The backup software is integrated with third-party LUN-masking software
and dynamically switches access to the tape LUN to the backup server.
This method also requires some extra intelligence on the part of the backup
software to coordinate multiple backup jobs running on different cluster
nodes when they're all trying to switch the tape LUN to their respective
server.

When a backup job is run, the backup software reserves the shared tape device
for its exclusive use. Only one backup job can reserve the tape device at a time. If
you have multiple backup jobs scheduled to run on different cluster nodes, each
one waits its turn to get exclusive access to the shared tape device. The benefit of
the floating tape method is that any cluster node can run a backup job for volumes
it has mounted at that time. Using a combination of the failover backup job
method and floating tape access, nodes back up whatever cluster-volumes they
have access to at the time the backup jobs are run and all cluster volumes are
backed up over the SAN.

If you have more than one shared tape device, partition the backup jobs so
mutually exclusive groups of nodes use different tape devices. For example,
suppose you have a four-node cluster and two shared tape devices. The backup
jobs you create for Node0 and Node1 access the first shared tape device while jobs
on Node2 and Node3 access the second tape device.

Implementing Floating Volume Backups

Use the floating volume backup method in any of the following scenarios:

▶ Your tape device is directly attached to one of the nodes in the cluster.

▶ Your tape device is dedicated to a single node in the cluster.

▶ Your backup hardware or software doesn't support the floating tape
method.

The server with access to the tape device is the designated backup node. Only
it will run scheduled backup jobs for cluster-enabled volumes. The backup node
has access to the tape device, but backing up a volume without going remote over
the local area network also requires direct file-level access to the volume. You
migrate the volume to the backup node, and the backup node can then back the
volume up. Think about the floating volume method in terms of temporarily
floating a volume from its most preferred node to the backup node, just for the

purpose of a running a backup job against that volume. The location of the tape device is fixed and volumes float to the tape to enable spontaneous backup.

NOTE   **Migrating a volume from its most preferred node to the backup node may affect some users. They will experience the equivalent of a cluster failover. You can plan to minimize the impact of this brief period of unavailability by scheduling the volume migration and backup during off-peak hours.**

To migrate a cluster-enabled volume from one cluster node to another node, use the ConsoleOne Cluster State View to select the corresponding cluster volume resource and migrate it to the backup node. Run the backup job once the volume is mounted on the backup node.

NOTE   **Novell Cluster Services 1.01 doesn't support command line cluster resource migration. This functionality is enabled with Novell Cluster Services 1.6 for NetWare 6.**

Automating this process requires a little bit of creativity when using Novell Cluster Services 1.01. Follow these steps:

1. For each cluster-enabled volume you want to back up, configure the corresponding cluster volume resource's preferred nodes list to identify the backup node as the second choice preferred node. In normal operation, each cluster volume is then located on their most preferred nodes, not the backup node.

2. For each cluster node, configure a server CRON job to have that node leave the cluster when it's time to run the backup job. Use the CLUSTER LEAVE command in the CRON job. Any cluster-enabled volumes located on the node at the time it leaves fail over to their second choice preferred node, which is the backup node. Once your cluster volumes are relocated to the backup node, they are backed up over the SAN, using a scheduled backup job.

3. For each cluster node, configure a server CRON job to have that node rejoin the cluster some time later. Use the CLUSTER JOIN command in the CRON job. Any cluster-enabled volumes located on the backup node will failback to their most preferred nodes. Ensure that nodes rejoin the cluster only after an amount of time has elapsed sufficient to allow backup jobs to complete on the backup node.

NOTE You must configure automatic failback for your cluster volume resources to enable the automatic return of cluster-enabled volumes to their most preferred nodes. However, the default setting, disable failback, is intended to reduce unnecessary downtime after a real failure-induced failover, should the most preferred node be restored to service. You must therefore trade off the benefits of automatic backup against the potential impact of failback at other times.

To automate this process when using Novell Cluster Services 1.6, follow these steps:

1. For each cluster-enabled volume you want to back up, configure a server CRON job on the backup node to migrate the volume from its current node to the backup node. Use the CLUSTER MIGRATE command in the CRON job. The CLUSTER MIGRATE command requires that you specify only the destination node; type in the name of your backup node.

2. Schedule backup jobs to run when cluster volumes are on the backup node. Your cluster volumes are backed up over the SAN.

3. Configure a server CRON job on the backup node to migrate volumes back to their most preferred nodes. Use the CLUSTER MIGRATE command and specify the desired destination node name. Alternatively, and depending on your backup software, you may be able to add the CLUSTER MIGRATE command to the "post-job" script. This way, you are assured the migration will happen only after successful completion of the backup job.

Backing Up Open Files on Cluster Volumes

A number of methods are available to back up open files on cluster volumes, including:

▶ Third-party open file managers (OFMs)

▶ Novell Storage Services File Copy on Write (COW)

▶ Application-specific Target Service Agents (TSAs)

TIP Because Cluster Services supports only Novell Storage Services (NSS) volumes, you should verify that your backup software or open file manager works with NSS.

File Copy on Write

Novell Storage Services enables open file backup via a feature called File Copy on Write (COW). File COW works by automatically generating a copy of a file at the time it is opened for write. The copy is a representation of the file's contents and state before it's opened. The original file is then actually opened and accessed or updated. To back up files using file COW, the backup engine ignores open files and backs up the corresponding COW copies instead.

It's safe to back up open files with COW because the automatically generated copies represent a consistent version of application-specific data at the time the files are opened by the application or client, before they have had a chance to modify anything.

There is, however, a caveat: If a file is held open by an application for a long period of time, every time a backup is run, only the data corresponding to the file's contents at the time it was opened is backed up. For example, if a file is opened but not closed for two weeks, no changes made to the file during that two-week period are backed up.

WARNING **File COW works very well with desktop productivity files like Office documents. However, do not use file COW with database applications like GroupWise. GroupWise never closes its database files, so the backup engine will never see any changes.**

To enable file COW on an NSS volume, type the following command:

```
NSS /FileCopyOnWrite=volName
```

To disable file COW on an NSS volume, type the following command:

```
NSS /NoFileCopyOnWrite=volName
```

After enabling COW, you must deactivate and reactivate (and mount) the volume to ensure that there are no existing open files without a COW copy. Open file backup works with SMS-compliant backup engines when using the NetWare file system target service agent (TSA500), which understands how to access COW volumes.

WARNING **We recommend you only use file COW if running NetWare 5.1 SP3 or later. Earlier versions had limitations and you should consult Novell's Technical Information Documents (TIDS) for advice if running an earlier version of NetWare.**

GroupWise Target Service Agent

New with GroupWise 6, the GroupWise Target Service Agent (GWTSA) provides reliable backups of a running GroupWise system by successfully backing up open files and locked files. GWTSA works with any SMS-compliant backup engine and enables online backup of GroupWise databases on cluster-enabled (NSS) volumes.

Implementing Cluster Volume Snapshot

Cluster volume snapshot is enabled by special storage array hardware and embedded firmware. Consider the cluster shown in Figure 17.4. Four nodes are all attached to a Storage Area Network. The shared storage array supports volume-level snapshot. Illustrated in the figure is a storage array employing disk-mirror based snapshot. The volume mirror comprises two sets of disks—primary and snapshot. Primary volume data is visible to cluster nodes, but snapshot data is hidden from view. The cluster is logically partitioned using storage array LUN masking: one partition contains a dedicated "standalone" backup node, the other partition contains active cluster nodes. The active nodes run Cluster Services software and share access to the storage array's primary LUNs. Active nodes are Node0, Node1, and Node2 in the figure. They do not have access to snapshot LUNs. Conversely, Node3, the standalone backup node, has access to snapshot LUNs, but not primary data LUNs. The tape drive, not shown, is accessible to the backup node.

Follow these steps to configure your cluster for volume snapshot:

1. Install Cluster Services on all nodes attached to the Storage Area Network.

2. Use LUN masking to logically partition the cluster. Grant active cluster nodes access to primary LUNs, and grant the standalone backup node access to the snapshot LUNs.

3. Disable Cluster Services on the standalone backup node so it does not run by default; comment out the LDNCS line in the server's AUTOEXEC.NCF file.

4. Load the TRUSTMIG utility on the standalone backup server; edit the server's AUTOEXEC.NCF file and add the following commands:

```
LOAD CLSTRLIB

LOAD TRUSTMIG
```

NOTE

If TRUSTMIG fails to load, you need to update your version of Cluster Services software to SP2. SP2 is the first version of Cluster Services that enables volume snapshot with an enhanced TRUSTMIG utility.

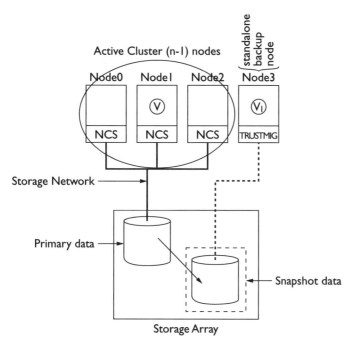

FIGURE 17.4 *Using storage array snapshot hardware with Novell Cluster Services*

Even though the standalone backup node doesn't run Cluster Services software, it must be configured in the same cluster as other active nodes because CLSTRLIB requires a cluster server license. The trustee migration utility will load only if CLSTRLIB is present. The standalone backup node doesn't run other Cluster Services NLMs because that would prevent it from using NSS to activate snapshot volumes. Because snapshot volumes are an identical block-for-block copy of the original volume, they share the same Novell Storage Services identifier that is used to acquire a distributed activation lock. By not running the other Cluster Services NLMs, the standalone backup node isn't subject to the distributed-volume locking rule as are the active nodes. It's very important, therefore, that the standalone backup node not have access to primary LUNs.

To perform a volume snapshot operation on a running cluster, follow these steps:

1. Use your storage array management tools to break the mirrored LUNs and create a snapshot corresponding to the cluster volume you want to back up. There are different interfaces for this operation depending on your storage array. EMC, for example, provides a command-line interface called SymCLI for NetWare that enables scripted automation of the snapshot procedure.

NOTE

Unless you temporarily deactivate the NSS volume, take the snapshot, then reactivate the volume, this procedure will generate a crash-consistent snapshot that may not contain recently cached file system updates. At the time of this writing, Novell is investigating the implementation of an online volume flush mechanism to enable consistent volume snapshots. We have seen some customers work around the current lack of online flush by adding snapshot commands to their cluster volume resource load scripts prior to the NSS/ACTIVATE=VOL command. This has the effect of taking a volume snapshot every time the load script is executed. This can be a desirable policy because it generates a snapshot anytime the volume fails over.

2. Assuming the standalone backup node has access to the snapshot LUNs, type the following commands at the server console:

```
SCAN FOR NEW DEVICES

NSS /ACTIVATE=volName

MOUNT volName

TRUSTMIG volName
```

NOTE

You use TRUSTMIG to migrate the volume's trustee assignments to the standalone backup node. This enables the same kind of trustee migration that happens during normal volume failover. The volume can be backed up once its trustees are migrated and valid on the backup node.

3. Use your backup software to back up the snapshot volume. Its name and contents are identical to the primary volume that remains accessible to the active cluster.

Summary

In this chapter, you learned how to back up a Novell Cluster Services Storage Area Network.

You reviewed the traditional server backup architecture of current production local area networks and looked at some of the problems faced by organizations when they try to protect their data via backup. The chapter then discussed the relative merits of file- versus volume-level backup. Traditional backup is file-oriented, whereas Storage Area Networks are block oriented and enable some new possibilities.

Next, you were introduced to backup concepts for Storage Area Networks — LAN-free backup and volume snapshot, for example. Finally, the chapter presented some tips for designing a successful backup strategy and gave you detailed steps for backing up Novell Cluster Services Storage Area Networks.

Protecting data via backup is a critical element of your high-availability strategy. The irony is that conventional client/server backup actually reduces availability because of the load placed on the local area network and file servers when moving huge amounts of data from remote server attached volumes to tape devices. Clustered SANs offer many solutions to both the bandwidth and data availability issues of today's LAN-based backup processes. Data need not travel over an already burdened LAN. By using a SAN, you back up data where it resides, direct from SAN disks and at full SCSI channel bandwidth. SANs enable flexible combining of tape devices and volumes for backup; you can float volumes to tape devices, or float tape access to cluster volumes, independent of file server availability. Block level snapshot can be used to enable online continuous backup that eliminates the need for conventional backup windows.

## CHAPTER 18

Applying Novell Cluster Services with Virus-Scanning Solutions

In this chapter, you learn how to virus scan clusters, and explore the benefits of virus scanning NetWare volumes that are physically located on Storage Area Network disks.

Symantec's Norton AntiVirus product for NetWare is the virus-scanning solution this chapter focuses on. You examine how to set up scheduled scan jobs for cluster volumes, folders, and files regardless of cluster membership — that is, regardless of what nodes are available to run virus-scanning services in your cluster at any given time. This chapter also includes steps to verify noninterrupted virus scanning during volume failover, enabling you to test your cluster in a simulated server failure scenario. Finally, the chapter examines the expected failover behavior of virus-scanning solutions and what you can expect from different products.

Virus scanning is an important element of your high availability strategy. If files are infected with a virus that spreads as a result of file sharing, then many users are potentially affected and the impact of having to clean up is significant. The file server may also have to be temporarily removed from service until the infected files are found and eliminated. Clustering enables high availability of access to files on SAN-shared volumes. By decoupling storage from servers, any server can scan any volume for viruses. This kind of flexibility enables dynamic management of virus protection. For example, because virus scanning is CPU-intensive, you can migrate volumes to heavy-duty processor nodes once a month to perform an extensive monthly virus check, and leave them on their default nodes for weekly virus checking. Cluster nodes are simply the place where volumes and CPU cycles coincide to scan for viruses. By reading on, you will learn how to scan your SAN volumes for viruses independent of specific host servers.

Virus Scanning Clusters

Your organization probably owns many NetWare servers hosting numerous applications, users, and data volumes. Users enjoy the freedom to access and share virus-free files. They can launch applications directly from public volumes. Running a virus scanner on each server is a particularly effective way to enable centralized virus protection for your entire organization. Every server scans its volumes and files for viruses.

Clusters enable high availability access to files (applications and network services). If an organization is willing to invest in clustering for high availability file access, chances are also reasonably good that those same files are required to be virus free when accessed. The factors that motivate high availability also motivate virus protection. Organizations desire highly available access to clean files. In fact, decreased system availability can be directly related to not providing virus protection. Mean Time to Repair can be the time spent searching for and eliminating multiple copies of a virus-infected file, for example. Virus scanning and clustering are complementary technologies that enable high availability and safe access to an organization's files.

Chapter 3 defines high availability and the related variables, Mean Time to Repair (MTTR) and Mean Time between Failures (MTBF).

X-REF

Clustering and Storage Area Networks invalidate some of the assumptions historically made by traditional file server software. For one thing, volumes are no longer statically tied to any particular server. Cluster volumes don't have a fixed host server. They are free to be mounted on any node as a function of availability and load. How do you provide virus protection for cluster volumes? Fortunately, the solution is quite straightforward, requiring no more than a minor adjustment of existing virus-scanning procedures.

Consider the three-node NetWare cluster depicted in Figure 18.1. Three nodes, named NODE1, NODE2, and NODE3, are attached to a SAN. Any node can access any shared disk via the SAN. All six NetWare volumes have been cluster-enabled for transparent failover. The volumes are named VOL1 through VOL6.

Novell Cluster Services enables access to files via whatever cluster nodes are currently available. By installing virus-scanning software on every node, you enable constant virus protection. All nodes virus scan whatever volumes are mounted on them. If any node should fail, Cluster Services fails over volumes to surviving nodes. NetWare clients automatically reconnect and regain access to their files. The virus-scanning software running on the surviving nodes immediately detects that new volumes are being mounted and starts scanning them for viruses.

Chapter 9 describes how to cluster enable a shared disk NSS volume and how to configure cluster-enabled volumes for automatic failover.

X-REF

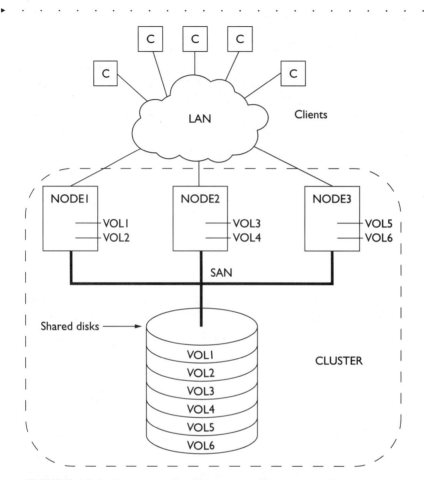

FIGURE 18.1 *Cluster comprising three nodes and six cluster-enabled volumes*

Why Virus Scan Clusters?

Following are some of the benefits of virus scanning a cluster:

▶ All nodes actively scan for viruses independent of other nodes. Nodes scan whatever volumes they have mounted. When you create new volumes on your SAN and assign them to cluster nodes, they are automatically scanned by whatever nodes they are assigned to, thereby reducing some of the overhead of managing virus protection on individual servers.

▶ If any node should fail, NetWare volumes failover to surviving nodes and continue to receive virus protection. If a node fails, client access to files and virus scanning continues uninterrupted. You don't have to worry that your volumes aren't receiving virus protection, as they will be scanned no matter what node they are mounted on.

▶ Clients are unaware of which node they connect to to access their files. They are similarly unaware that all nodes also provide highly available virus-scanning protection. When clients access files from the cluster, they are clean of viruses.

▶ If an additional node is installed into the cluster, it can take on some of the virus-scanning effort by simply migrating cluster-enabled volumes to it. The addition of a new cluster node doesn't require that others be rebooted. If you need to boost your virus scanning performance, you can add another server and spread your volumes more thinly over the available cluster nodes, thereby increasing overall performance — the same volumes are scanned in less time (assuming server CPU capacity is the bottleneck, not the I/O channel).

Introducing Symantec Norton Anti-Virus Corporate Edition

Symantec has offered an excellent virus-scanning solution for the NetWare platform for a number of years. Symantec's virus protection product for NetWare is called Norton Anti-Virus Corporate Edition (NAV-CE). In this chapter, we use NAV-CE 7.51 to demonstrate the principles and practice of virus scanning a cluster. These principles equally apply to most other virus-scanning products available for NetWare. For example, McAfee's NetShield for NetWare anti-virus product also supports Cluster Services.

Exploring the Major Features of NAV-CE 7.51

NAV-CE is robust enterprise software and a perfect companion to Cluster Services. The major features of NAV-CE 7.51 include the following:

▶ Improved uptime with automatic, reliable virus detection. Files are unavailable when they are infected. You increase uptime when you avoid viruses. Volumes are scanning in scheduled batch mode, or realtime mode, which enables detection of viruses as they enter the server.

▸ Centralized management from a single console allows you to create policies that keep servers up to date and properly configured, fully protecting files at all times.

▸ CPU utilization of the NetWare loadable module can be customized to minimize impact on server performance while providing optimal protection.

▸ Improves day-to-day server performance by eliminating redundant scanning — once Norton AntiVirus scans a file and finds it free of viruses, Norton AntiVirus will not scan it again until changes have been made.

Installing NAV-CE

You install and configure NAV-CE on a NetWare cluster the same way you install it on multiple standalone NetWare servers. Because this part of Symantec's solution remains unchanged, the complete installation steps aren't described in this chapter. Refer to Symantec's documentation for more detailed information.

TIP

It's recommended that you use NAV-CE's server group feature to manage the NetWare servers that correspond to a cluster. NAV-CE server groups and Novell clusters are very similar concepts. They both enable a single management domain for a collection of servers. Using the NAV-CE server group feature enables centralized management of virus scanning for all nodes in the same cluster. Whatever policies you apply to the server group are automatically replicated to all cluster nodes.

Figure 18.2 shows a screen from the NAV-CE installation wizard. This screen enables you to configure server groups and to install NAV-CE to all servers specified in the group. You give the server group a name. For convenience, give the server group a name that associates it with the NetWare cluster. Figure 18.2 shows a server group called Norton Anti-Virus Cluster. Although not listed, it contains three NetWare servers, NODE1, NODE2 and NODE3, all of which are also configured into a NetWare cluster called CLUSTER.

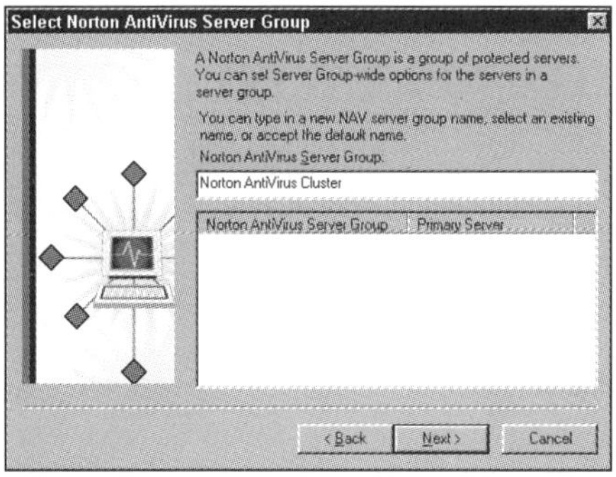

▶ · ◀

FIGURE 18.2 *Configure server groups to match the servers in your cluster.*

Configuring NAV-CE

You configure and manage NAV-CE via a utility called the Symantec System Center Console (SSCC). SSCC runs on a Windows NT workstation.

TIP

Install SSCC to the same workstation in which you have ConsoleOne and the cluster snapins installed. This enables you to manage your cluster and virus protection from a single workstation.

You manage virus protection by creating scheduled scan jobs for all servers in a server group or selected individual servers. Figure 18.3 shows the SSCC. The main console window is open and displays the status of a single server group called "Norton AntiVirus Cluster." The server group contains the three servers that are also members of a Novell Cluster Services cluster.

NAV-CE has no direct knowledge of cluster configuration. The virus-scanning agent software installed onto each server functions independently of the other servers. Agents scan files on volumes when given scheduled scan jobs to perform. Server group–based operation means that all agents share the group's configuration and scheduled scan jobs. But scan jobs can also be created and given to individual servers independent of groups.

NAV-CE supports two primary virus-scanning methods:

> ▸ *Realtime Scanning* — Enables constant scanning of files as they are accessed or modified. File operations are intercepted before reaching disk.

▸ *Scheduled Scanning* — Individual scan jobs are created and scheduled to run on various days of the week and at various times of the day. Different jobs have different parameters. You might create a weekly virus scan job to perform a thorough scan of all files on all volumes, together with daily scanning jobs that are less extensive, perhaps scanning only select volumes and files.

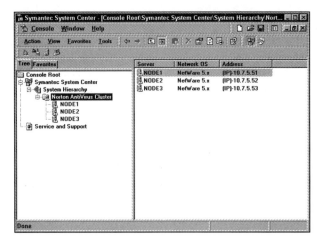

FIGURE 18.3 *Using Symantec System Center Console to manage server groups*

Realtime scanning and scheduled scan jobs can be configured for an entire server group or individual servers within a group. Individual server jobs support inclusion/exclusion of specific volumes, folders, and files, enabling you to ignore uninteresting volumes or folders. There might be no reason to scan every server's SYS volume if no changes are being made, for example.

Clustering NAV-CE

Configuring NAV-CE to virus scan cluster-enabled volumes requires a slight change of procedure compared to virus scanning traditional server attached volumes. From NAV-CE's perspective, specific volumes are associated with specific servers. You create a scan job by drilling down into a specific server, then selecting from whatever volumes it hosts. The configuration utility presents volumes as subordinate to servers; you first select a server, then you select a volume. In a cluster, however, volumes are promoted to a position higher than servers. The host server is less important than the volume itself. The goal is to create scan jobs for cluster-enabled volumes no matter what server they are mounted on.

Scanning All Cluster-Enabled Volumes

When you create a scan job for a server group, SSCC prevents you from selecting any specific volumes. Your scan job includes all volumes on all servers in the group.

TIP

Because server group–based scan jobs aren't volume specific, use server group jobs to enable scanning of all volumes on your cluster. NAV-CE gives the server group job to all virus-scanning agents on all servers. Each agent then scans all the volumes that are available to it on the server the agent is running on. You don't need to know anything about what nodes have what volumes mounted at the time you create the scan job. You create one scan job for the entire cluster, and all nodes scan all volumes.

Follow these steps to create a scheduled scan job for all volumes in your cluster:

1. Using SSCC, right-click the server group and select All Tasks ➪ Norton AntiVirus ➪ Scheduled Scans. The Scheduled Scans dialog box shown in Figure 18.4 is displayed.

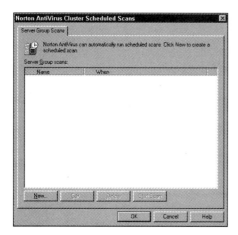

FIGURE 18.4 *Launching the Scheduled Scans dialog box for a server group*

2. Click New to launch the Scheduled Scan dialog box shown in Figure 18.5. Type a name for your scan job in the Name field and configure the various scheduling options. The new scan job in Figure 18.5 is called Cluster Scan and is set to run at 12:00 p.m. every day.

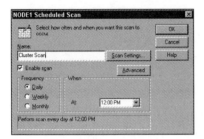

FIGURE 18.5 *Creating a new scheduled scan called Cluster Scan*

3. Click Scan Settings and the Select Items dialog box shown in Figure 18.6 is displayed. The dialog box states, "Multiple computers are selected. Item selection is not available. Norton AntiVirus will scan all files and all folders." Thus, the Cluster Scan job will scan all volumes on all nodes. By creating a single job, you enable virus protection for all volumes hosted by your cluster, regardless of which nodes are actually available.

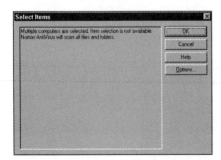

FIGURE 18.6 *Server group scheduled scans do not permit item selection.*

Scanning Select Cluster-Enabled Volumes

When you create a scan job for an individual server, SSCC lets you configure volumes, folders, and files for inclusion or exclusion from the scan job. This enables selective scanning of precisely the files you want. The goal in this case is to enable selective scanning of files on volumes independent of host servers. If you create a selective scan job for one server, you want to ensure that you are receiving identical virus protection no matter what node the volume is mounted on. To include a specific volume in a scan job on any node, you must create duplicate scan jobs for each node. Here's how:

1. Migrate the cluster-enabled volume to the node you wish to configure the job for. Using ConsoleOne, browse to and highlight the cluster container, then select View ⇨ Cluster View. Click the cluster volume resource to launch the Cluster Resource Manager dialog box. Migrate the cluster volume resource to the desired node by selecting the node from the list of available nodes and clicking Migrate. Figure 18.7 shows a cluster volume resource named VOL1_SERVER migrating to NODE1.

FIGURE 18.7 *Using the Cluster Resource Manager to migrate VOL1_SERVER to NODE1*

2. Using SSCC, right-click the server you just migrated the volume to and select All Tasks ⇨ Norton AntiVirus ⇨ Scheduled Scans. Figure 18.8 shows the Scheduled Scans dialog box for NODE1.

3. Click New to launch the Scheduled Scan dialog box shown in Figure 18.9. Type a name for your scan job in the Name field and configure the various scheduling options. The new scan job in Figure 18.9 is called VOL1 and is set to run at 12:00 p.m. every day.

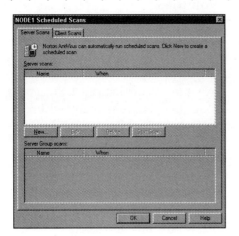

FIGURE 18.8 *Launching the Scheduled Scans dialog box for an individual server*

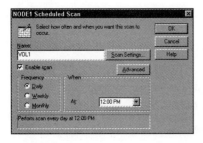

FIGURE 18.9 *Creating a new scheduled scan called VOL1*

4. Click Scan Settings to display the dialog box shown in Figure 18.10. Here you include the desired volumes in the scan job. If a volume is currently mounted on the node, it will be listed in this dialog box. Scanning of files on VOL1 is enabled in Figure 18.10. Scanning on SYS and NSS_ADMIN is disabled.

Always disable scanning of the NSS_ADMIN volume. This isn't a real volume and is used only for internal NSS file system management. There are no user files on NSS_ADMIN.

TIP

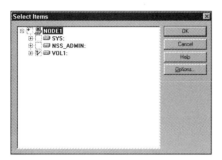

FIGURE 18.10 *Select volume, folders, and files to include in the scan job.*

5. Repeat steps 1 through 4 on every cluster node in the failover path of the volume you wish to scan.

Realtime Scanning

Realtime protection enables constant scanning of files as they are accessed or modified. You have two configuration options:

- ▶ Configure realtime scanning for all cluster volumes on all nodes.

- ▶ Configure realtime scanning for individual cluster volumes on each node.

NOTE

The goal is to use SSCC to enable realtime scanning of volumes no matter what node they might be mounted on. If scanning isn't enabled on one node, you risk the introduction of a virus while volumes are mounted on that node. By enabling scanning for all nodes, you don't need to worry about which nodes volumes might be mounted on at any given instant.

To configure realtime scanning for all cluster volumes on all nodes, follow these steps:

1. Using SSCC, right-click the server group and select All Tasks ➪ Norton AntiVirus ➪ Server Realtime Protection Options. The Server Realtime Protection Options dialog box (see Figure 18.11) appears.

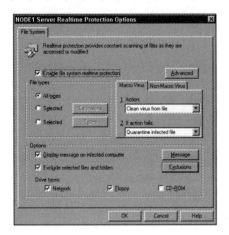

FIGURE 18.11 *Server Realtime Protection Options dialog box*

2. You are presented with various options including filters for file types and extensions. The Enable file system realtime protection checkbox is enabled by default for all volumes. Click OK to save settings for all volumes on all nodes. Because you selected a server group in step 1, the configuration is automatically applied to all servers configured in your server group — to all of your cluster nodes.

To configure realtime scanning for individual cluster volumes on each node, follow these steps:

1. Using SSCC, right-click an individual server and select All Tasks ⇨ Norton AntiVirus ⇨ Server Realtime Protection Options. The Server Realtime Protection Options dialog box appears.

2. Check "Exclude selected files and folders" to enable the Exclusions button.

3. Click Exclusions to display the Exclusions dialog box, shown in Figure 18.12. If the Files/Folders button is not present in the Exclusions dialog box, make sure you selected an individual server when launching the Realtime Protection Options dialog box.

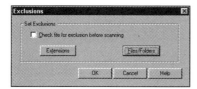

FIGURE 18.12 *The Exclusions dialog box showing the Files/Folders button*

4. Click the Files/Folders button to display the Select Items dialog box, shown in Figure 18.13. This is where you specify individual volumes, folders, or files to exclude from realtime scanning.

5. Use the volume tree browser to select individual folders and files or select entire volumes to exclude from realtime scanning. Figure 18.13 lists four volumes: SYS, NSS_ADMIN, VOL2, and VOL1. As seen in this figure, VOL1 and VOL2 are cluster volumes mounted on the node you select in step 1.

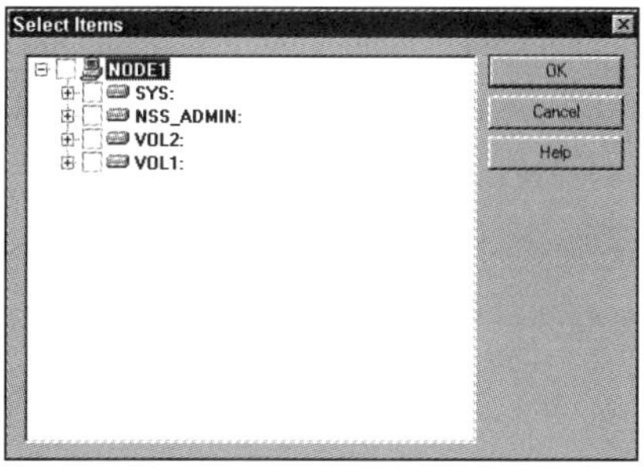

FIGURE 18.13 *Select volumes, folders, and files to exclude from realtime scanning.*

TIP

Realtime scanning processes only those files that are accessed or modified. Therefore, you should enable realtime scanning for the entire cluster by selecting a server group. With realtime scanning enabled for the entire cluster, when files are accessed on cluster volumes, they are scanned no matter what server the volume is mounted on. This is by far the easiest and most effective way to set up realtime scanning, because you don't need to select individual servers or volumes.

Testing NAV-CE Failover

You should test your virus-scanning services in normal and simulated failure scenarios so you can verify that your cluster volumes are scanned no matter what node they are mounted on.

It's recommended that you simulate a node failure to test that your cluster volumes are virus scanned when they fail over. Consider and test a worst-case failure scenario.

For example, simulate an unexpected node failure by power cycling NODE2. Figure 18.14 shows the result of a simulated node failure. Volume VOL3 failed over to NODE1 and volume VOL4 failed over to NODE3. Two nodes survived the failure: NODE1 and NODE3. They now have three volumes each.

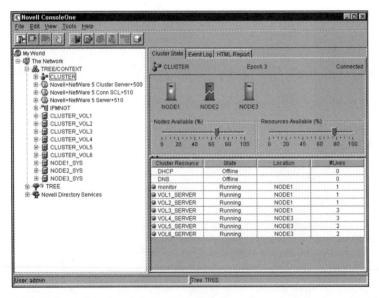

FIGURE 18.14 *ConsoleOne's Cluster State View shows the cluster state after NODE2 failed.*

Figure 18.15 shows NAV-CE's response to a client workstation copying files to VOL3. VOL3 was mounted on NODE2 before the simulated failure, but is now mounted on NODE1. Realtime scanning is enabled for the cluster, and the new files copied to VOL3 now mounted on NODE1 are scanned for viruses in the exact same way they were being scanned when mounted on NODE2.

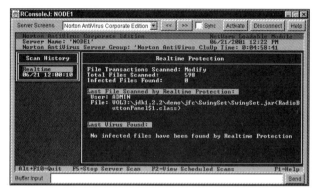

FIGURE 18.15 *VOL3 is scanned after it fails over to NODE1 from NODE2.*

Virus Scanning Failover Behavior

Virus-scanning agents run on all cluster nodes. Whenever Cluster Services mounts a volume on a node as a result of failover, failback, or migration, the virus-scanning agent detects the mount event and adds the newly mounted volume to its list of active volumes to process. Virus scanning is therefore considered Active/Active. A failover results in nothing more than a simple volume mount event from the perspective of a virus-scanning agent. The same behavior is required of the scanning agent when you dismount or mount a volume by hand, for example. There is no difference.

Most virus-scanning products handle dynamic volume mount and dismount and therefore function well in a cluster. A good virus-scanning solution enables scan job configuration independent of particular host servers. You are effectively managing your cluster, its storage, and virus protection as a single system. You can scan the entire cluster with a single scan job. It doesn't matter what nodes are available; you aren't required to create multiple jobs to handle different failure scenarios.

Summary

It cannot be stressed enough how important virus scanning is as an element of your high availability strategy. Infected files can spread a virus simply as a result of file sharing, potentially affecting many users, and causing a clean up that has significant impact on your system's availability. The file server may have to be temporarily removed from service until the infected files are found and eliminated.

In this chapter, you learned how to virus scan clusters and you explored the benefits of virus scanning NetWare volumes that are physically located on Storage Area Network disks.

Symantec's Norton AntiVirus product for NetWare was introduced, and you examined how to set up scheduled scan jobs for cluster volumes, folders, and files regardless of cluster membership, that is, regardless of what nodes are available to run virus-scanning services in your cluster at any given time.

You examined steps you can take to verify noninterrupted virus scanning during volume failover, which enables you to test your cluster in a simulated server failure scenario.

Finally, this chapter discussed the expected failover behavior of virus-scanning solutions and what you can expect from different products. In general, the failover characteristics of virus-scanning solutions are as follows:

CLUSTER FAILOVER CLASSIFICATION INDEX	
Transparency	Very transparent
Active/Active or Active/Passive	Active/Active
Time to failover	Same as a cluster-enabled volume

## CHAPTER 19

Exploring Novell Cluster Services 1.6 for NetWare 6

In this chapter, you learn about the newest version of Cluster Services software. Novell Cluster Services 1.6 is an enhanced version of Cluster Services software designed specially for NetWare 6–based server clusters and Storage Area Networks.

The goal of this chapter is to introduce you to Novell Cluster Services 1.6 and NetWare 6. Many of the clustering concepts and procedures described in this book apply equally to NetWare 6–based clustering. However, NetWare 6 includes a number of changes in the areas of storage and storage management that are significant enough to warrant more attention than we can devote in a single chapter. This chapter covers the basics, giving you enough detail to install and run your first NetWare 6 cluster.

In this chapter, you explore the new features, architecture, and operation of Novell Cluster Services 1.6, including information about NetWare 6 where necessary. You learn how to install Novell Cluster Services 1.6 onto a cluster of NetWare 6 servers. The chapter also covers the NetWare 5.x to NetWare 6 cluster upgrade process, including step-by-step instructions to perform a complete upgrade.

This chapter further includes an introductory tutorial on NetWare 6 storage management. You learn how to work with shared disk storage pools and logical volumes and how to cluster enable volumes for automatic client failover.

Finally, the chapter closes with information on Novell Cluster Services 1.6 cluster management and monitoring enhancements. This enables you to immediately start working with NetWare 6–based clusters.

Exploring Novell Cluster Services 1.6

Novell Cluster Services 1.6 is Novell's newest version of clustering software specially designed for Novell's newest version of NetWare: NetWare 6. A two-node version of Novell Cluster Services 1.6 is bundled with NetWare 6 at no additional cost, so you receive two-node clustering capability for free when purchasing NetWare 6. By purchasing additional cluster node licenses, you can create clusters containing up to 32 NetWare 6 nodes.

Both Novell Cluster Services 1.6 and NetWare 6 offer a number of significant enhancements compared with earlier product versions. In particular, NetWare 6 includes Novell Storage Services (NSS) 3.0, Novell's advanced 64-bit multiprocessor journaled file system. Novell Storage Services 3.0 enables the kind of file system scalability necessary for large-scale SAN environments containing hundreds of disks and terabytes of data. For example, one of many new features, built-in disk mirroring, enables protection from disk drive faults and disaster recovery when mirrored disks are located in storage arrays separated by long-distance links in the back end Storage Area Network. For the front-end local area network, NetWare 6 enables increased high availability with an updated multiprocessor TCP/IP protocol stack and built-in NIC load balancing and fault tolerance features.

In the broadest sense, the enhancements in NetWare 6 and Cluster Services 1.6 create a platform for simpler management of high availability network services and storage. Most of these enhancements fall into one of four categories:

- ▸ Integration with Novell Storage Services 3.0

- ▸ Cluster management and monitoring

- ▸ Cluster resource policies and control

- ▸ High availability TCP/IP protocol stack

Integration with Novell Storage Services 3.0

Novell Storage Services 3.0 has a number of new capabilities that are designed to simplify the task of creating and managing volumes on direct attached and Storage Area Network disks:

- ▸ Virtual disk partitions

- ▸ Storage pools

- ▸ Shared for clustering pools

- ▸ Logical volumes

- ▸ Globally unique identifiers

Figure 19.1 illustrates the relationship between disks, virtual disk partitions, storage pools, and logical volumes. NSS consumes disks presented by the storage network. Disks are then formatted according to the IBM DOS partition table standard. From a single DOS partition on a disk, NSS enables the creation of an unlimited number of virtual disk partitions and, in so doing, eliminates the traditional limit of four DOS partitions per disk.

Disk partitions are aggregated to create storage pools. Mirroring or other aggregation functions can be applied to create the illusion of a contiguous array of disk blocks that is a storage pool. Logical volumes are created inside storage pools Pools can contain many logical volumes. Logical volumes expand to a predetermined maximum size and shrink when space is released as folders and files are deleted. This dynamic space allocation occurs within the boundary of a pool. If a pool runs out of space for its logical volumes, additional virtual disk partitions can be added to the pool to increase its size. However, unlike a logical volume, a pool cannot shrink by giving up virtual disk partitions once they've been allocated to the pool.

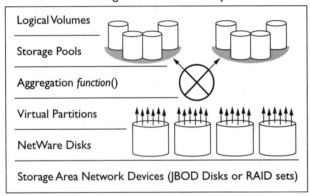

FIGURE 19.1 *Novell Storage Services 3.0 virtual disk partitions, storage pools, and logical volumes*

Virtual Disk Partitions

You can create up to four partitions on an IBM DOS–formatted disk drive. Novell Storage Services 3.0 uses virtual disk partitions to reduce the complexities that can arise from this four-partition limit. You can create an unlimited number of virtual disk partitions within a single DOS disk partition. Each virtual disk partition has a set of attributes that define how its contents are to be used. For example, virtual disk partitions can inherit a "sharable for clustering" attribute that marks storage pools created on these virtual disk partitions as participants in a shared disk cluster. Virtual disk partitions also have a mirroring attribute that enables you to mirror partitions across multiple devices.

Storage Pools

You aggregate individual virtual disk partitions into higher-layer objects called *storage pools*. Storage pools are chunks of disk space gathered from one or more virtual disk partitions physically located on one or more storage devices. For example, you can create a storage pool that consumes disk space from a number of Storage Area Network disks. To create a storage pool, you select space from multiple virtual disk partitions.

Conceptually, NetWare 6 Storage Pools are roughly equivalent to NetWare 5 Storage Groups.

TIP

Shared for Clustering Pools

To perform I/O to a storage pool, it must be activated. Novell Cluster and Storage Services work together to protect shared disks from uncoordinated access. NSS 3.0 helps protect your shared storage disks using a flag that labels the underlying disks as "sharable for clustering." Although set at the disk level, the sharable for clustering flag is inherited by all higher-layer disk objects that reference disk space on shared disks. When you create virtual disk partitions and then storage pools from a device that is marked sharable, the virtual disk partitions and storage pools also become sharable for clustering.

When NSS 3.0 detects a sharable for clustering pool, it will not activate the storage pool unless Novell Cluster Services 1.6 is also running. By default, NSS 3.0 enables activation of storage pools held on local (nonshared) direct attached disks only. Novell Cluster Services 1.6 provides protection against uncoordinated multiserver access to shared disks at the storage pool level. Cluster Services software intercepts and selectively vetoes NSS's requests to activate storage pools. The rule enforced by Cluster Services ensures that only one cluster node can activate a storage pool at a time. Many storage pools can exist on a Storage Area Network, but Cluster Services ensures that each pool is active on only one node at a time.

For NetWare 6, cluster failover occurs at the storage pool level. Individual storage pools fail over from one node to another. Contrast this with NetWare 5, which fails over volumes.

NOTE

Logical Volumes

Logical volumes are created from disk space inside storage pools. You can create an unlimited number of logical volumes on any storage pool. Logical volumes are containers for NetWare folders and files—they are regular file systems—the equivalent of a NetWare 5.x NSS volume.

Storage pools know nothing about the folders, files, or trustee rights associated with logical volumes. Likewise, the logical volumes that consume space from an underlying storage pool know nothing about the origins of that disk space.

When you create a logical volume, you assign a specific number of megabytes— a quota—that the logical volume cannot exceed. You can optionally allow a logical volume's quota to grow to the size of the storage pool that underlies the volume.

Rather than automatically consuming the amount of space specified in the quota, a logical volume takes only the amount of space that it needs. As users and applications add files to a logical volume, the volume uses space from the underlying storage pool to store those files. When users delete files, a logical volume returns the space to its storage pool.

Globally Unique Identifiers

For NetWare 6, Novell Storage Services and Novell Directory Services use a globally unique identifier (GUID) scheme to identify directory objects. All NDS objects have globally unique identifiers in addition to their fully distinguished NDS names. A user object has only one GUID, and this single GUID remains the same across all servers. As a result, when a NetWare 6 cluster fails over an NSS storage pool containing logical volumes, there is no longer any need to translate trustee IDs. Regardless of the node mounting a logical volume, the GUIDs corresponding to trustees of file system objects remain the same and are always intact and accessible in NDS. The same GUIDs that associate users with trustee assignments also identify user objects with the files they own. As a result, user space restrictions and file ownership also failover in NetWare 6 clusters. In NetWare 5.x–based clusters, only directory space restrictions failover.

Because Novell Cluster Services 1.6 no longer has to translate trustee IDs, failover is faster than with NetWare 5.x–based clusters. Gone is the need for a separate trustee migration utility. Consequently, the NetWare 5.x TRUSTMIG utility is no longer shipped with Novell Cluster Services 1.6.

In addition to efficiently failing over logical volumes and also enabling cluster user space restrictions, NetWare 6 clusters simplify volume snapshot processes. When you take a snapshot of a NetWare 5.x cluster volume, you have to migrate trustees to the node that you use for backup. In contrast, when you take a snapshot of a NetWare 6 cluster volume, you don't have to migrate trustees because the trustees and user space restrictions remain intact.

Cluster Management and Monitoring

Novell Cluster Services 1.6 enables the following new cluster management and monitoring capabilities:

- Single system image storage management

- Web browser cluster management interface

- Simple Network Management Protocol (SNMP) cluster alerts

- Simple Mail Transfer Protocol (SMTP) cluster alerts

- Command-line management interface

- Persistent cluster event log

Single System Image Storage Management

Novell Storage Services 3.0 provides a generic XML-based management interface. You implement all storage management operations by writing an XML-based description of the operation to special files located in the file system namespace. For example, if you wanted to extend the size of a pool by creating a new virtual disk partition, you would create an XML document to describe the operation and then save that document to a special file.

NetWare 6 storage is managed using ConsoleOne, NetWare Remote Manager, or any client- or server-side scripting language capable of generating XML documents. When you create a sharable for clustering storage pool using any of these management interfaces, Novell Storage Services ensures that the underlying storage devices are all shared. For example, it is not valid and therefore not possible to create a sharable for clustering storage pool that spans a mixture of locally attached (nonshared) and Storage Area Network disks. If it were possible to create such a hybrid local and shared storage pool, a portion of the storage pool corresponding to the local disks would be accessible only to the server with direct access to those local disks. Such restricted access would prevent failover, because the pool could be activated only on the server with the local disks. By enforcing the creation of only pure shared storage pools, NSS ensures that this invalid configuration cannot arise.

Because every cluster node attached to a Storage Area Network has equal block-level access to shared disks, any node can be used to manage shared storage. You do not need to know what servers are running or even connected to the storage network to manage storage.

You can enable single system image storage management in two ways:

▶ When you manage shared storage, the NetWare 6 storage management interface hides details of particular servers. Instead of managing storage attached to a server, you click the cluster object and manage storage attached to the cluster.

▶ When you reconfigure shared storage, all cluster nodes automatically refresh to the new view of available storage. For example, suppose you add a shared virtual disk partition to a storage pool, and all nodes in the cluster are updated to reflect the storage change. You don't have to manually visit each node, or worse, reboot each node, for it to update its view of available storage. NetWare 6 clusters enable dynamic online storage reconfiguration regardless of the number of nodes or external storage devices.

X-REF

NetWare 5.x also enables single system image storage management, but to a lesser degree. See Chapter 9 for details on how to manage shared disk storage and NSS volumes on NetWare 5 clusters. In NetWare 5, the cluster-aware NSS tools run on the server. But because you have to find an available cluster node to run the tools, you are exposed to the details of specific servers. NetWare 6, therefore, makes single system image storage management even easier.

Web Browser Cluster Management Interface

Novell Cluster Services 1.6 includes a NetWare Remote Manager snapin that allows you to manage NetWare 6 clusters from a Java-enabled Web browser. Formerly known as NetWare Portal Management, NetWare Remote Manager provides a fully functional alternative to ConsoleOne for configuring and managing NetWare 6 clusters.

Novell made the cluster management interface in NetWare Remote Manager match the ConsoleOne interface as closely as possible. For example, the Cluster Status screen in NetWare Remote Manager looks similar to the Cluster View screen in ConsoleOne. Both interfaces show the same details about the status of a cluster, including the following:

▶ The number and names of cluster nodes

▶ Which of the nodes is the master (indicated with a yellow dot)

▶ The names and locations of cluster resources

▶ The status of cluster resources (for example, running or offline)

The Cluster Status screen in NetWare Remote Manager and the ConsoleOne Cluster View screen also display an "Up Since" timestamp. This timestamp shows the start date and time of each cluster resource's current life.

You use NetWare Remote Manager to manage the cluster, regardless of which nodes are running, because Novell Cluster Services 1.6 has a special cluster-wide IP address. You create this cluster IP address when you install the clustering software. You can use either ConsoleOne or NetWare Remote Manager to edit this address later. When you enter and connect to this cluster IP address via your browser, you can manage any node or resource in your cluster without needing to know which node you are currently attached to.

During installation, Novell Cluster Services 1.6 also automatically generates a special cluster resource called the Master IP Address resource. The Master IP Address resource binds the cluster IP address and also binds this address to NetWare Remote Manager. After Novell Cluster Services 1.6 generates the Master IP Address resource, it runs on the master node and can't be controlled or modified except to change the IP address.

TIP

Think of the Master IP Address resource as a built-in (internal) cluster resource that controls the cluster IP address and enables cluster management via a single IP address regardless of which nodes are available. You can edit the cluster IP address (via cluster container properties) and the Master IP Address resource is automatically updated.

Simple Network Management Protocol Cluster Alerts

Novell Cluster Services 1.6 supports the Simple Network Management Protocol (SNMP) through cluster-specific management information base (MIB) extensions developed by Compaq Computer Corporation. The cluster MIB defines the cluster entities you can monitor using SNMP.

For example, the MIB enables you to use SNMP for cluster discovery (to detect the cluster's name as well as node names and IP addresses). In addition, the MIB enables you to monitor node traps such as when nodes join, leave, or fail. You can use any SNMP-compliant management software to listen for cluster-specific traps.

Simple Mail Transfer Protocol Cluster Alerts

The cluster MIB enables only node-specific alerts. Novell Cluster Services 1.6 uses the Simple Mail Transfer Protocol (SMTP) to extend the available event notification options to include cluster resource specific events. You can configure the cluster to send messages to up to eight e-mail addresses when various cluster events occur. For example, Novell Cluster Services 1.6 can notify you by e-mail when a node joins, leaves, or fails. Further, you can be notified any time the status of a cluster resource changes. For example, you might want to receive an e-mail when a cluster resource's state changes from loading to running.

Novell Cluster Services 1.6 sends either plain text or XML-formatted messages, depending on which format you select. The XML format is a forward-looking option. In the future, Novell plans to create intelligent software designed to take advantage of the XML management interface that NSS provides. Such software could receive XML-formatted e-mail messages from the clustering software and act on those messages by automatically making any necessary changes to the SAN file system.

Command-Line Management Interface

The command-line interface enables you to manage cluster resources from the console command line of any cluster node. Any cluster resource management you previously used ConsoleOne for is possible via command line. For example, the cluster command-line interface enables resource migration, online/offline, and response to management alerts.

TIP

Use the cluster command-line interface to script maintenance operations. For example, you can schedule cluster resource migrations with a CRON job by using the CLUSTER MIGRATE command. You can use the cluster command-line interface to automate many operations that previously were only possible using ConsoleOne.

Persistent Cluster Event Log

The persistent cluster event log is a cluster-wide log of cluster node and resource state changes that have been made since the cluster was first formed. The event log is persistent and survives node failure or restart. As long as one node remains in the cluster, the event log can be inspected via ConsoleOne or the NetWare Remote Manager user interfaces. Even if the entire cluster is restarted, the previous history is kept in the event log until cleared.

The cluster event log can be saved to an HTML file for offline viewing and can be quite helpful with contacting Novell Technical Support.

Cluster Resource Policies and Controls

Cluster resource policies and control options in Novell Cluster Services 1.6 include the following:

▶ *Cluster resource priorities* — Resource priorities enable the comparative ranking of cluster resources against each other. You use this to ensure that a high-priority cluster resource is started before a lower-priority one. For example, suppose you have two cluster resources: DHCP and GroupWise. DHCP might be considered higher priority because it's a critical network service. For example, if during a failover it's possible the DHCP service could be delayed by GroupWise if GroupWise loads first, then with cluster resource priorities, you can avoid this situation by configuring DHCP with a resource priority higher than that of GroupWise.

▶ *Online to specified cluster node* — When you online a cluster resource, you can optionally specify which node to online it to. This saves a step if you're onlining a cluster resource only to then migrate it to a different node. By default, a cluster resource is onlined on its most preferred node.

▶ *Automatic online at creation* — When you create a cluster resource, you have the option of automatically having the resource come online without having to switch to the Cluster State View to manually online the resource, as was the case with Novell Cluster Services 1.01.

These cluster resource policies and controls simplify cluster management and, in the case of cluster resource priorities, improve availability by ensuring that failover of critical cluster resources isn't delayed by less important cluster resources.

High Availability TCP/IP Protocol Stack

With the NetWare 6 TCP/IP protocol stack, you can optionally bind a single IP address to multiple network interface cards (NICs) to enable redundant network paths. Built-in multipathing enables fault tolerance for client/server and cluster heartbeat packets by masking NIC or Ethernet cable failures with redundant hardware.

By creating a redundant front end local area network to your cluster, you eliminate potential single points of failure that might otherwise cause cluster nodes to lose contact with each other or clients to lose contact with servers. This increases overall system availability by preventing service outages (services that become inaccessible to clients or cluster nodes that are forced to shut down because of split brain conditions).

Detailing Novell Cluster Services 1.6 Architecture

The architecture underlying Novell's clustering software necessarily had to change to support many of the enhancements in Novell Cluster Services 1.6. The basic structure remains essentially the same but, as Figure 19.2 shows, Novell Cluster Services 1.6 no longer requires the TRUSTMIG module because it no longer needs to translate trustee IDs during volume failovers. The revised architecture, depicted in Figure 19.2, has four new NetWare Loadable Modules (NLMs): CSS, CVB, PCLUSTER, and VIPX. Also of note is the event bus between Novell Cluster Services 1.6 and Storage Services 3.0. This event bus interface also exists in Novell Cluster Services 1.01, but is expanded for Novell Cluster Services 1.6 to enable distribution of storage reconfiguration events and storage pool access control.

Revised Architecture

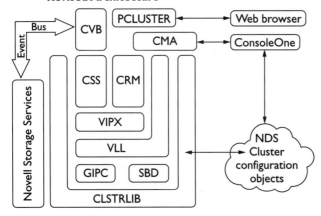

FIGURE 19.2 *Novell Cluster Services 1.6 architecture diagram*

See Chapter 4 for a complete description of the common NetWare 5 and NetWare 6 Cluster Services modules and their interrelationships.

X-REF

NetWare Loadable Modules

In Novell Cluster Services 1.6, the four new Cluster Services modules are as follows:

- Cluster System Services (CSS.NLM)

- Cluster Volume Broker (CVB.NLM)

- Portal Cluster (PCLUSTER.NLM)

- Virtual Interface Provider Library Extensions (VIPX.NLM)

Cluster System Services

The Cluster System Services (CSS) module provides a generic API that any distributed, cluster-aware application can use to enable distributed locking and distributed shared memory. Distributed locking protects cluster resources by ensuring that if one thread on one node gets a lock, then another thread on another node can't get the same lock. Distributed shared memory allows cluster-aware applications running across multiple servers to share access to the same data structures as though they were held in physically shared memory chips. CSS APIs are used by the cluster volume broker to implement a distributed database of shared storage pool access control information. In Novell Cluster Services 1.01, the distributed lock API was exported by the cluster resource manager (CRM). For Novell Cluster Services 1.6, CSS provides an integrated lock and shared memory API for distributed (cluster-aware) applications.

Cluster Volume Broker

The Cluster Volume Broker (CVB) is a cluster-aware application that provides the main interface between Novell Cluster Services and Novell Storage Services. NCS and NSS communicate via an asynchronous event bus. Events are generated under the following circumstances:

- Novell Storage Services requests permission to activate a shared storage pool.

- Storage (re)configuration requires that the event be published to all clustered nodes.

The Cluster Volume Broker provides two functions. First, it intercepts shared storage pool activation and deactivation events and selectively vetoes activation as a function of pool state. If the CVB receives an activation event on one node and another node holds the same pool in the active state, then CVB will veto the event and NSS will deny the activation on the first node. The second function of CVB enables distribution of storage configuration changes across the cluster. If one node changes the configuration of a storage object, the CVB distributes the reconfiguration event to all nodes so they are all refreshed.

Portal Cluster

The Portal Cluster (PCLUSTER) module is a NetWare Remote Manager extension that enables you to manage your cluster from any browser-equipped computer. You can use NetWare Remote Manager, PCLUSTER, and a Web browser for any cluster management possible with ConsoleOne. When you point your Web browser at the cluster IP address, the NetWare Remote Manager running on the corresponding cluster master node responds with the default NetWare server management home page. The PCLUSTER module adds two management options to the NetWare server management home page: Cluster Configuration and Cluster Management.

Virtual Interface Provider Library eXtensions (VIPX)

The VIPX module is a Novell extension of the industry-standard programming interface to the Virtual Interface (VI) Architecture specification. The programming interface is called the VI Provider Library (VIPL). The VI Architecture specification defines an industry-standard architecture for communication within clusters of servers.

X-REF

For more information about the VI Architecture specification, see http://www.viarch.org.

The VIPX makes it easier to write programs for Novell Cluster Services using the standard VI Provider Library. The VIPX module is used by the Cluster System Services and Cluster Resource Manager modules.

Cluster-Enabled Volumes

Whether a storage pool contains only one volume or many volumes, if you wish to cluster enable a volume, you can independently cluster enable each individual logical volume in a storage pool. Cluster enabling a volume ensures that NetWare client access to the volume remains uninterrupted during a failover. Even though storage pools are the managed unit of failover in Novell Cluster Services 1.6, you still have to cluster enable individual logical volumes on storage pools.

You cluster enable a volume in a NetWare 6 cluster basically the same way you cluster enable volumes in a NetWare 5 cluster. When you cluster enable a volume, a virtual NCP server is created on which to mount that volume. This virtual server ensures that the volume remains accessible to clients regardless of the physical cluster node on which the volume is mounted.

The NDS schema relationship between cluster volumes, virtual NCP servers, and cluster volume resources remains unchanged. Novell Storage Services 3.0 introduces a new NDS object to represent a storage pool. Every storage pool has a corresponding NDS object. NDS storage pool objects contain the following attributes:

- *Host server* — Fully distinguished name of the pool's host server

- *Host resource name* — Physical name of the pool known by server software

- *Shared flag* — Copy of the sharable for clustering flag

The cluster management tools prevent a volume from being cluster enabled if it is not located on a shared storage pool.

When a logical volume is cluster enabled, the NDS schema relationship between volume and server objects is adjusted. Figure 19.3 illustrates the relationship between cluster volumes, virtual NCP servers, cluster volume resources, and storage pools after a volume is cluster enabled. A cluster volume resource is created under the cluster container. It contains the load and unload scripts for the cluster-enabled volume. The cluster-enabled volume object has its Host Server attribute altered to point to a new virtual NCP server object that is created in the same context as the volume object. There are cross links between the cluster volume, virtual NCP server, and cluster volume resource objects. The cluster volume object has an nssfsPool attribute that points to the storage pool. The storage pool has a Host Server attribute that points back to the virtual NCP server. Because a storage pool can have many logical volumes, when each subsequent volume is created on a pool containing an already cluster-enabled volume, the new volume is added to the existing cluster-enabled volume and inherits its virtual NCP server and cluster volume resource objects. All cluster-enabled volumes held on the same storage pool share the same IP address of the single virtual NCP server and all cluster-enabled volumes therefore failover together, with the storage pool and its virtual NCP server.

With Novell Cluster Services 1.6, you can optionally customize the names of virtual servers. In contrast, Novell Cluster Services 1.01 assigns virtual server names that cannot be customized. These default virtual server names include an underscore character that some Domain Naming System (DNS) servers don't support and, therefore, are problematic in some cases. By enabling you to customize virtual server names, Novell Cluster Services 1.6 eliminates any such potential problems.

Schema Relationship

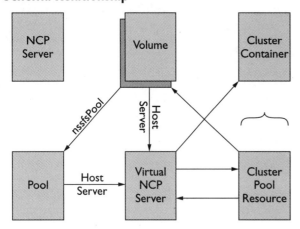

FIGURE 19.3 *NDS schema relationship for cluster-enabled volumes on shared storage pools*

NOTE

The ability to customize virtual NCP server names is enabled by the ConsoleOne cluster snapins. At the time of this writing, the snapins developed for Novell Cluster Services 1.6 also support Novell Cluster Services 1.01. You can manage both kinds of cluster in the same NDS tree from a single ConsoleOne session. The new snapins are available for download at the Novell Web site (www.novell.com/download**).**

For Novell Cluster Services 1.6, the default naming convention for cluster-enabled volumes is as follows. For example, suppose you have a cluster named CLUSTER. Also, suppose you create a logical volume called MYVOL on a shared pool called MYPOOL. NDS cluster objects are created with the following default names:

- *Virtual NCP server* — CLUSTER_MYPOOL_SERVER. This NDS object is created in the same context as the cluster-enabled volume object.

- *Cluster volume resource* — CLUSTER_MYPOOL_SERVER. This NDS object is created in the cluster container.

The existing NDS logical volume and pool objects are renamed as follows:

- *Volume* — CLUSTER_MYVOL

- *Pool* — CLUSTER_MYPOOL_POOL

The Novell Cluster Services 1.6 default naming convention uses the name of the host pool corresponding to a logical volume as the basis from which to derive names for the virtual NCP server and cluster volume resource objects. Unchanged is the naming convention for cluster volume objects. NDS volume objects are renamed to eliminate any particular host server name from the name of the NDS object. In our example, when a volume named MYVOL is cluster-enabled, its NDS volume object is renamed to CLUSTER_MYVOL. NDS pool objects are also renamed to eliminate any particular host server from their name.

Installing Novell Cluster Services 1.6

Novell Cluster Services 1.6 is integrated with NetWare 6. Clustering is optional. Following the installation of NetWare 6, if you have two or more servers you want to cluster together, you run the Cluster Services installation from the NetWare 6 CD. Cluster Services is installed using the Novell NetWare Deployment Manager utility. NetWare Deployment Manager is a single integrated utility that has a number of NetWare 6 product installation and upgrade tools, including:

- Preupgrade tool for NetWare 5 clusters

- NetWare 6 installation, upgrade, and migration tools

- Installation tools for optional NetWare 6 products

X-REF

The procedure to install Cluster Services on NetWare 6 servers is almost identical to NetWare 5.x–based clusters. See Chapter 6 for detailed instructions on how to install a cluster. For NetWare 6, the way you launch the cluster installer is different because it's integrated with the NetWare Deployment Manager.

To install a NetWare 6 cluster, you must first install NetWare 6 on your servers. To do this, insert the NetWare 6 CD in the CD drive of the server you want to install. You upgrade existing NetWare 5.x servers to NetWare 6 using the Deployment Manager. If you already have a NetWare 5.x cluster, follow the steps in the section "Upgrading to Novell Cluster Services 1.6" later in this chapter to upgrade your NetWare 5.x servers to NetWare 6 and your Cluster Services software to version 1.6. If your servers are all running NetWare 6 and you want to install a brand-new Novell Cluster Services 1.6 cluster, follow these steps:

1. Insert the NetWare 6 CD into a client workstation CD drive. The client must be running Novell client software.

2. Browse to the root of the NetWare 6 CD and locate the Novell NetWare Deployment Manager — nwdeploy.exe.

3. Run nwdeploy from the root of the NetWare 6 CD.

4. Double-click Post-Installation Tasks. The NetWare Deployment Manager is shown in Figure 19.4. You have a number of choices when you select Post-Installation Tasks: Install NetWare 6 products, Use DSREPAIR to check NDS and schema status, and Enable a NetWare Cluster. These are all considered to be postinstallation tasks assuming you have already installed NetWare 6 on your servers.

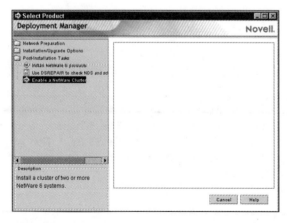

FIGURE 19.4 *Using the NetWare Deployment Manager to start the cluster installer*

5. Click Enable a NetWare Cluster to start the cluster installation utility.

6. Click Next to skip past the introduction screen and display the NCS Action screen. Figure 19.5 shows the available installation options: Create new cluster, Add new nodes to existing cluster, and Upgrade software in existing cluster. The Skip the file copy option is enabled by default and instructs the installer to skip the copy of cluster software files to each server during installation. Cluster software is automatically copied to NetWare 6 servers during NetWare 6 installation. Copying the cluster files again is optional.

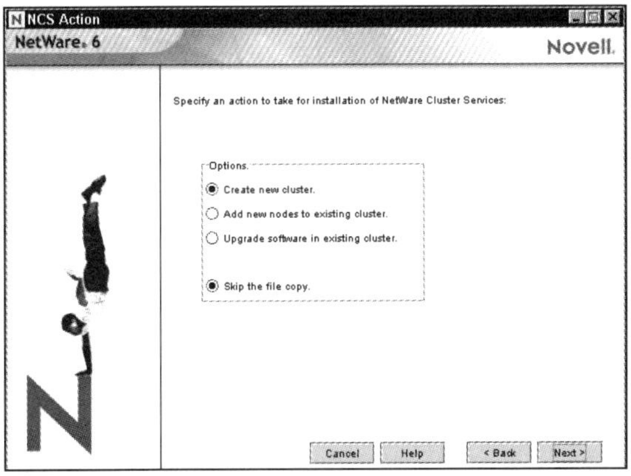

FIGURE 19.5 *The cluster installation utility started from the NetWare Deployment Manager*

7. Select Create new cluster, then click Next. The NCS Cluster Selection screen shown in Figure 19.6 is displayed. On this screen, you type a name for your cluster in the Cluster Object Name field. You also select an NDS tree and context. Figure 19.6 shows a cluster named clus628 being created at context novell in a tree called 3NCPQ_TR. Click Next when you're done.

8. On the NCS Cluster Node Modification screen (see Figure 19.7), select the servers to add to the cluster. By clicking the server browser button, you can select multiple servers at once. Figure 19.7 shows three servers named CPQ2, CPQ3, and CPQ4 being added to the cluster. Their IP addresses are also shown in the IP Address column of the multiple server selection table. Click Next when you're done.

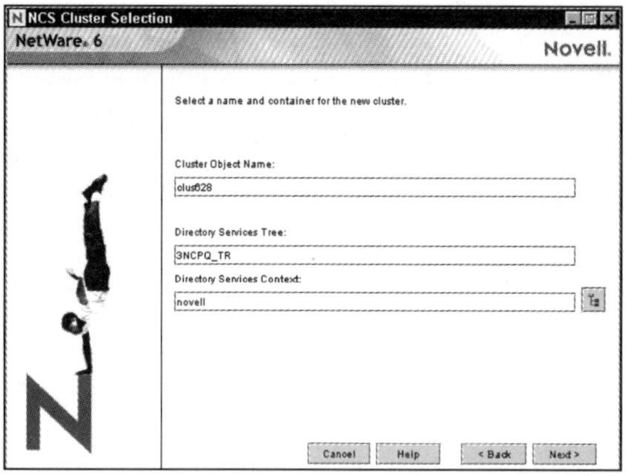

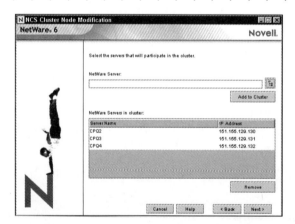

FIGURE 19.6 *Use the NCS Cluster Selection screen to configure the name and location of your cluster relative to an NDS tree and a context.*

FIGURE 19.7 *Use the NCS Cluster Node Modification screen to select servers to add to your cluster.*

9. The next screen, Cluster IP Address Selection, is new for Novell Cluster Services 1.6. It is shown in Figure 19.8. This is where you must provide a unique IP address to be used for cluster management. Choose a unique IP address for your cluster. The value you choose must be appropriate given the IP subnet used by each cluster node for heartbeat traffic. We

recommend that you make note of the IP address because you need it later when managing your cluster via a Web browser. The IP address chosen for the cluster in Figure 19.8 is 151.155.129.134. Note also that the installer displays the corresponding IP subnet information it retrieved from the heartbeat network. In this example, the subnet is 255.255.252.0. Click Next when you're done.

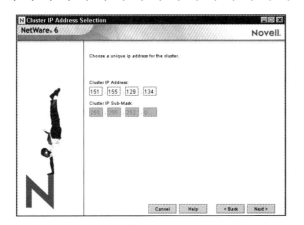

FIGURE 19.8 *Use the Cluster IP Address Selection screen to enter a unique IP address for your cluster.*

10. The next screen, NCS Shared Media Selection, identifies autodetected shared devices. The installer creates the special Cluster Services split brain detection partition on the device you select. If you have a Storage Area Network or other shared disks, then the "Does the cluster have shared media?" selector should be marked Yes. Figure 19.9 shows the NCS Shared Media Selection screen. Shared devices have been found, and the installer will create the Cluster Services partition on device [V502-A2-D0:0] Compaq RA4x00 Disk 0 NFT. Click Next when you're done.

NOTE

The Novell Cluster Services 1.6 installer detects and marks all shared devices "sharable for clustering" and in so doing automatically configures your shared storage to be cluster ready.

11. The next screen, Start Clustering, is also new for Novell Cluster Services 1.6. You are no longer required to reboot servers after installation. Instead, you have the option to automatically start Cluster Services at the end of the installation or defer starting Cluster Services until you are ready to manually start the software. Figure 19.10 shows the new choice. Click Next when you're done.

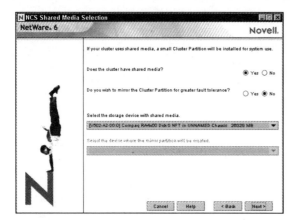

FIGURE 19.9 *The installer automatically detects shared devices and creates the Cluster Services split brain detection partition on the device you select.*

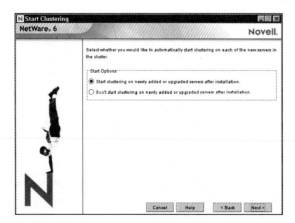

FIGURE 19.10 *Use the Start Clustering screen to decide whether to start Cluster Services immediately after installation is complete.*

12. Install licenses at the next Licenses screen. You have the option to install without licenses, although you will have to install licenses later if you select this option. Click Next when you're done.

13. The final Summary screen now displays. The Summary screen details the products to be installed — Novell Cluster Services in this case. Click Finish to complete the installation wizard and start installing Cluster Services.

14. If you selected "Start clustering on newly added or upgraded servers after installation" in step 11, Cluster Services automatically loads and starts when the installation is complete. If you selected "Don't start clustering . . ." you can start Cluster Services manually. At the server console of each cluster node, type LDNCS to load and start Cluster Services software.

The Novell Cluster Services 1.6 installation performs the following actions:

▶ Verifies that all servers share at least one IP subnet in common and configures the cluster software to use that IP subnet for cluster heartbeat traffic. Because a common IP subnet is required by Cluster Services, if this check fails, installation is aborted.

▶ Verifies that all servers share access to Storage Area Network or other shared disks. If you don't have a Storage Area Network or other shared disks, you can still create a nonshared disk cluster for failing over network services like DHCP that don't need shared disks.

▶ Creates the Cluster Services split brain detection partition on a shared disk.

▶ Automatically sets the sharable for clustering flag on all shared disks.

▶ Creates the cluster container object in the NDS tree at the context you specify.

▶ Creates the Master IP Address resource with the cluster IP address you specify.

▶ Populates the cluster container with node and cluster resource template objects.

▶ Edits the server AUTOEXEC.NCF file on each node to add the command LDNCS.NCF so Cluster Services is automatically started the next time the server is rebooted.

▶ Edits the server SNMP configuration file SYS:\ETC\TRAPTARG.CFG to add the cluster IP address as an SNMP trap target.

Upgrading to Novell Cluster Services 1.6

Before providing step-by-step instructions on how to upgrade a cluster running NetWare 5.x and Novell Cluster Services 1.01 to NetWare 6 and Novell Cluster Services 1.6, this section first details the overall four-phase upgrade process.

TIP

You should be sure you understand the upgrade process in detail before attempting to upgrade a production cluster and SAN to NetWare 6 and Novell Cluster Services 1.6. Furthermore, you should perform this process in a lab environment until you feel fully comfortable with all aspects of the upgrade procedure.

Detailing the Upgrade Process

One significant difference between NetWare 5.x and NetWare 6 is the format of Novell Storage Services file system disk structures. NetWare 5.x NSS volumes have a different disk format than NetWare 6 NSS volumes. Also changed for NetWare 6 is the way trustee information is held on NSS volumes. Both changes directly affect upgrade of cluster nodes and Storage Area Network shared disks from NetWare 5.x to NetWare 6.

To protect against uncoordinated shared disk access on NetWare 5.x clusters, Cluster Services software runs across all nodes and interacts with Novell Storage Services to lock individual volumes for exclusive I/O access on specific nodes. A number of assumptions are made in NetWare 5.x clusters to ensure volumes aren't corrupted as a result of multiple-server access:

▶ All nodes with access to shared disks must run Cluster Services software.

▶ No node can run software that directly interacts with shared storage devices unless Novell Storage Services and Cluster Services software coordinates that access.

▶ When data is written to a shared disk, any server with access to that data must be running a consistent version of software such that data written by one server is identically understood by software running on other servers. This assumption applies at many levels. For example, multiple servers must use an identical disk block format for file system structures. At a higher level, all servers must share a common interpretation of file system metadata such as trustee assignments.

Without proper software control, these rules could be violated during a NetWare 5.x–to–NetWare 6 upgrade. For example, suppose you upgrade one clustered NetWare 5.x server to NetWare 6. When that server runs NetWare 6, suppose it has access to all shared disk data, unaware of the existence of other NetWare 5.x servers that potentially also access the same shared disks. This kind of conflicting I/O access will corrupt shared disk volumes. Novell's NetWare 5.x–to–NetWare 6 cluster upgrade process is designed to eliminate the potential for disk corruption.

The process to upgrade a NetWare 5.x–based cluster to NetWare 6 comprises four main phases and is designed to safely upgrade Storage Area Network shared disk data, NetWare, and Cluster Services software on all servers:

1. Preupgrade the NetWare 5.x cluster.

2. Upgrade cluster nodes from NetWare 5.x to NetWare 6.

3. Upgrade to Novell Cluster Services 1.6.

4. Upgrade cluster volumes to Novell Storage Services 3.0.

Preupgrading a NetWare 5.x Cluster

To preupgrade a NetWare 5.x cluster, you run the NetWare Deployment Manager against a running cluster. The deployment manager preupgrade performs the following actions:

▶ Rather than migrating trustee assignments from one internal format to another, they are backed up and removed from cluster-enabled volumes Trustee assignments are saved in an XML-formatted file named `trustees.xml` and located at the root of each cluster-enabled volume.

▶ Access to shared-disk storage using NetWare 5.x server software is then disabled. The method used to disable shared disk storage prevents NetWare 5.x from recognizing and therefore accessing shared disk partitions in the future. All shared disks are also marked "sharable for clustering," ready for NetWare 6.

▶ Finally, Cluster Services software is shut down and disabled by removing the `LDNCS` command line from each cluster node's `AUTOEXEC.NCF` server startup file.

Upgrading from NetWare 5.x to NetWare 6

Contingent upon having completed the preupgrade phase, you run the NetWare Deployment Manager to upgrade every server in the cluster from NetWare 5.x to NetWare 6. This upgrade task is no different than upgrading multiple standalone (nonclustered) servers from NetWare 5.x to NetWare 6. You can upgrade servers in any order.

Because all shared disks are marked "sharable for clustering" during the preupgrade phase, they are subsequently ignored by Novell Storage Services 3.0 when servers reboot to NetWare 6 after upgrade. If at any time a server reboots back to NetWare 5, shared disk data is protected because disks are disabled by the preupgrade in such a way that the data they hold becomes invisible to NetWare 5.x.

Upgrading to Novell Cluster Services 1.6

Once at least two servers are running NetWare 6, you run the NetWare Deployment Manager a final time to upgrade and enable Cluster Services on NetWare 6. This phase upgrades NDS cluster objects including the cluster container and cluster resources. During this phase, the following occurs:

► Cluster resource load and unload scripts are upgraded from NetWare 5.x command syntax to NetWare 6 command syntax. Table 19.1 lists the command translation rules applied by the cluster upgrade utility.

TABLE 19.1

Command Syntax Translation during Upgrade

NETWARE 5.X COMMANDS	NETWARE 6 COMMANDS
CLUSTER_START *	CLUSTER *
NUDP ADD *	Unchanged
NUDP DEL *	Unchanged
ADD SECONDARY IPADDRESS *	Unchanged
DEL SECONDARY IPADDRESS *	Unchanged
CVSBIND ADD *	CLUSTER CVSBIND ADD *
CVSBIND DEL *	CLUSTER CVSBIND DEL *
NSS /ACTIVATE=*name*	NSS /POOLACTIVATE=*name*
NSS /FORCEDEACTIVATE=*name*	NSS /POOLDEACTIVATE=*name* /OVERRIDE=QUESTION

NETWARE 5.X COMMANDS	NETWARE 6 COMMANDS
`MOUNT name`	Unchanged
`MOUNT name VOLID=N`	Unchanged
`DISMOUNT name /FORCE`	Removed
`TRUSTMIG *`	Removed

- ▶ The special master IP address resource is created from an IP address you supply to the cluster upgrade utility.
- ▶ The NDS schema relationship is upgraded for every cluster-enabled volume.

X-REF

> **See the section "Cluster-Enabled Volumes" earlier in this chapter for a description of the Novell Cluster Services 1.6 NDS schema relationship.**

- ▶ Every cluster volume resource load script receives two additional commands to upgrade NetWare 5.x volumes to Novell Storage Services 3.0 storage pools and to restore trustee assignments from the `trustees.xml` file located at the root of each volume. The commands are as follows:

```
nss /ZLSSVolumeUpgrade=VOL

load protected trustbar VOL:trustees.xml -r
```

- ▶ Finally, Cluster Services software is enabled by adding the `LDNCS` command line to each cluster node's `AUTOEXEC.NCF` server startup file.

Upgrading Cluster Volumes to Novell Storage Services 3.0

When Cluster Services software is restarted on NetWare 6, cluster resources are loaded on their most preferred nodes as normal. For cluster-enabled volumes, the additional upgrade-specific commands added to the load script during cluster upgrade are executed. These commands automatically complete the upgrade process:

- ▶ The `NSS /ZLSSVolumeUpgrade` command upgrades NetWare 5.x format volumes to NetWare 6 storage pools. Each pool contains a single logical volume. The storage pool and logical volume names are identical and are the same as the original NetWare 5.x volume.
- ▶ Trustee assignments are restored to volumes using the `TRUSTBAR` utility.

Both commands are effective only once. The first time each cluster volume load script is executed, the commands do real upgrade work. They become ineffective subsequently.

Preupgrading a NetWare 5.x Cluster

Now that you understand what happens during each phase of the upgrade, you are ready to try it. You start by pre-upgrading a NetWare 5.x cluster. You preupgrade an existing NetWare 5.x cluster using the NetWare Deployment Manager. Your cluster must be operational and all cluster-enabled volumes must be in the running state before you begin the preupgrade. If a cluster-enabled volume is not in the running state, the deployment manager fails to back up that volume's trustee assignments. Follow these steps to preupgrade a NetWare 5.x cluster:

1. Insert the NW6 CD into a client workstation CD drive. The client must be running Novell client software.

2. Browse to the root of the NetWare 6 CD and locate the Novell NetWare Deployment Manager — nwdeploy.exe.

3. Run nwdeploy from the root of the NetWare 6 CD.

4. Double-click Network Preparation. The NetWare Deployment Manager is shown in Figure 19.11. You have a number of choices when you select Network Preparation: Backup data, View and update NDS versions, Prepare for NDS eDirectory 8.6, Pre-upgrade a NetWare Cluster, and Prepare for server with NDS7 and NSS. These are all considered network preparation tasks to ready your network and servers for upgrading to NetWare 6.

5. Click Pre-upgrade a NetWare Cluster to start the Cluster preupgrade utility.

6. Click Next to skip past the introduction screen and display the NCS Cluster Selection screen shown in Figure 19.12. On this screen, you identify your existing NetWare 5.x cluster to be preupgraded. Use the browser button to open an NDS tree browser and select your cluster container object, or type in your cluster's name in the Cluster Object Name field, and the NDS tree and context names in the Directory Services Tree and Directory Services Context fields. Figure 19.12 shows a cluster named CLUSTER at context CONTEXT in a tree called TREE. Click Next when you're done.

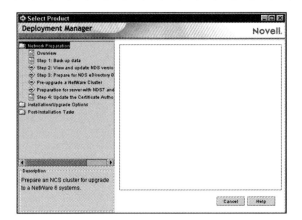

FIGURE 19.11 *Using the NetWare Deployment Manager to start the cluster preupgrade utility*

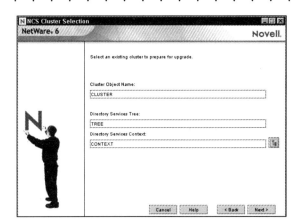

FIGURE 19.12 *Use the NDS cluster selection screen to identify an existing NetWare 5.x cluster to preupgrade.*

7. The next screen, Down Server(s), is where you choose whether to down your servers after preupgrade or leave them running. Your choices are shown in Figure 19.13. The default action is "Take the cluster servers down after the pre-upgrade." Note also how the screen includes a recommendation to always down servers after preupgrade. Downing your servers after preupgrade ensures that shared-disk volumes are properly dismounted and deactivated prior to NetWare 6 upgrade. The preupgrade process begins when you click Next.

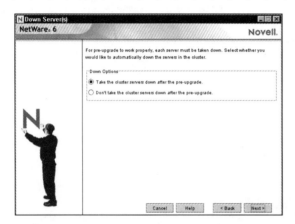

FIGURE 19.13 *The Down Server(s) screen enables you to choose whether to down servers after preupgrade is complete.*

8. The preupgrade utility processes every cluster-enabled volume by backing up and removing trustee assignments. Trustee assignments are saved in a file named trustees.xml located at the root of each volume. Figure 19.14 shows trustee backup of a cluster-enabled volume, Trees/TREE/CLUSTER_VOL1.CONTEXT. Note how the preupgrade utility processes cluster-enabled volumes independent of which cluster nodes are currently hosting the volumes.

FIGURE 19.14 *The preupgrade utility backs up trustee assignments on a cluster-enabled volume, Trees/TREE/CLUSTER_VOL1.CONTEXT.*

9. If a cluster-enabled volume is inaccessible when you're backing up trustee assignments, the preupgrade utility displays a warning dialog box and enables you to bring the volume online so that its trustees can be successfully backed up. Figure 19.15 shows the warning dialog box. The installer is unable to back up trustees on volume Trees/TREE/CLUSTER_VOL1.CONTEXT. You have two choices: Ignore the failure and move on to the next cluster-enabled volume, or retry the backup. The Retry option enables you to bring the volume online to retry the backup.

FIGURE 19.15 *If a cluster-enabled volume is offline, the preupgrade utility fails to back up its trustee assignments. Use the Retry button to try again later when the cluster volume becomes available.*

If you ignore a preupgrade failure to back up trustee assignments on a cluster-enabled volume, you will lose trustee assignments or experience corrupt trustees when clustered NetWare 5.x servers are upgraded to

WARNING NetWare 6.

10. The preupgrade is complete when trustee assignments on all cluster-enabled volumes are backed up. The dialog box shown in Figure 19.16 is displayed. The cluster named CLUSTER.CONTEXT is now ready for NetWare 6 upgrade. When you click OK, all servers in the cluster will be downed to ensure that cluster-enabled volumes are properly dismounted and deactivated.

FIGURE 19.16 *The preupgrade utility has completed its processing. Click OK to down all clustered servers that are ready for NetWare 6 upgrade.*

Upgrading from NetWare 5.x to NetWare 6

To upgrade your cluster from NetWare 5.x to NetWare 6, follow Novell's instructions for upgrading NetWare on individual (nonclustered) servers. You can upgrade servers in any order. Because the cluster preupgrade disables shared disk NSS volumes, the NetWare 5.x to NetWare 6 server upgrade does not interact with shared storage in any way. If you do not run the cluster preupgrade, you will receive an error when attempting to upgrade any server that is configured in a cluster. Running the preupgrade is a mandatory step that must be performed before you attempt to upgrade any clustered servers. You are ready to upgrade your cluster to Novell Cluster Services 1.6 only after servers have been upgraded from NetWare 5.x to NetWare 6.

NOTE

The generic NetWare 5.x to NetWare 6 upgrade instructions are not included here. They are fairly detailed and beyond the scope of this book. Visit Novell's NetWare Deployment Guides Web site at `www.novell.com/` `products/netware/deployment_solutions/` **for more details.**

Upgrading to Novell Cluster Services 1.6

You upgrade Novell Cluster Services to version 1.6 on NetWare 6 servers using the NetWare Deployment Manager. To upgrade Novell Cluster Services to version 1.6 on NetWare 6 servers, follow these steps:

1. Insert the NW6 CD into a client workstation CD drive. The client must be running Novell client software.

2. Browse to the root of the NetWare 6 CD and locate the Novell NetWare Deployment Manager — `nwdeploy.exe`.

3. Run `nwdeploy` from the root of the NetWare 6 CD.

4. Double-click Post-Installation Tasks. The NetWare Deployment Manager is shown in Figure 19.17. You have a number of choices when you select Post-Installation Tasks: Install NetWare 6 products, Use DSREPAIR to check NDS and schema status, and Enable a NetWare Cluster. These are all considered postinstallation tasks, assuming you have already upgraded your servers from NetWare 5.x to NetWare 6.

5. Click Enable a NetWare Cluster to start the Cluster installation utility.

6. Click Next to skip past the introduction screen and display the NCS Action screen. Figure 19.18 shows the available installation options. They are

Create new cluster, Add new nodes to existing cluster, and Upgrade software in existing cluster. The Skip the file copy option is enabled by default and instructs the installer to skip the copy of cluster software files to each server during upgrade. Cluster software is automatically copied to servers during the NetWare 5.x to NetWare 6 upgrade. Copying the cluster files again is optional.

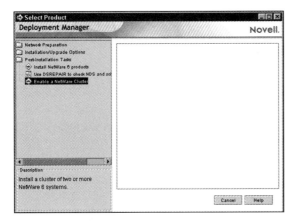

FIGURE 19.17 *Using the NetWare Deployment Manager to start the cluster installer*

FIGURE 19.18 *The cluster installation utility started from the NetWare Deployment Manager*

7. Select Upgrade software in existing cluster, then click Next. The NCS Cluster Selection screen shown in Figure 19.19 is displayed. On this screen, you identify your existing cluster to upgrade. Use the browser button to open an NDS tree browser and select your cluster container object, or type in your cluster's name in the Cluster Object Name field, and the NDS tree and context names in the Directory Services Tree and Directory Services Context fields. Figure 19.19 shows a cluster named CLUSTER at context CONTEXT in a tree called TREE. Click Next when you're done.

FIGURE 19.19 *Use the NCS Cluster Selection screen to identify your existing cluster to upgrade.*

8. The next screen, Cluster IP Address Selection, is shown in Figure 19.20. This is where you must provide a unique IP address to be used for cluster management. Choose a unique IP address for your cluster. The value you choose must be appropriate given the IP subnet used by each cluster node for heartbeat traffic. You should make note of the IP address, because you need it later when managing your cluster via a Web browser. The IP address chosen for the cluster in Figure 19.20 is 10.7.5.15. Note also that the installer displays the corresponding IP subnet information it retrieved from the heartbeat network. In this example, the subnet is 255.255.255.0. Click Next when you're done.

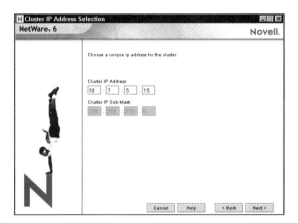

FIGURE 19.20 *Use the Cluster IP Address Selection screen to enter a unique IP address for your cluster.*

9. The next screen, Start Clustering, is shown in Figure 19.21. You have the option to automatically start Cluster Services at the end of the upgrade or defer starting Cluster Services until you are ready to manually start the software. Figure 19.21 shows the two choices. Click Next when you're done.

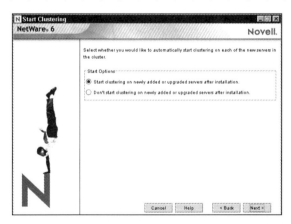

FIGURE 19.21 *Use the Start Clustering screen to decide whether to start Cluster Services immediately after the upgrade is complete.*

10. The final Summary screen is displayed. The Summary screen details the products to be upgraded — Novell Cluster Services in this case. Click Finish to complete the upgrade wizard and to start upgrading Cluster Services on your servers.

11. If you selected "Start clustering on newly added or upgraded servers after installation" in step 9, Cluster Services automatically loads and starts when the upgrade is complete. If you selected "Don't start clustering . . ." you can start Cluster Services manually. At the server console of each cluster node, type LDNCS to load and start Cluster Services software.

When the cluster upgrade is complete and LDNCS has been run on each of your servers, Cluster Services software starts and forms a cluster. Your cluster resources are then loaded on their most preferred nodes in exactly the same way a rebooted cluster first starts running — quorum and preferred node policies are applied. Because each cluster resource load script is modified with upgrade-specific commands, the final phase of cluster upgrade occurs when the cluster resource load scripts run. On all your nodes, cluster resources run in parallel and complete the upgrade. NSS volumes are upgraded via the NSS /ZLSSVolumeUpgrade command and trustee assignments are restored via the load protected TrustBar command. You can check the status of individual resources using ConsoleOne or NetWare Remote Manager.

Managing Novell Cluster Services 1.6

You have a choice of using ConsoleOne or NetWare Remote Manager to manage Novell Cluster Services 1.6 clusters. Both enable identical functionality and are designed to offer a similar look and feel whether you use a Web browser or the Java-based ConsoleOne management utility. A third management option is enabled via new console commands. Cluster commands correspond to all of the cluster resource operations available from ConsoleOne or NetWare Remote Manager. For example, you can migrate a cluster resource from one node to another node using a console command.

ConsoleOne Cluster Snapins

ConsoleOne cluster snapins are distributed with NetWare 6 software. The snapins are installed in the standard ConsoleOne snapins directory on the SYS volume of every NetWare 6 server whether or not that server is configured in a cluster. The location of the cluster snapins is as follows:

```
SYS:\PUBLIC\MGMT\CONSOLEONE\1.2\SNAPINS\NCS\NCS.JAR
```

```
SYS:\PUBLIC\MGMT\CONSOLEONE\1.2\RESOURCES\NCS\NCSRES.JAR
```

You can use ConsoleOne to manage a Novell Cluster Services 1.6 cluster the same way as earlier versions of Novell Cluster Services. The ConsoleOne snapins developed for Novell Cluster Services 1.6 also support Novell Cluster Services 1.01. You can manage both kinds of clusters located in the same or different NDS trees from a single ConsoleOne session.

See Chapters 7 and 8 for details on how to use ConsoleOne to manage Cluster Services.

X-REF

NetWare Remote Manager

All you need is a Web browser to manage NetWare 6 and Novell Cluster Services 1.6. Point your browser at the cluster IP address. For example, if your cluster's IP address is 151.155.129.134, point your browser to http://151.155.129.134:8008. Port 8008 is the default port for NetWare Remote Manager. When you use a browser with NetWare Remote Manager, you will have to accept a security certificate from the server and then log in with administrator rights. Use your NDS user name and password to log in. You are then securely reconnected to https://151.155.129.134:8009.

When you connect via the cluster IP address, you are taken to whichever node is currently the cluster master node. The cluster IP address is always bound to the cluster master node. To manage the cluster, you don't need to know which nodes are available — simply point your browser to the cluster IP address.

If the cluster software isn't running, the browser fails to connect to the cluster IP address. You can still create and edit cluster resources even if the cluster isn't running. Simply point your browser to the IP address of any server installed into the cluster. This is also the standard way for managing servers that aren't part of a cluster.

TIP

Figure 19.22 shows the default NetWare Remote Manager screen when you first connect with a Web browser. The user interface consists of two main parts. The left-hand panel is a list of supported management operations. Each operation is a hypertext link; clicking on the link takes you to the corresponding management screen. The right-hand panel is the main management interface. Its contents change when you click management links in the left-hand panel. When the NetWare server you connect to is configured in a cluster, the left-hand panel includes clustering links. Shown in the lower left-hand corner of Figure 19.22 are the Cluster Config and Cluster Management links, under the heading "Clustering."

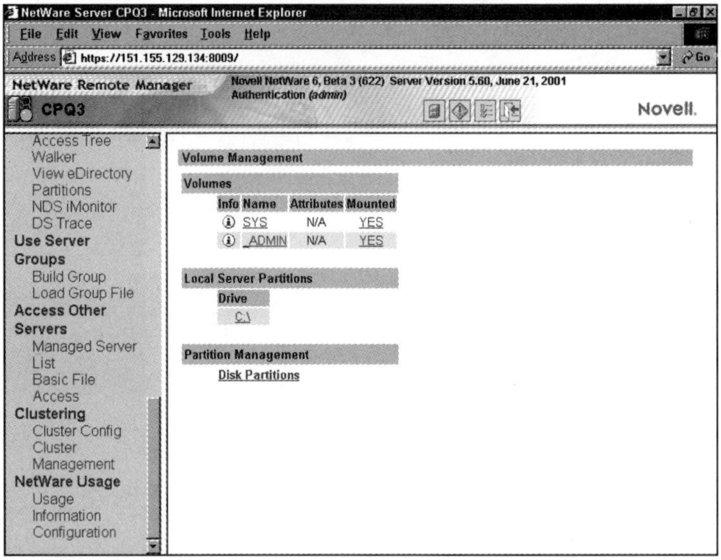

FIGURE 19.22 *NetWare Remote Manager running on a cluster node with Cluster Config and Cluster Management links*

Cluster Config

When you select Cluster Config, the screen shown in Figure 19.23 displays. Each cluster object has a hypertext link to the various management operations enabled by the screen. You can click the cluster, cluster node, or cluster resource links to bring up further task-specific management screens. The management tasks enabled by the Cluster Config screen are identical to those enabled with ConsoleOne's main view. You create and edit cluster resources, configure cluster protocol settings, and cluster enable volumes from the Cluster Config screen. Figure 19.23 shows a cluster called clus628. It has three nodes named CPQ2, CPQ3, and CPQ4. The cluster Master IP Address resource has a purple pyramid icon. Other cluster resources have green pyramid icons. There are two cluster volume resources named SHP1_SERVER and SHP2_SERVER. By clicking the New Cluster Volume link, you cluster enable a new volume.

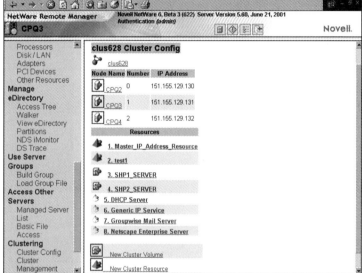

FIGURE 19.23 *The NetWare Remote Manager Cluster Config screen enables cluster configuration.*

Cluster Management

When you select Cluster Management, the screen shown in Figure 19.24 appears. The screen is intended to look like the ConsoleOne Cluster State View. Again, there are hypertext links to the various management operations enabled by the screen. You can click cluster resource links to bring up further task-specific management screens. The management tasks enabled by the Cluster Management screen are identical to those enabled with ConsoleOne's Cluster State View. Figure 19.24 shows the status of a cluster called clus628. All three of its nodes, CPQ2, CPQ3, and CPQ4 are available. Clus628 is running four cluster resources that are listed in the Cluster Resource table. For example, the Master IP Address resource is shown running on CPQ3. You online, offline, or migrate cluster resources by clicking their links. Also shown is the Event Log link. To view the cluster event log, click this link.

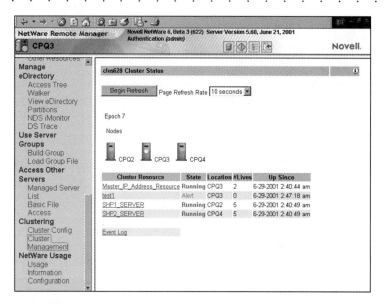

FIGURE 19.24 *The NetWare Remote Manager Cluster Management screen enables cluster management.*

Cluster Console Commands

Figure 19.25 lists the available cluster console commands. Type **HELP CLUSTER** at the console of any clustered server to display this help screen.

The cluster console commands are effective on all nodes. For example, if you want to offline a cluster resource that is currently running on one node, you type the command **CLUSTER OFFLINE** *resource* on any node currently in the cluster membership. You don't have to type the command on the node that is running the cluster resource. The cluster commands can be used on any node to work with any cluster resource.

Figure 19.26 illustrates use of cluster commands to first inspect the status of all cluster resources and to then migrate a cluster resource called SHP1_SERVER to a cluster node named CPQ3. The CLUSTER MIGRATE command is used to migrate a cluster resource initially located on node CPQ2 to node CPQ3. Note how CPQ3's server console is used to run the CLUSTER MIGRATE command even though SHP1_SERVER was originally running on CPQ2.

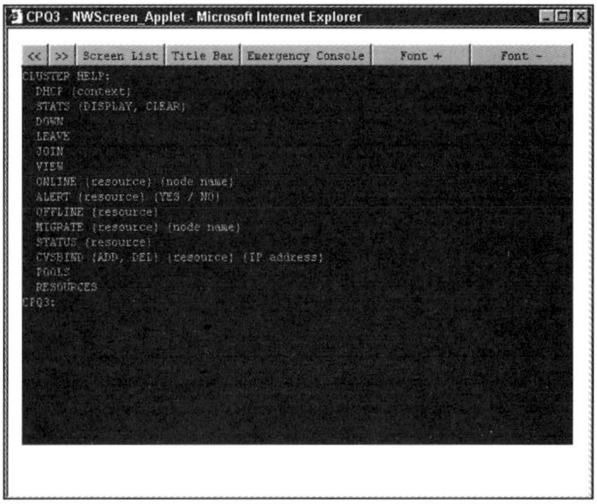

FIGURE 19.25 *Type **HELP CLUSTER** to get a list of cluster-specific console commands.*

FIGURE 19.26 *Using cluster commands to list resource states and to then migrate a resource to another node*

CLUSTER DHCP (context)

This is identical to the Novell Cluster Services 1.01 command CLUSTER_START DHCP.

See Chapter 15 for information about applying DHCP with Cluster Services.

X-REF

CLUSTER STATS (DISPLAY, CLEAR)

This is a revised version of the Novell Cluster Services 1.01 commands CLUSTER_START DISPLAYSTATS and CLUSTER_START CLEARSTATS.

CLUSTER DOWN

Use this command to shut down the cluster, same as in Novell Cluster Services 1.01.

CLUSTER LEAVE

Use this command to have a node leave the cluster, same as in Novell Cluster Services 1.01.

CLUSTER JOIN

Use this command to have a node join a cluster, same as in Novell Cluster Services 1.01.

CLUSTER VIEW

Use this command to inspect the state of the current cluster membership, same as in Novell Cluster Services 1.01.

CLUSTER ONLINE (resource) (node name)

Use this command to online a cluster resource to a specific node. If the resource is in the offline state, it is onlined to the specific node. If you omit the node name, the resource is onlined to its most preferred node. Node name must be one of the nodes configured in the resource's preferred nodes list.

CLUSTER ALERT (resource) (YES / NO)

Use this command to acknowledge a cluster resource in the alert state. The CLUSTER ALERT command has two forms:

- ► CLUSTER ALERT *resource* YES — Confirm the alert and allow the resource to change state.

- ► CLUSTER ALERT *resource* NO — Deny the alert and force the resource to stay in the same state or go offline if the alert is start mode manual.

CLUSTER OFFLINE (resource)

Use this command to offline a cluster resource. If the resource is in the online state, it is unloaded wherever it is running.

CLUSTER MIGRATE (resource) (node name)

Use this command to migrate a cluster resource from one node to another node. The cluster resource is unloaded where it is running, then loaded on the specified node. Node name must be one of the nodes configured in the resource's preferred nodes list.

CLUSTER STATUS (resource)

Use this command to display the status of the given cluster resource. The returned cluster resource status includes the node it is currently running on if online, and the number of lives since the resource first came online.

CLUSTER CVSBIND (ADD, DEL) (resource) (IP address)

Cluster Services automatically adds the CLUSTER CVSBIND command to cluster volume resource load and unload scripts when cluster enabling a volume. In normal circumstances, you never use this command. The CLUSTER CVSBIND command adds and deletes virtual server name–to–IP address bindings to enable advertising of virtual NCP servers in the bindery namespace.

CLUSTER POOLS

Use this command to display the state of all "sharable for clustering" Novell Storage Services storage pools managed by Cluster Services. CLUSTER POOLS lists the name of each pool, the status of the pool (whether active or deactive), and the name of the node it is currently active on, if in the active state.

CLUSTER RESOURCES

Use this command to display the status of all cluster resources. This command returns the same information as the CLUSTER STATUS command, but for all cluster resources.

Working with Shared Disk NSS Pools

This section gives you an introduction to working with shared disk NSS storage pools and logical volumes in the context of Novell Cluster Services 1.6 and NetWare 6. For NetWare 6, all storage management is performed via ConsoleOne (or NetWare Remote Manager). The NWCONFIG and NSS /MENU utilities no longer exist to support storage management.

X-REF

Chapter 9 includes detailed instructions on working with NetWare 5.x shared disk NSS volumes. Whereas the concepts of Storage Area Network shared disks are identical in both NetWare 5.x and NetWare 6, the management tools used to create storage pools and logical volumes are very different for NetWare 6. However, the method by which you cluster enable volumes is identical for NetWare 5.x or NetWare 6.

To manage the storage attached to a NetWare 6 server or cluster, run ConsoleOne and select the corresponding server or cluster container object in the NDS tree. Right-click to bring up the property book for the server or cluster. You'll see a new Media property page tab. From this single tab, you manage the following storage objects:

▶ Devices

▶ RAID Devices

▶ Free Space

▶ Partitions

▶ NSS Pools

▶ NSS Logical Volumes

Figure 19.27 shows the Media tab corresponding to a cluster named clus628. When you right-click on the Cluster container to launch the property book, the first page displayed is Quorum Triggers. The new Media tab is shown in the figure, positioned between the Notification and NDS Rights property page tabs. From the Media tab drop-down menu (shown in the figure), select from Devices, RAID Devices, Free Space, Partitions, NSS Pools, or NSS Logical Volumes and the corresponding page will be displayed (not shown in the figure).

From the cluster container Media tab, you manage storage attached to the cluster without needing to know particular details of which servers are currently available. This is transparent because the ConsoleOne snapins communicate with whatever node is the cluster master node at the time you launch ConsoleOne. If the master node should fail over, ConsoleOne reconnects to the new master node. All of this is hidden behind the cluster Media tab.

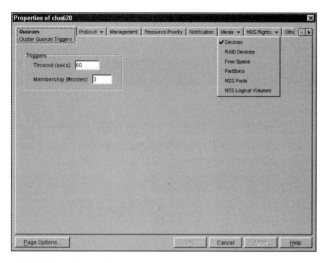

FIGURE 19.27 *Selecting the Media tab via the cluster container property book enables single system image storage management for your cluster.*

Cluster Enabling Volumes on Shared Storage Pools

There are many aspects to the new ConsoleOne-based storage management interface and many corresponding screens and options. By following an example of the steps to create shared virtual disk partitions, storage pools, and logical volumes, you will be introduced to most of the important elements of the storage management user interface.

Use the following steps to create cluster-enabled volumes from a NetWare 6 sharable for clustering storage pool. You use ConsoleOne for all of the steps— you no longer have to switch between server- and client-side tools. Storage management for the entire cluster is enabled from the cluster container's Media tab.

1. Create a disk partition on a sharable for clustering disk.

2. Create a storage pool from a shared disk partition.

3. Create a logical volume on a shared storage pool.

4. Cluster enable the logical volume for transparent client failover.

NOTE

To emulate the cluster-enabled volume failover behavior of NetWare 5.x Cluster Services, create a single logical volume per storage pool. Because storage pools are the unit of failover for NetWare 6, by having a single logical volume per storage pool, you enable the equivalent flexibility of being able to configure any logical volume to fail over to any node independent of other logical volumes. If you create multiple logical volumes on a single pool, they all have to fail over to the same node.

Creating a Disk Partition on a Sharable for Clustering Disk

Select the Cluster container and right-click to launch the property book. Starting at the cluster Media tab, follow these steps:

1. Select the Partitions menu item from the drop-down Media tab. The Partitions dialog box is displayed in Figure 19.28. Existing partitions are listed in the left-hand panel. The center panel displays information corresponding to individual partitions selected via the left-hand panel, including Device ID, Name, Type, Share State, and Total Space. The server's local DOS partition is highlighted. It is not sharable for clustering.

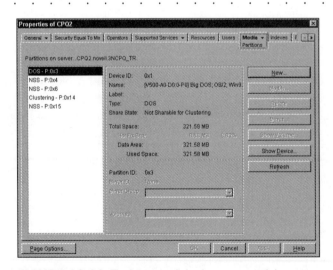

FIGURE 19.28 *The Partitions dialog box manages disk partitions.*

2. Click New to create a new partition. The Create a new partition dialog in Figure 19.29 appears. Existing disk devices are listed in the left-hand panel. Select a disk device to create your new partition and specify a size for the new partition using the Size field. In Figure 19.29, the size of the new partition is 13.4GB. Click OK to create the partition.

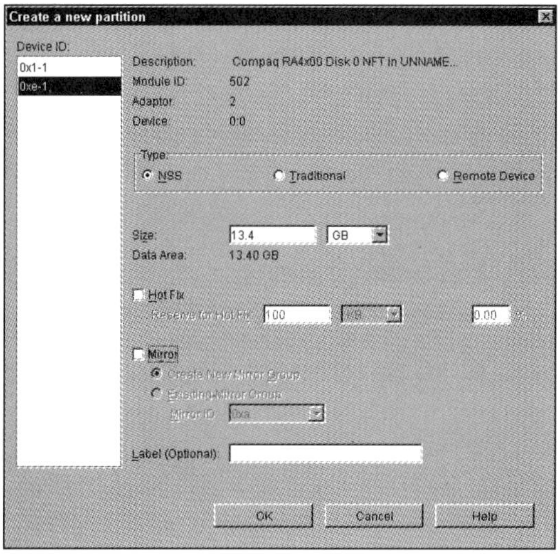

FIGURE 19.29 *Using the Create a new partition dialog box to create a new disk partition*

Creating a Storage Pool from a Shared Disk Partition

Select the Cluster container and right-click to launch the property book. Starting at the cluster Media tab, follow these steps:

1. Select the NSS Pools menu item from the Media tab. The Pools dialog box shown in Figure 19.30 is displayed. Existing pools are listed in the left-hand panel. The center panel displays information corresponding to individual pools selected in the left-hand panel, including State, Share State, and Total Space. A pool named SHP2 is highlighted in Figure 19.30. Total Space is 12GB and its Share State is Sharable for Clustering.

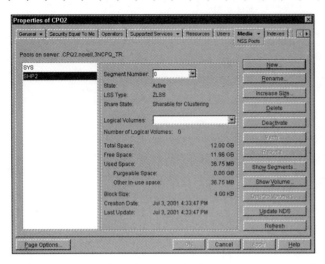

FIGURE 19.30 *The NSS Pools dialog box manages storage pools.*

2. Click New to create a new pool. The first screen of the Create a New Pool
wizard, shown in Figure 19.31, appears. Type a name for your new pool in
the Name field. The new pool in Figure 19.31 is called SHP1, presumably
shorthand for "shared pool 1." You can name your pools anything you like
provided you follow the rules shown on the screen. The default value for
the LSS (Loadable Storage Services) Type is ZLSS and cannot be changed.
Click Next when you're done.

3. The second screen of the Create a New Pool wizard, shown in Figure 19.32,
is where you configure storage for the pool. Follow the instructions
shown on the screen — select storage objects, then edit the number in
the Used column for each object. All the space in the storage object
NSS - P:0x12-1 is used to create the SHP1 pool, with a total pool size
of 13,722MB. Click Next when you're done.

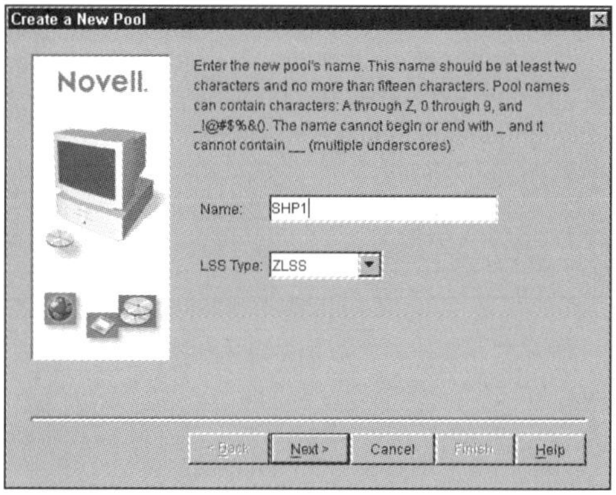

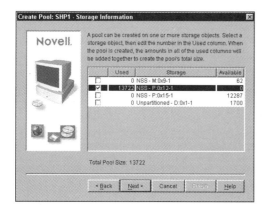

FIGURE 19.31 *The first screen of the Create a New Pool wizard is where you give the pool a name.*

FIGURE 19.32 *The second screen of the Create a New Pool wizard is where you configure the pool's storage.*

4. The third and final screen of the Create a New Pool wizard is shown in Figure 19.33. Here you determine whether the new pool should be activated after being created. To create logical volumes on a pool, it must be active. Accept the default choice and click Finish to create and activate the new pool.

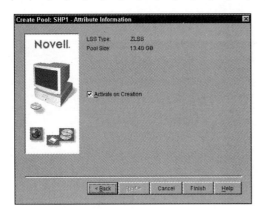

FIGURE 19.33 *The final screen of the Create a New Pool wizard is where you decide to activate the pool after creating it.*

Creating a Logical Volume on a Shared Storage Pool

Select the Cluster container and right-click to launch the property book. Starting at the cluster Media tab, follow these steps:

1. Select the NSS Logical Volumes menu from the Media tab. The Logical Volumes dialog box shown in Figure 19.34 is displayed. Existing logical volumes are listed in the left-hand panel. The center panel displays information corresponding to individual logical volumes selected in the left-hand panel, including Host Pool, State, Quota, and Available Space. A logical volume named SYS is highlighted in Figure 19.34. Available Space is 1499.18MB and its State is Active and Mounted Note the Host Pool is SYS. All logical volumes have a Host Pool; in this case, the Host Pool and logical volume it contains have the same name — SYS.

2. Click New to create a new logical volume. The first screen of the Create a New Logical Volume wizard, shown in Figure 19.35, is displayed. Type a name for your new logical volume in the Name field. The new logical volume in Figure 19.35 is called SHP1V1, presumably shorthand for "shared pool 1 - volume 1." You can name your logical volumes anything you like provided you follow the rules shown on the screen. Click Next when you're done.

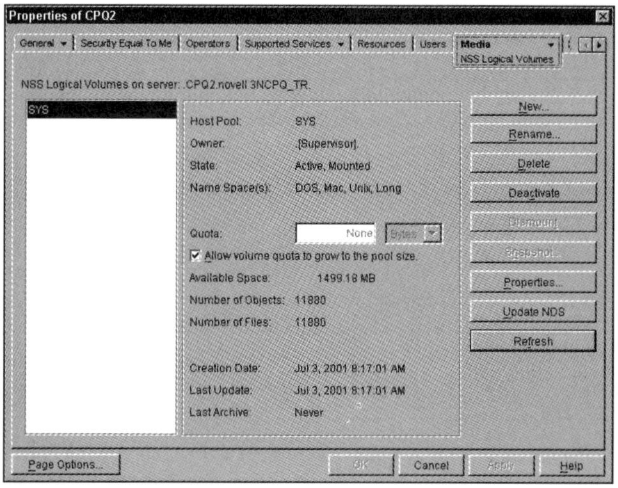

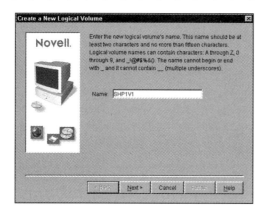

FIGURE 19.34 *The NSS Logical Volumes dialog box manages logical volumes.*

FIGURE 19.35 *The first screen of the Create a New Logical Volume wizard is where you give the logical volume a name.*

3. The second screen of the Create a New Logical Volume wizard, shown in Figure 19.36, is where you configure storage for the logical volume. Follow the instructions shown on the screen — you create a logical volume from an existing pool or free space device. Once you select where you want to create the logical volume, enter a space quota in the Volume Quota field. By optionally checking Allow volume quota to grow to the pool size, you give the logical volume an unlimited quota. Figure 19.36 shows a storage pool called SHP1 being used to create the new logical volume (named SHP1V1).

NOTE

For more information on Novell Storage Services 3.0 features, such as Data Shredding and File Level Snapshot, visit Novell's NSS Web site at www.novell.com/products/nss/

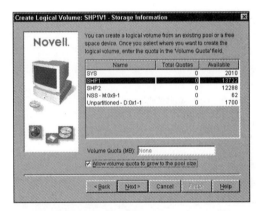

FIGURE 19.36 *The second screen of the Create a New Logical Volume wizard is where you configure the logical volume's storage.*

4. The third and final screen of the Create a New Logical Volume wizard is shown in Figure 19.37. Here you configure various volume attributes, including Data Shredding, File Level Snapshot, User Space Restrictions, and so forth. You also determine whether the new logical volume should be activated and mounted after being created. Accept the default choices and click Finish to create, activate, and mount the new logical volume. When you create a new logical volume, an NDS volume object is created in the NDS tree.

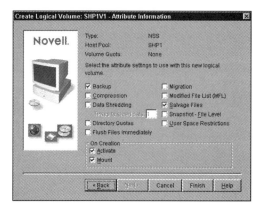

FIGURE 19.37 *The final screen of the Create a New Logical Volume wizard is where you configure various volume attributes and decide to activate the logical volume after creating it.*

Cluster Enabling a Logical Volume for Transparent Client Failover

Select the cluster container object and follow these steps:

1. Click the New Cluster Volume button or select File ➪ New ➪ Cluster ➪ Cluster Volume. The New Cluster Volume dialog box shown in Figure 19.38 is displayed. Use the NDS tree browser to select the NDS volume object corresponding to your newly created logical volume. The New Cluster Volume dialog box automatically fills in the Volume, Virtual Server Name, and Cluster Volume Name fields from the volume you select. The New Cluster Volume dialog also verifies that the logical volume is eligible for clustering — it must be held on a shared storage pool attached to the servers in your cluster. Figure 19.38 shows a logical volume named CPQ2_SHP1V1.novell. The virtual NCP server name is derived from the cluster name and the logical volume's host pool name. The cluster name is clus628 and the host pool name is SHP1. The default virtual

NCP server name is, therefore, `clus628_SHP1_SERVER`. The default cluster volume name is derived from the cluster name also — it is `clus628_SHP1V1`.

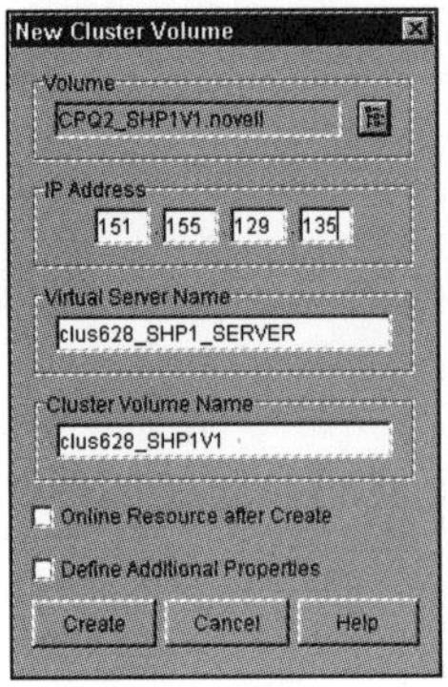

FIGURE 19.38 *Using the New Cluster Volume dialog box to cluster enable a logical volume*

2. You must provide a unique IP address to cluster enable a volume. Type the IP address in the IP Address field and click Create to cluster enable the volume. If you check Online Resource after Create, the cluster volume resource is started automatically.

Before starting the cluster volume resource, ensure that the corresponding logical volume and its host pool are deactivated. If not, Cluster Services will detect the pool is already active and the cluster volume resource will be forced into the Comatose state. If this happens, offline the resource, then online it again.

NOTE

Using Novell Storage Services Console Commands

Novell Storage Services 3.0 provides new console commands to enable management of storage pools and logical volumes from the server console. They are as follows:

▸ `NSS POOLS` — Displays the status of all storage pools.

▸ `NSS /POOLACTIVATE=POOL` — Activates a storage pool on the server.

- NSS /POOLDEACTIVATE=POOL — Deactivates a storage pool on the server.

- NSS VOLUMES — Displays the status of all logical volumes.

- NSS /ACTIVATE=VOLUME — Activates a logical volume on a storage pool.

- NSS /DEACTIVATE=VOLUME — Deactivates a logical volume on a storage pool.

To activate and mount a logical volume, its underlying storage pool must be in the active state. If a storage pool is not in the active state, it's not possible to identify the names of logical volumes on that pool. You must first activate a pool to list its logical volumes.

An example of using the new commands is shown in Figure 19.39. The NSS POOLS command displays the status of three storage pools: SYS, SHP1, and SHP2. The storage pools SHP1 and SHP2 are both sharable for clustering. They are in the deactive state on cluster node CPQ3. The CLUSTER POOLS command reveals that pool SHP1 is in the active state on node CPQ2 and pool SHP2 is in the active state on node CPQ4.

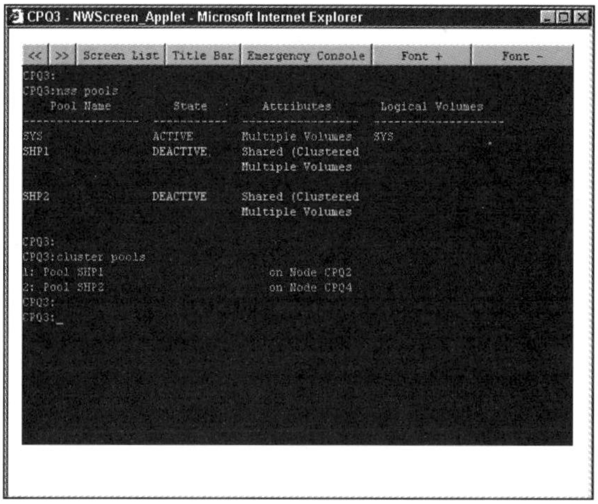

FIGURE 19.39 *Using the NSS and CLUSTER POOLS commands to discover the state and location of storage pools*

Monitoring Novell Cluster Services 1.6

Novell Cluster Services 1.6 enables three methods for monitoring an operational cluster:

- SNMP-based cluster node alerts

- SMTP-based cluster node and resource alerts

- Persistent cluster event log

SNMP-Based Cluster Alerts

Cluster Services 1.6 enables SNMP-based cluster management and traps conformant with Compaq Computer Corporation's "Common Cluster Management MIB version 2.0 — svrclu.mib" (Compaq's specification of a base MIB that enables a standard way to manage clusters).

By default, Novell Cluster Services 1.6 generates SNMP traps corresponding to cluster node join, leave, and fail events.

To monitor a cluster using SNMP, configure your SNMP management console to listen for cluster-specific SNMP traps.

SMTP-Based Cluster Alerts

In addition to SNMP-based cluster node event notification, Cluster Services enables cluster resource–specific events via Simple Mail Transfer Protocol. Cluster Services will optionally send e-mail messages containing cluster node and cluster resource state change information.

Unlike SNMP, to generate an SMTP-based cluster alert, Cluster Services requires a destination e-mail address. To configure Cluster Services to generate SMTP-based cluster node and resource alerts, use ConsoleOne or NetWare Remote Manager to set up destination e-mail addresses for individuals or third-party management software to receive e-mail based event notification. If you have Internet access, you can also configure Cluster Services to send cluster event e-mails to any mailbox on the Internet, including, for example, admin@yourcompany.com.

To set up notification e-mail addresses using ConsoleOne, select the cluster container object and right-click to display cluster properties. Select the Notification property page tab. Figure 19.40 shows the Notification page for a cluster named clus628. You can specify up to eight notification e-mail addresses. You have options to filter cluster events by severity (Receive Only Critical Events, for example), and to generate either Verbose or XML-formatted e-mail messages. The XML option generates e-mail messages using an XML-based encoding of the node or resource event. Even though these e-mail messages are human readable, the XML option is designed for e-mail messages sent to mailboxes that are read using automated management software.

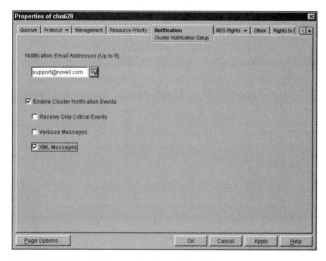

FIGURE 19.40 *Using the ConsoleOne Notification page to configure SMTP-based cluster event notification*

Persistent Cluster Event Log

The persistent cluster event log is a cluster-wide log of cluster node and resource state changes since the cluster was first formed. The event log is persistent and survives node failure or restart. Figure 19.41 shows the persistent cluster event log when viewed using NetWare Remote Manager. Every event carries a date and time stamp, the name of the affected cluster node or cluster resource, and an event description. Significant events are annotated in a bold colored font. For example, in Figure 19.41, a cluster resource named Master_IP_Address_Resource entered the Running state on node CPQ3 on June 28 at 2:23:29 a.m.

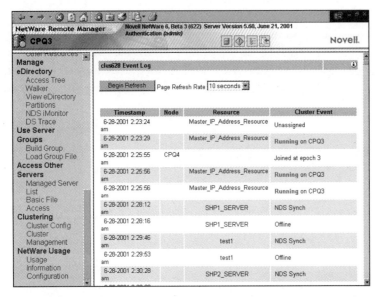

FIGURE 19.41 *Using NetWare Remote Manager to view the persistent cluster event log*

Summary

In this chapter, you learned about the newest version of Cluster Services software. Novell Cluster Services 1.6 is an enhanced version of Cluster Services software designed specially for NetWare 6–based server clusters and Storage Area Networks.

You explored the new features, architecture, and operation of Novell Cluster Services 1.6 in this chapter, including information about NetWare 6 where necessary. You learned how to install Novell Cluster Services 1.6 onto a cluster of NetWare 6 servers in this chapter. The NetWare 5.*x* to NetWare 6 cluster upgrade process was described, with step-by-step instructions for performing a complete upgrade. This chapter also had an introductory tutorial on NetWare 6 storage management, which showed you how to work with shared disk storage pools and logical volumes and how to cluster enable volumes for automatic client failover.

Finally, the chapter concluded with information on Novell Cluster Services 1.6 cluster management and monitoring enhancements. With this knowledge, you should now be able to start working with NetWare 6–based clusters.

## CHAPTER 20

Applying Novell Cluster Services with GroupWise 6

In this chapter, you learn about Novell's latest enterprise messaging system — GroupWise 6.0. This chapter builds on the clustering GroupWise foundation established in Chapters 11 and 12; most of the topics covered in those chapters also apply to GroupWise 6. If you haven't already read Chapters 11 and 12, you should start there before proceeding with this chapter.

In this chapter, you are introduced to GroupWise 6 and the new enhancements offered since GroupWise 5.5. Such information can help you decide if upgrading to GroupWise 6 is right for your organization.

Next, you learn about the clustering enhancements made to GroupWise 6 and how they affect implementation. You then examine how to create a brand-new GroupWise 6 system configured as a fault-tolerant service using Novell Cluster Services. This includes a summary of the key topics of clustering GroupWise 5.5 (which, again, are found in Chapters 11 and 12). You also explore how to upgrade an existing GroupWise 5.5 clustered system to GroupWise 6.

Finally, the chapter ends by explaining what to expect when a GroupWise component is migrated or a node running GroupWise fails.

▶   ·   ◀

Introducing GroupWise 6

GroupWise 6 includes many new enhancements that might benefit your organization. Although this book can't cover all of the details of GroupWise 6, some of the new administration benefits worth noting are listed in Table 20.1, and specific improvements to individual components are listed in the sections that follow.

NOTE

The lists offered in this chapter are not inclusive of all GroupWise 6 new features, but rather include some of the features that are most important to this discussion of Storage Area Networks and clustering.

T A B L E 20.1

GroupWise 6 New Administration Features

FEATURE	DESCRIPTION
ConsoleOne Administration	All GroupWise 6 administration is done using ConsoleOne.
Enhanced Backup and Restore	The new GroupWise 6 Target Service Agent (TSA) can ensure that GroupWise items are not purged from the system before they are backed up. In addition, the new TSA allows for online backups of the database and provides a new mechanism for restoring user data.
Disk Space Management	Administrators can now control how much disk space clients are allowed to use. Clients are able to easily monitor how much space they are using, and a new cleanup utility assists the client in cleaning up their mailbox.
Enhanced Maintenance	The Mailbox/Library Maintenance tasks are now multithreaded to allow significantly improved performance, especially on large databases.
More Accessible GroupWise Check	GWCHECK is now included with the client software so users can use it to correct problems with the remote and/or caching database.
Enhanced User Moves	Moving users from one Post Office to another now uses a live mode method, which uses a client/server thread to communicate between the POs. This makes moves more efficient and prevents many problems related to moving users that you may have experienced in the past.

Exploring New Agent Features

The GroupWise 6 NLMs and Windows NT/2000 agents have been enhanced to include the new features listed in Table 20.2.

TABLE 20.2	
GroupWise 6 New Agent Features	
FEATURE	**DESCRIPTION**
Novell Cluster Services	The MTA and POA agents have been optimized for enhanced failover behavior with GW6.
Enhanced Message Transfer	The GroupWise 6 Message Transfer Protocol (MTP) has been optimized to provide significantly faster message transfer across slow WAN links.
Message Size Restriction	Message size restrictions can now be enforced at the POA level.
Mailbox Size Monitoring	The POA now monitors mailbox sizes at the mailbox level and provides this information to the clients. You can now enforce size limits to prevent sending and/or receiving mail based on thresholds.
Improved Web Consoles	The HTML-based agent Web consoles have been improved to provide detailed thread status and message queue information and to modify certain agent settings.
POA Disk Space Management	The POA can now be configured to stop processing messages if the Post Office is critically short on disk space.

Exploring New Client Features

The new GroupWise 6 client has been significantly improved with the enhancements listed in Table 20.3.

TABLE 20.3	
GroupWise 6 New Client Features	
FEATURE	**DESCRIPTION**
Enhanced performance with Novell Cluster Services	The GroupWise 6 client detects if it is connected to a clustered Post Office, and if so, it becomes more patient when the POA doesn't respond.
Client Caching Mode	This new mode of operation provides a local cache of the user's mailbox, which makes for significantly fewer communications with the POA. This allows for much larger Post Offices using the same hardware.

FEATURE	DESCRIPTION
Mailbox Mode Switching	A drop-down box allows users to quickly switch between Online, Caching, and Remote mailbox modes.
Disk Space Management	Users can now see how much space they are using on the Post Office and receive warnings as they approach limits, and a new clean-up program assists in managing the mailbox size.
Network News Transport Protocol (NNTP) Support	The GroupWise client now supports an NNTP folder, allowing you to view your newsgroups within the GroupWise 6 universal mailbox.
Multiple Account Signatures	GroupWise 6 now allows you to use a different signature for each messaging type, such as POP3, IMAP4, and NNTP.
Backup and Restore of Deleted Items	If configured by the administrator, the user can open a backup of their mailbox and restore to their restore area to find missing items deleted since the backup set.
More Secure Internet Messaging	GroupWise 6 includes many enhancements for S/MIME secure messages.
Enhanced Calendar Printing	The GroupWise 6 client includes many enhancements to provide more control when printing calendar information.
Enhanced Remote Mode	The GroupWise 6 client includes more functionality while in Remote mode, such as Archive, Notify, Backup, and password management.
Enhanced Address Book	The GroupWise 6 client now provides a Quick Info feature, which provides detailed information by mousing over the TO, CC, BC, or FROM boxes of a message.
Improved Notification	GroupWise Notify now includes the ability to forward alarms to a pager, is available in caching and remote modes, can automatically start when GroupWise starts, and includes a snooze time for alarms.
Windows Time Zone Integration	GroupWise now uses the current Windows time zone of the local machine to display appointments, messages, and so on.

Exploring New Internet Agent Features

The GroupWise 6 GWIA has been enhanced with the new features listed in Table 20.4.

TABLE 20.4

GroupWise 6 New GWIA Features

FEATURE	DESCRIPTION
ESMTP support	GWIA supports ESMTP, including SIZE (message size restrictions), DSNs (delivery status notifications), and STARTTLS (SSL/TLS support in SMTP).
Secure POP3/IMAP4	GWIA now supports SSL in POP3 and IMAP4 for secure Internet e-mail.
Enhanced Access Control	New access control methods allow for improved control against spamming and unauthorized relaying.
Enhanced IMAP compliance	Improvements were made to the GWIA to more fully comply with the IMAP specifications.

Exploring New WebAccess Features

The GroupWise 6 WebAccess Agent has been enhanced with the new features listed in Table 20.5.

TABLE 20.5

GroupWise 6 New WebAccess Agent Features

FEATURE	DESCRIPTION
Wireless Application Protocol (WAP) Support	GroupWise 6 WebAccess supports WAP-enabled wireless devices with microbrowsers, which support Handheld Device Markup Language (HDML) or Wireless Markup Language (WML) (such as Windows CE, PocketPC, and AvantGo).
SNMP Management	WebAccess now includes SNMP support for enhanced management and notification.
Enhanced Novell Cluster Services Support	The WebAccess agent has been optimized for enhanced failover with Novell Cluster Services.
Enhanced Client Features	WebAccess has been enhanced with a new improved look and feel and with new functions including read later, add a signature, share folders, enable or disable rules, modify personal address books, search on all available address book fields, and adjust to the current time zone rather than the Post Office time zone.

Exploring the New Clustering Features

GroupWise 6 includes a few enhancements to improve support of Novell Cluster Services. The GroupWise 6 Support Pack One (due to ship about the same time this book is due to be published) will include even more enhancements to support clustering.

The new features in GroupWise 6 that improve Novell Cluster Services support are as follows:

▸ The Agent installation program now asks if you are installing into a cluster. If you are, the installation program makes the appropriate changes to the startup files (.MTA and .POA) to support clustering. Instead of using a UNC path in the /HOME switch, the installation program automatically uses legacy file system syntax without including a server name.

▸ Client automatically detects when it is connected to a cluster and increases its timeout value if it is.

In addition to the GroupWise 6 enhancements, NetWare 6 will add an additional ABEND option that will allow the core operating system to flush the GroupWise database cache in the event of an ABEND. Although this is not technically a GroupWise 6 enhancement, it does assist in preventing GroupWise database corruption.

In addition to these changes, Novell Cluster Services in NetWare 6 provides a new API that will further assist in the detection of services running on a cluster, even if these services are running in protected memory.

For more information on NetWare 6 and its use with Novell Cluster Services, see Chapter 19.

X-REF

Table 20.6 summarizes some of the key operating system and GroupWise enhancements that have been made to support Novell Cluster Services.

	T A B L E 20.6
	GroupWise and NetWare Enhancements that Support Novell Cluster Services

VERSION	ENHANCEMENT
GroupWise 5.5 EP SP1 and later	GroupWise agent tells the client that it is running in a cluster.
GroupWise client version 5.5 EP SP1 or later	GroupWise client is more tolerant of lost connections to the Post Office when it is running in a cluster.
GroupWise 6 and later	Installation option to install into a cluster. This option strips the server name off the /home switch in MTA and POA startup files; does not update the AUTOEXEC.NCF to load GroupWise; and adds the /cluster switch to the POA startup file.
GroupWise 6 SP1*	Home switches support UNC path with virtual server names.
	All agents understand UNC paths through virtual server for all paths.
	POA understands UNC paths through virtual servers to communicate with software distribution directory.
	version 5.5 EP SP1 The /cluster switch is available for all agents (MTA, POA, GWIA, GWINTER).
NetWare 5.1 SP3 and later	New ABEND recovery option to flush the GroupWise database for enhanced database integrity.
	New APIs in clustering to support detection of a cluster from ring-3 (protected memory). This allows GroupWise to autodetect if the agents are running on a cluster.

*Starred item was not yet implemented at the time of this writing, but was scheduled to be included in the Support Pack.

► . . . . ◄

Cluster Enabling GroupWise 6

The process of creating a cluster-enabled GroupWise 6 system is virtually identical to the process with GroupWise 5.5. All of the guidelines provided in GroupWise 5.5 still apply, such as:

- ▶ Use cluster-enabled volumes for the GroupWise Domains.

- ▶ Configure each GroupWise Gateway (GWIA, WebAccess) as a cluster resource with its dedicated GroupWise Domain.

- ▶ Run the MTA and POA in protected memory.

WARNING

With GroupWise 6, if the MTA is running in protected memory, the GWIA and/or WebAccess Agent (GWINTER) must also be running in the same protected memory space, or they will not properly communicate with their MTA running on the same server.

- ▶ Startup files should not use UNC paths in the /home switches (the installation program now automatically does this as long as you tell the program you are installing to a cluster).

- ▶ Use cluster-unique ports for all resource components (MTA, POA, GWIA, HTML consoles, and so on).

- ▶ Use Client/Server mode only for the Post Offices.

- ▶ Configure all links within the cluster as direct TCP/IP links.

- ▶ Fully consider TCP/IP name resolution.

- ▶ Use CVSBIND for each cluster-enabled volume.

- ▶ Place the agent startup files on the shared volume.

- ▶ Consider placing the NLMs on the shared volume.

X-REF

Each of these recommendations is thoroughly discussed in Chapters 11 and 12.

Introducing the GroupWise 6 Target Service Agent

In addition to new features, GroupWise 6 now offers a Target Service Agent (TSA) for backing up the GroupWise database while it is online. This TSA (GWTSA.NLM) is a GroupWise-specific API, which can be accessed by various backup software packages such as Novell's Storage Management Services (SMS) and Veritas's Backup Exec for NetWare.

The TSA allows the database files to be backed up while the agents are online. It supports backing up the Domain database, Post Office database, gateway databases (ASYNC, GWIA, WebAccess), Document Management database,

OFFILES directories, and so on. In addition, the TSA allows for a new option that prevents GroupWise from purging items that have not yet been backed up.

The TSA is loaded with a /home parameter for every database that you wish to back up. Each database must be referenced in the same load statement for the TSA. The TSA supports multiple /home parameters in the load command to allow you to back up multiple databases with a single instance of the TSA. For example, you can issue the following command to have the TSA available to back up the GWDOM1 Domain and the GWPO1 Post Office:

```
LOAD GW1:\SYSTEM\GWTSA /HOME-GW1:\GWDOM1 /HOME-GW1:\GWPO1
```

When you install a GroupWise 6 agent, it automatically creates a GWTSA.NCF file, which includes the commands to load the TSA and back up that agent's database.

If the GWTSA loads and the databases specified in the /HOME switch are not available, the TSA will remember them as available for backup. However, when you schedule your backup job using the TSA-compliant backup software, the TSA will only make available the databases that are currently active on the host at the time you are scheduling your job. This means that you have to do some extra planning to utilize the TSA in the event that a GroupWise database is not where you expect it to be. You can load the TSA with all the potential database paths listed in the /HOME parameter so that they will be available if they happen to reside on that server at the time of the backup.

This leaves you with the same issue you face in backing up the file system: do you set up backup jobs for every conceivable possibility, then have many fail each night, or do you only set up backup jobs based on the preferred nodes and modify the jobs in case of a migration? In essence, this is a preference, rather than a technology, issue, since either method will work.

If you want to set up a backup job for every possibility, you must migrate all potential (GroupWise) cluster resources to each node and configure the backup job with all resources on that node. Once you configure the job for that node, migrate the resources to the next node and configure the backup job. Although this is a tedious process, each time the backup job runs for a specific node, it will back up whatever databases reside on the node at the time the backup job starts (all other jobs will fail).

Creating a New GroupWise 6 System

This section assumes that you are creating a brand-new GroupWise system, and walks you through the complete installation process. It also assumes that you are creating your Primary Domain resource with a single Post Office as part of the same cluster resource. This configuration is not required. You can have multiple POs as separate resources from the Primary Domain, or you can have an empty Primary Domain. However, by walking through the steps to create a combined resource, you can modify these steps to create whichever subcomponents you wish.

If you already have a GroupWise 6 Primary Domain, jump ahead to the section "Creating a Secondary Domain and Post Office Resource" later in this chapter. If you have a GroupWise 5.x Primary Domain, jump ahead to the "Upgrading from an Existing GroupWise 5.5 Cluster" section later in this chapter.

X-REF

Creating the New System

To create a new GroupWise 6 system, do the following:

1. Create a cluster-enabled volume for the GroupWise MTA/POA (for this example, "GW1" is the volume name).

Chapter 9 discusses the process of creating cluster-enabled volumes.

2. Modify each server's SYS:ETC\HOSTS file by adding an entry for the newly created virtual servers. Also add these entries to your DNS configuration.

X-REF

3. Online the GroupWise cluster-enabled volume (GW1_SERVER) resource and map a drive to it. In this example, drive M: is mapped to this cluster-enabled volume.

4. Optionally, create a directory named SYSTEM on the cluster-enabled volume. You can choose to install the NLMs to this SYSTEM directory, or you can install them to the SYS volume of each server in the resource failover path. You do not need to create this directory in advance, as the installation program can create it for you.

The directory name does not need to be named SYSTEM for the Domain to function. However, naming it SYSTEM does help the administrator recognize the purpose of the directory.

TIP

5. Insert the GroupWise 6 installation CD into your workstation.

6. If the CD does not automatically start the installation, execute the SETUP.EXE file at the root of the CD.

7. From the main menu, select Create or update a GroupWise system.

8. From the Software License dialog box, click Yes to accept the terms of the software license.

9. From the Welcome to GroupWise Install dialog box, click Next to begin the installation.

10. From the Plan your System dialog box, click Next. Optionally, you can click the Installation Guide button for help in planning your installation.

11. In the Administration Options dialog box, verify that the Create a new system or update an existing system check box is selected, and then click Next.

12. Select the NDS tree that you are installing into, and then click Next.

13. From the NDS Will Be Extended dialog box, click Next to extend the schema for GroupWise 6.

14. From the NDS Has Been Extended dialog box, click Next to continue.

15. In the Select Languages dialog box, choose all languages to install (if applicable), and then click Next.

16. In the ConsoleOne path dialog box, do one of the following:

- If you don't already have ConsoleOne version 1.2d or later installed, click the Install ConsoleOne dialog box, and follow the wizard to install ConsoleOne to your local workstation.

- If you already have ConsoleOne version 1.2d or later installed, verify that the path to the ConsoleOne directory is correct, and then click Next.

TIP

All GroupWise 6 administration is done from ConsoleOne at a workstation. You cannot use NetWare Administrator to administer GroupWise 6.

17. In the Software Distribution Directory dialog box, enter or browse to the location that you wish to use for the software distribution. You should place this on a cluster-enabled volume that your users can access to install the GroupWise client software. You should also be sure not to install on top of your existing GroupWise 5.5 software distribution directory so that you will still have it available if needed later. Once you've entered the location, click Next to continue.

18. In the Select Software dialog box, click the Select All button to install all components to the software distribution directory, and then click Next. By selecting all components, your software distribution directory will be complete, allowing you the most flexibility to add components in the future.

19. In the Ready to Install dialog box, click Install.

20. Once all the files have been installed, the installation program displays the Novell GroupWise Partner Page. From this dialog box, you can click the Go to GroupWise Partner Page button, which will bring you to a Web site full of useful information about third-party products that integrate with GroupWise. If desired, review the partner page, otherwise click Next to continue to the new system creation process.

21. From the Determine the Next Step dialog box, select Creating a new GroupWise system, and then click Next.

22. From the Run ConsoleOne dialog box, click Run. This will launch ConsoleOne and start the new GroupWise system creation process. After ConsoleOne loads, you'll see a GroupWise System Setup dialog box. This begins the wizard that creates the new GroupWise system.

23. From the GroupWise Setup Progress dialog box, press Next.

24. From the Software Distribution Directory dialog box, confirm that the software directory is correct for your new system. Once you have confirmed the location, click Next.

25. In the NDS Tree dialog box, confirm that the correct NDS tree appears, and then click Next.

26. In the System Name dialog box, enter a unique name for your GroupWise system, and then click Next. Once you name your GroupWise system, the name cannot be changed.

27. In the Primary Domain dialog box, enter a name for your Primary GroupWise Domain, and then click Next.

28. In the Domain Directory dialog box (shown in Figure 20.1), enter or browse to the path you wish to use for your Domain's directory, and then click Next. Make sure you use either a UNC path through the virtual server or a drive mapped to the cluster-enabled volume to select the Domain directory. If you use a drive mapped through the server that is currently hosting the volume, then the NDS property for the Domain directory will include a tie to a physical server instead of the virtual path. For instance, the following examples illustrate the right and wrong ways to configure your Domain directory:

- Right — \\CLUSTER_GW1_SERVER\GW1\GWDOM1

- Right — M:\GW1\GWDOM1 (assuming drive M: is mapped to the cluster-enabled volume)

- Wrong — \\NODE1\GW1\GWDOM1

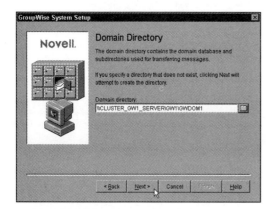

FIGURE 20.1 *Domain Directory dialog box*

29. In the Domain Context dialog box, enter or browse to the NDS context you wish to create your GroupWise objects in, and then click Next.

30. In the Domain Language dialog box, select the language to utilize for the Primary Domain, and then click Next.

31. In the Domain Time Zone dialog box, select the time zone to utilize for the Domain, and then click Next.

32. In the Post Office Name dialog box, enter a name for the first Post Office, and then click Next.

TIP

The wizard requires that you create a Post Office. You can delete this later if you don't want a Post Office assigned to the Primary Domain.

33. Enter or browse to the directory you wish to use for the Post Office database, and then click Next. If you are configuring the Post Office as the same cluster resource as the Domain, make sure that this is on the same volume as the Domain.

34. In the Post Office Context dialog box, either accept the default NDS context or browse to the context you wish to use for the Post Office, and then click Next.

35. In the Post Office Language dialog box, select the language to utilize for the Post Office, and then click Next.

36. In the Post Office Link dialog box, change the link to TCP/IP, and then click Next. Recall that all links within the cluster must be configured as TCP/IP for optimal operations in the cluster.

37. In the POA Network Address dialog box (shown in Figure 20.2), do the following:

   a. In the TCP/IP Address field, enter the secondary TCP/IP address that you used for the cluster-enabled volume for this resource.

TIP

You do not need to use another IP address for the POA; since it is in the same cluster resource as the cluster-enabled volume, wherever the volume goes, the POA will also go. There is no reason why these components (as well as the MTA) can't all share the same TCP/IP address, as long as they are all in the same cluster resource.

   b. In the Client/Server Port field, enter the cluster-unique port this POA will use.

   c. In the Message Transfer Port field, enter the cluster-unique port this POA will use for message transfer.

   d. In the HTTP Port field, enter the cluster-unique port this POA will use for the HTTP management console.

   e. Click Next to continue.

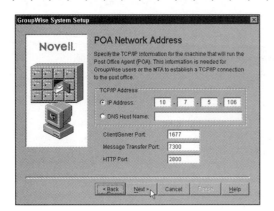

FIGURE 20.2 *POA Network Address dialog box*

38. In the MTA Network Address dialog box (shown in Figure 20.3), do the following:

   a. In the TCP/IP Address field, enter the secondary TCP/IP address that you used for the cluster-enabled volume for this resource.

   b. In the Message Transfer Port field, enter the cluster-unique port this MTA will use for message transfer.

   c. In the HTTP Port field, enter the cluster-unique port this MTA will use for the HTTP management console.

   d. Click Next to continue.

39. In the Post Office Users dialog box, click the Add button and then browse for all of the NDS users you wish to add to this Post Office. Once you have added all the desired users, click the Next button.

40. The GroupWise Setup Progress dialog box should now be on your screen. Click the Next button, which will display a summary of all your configuration choices.

41. In the Summary dialog box, confirm that your selections are correct, and then click Next to create the new GroupWise system.

42. Once you receive the message that the system is installed, click Next to return to the GroupWise System Progress dialog box.

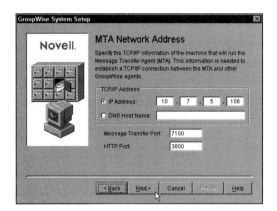

FIGURE 20.3 *MTA Network Address dialog box*

43. From the GroupWise System Progress dialog box, click Next to begin the GroupWise Agent installation.

44. In the Select Platform dialog box, confirm that NetWare is selected, and then click Next.

45. In the Installation Path dialog box, do the following:

  a. Change the Installation path to M:\SYSTEM, assuming that you mapped the M: drive to the shared volume that you wish to use for GroupWise, and assuming that you wish to install the agents on the shared storage. If you wish to install the agents to each server's SYS volume, enter a UNC path to the first server's SYS:\SYSTEM volume instead.

  b. Select the check box Configure GroupWise Agents for Clustering.

NOTE

The Configure GroupWise Agents for Clustering check box alters three things about the installation. First, it uses legacy file system syntax in the agent startup files instead of UNC paths for quicker agent initialization. Second, it does not update the AUTOEXEC.NCF **file with the GRPWISE.NCF file; you want to control starting GroupWise with a cluster resource, not have it automatically start on each node. Last, it automatically adds the** /cluster **switch to the POA startup file, which lets the POA inform the client that it is running in a cluster.**

  c. Click Next.

46. In the Web Console Information dialog box, either:

- Verify that the Enable Web console check box is selected, then enter a user name (not an NDS user) and password for the Web console user and click Next.

or

- Deselect the Enable Web console check box to disable Web console, and then click Next.

Since the Web Console passwords are transmitted in the clear and can be fairly easily captured, you don't want to use a valid NDS user for Web Console.

TIP

47. In the Language dialog box, select the language to utilize for the GroupWise agents, and then click Next.

48. In the Summary dialog box, click Install to install the agents.

49. In the Installation Complete dialog box, deselect the Launch GroupWise agents now option, and then click Next. You will launch the GroupWise agents using ConsoleOne once you configure the cluster resource load script.

50. In the GroupWise Setup Progress dialog box, click Next to begin the GroupWise 6 client installation. This launches the client installation wizard.

At this point, you have the new GroupWise system created and the agents installed to either one node or to the shared storage. If you installed the agents to the shared storage, you are ready to install the GroupWise client, modify the startup files, and then modify the cluster resource to start GroupWise.

If you installed the agents to the SYS volume of one node, you must also install the agents to the other nodes in the failover path. To do this, follow the procedure for installing the GroupWise agents found in the "Creating a Secondary Domain and Post Office Resource" section of this chapter.

Installing the GroupWise Client

To install the GroupWise client, perform the following steps:

1. In the Client Installation Welcome dialog box, click Next to begin the client installation.

2. In the Setup Options dialog box, either select Standard Install to install to your local hard drive, or select Workstation Install to run the client from a server. Then click Next to continue.

3. In the Destination Directory dialog box, select the directory to install GroupWise to, and then click Next to continue.

4. In the Select Optional Components dialog box, select any desired optional components, and then click Next.

5. In the Select Program Folder dialog box, enter the name of the Windows program group you wish to use for the GroupWise icons, and then click Next.

6. In the Select Startup Folder Software dialog box, select Notify if you wish GroupWise Notify to run every time you start Windows, or deselect it if you do not wish it to automatically run. Click Next to continue.

7. In the Language Selection dialog box, select the language to use for the GroupWise client, and then click Next to continue.

8. In the Software Integrations dialog box, select any installed software packages shown that you wish to integrate with GroupWise Document Management, and then click Next.

9. In the Start Copying Files dialog box, confirm that your options are correct, and then click Next to install the client.

10. In the Restart Windows dialog box, click OK to restart your workstation.

Obviously, you must also deploy the client to your end-user community. We recommend using ZENworks application deployment features to automatically install or update your client workstations.

Modifying the GroupWise Startup Files

GroupWise 6 automatically makes the minimum required modifications to the startup files to support clustering. Specifically, the MTA startup file includes the /home switch, which the installation program modifies by stripping off the server name and using legacy file system syntax. For example:

```
/home-GW1:\GWDOM1
```

The POA startup file has two parameters by default: the /home switch and the /cluster switch. As with the MTA file, the /home switch is automatically modified to strip off the server name and use legacy file system syntax. The /cluster switch is also automatically added so that the POA can inform the client that it is running on a cluster, even if it is running in protected memory.

TIP

If the POA is not running in protected memory, the /cluster **switch is not required. The POA uses Novell Cluster Services APIs to determine if it is running in a cluster, but these APIs are not accessible to the POA from protected memory. The cluster switch is used to tell the POA that it is running in a cluster even if it can't detect the cluster. Novell Cluster Services 1.01 Support Pack 2 or later includes new APIs that allow the POA to detect the cluster even from protected memory.**

You should add the /IP switch to the POA startup file. By using the /IP switch, the POA will bind to the correct secondary IP address instead of the server's primary IP address. You can confirm which address the POA binds to by reviewing the log file and looking for the entry under the Client/Server Settings under the IP Address entry.

Configuring the Cluster Resource

Once you have installed the new system and the agents, you must configure the cluster resource to start and stop GroupWise. If you are using a cluster-enabled volume, you must modify the resource for this volume. To configure the cluster resource, do the following:

1. Using ConsoleOne, change to the Console view and select your cluster-enabled volume cluster resource object — for example, GW1_SERVER.

2. Right-click the resource, and then select properties.

3. Select the Load tab, then verify that the following commands are included:

   nss /activate=<volume>

   mount <volume> VOLID=<xxx>

   trustmig <volume> watch

   NUDP ADD CLUSTER_<volume>_SERVER <IP Address>

   add secondary ipaddress <IP Address>

4. If desired, remove the TRUSTMIG line. Because you are operating in Client/Server mode only, you do not need to utilize file system trustees on the GroupWise volume. Removing TRUSTMIG may speed resource startup.

5. If desired, add the `CVSBIND` command to propagate the virtual server into SLP. This is not required, but is highly recommended. The command should go before the `NUDP ADD CLUSTER_<volume>_SERVER <IP Address>` line. For example:

```
CVSBIND ADD CLUSTER_<volume>_SERVER <IP Address>
```

6. Add the commands to load GroupWise using protected memory. For example:

```
LOAD ADDRESS SPACE=GW1 GW1:SYSTEM\GWMTA @GWDOM1.MTA

LOAD ADDRESS SPACE=GW1 GW1:SYSTEM\GWPOA @GWPO1.POA

PROTECTION RESTART GW1
```

TIP

With GroupWise 6, the NDS Synchronization event does not work if the MTA is running in protected memory because it cannot communicate properly with the `DSAPI.NLM` **running in conventional memory. To work around this issue, you can also load** `DSAPI` **in the same protected memory space as the MTA. To do this, add another line before the MTA load to load** `DSAPI.NLM`**. For example:** `LOAD ADDRESS SPACE=GW1 DSAPI.NLM`**.**

7. When satisfied with the load script, click Apply. The entire load script should now look like Figure 20.4.

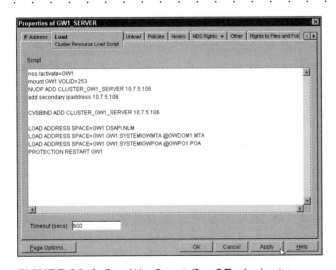

FIGURE 20.4 *GroupWise Domain/Post Office load script*

8. Click the Unload tab to modify the unload script.

9. At the beginning of the unload script, add the commands to unload GroupWise from protected memory. After the unload commands, add a command to delay processing for about 5 to 10 seconds, then kill the address space. The delay time will vary based on your system — allow enough time for the MTA to unload gracefully before removing the address space. For example, add these commands:

```
UNLOAD ADDRESS SPACE=GW1 GWMTA

UNLOAD ADDRESS SPACE=GW1 GWPOA

LOAD DELAY

DELAY 10

UNLOAD KILL ADDRESS SPACE=GW1
```

TIP

If you loaded `DSAPI.NLM` **in protected memory, you should also unload this prior to unloading the** `GWMTA`**. If you removed the** `TRUSTMIG` **command from the load script, you must also remove it from the unload script.**

10. Add the command to remove the `CVSBIND SLP` propagation just before the `DEL SECONDARY IPADDRESS` line. For example:

```
CVSBIND DEL CLUSTER_GW1_SERVER 10.7.5.106
```

11. Once you're satisfied with the unload script, click the Apply button. The unload script should now look like Figure 20.5.

12. Offline the cluster-enabled volume. This allows the changes to the load and unload scripts to take effect.

13. Online the cluster-enabled volume. Verify that GroupWise loads and functions properly.

At this point, you should have a fully functioning fault-tolerant GroupWise system! Before you finish, make sure that you migrate the resource to all nodes in the resource failover path. On each node, test all functions of GroupWise — better to find a problem before users start utilizing the system.

Next, you will probably want to add to this system — you may want to add more Domains and/or Post Offices, or you may want to connect the system to the Internet. The following sections provide the procedures to add these components to your cluster.

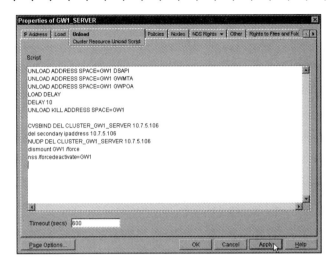

FIGURE 20.5 *GroupWise Domain/Post Office unload script*

Creating a Secondary Domain and Post Office Resource

This section walks you through the process of creating a Secondary Domain and Post Office as a single cluster resource. You can easily modify the process to create just a Secondary Domain or just a Post Office resource. If you are creating a Domain in the cluster resource, then be sure to cluster enable the volume for ease of administration without needing to worry about where the resource is actually running. If you are creating a resource with just a Post Office (or multiple Post Offices), then you don't need to cluster enable the volume.

Cluster enabling the volumes for GroupWise is thoroughly discussed in Chapter 11.

X-REF

Creating and Configuring the GroupWise Domain Object

When configuring a Secondary Domain in the cluster, you must first use ConsoleOne to create the Domain object. If you are just clustering a Post Office, skip this section and jump to "Creating and Configuring the GroupWise Post Office Object."

To create the Secondary Domain, do the following:

1. Create a cluster-enabled volume for the GroupWise Domain.

X-REF

Chapter 9 discusses the process of creating cluster-enabled volumes.

2. Modify each server's SYS:ETC\HOSTS file by adding an entry for the newly created virtual server. Also add this entry to your DNS configuration.

3. Online the GroupWise cluster-enabled volume resource (for this example, GW2_SERVER is used), and map a drive to it. In this example, drive N: is mapped to this cluster-enabled volume.

4. Optionally, create a directory named SYSTEM on the cluster-enabled volume. You can choose to install the NLMs to this SYSTEM directory, or you can install them to the SYS volume of each server in the resource failover path. You do not need to create this directory in advance, as the installation program can create it for you.

TIP

The directory name does not need to be named SYSTEM for the Domain to function. However, naming it SYSTEM does help the administrator recognize the purpose of the directory.

5. Launch ConsoleOne, and make your GroupWise connection to the Primary Domain.

6. Right-click the container you want to create the Domain in, and then select New ⇨ Object.

7. From the New Object dialog box, select GroupWise Domain.

8. From the Create GroupWise Domain dialog.box, shown in Figure 20.6, do the following:

a. In the Domain name field, enter the name of the new GroupWise Domain.

b. In the Domain Database Location field, enter or browse to the location you wish to create the new domain in. Be sure to use a drive mapped to the cluster-enabled volume or UNC syntax using the virtual server. This will ensure that the NDS Domain Path property is populated correctly.

c. In the Language field, select the language for this GroupWise Domain.

d. In the Time Zone field, select the time zone for this GroupWise Domain.

e. In the Link To Domain field, select the Primary GroupWise Domain.

f. Click the OK button to create the Domain.

▶ . . . . ◀

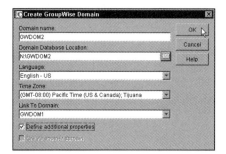

FIGURE 20.6 *Create GroupWise Domain dialog box*

9. Double-click the Domain's MTA object to modify its properties.

10. In the Network Address field, click the pencil to the right of the field. This will allow you to configure the MTA's TCP/IP address and port.

11. In the Edit Network Address dialog box, do the following:

a. In the TCP/IP Address field, enter the secondary TCP/IP address used for the cluster-enabled volume.

b. In the Message Transfer Port field, enter the cluster-unique port this MTA will use for message transfer.

c. In the HTTP Port field, enter the cluster-unique port this MTA will use for the HTTP Web Console administrative utility.

X-REF

TCP/IP addresses and port planning are thoroughly discussed in Chapter 11.

d. Click OK to accept your changes.

TIP

You should enter a description for the MTA in the Description field found on the Identification tab. This description should include the IP address and all ports used by the MTA. For example: GWDOM2; 10.7.5.107; 7101; 3801. This description will show on the server's MTA screen, which makes it easier to troubleshoot.

12. Right-click the Domain object, and then select GroupWise Utilities ➪ Link Configuration to edit the MTA links to any other Domains within the cluster. Following Novell's recommendations for links within the same WAN site, all Domain links should be configured as Direct TCP/IP links within the cluster. Links to Domains outside of the cluster should follow normal GroupWise link configuration guidelines based on the WAN topology.

13. Double-click each outbound link, and then do the following:

   a. Verify that the Link Type is direct.

   b. Change the Protocol to TCP/IP.

   c. Verify that the TCP/IP address and port are correct for this link.

   d. Click OK to make these changes.

14. Double-click each inbound link, and then do the following:

   a. Verify that the Link Type is direct.

   b. Change the Protocol to TCP/IP.

   c. Verify that the TCP/IP address and port are correct for this link.

   d. Click OK to make these changes.

15. Close the Link Configuration tool, and click Yes to accept the changes.

16. Since this Domain was not active when you modified the network properties and the link configuration, there was no way for the administrative messages to reach the Domain. Therefore, you must rebuild the GroupWise Domain prior to activating it for these changes to be properly registered. To rebuild the Domain, do the following:

   a. Right-click the GroupWise Domain object, and then select GroupWise utilities ➪ System Maintenance.

· · · · ·

b. Select Rebuild Database, and then click Run to start the database rebuild process.

c. Verify that the path to the database is correct. This should show as a UNC path through the virtual server, for example:

```
\\CLUSTER_GW2_SERVER\GW2\GWDOM2
```

d. Click OK to begin the actual rebuild. Once the rebuild completes successfully, you'll receive a message confirming the successful rebuild. Click OK to acknowledge this message.

e. Click Close to close the System Maintenance dialog box.

If you are creating a Post Office as part of this cluster resource, you are now ready to complete the "Creating and Configuring the GroupWise Post Office Object" procedure discussed in the next section. If you are not creating a Post Office, skip to the "Installing the GroupWise Agents" section to complete that procedure.

Creating and Configuring the GroupWise Post Office Object

Creating the GroupWise Post Office involves steps very similar to creating the Domain. To create the Post Office, do the following:

1. Launch ConsoleOne, and verify your GroupWise connection to the Secondary Domain that this Post Office will belong to. If your connection is incorrect, right-click the Secondary Domain in the GroupWise view, and then select Connect.

2. Right-click the container you want to create the Post Office in, and then select New ⇨ Object.

3. From the New Object dialog box, select GroupWise Post Office.

4. From the Create GroupWise Post Office dialog box, shown in Figure 20.7, do the following:

a. In the Post Office name field, enter the name of the new GroupWise Post Office.

b. In the GroupWise Domain field, verify that the correct Domain is already shown. If the wrong Domain is shown, browse to the Domain that you want this Post Office associated with.

c. In the Post Office Database Location field, enter or browse to the location you wish to create the new Domain in. If the Post Office resides on a cluster-enabled volume, be sure to use a drive mapped to the cluster-enabled volume or a UNC path through a cluster-enabled volume so that the Post Office path property will be correct.

TIP

Post Offices do not need to reside on cluster-enabled volumes, but if you are combining the Post Office with a Domain that is cluster enabled, it is beneficial to have the path correct. With the path correct through the virtual server, if you ever do system maintenance on the Post Office, the path to the Post Office will be correct no matter which node the POA is running on.

d. In the Language field, select the language for this GroupWise Post Office.

e. In the Time Zone field, select the time zone for this GroupWise Post Office.

f. In the Software Distribution Directory field, select the software distribution directory that is closest to the users of this Post Office so that they will have local LAN access to the directory (if possible).

g. If desired, you can also create a Document Management System Library.

h. Click the OK button to create the Post Office.

FIGURE 20.7 *Create GroupWise Post Office dialog box*

5. Double-click the Post Office's POA object to modify its properties.

6. In the Network Address field, click the pencil to the right of the field. This will allow you to configure the POA's TCP/IP address and port.

7. In the Edit Network Address dialog box, do the following:

    a. In the TCP/IP Address field, enter the secondary TCP/IP address used for the cluster-enabled volume. If you aren't using a cluster-enabled volume for the Post Office, enter the secondary IP address that you will use for this cluster resource.

    b. In the Message Transfer Port field, enter the cluster-unique port this POA will use for message transfer.

    c. In the HTTP Port field, enter the cluster-unique port this POA will use for the HTTP Web Console administrative utility.

    d. In the Client/Server Port field, enter the cluster-unique port this POA will use for client/server access.

X-REF

TCP/IP addresses and port planning are thoroughly discussed in Chapter 11.

    e. Click OK to accept your changes.

TIP

You should enter a description for the POA in the Description field found on the Identification tab. This description should include the IP address and all ports used by the POA. For example: GWPO2; 10.7.5.107; 7202; 2802. This description will show on the server's POA screen, which makes it easier to troubleshoot.

8. Next, you need to modify the Post Office to use Client/Server only (the default is Client/Server and Direct). Direct connections to the Post Office are less efficient and can lead to database errors if the Post Office is not shut down cleanly. To change the PO to Client/Server only, do the following:

    a. Right-click the Post Office object (not the POA), then select Properties.

    b. In the GroupWise tab, click the down arrow and select Post Office Settings.

    c. In the Access Mode field, change the mode to Client/Server only.

    d. Click the Apply button to accept your changes.

    e. Click Close to close the Post Office properties page.

9. Right-click the GroupWise Domain object that this Post Office belongs to, and then select GroupWise Utilities ⇨ Link Configuration to edit the Domain link to the Post Office. The Domain link should be configured as Direct TCP/IP to any Post Office within the cluster.

10. Click the Post Office Links icon, or from the menu, select View ⇨ Post Office Links.

11. Double-click the Post Office link, and then do the following:

   a. Change the Protocol to TCP/IP.

   b. In the Post Office Agent field, select POA.

   c. Verify that the TCP/IP address and port are correct for this link.

   d. Click OK to make these changes.

12. Close the Link Configuration tool, and click Yes to accept the changes.

13. Since this Post Office was not active when you modified the network properties and the link configuration, there was no way for the administrative messages to reach the POA. Therefore, you must rebuild the GroupWise Post Office prior to activating it for these changes to be properly registered. To rebuild the Post Office, do the following:

   a. Right-click the GroupWise Post Office object, and then select GroupWise utilities ⇨ System Maintenance.

   b. Select Rebuild Database, and then click Run to start the database rebuild process.

   c. Verify that the path to the database is correct. If you are using a cluster-enabled volume, this should show as a UNC path through the virtual server, for example:

   ```
   \\CLUSTER_GW2_SERVER\GW2\GWPO2
   ```

   d. Click OK to begin the actual rebuild. Once the rebuild completes successfully, you'll receive a message confirming the successful rebuild. Click OK to acknowledge this message.

   e. Click Close to close the System Maintenance dialog box.

Now that you have the Post Office created in NDS and the GroupWise system, you are ready to install the GroupWise agents. Just as you did with the new system, you must make a choice regarding the location of the agents. Installing the agents to the SYS volume means installing them to each cluster node, while installing them on the shared storage means installing them once.

Installing the GroupWise Agents

This section walks you through the process of installing the GroupWise agents, assuming you are creating a resource with both an MTA and POA. If you are just creating an MTA, or just a POA resource, you can easily modify these steps by removing the unneeded component in your resource.

If you installed the new system agents on the SYS volume of each cluster node, we recommend you continue this standard on all resources in the cluster. Likewise, if you install the agents to the shared storage, then do this for all resources in your cluster. You do not want any confusion about where the agents are, so be sure that you are consistent.

To install the agents, do the following:

1. From the software distribution directory, browse to the Agents subdirectory and run INSTALL.EXE.

2. In the Software License Agreement dialog box, click Yes to accept the terms of the license agreement.

3. In the Overview dialog box, click Next to continue.

4. In the Install/Uninstall dialog box, confirm that the Install radio button is selected, and then click Next to continue.

5. In the Select Platform dialog box, confirm that NetWare is selected, and then click Next to continue.

6. In the Installation Path dialog box, browse to the location in which you want to install the agent NLMs and startup files. If you install the agents to the SYS volume, you must make sure that you install them on all servers that will be in the resource failover path. Once you have the path correct, select the Configure GroupWise Agents for Clustering check box, and then click Next to continue.

Chapters 11 and 12 discuss the pros and cons of installing the agents on the SYS volume or the shared volume.

X-REF

7. In the Web Console Information dialog box, configure the Web Console information as desired by enabling Web Console with the appropriate user name and password or by disabling it. When you're done, click Next to continue.

8. In the Language dialog box, select the appropriate installation language(s), and then click Next to continue.

9. In the Domains/Post Offices dialog box, shown in Figure 20.8, do the following:

   a. Click the Add button to add the GroupWise Domain. Be sure that you select the path to the GroupWise Domain using the cluster-enabled volume, either using the UNC path through the virtual server or by the drive letter you mapped to the drive. In this example, N:\GWDOM2 is entered.

   b. Click the Add button to add any GroupWise Post Offices that run in this cluster resource. If these also reside on cluster-enabled volumes, be sure to use a drive mapped to the cluster-enabled volume or a UNC path using the virtual server name.

   c. Click Next to Continue.

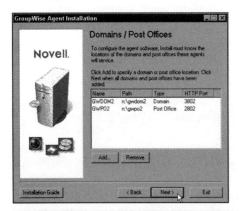

FIGURE 20.8 *The Domains/Post Offices dialog box for GroupWise agent installation*

10. From the Summary dialog box, click Install to continue.

11. From the Installation Complete dialog box, deselect all options, and then click Finish.

12. Open the .MTA and .POA files and verify that all of your desired options are set. By virtue of your using the Configure GroupWise Agents for Clustering check box in step 6, the /home switch should use the proper syntax of volume:path. For example:

/home-GW2:\GWDOM2

TIP

By selecting the option to configure the agents for clustering, the .MTA and .POA should be complete with the exception of the POA /IP switch. You should add the /IP switch with the resource IP address to the POA startup file so that the POA binds to the correct secondary IP address instead of the server's primary network address.

Once you have installed the agents, you are ready to configure your cluster resource object.

Configuring the Cluster Resource Object

Once you have created the NDS objects and installed the appropriate agents for the components you wish to cluster, you are ready to configure the cluster resource object. If you are using a cluster-enabled volume, you will modify the resource object that you already created by cluster enabling the volume (this is the assumption for this procedure). If you are creating a Post Office resource without a cluster-enabled volume, then you will need to create a new cluster resource object for this resource.

The steps to create the cluster resource object for a Secondary Domain and Post Office resource are identical to the steps in the Primary Domain. Refer back to the section "Configuring the Cluster Resource" for step-by-step instructions.

Installing a New GroupWise Internet Agent into Your Cluster

Just like a GroupWise 5.5 system, the GroupWise 6 GWIA should be installed into a Secondary Domain dedicated to the GWIA. This Domain and GWIA combination should reside on a cluster-enabled volume for ease of administration and be configured as a single cluster resource.

You should meet all of the GWIA prerequisites before you install the GWIA into a cluster. For example, configure your MX records (using the virtual server's IP address), have Internet connectivity, and have a properly configured DNS system prior to installing the GWIA.

The first step to clustering the GWIA is to create a Secondary Domain cluster resource, activate it, and test the configuration. Follow the procedure "Creating a Secondary Domain and Post Office Resource" earlier in this chapter, omitting the Post Office. This should be done on a cluster-enabled volume for ease of administration.

The reasons for using a cluster-enabled volume are explained in more detail in Chapter 11.

X-REF

The primary difference between clustering the GWIA in GroupWise 6 and clustering it in GroupWise 5.5 is that with GroupWise 6, if the GWIA's MTA is running in protected memory on the same server as the GWIA, the GWIA must also run in the same protected memory space.

Once you have installed and configured the dedicated Secondary Domain for the GWIA, you are ready to install the GWIA into your cluster. To install the GWIA, do the following:

1. Using ConsoleOne, make sure you are connected to the Domain into which you will install the GWIA.

2. Browse the software distribution directory, and run INSTALL.EXE from the \internet\gwia directory.

3. Press the Yes button to accept the software license agreement.

4. From the Welcome screen, click Next to begin the installation.

5. Select NetWare as the software platform, and then click Next to continue.

6. In the Installation Path dialog box, do the following:

   a. Enter or browse to the location that you wish to install the GWIA agent NLM files to.

   b. Enter or browse to the location that you wish to install the GWIA startup files.

   c. Deselect the option to update the AUTOEXEC.NCF file.

   d. Select the option to install into an existing cluster.

   e. Click Next to continue.

7. In the Web Console dialog box, either disable Web console, or enter the appropriate user name, password, and port that you use for Web Console. Remember that the port must be unique across the cluster for each agent.

8. In the Relay Host dialog box, enter the appropriate method for the GWIA to send mail to the Internet, then click Next.

9. In the GroupWise Domain Directory dialog box, do the following:

   a. Enter or browse to the GroupWise Domain that houses the GWIA. Be sure to use the UNC path through the virtual server or a drive mapped to the cluster-enabled volume so that the path property properly reflects the virtual path.

   b. Enter the correct name of the subdirectory that the GWIA was installed into.

   c. Click Next to continue.

10. In the Internet Mail Domain Name dialog box, enter the DNS zone that you wish to have this GWIA service, and then click Next.

11. From the Ready to Install dialog box, click Install.

12. At the conclusion of the installation, you will see a Post Installation task list. Be sure to complete any items listed in this list. After viewing the list, click Finish to end the installation.

13. If you installed the NLMs to the SYS volume, repeat these steps for each server in the failover path.

14. Review the `GWIA.CFG`, `EXEPATH.CFG`, and `GWIA.NCF`.

X-REF

Detailed information on these files is provided in Chapter 12.

15. Add the commands to the Cluster Load script to launch the GWIA. At the end of the current load script, add the following:

```
LOAD DELAY.NLM

DELAY <XX>

SEARCH ADD <Volume>:\<Path>

LOAD ADDRESS SPACE=<name> <Volume>:\<Path>\GWIA.NLM
@<Volume>:\<Path>\GWIA.CFG
```

NOTE

All of the LOAD ADDRESS SPACE parameters must appear on the same line in the Load script.

If you have the `DELAY.NLM` load in the `AUTOEXEC.NCF` file, then you can omit it here. You must add a delay value of sufficient time to allow the Domain MTA to fully load prior to loading the GWIA. Substitute the correct path to the GWIA.NCF — for example, `GWGWIA:\SYSTEM\GWIA.NCF`. The entire load script appears in Figure 20.9.

```
Properties of GWGWIA_SERVER

IP Address | Load                          | Unload | Policies | Nodes | NDS Rights ▼ | Other | Rights to Files and Folo
             Cluster Resource Load Script

Script

nss /activate=GWGWIA
mount GWGWIA VOLID=251
NUDP ADD CLUSTER_GWGWIA_SERVER 10.7.5.112
add secondary ipaddress 10.7.5.112

CVSBIND ADD CLUSTER_GWGWIA_SERVER 10.7.5.112

LOAD ADDRESS SPACE=GWIA DSAPI
LOAD ADDRESS SPACE=GWIA GWGWIA:\SYSTEM\GWMTA @GWIADOM.MTA

LOAD DELAY
DELAY 10
SEARCH ADD GWGWIA:\SYSTEM
LOAD ADDRESS SPACE=GWIA GWGWIA:\SYSTEM\GWIA @GWGWIA:\SYSTEM\GWIA.CFG


Timeout (secs)  600

Page Options...              OK     Cancel    Apply     Help
```

FIGURE 20.9 *GroupWise GWIA load script*

TIP

With the current version of GroupWise 6 (no support packs), if you load the MTA in protected memory, you must also load the GWIA in the same protected memory space.

16. Add the commands to the unload script to unload GWIA. At the beginning of the script, add this command:

```
UNLOAD ADDRESS SPACE=<name> GWIA
```

The entire unload script is shown in Figure 20.10.

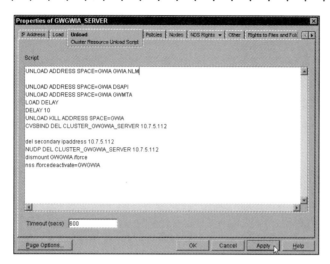

FIGURE 20.10 *GroupWise GWIA unload script*

17. Next you must modify your system addressing so that the GWIA can service your GroupWise system. To do this, follow these steps:

   a. Launch ConsoleOne.

   b. From the menu, select Tools ➪ GroupWise Systems Operations ➪ Internet Addressing.

   c. Select the desired Internet Addressing format, such as userID@Internet Domain Name.

   d. Click the Create button to create a new Internet Domain Name.

   e. Enter the name of the DNS zone or zones this GWIA will service, such as `consulting.novell.com`.

   f. Click OK to close the Internet Domain Name dialog box.

   g. Click OK to close the Internet Addressing dialog box.

18. After you have fully configured the GWIA, offline the GWIA resource, and then online it again. This will allow all of your load and unload script changes to take effect.

Simply migrating the resource to a new node is not sufficient for your script changes to take effect. You must offline and online the resource.

TIP

19. If you install the agent files to the SYS volume, install the agents to each server in the preferred nodes list.

Once you have installed the GWIA, be sure to test all operations of the GWIA on each node in the preferred nodes list. Don't simply make sure that the GWIA loads! Be sure to test all components of the GWIA that you are using, such as IMAP, POP3, SMTP, and so on. Each component should be tested on each node in the failover path.

Installing a New WebAccess Resource into Your Cluster

WebAccess consists of two components: the WebAccess Agent (GWINTER.NLM) and the Web Server Servlet. These components can be clustered together in a single resource, or they can be separated into multiple resources and clustered separately. For purposes of this procedure, separate these two into two resources, with the Servlet configured in an Active/Active Web server configuration. This is not to imply that this configuration is required, or even the best practice. This configuration simply highlights the component differences and makes it easier to understand the dependencies of each subcomponent of the WebAccess application.

Installing the WebAccess Agent into Your Cluster

The WebAccess Agent should be configured as a resource with a Secondary Domain dedicated to this gateway. This Domain should be configured on a cluster-enabled volume for ease of administration of the Domain.

The biggest difference between clustering the WebAccess Agent in GroupWise 6 and clustering it in GroupWise 5.5 is that with GroupWise 6, if the WebAccess Agent's MTA is running in protected memory on the same server as GWINTER, then GWINTER must also run in the same protected memory space.

To install the WebAccess Agent, follow these steps:

1. Follow steps 1 through 16 in the "Creating and Configuring the GroupWise Domain Object" section earlier in this chapter to create a new Secondary GroupWise Domain for the WebAccess Agent.

2. Follow steps 1 through 12 in the "Installing the GroupWise Agents" section earlier in this chapter to install the GroupWise agents for the Secondary Domain.

3. Follow steps 1 through 13 in the "Configuring the Cluster Resource" section earlier in this chapter to modify the cluster resource object for the Secondary GroupWise Domain.

4. Use ConsoleOne to make your GroupWise connection to the Domain that holds the WebAccess Gateway.

5. Browse the software distribution directory, and run SETUP.EXE from the \internet\webaccess directory.

6. Press the Yes button to accept the software license agreement.

7. From the WebAccess Components screen, select the GroupWise WebAccess Agent item and deselect all other options, then click Next to begin the installation.

8. Select NetWare as the software platform; enter or browse to the correct path to install the NLMs to, and then click Next to continue.

TIP

If you place the NLMs on the shared volume, you need to install the WebAccess Agents only once. If you place them on the SYS volume of each node, you must install these to each node that will be in the WebAccess Agent failover path.

9. You will receive a notice that all agents must be stopped to install WebAccess. Either click Yes to have the installation program stop them for you, or click No to stop the agents yourself.

10. In the Server Information dialog box shown in Figure 20.11, do the following:

    a. For the IP address field, enter the secondary IP address used for the WebAccess gateway cluster resource.

    b. For the Port field, enter the TCP/IP port the resource is using.

    c. Select the Configure GroupWise agents for clustering check box.

    d. Click Next to continue.

FIGURE 20.11 *GroupWise WebAccess Agent: Server Information dialog box*

11. In the Gateway Directory dialog box, do the following:

a. Enter or browse to the Domain directory path.

b. Either accept the default Gateway Directory name, or enter a new name to use to create the Gateway Directory.

c. Click Next to continue.

12. In the Gateway Object Name dialog box, either accept the name WEBAC60A, or enter a new name for the NDS WebAccess Gateway object to create an NDS object for the gateway.

13. In the NDS Authentication dialog box, do the following:

a. Enter the distinguished name of an NDS user object to be used by the WebAccess Gateway to access the Domain directory.

b. Enter and confirm the NDS user's password.

c. Click Next to continue.

14. In the Web Console dialog box, either disable Web Console or enter the appropriate credentials for Web Console. Then click Next to continue.

15. In the WebPublisher dialog box, either disable WebPublisher by clicking Next to continue, or do the following:

    a. Select the Enable WebPublisher check box.

    b. Enter a mailbox ID to use for Web Publisher.

    c. Enter and confirm the mailbox password.

    d. Click Next to continue.

16. From the Summary dialog box, click Next to install.

17. In the Start Applications dialog box, select the Launch Installation Summary to see details on the installation. Deselect Start GroupWise Agents now, and then click Finish to end the installation.

18. If you installed the NLMs to the SYS volume, repeat these steps for each node in the WebAccess Agent failover path.

19. Copy the `STRTWEB.NCF` and `STOPWEB.NCF` files from the SYS:SYSTEM volume to your shared volume. Even when you select the shared volume to install the agents to, these startup files are placed on the SYS volume of the server that was hosting the domain that you installed to.

20. With GroupWise 6, the WebAccess Agent must be running in the same memory space as its MTA. Since you must use protected memory for the MTA in a cluster, you must also modify the `STRTWEB.NCF` file to load the `GWINTER` module in the same address space as you are using for the MTA. Modify the `STARTWEB.NCF` file and change the `load` command as follows:

```
load ADDRESS SPACE=GWWEB GWWEB:system\gwinter
```

21. Next, you must modify the cluster resource object to load the WebAccess agent, as shown in Figure 20.12. To modify the resource, do the following:

    a. Right-click your cluster resource object, and then select Properties.

    b. Click the Load tab, and add the following commands to the end of the load script:

```
LOAD DELAY.NLM

DELAY 10

SEARCH ADD GWWEB:\SYSTEM

GWWEB:\SYSTEM\STRTWEB.NCF
```

    c. Click the Apply button.

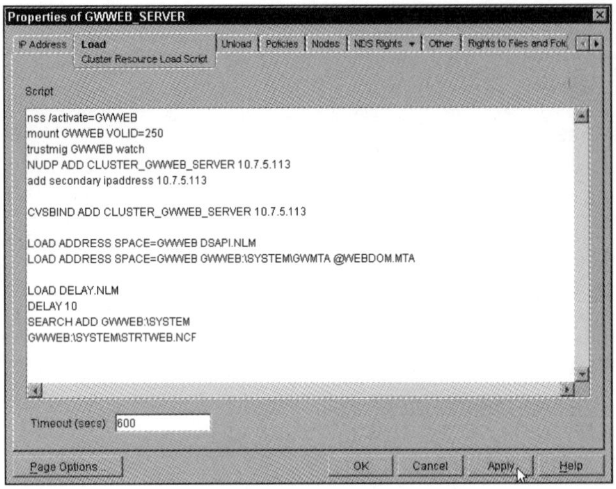

FIGURE 20.12 WebAccess load script

22. Next, you must modify the cluster resource object to unload the WebAccess Agent, as shown in Figure 20.13. To modify the resource, do the following:

    a. Click the Unload tab.

    b. Add the following command to the start of the unload script:

```
UNLOAD ADDRESS SPACE=GWWEB GWINTER
```

    c. Click the Apply button.

    d. Click the Close button to close the cluster resource object.

23. Offline the WebAccess Agent cluster resource, then online it again.

Now that you have the WebAccess Agent installed, you are ready to install the Servlet into the cluster. Remember that the WebAccess Agent is a component of the GroupWise Domain, while the Servlet is a component of the Web Server. Because the Servlet is tied to a Web Server with SYS volume dependencies, you must install it to each node in the Servlet failover path (even if this is configured as the same cluster resource as the WebAccess Agent).

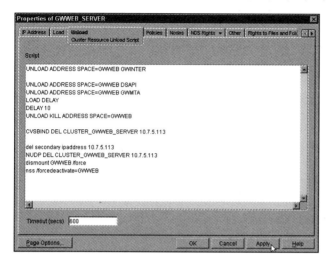

FIGURE 20.13 *WebAccess unload script*

Installing the WebAccess Servlet into Your Cluster

The WebAccess Servlet is a plug-in component to the Novell Enterprise Web Server and runs as a Java application. This component does not understand virtual servers and has SYS volume dependencies. For these reasons, do not cluster enable a volume for the WebAccess Servlet.

To install the WebAccess Servlet, do the following:

1. Follow the directions in Chapter 13 to create an Active/Active Web server resource. You do not need to create a volume for any content; the content can reside on the SYS volume of each node, since you must install to each node anyway.

2. Follow the directions in the "Installing the WebAccess Agent into Your Cluster" section earlier in this chapter.

3. Use ConsoleOne to make your GroupWise connection to the Domain that holds the WebAccess Gateway.

4. Unload the Web server, Web Manager, and Java from the server that you are installing to.

TIP You should migrate any Web or Java resources that are running on this server to other nodes in your cluster before unloading the Web Server and Java.

5. Browse the software distribution directory and run SETUP.EXE from the \internet\webaccess directory.

6. Press the Yes button to accept the software license agreement.

7. From the WebAccess Components screen, deselect the GroupWise WebAccess Agent, select the GroupWise WebAccess Application item and the GroupWise WebPublisher Application (if you wish to install WebPublisher), and then click Next to begin the installation.

8. In the Gateway Directory dialog box, enter or browse to the path to the WebAccess Domain directory. Be sure to select the \WPGATE\WEBAC60A (substitute the name of your gateway for WEBAC60A) subdirectory, and then click Next.

9. In the Web Server Information dialog box, do the following:

   a. Verify that Netscape Enterprise Server for NetWare is selected.

   b. In the path to the Web server's root directory, enter or browse to the SYS:\NOVONXY\SUITESPOT directory of the server you are installing the Servlet to. You must install this to the server's SYS volume.

   c. Click Next to continue.

10. In the second Web Server Information dialog box, do the following:

   a. Enter the secondary TCP/IP address used by the Web server's cluster resource. This is the address you used in step 1 for your Active/Active Web server resource.

   b. Either select Uses SSL or Does Not Use SSL.

   c. If necessary, change the TCP/IP port to use by the Servlet.

11. Specify whether or not you want to replace the Web server's default home page with GroupWise WebAccess, and then click Next to continue.

12. In the Novell root directory, specify a path for the configuration and log files. This path cannot use cluster-enabled volume syntax. If you are configuring an Active/Active Web server, this path must be the SYS volume

of each server. When NSWEB runs on the server, this volume must be accessible, or the Servlet will not start properly. If you are configuring an Active/Passive Web server, you can choose a volume on the shared storage and make sure your load script mounts the volume before NSWEB is run.

13. Specify whether to use the Novell Servlet Engine or a third-party engine, and then click Next to continue. Novell recommends using the Novell Servlet Engine.

14. Specify an arbitrary user name and password to limit access to the Servlet gateway, and then click Next.

15. Select the default language for the Servlet, and then click Next to continue.

16. In the NDS Object Configuration dialog box, verify or enter the NDS tree and context to store WebAccess application information, and then click Next.

17. In the Summary dialog box, confirm the information presented, and then click Next.

18. If prompted to replace the Servlet Gateway, review the dates of the gateways presented and be sure to use the newest gateway.

19. If promoted to replace the Java Virtual Machine (JVM), review the dates of the JVMs presented and be sure to use the newest JVM.

20. In the Start Applications dialog box, select Launch Installation Summary, deselect Restart Web Server, and then click Finish.

21. Restart Java, the Web server, and the Web Manager.

22. If you created a volume on the shared storage for the hardware virtual server for WebAccess, copy the SYS:\NOVONYX\SUITESPOT\DOCS\COM directory from the server you installed the Servlet on to the document root directory of the hardware virtual server. For example, we created a hardware virtual server on the WEB volume, pointing to a Docs subdirectory as the document root. In this case, we copy the COM directory and all its components to WEB:\Docs\COM.

23. Offline and then online the Web server resource, and any other Web servers that were running on this node. This is necessary if you are using Active/Active Web servers, since starting the Web server will delete all of your secondary IP addresses.

24. Repeat these steps for all Web servers in the failover path of the WebAccess Servlet resource.

25. Test WebAccess functionality for all combinations of resources. For example, migrate the Web Servlet component to each of its preferred nodes. Each time you migrate the Servlet, test while the WebAccess Agent is on each of its preferred nodes, then move the Servlet to the next node.

TIP **Remember that any time the server configuration changes (such as when you change the WebAccess Agent's IP address), you must recopy the `commgr.cfg` file from the `Domain\wpgate\webac60A` subdirectory to each Servlet server's `SYS:NOVELL\WebAccess` directory.**

Upgrading from an Existing GroupWise 5.5 Cluster

If you already have GroupWise 5.5 installed in your cluster and just wish to upgrade to GroupWise 6, you'll be glad to hear that it is a fairly straightforward process that is not that different from upgrading a nonclustered system.

As with a nonclustered upgrade, you must start the upgrade by upgrading the Primary GroupWise Domain. This is true whether this Domain is part of the cluster or not. During the process of upgrading the Primary Domain, you extend the NDS schema for the new GroupWise 6 attributes, and you either create a new software distribution directory or upgrade your existing software distribution directory.

TIP **You should create a new Software Distribution Directory so that you can maintain your GW 5.5 software directory for any remaining GW 5.5 components you might still have.**

Once you upgrade the Primary Domain, you can either next upgrade the Post Offices in that Domain, or you can start upgrading your Secondary Domains. The first time a GW6 agent is run against a GW 5.x Domain or Post Office, the agent will automatically rebuild that database and upgrade it.

At the time of this writing, Novell does not have an official stance regarding mixed versions of GroupWise within a cluster. It is quite possible that this configuration will not be supported, since you would never want to load a GroupWise 5.5 agent against a GroupWise 6 database. It is also not clear in the long term what occurs if you have two different versions of the same NLM running on the same server (protected memory allows you to do this). It is quite possible that running a GroupWise 5.5 MTA on the same server as a GroupWise 6 MTA might eventually lead to problems. Unless Novell officially supports this configuration, you should thoroughly test your configuration in a lab prior to implementing in production.

Upgrading the Primary Domain

The first Domain that you upgrade must be the Primary Domain. If you have a cluster resource with the Primary Domain and additional Domains or Post Offices in the same cluster resource, you should also upgrade these components at the same time. If the Primary Domain has Post Offices that are not in the same cluster resource, you can choose to upgrade those at a later time.

In this example configuration, GWDOM1 is the primary GroupWise Domain. It has two Post Offices, GWPO1 and GWPO2. GWPO1 is in the same cluster resource as the Primary Domain on a cluster-enabled volume, whereas GWPO2 is a separate cluster resource on a non–cluster-enabled volume.

To upgrade an existing GroupWise 5.5 Domain configured in a cluster, do the following:

1. Map a drive to the Primary GroupWise Domain database. If this is a cluster resource, make sure you map a drive using the cluster-enabled volume. In our example, the Primary Domain is GWDOM1, and we map drive M: to \\CLUSTER_GW1_SERVER\GW1.

2. From the server console screen of the node that is running the Primary Domain (and any Post Offices or Gateways on the same cluster resource or in this Domain), switch to the agent screen and press F7 to unload the agent. The agents should not be running while you upgrade their databases.

TIP
Normally it's recommended that you never stop a resource without using ConsoleOne and offlining the resource. However, in this case the cluster-enabled volume needs to be active, but the GroupWise agents themselves need to be stopped.

3. Insert the GroupWise 6 CD. The CD will automatically run the GroupWise Welcome screen. From this screen, you can read the GroupWise documentation on how to install and upgrade GroupWise systems.

4. From the Welcome screen, click the Install Products link.

5. From the list of products to install, click GroupWise Administration.

6. From this GroupWise Administration screen, click Install GroupWise Administration.

7. Click Yes to accept the GroupWise 6 license agreement.

8. From the Welcome to GroupWise Install screen, click the Next button to begin the installation.

9. From the Plan Your System dialog box, click Next to proceed. If you need help planning your system, you can first click the Installation Guide button for detailed help on planning your GroupWise system.

10. From the Installation Options dialog box, click Next to continue.

11. From the Select Trees dialog box, select the NDS tree that you wish to install GroupWise into. This allows the installation program to determine if the NDS schema needs to be extended.

12. If your schema has not already been upgraded, you receive a message that the installation program must modify the NDS schema. If this is the case, click Next to modify the schema for GroupWise 6. If you had already modified the schema, you receive a message that the schema is ready for GroupWise 6. In this case, click Next to continue.

13. If applicable, you receive a dialog box telling you the NDS schema has now been extended. Click Next to continue.

14. Select the appropriate language for installation, and then click Next to continue.

15. In the ConsoleOne Path dialog box, do one of the following:

- If you have not already installed ConsoleOne 1.2d or later to your Management workstation, click the Install ConsoleOne button, then follow the prompts to install ConsoleOne to your local workstation.

- If you have already installed ConsoleOne 1.2d or later, verify that the path to ConsoleOne Directory is correct. Once it's correct, click Next to continue. This will install the appropriate GroupWise 6 snapins to ConsoleOne to allow you to administer GroupWise.

16. In the Software Distribution Directory dialog box, browse to the location that you wish to install the Software Distribution files to. If you select your existing Software Distribution Directory, it will be upgraded for GW6. If you select a new location, a new Software Distribution Directory will be created. If you still have GroupWise 5.x components in your tree, you should create a new software distribution directory in case you later need the GroupWise 5.x software distribution directory for some reason.

17. In the Select Software dialog box, check all of the software that you wish to have available in the software distribution directory. By checking all available components, you will make a complete distribution directory. Once you've selected the components you desire, click Next to continue.

18. The installation program now reviews your installed files to determine the work it must do. This review may take several minutes, but nothing is actually being upgraded at this time. Once the review is done, click Install to perform the file modifications.

19. Once the files are copied, the installation program displays a Partner information screen. From this screen, you can click the Go to GroupWise Partner Page button, which takes you to a Web site with partner information. Otherwise, click Next to continue the installation.

20. The installation program now brings you to the Determine the Next Step dialog box. From here you can choose to Create a New GroupWise System, or to upgrade an existing system to GroupWise 6. To upgrade, make sure the Upgrade an Existing GroupWise 5.x system is selected, and then click Next.

21. In the Update GroupWise System dialog box, browse to the Primary Domain database using the drive mapped to the cluster-enabled volume, as shown in Figure 20.14, and then click Update.

22. Step 20 launches the Agent installation program. From the GroupWise Agent Installation Overview dialog box, click Next to continue the installation.

23. In the Install/Uninstall dialog box, verify that Install is selected, and then click Next.

24. In the Select Platform dialog box, verify that NetWare is selected and then click Next.

▶ · ◀

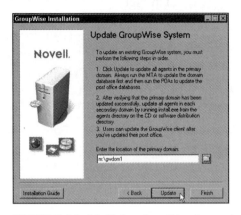

FIGURE 20.14 *Update GroupWise System dialog box*

25. In the Installation Path dialog box, browse to the location that you want to install the Agent NLMs and startup files. If you install the agents to the SYS volume, you must make sure that you install them on all servers that will be in the resource failover path. Once you have the path correct, select the Configure GroupWise Agents for Clustering check box, and then click Next to continue.

Chapters 11 and 12 discuss the pros and cons of installing the agents on the SYS volume or the shared volume.

X-REF

If you are installing the agents to the SYS volume, note that you will be upgrading all resources on that server. This could cause database problems if the resource is later migrated to a server that does not have the NLMs upgraded.

WARNING

26. In the Web Console Information dialog box, configure the Web Console information as desired by enabling Web Console with the appropriate user name and password, or disabling it. When you're done, click Next to continue.

27. In the Language dialog box, select the appropriate installation language(s), and then click Next to continue.

28. In the Domains/Post Offices dialog box (shown in Figure 20.15), do the
following:

    a. Click the Add button to add the GroupWise Domain. Be sure that you
select the path to the GroupWise Domain using the cluster-enabled
volume, either using the UNC path through the virtual server or by the
drive letter you mapped to the drive.

    b. Click the Add button to add any GroupWise Post Offices that run in
this cluster resource.

    c. Click Next to continue.

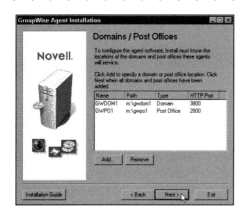

FIGURE 20.15 *GroupWise Agent Installation Domains/Post Offices dialog box*

29. From the Summary dialog box, click Install to continue.

30. Since you are upgrading this resource, you will be prompted that the
GRPWISE.NCF file already exists. The installation program asks if you want
to overwrite the existing file, to append to the existing file, or to create a
GRPWIS1.NCF file. If you followed the directions in Chapters 11 and 12,
then you don't use the GRPWISE.NCF file anyway; instead, you place all of
the commands that are normally in this file into the cluster resource load
script. Because you don't use this file, it doesn't matter how you answer this
prompt, just make a selection and click OK. You can choose to create a
GRPWIS1.NCF file so that you can compare the commands and look for any
differences.

31. From the Installation Complete dialog box shown in Figure 20.16, deselect all options, and then click Finish.

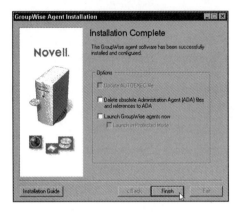

FIGURE 20.16 *Installation Complete dialog box*

32. If the installation program doesn't toggle you back to the GroupWise Installation/Update GroupWise System dialog box, then press Alt+Tab until this dialog box is active.

33. Click the Finish button.

34. Open the .MTA and .POA files and verify that all of your desired options are set. By using the Configure GroupWise Agents for Clustering check box in step 25, the /home switch should use the proper syntax of *volume:path*, for example:

/home-GW1:\GWDOM1

TIP
By selecting the option to configure the agents for clustering, the .MTA and .POA should be complete, with the exception of the POA /IP switch. You should add the /IP switch with the resource IP address to the POA startup file so that the POA correctly binds to the resource secondary IP address instead of the server's primary network address.

35. Once you are satisfied that your startup files are correct, offline the cluster resource.

36. If the GroupWise installation created new `.MTA` and `.POA` files with different names, you need to change the cluster startup switches to match the new file names. For example, the installation program created a `GWDOM1.MT1` file for the MTA startup file. Therefore, change the MTA and POA load lines as follows and as shown in Figure 20.17:

```
LOAD ADDRESS SPACE=GW1 GW1:SYSTEM\GWMTA @GWDOM1.MT1

LOAD ADDRESS SPACE=GW1 GW1:SYSTEM\GWPOA @GWPO1.PO1
```

Properties of GW1_SERVER

IP Address | **Load** | Unload | Policies | Nodes | NDS Rights ▾ | Other | Rights to Files and Folders ◄ ►
Cluster Resource Load Script

Script

```
nss /activate=GW1
mount GW1 VOLID=250
NUDP ADD CLUSTER_GW1_SERVER 10.7.5.106
add secondary ipaddress 10.7.5.106

CVSBIND ADD CLUSTER_GW1_SERVER 10.7.5.106
LOAD ADDRESS SPACE=GW1 GW1:SYSTEM\GWMTA @GWDOM1.MT1
LOAD ADDRESS SPACE=GW1 GW1:SYSTEM\GWPOA @GWPO1.PO1
PROTECTION RESTART GW1
```

Timeout (secs) 600

Page Options...   OK   Cancel   Apply   Help

FIGURE 20.17 *GroupWise Domain/POA load script*

TIP

With GroupWise 6, the NDS Synchronization event does not work if the MTA is running in protected memory because it cannot communicate properly with the `DSAPI.NLM` running in conventional memory. To work around this issue, you can also load `DSAPI` in the same protected memory space as the MTA. To do this, add another line before the MTA load line to load `DSAPI.NLM`—for example, `LOAD ADDRESS SPACE=GW1 DSAPI.NLM`.

37. Once you are satisfied with the load script and startup files, online the GroupWise resource.

Upgrading Subsequent Secondary Domains and Post Offices

Once you have the Primary Domain upgraded to GroupWise 6, you can start upgrading the Secondary Domains and the Post Offices. Before upgrading a Post Office to GroupWise 6, first upgrade the Domain that holds that Post Office. You should always upgrade all agents involved in a single cluster resource at the same time. Thus, if you have a cluster resource with a Domain and a Post Office, upgrade both at once.

Technically, to upgrade the Secondary Domains and Post Offices, all you really need to do is load the GroupWise 6 NLMs against the GroupWise 5.5 database; the NLM will rebuild the database with the new structure. To ease the installation, Novell provides an agent installation program located in the GroupWise 6 software distribution directory. Running this program upgrades all of the NLMs, as well as creates new startup files that are documented with the GroupWise 6 settings. Be sure to document your current settings before replacing the startup files.

To upgrade a Secondary Domain and Post Office resource, do the following:

1. Map a drive to the Secondary GroupWise Domain database. If this is a cluster resource, make sure you map a drive using the cluster-enabled volume. In this example, the Secondary Domain is GWDOM3, and drive N: is mapped to \\CLUSTER_GW3_SERVER\GW3.

2. From the server console screen of the node that is running the Secondary Domain (and any Post Offices or Gateways on the same cluster resource or in this Domain), switch to the agent screen and press F7 to unload the agent. The agents should not be running while you upgrade their databases.

TIP

Normally it is recommended that you never stop a resource without using ConsoleOne and offlining the resource. However, in this case the cluster-enabled volume needs to be active, but the GroupWise agents themselves need to be stopped.

3. Browse the GroupWise 6 Software Distribution Directory to the \agents subdirectory, and run INSTALL.EXE.

4. Click Yes to accept the license agreement.

5. Step 4 launches the Agent installation program. From the GroupWise Agent Installation Overview dialog box, click Next to continue the installation.

6. In the Install/Uninstall dialog box, verify that Install is selected, and then click Next.

7. In the Select Platform dialog box, verify that NetWare is selected and then click Next.

8. In the Installation Path dialog box, browse to the location to which you want to install the Agent NLMs and startup files. If you install the agents to the SYS volume, you must make sure that you install them on all servers that will be in the resource failover path. Once you have the path correct, select the Configure GroupWise Agents for Clustering check box, and then click Next to continue.

Chapters 11 and 12 discuss the pros and cons of installing the agents on the SYS volume or the shared volume.

X-REF

If you are installing the agents to the SYS volume, note that you will be upgrading all resources on that server. This could cause database problems if the resource is later migrated to a server that does not have the NLMs upgraded.

WARNING

9. In the Web Console Information dialog box, configure the Web Console information as desired by enabling Web Console with the appropriate user name and password, or disabling it. When you're done, click Next to continue.

10. In the Language dialog box, select the appropriate installation language(s), and then click Next to continue.

11. In the Domains/Post Offices dialog box (shown in Figure 20.18), do the following:

    a. Click the Add button to add the GroupWise Domain. Be sure that you select the path to the GroupWise Domain using the cluster-enabled volume, either using the UNC path through the virtual server or by the drive letter you mapped to the drive. In this example, enter N:\GWDOM3.

    b. Click the Add button to add any GroupWise Post Offices that run in this cluster resource.

    c. Click Next to continue.

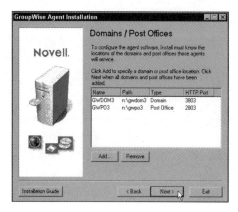

FIGURE 20.18 *GroupWise Agent Installation Domains/Post Offices dialog box*

12. From the Summary dialog box, click Install to continue.

13. Since you are upgrading this resource, you will be prompted that the GRPWISE.NCF file already exists. The installation program asks if you want to overwrite the existing file, append to the existing file, or create a GRPWIS1.NCF file. If you followed the directions in Chapters 11 and 12, then you don't use the GRPWISE.NCF file anyway; instead, you place all of the commands that are normally in this file into the cluster resource load script. Because you don't use this file, it doesn't matter how you answer this prompt—just make a selection and click OK. You can choose to create a GRPWIS1.NCF file so that you can compare the commands and look for any differences.

14. From the Installation Complete dialog box, deselect all options, and then click Finish.

15. Open the .MTA and .POA files and verify that all of your desired options are set. By using the Configure GroupWise Agents for Clustering check box in step 8, the /home switch should use the proper syntax of *volume:path*, for example:

```
/home-GW3:\GWDOM3
```

16. Once you are satisfied that your startup files are correct, offline the cluster resource.

17. If the GroupWise installation created new `.MTA` and `.POA` files with different names, you need to change the cluster startup switches to match the new filenames. For example, the installation program created a `GWDOM3.MT1` file for the MTA startup file. Therefore, we changed the MTA and POA load lines as follows and as shown in Figure 20.19:

```
LOAD ADDRESS SPACE=GW3 GW3:SYSTEM\GWMTA @GWDOM3.MT1

LOAD ADDRESS SPACE=GW3 GW3:SYSTEM\GWPOA @GWPO3.PO1
```

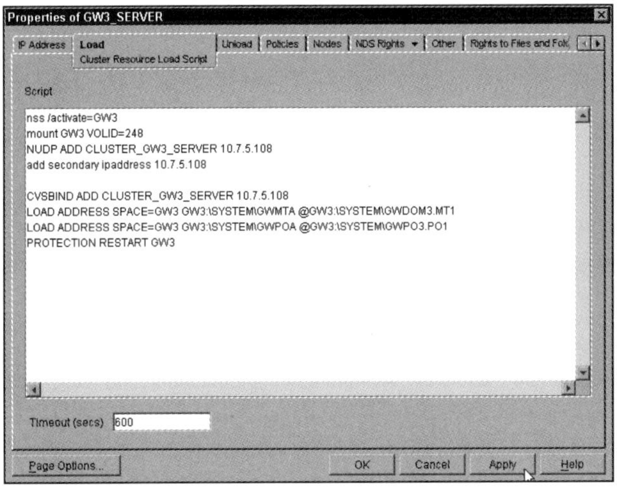

FIGURE 20.19 *GroupWise Domain/POA load script*

Once you are satisfied with the load script and startup files, online the GroupWise resource and thoroughly test all functionality with the resource on each node in the failover path. Remember, you need to do more than simply watch the NLMs load — you must test all functionality!

Upgrading the GWIA

The GroupWise 5.5 GWIA can fully operate for both users in GroupWise 5.5 Domains and Post Offices and those in GroupWise 6 Domains and Post Offices. However, the GroupWise 6 GWIA can only fully operate for users in GroupWise 6 Domains and Post Offices. The GroupWise 6 GWIA will not function for GroupWise 5.x POP3 and IMAP4 clients, but will support SMTP messaging using the GroupWise client.

This means that you should not upgrade the GWIA until all users of Domains and Post Offices have been upgraded, especially if the users need Internet services beyond simply sending and receiving Internet messages while using the GroupWise client.

To upgrade the GWIA, do the following:

1. Follow steps 1 through 17 in the "Upgrading Subsequent Secondary Domains and Post Offices" section earlier in this chapter. Do not bring the resource online when you are done; you will install the new GWIA before onlining the resource.

2. Browse the software distribution directory and run INSTALL.EXE from the \internet\gwia directory.

The GroupWise 6 GWIA installation program also has a /copyonly **switch that bypasses many of the unnecessary options. To use this instead of the full installation, run** \internet\gwia\install.exe/copyonly.

TIP

3. Press the Yes button to accept the software license agreement.

4. From the Welcome screen, click Next to begin the installation.

5. Select NetWare as the software platform, and then click Next to continue.

6. In the Installation Path dialog box shown in Figure 20.20, do the following:

   a. Enter or browse to the location of the GWIA agent NLM files.

   b. Enter or browse to the location of the GWIA startup files.

   c. Deselect the option to update the AUTOEXEC.NCF file.

d. Select the option to install into an existing cluster.

e. Click Next to continue.

7. In the Web Console dialog box, either disable Web Console or enter the appropriate user name, password, and port that you use for Web Console. Remember that the port must be unique for each agent.

8. In the Relay Host dialog box, enter the appropriate method for the GWIA to send mail to the Internet, then click Next.

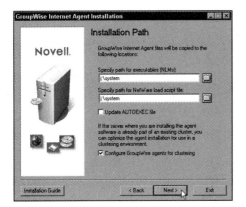

FIGURE 20.20 *GroupWise Internet Agent Installation Path dialog box*

9. In the GroupWise Domain Directory dialog box, do the following:

a. Enter or browse to the GroupWise Domain that houses the GWIA. Be sure to use the UNC path through the virtual server or a drive mapped to the cluster-enabled volume so that the path property properly reflects the virtual path.

b. Enter the correct name of the subdirectory that the GWIA was installed into.

c. Click Next to continue.

10. From the Ready to Install dialog box, click Install.

11. At the conclusion of the installation, you will see a Post Installation task list. Be sure to complete any items listed in this list. After viewing the list, click Finish to end the installation.

12. If you installed the NLMs to the SYS volume, repeat these steps for each server in the failover path.

13. Review the GWIA.CFG, EXEPATH.CFG, and GWIA.NCF. When you're satisfied that all paths are correct, offline the GWIA cluster resource and then online it.

Detailed information on these files is provided in Chapter 12.

X-REF

Upgrading GroupWise WebAccess

Upgrading WebAccess requires upgrading the various components, which may be installed and running separately. You must plan for upgrading the WebAccess Agent (GWINTER) and the Web Server Servlet. This is most critical if you have clustered the Web Server Servlet component as a separate cluster resource as the WebAccess Agent.

Upgrading WebAccess involves upgrading two components: the WebAccess Agent (GWINTER) and the WebAccess Servlet. These two components can be configured as the same cluster resource, or they can be configured as separate resources. In our example, they are configured separately, although in this case that doesn't necessarily mean this is the preferred method.

The WebAccess Agent should be installed with a dedicated Secondary Domain just for WebAccess. To facilitate GroupWise administration, this should be installed to a cluster-enabled volume.

The WebAccess Servlet is installed as a component of the Enterprise Web Server and does not understand cluster-enabled volumes. When installing and configuring the Servlet, you must install this to each Web server, and you must configure the path to the Servlet without using the virtual server information. Because of the potential confusion in keeping these components straight, the following sections run through the installation in two phases — the first for the WebAccess Agent, and the second for the Servlet.

Upgrading the WebAccess Agent

Generally speaking, GroupWise WebAccess agents can service only Domains and Post Offices of the same version. Whenever you upgrade a Domain that contains a WebAccess Agent, you should also upgrade the agent simultaneously. If some of your users will remain on GroupWise 5 while others will be upgraded to GroupWise 6, then you need to have two WebAccess Agents — one on version 5 for the 5.*x* users, and the other on version 6 for the 6.*x* users.

The GroupWise 5.5 Enhancement Pack WebAccess Agent running Service Pack 3 is one exception to this rule. This version agent can service both GroupWise 5.*x* and GroupWise 6 users.

After conferring with the GroupWise Product Management and developers, we do not recommend performing an upgrade to the existing agents in the same directory and NDS object. Instead, install a new WebAccess agent in a new directory and NDS object following the same procedure given in the "Installing a New WebAccess Agent into Your Cluster" section of this chapter. Once the new WebAccess agent is installed, configured, and tested, delete the old WebAccess NDS object and file system structure. This provides the cleanest upgrade path.

Upgrading the WebAccess Servlet

The GroupWise 6 WebAccess Agent (GWINTER) can communicate with GroupWise 5.5, GroupWise Enhancement Pack, and GroupWise 6 WebAccess Servlets (the component that runs on the Web Server). This allows you to upgrade your WebAccess Agent independently of the WebAccess Servlet, assuming you are running GW 5.5 or later.

The GroupWise 6 WebAccess Agent (GWINTER) cannot communicate with Servlets prior to GW 5.5.

To upgrade the WebAccess Servlet, simply follow the same steps as provided in the "Installing a New WebAccess Servlet into Your Cluster" section of this chapter. Install on top of the existing Servlet, or rename the SYS:\NOVELL and SYS:NOVONYX\SUITESPOT\DOCS\COM directories and then reinstall the WebAccess Servlet.

Upgrading the GroupWise Client

The GroupWise 5.*x* client can be used to access a GroupWise 6 Domain and Post Office. However, the GroupWise 6 client cannot be used to access a GroupWise 5.*x* Domain and Post Office. GroupWise 5.*x* clients will not have access to the new GroupWise 6 features, such as disk space management and the caching mode, but they will have all of the functionality they had with GroupWise 5.*x*.

Therefore, you should upgrade the client only after the user's Domain and Post Office have been upgraded to GroupWise 6.

► · ◄

Migration/Failover Characteristics

This section discusses how the various GroupWise components discussed in this chapter normally behave when they are migrated to another node or when the node they are running on fails. Recall that a migration involves a voluntary process by the administrator to move a resource from one node to another, while a failover involves a hardware or software fault that causes a node to fail.

The section gives you a baseline of what to expect from each of the components, including the gateways and the clients, for the migration or failover event. Actual time taken for these events will naturally vary from system to system based on configuration and usage.

MTA Failover Behavior

The GroupWise MTAs failover and migrate relatively rapidly, but your time will vary according to the size of your system and the Domain database. In a failure scenario, the MTA may need to repair the database prior to starting message flow, which can significantly add to the startup time. The good news here is that the primary noticeable functions of GroupWise still function during this time; the user is able to make the client/server connection to the Post Office, but mail entering or leaving the Post Office is queued until the MTA fully starts.

Migrations of resources take significantly longer than a server failure, as closing the Domain database can take some time to process.

Once the MTA comes up on the new node, it is common for the initial startup to leave many of the other Domains and possibly Post Offices and Gateways in a closed state. This is normal and expected behavior, and in a properly configured system, it will be resolved in 10 minutes when the MTA does its automatic restart. This means that the first 10 minutes after a migration or failure, you may not have MTA-to-MTA message flow, even though users are accessing their mailboxes normally. If you cannot wait the 10 minutes, manually restart the MTA by using the F6 key at the server console.

POA Failover Behavior

Post Office behavior is very similar to the MTA behavior; failures are relatively quick, whereas a manual migration may take some time for the Post Office to unload. Again, the larger the Post Office, the more significant delay you will see in the startup and shutdown times.

Like the MTA, if the POA database goes down dirty, it may need to perform some repairs when restarted. This is the primary reason to insist on client/server connections only; if you had users connecting Direct to the Post Office, your risk of data corruption is significantly increased.

The Post Office will generally be up and ready to go long before the MTA is fully communicating. From the users' perspective, users are able to connect (or reconnect) to the Post Office and send mail very quickly once the POA starts backup, and unless they are on the phone talking to the person sending them a message, they will probably not even be aware that the MTA is not fully communicating.

Gateways Failover Behavior

Like the MTA and POA, resource migrations on the Gateways are much slower than the recovery time should a server actually fail. This is especially true and painful with the GWIA, which can be extremely slow to shut down as it finishes processing all of its threads (we have seen heavily used GWIAs take more than 10 minutes to shut down).

During the GWIA migration or failover, POP3, IMAP4, and LDAP clients receive a TCP/IP error message stating that the server is not available. The actual errors vary depending on the client software used, but most of these clients do not automatically reconnect, which requires the user to close down the client and reopen it.

The WebAccess symptoms depend on whether it is the Web Server (Servlet) that fails/migrates or the WebAccess Gateway itself. The Servlet caches the user's credentials, so if the WebAccess Gateway server (GWINTER.NLM) fails or migrates, the user receives an error message that the agent is not available. Once the agent has started again, the user is able to reconnect, as the Servlet passes the user credentials back to the agent. If it is the Servlet that fails or migrates, the user needs to reauthenticate, as the cached credentials do not survive a Servlet failure.

Both the GWIA and the WebAccess agent are pretty quick to start up, so in the event of a server failure, resources are quickly reestablished.

Client Failover Behavior

The GroupWise 6 client has been enhanced to detect when it is connected to a cluster, and it modifies its behavior appropriately. If the user is not actively sending messages during a Post Office migration, they never know anything happened.

The only time the client produces an error is if the client is in the process of sending a message when the POA is not up, and the client needs to do an address book search. In this case, the client receives an error, and the user is forced to shut down the GroupWise client (not the workstation) and start it again.

The GroupWise 6 Notify program is also significantly better at handling failover than the GroupWise 5.x version. The new Notify waits much longer to produce an error, and when it does notice a communications failure, it displays the message shown in Figure 20.21. If the user selects No to exiting Notify, the program remains running and attempts to reconnect to the POA when it comes back online.

FIGURE 20.21 *GroupWise Notify dialog box*

Active/Active versus Active/Passive

Just like those in GroupWise 5.5, all GroupWise 6 components function in an Active/Passive manner. Only one server can have the database volume mounted and the agent loaded, so migrating a resource requires starting all of the appropriate NLMs on the destination node.

Summary

In this chapter, you learned about GroupWise 6 and its improvements over GroupWise 5.5.

You examined the clustering enhancements made to GroupWise 6 and how they affect implementation. You also learned about planned enhancements for GroupWise 6 Support Pack 1 that were not yet committed as this book was being written.

You learned how to create a brand-new GroupWise 6 system configured as a fault-tolerant service using Novell Cluster Services. This included a summary of the key topics in Clustering GroupWise 5.5, which were introduced in Chapters 11 and 12. You also learned how to upgrade an existing GroupWise 5.5 clustered system to GroupWise 6.

Finally, you explored what to expect when a GroupWise component is migrated or a node running GroupWise fails. GroupWise 6 migration and failover characteristics are as follows:

CLUSTER FAILOVER CLASSIFICATION INDEX	
Transparency	Client is very transparent unless doing an address book search.
Active/Active or Active/Passive	Active/Passive
Length to failover	Each component is different. Post Office is quick, while MTA can be slow. Migrations are much slower than failovers.

## CHAPTER 21

Applying Novell Cluster Services — Case Studies

This chapter examines the following real-world clustered Storage Area Networks running Novell Cluster Services software and other Novell products and services:

- University of Idaho

- Frankfurt Airport

- COMDEX/Fall 1999

- MobilCom Communicationstechnik GmbH

- Tenet Healthcare Corporation

University of Idaho

The University of Idaho in Moscow, Idaho, was founded in 1889 as a land grant research university. At that time the school had only 40 students and one professor. Today more than 11,500 students are enrolled, and more than 850 faculty members are involved in teaching and research. The university is a leader in leveraging information technology (IT) to enhance learning and streamline business operations. In 2000, *Yahoo Magazine* ranked the university number 13 among the nation's 100 most wired campuses. More than 11,500 users rely on the university network for essential activities, ranging from registering for classes and posting grades to teaching and conducting research. In late 1999, Information Technology Services (ITS) implemented Novell Cluster Services running on Dell PowerEdge servers to help meet the 24/7 network availability requirements of the university's user community.

According to Kenneth Fingerlos, Server Systems Supervisor in ITS, maintaining service levels was becoming increasingly difficult. Any time a server went down, many people were negatively affected. If a server hosting the front-end applications for the enterprise resource planning (ERP) system failed or required maintenance, day-to-day business operations such as issuing invoices, paying bills, and registering students were disrupted. In addition, faculty members who relied on ITS systems for instructional purposes couldn't teach their classes effectively. The ITS staff began looking at options to improve availability. "Although we could improve the situation by purchasing more reliable servers and software, we realized that we needed physical redundancy to ensure maximum availability," Fingerlos recalls. "But the overhead of eight backup servers sitting next to the active ones would have been a very expensive path to take." In early

1999, the staff saw a demonstration of Novell Cluster Services, a solution that enables organizations to group multiple NetWare 5 servers into a single cluster to increase availability, scalability, and manageability. All servers in the cluster are active and each server provides failover support for the others. Typically, clusters contain two to seven nodes, although Dell and Novell have demonstrated the ability to support up to 32 nodes in a single cluster.

After seeing the prerelease version, Fingerlos contacted Novell and asked to participate in the beta program. "Our next step was to find a hardware vendor. It's difficult, though, to find a vendor who will provide support when you're running beta software. Dell was actually very enthusiastic about the project." In July 1999, the ITS staff began beta testing the clustering solution, which comprises five Dell PowerEdge 4350 servers running NetWare 5 and Novell Cluster Services. The cluster provides essential file and print services, and it provides data storage for a variety of important applications, including the ERP system. Currently, the cluster supports 287 printers. Novell Distributed Print Services (NDPS) provides intelligent, bidirectional communications between users, printers, and administrators and offers plug-and-print capabilities to simplify administration and user access. The cluster includes a PowerVault 650F disk array, Dell's PowerVault Storage Area Network (SAN) technology.

With the SAN technology, the university enjoys the advantages of a highly available centralized storage environment. SAN technology improves application performance across a network, delivers virtually uninterrupted access to data, enhances disaster protection and data management, and costs less than traditional storage technologies. Total storage capacity at the university is 360GB, with approximately 290GB available for online storage. An external tape library provides backup for the content of the shared storage. Testing went smoothly, and by the end of December, all faculty and administrative personnel were using the clustering solution. Then in July 2000, the staff deployed a three-node cluster for student data and applications. This second cluster is based on the same hardware and software configuration as the first one. It supports 37 printers and shares the backup tape library with the first cluster.

Novell Cluster Services and the Dell PowerEdge servers have increased service availability substantially, while easing the burden on the ITS staff. To further increase availability, the staff has configured servers with redundant network interfaces—using one fast Ethernet interface and a 1-gigabit Ethernet interface. "Recently we had a situation in which the UPS (uninterruptible power supply) devices attached to two servers had been turned off inadvertently," Fingerlos recalls. "The Novell/Dell clustering solution automatically restarted the resources on another node. Our users experienced a brief interruption of only a few seconds."

Clustering benefits the university in other ways as well. Hardware costs are substantially lower, and maintenance and administration have been simplified. Moreover, the staff can now fix problems and perform routine maintenance during normal business hours. "We don't have to come in at midnight to get a server up and running," Fingerlos notes. "And we don't have to plan routine maintenance tasks for nights and weekends." A staff member can even dial in remotely at night to take a server offline in preparation for maintenance the next day.

The combination of Novell Cluster Services and the Dell PowerEdge servers is proving to be a cost-effective, easy-to-manage solution for improving network reliability for the University of Idaho. Fingerlos says, "It's easy to install, configure, and administer. In short, the product does what we need it to do."

Table 21.1 details the University of Idaho's two clusters—one containing five nodes, the other three nodes.

TABLE 21.1

University of Idaho's Five- and Three-Node NetWare Clusters

CONFIGURATION	DETAILS (CLUSTER #1)	DETAILS (CLUSTER #2)
Nodes	5	3
Users	3,500 faculty and staff	11,000 students
Server software	NetWare 5.0 and Novell Cluster Services 1.01	NetWare 5.0 and Novell Cluster Services 1.01
Server hardware	Dell PowerEdge 4350 servers	Dell PowerEdge 4350 servers
Storage Area Network	Dell PowerVault 650F disk array	Dell PowerVault 650F disk array
	Dell PowerVault 630F disk chassis	Dell PowerVault 630F disk chassis
	Twenty 18GB hard disks configured as two logical units (Total: 360GB)	Twenty 18GB hard disks configured as two logical units (Total: 360GB)
	Two hard disks configured as Hot Spares	Two hard disks configured as Hot Spares
	QLogic 2100 Fibre Channel Host Bus Adapters	QLogic 2100 Fibre Channel Host Bus Adapters
	Dell PowerVault 50F Fibre Channel Switch	Dell PowerVault 50F Fibre Channel Switch

CONFIGURATION	DETAILS (CLUSTER #1)	DETAILS (CLUSTER #2)
Backup	LAN-based backup via Shared Spectralogic tape library	LAN-based backup via Shared Spectralogic tape library
Cluster resources	File	File
	Print (NDPS)	Print (NDPS)
	287 Printers	37 Printers

Frankfurt Airport

"To operate thousands of flights daily, including keeping airlines and passengers constantly informed, we require a complex, multiapplication system that relies on a wide array of computers, communications connections, and people to operate," said Norbert Richter, system planner for Frankfurt Airport. "This massive, widely distributed system uses Novell software and services to tie it all together securely, leveraging our existing technology investment so we can better serve our customers and partners while keeping costs down."

The reason Frankfurt Airport selected a Novell Cluster Services configuration was to migrate from Novell NetWare SFTIII and IPX to Novell Cluster Services and TCP/IP. The goal was to achieve maximum availability for Btrieve database applications and data in an environment that supports failover.

Airport operations are supported by five critical applications. The applications are based on Btrieve databases and enable central operations management. With these critical applications, the airport controls nearly everything that is going to or leaving an aircraft. Each application is running on a cluster-enabled volume using Pervasive's SP3 update for SQL 2000i running against a cluster-enabled volume's virtual server. The Novell NetWare client for Windows NT desktop version 4.8 SP1 and the Btrieve 32-bit requester run the application via a DOS command shell.

"Because several Btrieve applications can run on the same cluster node, the failover design was not complicated," says Richter. Every application is assigned to three nodes via its cluster resource preferred nodes list. By default, every application is running on its own node. Active/Active failover happens when an application fails over to a node that is already running another Btrieve application.

All kinds of failover scenarios were tested, first with test data and finally with live production data directly from a Tandem mainframe host. To understand how this works: the central Tandem host pushes every change to a special gateway machine. The gateway machine is a Windows NT workstation logged in to the cluster via a special gateway user identity. It pushes data directly into the Btrieve databases located on cluster-enabled volumes. To optimize client reconnect after a failover, the Microsoft Windows TCP stack connect and data retransmission parameters were altered. Novell's special two-node split-brain patch was applied, together with Compaq's teaming NIC solution.

The cluster has been operational for six months without problems.

Storage Area Networks are considered a strategic part of Frankfurt Airport's global infrastructure. SANs are used to host other operating systems in addition to NetWare clusters. The goal is to consolidate all storage on a common Storage Area Network.

Table 21.2 details Frankfurt Airport's six-node cluster.

TABLE 21.2

Frankfurt Airport's Six-Node NetWare Cluster

CONFIGURATION	DETAILS
Nodes	6
Server software	NetWare 5.1 and Novell Cluster Services 1.01
Server hardware	Compaq Proliant DL380
Storage Area Network	Compaq Storage Works RA4100
	Twelve 18GB hard disks
	(Total: 216GB)
	Compaq Fibre Channel Host Bus Adapter
	Compaq Fibre Channel Storage HUB12
Cluster resources	File
	Pervasive Btrieve SQL 2000
	Print (NDPS)

COMDEX/Fall 1999

Novell Connecting Points (NCP) is the messaging system that the Novell Corporate Events Team designs and configures before packing, shipping, and setting up at trade shows all over the world. From BrainShare U.S. in Salt Lake City, Utah, to NetWorld+Interop in Tokyo, Japan, NCP travels the globe in various sizes and configurations. Despite its changing locale and design, NCP's purpose remains the same: to provide individual e-mail accounts that trade-show attendees can use to exchange e-mail messages.

Of all of the trade shows that have featured NCP, COMDEX/Fall 1999 was one of the largest. By the last day of this five-day show, more than 300,000 attendees had crowded the halls of the Las Vegas Convention Center (LVCC), the neighboring Sands Expo and Convention Center, and the Venetian Resort in Las Vegas, Nevada.

This largest show also claimed the smallest footprint for an NCP at COMDEX. Due to the inclusion of Novell Cluster Services, NCP at COMDEX/Fall 1999 required considerably less hardware than NCPs at any previous COMDEX. For example, for COMDEX/Fall 1998, the NCP team hauled 44 servers from Novell headquarters in Orem, Utah, to the show floor in Las Vegas. In contrast, for COMDEX/Fall 1999, the team took only 14 servers for the back end.

NOTE

The NCP featured at COMDEX/Fall 1999 was not the first NCP to run Novell Cluster Services — and it wasn't the last. The team first ran Novell Cluster Services on the NCP at the Fall 1999 NetWorld+Interop, which holds the record for having the smallest footprint of an NCP at any show. This NCP's back-end system consisted of one nine-node cluster, which provided the usual NCP services for 60,000 attendees.

By utilizing Novell Cluster Services, the team simultaneously managed to shrink NCP's footprint and improve NCP's reliability and performance. During the show, the back-end NCP servers experienced ABENDs only twice, and both of these failures went unnoticed by the COMDEX attendees who used NCP. In fact, the team members themselves did not learn about the ABENDs until after the fact and, even then, were nonplussed. Brian Petersen, Novell field marketing specialist at the time, explains that he corrected the problem "when [he] felt the need to," which was at the end of the day, long after attendees had gone home. In the meantime, NCP at COMDEX/Fall 1999 continued offering its services — uninterrupted.

NCP at COMDEX/Fall 1999 featured a back-end system consisting of three clusters. Six Compaq 1850R servers running Novell Cluster Services formed Cluster 1. Clusters 2 and 3 were also built on Compaq 1850R servers, four each, running Novell Cluster Services.

Fourteen nodes, says Petersen, who designed this back-end system, was the smallest number of nodes he "felt comfortable with." Mounted on one rack, these 14 nodes were centrally located in the NCP Network Operations Center (NOC).

Originally, Petersen planned to design one 14-node fibre channel arbitrated loop clustered–SAN. However, after speaking with Novell's clustering development group, Petersen and other members of the team decided that a single FC-AL SAN might not be able to handle some of the after-hours maintenance routines. For example, the team was particularly concerned that a single FC-AL SAN might not perform satisfactorily on the first, second, and third nights of the show, when the team planned to distribute messages to each of the 300,000 NCP users.

"Our big concern was input/output," Petersen explains. "We only have a few hours at night to distribute mail and were concerned that the shared pipe from the cluster to the data stores would not be big enough to get the performance we needed."

The system's data stores to which Petersen refers were on shared volumes that Petersen set up on three Compaq RAID Array 4000 storage subsystems—one array for each cluster. These arrays were connected to the clusters by way of three Compaq Fibre Channel hubs—one for each array and cluster. The connection was made over fiber optic cable at a rate of 1 gigabit per second. Both the hubs and the arrays were mounted in a rack that sat next to the rack of cluster nodes. Figure 21.1 illustrates the rack mount configuration. The left-hand rack contained the Fibre Channel storage arrays and arbitrated loop hubs. The right-hand rack housed the fourteen servers. Each server in Figure 21.1 has a label identifying its primary role. For example, server NCP-D088 is Node 14 in Cluster 3 and ran six GroupWise post office agents (POAs), one message transfer agent (MTA) and one copy of GroupWise WebAccess.

Running Novell Cluster Services was relatively new to the team, who had run the clustering software only once before during the Fall 1999 NetWorld+Interop held in Atlanta, Georgia. A pair of microwave towers that established the wireless, Fast Ethernet connection between the clusters and NCP workstations in the Sands and the Venetian Resort was also new to NCP. Although these and other technologies that kept Novell Cluster Services connected and running were new to NCP, the resources NCP provided at COMDEX/Fall 1999 were essentially the same services that NCP had provided for other trade shows.

For example, NCP at COMDEX/Fall 1999 ran Novell Directory Services (NDS), as have all NCPs in the past. However, NCP at COMDEX/Fall 1999 ran NDS 8 on Nodes 1, 2, 3, 4, 5, and 6. Running NDS 8, which can support one billion (or more) objects in a single NDS tree, enabled the team to place User objects for all 300,000 users in one Organizational Unit (OU) object.

Like other NCP users, NCP users at COMDEX/Fall 1999 could use NCP print services. The team ran Novell Distributed Print Services (NDPS) 2.0 on Node 3. NDPS enabled NCP users to print to any one of the eight Hewlett-Packard 4000tn printers available on the show floor. (Each NCP location had two printers.)

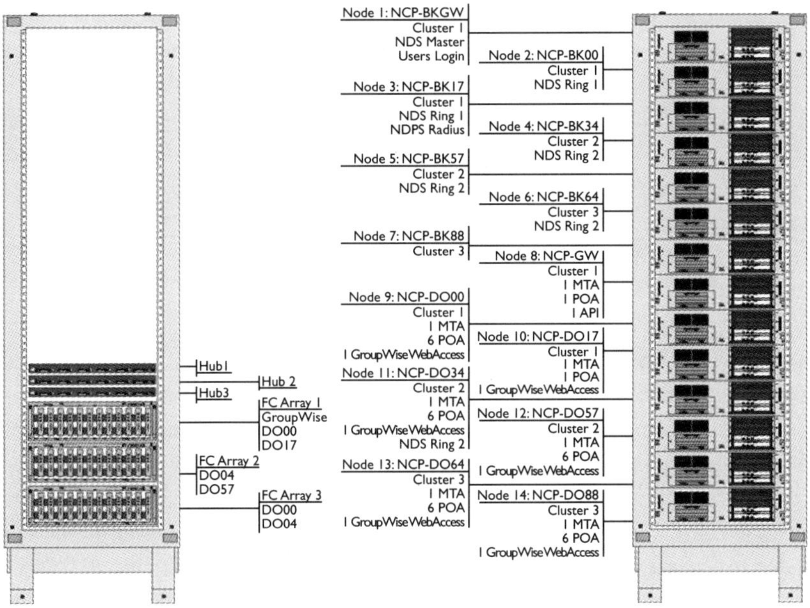

Node 1: NCP-BKGW
Cluster 1
NDS Master
Users Login

Node 2: NCP-BK00
Cluster 1
NDS Ring 1

Node 3: NCP-BK17
Cluster 1
NDS Ring 1
NDPS Radius

Node 4: NCP-BK34
Cluster 2
NDS Ring 2

Node 5: NCP-BK57
Cluster 2
NDS Ring 2

Node 6: NCP-BK64
Cluster 3
NDS Ring 2

Node 7: NCP-BK88
Cluster 3

Node 8: NCP-GW
Cluster 1
1 MTA
1 POA
1 API

Node 9: NCP-DO00
Cluster 1
1 MTA
6 POA
1 GroupWise WebAccess

Node 10: NCP-DO17
Cluster 1
1 MTA
1 POA
1 GroupWise WebAccess

Node 11: NCP-DO34
Cluster 2
1 MTA
6 POA
1 GroupWise WebAccess

Node 12: NCP-DO57
Cluster 2
1 MTA
6 POA
1 GroupWise WebAccess

Node 13: NCP-DO64
Cluster 3
1 MTA
6 POA
1 GroupWise WebAccess

Node 14: NCP-DO88
Cluster 3
1 MTA
6 POA
1 GroupWise WebAccess

NDS Ring 2

Hub 1
Hub 2
Hub 3

FC Array 1
GroupWise
DO00
DO17

FC Array 2
DO04
DO57

FC Array 3
DO00
DO04

FIGURE 21.1 *For NCP at COMDEX/Fall 1999, the Novell Corporate Events Team set up three Novell Cluster Services clusters with a total of 14 nodes. Each cluster was connected to a dedicated storage array via Fibre Channel arbitrated loop (hub).*

Of course, the star of NCP, as always, was GroupWise. For COMDEX/Fall 1999, the team ran GroupWise 5.5 Enhancement Pack on Nodes 8, 9, 10, 11, 12, 13, and 14.

The team ran the GroupWise WebAccess component on Nodes 9 through 14. When users launched Netscape Navigator running on an NCP workstation, the browser opened automatically to the NCP home page. From this page, users could click the GroupWise WebAccess icon to open the WebAccess home page.

By running Novell Cluster Services, the team was able to provide these same services—without interruption—using far fewer servers than NCP implementations have required in the past. Before the team ran Novell Cluster Services, Petersen explains, "we managed to failsafe our system only with hardware-heavy designs." To ensure that NCP services remained available for the duration of a trade show, the team set up "spare servers," which were kept "online, ready to do whatever [the team] needed them to do."

More specifically, the team previously ran system services, processes, and applications on separate servers. For example, the team set up dedicated servers that ran only the data stores, other servers that ran only the GroupWise Message Transport Agent (MTA) and Post Office Agent (POA) NetWare Loadable Modules (NLMs), other servers that ran only the GroupWise WebAccess Gateway, and still other servers that ran only the GroupWise Internet Access (GWIA) Gateway. By using this design, Petersen explains, "if a server running the GroupWise agent NLMs failed, the servers running the data stores would remain up."

In the past, for each dedicated server, the team configured another identical server. Having to set up dedicated servers and identical twin servers created a hardware-heavy system.

With Novell Cluster Services, "there's no need for such redundancy," Petersen says. A Novell Cluster Services node can run several services and applications without the threat of one of them downing the system. If a node fails, Novell Cluster Services detects the failure and begins a failover process: Novell Cluster Services moves the failed node's resources and associated IP addresses to one surviving node or distributes them among several surviving nodes.

Petersen's failover plan centered on the GroupWise system, which comprised a total of seven domains: one primary domain, named NCP-GW, and six user domains, named NCP-DO00, NCP-DO17, NCP-DO34, NCP-DO57, NCP-DO64, and NCP-DO88.

The numbers included in the domain names were arbitrarily generated by a user import utility. This utility divided the number of post offices so that each of the six domains had six post offices, for a total of 36 post offices. The utility then divided the number of user accounts equally among these 36 post offices. Each post office held approximately 7,500 user accounts.

For the NCP clusters at COMDEX/Fall 1999, Petersen configured Novell Cluster Services to move all of a failed node's resources and associated IP addresses to a predetermined surviving node. The resources included the GroupWise agents and gateways within the domain for which the failed node was responsible.

Petersen configured Novell Cluster Services to fail over resources (including the GroupWise agents and gateways) running on Cluster 1, Nodes 8, 9, and 10 to Cluster 1, Nodes 1, 2, and 3. Similarly, Petersen configured Novell Cluster Services to fail over the resources on Cluster 2, Nodes 11 and 12 to Cluster 2, Nodes 4 and 5. Finally, Petersen configured Novell Cluster Services to fail over the resources on Cluster 3, Nodes 13 and 14 to Cluster 3, Nodes 6 and 7.

Finally, Petersen configured Novell Cluster Services so that all nodes had access to the system's data stores, which were stored on cluster-enabled volumes set up on the system arrays. Anything users were working on (and had saved) at the time of a failure would be on the cluster-enabled volumes to which all nodes had access. Consequently, if one node failed, the failover node accessed the data on the cluster-enabled volume and simply picked up where the failed node left off.

During COMDEX/Fall 1999, the team twice witnessed the success of Petersen's failover plan because two of the servers experienced ABENDs during the show. Two ABENDs during a five-day show is a "very low" number of ABENDs, Petersen says. Petersen attributes the low number to the memory patches provided by the WebAccess Enhancement component for the GroupWise 5.5 WebAccess Gateway.

When the two nodes experienced ABENDs, the resources on those nodes failed over as planned. Consequently, team members noticed the ABENDs only later, when they checked the Cluster View screen. Because the Cluster View screen showed that resources from the failed nodes were still running, there was little cause for worry, let alone action. Petersen casually investigated the failed nodes to determine the cause of the ABENDs; he then restored these nodes and returned their resources only at the end of the day, when he had the time to do so.

When ABENDs occurred on back-end servers before NCP ran Novell Cluster Services, the sequence of events that followed was not nearly as simple — and the team's response was not nearly as casual. In the days before Novell Cluster Services, users who were accessing their GroupWise account by way of the WebAccess gateway saw an error message when the server running that gateway ABENDed. "Then they'd turn around and look at us," Petersen begins. "And at that point, I would throw my hands in the air and start trying to figure out what happened."

Determining what happened was a lot more difficult than simply glancing at a cluster status screen displayed on a monitor. Instead, Petersen or another team member would open the console for each of the servers, guessing at the possible failure and its probable cause. After determining which server failed, the team member downed the server immediately, fixed the problem, and restarted the server, all the while knowing users were waiting.

In addition to making server failures inconsequential, Novell Cluster Services helped decrease the time required for the team's nightly maintenance routine. Every night during a show, the team backs up both the e-mail system and the NDS files. In the past, this backup could take anywhere from six to eight hours. At COMDEX/Fall 1999, backing up the e-mail system and the NDS files took only about three hours.

On three of the show's five nights, the team distributed e-mail messages to each of the show's attendees. For example, on the first night — the night of the largest mail distribution — the team distributed five e-mail messages to each of the show's then expected 265,000 attendees in only $1\frac{1}{2}$ hours. At COMDEX/Fall 1998, distributing the same number of messages took more than 5 hours.

Why did the nightly maintenance routine take so much longer in the past? Without Novell Cluster Services, the team did not use SAN storage arrays for GroupWise data stores because the arrays, without Novell's clustering software, offered little more than a large storage area. Instead, the GroupWise data stores were distributed among server volumes throughout the system. As a result, the speed of backups and mail distributions depended on the speed of the network and the speed of the servers running the volumes.

Novell Cluster Services sped things up because it enabled the team to incorporate the SAN storage arrays into the back-end system and to use them in a failover plan. Novell Cluster Services also supported the fibre channel pipe that provided the 1 gigabit-per-second connection between the arrays and the cluster nodes. A fast pipe between the clusters and their arrays meant a fast pipe between source and destination locations for backups and mail distributions.

MobilCom Communicationstechnik GmbH

Over a very short period of time, MobilCom has become the leading telecommunications firm in Germany. MobilCom launched its business in the summer of 1992, marketing cell phone connections as a private service provider. The company soon offered a complete range of fixed network services. Through its introduction of reasonably priced Internet access, MobilCom made telecommunications more practical and easier to use for everyone throughout Germany. As a result, the company now boasts more than 11 million active customers.

As a telecommunications firm, MobilCom required round-the-clock operation. For several years, company management felt the need to reduce network downtime. "There was just nothing out there we could use or the solutions were too expensive," said Thorsten Glodde, Team Leader of Networks and Administration of MobilCom Communicationstechnik GmbH. Then one day, it happened—a server failed due to a hardware defect. Essential LAN services were no longer available, and customer hotline calls could be answered only on a limited basis. "A workstation PC can be quickly replaced and started up, but that's not the case with a server computer. The importance to the LAN and the amount of money and time it costs when you're not prepared for something like this was made crystal clear," adds Glodde. "So we discussed at great length how this single point of failure could be avoided in the future."

Novell's Net services software had already played an impressive role at MobilCom Communicationstechnik GmbH. "We have always used NetWare because it's a system that works efficiently and offers a large amount of uses at a reasonable price," said Glodde. MobilCom had been very pleased with the file-and-print services of NetWare and the efficient, single-location management of Novell Directory Services (NDS) up to that point. "Every week we get a large number of new employees and our structure changes from time to time," said Glodde. "NetWare and NDS have efficiently handled all of these changes."

Based on their favorable experiences with Novell, Glodde and his colleagues began to scrutinize Novell Cluster Services in May of 2000. This server clustering system ensures high availability and manageability of critical network resources including data (volumes), applications, server licenses, and services. With Novell Cluster Services, it is no longer important which server within the cluster handles tasks, nor does it matter if a certain server even stops functioning momentarily due to a hardware defect or maintenance work, because a second server automatically takes over within seconds if the first server should fail. The cluster itself remains available and therefore guarantees continuous and uninterrupted operation.

In August of 2000, MobilCom Communicationstechnik GmbH decided to introduce Novell Cluster Services to ensure 24-hour availability. All 20 NetWare servers, including all active services in Novell Cluster Services 1.01, would be converted and a new Novell cluster with a total of 10 server nodes, based on NetWare 5.1, would be created. "Although fewer servers are required for Novell Cluster Services, in view of our steady growth and the resulting increased demand on the LAN servers, we wanted to be fully equipped. Our cluster is actually larger than what is required, but we want sufficient server reserves for the coming years," says Glodde. "We simply do not want to have to worry about server failures anymore."

Server hardware and software defects are no longer a concern to MobilCom because Novell's solution guarantees uninterrupted and long-term operation of the local network and services.

"We are extremely happy with the Novell cluster," says Glodde. "The local network and its services are available around the clock. Even a serious incident caused by an overloaded fuse had no permanent effect whatsoever on the MobilCom LAN operation."

The company's conversion to ZENworks for Desktops 3 for centralized desktop configuration is underway, along with integrating Novell Cluster Services to take advantage of the high level of availability. MobilCom Communicationstechnik's future goal is to minimize on-site support by remotely managing all PC workstations. This is yet another area in which Novell Cluster Services can reduce downtime, even in unusual circumstances.

Table 21.3 details MobilCom's ten-node cluster and fully redundant dual-path Storage Area Network.

TABLE 21.3

MobilCom Communicationstechnik Ten-Node NetWare Cluster

CONFIGURATION	DETAILS
Nodes	10
Server software	NetWare 5.1 and Novell Cluster Services 1.01
Server hardware	Acer Altos 21000 Server System
Storage Area Network	MetaStor E4400 Enterprise Storage System
Fully redundant dual-path SAN	Fifty-two 36GB hard disks
	(Total: 1.8TB)
	Dual Fibre Channel RAID Controllers
	Dual QLogic QLA2200F/66 per server Fibre Channel Host Bus Adapter
	Dual Gadzoox Capellix 3000 HA Novell Directory Services enabled Fibre Channel Switch
Cluster resources	File
	Print (NDPS)
	DHCP/DNS
	ZENworks for Desktops 3

Tenet Healthcare Corporation

For Tenet Healthcare Corporation, good planning and employee dedication are largely responsible for the company's recent surge of success. Tenet is a nationwide provider of healthcare services. The $11.4 billion company owns or operates 110 acute care hospitals and related businesses through its subsidiaries. Central support services are provided to Tenet's hospitals from its Dallas-based operations center.

Tenet's healthy bottom line has been attributed to both innovation and commitment displayed by employees and managers in carrying out long-term performance initiatives — qualities equally valued by its MIS department. Jeff Lett, Tenet's director of telecommunications and technology, and the staff at the Dallas operations center are dedicated to maintaining an uninterrupted flow of information among the company's 750 computer users. And doing that takes innovative thinking.

A move to new quarters, along with an operating system upgrade to NetWare 5.1, prompted the MIS department to evaluate its network storage capacity. "Before that, we didn't have a storage area network," says Lett. "We relied on individual servers, and were always having to add expensive server storage. We wanted to make our move without interrupting network service."

Tenet runs Novell Cluster Services, which allows combining all four of their Dell PowerEdge servers in a cluster formation for continuous network availability. According to Peter Stadigh, Tenet's LAN administrator, "Our 750 workstations are all linked to the virtual drives that reside on the Storage Area Network, running printing and file applications. Shared NSS volumes and NDPS printing are configured for failover so that even in a multi-node failure, another network servers will automatically take over the resources and services."

Tenet wanted a SAN solution with built-in redundancy for extra assurance of uptime. "We went with the XIOtech MAGNITUDE because it offered the best combination of performance and price," Lett says.

The MAGNITUDE is XIOtech's scalable, multiplatform, centralized storage solution. What sets the MAGNITUDE apart is its ease of operation and expansion, made possible by an exclusive storage virtualization process, which allows a dynamic reallocation of storage space. Virtualization technology eliminates investment in costly server-attached storage to accommodate growth. Virtual storage capacity can be created or expanded in a matter of seconds, without ever going offline.

The bar has never been higher for network uptime and performance. Expectations for continuous data availability and reliability are no longer limited to high-end computing environments. And those standards don't yield to system installation, upgrades, or migration. "Our migration was accomplished without any service outage at all—it was totally seamless to users. Ever since installing Novell Cluster Services and the MAGNITUDE we've maintained 99.999% data availability," Lett recalls. "And with Novell Cluster Services, we can load balance in Active/Active mode (which we can't do with Microsoft) reliably."

Tenet's MIS staff feels certain it made the right choice. Says Stadigh, "The MAGNITUDE has proven to be a reliable and stable SAN solution for Novell Cluster Services. Response time from the MAGNITUDE has always been great. And adding storage is easy and can be easily fit into our monthly maintenance window."

Table 21.4 details Tenet Healthcare's four-node cluster.

TABLE 21.4

Tenet Healthcare Four-Node NetWare Cluster

CONFIGURATION	DETAILS
Nodes	4
Server Software	NetWare 5.1 and Novell Cluster Services 1.01
Server Hardware	Dell PowerEdge
Storage Area Network	XIOtech MAGNITUDE
	(Total: 1.4TB)
Cluster Resources	File
	Print (NDPS)

Summary

This chapter examined several real-world clustered Storage Area Networks running Novell Cluster Services software and other Novell products and services:

- ▸ University of Idaho

- ▸ Frankfurt Airport

- ▸ COMDEX/Fall 1999

- ▸ MobilCom Communicationstechnik GmbH

- ▸ Tenet Healthcare Corporation

As these case studies demonstrate, Novell Cluster Services is a robust and scalable solution ready for use in any size enterprise. High availability and simplified storage management is a requirement in many industry sectors, including those represented by the case studies in this chapter, namely education, transportation, communications and healthcare.

## CHAPTER 22

Troubleshooting Novell Cluster Services

This chapter is designed to help you avoid calling Novell Technical Support for some of the most common problems experienced by Novell customers. The issues discussed in this chapter are based on Novell Consulting's experience in the field, the Novell Technical Support forum for Novell Cluster Services, and many of the support incidents in Novell's Technical Support database.

This chapter is an excellent resource if you are having a problem with your cluster, and an even better resource to read before you implement Novell Cluster Services to help you avoid some of the more common problems you may experience.

In this chapter, you examine various troubleshooting methodologies and solutions to common problems experienced with Novell Cluster Services.

The chapter begins with the most common troubleshooting issues, those with poison pill ABENDs. This includes an in-depth explanation of various issues surrounding poison pill ABENDs, as well as an exploration of tools to help determine the cause of the poison pill ABENDs. The chapter also discusses server parameter settings that can help in avoiding or isolating the problems.

Next, the chapter reviews many of the most common issues that Novell customers have experienced related to Novell Cluster Services. The first of these issues is the comatose resource issue, why it occurs, and how to troubleshoot it.

The chapter also surveys troubleshooting issues related to Novell Cluster Services failing to start. A methodology for troubleshooting startup issues is provided, as are common reasons why Novell Cluster Services may fail to start.

Then you learn about troubleshooting drive-mapping issues, which are broken into two categories — problems with trustees and problems with TCP/IP name resolution. The chapter concludes by explaining how to re-create the cluster services Split Brain Detection partition.

Troubleshooting Poison Pill ABENDs

One of the most frustrating issues to troubleshoot with Novell Cluster Services is random poison pill ABENDs. So before you get into the details of how to troubleshoot these problems, you should first understand the poison pill and why this is such an important *intentional* feature to include with Novell Cluster Services.

X-REF

Split brain conditions and poison pills are discussed in Chapter 4 as well.

A *split brain condition* is a condition in which a single node or group of nodes becomes isolated from other nodes in the cluster. Consider, for example, a case where three nodes are plugged into one switch, while six nodes are plugged into a different switch. If the cross-connect between the two switches were to fail, a split brain condition would then exist where the three nodes thought that the six nodes failed, and the six nodes would believe that the three-node group failed.

If this condition were allowed to continue, the group of three nodes would start activating and mounting the resources that were currently running on the group of six nodes. Meanwhile, the group of six would start activating and mounting the resources that were currently running on the group of three. Because Novell Cluster Services does not support a distributed file lock across the cluster, if two nodes were to simultaneously activate, mount, and write to the same volume, then file system corruption would occur.

TIP

Novell Cluster Services does include a distributed file lock for the Split Brain Detection partition used by the clustering software. It does not support a lock across cluster nodes for user data, so if two servers were allowed to write to the same volume at the same time, there would be no support to prevent file system corruption.

To prevent this file system corruption, Novell Cluster Services uses the Cluster Services partition on the shared storage. Each node is assigned their own scratchpad on this partition, and the nodes perform periodic heartbeats to this scratchpad. In addition to writing to their area, they can read the scratch pad information from all the other nodes. If a cluster node can no longer access the Cluster Services partition, it removes itself from the cluster.

In this three-node/six-node example, suppose both the three-node group and the six-node group still had access to the Cluster Services partition. In that case, they could also see that while the other group is no longer communicating on the LAN, the group is still active in the cluster. This causes the split brain algorithm to force a vote, in which case the group of six nodes wins and the group of three nodes loses. Each node on the losing side then "eats the poison pill," meaning it causes a self-inflected ABEND to remove it from the cluster, and stop all processes on the server.

At first you might question the need for such a dramatic event. Why not just have the servers perform a cluster leave, or even a DOWN command? There are actually many reasons why it is preferable to immediately remove the server. The two most important reasons are as follows:

▸ To allow client reconnections, the services must be migrated very quickly. If a cluster node has 10 services running on it, it might take several minutes to gracefully stop all these services. This would be far too slow for a clean client reconnection.

▸ If a node is being removed from the cluster, there must be some problem with the node. There would be no way to guarantee that the console hasn't already hung, or some processes are hung while others are not. If a partially functioning server were to fail to gracefully leave the cluster, it may still have services writing to the shared storage, which could cause file system corruption.

So although a poison pill decreases the availability of a single node in the cluster, it actually improves overall availability of the actual services by quickly restarting these services on nodes that are not experiencing problems.

Exploring the Heartbeat Process

The first node that joins the cluster automatically becomes the *cluster master node*. Subsequent nodes that join the cluster become *slave nodes*. The slave nodes periodically perform a heartbeat based on the heartbeat parameter configured for the cluster by sending a unicast TCP/IP packet to the master node. The master node periodically performs a heartbeat across the LAN based on the master watchdog parameter by sending a multicast packet to all slave nodes.

Heartbeat parameters are discussed in detail in Chapter 7. Additionally, Chapter 7 discusses the cluster statistical tools that help troubleshoot the heartbeat process.

X-REF

In addition, each node performs a heartbeat across the SAN by periodically (based on one half of the tolerance parameter) increasing a counter value stored in its own section of the cluster services partition. Each node writes in its own space and reads all other nodes' sectors prior to writing its own update.

By default, the master and slave heartbeats take place every second, with a tolerance of eight seconds.

NOTE

The failure detection algorithm is initiated any time a node experiences a continuous failure to heartbeat equal to the tolerance parameter. The master and slave nodes then communicate over the LAN to form a new cluster based on the nodes that win the failure detection algorithm. A new master node is also elected during this phase, although this could be the same node as before the failure.

Because only one node is allowed to control any given cluster resource at a time, any node that fails to perform the heartbeat is removed from the cluster.

LAN Failure or Congestion Issues

A frequently asked question is whether or not a cluster should have a dedicated TCP/IP network for the heartbeat traffic. Because the heartbeat traffic is very light, the heartbeat process itself does not necessitate a dedicated network. Additionally, you may not want a dedicated network for several reasons:

▶ Production LAN card failures will not be noticed if you're using a heartbeat network, so nodes can't be removed when they should.

▶ A heartbeat LAN failure with the production LAN still functioning will cause a poison pill even though the node was actively servicing clients.

▶ The ConsoleOne management workstation needs to have a route to the heartbeat network to manage the cluster.

Because of these and possibly other issues, many clients decide not to implement a heartbeat network. This may be fine, but you need to understand your production network environment and the heartbeat tuning parameters before you can decide if this will work for you. Based on the defaults, if eight seconds of consecutive heartbeat packets are dropped, a node will be removed. If your network is congested, or your VLAN includes multiple switches between the cluster nodes, you may have cases where nodes are removed from the cluster simply because the heartbeats didn't get through your network.

If your network is too congested to support the default settings, you can decide to increase the heartbeat tolerance. If you decide to do this, keep in mind that this might hamper transparent client reconnections. As a general rule, if the client can't reconnect within 60 seconds, it probably won't without performing a new login. You should calculate how long it takes your resources to migrate and determine how much room you have to increase the tolerance. If you can't increase the tolerance sufficiently enough to overcome your LAN congestion, then you must either resolve the LAN congestion or implement a dedicated heartbeat network.

LAN Card Issues

One of the most important things you can do to resolve poison pill issues is to ensure that you are using the latest NetWare support packs, as well as the latest vendor-supplied LAN drivers. In many cases, updating the LAN drivers has been known to resolve poison pill issues.

If you're using the Intel CE100B card, ensure the driver is version 3.29 or later.

TIP

In addition, you should always manually set the LAN card driver to the same speed and duplex as used on your switch and manually set the switch to the proper speed and duplex for your network. Avoid using automatic speed or duplex detection on servers or the switch ports the servers are plugged into. This is even more important if you are mixing hardware vendors — for example, using an Intel NIC with a 3COM switch.

Another LAN card issue deals with the proper implementation of the link indicating counters. In a two-node cluster, Novell Cluster Services watches the following counters to determine if a node is communicating on the LAN:

- ► If using Ethernet:

  - MLID_NUM_GENERIC_COUNTER

  - NUM_GENERIC_MLID_COUNTERS

  - NUM_ETHERNET_SPECIFIC_COUNTERS

  - ETH_TX_ABORT_CARRIER_SENSE

- ► MLID_TOTAL_TX_PACKET_COUNT — This should increment after the heartbeat packet is transmitted.

- ► MLID_TOTAL_TX_OK_BYTE_COUNT_LOW — This should change after the heartbeat packet is transmitted.

- ► MLID_PACKET_TX_MISC_ERROR_COUNT — This is monitored to see if it changes after the heartbeat is transmitted.

In a two-node cluster, Novell Cluster Services needs to determine the proper node to kill in the event the heartbeats are not getting through; it can't just assume that the master node is the good node and kill the slave. It determines which node is good by monitoring the LAN counters and ascertaining which node is actively communicating. If it can't determine which node is good, then it will kill the slave node. Unfortunately, not all LAN drivers actually implement these counters. If the LAN driver doesn't implement the counters, then the master node will always survive, and the slave node will always fail when the heartbeat does not get through.

The logic to detect LAN traffic was added to the Novell Cluster Services 1.01 two-node tiebreaker patch. Without this patch, the master node always wins.

NOTE

Tuning Server Configuration to Avoid Poison Pills

NetWare servers by default are tuned to support 200 to 400 client connections. If you have more connections than the default, then you will want to modify several parameters to help avoid poison pill issues. Some of the parameters you may wish to increase are listed in Table 22.1.

TABLE 22.1

Tuning Parameters to Avoid Poison Pills

PARAMETER	EXPLANATION
Service Processes	If the server does not have enough service processes for all the processes running, performance may degrade to the point that the heartbeat is not performed fast enough.
Packet Receive Buffers	If the server does not have an available packet receive buffer when an incoming packet arrives, the server drops the packet and increments the packet receive buffers until it reaches the maximum. Once at the maximum, it drops packets until it catches up and empties the buffer. By default, dropping eight seconds of consecutive packets would be enough to assume the monitored server is down.
LAN Speed	If the switch is set to 100mb and the server is set to 10mb (or vice versa), sporadic communications occur, which most likely eventually cause a poison pill.
LAN Duplex	If a server is set to full duplex, but the switch is set to half (or vice versa), slow and sporadic communications occur, which most likely eventually cause a poison pill.

In addition to the set parameters, other common issues that may contribute to poison pills include:

- LAN switch delays or drops of multicast/broadcast packets

- Extremely high LAN utilization such as a broadcast or multicast storm

- Unstable LAN drivers

- Using a LAN card on a low-priority interrupt, or on IRQ 2/9

- Software that hogs the CPU

- Nonoptimal placement of the LAN card on the PCI bus

- Misbehaving NIC that transmits but won't receive packets

- Use of any Real Mode drivers

If you are having poison pill problems, systematically go through the above list to eliminate each of these items as a potential cause of the problem. While most of these items are self-explanatory, the next section further discusses the issues related to CPU Hogs.

Diagnosing CPU Hog Issues

As the bulleted list in the previous section mentioned, applications that hog the CPU can contribute to poison pills. This issue deserves further explanation because, unless you make some modifications to your configuration, you will never know the problem is a CPU Hog, or which module is causing the problem. An application is considered a CPU Hog if it fails to voluntarily release the CPU as required. If an application fails to release the CPU for a period longer than the heartbeat tolerance, a poison pill will occur because the cluster was not allowed to perform the required heartbeats. Since the default CPU Hog timeout interval is set to 60 seconds, you would never know that the cause of the ABEND was a specific application hogging the CPU.

To help determine if one of your applications is hogging the CPU too long, adjust the server parameter CPU Hog Timeout Amount to a value less than the heartbeat tolerance parameter. This way, the servers will ABEND with a CPU hog in the problematic module rather than ABENDing due to a poison pill. Once you identify the problematic module, you can determine the best way to resolve the problem.

Due to the single-threaded nature of bindery services, you should also eliminate bindery emulation on all of your cluster nodes. Excessive bindery contexts and use could contribute to a CPU hog issue, but would not point you to a specific module that is causing the problem.

To deal with a CPU hog of another sort, it's highly recommended that you eliminate IPX from your cluster nodes since all resources must be serviced via TCP/IP to allow automatic reconnection. If you cannot eliminate IPX, then you should at least eliminate the use of the IPXRTR module. This module has a tendency to periodically hog the CPU for 10 or more seconds, which normally would not be a major issue, but with a cluster is sufficient to cause false poison pills. We have seen cases where clusters with stability problems were completely resolved by eliminating the use of IPXRTR.

TIP

Using INETCFG **to disable IPX routing does not remove the** IPXRTR **module. Consider placing the** load **and** bind **commands for IPX in the** AUTOEXEC.NCF **instead of using** INETCFG **if you can't eliminate IPX altogether.**

Categorizing the Four Types of Poison Pill Conditions

In general, poison pill conditions fall into one of four categories:

► Fatal SAN errors

► False node failure detections

► Stalled self leave

► Split brain conditions

For each of these categories, the following sections provide some basic troubleshooting ideas.

Fatal SAN Errors

Any cluster node that cannot read or write to the shared storage is essentially useless to the cluster and must be removed. If the node cannot read or write to the split brain detection partition, it will intentionally remove itself by eating one of the following poison pills:

► CLUSTER: Node castout, fatal SAN read error

► CLUSTER: Node castout, fatal SAN write error

► CLUSTER: Node castout, fatal SAN device alert

Each of these ABENDs is caused by a fatal I/O error or device alert, which is signaled by the SAN device driver when invoked by the SBD.NLM module. As with nodes that can't communicate on the LAN, clean shutdowns to misbehaving nodes are problematic, so the node must force itself out of the cluster immediately by eating a poison pill. If you are receiving these fatal SAN errors, start by troubleshooting your hardware and the device drivers. These ABENDs are caused by the device driver passing a fatal error to Novell Cluster Services, which means that you either have a hardware fault or a problem with the driver. Check with the hardware manufacturer for any tools to help you troubleshoot the hardware devices.

Since a fatal SAN error generally signifies an error with the SAN hardware or the SAN driver in the server, when you receive such an error, check the following:

- Are the GBICs properly seated and fully connected to the switch and fibre card?

- Are there any error lights on the switch or fibre card?

- Is the fibre cable compromised? Try replacing with a new cable.

- Is a GBIC the problem? GBICs do go bad. Try switching with a different node if a spare GBIC is not available.

- Is a fibre switch port the problem? Fibre switch ports can go bad as well. Try switching to a different port.

- Are the laser light components working properly? Try cleaning the laser light components.

- Are there any version issues? Verify that the SAN devices and drivers are certified for the version of NetWare.

Your hardware vendor should be able to provide vendor-specific SAN diagnostics (based on the model of hardware). You might also need to disable the BIOS on the fibre channel card if you are not booting from the SAN, or enable the BIOS if you are.

In some cases, the fibre channel card tries to use High Memory, which causes major instability. Increasing the FILES and/or BUFFERS statements in the CONFIG.SYS beyond 100 to 150 prevents the cards from doing this and stabilizes the system.

Another common error with SAN implementations is a failure to match the fibre channel HBA to the SAN topology. Many vendors have generic cards that work for PPP, FC-AL, and Fabric SAN implementations. In these cases, you may have a jumper or BIOS setting to tell the card the proper SAN topology. In other cases, the hardware vendor requires different cards to match the topology. In this case, you can't use a PPP card if your server is attached to a fabric switch.

Storage Area Network topologies are discussed in Chapter 2.

X-REF

Check with your hardware vendor to make sure you have the right card and the right configuration settings for the topology you have implemented.

False Node Failure Detection

False node failure detection is different than a split brain condition in that the cluster thinks the node is dead due to a lack of heartbeat packets when, in fact, the node is alive. In a classical split brain condition, each side of the split brain thinks that the other side has failed and that it needs to start the other side's resources. In a false split brain condition, one side believes the other side has failed, while the other side thinks everything is fine. There are two categories of false node failure detection:

▶ The node goes to sleep for a period of time, the cluster removes it, and then it wakes up thinking it's still in the cluster (sleepy node syndrome).

▶ The cluster thinks the node is dead, while the node still sees the cluster (divergent view syndrome).

Sleepy Node Syndrome We currently know of two circumstances where a node can appear to have failed, not perform its required ABEND, and then appear to come back to life. You should be aware of these situations and be sure to avoid them. Because other nodes take over the resources from the node that appeared to fail, if the node comes back to life and continues on, file system corruption will likely occur because the node believes it is still a member of the previous cluster and has no reason to believe it doesn't still own the resources it had prior to going to sleep. (Actually, the node continues on as before until the next time it heartbeats to the shared storage, four seconds by default, at which time the node will realize that it was given a poison pill and ABEND itself.) However, since there is potential for data corruption (by this node writing to a volume that is mounted elsewhere), the two known causes of this occurring should be avoided.

The first case of a "sleepy node" occurs when a node enters and stays in real mode for a period of time equal to or greater than the heartbeat threshold parameter. Because the NetWare floppy disk driver can execute in real mode longer than the threshold period, avoid using the floppy drive from a cluster node. If you must use the floppy disk, copy any NLMs from the floppy to the server, and then run them from the server. Loading a module directly from a floppy has a very good chance of leaving the server in Real Mode too long to answer the heartbeats and will likely cause a false node failure detection issue.

The second case occurs when an administrator suspends a node by bringing it into the system kernel debugger, and then restarts the node after the threshold parameter has passed. If you need to use the kernel debugger, use the cluster console command CLUSTER DEBUG, which halts all nodes. Or use the HTML-based NetWare Management Portal and its nonintrusive debugging tools. If you switch to the system kernel debugger, make sure you either leave the cluster first, with the CLUSTER LEAVE command, or execute the Quit (Q) command to exit to DOS.

Divergent View Syndrome   The second category of false node failure detection is the case where the cluster doesn't see the node's heartbeat, but the node does see the rest of the cluster. This can be caused when the node's LAN transmit is not functioning, but the receive is. Similar issues could arise if the master's multicasts can't get through a switch, but the slave's unicast packets can (this would result in the slaves thinking the master is dead, while it sees all of the slaves as alive).

This situation typically results in an ABEND like "Ate poison pill in *xxx* given by some other node," where *xxx* may vary depending on the specifics of the communications issue. For example:

```
Ate poison pill in sbdWriteNodeTick given by some other node
```

For this situation, consider the following potential solutions:

- ▸ Replace the misbehaving node's NIC.
- ▸ Replace the misbehaving node's LAN cable.
- ▸ Verify that spanning tree is not interfering in the communications.
- ▸ Use a protocol analyzer to help pinpoint the communications issue.

Stalled Self-Leave
When a node voluntarily leaves the cluster, either from the DOWN command or the CLUSTER LEAVE command, it attempts to gracefully shut down all of its resources so that other nodes can begin servicing them. Even though this node is

leaving the cluster, there is still potential for file system corruption if some event were to occur that caused another node to start resources before this server actually released them.

Because of this, the node monitors the resources as they shut down, and if a problem is detected that appears to prevent the graceful shutdown, the node administers one of several stalled self-leave ABENDs. These ABENDs are preferable to having a server that hangs during the leave process that never finishes, and resources that never start on other nodes. Once again, reducing availability of this single server actually increases availability of the resources running in your cluster.

To troubleshoot stalled self-leaves, you must determine what caused the server to hang during the leave process. Many times these are due to errors with the unload scripts and can be diagnosed by watching the server console during the unload/leave process and analyzing the system console log.

Other troubleshooting tips for stalled self-leaves include the following:

▸ Check the cluster resource event log to determine the most recent resource status.

▸ Cross-check the resource's unload script commands with the server console log and verify that the commands executed properly.

▸ Check the server console log for the last commands executed before the stall/ABEND and see if that points you toward the cause. Is this always the same command? You should make sure that the CONLOG.NLM is loaded in the AUTOEXEC.NCF file and never unloaded so that you have a complete console log.

▸ Identify the resource that caused the stall and offline that resource. Does this produce any errors? Did it take an excessive amount of time to shut down? Did it execute in the wrong order — for example, did you dismount the volume before the application shut down, so that the application is trying to write to a nonexistent volume?

Split Brain Conditions

Split brain conditions generally occur as a result of LAN hardware or software problems. Recall that a split brain is a condition where not all of the nodes agree on what the cluster membership is; there is a split in agreement on the view of the cluster membership, with each side of the split thinking that the other side failed.

WARNING **If you ever have a split brain condition without the SBD.NLM loaded, you will not have a poison pill ABEND, and you are sure to have data corruption to follow. Never selectively unload any Novell Cluster Services module—use the ULDNCS.NCF command to stop clustering, or you may defeat the failsafe features. Additionally, if you install Novell Cluster Services without shared storage, the SBD module will not be included. If you later add shared storage, you must add the SBD support and create the SBD Partition.**

To troubleshoot split brain conditions, review the following:

▸ Check on the server's LAN driver and protocol stack statistics with the LSLSTAT command. Look for excessive NO ECB Available, as well as any type of packet errors.

▸ Check all of the connectivity devices between the cluster nodes.

- Are the cables properly seated and connected?

- Are all the hubs powered on?

- Did an administrator change the configuration of a switch, which required the switch to shut down and restart?

▸ Check the LAN switch for settings that can delay packets.

- Is the switch port manually set for speed and duplex?

- Does the switch port configuration match the settings on the server's driver?

- Is PortFast/spanning tree configured properly for your environment?

- Did spanning tree reset all bridge ports and cause packet delay?

▸ Check to make sure the server has sufficient resources to communicate on the LAN.

- Are packet receive buffers at their maximum? If so, increase the maximum.

- Are service processes at their maximum? If so, increase the maximum.

TIP

Just as dual-paths to the Storage Area Network provide additional fault tolerance for the server to attach to the storage, NIC teaming provides fault tolerance for the server's connection to the LAN. Using NIC teaming can help prevent split-brain conditions. Many third-party hardware vendors have NIC teaming support, and NetWare 6 is expected to include this natively.

In addition to the above configuration issues, also check and resolve any LAN connectivity issues. Use the appropriate diagnostic tools for your LAN (sniffer, probes, and so on) to determine if your LAN is causing delays due to congestion, misbehaving hosts, or so forth.

You can also try increasing the cluster tolerance and slave watchdog parameters, which cause the servers to be more tolerant of delayed packets. However, keep in mind that increasing these too much may negatively affect automatic client reconnection.

If you can't diagnose or resolve any of these potential issues, consider implementing a dedicated heartbeat network to isolate the heartbeat traffic. You might simply have too much on the production LAN for the heartbeat to function efficiently.

NetWare 5.1 includes a new diagnostic tool that can help you troubleshoot LAN errors at the LSL layer. This tool produces an LSL Statistics Monitor screen, as shown in Figure 22.1, that can help you determine if you are having issues with dropped packets due to Event Control Block issues.

FIGURE 22.1 *LSL Statistics Monitor*

Categorizing Various Poison Pill ABENDs

Table 22.2 lists some of the more common poison pill ABENDs, what category they fall into, and an explanation of what happens with them.

TABLE 22.2

Common Poison Pill ABENDs

ABEND	CATEGORY	EXPLANATION
CLUSTER: Node castout, fatal SAN read error	Fatal SAN error	The SAN device driver detects a fatal (nonrecoverable) error while reading from the shared storage.
CLUSTER: Node castout, fatal SAN write error	Fatal SAN error	The SAN device driver detects a fatal (nonrecoverable) error while writing to the shared storage.
CLUSTER: Node castout, fatal SAN device alert	Fatal SAN error	The SAN device driver detects a fatal (nonrecoverable) error while communicating or attempting to communicate with a shared storage device.
Ate poison pill in sbdProposeView given by some other node	False Node Failure Detection	Communications issues cause a divergent view between this node and the cluster.
Ate poison pill in sbdWriteNodeTick given by some other node	False Node Failure Detection	Communications issues cause a divergent view between this node and the cluster.
Ate poison pill. Link is down. Other node is alive and ticking.	Split Brain Condition	This is a two-node cluster condition where the LAN counters are are incrementing on the other node, but aren't incrementing on this node. This indicates a LAN card or driver failure.
This node is in the Minority partition and the node in the Majority partition is alive.	Split Brain Condition	This is a split brain condition where this server is on the losing side of the vote. All nodes in the minority eat the poison pill.

ABEND	CATEGORY	EXPLANATION
At least one of the nodes is alive in the old master's node partition. This node is not in the old master's node partition.	Split Brain Condition	This is a split brain condition where there is a tie. In the case of a tie, the side with the master node wins, and this server is in the side that does not contain the master node.
The alive partition with the highest node members should survive. This node is not in the alive partition with highest node number.	Split Brain Condition	This is a split brain condition where the master node is not available because it left the cluster or failed. The side that contains the most nodes wins, and this server is not on that side.
This cluster node failed to process its self-leave event in a timely fashion and will be forced out of the cluster.	Stalled self-leave	The node tries to leave the cluster, but for some reason stalls. Because it does not leave cleanly, it is impossible to guarantee that the resources are safe to start on new nodes, so the node must kill itself to safely start the resources elsewhere in the cluster.
CRM: CRMSelfLeave: Some resources went in comatose state while SelfLeave.	Stalled self-leave	This situation is similar to the previous one, except that a failure is detected while running a resource unload script. Again, it isn't safe to assume this node cleanly stopped the resources, so it removes itself via an ABEND to allow the clean start of resources on another node.

Troubleshooting Comatose Resources

A resource goes into the comatose state when it encounters an error during a load or unload script execution, or when the scripts do not complete within the load or unload script timeout parameter.

Comatose issues are almost always caused by one of the following two reasons:

- Error/typo in the load/unload script
- Administrator's manual intervention interfered in the cluster

Troubleshooting Errors/Typos in the Script

An error or typo in the load or unload script is the number one cause of comatose resources. Common typos to look for include:

- Misspelled volume name
- An IP address is already in use somewhere
- Commands with prerequisites in the wrong order — dependent module or volume was not available for a command to complete

The best way to determine the cause is to watch the server console screen while you online or offline the resource. Watch for any error messages or warnings on the screen; these will most likely reveal the cause of the error.

Troubleshooting Administrators Intervention

The second most common cause for comatose resources is an administrator's manually starting or stopping cluster resources without using ConsoleOne. For example, if one administrator moves a resource from one node to another by manually typing the commands at the server console, the next time a different administrator tries to use ConsoleOne to manage the resource, or the next time a server fails and causes a migration, the resource will go comatose because the volume and/or IP address is active elsewhere in the cluster.

Always use ConsoleOne to manage your resources. Never manage manually at the server console!

TIP

Again, the best way to troubleshoot this is to look at the server console screen for error messages.

Corrupting the File System with Duplicate Volume Names

Another potential cause of comatose resources is duplicating the shared volume names locally. For example, say you have a shared volume named VOL1 in your SAN. If one of your cluster nodes also has a local volume named VOL1, and the shared volume is moved to or from this volume, file system corruption will likely occur. The one server with the local volume will see this as a volume with multiple segments. However, the other servers that don't have this volume (or worse yet, also have local volumes with the same name) will encounter problems when you try to access files written to the volume.

This issue may or may not cause comatose problems when the cluster resource is migrated or brought online. More often, you simply have data corruption issues, as users try to access files that just don't exist on the shared volume.

Unfortunately, recovering from this event requires deleting the volume and restoring from your last good backup. The best advice here is to have only SYS volumes locally on your servers; do not store any data other than the NetWare Operating System locally on any cluster node.

Problems with Resource Names Beginning with a Number

Never name a cluster resource with a number as the first character. One of two things will occur:

- ▸ The resource will never leave the NDS Sync resource state.
- ▸ The resource will go comatose and never actually start.

When the resource never leaves the NDS Sync state, you will see continuous error messages on the server console screen, as in Figure 22.2.

As an interesting test, create a resource with the same name as another cluster resource, but put a number in front of the name. For example, create a real cluster resource named DNS, and then create another resource named 2DNS. You will see both resources go comatose, and you won't be able to online or offline the DNS resource until you delete the 2DNS resource object.

There isn't much troubleshooting to do here; just don't name your cluster resources (including cluster-enabled volumes) with a number as the first character.

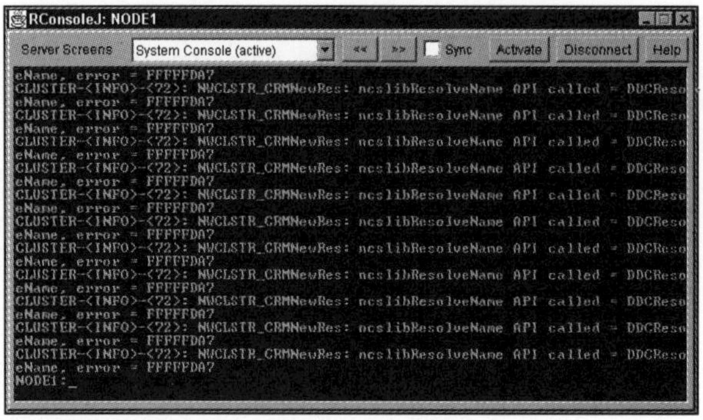

FIGURE 22.2 *CLUSTER-<INFO>-<72> error*

Troubleshooting Failures to Start Novell Cluster Services

Sometimes you might try to start your cluster and for any number of reasons the cluster will not start. Usually what you see on the screen after the LDNCS.NCF file loads is a series of public symbol errors. This is because the module that usually prevents cluster services from starting is first in the load order (CLSTRLIB.NLM), and if it fails to load, all other modules fail to load due to missing public symbols contained in the CLSTRLIB module.

To troubleshoot cluster startup failures, first make sure that the NDS and Time Synchronization are functioning properly. Follow TID 10060600 to perform an NDS Health Check, and verify that Time is in synchronization.

Next, manually load the files contained in LDNCS.NCF in the following order:

- CLSTRLIB
- SBDLIB
- VLL
- GIPC
- SBD
- CRM

- ► `TRUSTMIG`

- ► `CMA`

- ► `CMON`

- ► `CVSBIND` (optional)

Watch the server console screen as you load each module and see if you can determine the cause of the error based on the console messages. Three common startup problems are listed in Table 22.3.

T A B L E 22.3

Common Failures in Loading Novell Cluster Services

ERROR	CAUSE	REMEDY
`CLSTRLIB FFFFFDA5`	Missing NDS property	One of the cluster nodes has lost its association with the cluster container. Go to each server object in ConsoleOne, and select the Other properties tab. Verify that the `NCS:NetWare Cluster` property is associated with the cluster container. You may have to click the Add button to see this property.
`CLSTRLIB <FATAL>-<51> NcslibResolveName failed`	NDS corruption	Attempt to repair the NDS corruption (may need to call Novell Technical Support).
	Excessive NICs or bindings	Remove multiple bindings and simplify the networking configuration, or apply the latest NetWare support pack, which resolves this issue.
`CLUSTER-<INFO>-<2090>: Join retry, some other node acquired the cluster lock`	LAN communications	Check all LAN hardware, drivers, and so on.
	SBD partition corruption	Do a `SBD VIEW ALL` from the master node to look for clues.
		Rebuild the SBD partition.

Also, Novell Cluster Services currently limits the load and unload scripts to a maximum of 600 characters (including spaces). However, the interface does not warn you if you exceed this number of characters. When you exceed 600 characters on any resource, you receive a continuous stream of errors on the master node, as shown in Figure 22.3.

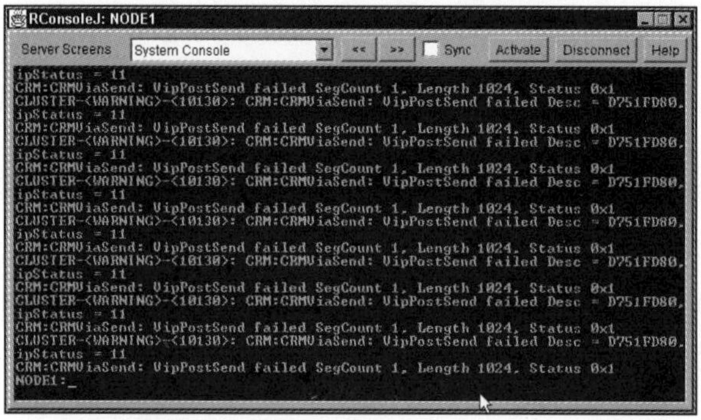

FIGURE 22.3 *Load/unload script overflow error*

To resolve this error, reduce the number of characters in the load/unload scripts. You can call NCF files from the load or unload scripts, so if you need very long scripts, put them in an NCF file and call the NCF file from the scripts. If you take this action, however, be sure to place the NCF file on the shared storage so that you don't have multiple files to maintain.

Troubleshooting Drive-Mapping Issues

Another common problem that requires troubleshooting is the inability to map drives to cluster-enabled volumes. The two most common issues are:

- Loss of file system trustees
- TCP/IP name resolution

Troubleshooting Trustee Issues

Each server tracks file system trustees based on the Object ID of the trustee. With NetWare 5.*x*, each server has its own view of Object IDs; any given NDS object will have a different Object ID depending on which server refers to this object. Because Object IDs are server-centric, when you move a volume from one server to another, Novell Cluster Services must adjust the Object IDs of the trustees based on the new server's prospective. To achieve this, Novell uses the TRUSTMIG.NLM module.

NOTE

NetWare 6 will use globally unique Object IDs, so it will no longer need to use TRUSTMIG.NLM.

TRUSTMIG.NLM does a good job accounting for and updating file system trustees. However, there may be times when something occurs to cause trustee errors. Some of the more common problems include the following:

▶ An administrator manually moves a volume to another server without using the TRUSTMIG utility.

▶ A server fails in the middle of a trustee migration process.

▶ A trustee is updated while TRUSTMIG is not watching the volume.

▶ An NDS object that has file system trustee assignments is deleted or moved while TRUSTMIG is not watching a volume (perhaps because the volume resource was offline) but the volume was mounted.

▶ NSS corruption occurs on the volume.

▶ An administrator has removed the TRUSTMIG command or the WATCH parameter from the load script.

Exploring What TRUSTMIG Does

To help troubleshoot trustee issues, it is first useful to discuss what TRUSTMIG.NLM does in a cluster. NetWare stores file system trustees in the metadata of the NSS volumes as a 4-byte Trustee ID (TID). These IDs are then resolved back to NDS objects based on the Entry ID table stored in the SYS:_NETWARE directory of the server. Each server has its own Entry ID table, which is different from one server to the next.

When a volume is moved from one server to another, the TIDs in the metadata are not valid for the new server. TRUSTMIG resolves this issue by keeping a

TRUSTMIG.FIL file in a hidden _NETWARE directory on each shared volume that it is configured to watch. The header record in this TRUSTMIG.FIL has a marker that tells it which cluster node the file is currently valid on. It also contains a state marker, which tells the server the current migration status (this is used to recover from a crashed migration). Finally, it contains a list of all the Distinguished Names (DNs) of trustees on this volume, along with the trustee assignment.

When a volume is mounted on a new server, TRUSTMIG goes through a routine to translate all of the DNs to the new server's TIDs. This process first produces temporary TIDs, then produces the actual TIDs, thus giving it the ability to recover even if the server were to crash in the middle of a migration.

Recovering from a Partially Migrated Volume

Any time a volume crashes in the middle of a trustee migration, Novell Cluster Services forces you to bring that volume back to the previous host server where the trustees were valid. This is necessary only when a node fails in the middle of the trustee migration process, which can happen only when a volume load script is being run on a node and that node fails — for example, a volume fails over from one node to another, and then the second node also fails. You have to fix the trustees with the volume on either the first or second node, not any other node.

The problem happens only with a double node fault — that is, one node fails, the second node runs TRUSTMIG, and then it, too, fails. The volume has to be restored on node 1 or node 2. If this does happen, you will see an error on the console of the node you are attempting to mount the volume on that is similar to the following:

```
CLUSTER-<FATAL>-<18008>: You can't go to another node. Go back to either
NODE1 or NODE2
```

It's extremely rare to get a double node failure and, furthermore, rarer still that the second failure happens right in the middle of TRUSTMIG. But Cluster Services is designed to deal with this kind of double-node failure; you simply move the volume back to the first node, and then take the following steps:

1. Offline the cluster resource.

2. Run the TRUSTOOL utility to finish the partial migration back to the previous host server. This allows the migration to finish if run on the server where the volume was being moved to, or it will back out of the migration if run on the server that hosted the volume prior to the failure. If it is run on a server other than the two just listed, the tool tells the administrator which server it must be run from. To do this, execute the following command:

```
TRUSTOOL <VOLUME> FIX
```

TIP

TRUSTOOL FIX **deactivates the volume if it isn't already deactivated. You should make sure to offline the resource before performing this action.**

3. Activate and mount the volume.

4. Create a Trustool dump file by executing the following command:

TRUSTOOL <VOLUME> DUMP

This command echoes all DNs and their migration status to the server console screen, as well as to a file, SYS:ETC\TRUSTDMP.TXT.

5. Use the above text file to verify that the trustees are correct. You can also use NetWare Administrator, ConsoleOne, or Windows Explorer to validate trustees, but at this point you must manually connect to the volume through the server that has it mounted since you haven't yet onlined the cluster-enabled volume.

6. If necessary, adjust any missing trustees.

7. Purge any bad trustees. The purging process deletes any bad DNs in the TRUSTMIG.FIL file. First it creates the TRUSTMIG.BAK file; then it re-creates the TRUSTMIG.FIL after purging the bad DNs. Bad DNs occur whenever you delete an NDS object without first removing their file system trustee assignment, or when NDS doesn't synchronize quickly enough after new users with trustee assignments are created in the tree. To purge the bad trustees, execute the following command:

TRUSTOOL <VOLUME> PURGE

8. Create a new Trustool dump file by executing the following command:

TRUSTOOL <VOLUME> DUMP

9. Use the above text file to verify that the trustees are correct.

10. Dismount and deactivate the volume.

11. Online the volume using ConsoleOne.

12. Verify once again that the trustees are correct.

13. Migrate the volume to the server that you wish it to run on.

14. Run a TRUSTOOL DUMP on the new server, and compare the dump files to the good file you created in step 8.

Covering Yourself in Case of Catastrophic Trustee Loss

Although the TRUSTMIG and TRUSTOOL utilities provide a great deal of protection and recovery in the event of trustee loss, you should still back up your trustees periodically just in case you have a serious volume error that prevents TRUSTOOL from recovering your trustees. Since these utilities rely on the TRUSTMIG.FIL file, any serious error that corrupts this file can cause irreversible loss of trustees.

Novell has an unsupported utility, TBACKUP.EXE, found at http://support.novell.com/misc/patlst.htm#tools, which you can use to periodically back up your trustees. Many third-party companies also have tools that can back up your trustees, including the DreamLAN-supported utility FSTRUST by DreamLAN Network Consulting Ltd., found at http://www.dreamlan.com/main.htm.

TIP

Your backup software probably backs up trustees for you, so you may think this recommendation isn't worthwhile. You should be aware that the backup program is subject to the same object ID problems that cause us to use TRUSTMIG in the first place — the backup may only correctly restore trustees if the volume is mounted on the same server that it was on when backed up. Using another utility that creates an NDS-object-based backup such as TBACKUP or FSTRUST is an excellent way to protect yourself from the server-centric Object ID issue with trustees.

Periodically back up your trustees using your preferred method at intervals based on how often you change file system trustees. If you have a lot of file system trustee activity, you might consider backing up your trustees weekly or even daily. For less active sites, consider doing this monthly.

Understanding the Importance of TCP/IP Name Resolution

Novell Cluster Services requires NetWare 5.x servers and TCP/IP-based connections. This is easy enough to understand, but you may not understand the ramifications if you are not already familiar with accessing resources in an IP-based world.

With IPX, there is rarely a problem finding resources — you ask for a list, and there everything is! With TCP/IP, this may not be the case. With IPX, every server and every router automatically tells the world about everything it knows. TCP/IP does not take this active an approach to advertising resources, so you don't necessarily see everything on the network, even if it is properly configured.

Figure 22.4 shows the Novell Client's Protocol Preferences tab. This section briefly discusses each of the resolution methods shown on this tab and how they each relate to finding Novell Cluster Services resources.

FIGURE 22.4 *Novell Client Protocol Preferences tab*

NDS

NDS is a valid name resolution protocol that resolves names to IP and/or IPX addresses. However, when using NDS as a name resolution protocol, you must remember to consider context in the resolution process. Suppose you want to resolve the virtual server GW1_SERVER.CONTEXT using NDS. If your current context is USERS.CONTEXT, and you tried to resolve GW1_SERVER, would you be successful? No, you wouldn't! This is a common sticking point in using NDS for short name resolution; it relies on the current context being the same as the context of the resource.

More commonly, you use NDS to resolve an NDS volume object. In the GW1 example, assume you wish to map your M: drive to the cluster-enabled GW1 volume. If your NDS volume object is CLUSTER_GW1, and it is in the CONTEXT container, you can issue the following MAP command:

```
MAP M: = .CLUSTER_GW1.CONTEXT:\
```

Mapping drives to the NDS volume object is the preferred method with Novell Cluster Services. Using this method provides the best automatic client reconnection performance.

HOSTS Files

The next available IP name resolution method is the HOSTS (or NWHOST) file. For Windows 9x clients, create a NWHOST file in the \NOVELL\CLIENT32 directory with your TCP/IP name–to–IP address mappings. For Windows NT or Windows 2000, use the standard HOSTS file in \WINNT\SYSTEM32\DRIVERS\ETC for these mappings. Using HOSTS files at client workstations is tedious and difficult to maintain on all users' workstations and, therefore, is not the preferred method for TCP/IP name resolution (except perhaps for the administrator's workstation).

If you decide to maintain HOSTS files for users, you can use Novell's ZENworks to easily distribute the updated files.

TIP

NetWare servers can also use a HOSTS file for IP name resolution. Whenever you cluster enable a volume, it is a good practice to add the virtual NCP server to the HOSTS file of all servers in the cluster, thus allowing the servers to resolve virtual server names to IP addresses. Modify the SYS:ETC\ HOSTS file by adding each virtual server in your cluster, as shown in Figure 22.5.

```
hosts - Notepad
File  Edit  Format  Help
10.7.5.51    NODE1.CLUSTER.NOVELL.COM    NODE1
10.7.5.52    NODE2.CLUSTER.NOVELL.COM    NODE2
10.7.5.53    NODE3.CLUSTER.NOVELL.COM    NODE3

10.7.5.101   CLUSTER_PUB_SERVER.CLUSTER.NOVELL.COM    CLUSTER_PUB_SERVER
10.7.5.102   CLUSTER_APPS_SERVER.CLUSTER.NOVELL.COM   CLUSTER_APPS_SERVER
10.7.5.103   CLUSTER_USERS_SERVER.CLUSTER.NOVELL.COM  CLUSTER_USERS_SERVER

10.7.5.105   CLUSTER_NDPS_SERVER.CLUSTER.NOVELL.COM   CLUSTER_NDPS_SERVER
10.7.5.106   CLUSTER_GW1_SERVER.CLUSTER.NOVELL.COM    CLUSTER_GW1_SERVER
10.7.5.108   CLUSTER_GW3_SERVER.CLUSTER.NOVELL.COM    CLUSTER_GW3_SERVER
10.7.5.109   CLUSTER_GW4_SERVER.CLUSTER.NOVELL.COM    CLUSTER_GW4_SERVER
10.7.5.110   CLUSTER_GW5_SERVER.CLUSTER.NOVELL.COM    CLUSTER_GW5_SERVER
10.7.5.111   CLUSTER_GW6_SERVER.CLUSTER.NOVELL.COM    CLUSTER_GW6_SERVER
10.7.5.112   CLUSTER_GWGWIA_SERVER.CLUSTER.NOVELL.COM CLUSTER_GWGWIA_SERVER
10.7.5.113   CLUSTER_GWWEB_SERVER.CLUSTER.NOVELL.COM  CLUSTER_GWWEB_SERVER
```

FIGURE 22.5 *Sample HOSTS file*

DNS

Perhaps the most common IP name resolution option is Domain Name Service (DNS). As it was with the HOSTS file, it is a good practice to place all of your virtual servers into DNS, as well as any cluster resources that users connect to using a name, thus allowing the server to use DNS to resolve virtual server names to IP addresses.

However, placing virtual servers in DNS requires that your DNS server support the underscore (_) character, which may or may not be the case.

NOTE **The next version of Novell Cluster Services will allow you to name your virtual servers however you want, so you will be able to avoid this issue.**

Also note that the DNS entry does not need to match the actual resource. For example, you can put `CLUSTER-PUB` in DNS using the TCP/IP address of the `CLUSTER_PUB_SERVER` virtual server. Clients can then map drives using the DNS name.

For short name resolution to work using DNS, the client workstation must either belong to the same DNS zone as the resource, or the resource zone must be configured in the client's DNS suffix search path.

With the virtual servers configured in DNS, the clients can use DNS to map drives using UNC paths. For example:

```
MAP F: = \\CLUSTER_PUB_SERVER.CLUSTER.COM\PUB\PUBLIC
```

Or, assuming the client's DNS zone is the same as the resource:

```
MAP F: = \\CLUSTER_PUB_SERVER\PUB\PUBLIC
```

Or, with the example mentioned earlier in this section where the DNS entry doesn't match the resource (in this case, the DNS entry is configured with a host name of `CLUSTER-PUB.CLUSTER.COM`):

```
MAP F: = \\CLUSTER-PUB.CLUSTER.COM\PUB\PUBLIC
```

DNS is the most common TCP/IP name resolution protocol, which makes this method vital to resolving virtual server names as well as physical server names.

SLP

NetWare 5.x uses the IETF standard Service Location Protocol (RFC 2165) to advertise service information across TCP/IP-based networks. SLP does for a TCP/IP network what SAP does for an IPX network, thus providing short name resolution of TCP/IP-based resources within your network.

Novell Cluster Services versions 1.0 and 1.01 do not propagate virtual server information into SLP by default (the next version of clustering will automatically add this support).

If you wish to propagate virtual server information to SLP, download the `CVSBIND` utility (`http://support.novell.com/cgi-bin/search/searchtid.cgi?/`

2957434.htm). After installing the utility according to the included directions, you add the following command to your cluster load scripts:

```
CVSBIND ADD <NAME> <IP ADDRESS>
```

where `<NAME>` represents the name of the virtual server and `<IP ADDRESS>` is the address of this virtual server. This command adds the virtual server into the `bindery.novell` SLP service within your existing SLP infrastructure.

To your unload scripts, add the following command:

```
CVSBIND DEL <NAME> <IP ADDRESS>
```

The primary advantage of using CVSBIND is that it gives you TCP/IP short name resolution regardless of a user's context or DNS zone. This allows UNC paths to be valid using only the short names of the virtual server.

It's strongly recommended that you use CVSBIND for all of your cluster-enabled volumes, because TCP/IP name resolution to your virtual server(s) is critical for any connections to these virtual servers, and CVSBIND gives you short-name resolution without regard to context or DNS zone.

Based on these name resolution options, the simplest method to guarantee short name resolution is using CVSBIND and SLP. However, from a fault-tolerance perspective, the more functioning name resolution methods you have available, the greater your ability to resolve names to IP addresses.

DHCP NDS

This option is not actually a name resolution method, but enabling it tells the client to utilize DHCP to receive SLP information including the SLP Directory Agent, SLP Scope(s), and Compatibility Mode Migration Agents.

Determining If You Have a Name Resolution Issue

If you cannot connect to a cluster resource by using its name, try connecting using the secondary IP address. If you can connect via IP address, but not by name, then you have a name resolution issue.

Re-creating the Split Brain Partition

Occasionally, it may be necessary to re-create the split brain partition (SBD or cluster services partition). A corrupt SBD is generally indicative of problems with the hardware/fibre channel devices and can be corrected without your having to reinstall Novell Cluster Services. Since cluster-specific information is stored in the

SBD, recreating the SBD involves executing a process on *one* of the cluster nodes. This process will work as long as the cluster name does not change.

The following commands are used to re-create the split brain partition:

1. Unload Novell Cluster Services if it is already loaded.

    a. Make sure all resources are offline.

    b. Enter CLUSTER DOWN on the console of one of the cluster nodes.

    c. Enter ULDNCS on the console of each of the cluster nodes.

2. Load CLSTRLIB.

3. Load VLL.

4. Load SBD.

5. Enter the following command:

    SBD INSTALL

6. Follow the prompts to create the partition and mirror the partition (if desired).

Summary

This chapter is a good resource to help you avoid running into some of the more common issues with Novell Cluster Services, as well as to help you recover from these issues should you encounter them. It provided a good set of tools to help you avoid a call to Novell Technical Support should you encounter problems with your cluster. Keep in mind that you can access the Novell Technical Support forum using a NNTP-enabled newsreader at support-forums.novell.com and subscribing to the novell.support.high-availablity.cluster-services forum, or by visiting the knowledge base at http://support.novell.com.

In this chapter, you learned various troubleshooting methodologies and solutions to common problems experienced with Novell Cluster Services.

You learned how to troubleshoot the most common issues, issues with poison pill ABENDs. This included an in-depth explanation of various issues surrounding poison pill ABENDs, as well as tools to help determine the cause of the poison pill ABENDs. The chapter also discussed server parameter settings that can help you avoid or isolate these kinds of problems.

The chapter delved into the four categories of poison pills, the qualities of each category, as well as specific troubleshooting techniques to resolve each type of ABEND.

You looked at many of the most common issues that Novell customers have experienced related to Novell Cluster Services. The first of these is the comatose resource issue; the chapter explored why it occurs and how to troubleshoot it. Further, the chapter discussed issues related to Novell Cluster Services failing to start, including causes of a failure to start and a methodology to troubleshoot those failures. Troubleshooting drive-mapping issues was also discussed, broken into two categories — problems with trustees, and problems with TCP/IP name resolution. Finally, you learned how to re-create the cluster services partition.

Third-Party SAN Products for NetWare

This appendix contains a compendium of available third-party Storage Area Network solutions for NetWare — hardware and software products that work with NetWare and Novell Cluster Services. This appendix was compiled with help from Novell's SAN partners, Novell "YES, Tested and Approved" product certification bulletins posted by Novell's DeveloperNet group, and publicly available Web site information. Included are details of products known to work with NetWare and Novell Cluster Services.

Remembering that operating system software is independent of Storage Area Network hardware, the only real requirement for NetWare SAN support is the availability of a host bus adapter and device driver software. Beyond the HBA, the fibre channel specification ensures device interoperability. Fibre channel ports and SCSI LUNs are OS neutral.

TIP

For the most up-to-date information, you should visit the SAN vendor's Web site and also check Novell "YES, Tested and Approved" certification bulletins posted at `http://developer.novell.com/prodcert`.

Several companies offer complete SAN solutions that include everything you need to deploy a SAN. For example:

- *Storage Works* — Compaq Computer Corporation

- *PowerVault* — Dell Computer Corporation

- *Enterprise Storage Network* (ESN) — EMC Corporation

- *FAStT* — IBM

- *MAGNITUDE* — XIOtech

Other vendors provide a subset of devices necessary to build a SAN. For example, some vendors sell only HBAs or storage array products.

When you design a traditional local area network, you are free to purchase devices from different vendors safe in the knowledge that they will interoperate when deployed. Fibre channel SANs are based on industry standards but at the time of this writing, the SAN industry hasn't quite achieved the same level of interoperability that is enjoyed by the classic local area networking market.

TIP

SANs are generally no longer considered bleeding-edge technology, but you should still work with SAN vendors to ensure that the products you are purchasing have been tested and work together. The results of interoperability tests are usually provided by SAN vendors and third-party test labs on their Web sites.

A large number of SAN products support NetWare and Novell Cluster Services. The three main categories of SAN products are as follows:

▸ *Server attachment* — Host bus adapters (HBAs).

▸ *Network connectivity* — Loop hubs, fabric switches, bridges/routers, and LUN masking appliances (sometimes called block-level gateways or just gateways).

NOTE

Fibre channel bridges and fibre channel routers enable the same basic capability of converting fibre channel to SCSI. The terms *bridge* and *router* are generally used interchangeably. The terms *gateway* and *LUN-masking appliance* are also used interchangeably. A LUN-masking appliance is a device that presents the illusion of being a storage array to servers, but is actually a block-level client of multiple back end storage arrays.

▸ *Storage devices* — JBOD/RAID arrays and tape units.

In this appendix, SAN product information is organized in the following way:

▸ Cross-reference of companies offering products in each category.

▸ Per-category listings of companies and specific product information.

▸ Links to fibre channel information and resources on the Web.

At the time of this writing, double-rate fibre channel products are starting to appear on the market. These products enable double the base rate 100 megabytes per second per-link bandwidth. On a single fibre channel cable, it will now be possible to achieve 200 megabytes per second (2 gigabits per second) unidirectional bandwidth and therefore 400 megabytes per second full duplex (200 megabytes per second on both input and output links).

TIP

If you are purchasing double-rate equipment, be sure to check for interoperability between single- and double-rate devices. Most of the new 200 megabytes per second products support both link bandwidths, but it's worth checking, especially if you have older equipment you'd still like to use.

▶ · ◀

SAN Product Cross-Reference

Table A.1 is a cross-reference of companies offering products in each category. *OEM* means the company resells an original equipment manufacturer's (OEM) product under their own brand. For example, Compaq sells Brocade switches with a Compaq logo.

T A B L E A . 1			
Cross-Reference of Companies Offering Products in Each Category			
COMPANY NAME	SERVER ATTACH: HOST BUS ADAPTERS	NETWORKING: HUBS, SWITCHES, BRIDGES/ROUTERS, GATEWAYS	STORAGE ARRAYS: JBOD, RAID, TAPE LIBRARIES
Adaptec, Inc. www.adaptec.com	✓		
ADIC www.adic.com		Routers Gateways	Tape
ATL Products, Inc. www.atlp.com			Tape
ATTO Technology, Inc. www.attotech.com		Hubs Bridges	
Brocade Communications Systems, Inc. www.brocade.com	Switches		
Chaparral Network Storage, Inc. www.chaparralnet.com		Routers	RAID
Compaq Computer Corporation www.compaq.com/ products/storageworks/ SAN/index.html	✓	OEM	✓

COMPANY NAME	SERVER ATTACH: HOST BUS ADAPTERS	NETWORKING: HUBS, SWITCHES, BRIDGES/ROUTERS, GATEWAYS	STORAGE ARRAYS: JBOD, RAID, TAPE LIBRARIES
Crossroads Systems, Inc. www.crossroads.com		Routers Switches	
Dell Computer Corporation www.dell.com/us/en/ esg/topics/segtopic_ storage_storage_ main.htm	OEM	OEM Gateways	OEM
Dot Hill Systems Corporation. www.dothill.com			✓
EMC Corporation www.emc.com		Switches	✓
Emulex Corporation www.emulex.com	✓	Hubs	
Eurologic www.eurologic.com			JBOD RAID
Fujitsu Technology Solutions Inc. http://storage- system.fujitsu. com/global www.fujitsu.com			JBOD RAID
Gadzoox Networks, Inc. www.gadzoox.com		Hubs Switches	
Hewlett-Packard Company www.hp.com	✓	OEM	OEM
Hitachi Data Systems www.hds.com			JBOD RAID

Continued

TABLE A.1			
Cross-Reference of Companies Offering Products in Each Category (continued)			
COMPANY NAME	SERVER ATTACH: HOST BUS ADAPTERS	NETWORKING: HUBS, SWITCHES, BRIDGES/ROUTERS, GATEWAYS	STORAGE ARRAYS: JBOD, RAID, TAPE LIBRARIES
IBM www.ibm.com	OEM	OEM	✓
ICP Vortex www.icp-vortex.com	✓		
Interphase www.iphase.com	✓		
JNI Corporation www.jni.com	✓		
LSI Logic Corporation www.lsilogic.com	✓		JBOD RAID
McData Corporation www.mcdata.com		Switches	
MTI Corporation www.mti.com			RAID
nStor Technologies www.nstor.com			JBOD RAID
QLogic Corporation www.qlogic.com	✓	Switches	
Raidtec Corporation www.raidtec.com			JBOD RAID
Spectra Logic www.spectralogic.com			Tape
StorageTek www.network.com		Hubs Switches	✓

COMPANY NAME	SERVER ATTACH: HOST BUS ADAPTERS	NETWORKING: HUBS, SWITCHES, BRIDGES/ROUTERS, GATEWAYS	STORAGE ARRAYS: JBOD, RAID, TAPE LIBRARIES
Vixel Corporation		Hubs	
www.vixel.com		Switches	
XIOtech Corporation	✓		JBOD
www.xiotech.com			RAID
Xyratex			JBOD
www.xyratex.com			RAID

Table A.2 provides a list of companies offering HBAs and their respective product information.

TABLE A.2

Host Bus Adapters

COMPANY NAME	PRODUCT	DESCRIPTION
Adaptec, Inc.	AFC-9210	1 and 2 Gbps
Compaq Computer Corporation	Host Bus Adapter	1 Gbps
Emulex Corporation	LP850	33 MHz PCI 1 Gbps
	LP8000	33 MHz PCI 1 Gbps
	LP9000	66 MHz PCI 1 Gbps
	LP9002	66 MHz PCI 2 Gbps
Hewlett-Packard Company	D8602A	Single port 1 Gbps
ICP Vortex	GDT7619RN	Single port 1 Gbps
	GDT7629RN	Dual port 1 Gbps
Interphase	PowerSAN range	Dual port 2 Gbps
JNI Corporation	FCE-3210	32-bit PCI single port
	FCE-6410/6412	64-bit PCI dual port
QLogic Corporation	SANblade 2100 series	33 MHz PCI 1 Gbps
	SANblade 2200 series	66 MHz PCI 1 Gbps
	SANblade 2300 series	133 MHz PCI-X 2 Gbps

Table A.3 lists companies offering hubs, switches, bridge/routers, and gateways, and their respective product information.

T A B L E A.3		
Hubs, Switches, Bridge/Routers, and Gateways		
COMPANY NAME	**PRODUCT**	**DESCRIPTION**
ADIC	SAN Gateway	Gateway: 6 ports to 4 or 6 SCSI buses
	SAN Router	Router: 2 ports to 2 SCSI buses
ATTO Technology, Inc.	FibreCenter series	Hub: 5 ports
	FibreBridge series	Bridge products
Brocade Communications Systems, Inc.	Silkworm 2800	Switch: 16 ports
	Silkworm 12000	Switch: 128 ports
Chaparral Network Storage, Inc.	FS2620	Router: 1 port to 1 to 6 SCSI buses
	FS1310	Router: 1 port to 1 to 3 SCSI buses
Crossroads Systems, Inc.	ConXsan 4x50	Router: 1 port to 1 to 4 SCSI buses
Dell Computer Corporation	PowerVault 530F	Gateway: 24 ports
Emulex Corporation	LH1005	Hub: 5 ports
	LH5000	Hub: 10 ports
Gadzoox Networks, Inc.	Gibraltar GL & GS	Hub: 6 or 12 ports
	Capellix 2000	Switch: 8 to 11 ports
	Capellix 3000	Loop switch: to 24 ports
	Slingshot 4218	Switch: to 18 ports
McData Corporation	ED-6064	Switch: 64 ports
QLogic Corporation	SANbox-8	Switch: 8 ports
	SANbox-16	Switch: 16 ports
	SANbox-64/128	Switch: 128 ports

COMPANY NAME	PRODUCT	DESCRIPTION
StorageTek	Access Hub	Hub: 32 ports
	SN 1500/2000	Hub: 14 ports
	Storage Net 3250	Router: 1 port to 1 SCSI bus
	Storage Net 6000	Gateway: to 64 ports
	4100 Series Switch	Switch: to 16 ports
Vixel Corporation	2100	Hub: 8 ports
	7100	Switch: 8 ports
	7200	Switch: 16 ports

Table A.4 lists companies offering JBOD/RAID storage arrays and tape units and their respective product information.

T A B L E   A . 4

JBOD, RAID Storage Arrays, and Tape Units

COMPANY NAME	PRODUCT	DESCRIPTION
ADIC	Tape Units	Broad range of fibre channel tape units and libraries
ATL Products, Inc.	Tape Units	Broad range of fibre channel tape units and libraries
Chaparral Network Storage, Inc.	A-series	Rack mount fibre channel RAID controllers (no disks)
	K-series	External fibre channel RAID controllers (no disks)
Compaq Computer Corporation	Tape Units	Broad range of fibre channel tape units and libraries
	RAID Array 4100	FC RAID Array
	RAID Array 8000	FC RAID Array
	RAID Array 12000	FC RAID Array

Continued

TABLE A.4		
JBOD, RAID Storage Arrays, and Tape Units (continued)		
COMPANY NAME	**PRODUCT**	**DESCRIPTION**
Dell Computer Corporation	Tape Units	Broad range of fibre channel tape units and libraries
	PowerVault 650F	to 730GB
	PowerVault 660F	to 730GB
Dot Hill Systems Corporation	SANnet RAID arrays	Range of fibre channel JBOD, RAID, and tape units and libraries
	TANnet tape libraries	
EMC Corporation	CLARiiON FC5700	180GB to 3.6TB
	Symmetrix 3630	144GB to 1.158TB
	Symmetrix 8430	288GB to 8.577TB
	Symmetrix 8730	288GB to 34TB
Eurologic	SANbloc series	Modular FC RAID arrays
	XL series	FC RAID arrays
	Voyager series	FC RAID arrays
Fujitsu Technology Solutions, Inc.	GR series	100GB to 64TB
Hitachi Data Systems	Freedom 9900	90GB to 37TB
	Freedom 9200	72GB to 7.2TB
IBM	Tape Units	Broad range of fibre channel tape units and libraries
	FAStT series	FC RAID arrays
	Enterprise Storage Server	FC RAID array
LSI Logic Corporation	MetaStor E2400	90GB to 3TB
	MetaStor E3300	90GB to 10TB
	MetaStor E4400	90GB to 16TB
MTI Technology Corporation	Vivant 25	to 1.76TB
	Vivant 35	to 13.6TB
nStor Technologies	NexStor	FC RAID arrays

COMPANY NAME	PRODUCT	DESCRIPTION
Raidtec Corporation	FibreArray series	FC RAID arrays
Spectra Logic	Tape Units	Broad range of fibre channel tape units and libraries
	917x Disk Array	to 14.4TB
	9500 Shared Virtual Array	170GB to 3.7TB
StorageTek	Tape Units	Broad range of fibre channel tape units and libraries
XIOtech Corporation	MAGNITUDE	18GB to 11.5TB
Xyratex	SR and SS series	FC JBOD/RAID arrays

Web Resources

If you want to do more reading on Fibre Channel and SAN technology, you can find more information at the following Web sites:

- Fibre Channel Industry Association at www.fibrechannel.com
- FibreAlliance at www.fibrealliance.org
- Storage Networking Industry Association at www.snia.org
- ANSI T11 organization at www.T11.org

Many SAN vendors include excellent tutorials about SAN technology and architecture on their Web sites. You may also want to check out the following Web sites:

- Brocade Communications Systems, Inc., at www.brocade.com/SAN
- Gadzoox Networks, Inc., at www.gadzoox.com/san_library

Application Configuration
Checklists

This appendix contains easy-to-follow checklists for many of the procedures discussed in Part II of the book. If you are working with Novell Cluster Services and just need a reminder of what steps to take when, or what you still need to cover before you are finished, these checklists should prove a handy reference to follow. If, however, you want more detailed information about a procedure, then see the specific chapter in the book that describes that procedure.

Working with Shared Disk NSS Volumes

For more detailed information about dealing with shared disk NSS volumes, see Chapter 9.

To create a shared disk NSS storage group:

❑ At one server console, type **NWCONFIG,** then press Enter.

❑ Select NSS Disk Options, then press Enter.

❑ Select Storage and press Enter.

❑ Select Update provider information and press Enter.

❑ Select MMPRV, then press Enter. Press Esc to return to the Available NSS Storage Options menu.

Steps 4 and 5 (that is, selecting Update provider information and selecting MMPRV) are optional. You should perform these steps only if you have added or deleted from LUNs on your SAN using external SAN management software.

TIP

❑ Select Assign ownership and press Enter.

❑ Select a shared storage LUN, then press Enter.

❑ Enter the size to create the NSS partition, then press Enter.

You can have only four partitions per disk with NetWare 5.x, so carefully plan how you use the available free space on this disk.

TIP

❑ At the Confirm Message dialog box, select Yes, then press Enter.

❑ After returning to the Available NSS Options menu, select NSS Volume Options, then press Enter.

❑ If prompted, enter the administrator name and password of a user with the appropriate rights to create the volume in NDS, then press Enter.

❑ From the Available NSS Volume Options menu, select Create, then press Enter.

❑ Select Storage Group and press Enter.

❑ Select the NSS partition from which you wish to create the storage group, then press Enter.

❑ Select Yes to confirm the storage group creation, then press Enter.

To create a shared disk NSS volume on a storage group, follow these steps:

❑ At one server console, type **NWCONFIG**, then press Enter.

❑ Select NSS Disk Options, then press Enter.

❑ Select NSS Volume Options, then press Enter.

❑ If prompted, enter the administrator name and password of a user with the appropriate rights to create the volume in NDS, then press Enter.

❑ From the Available NSS Volume Options menu, select Create, then press Enter.

❑ Select NSS Volume, then press Enter.

❑ Select the shared disk storage group on which you wish to create the volume, then press Enter.

❑ Enter the size you wish to make the volume and press Enter.

❑ Enter the name you wish to assign to this volume and press Enter.

❑ Select Yes to confirm the volume creation, then press Enter.

❑ When the volume is successfully created and you are prompted, press any key to continue.

To cluster enable an NSS volume, follow these steps:

❑ Using ConsoleOne, browse and select the Cluster object, then click the New Cluster Volume button.

❑ In the New Cluster Volume dialog box that appears, browse to the volume you created and enter a unique IP address, then click Create.

❏ Select the Cluster object and change to the Cluster State View by selecting View ➪ Cluster State from the menu.

❏ Click once on the cluster volume resource you created.

❏ In the Cluster Resource Manager dialog box that appears, click the Online button to start the cluster volume resource.

To expand a volume:

❏ At the console of the server where the volume is in the active state or any server if the volume isn't active anywhere in the cluster, type **NWCONFIG** and then press Enter.

❏ Select NSS Disk Options, then press Enter.

❏ Select NSS Volume Options, then press Enter.

❏ If prompted, enter the administrator name and password of a user with the appropriate rights to create the volume in NDS, then press Enter.

❏ Select Modify, then press Enter.

❏ Select Increase NSS Volume Size, then press Enter.

❏ Select the volume you wish to expand, then press Enter.

❏ Select a storage group that has free space, then press Enter.

❏ Specify how much free space to take from the storage group to add to your volume, then press Enter.

❏ Select Yes to confirm the volume expansion, then press Enter.

To delete an NSS volume:

❏ At the console of the server where the volume is in the active state or any server if the volume isn't active anywhere in the cluster, type **NWCONFIG**, then press Enter.

If you are deleting a cluster-enabled NSS volume, you should first offline and then delete the corresponding cluster volume resource.

WARNING

❏ Select NSS Disk Options, then press Enter.

❏ Select NSS Volume Options, then press Enter.

❏ If prompted, enter the administrator name and password of a user with the appropriate rights to create the volume in NDS, then press Enter.

❏ Select Delete, then press Enter.

❏ Select NSS Volume, then press Enter.

❏ Select the volume you wish to delete, then press Enter.

❏ Select Yes to confirm the volume deletion, then press Enter.

❏ When the volume is successfully deleted and you are prompted, press any key to continue.

To offline a cluster volume resource and delete the NDS objects corresponding to a cluster-enabled NSS volume:

❏ Using ConsoleOne, browse and select the Cluster object.

❏ Change to the Cluster State View by selecting View ⇨ Cluster State from the menu bar.

❏ Click once on the cluster volume resource.

❏ In the Cluster Resource Manager dialog box that appears, click the Offline button to stop the cluster volume resource.

❏ Return to the Console View by selecting View ⇨ Console View from the View menu bar.

❏ Right-click once on the cluster volume resource.

❏ Select Delete NDS Object and click once.

▶ • ◀

Cluster Enabling NDPS

For more detailed information on cluster enabling NDPS, see Chapter 10. To cluster enable NDPS:

❏ First create an NSS Partition and Storage Group on the shared storage for NDPS by following these steps:

If you already have a Storage Group with available space for the NDPS volume, skip this step.

TIP

❏ On one node in the cluster, load NWCONFIG.NLM.

❏ Select NSS Disk Options.

❏ Select Storage (Configure NSS Storage).

❏ Select Update provider information (optional).

❏ Select MMPRV.

❏ Select Assign ownership.

❏ Select an area of available free space.

❏ Enter the desired NSS partition size.

❏ Return to the Available NSS options menu, and select NSS Volume Options.

❏ Select Create.

❏ Select Storage Group.

❏ Select the NSS partition you wish to use for the Storage Group.

❏ Next, create an NSS volume on the shared storage for NDPS by following these steps:

❏ On one node in the cluster, load NWCONFIG.NLM.

❏ Select NSS Disk Options.

❏ Select NSS Volume Options.

❏ From the Select Create Option menu, select NSS Volume.

❏ Enter the size to use for the volume.

❏ Enter the name for the volume.

❏ Activate and mount the NSS volume.

❏ From the Directory Options menu of NWCONFIG.NLM, select Upgrade mounted volumes into the Directory, and upgrade this volume into NDS.

WARNING

> **If you don't mount the volume and upgrade it into the Directory before you cluster enable it, NDPS will not work on this volume.**

❏ Now cluster enable the NSS volume and online the cluster resource by following these steps:

  ❏ Launch ConsoleOne and browse to your Cluster container object.

  ❏ Click the New Cluster Volume button from the toolbar.

  ❏ Browse to the volume you created for the NDPS resource, and enter an IP address for the NDPS resource.

  ❏ Change to the Cluster State View.

  ❏ Click the NDPS resource, then click the Online button.

❏ Now create the NDPS Broker:

  ❏ Map a drive to the cluster-enabled volume.

  ❏ Copy the NDPS directory from the server you initially installed NDPS on to the root of the cluster-enabled volume.

  ❏ Modify the HOSTS file on all cluster nodes to include an entry for the NDPS virtual server.

  ❏ Launch NetWare Administrator and select the container you wish to use for the NDPS Broker.

  ❏ Click the Create button and select NDPS Broker.

  ❏ Do the following: Enter the desired NDPS Broker name; check each service you wish to enable; for the RMS Volume, browse to the cluster-enabled volume object; then click the Create button.

❏ Create the NDPS Manager:

  ❏ Launch NetWare Administrator and select the container you wish to use for the NDPS Manager.

  ❏ Click the Create button and select NDPS Manager.

  ❏ Do the following: Enter the desired NDPS Manager name; for the Resident Server, browse to the NDPS virtual server object; for the Database Volume, browse to the NDPS cluster-enabled volume object; then click the Create button.

❑ Next, modify the NDPS resource for the NDPS services:

❑ Launch ConsoleOne.

❑ Right-click the NDPS resource object for the cluster-enabled volume resource, and then select Properties.

❑ Click the Load Script tab.

❑ At the end of the load script, enter the following two commands:

```
LOAD BROKER .BROKER.CONTEXT /ALLOWDUP

LOAD NDPS .MANAGER.CONTEXT /DBVOLUME=NOCHECK
```

NOTE

Substitute the correct distinguished name for the NDPS Broker and NDPS Manager.

❑ Click the Unload Script tab.

❑ At the beginning of the unload script, enter the following two commands:

```
UNLOAD NDPSM

UNLOAD BROKER
```

❑ Click the Policies tab and modify the Startup, Failover, and Failback modes as desired.

❑ Click the Nodes tab and modify the Assigned order as desired.

❑ Now offline and online the resource so your changes take effect.

❑ Create printer agents for each NDPS printer.

Cluster Enabling GroupWise 5.5 Domains and Post Offices

For more detailed information about cluster enabling GroupWise Domains and Post Offices, see Chapter 11.

Creating a New System with an MTA/POA as One Resource

To prepare the system:

❏ Create a cluster-enabled volume for the GroupWise resource.

❏ Modify all nodes' HOSTS files to include the GroupWise cluster-enabled volume virtual server.

❏ Online the cluster-enabled volume resource, and map a drive to it.

❏ Create a directory named SYSTEM in the new cluster-enabled volume (unless you are installing the agents to the SYS volume of each node).

To create the GroupWise system:

❏ Insert the GroupWise Enhancement Pack CD (it will autorun if enabled).

❏ Click Install Products.

❏ Click GroupWise Administration.

❏ Click Install GroupWise Administration.

❏ Walk through the installation wizard to install snapins and ConsoleOne.

❏ When installation is complete, launch NetWare Administrator.

❏ Acknowledge any GroupWise snapin errors.

❏ Select Tools ➪ GroupWise Utilities ➪ New GroupWise System.

❏ Enter your software distribution directory path.

❏ Enter your tree name.

❏ Enter the system name.

❏ Enter the Primary Domain name.

❏ Enter the path to the Primary Domain.

TIP

> **Use the UNC path through the virtual server or your drive mapped to the cluster-enabled volume to select the path to the Primary Domain.**

❏ Enter the NDS Context to create the GroupWise objects.

❏ Enter the Post Office name, path to the Post Office, and context.

❏ Walk through the wizard to create the Domain and Post Office.

TIP

Make sure you use cluster-unique ports for all of the GroupWise agents.

❏ Install the GroupWise agents.

❏ Walk through the wizard selecting the path for the GroupWise agents.

TIP

If desired, you can install the agents to the shared volume by creating a SYSTEM **directory.**

❏ Do not update the AUTOEXEC, and do not start agents now.

❏ If you installed to the SYS volume, either copy the agents or run through the wizard again for every other node in the cluster on which you might run GroupWise.

❏ Install the GroupWise client if it hasn't already been installed.

To modify the configuration for Novell Cluster Services:

❏ Modify the GroupWise start-up files (.MTA and .POA) to remove any server name dependencies (for example, /home-gw1:\gwdom1).

❏ Add the appropriate POA switches:

    ❏ /ip-   (required)

    ❏ /port- (optional)

    ❏ /mtpinip- (optional)

    ❏ /mtpinport (optional)

    ❏ /cluster- (required)

❏ If you didn't install the agents to the shared volume, move the startup files from the SYS volume to the shared volume.

To modify the cluster resource:

❏ Launch ConsoleOne, and modify your cluster-enabled volume resource object.

❏ Change the load script to match the following, substituting the appropriate volume names and IP addresses for your environment:

```
NSS /ACTIVATE=<volume>

MOUNT <volume>

TRUSTMIG <volume> WATCH      (Optional)

NUDP ADD <cluster name>_<volume>_SERVER <IP Address of resource>

ADD SECONDARY IPADDRESS <IP Address of resource>


CVSBIND ADD <cluster name>_<volume>_SERVER <IP Address of resource>

LOAD ADDRESS SPACE=<name> <volume>:\SYSTEM\GWMTA @<domain>.MTA

LOAD ADDRESS SPACE=<name> <volume>:\SYSTEM\GWPOA @<PO>.POA PROTECTION RESTART
<name>
```

TIP

Also load DSAPI.NLM in the same protected memory space as the MTA if this MTA will perform the NDS User Synchronization event. Be sure to unload it in the unload script if you load it in the load script.

❑ Change the unload script to match the following, substituting the appropriate volume names and IP addresses for your environment:

```
UNLOAD ADDRESS SPACE=<name> GWMTA

UNLOAD ADDRESS SPACE=<name> GWPOA

UNLOAD ADDRESS SPACE=<name> GWENN2

LOAD DELAY.NLM

DELAY 10

UNLOAD KILL ADDRESS SPACE=<name>

CVSBIND DEL CLUSTER1_GW1_SERVER <IP Address of resource>


DEL SECONDARY IPADDRESS <IP Address of resource>

NUDP DEL CLUSTER1_GW1_SERVER <IP Address of resource>

TRUSTMIG <volume> unwatch      (Optional)

DISMOUNT <volume> /FORCE

NSS /FORCEDEACTIVATE=<volume>
```

❏ Change the resource policies and Node order as desired.

❏ Offline, then online the resource, and test GroupWise.

Creating a POA-Only Resource

To prepare the system:

❏ Create a volume on the shared storage for the GroupWise resource, but do not cluster enable it.

❏ Activate and mount the volume.

❏ Create a directory named SYSTEM in the new cluster-enabled volume.

❏ Make your GroupWise connection to the Domain you will install the Post Office into.

To create the GroupWise Post Office:

❏ Launch NetWare Administrator, browse to the desired context, and create a GroupWise Post Office.

❏ Enter the Post Office name, Domain, and location.

❏ Walk through the wizard and complete the required information to finish creating the Post Office.

❏ Open the Post Office object, and change the delivery mode to Client/Server.

❏ Open the POA object, and add the network address information.

❏ Rebuild the Post Office.

❏ Modify the Domain links to the Post Office to be TCP/IP.

To install and configure the agents:

❏ From the software distribution \agents directory, run INSTALL.EXE.

❏ Complete the wizard screens, entering your specific information.

❏ Do not update the AUTOEXEC.NCF, and do not launch the agents now.

❑ If you didn't install the agents to the shared volume, repeat these steps (to install the agent to SYS) for each node that might run the Post Office.

❑ Modify the GroupWise start-up files (.POA) to remove any server name dependencies (for example, /home-gw1:\gwdom1).

❑ Add the appropriate POA switches:

  ❑ /ip- (mandatory)

  ❑ /port- (mandatory)

  ❑ /MTPinip- (optional)

  ❑ /MTPinport (optional)

  ❑ /cluster- (mandatory)

❑ If you didn't install the agents to the shared volume, move the startup files from the SYS volume to the shared volume.

To create the cluster resource:

❑ Launch ConsoleOne, browse to your cluster, and create a new cluster resource.

❑ Enter the name, and select to inherit from the GroupWise Mail Server Template.

❑ Change the load script to match the following, substituting the appropriate volume names and IP addresses for your environment:

```
NSS /ACTIVATE=<volume>

MOUNT <volume>

ADD SECONDARY IPADDRESS <IP Address of resource>


LOAD ADDRESS SPACE=<name> <volume>:\SYSTEM\GWPOA @GWPO1.POA

PROTECTION RESTART <name>
```

❏ Change the unload script to match the following, substituting the appropriate volume names and IP addresses for your environment:

```
UNLOAD ADDRESS SPACE=<name> GWPOA

UNLOAD ADDRESS SPACE=<name> GWENN2

LOAD DELAY.NLM

DELAY 10

UNLOAD KILL ADDRESS SPACE=<name>


DEL SECONDARY IPADDRESS <IP Address of resource>

DISMOUNT <volume> /FORCE

NSS /FORCEDEACTIVATE=<volume>
```

❏ Change the resource policies and Node order as desired.

❏ Online the resource and test GroupWise.

Creating a New Secondary Domain and POA as One Resource

To prepare the system:

❏ Create a cluster-enabled volume for the GroupWise resource.

❏ Modify all nodes' HOSTS files to include the GroupWise cluster-enabled volume virtual server.

❏ Online the cluster-enabled volume resource, and map a drive to it.

❏ Create a directory named SYSTEM in the new cluster-enabled volume (unless you are installing the agents to the SYS volume of each node).

To create the GroupWise NDS objects:

❏ Launch NetWare Administrator, and connect to the Primary GroupWise Domain.

❏ Create a new GroupWise Domain object.

❑ Browse to the path to the Domain object using the UNC path through the virtual server or your drive mapped to the cluster-enabled volume.

❑ After creating the Domain object, modify the object by adding an administrator and verifying that the path is the UNC through the virtual server.

❑ Modify the MTA object and add the network address information. Be sure to use cluster-unique ports for the MTP and HTTP ports.

❑ Modify the Domain's links to all other Domains and make all links Direct TCP/IP, with no indirect or UNC links.

❑ Rebuild the GroupWise Domain.

❑ Connect to the GroupWise Domain that you just created (where you will create the Post Office).

❑ Create a new Post Office object.

❑ Configure the Post Office object as appropriate for your environment.

❑ After creating the Post Office object, modify the object and change the Access Mode to Client/Server.

❑ Modify the POA object by adding the Network Address and cluster-unique ports for Client/Server, MTP, and HTTP.

❑ Rebuild the Post Office.

❑ Modify the Domain links to the Post Office to be TCP/IP.

To install and configure the agents:

❑ From the software distribution \agents directory, run INSTALL.EXE.

❑ Complete the wizard screens, entering your specific information.

❑ Do not update the AUTOEXEC.NCF, and do not launch the agents now.

❑ If you didn't install the agents to the shared volume, repeat these steps for each node that might run the Post Office.

❑ If you didn't install the agents to the shared volume, move them from the SYS volume to the shared volume.

❑ Modify the GroupWise start-up files (.MTA and .POA) to remove any server name dependencies (for example, /home-gw1:\gwdom1).

❑ Add the appropriate POA switches:

   ❑ `/ip-`   (mandatory)

   ❑ `/port-` (optional)

   ❑ `/mtpinip-` (optional)

   ❑ `/mtpinport` (optional)

   ❑ `/cluster-`   (mandatory)

❑ If you didn't install the agents to the shared volume, move the startup files from the SYS volume to the shared volume.

To modify the cluster resource:

❑ Launch ConsoleOne, and modify your cluster-enabled volume resource object.

❑ Change the load script to match the following, substituting the appropriate volume names and IP addresses for your environment:

```
NSS /ACTIVATE=<volume>

MOUNT <volume>

TRUSTMIG <volume> WATCH     (Optional)

NUDP ADD <cluster name>_<volume>_SERVER <IP Address of resource>

ADD SECONDARY IPADDRESS <IP Address of resource>


CVSBIND ADD <cluster name>_<volume>_SERVER <IP Address of resource>

LOAD ADDRESS SPACE=<name> <volume>:\SYSTEM\GWMTA @<domain>.MTA

LOAD ADDRESS SPACE=<name> <volume>:\SYSTEM\GWPOA @<PO>.POA

PROTECTION RESTART <name>
```

Also load DSAPI.NLM in the same protected memory space as the MTA if this MTA will perform the NDS User Synchronization event. Be sure to unload it in the unload script if you load it in the load script.

TIP

❑ Change the unload script to match the following, substituting the appropriate volume names and IP addresses for your environment:

```
UNLOAD ADDRESS SPACE=<name> GWMTA

UNLOAD ADDRESS SPACE=<name> GWPOA

UNLOAD ADDRESS SPACE=<name> GWENN2

LOAD DELAY.NLM

DELAY 10

UNLOAD KILL ADDRESS SPACE=<name>

CVSBIND DEL CLUSTER1_GW1_SERVER <IP Address of resource>


DEL SECONDARY IPADDRESS <IP Address of resource>

NUDP DEL CLUSTER1_GW1_SERVER <IP Address of resource>

TRUSTMIG <volume> unwatch     (Optional)

DISMOUNT <volume> /FORCE

NSS /FORCEDEACTIVATE=<volume>
```

❑ Change the resource policies and Node order as desired.

❑ Offline, then online the resource, and test GroupWise.

❑ Test the configuration with the GroupWise resource migrated to each cluster node.

Cluster Enabling GroupWise 5.5 Gateways

For more detailed information about cluster enabling GroupWise Gateways, see Chapter 12.

Creating a New Secondary Domain and GWIA as One Resource

To prepare the system:

❏ Create a new cluster-enabled Secondary Domain and verify operations (use the checklist in this appendix in the "Creating a New Secondary Domain and POA as One Resource" section, but omit the Post Office).

❏ Verify that all TCP/IP and DNS configurations are correct, and that you have an MX entry for the GWIA using the secondary IP address that you plan on using for this cluster resource.

To install the GWIA:

❏ From the software distribution \internet\gwia directory, run INSTALL.EXE.

❏ Complete the installation wizard, noting the following:

    ❏ NLMs can be installed once to the shared storage, or once to each server's SYS volume.

    ❏ Be sure that you select the path to the Domain using a UNC path through the virtual server, or through a drive mapped to the cluster-enabled volume.

❏ If you installed to each server's SYS volume, move the start-up file (GWIA.CFG) to the shared volume.

❏ Modify the start-up file (GWIA.CFG), replacing the /Home and /Dhome paths with server-generic paths such as the following:

/Home-GWGWIA:\GWGWIA\WPGATE\GWIA

/DHome-GWGWIA:\GWGWIA\WPGATE\GWIA

To modify the cluster resource:

❏ Launch ConsoleOne and modify your cluster-enabled volume resource object.

❏ Change the load script to match the following, substituting the appropriate volume names and IP addresses for your environment:

```
NSS /ACTIVATE=<volume>

MOUNT <volume>

TRUSTMIG <volume> WATCH     (Optional)

NUDP ADD <cluster name>_<volume>_SERVER <IP Address of resource>

ADD SECONDARY IPADDRESS <IP Address of resource>


CVSBIND ADD <cluster name>_<volume>_SERVER <IP Address of resource>LOAD
ADDRESS SPACE=<name> <volume>:\SYSTEM\GWMTA @<domain>.MTA

<volume>:\SYSTEM\GWIA.NCF

PROTECTION RESTART <name>
```

❏ Change the unload script to match the following, substituting the appropriate volume names and IP addresses for your environment:

```
UNLOAD GWIA

UNLOAD ADDRESS SPACE=<name> GWMTA

UNLOAD ADDRESS SPACE=<name> GWPOA

UNLOAD ADDRESS SPACE=<name> GWENN2

LOAD DELAY.NLM

DELAY 10

UNLOAD KILL ADDRESS SPACE=<name>

CVSBIND DEL CLUSTER1_GW1_SERVER <IP Address of resource>


DEL SECONDARY IPADDRESS <IP Address of resource>

NUDP DEL CLUSTER1_GW1_SERVER <IP Address of resource>

TRUSTMIG <volume> unwatch

DISMOUNT <volume> /FORCE

NSS /FORCEDEACTIVATE=<volume>
```

❏ Change the resource policies and Node order as desired.

❏ Offline, then online the resource, and test GroupWise.

To configure final NDS objects:

❏ Modify the System Addressing to use this GWIA, and specify the Internet Domain name.

❏ Add a Gateway Administrator with at least the Postmaster role.

❏ Configure the Hostname/DNS "A record" property.

❏ Configure the Post Office links for TCP/IP.

To configure the firewall:

❏ Allow the secondary IP address for the GWIA in on all ports for the services it will provide.

❏ Allow all nodes' primary IP addresses out for port 25.

Creating a New Secondary Domain and Web Access Gateway as One Resource

To prepare the system:

❏ Create a new cluster-enabled Secondary Domain and verify operations (use the checklist in the "Creating a New Secondary Domain and POA as One Resource" section, but omit the Post Office).

❏ If you wish to have the Web Server be fault tolerant as well, configure the Web Server cluster resource, as described in Chapter 13.

❏ Make your GroupWise connection to the Domain into which you will install the Web Access Agent.

Install the Web Access Gateway:

❏ From the software distribution \internet\WebAccess directory, run SETUP.EXE.

❑ Complete the installation wizard, noting the following:

  ❑ NLMs can be installed once to the shared storage or multiple times to each SYS volume.

  ❑ Be sure that you select the path to the Domain using a UNC path through the virtual server or through a drive mapped to the cluster-enabled volume.

  ❑ If you are installing with the Novell Enterprise Web Server, you must select the WebAccess Servlet, WebAccess/WebPublisher Agent, and the GroupWise Administrator files as the minimum components to install.

  ❑ Do not replace a newer Servlet gateway or Java Virtual Machine (JVM) with the ones that ship with the Web Access Gateway.

  ❑ Web Access requires configuration with an NDS user object that has rights to all of the Post Offices the agent will service.

TIP

In several cases, the NDS Tree Admin account was used for this purpose. Instead, you should create a separate account with only the necessary rights to the Post Offices. This user account and password is stored unencrypted in the agent start-up file, so it should not have excessive rights.

❑ If you installed to each server's SYS volume, move the start-up file (STRTWEB5.NCF) to the shared volume.

❑ Modify the start-up file (STRTWEB5.NCF), replacing the /ph (path) switch's path to a server-generic path such as:

/ph=gwweb:gwweb\WPGATE\WEBAC55A

❑ Issue the following commands on all Web Servers into which you installed the WebAccess agent:

NSWEBDN

NSWEB

SPELLSRV

❑ Modify the AUTOEXEC.NCF file of all servers that will be in the failover path for the Web Server to include the command SPELLSRV.

TIP

The Web Server resource should use a different IP address than the Web Access Gateway, and it may have completely different failover paths. It communicates with the Gateway via TCP/IP.

To modify the cluster resource:

❑ Launch ConsoleOne and modify your cluster-enabled volume resource object.

❑ Change the load script to match the following, substituting the appropriate volume names and IP addresses for your environment:

```
NSS /ACTIVATE=<volume>

MOUNT <volume>

TRUSTMIG <volume> WATCH     (Optional)

NUDP ADD <cluster name>_<volume>_SERVER <IP Address of resource>

ADD SECONDARY IPADDRESS <IP Address of resource>


CVSBIND ADD <cluster name>_<volume>_SERVER <IP Address of resource>

LOAD ADDRESS SPACE=<name> <volume>:\SYSTEM\GWMTA @<domain>.MTA

<volume>:\SYSTEM\STRTWEB5.NCF

PROTECTION RESTART <name>
```

❑ Change the unload script to match the following, substituting the appropriate volume names and IP addresses for your environment:

```
UNLOAD GWINTER

UNLOAD ADDRESS SPACE=<name> GWMTA

UNLOAD ADDRESS SPACE=<name> GWENN2

LOAD DELAY.NLM

DELAY 10

UNLOAD KILL ADDRESS SPACE=<name>

CVSBIND DEL CLUSTER1_GW1_SERVER <IP Address of resource>
```

```
DEL SECONDARY IPADDRESS <IP Address of resource>

NUDP DEL CLUSTER1_GW1_SERVER <IP Address of resource>

TRUSTMIG <volume> unwatch     (Optional)

DISMOUNT <volume> /FORCE

NSS /FORCEDEACTIVATE=<volume>
```

❑ Change the resource policies and Node order as desired.

❑ Offline, then online the resource.

To configure NDS objects:

❑ Configure the Post Office links for TCP/IP.

❑ Add a Gateway Administrator with at least the Postmaster role.

❑ Change the WebAccess/WebPublisher Agent disk cache subdirectory to remove any server names, for example:

```
GWWEB:\SYSTEM\CACHE
```

❑ If you are using the EWS and hardware virtual servers, copy the `SYS:\NOVONYX\SUITESPOT\DOCS\COM` subdirectory and its contents to the shared volume you are using for the Web content, right below the document root.

❑ Copy the `COMMGR.CFG` file from the `Domain\WPGATE\WEBAC55A` directory to each Enterprise Web Server's `SYS:\NOVELL` directory.

❑ Test, test, and test again.

Cluster Enabling Enterprise Web Server

For more detailed information about cluster enabling Enterprise Web Server, see Chapter 13.

Active/Active Checklist

To cluster enable Enterprise Web Server (EWS) in the Active/Active configuration:

❑ Create an NSS Partition and Storage Group on the shared storage for EWS if you don't already have a storage group with free space.

❑ Create the volume for the Web content (do not cluster enable it).

❑ Install the Enterprise Web Server to every node that will be in the failover path.

❑ At each server, do the following:

    ❑ Add the secondary IP address to use for this resource.

    ❑ Activate and mount the volume for this resource.

    ❑ Using your Web browser, connect to the server's primary address and administration port — for example, `https://10.7.5.51:2200`.

    ❑ Authenticate to the Web Manager using your NDS admin account.

    ❑ Click the NetWare Enterprise Web Server button corresponding to your Web Server.

    ❑ Click the Content Management link.

    ❑ Click the Hardware Virtual Servers link.

    ❑ Enter the secondary IP address, port number, and document root path for this hardware virtual server.

The hardware virtual server path must be in the *volume*:/*path* **syntax — for example,** `web:/docs`. **And remember, the path is case-sensitive.**

TIP

    ❑ Click OK.

    ❑ Click Save and Apply.

    ❑ At the success dialog box, click OK.

    ❑ Click the Server Preferences link.

❑ Click the Restrict Access link.

❑ Click the Insert button to insert a new public directory.

❑ Enter the document root path, then click Save.

❑ Use the `NSWEBDN` and `NSWEB` NCF files to restart your Web Server.

❑ Modify your `NSWEB.NCF` file as follows:

At the beginning, add these lines:

```
SET ALLOW IP ADDRESS DUPLICATES=ON
ADD SECONDARY IPADDRESS <IP ADDRESS>
```

At the end, add these lines:

```
LOAD DELAY.NLM
DELAY 10
DEL SECONDARY IPADDRESS <IP ADDRESS>
SET ALLOW IP ADDRESS DUPLICATES=OFF
```

❑ Add the `NSWEB.NCF` command to your `AUTOEXEC.NCF` file.

❑ Create a new cluster object using the Netscape Enterprise Server template.

❑ Add or modify these commands to the load script:

```
NSS /ACTIVATE = <Volume>
MOUNT <Volume>
ADD SECONDARY IPADDRESS <IP ADDRESS>
```

❑ Add or modify these commands to the unload script:

```
DISMOUNT <volume> /FORCE
NSS /FORCEDEACTIVATE=<volume>
DEL SECONDARY IPADDRESS <IP Address>
```

> **Remove the** `NSWEB.NCF` **command from the load script and the** `NSWEBDN.NCF` **from the unload script for an Active/Active Web resource.**
>
> TIP

❏ Copy your content to the shared volume.

❏ Activate and test your Web Server.

Active/Passive Checklist

To cluster enable Enterprise Web Server in the Active/Passive configuration:

❏ Create an NSS Partition and Storage Group on the shared storage for EWS if you don't already have a Storage Group with sufficient free space for the Web content volume.

❏ Create the volume for the Web content (do not cluster enable it).

❏ Install the Enterprise Web Server to every node that will be in the failover path.

❏ At each server, do the following:

  ❏ Using your Web browser, connect to the server's primary address and administration port — for example, `https://10.7.5.51:2200`.

  ❏ Authenticate to the Web Manager using your NDS admin account.

  ❏ Click the NetWare Enterprise Web Server button that corresponds to your Web Server.

  ❏ Enter the path to the document root on the shared storage in the Primary Directory field.

  ❏ Click OK.

  ❏ Click Save and Apply.

  ❏ At the success dialog box, click OK.

  ❏ Confirm that the `NSWEB.NCF` file is not called in the `AUTOEXEC.NCF` file on the server.

❏ Create a new cluster object using the Netscape Enterprise Server template.

❏ Add or modify these commands to the load script:

```
NSS /ACTIVATE = <Volume>

MOUNT <Volume>

ADD SECONDARY IPADDRESS <IP ADDRESS>

NSWEB.NCF
```

If you are using secure content using NDS-based file system rights, add TRUSTMIG <Volume> /watch **to the load script, and** TRUSTMIG <Volume>/ unwatch **to the unload script.**

TIP

❏ Add or modify these commands to the unload script:

```
NSWEBDN.NCF

NSS /ACTIVATE = <Volume>

MOUNT <Volume>

ADD SECONDARY IPADDRESS <IP ADDRESS>
```

❏ Copy your content to the shared volume.

❏ Activate and test your Web Server.

Cluster Enabling the NetWare FTP Server

For more detailed information about cluster enabling FTP services, see Chapter 14.

Active/Passive Checklist

To cluster enable the NetWare FTP Server in the Active/Passive configuration:

❏ Create or use an existing cluster-enabled volume (cluster volume resource).

❏ Create an FTP Server configuration file. Using the default FTP Server configuration file found in SYS:\ETC\FTPSERV.CFG as a starting point, make the following edits:

❏ Set HOST_IP_ADDR to the IP address of your cluster-enabled volume.

❏ If you desire a different default anonymous home directory, set
ANONYMOUS_HOME to a directory on your cluster-enabled volume.

❏ If you desire a different default user home directory, set
DEFAULT_USER_HOME to a directory on your cluster-enabled volume.

TIP

You must use the forward slash "/" to configure a home directory, not backslash "\".

❏ Save your changes to a new configuration file dedicated to this instance of the FTP Server.

❏ Ensure that the new FTP Server configuration file is copied to the
SYS:\ETC directory of every cluster node that might run the FTP Server cluster resource.

❏ Extend the cluster volume resource by adding FTP Server startup and shutdown commands to its load and unload scripts. Add commands to your cluster volume resource's load and unload scripts to start up and shut down the FTP Server software:

❏ Launch ConsoleOne, then browse to the cluster container object.

❏ Right-click the Cluster Volume Resource, then select Properties.

❏ Select the Load tab, then add the following command to the *end* of the load script:

```
nwftpd -c <instance.cfg>
```

NOTE

Change <instance.cfg> **to match the FTP Server configuration filename of your Active/Passive FTP Server.**

❏ Select the Unload tab, then add the following command to the *start* of the unload script:

```
unload nwftpd
```

❏ Modify the Policies and Nodes configuration as desired, then click OK.

Active/Active Checklist

To cluster enable the NetWare FTP Server in the Active/Active configuration:

❏ Create or use an existing cluster-enabled volume (cluster volume resource).

❑ Create an FTP Server configuration file. Using the default FTP Server configuration file found in SYS:\ETC\FTPSERV.CFG as a starting point, make the following edits:

   ❑ Set HOST_IP_ADDR to the IP address of your cluster-enabled volume.

   ❑ If you desire a different default anonymous home directory, set ANONYMOUS_HOME to a directory on your cluster-enabled volume.

   ❑ If you desire a different default user home directory, set DEFAULT_USER_HOME to a directory on your cluster-enabled volume.

You must use the forward slash "/" to configure a home directory, not backslash "\".

TIP

   ❑ Save your changes to a new configuration file dedicated to this instance of the FTP Server.

   ❑ Ensure that the new FTP Server configuration file is copied to the SYS:\ETC directory of every cluster node that will run the FTP Server cluster resource.

❑ Load a disabled instance of the FTP Server on all cluster nodes. On all cluster nodes that could potentially run your Active/Active FTP Server, add the following commands to the server's AUTOEXEC.NCF start-up file. Ensure you add these commands before the LDNCS command used to start Cluster Services:

```
SET ALLOW IP ADDRESS DUPLICATES=ON
#
ADD SECONDARY IPADDRESS <ipaddress>


# Load FTP Server instance(s)
nwftpd -c <instance.cfg>


LOAD DELAY.NLM
```

```
DELAY 10


DEL SECONDARY IPADDRESS <ipaddress>


SET ALLOW IP ADDRESS DUPLICATES=OFF
```

NOTE

Change `<ipaddress>` **and** `<instance.cfg>` **to match the secondary IP address and FTP Server configuration filename of your Active/Active FTP Server. For each additional Active/Active FTP Server you create, add additional commands to add the secondary IP address, start** `nwftpd` **with the configuration file, and delete the secondary IP address.**

Creating Cluster-Enabled DHCP Service

For more detailed information about cluster enabling DHCP, see Chapter 15. To cluster DHCP Services:

❑ Install DHCP services in the tree.

❑ Configure the DHCP settings, including Subnets, Scopes, Subnet Address Ranges, and so on.

❑ Configure each server as a DHCP server using the DNSDHCP Console.

❑ Pick a server to use as the configuration server — use this server in all the scopes, and so on.

❑ Launch ConsoleOne, select the Cluster Container object, and click New Cluster Resource.

❑ Name the resource, and browse to the DHCP Server Template. Check the Define Additional Properties box, and click Create.

❑ Select the Load Script tab, and configure the load script as follows:

```
CLUSTER_START DHCP CN=<Distinguished name including tree of the
NDS Server Object of the node you configured as the DHCP Server>

LOAD DHCPSRVR

ADD SECONDARY IPADDRESS <IP ADDRESS>
```

It is critical that you use the NDS object of the server you configured, not the DHCP Server object.

TIP

❑ Select the Unload Script tab, and configure the unload script as follows:

```
UNLOAD DHCPSRVR

DEL SECONDARY IPADDRESS <IP ADDRESS>
```

❑ Select the Policies tab, and configure the policies for Start Mode, Failover Mode, and Failback Mode.

❑ Select the Nodes tab, and modify the Assigned Nodes and node order for this resource.

❑ Online the resource from the ConsoleOne Cluster State View.

Creating Cluster-Enabled DNS

For more detailed information about cluster enabling DNS, see Chapter 15. To cluster enable DNS:

❑ Create the DNS zone information using the DNSDHCP Console.

❑ Create a DNS Server object for all servers you wish to be in the failover path.

❑ Assign all servers you wish to be in the failover path to all the zones you wish fault tolerance on.

❑ Launch ConsoleOne, select the Cluster Container object, and click the New Cluster Resource button.

❑ Name the resource, select Define Additional Properties, and click Create.

❑ For the load script, enter the following commands:

```
ADD SECONDARY IPADDRESS <IPADDRESS>

LOAD NAMED
```

❑ For the unload script, enter the following commands:

```
UNLOAD NAMED

DEL SECONDARY IPADDRESS <IPADDRESS>
```

❑ Modify the policies for Start Mode, Failover Mode, and Failback Mode.

❑ Modify the Assigned Nodes and node order for this resource.

❑ Online the resource from the ConsoleOne Cluster State View.

❑ Use the assigned secondary IP address for the client's DNS server either via DHCP or manual workstation assignment.

Cluster Enabling BorderManager

For more detailed information about cluster enabling BorderManager, see Chapter 16.

To cluster enable BorderManager:

❑ Create an NSS Partition and Storage Group on the shared storage for the BorderManager Cache if you don't already have sufficient free space within an existing Storage Group for the BorderManager Cache volume.

❑ Bind the secondary IP address to be used for the resource to each node prior to installing BorderManager so that you can designate the private IP address.

❑ Install BorderManager on each cluster node, selecting Firewall/Caching services.

❑ Configure the tree Login Policy if it hasn't already been configured (and if needed).

❑ Configure each BorderManager Server:

❑ Add the cluster resource secondary IP address.

❑ Load BRDSRV so that the NDS Configuration page is active.

❑ Launch NetWare Administrator, and select the NCP Server object of the server you wish to configure.

❑ Enable the Proxy Services you wish to use.

❑ Configure the Cache Location and number of Cache Directories desired.

❑ Verify the IP address configuration.

❑ Enable NDS Authentication and configure as desired.

❑ Configure the logging parameters as desired.

❑ Create the cluster resource:

    ❑ Launch ConsoleOne and create a new cluster resource.

    ❑ Configure the load script as follows:

```
NSS /ACTIVATE=<Volume Name>

MOUNT <Volume Name>

ADD SECONDARY IPADDRESS <IP Address>

LOAD BRDSRV
```

    ❑ Configure the unload script as follows:

```
UNLOAD PROXY

UNLOAD IPXIPGW

UNLOAD BRDMON

UNLOAD PROXYCFG

UNLOAD ACLCHECK

UNLOAD NBMALERT

UNLOAD BRDSRV

DEL SECONDARY IPADDRESS <IP Address>

DISMOUNT <Volume Name> /FORCE

NSS /DEACTIVATE = <Volume Name>
```

    ❑ Configure the policies as desired.

    ❑ Configure the Preferred nodes as desired.

    ❑ Unload BorderManager from all nodes, delete the secondary IP addresses, and dismount the shared cache volume.

    ❑ Online the resource and test.

▶ · ◀

Cluster Enabling GroupWise 6

For more detailed information about cluster enabling GroupWise 6, see Chapter 20.

Creating a New System with an MTA/POA as One Resource

To prepare the system:

❑ Create a cluster-enabled volume for the GroupWise resource.

❑ Modify all nodes' HOSTS files and DNS to include the GroupWise cluster-enabled volume virtual server.

❑ Online the cluster-enabled volume resource, and map a drive to it.

❑ Create a directory named SYSTEM in the new cluster-enabled volume (unless you are installing the agents to the SYS volume of each node).

To create the GroupWise system:

❑ Insert the GroupWise 6 CD (it will auto-run if enabled).

❑ Click Create or update a GroupWise system.

❑ Walk through the installation wizard to install snapins and ConsoleOne.

❑ When installation is complete, launch ConsoleOne.

❑ Enter your software distribution directory path and select all components to install.

❑ Enter your tree name, system name, and Primary Domain name.

❑ Enter the path to the Primary Domain.

For the path to the Primary Domain, use the UNC path through the virtual server or your drive mapped to the cluster-enabled volume.

TIP

❑ Enter the NDS Context to create the GroupWise objects.

❑ Enter the Post Office name, path to the Post Office, and context.

❑ Walk through the wizard to create the Domain and Post Office.

TIP

Make sure you use cluster-unique ports for all of the GroupWise agents.

❏ Install the GroupWise Agents.

❏ Walk through the wizard selecting the path for the GroupWise agents.

TIP

If desired, you can install the agents to the shared volume by creating a SYSTEM **directory.**

❏ Make the Post Office link a TCP/IP link instead of Direct.

❏ Be sure to check the Configure GroupWise Agents for Clustering check box.

❏ Do not update the AUTOEXEC, and do not start agents now.

❏ If you installed to the SYS volume, either copy the agents or run through the wizard again for every other node in the cluster that you might run GroupWise on.

❏ Install the GroupWise client if it hasn't already been installed.

To modify the configuration for Novell Cluster Services:

❏ If you didn't install the agents to the shared volume, move the start-up files (.MTA and .POA) from the SYS volume to the shared volume.

❏ Modify the GroupWise start-up files (.MTA and .POA) to remove any server name dependencies (for example: /home-gw1:\gwdom1). As long as you selected Configure GroupWise Agents for Clustering, this is already done for you.

❏ Add the appropriate POA switches:

   ❏ /ip-

   ❏ /port- (optional)

   ❏ /mtpinip- (optional)

   ❏ /mtpinport (optional)

To modify the cluster resource:

❏ Launch ConsoleOne, and modify your cluster-enabled volume resource object.

❑ Change the load script to match the following, substituting the appropriate volume names and IP addresses for your environment:

```
NSS /ACTIVATE=<volume>

MOUNT <volume>

TRUSTMIG <volume> WATCH      (Optional)

NUDP ADD <cluster name>_<volume>_SERVER <IP Address of resource>

ADD SECONDARY IPADDRESS <IP Address of resource>


CVSBIND ADD <cluster name>_<volume>_SERVER <IP Address of resource>


LOAD ADDRESS SPACE=<name> DSAPI.NLM (Only required if the agent will run the
NDS User Synchronization scheduled event)

LOAD ADDRESS SPACE=<name> <volume>:\SYSTEM\GWMTA @<domain>.MTA

LOAD ADDRESS SPACE=<name> <volume>:\SYSTEM\GWPOA @<PO>.POA PROTECTION RESTART
<name>
```

❑ Change the unload script to match the following, substituting the appropriate volume names and IP addresses for your environment:

```
UNLOAD ADDRESS SPACE=<name> DSAPI (Only if you loaded it)

UNLOAD ADDRESS SPACE=<name> GWMTA

UNLOAD ADDRESS SPACE=<name> GWPOA

LOAD DELAY.NLM

DELAY 10

UNLOAD KILL ADDRESS SPACE=<name>


CVSBIND DEL <cluster name>_<volume>_SERVER <IP Address of resource>

DEL SECONDARY IPADDRESS <IP Address of resource>

NUDP DEL CLUSTER_GW1_SERVER <IP Address of resource>
```

```
TRUSTMIG <volume> unwatch    (Optional)

DISMOUNT <volume> /FORCE

NSS /FORCEDEACTIVATE=<volume>
```

❑ Change the resource policies and Node order as desired.

❑ Offline, then online the resource, and test GroupWise.

Creating a New Secondary Domain and POA as One Resource

To prepare the system:

❑ Create a cluster-enabled volume for the GroupWise resource.

❑ Modify all nodes' HOSTS files and DNS to include the GroupWise cluster-enabled volume virtual server.

❑ Online the cluster-enabled volume resource, and map a drive to it.

❑ Create a directory named SYSTEM in the new cluster-enabled volume (unless you are installing the agents to the SYS volume of each node).

To create the GroupWise NDS objects:

❑ Launch ConsoleOne, and connect to the Primary GroupWise Domain.

❑ Create a new GroupWise Domain object.

❑ Browse to the path to the Domain object using the UNC path through the virtual server or your drive mapped to the cluster-enabled volume.

❑ After creating the Domain object, modify the object by adding an administrator and verifying that the path is UNC through the virtual server.

❑ Modify the MTA object and add the network address information. Be sure to use cluster-unique ports for the MTP and HTTP ports.

❑ Modify the Domain's links to all other Domains; make all links Direct TCP/IP, with no indirect or UNC links.

❑ Rebuild the GroupWise Domain.

❑ Connect to the GroupWise Domain that you just created (where you will create the Post Office).

❑ Create a new Post Office object.

❑ Configure the Post Office object as appropriate for your environment.

❑ After creating the Post Office object, modify the object and change the Access Mode to Client/Server.

❑ Modify the POA object by adding the Network Address and cluster-unique ports for Client/Server, MTP, and HTTP.

❑ Modify the Domain links to the Post Office to be TCP/IP.

❑ Rebuild the Post Office.

To install and configure the agents:

❑ From the software distribution \agents directory, run INSTALL.EXE.

❑ Complete the wizard screens, entering your specific information.

❑ Be sure to check the Configure GroupWise Agents for Clustering check box.

❑ Do not update the AUTOEXEC.NCF file, and do not launch the agents now.

❑ If you didn't install the agents to the shared volume, repeat the agent installation for each node that might run the Post Office.

❑ If you didn't install the agents to the shared volume, move the start-up files from the SYS volume to the shared volume.

❑ Modify the GroupWise start-up files (.MTA and .POA) to remove any server name dependencies (for example: /home-gw1:\gwdom1).

❑ Add the appropriate POA switches:

  ❑ /ip-

  ❑ /port- (optional)

  ❑ /mtpinip- (optional)

  ❑ /mtpinport- (optional)

  ❑ /cluster

To modify the cluster resource:

❏ Launch ConsoleOne, and modify your cluster-enabled volume resource object.

❏ Change the load script to match the following, substituting the appropriate volume names and IP addresses for your environment:

```
NSS /ACTIVATE=<volume>

MOUNT <volume>

TRUSTMIG <volume> WATCH      (Optional)

NUDP ADD <cluster name>_<volume>_SERVER <IP Address of resource>

ADD SECONDARY IPADDRESS <IP Address of resource>


CVSBIND ADD <cluster name>_<volume>_SERVER <IP Address of resource>


LOAD ADDRESS SPACE=<name> DSAPI.NLM (Only required if the agent will run the
NDS User Synchronization scheduled event)

LOAD ADDRESS SPACE=<name> <volume>:\SYSTEM\GWMTA @<domain>.MTA

LOAD ADDRESS SPACE=<name> <volume>:\SYSTEM\GWPOA @<PO>.POA

PROTECTION RESTART <name>
```

❏ Change the unload script to match the following, substituting the appropriate volume names and IP addresses for your environment:

```
UNLOAD ADDRESS SPACE=<name> DSAPI (Only if you loaded it)

UNLOAD ADDRESS SPACE=<name> GWMTA

UNLOAD ADDRESS SPACE=<name> GWPOA

LOAD DELAY.NLM

DELAY 10

UNLOAD KILL ADDRESS SPACE=<name>
```

```
CVSBIND DEL <cluster name>_<volume>_SERVER <IP Address of resource>

DEL SECONDARY IPADDRESS <IP Address of resource>

NUDP DEL CLUSTER_GW1_SERVER <IP Address of resource>

TRUSTMIG <volume> unwatch    (Optional)

DISMOUNT <volume> /FORCE

NSS /FORCEDEACTIVATE=<volume>
```

❏ Change the resource policies and Node order as desired.

❏ Offline, then online the resource, and test GroupWise.

Creating a New GWIA Cluster Resource

To prepare the system:

❏ Create a new cluster-enabled Secondary Domain and verify operations (use the checklist for creating the Domain and Post Office as a single resource, but omit the Post Office).

❏ Verify that all TCP/IP and DNS configurations are correct, and you have an MX entry for the GWIA.

To install the GWIA:

❏ From the software distribution \internet\gwia directory, run INSTALL.EXE.

❏ Complete the installation wizard, noting the following:

  ❏ NLMs can be installed once to the shared storage, or multiple times to each SYS volume.

  ❏ Be sure that you select the path to the Domain using a UNC path through the virtual server, or through a drive mapped to the cluster-enabled volume.

❏ If you installed multiple times to each server's SYS volume, move the start-up file (GWIA.CFG) to the shared volume.

❏ Be sure to check the Configure GroupWise Agents for Clustering check box so that the /Home and /DHome switches are correct.

To modify the cluster resource:

❑ Launch ConsoleOne, and modify your cluster-enabled volume resource object.

❑ Change the load script to match the following, substituting the appropriate volume names and IP addresses for your environment:

```
NSS /ACTIVATE=<volume>

MOUNT <volume>

TRUSTMIG <volume> WATCH     (Optional)

NUDP ADD <cluster name>_<volume>_SERVER <IP Address of resource>

ADD SECONDARY IPADDRESS <IP Address of resource>


CVSBIND ADD <cluster name>_<volume>_SERVER <IP Address of resource>


LOAD ADDRESS SPACE=<name> <volume>:\SYSTEM\GWMTA @<domain>.MTA

LOAD DELAY.NLM

DELAY <XXX>

LOAD ADDRESS SPACE=<name><volume>:\SYSTEM\GWIA.NCF

PROTECTION RESTART <name>
```

TIP

With GroupWise 6, the GWIA must be loaded in the same address space as its MTA.

❑ Change the unload script to match the following, substituting the appropriate volume names and IP addresses for your environment:

```
UNLOAD ADDRESS SPACE=<name> GWIA

UNLOAD ADDRESS SPACE=<name> GWMTA

UNLOAD ADDRESS SPACE=<name> GWPOA

LOAD DELAY.NLM

DELAY 10

UNLOAD KILL ADDRESS SPACE=<name>
```

```
CVSBIND DEL CLUSTER_GW1_SERVER <IP Address of resource>


DEL SECONDARY IPADDRESS <IP Address of resource>

NUDP DEL CLUSTER_GW1_SERVER <IP Address of resource>

TRUSTMIG <volume> unwatch     (Optional)

DISMOUNT <volume> /FORCE

NSS /FORCEDEACTIVATE=<volume>
```

❑ Change the resource policies and Node order as desired.

❑ Offline, then online the resource, and test GroupWise.

To configure final NDS objects:

❑ Modify the System Addressing to use this GWIA, and specify the Internet Domain name.

❑ Add a Gateway Administrator with at least the Postmaster role.

❑ Configure the Hostname/DNS "A record" property.

❑ Configure the Post Office links for TCP/IP.

To configure the firewall:

❑ Allow the secondary IP address for the GWIA in on all ports for the services it will provide.

❑ Allow all nodes' primary IP addresses out for port 25.

Creating a New Secondary Domain and WebAccess Gateway as One Resource

To prepare the system:

❑ Create a new cluster-enabled Secondary Domain and verify operations (use the checklist for creating the Domain and Post Office as a single resource, but omit the Post Office).

❑ If you wish to have the Web Server be fault tolerant as well, configure the Web Server cluster resource as described in Chapter 13.

❑ Make your GroupWise connection to the Domain into which you will install the WebAccess Agent.

To install the WebAccess Gateway (GWINTER):

❑ From the software distribution \internet\WebAccess directory, run SETUP.EXE.

❑ Complete the installation wizard, noting the following:

   ❑ NLMs can be installed once to the shared storage, or multiple times to each SYS volume.

   ❑ Be sure that you select the path to the Domain using a UNC path through the virtual server or a drive mapped to the cluster-enabled volume.

   ❑ Assuming you are installing with the Novell Enterprise Web Server, select the WebAccess/WebPublisher Agent as the minimum components to install.

   ❑ WebAccess requires configuration with an NDS user object that has rights to all of the Post Offices the agent will service.

TIP **In several cases, the NDS Tree Admin account was used for this purpose. Instead, you should create a separate account with only the necessary rights to the Post Offices. This user account and its password are stored unencrypted in the agent start-up file, so that account should not have excessive rights.**

❑ Be sure to check the Configure GroupWise Agents for Clustering option.

❑ Move the start-up file (STRTWEB.NCF) to the shared volume.

❑ Modify the start-up file (STRTWEB.NCF), replacing the /ph (path) switch's path to a server-generic paths such as:

/ph=gwweb:webdom\WPGATE\WEBAC60A

❑ Modify the start-up file to load the GWINTER module into the same protected memory space as the WebAccess Agent's MTA.

TIP **With GroupWise 6, the WebAccess Agent must be loaded in the same address space as its MTA.**

To modify the cluster resource:

❏ Launch ConsoleOne, and modify your cluster-enabled volume resource object.

❏ Change the load script to match the following, substituting the appropriate volume names and IP addresses for your environment:

```
NSS /ACTIVATE=<volume>

MOUNT <volume>

TRUSTMIG <volume> WATCH      (Optional)

NUDP ADD <cluster name>_<volume>_SERVER <IP Address of resource>

ADD SECONDARY IPADDRESS <IP Address of resource>


CVSBIND ADD <cluster name>_<volume>_SERVER <IP Address of resource>


LOAD ADDRESS SPACE=<name> <volume>:\SYSTEM\GWMTA @<domain>.MTA

LOAD DELAY.NLM

DELAY <XXX>

<volume>:\SYSTEM\STRTWEB.NCF

PROTECTION RESTART <name>
```

❏ Change the unload script to match the following, substituting the appropriate volume names and IP addresses for your environment:

```
UNLOAD ADDRESS SPACE=<name> GWINTER

UNLOAD ADDRESS SPACE=<name> GWMTA

LOAD DELAY.NLM

DELAY 10

UNLOAD KILL ADDRESS SPACE=<name>
```

```
CVSBIND DEL CLUSTER_GW1_SERVER <IP Address of resource>
```

```
DEL SECONDARY IPADDRESS <IP Address of resource>
```

```
NUDP DEL CLUSTER_GW1_SERVER <IP Address of resource>
```

```
TRUSTMIG <volume> unwatch     (Optional)
```

```
DISMOUNT <volume> /FORCE
```

```
NSS /FORCEDEACTIVATE=<volume>
```

❏ Change the resource policies and Node order as desired.

❏ Offline, then online the resource.

To configure final NDS objects:

❏ Configure the Post Office links for TCP/IP.

❏ Add a Gateway Administrator with at least the Postmaster role.

❏ Change the WebAccess/WebPublisher Agent disk cache subdirectory to remove any server names — for example:

```
GWWEB:\SYSTEM\CACHE
```

❏ If using the EWS and hardware virtual servers, copy the `SYS:\NOVONYX\ SUITESPOT\DOCS\COM` subdirectory and its contents to the shared volume you are using for the Web content, right below the document root.

❏ Copy the `COMMGR.CFG` file from the `Domain\WPGATE\WEBAC55A` directory to each Enterprise Web Server's `SYS:\NOVELL` directory.

❏ Test, test, and test again.

To install the WebAccess Servlet into your cluster (as an Active/Active Web Server resource):

❏ Follow the directions in Chapter 13 to create an Active/Active Web Server resource.

❑ Use ConsoleOne to make your GroupWise connection to the Domain that holds the WebAccess Gateway.

❑ Unload the Web Server, Web Manager, and Java from the server that you are installing to.

You should migrate any Web or Java resources that are running on this server to other nodes in your cluster before unloading the Web Server and Java.

TIP

❑ Browse the software distribution directory, and run `SETUP.EXE` from the `\internet\WebAccess` directory.

❑ Select the components to install as GroupWise WebAccess Application and the GroupWise WebPublisher Application (if you wish to install WebPublisher), and deselect the GroupWise WebAccess Agent.

❑ Install the Servlet to `SYS:\NOVONXY\SUITESPOT` on each cluster node in the preferred nodes list.

❑ In the Web Server Information dialog box, use the secondary IP address assigned to the Web Server's cluster resource object as the Web Server's IP address.

❑ In the Novell Root Directory, specify a path for the configuration and log files as `\\<This Server>\SYS\NOVELL`. For the Active/Active cluster resource, this must be installed to the SYS volume of each node in the failover path.

❑ When the installation is complete, restart Java, the Web Server, and the Web Manager.

❑ If you created a volume on the shared storage for the hardware virtual server for WebAccess, copy the `SYS:\NOVONYX\SUITESPOT\DOCS\COM` directory from the server you installed the Servlet on to the document root directory of the hardware virtual server.

❑ Offline and then online the Web Server resource, and any other Web Servers that were running on this node.

❑ Repeat these steps for all Web Servers in the failover path of the WebAccess Servlet resource.

❑ Test, test, and test again.

Glossary

This glossary includes a listing of many of the terms used in this book. For a more complete listing of Storage Area Network terms, see the Storage Networking Industry Association (SNIA) online technical dictionary at `www.snia.org/English/Help/SiteMap_FS.html`.

Active/Active When referring to a high-availability server, Active/Active signifies that each server is able to actively run services rather than passively wait for another server to fail.

When referring to a service such as the Novell Enterprise Web Server, Active/Active signifies that each node can actively run the application, so if another node fails, the application is already running and all the node has to do is start an instance of the application, thus making failover/migrations happen quickly.

Active/Passive When referring to a high-availability server, Active/Passive signifies that each server is *not* able to actively run services; instead, they passively wait for another server to fail.

When referring to a service such as the Novell Enterprise Web Server, Active/Passive signifies that each node *cannot* actively run the application, so if another node fails, the application must first load before starting the instance or session.

Alert The resource state that requires administrative intervention, typically seen when manual failover or failback has been set.

Availability The amount of time a system is usable, usually expressed as a percentage. The higher a system's mean time between failure (MTBF) and the lower its mean time to repair (MTTR), the higher its availability.

Cluster The combination of hardware and software that enables you to connect two or more servers into a single logical system. Clusters increase overall availability by allowing one server to take over the work of another in the event of a hardware or software failure.

Cluster Configuration Library An NLM that provides the interface between Novell Cluster Services and Novell Directory Services.

Cluster Container An NDS object that represents each group of nodes in the cluster and all NDS cluster resource objects. The cluster container facilitates the configuration of the cluster's configuration parameters.

Cluster Management Agent (CMA) The CMA is an asynchronous, proprietary protocol that runs between the cluster and the client workstation running ConsoleOne. The CMA interacts with ConsoleOne to facilitate control of the cluster's current state, configure the cluster settings stored in NDS, and display the current state of the cluster.

Cluster Membership The subset of installed nodes that are currently joined to the cluster and are currently available to run cluster resources.

Cluster Node A server in a cluster. Also known as a *cluster server* or *node*.

Cluster Resource The data volumes, applications, and services that run on cluster nodes and whose state is monitored by the Cluster Resource Manager.

Cluster Resource Manager (CRM) An NLM that runs on every cluster server and determines where and when to execute cluster resources.

Cluster Server A server that has been grouped together with other servers to comprise a cluster. Also known as a *cluster node* or *node*.

Cluster Services Partition (also known as Cluster Partition, Split Brain Partition, and Split Brain Detection Partition) The special partition created on the shared storage during the Cluster Services installation that is used to implement the atomic cluster-wide lock and used for the nodes to perform periodic heartbeats. This partition ensures that only one master node exists and is used in the split brain algorithm to recover from split brain events.

Cluster-Enabled Volume A volume that is not permanently bound to a physical server, but is instead tied to a virtual NCP server within the cluster.

Comatose The resource state that occurs when a runtime failure is detected, typically during the load phase.

Epoch Number A number that indicates how often the state of the cluster membership changes (for example, when a node joins or leaves the cluster).

Failback The process of returning resources to the server they were on before a failover. Failback occurs when a cluster resource returns to its preferred node after the node rejoins the cluster. This process can be automatic, manual, or disabled.

Failed The state of a node that has been cast out of the cluster membership by surviving nodes because it failed to respond to the heartbeat protocols either on the LAN or on the split brain partition.

Failover   The action that occurs when Novell Cluster Services software detects a node failure, which involves determining the next most preferred node for each resource, and starting that resource on the appropriate node.

Fan-Out Failover   The process of moving cluster resources from one failed node to multiple (different) surviving nodes, thus spreading the work out among the survivors.

Fibre Channel   Fibre Channel (FC) is a technology standard that allows data to be transferred from one network node to another at very high speeds. Current implementations transfer data at 100MB per second, while 200MB per second and 400MB per second data rates have been tested. It currently supports Point-to-Point, Arbitrated Loop, and Switched topologies. It can utilize either copper or fiber-optic as a transport medium.

The FC standard is backed by a consortium of industry vendors and has been accredited by the American National Standards Institute (ANSI). It is an architecture used to carry many protocols at the same level on the standard FC transport. Like Ethernet, where IP, NetBIOS, and SNA are all used simultaneously over a single Ethernet adapter because they all have mappings to Ethernet, FC has many protocol mappings, including IPI, IP, FICON, FCP (SCSI), and others.

Group Interprocess Protocol (GIPC — pronounced "gypsy")   An NLM that tracks cluster membership changes (for example, when a node leaves or joins the cluster).

Heartbeat(s)   The periodic "I'm alive" signal sent out by each cluster node, both on the LAN and on the shared storage to the cluster services partition. The master node multicasts its heartbeat to all slave nodes, and the slave nodes unicast a heartbeat to the master.

Heartbeat Network/Subnet   The subnet utilized for Novell Cluster Services communication protocols. This can also be the production subnet, or it can be a dedicated subnet reserved only for the clustering protocols.

High-Availability System   A system that provides users with constant access to data, applications, and services on the network. A system that provides availability of 99.9 percent or higher is considered a high-availability system.

Joined   The state of a node when it has acknowledged the cluster, been accepted, and is ready to run cluster resources.

Left   The state of a node when it is no longer eligible to run cluster resources.

Load Script   The set of commands associated with a cluster resource that are executed any time that a resource starts or is brought online.

Loading   The state of a resource that is currently being brought online, but has not yet finished executing its load script.

Location Transparency   The concept that insulates clients from knowing or caring which physical server is servicing the application or file system being accessed.

Logical Unit Number (LUN)   A logical number that is assigned to either a physical or a virtual disk drive or other storage device such as a tape drive, SCSI adapter, and so on.

Master Node   The first node to join the cluster. The master node is responsible for determining the true status of the cluster membership, as well as notifying the cluster nodes about changes made in NDS.

Metadata   NSS control information that describes user data such as volume free space lists, directory entries, file attributes, and so on.

Migration   The process of moving resources from one server to other servers in the cluster. Cluster resources are migrated when a node fails (automatic migration), to balance workloads (manual migration), or to perform scheduled maintenance on a node (also manual migration).

NDS Sync   The state of a resource that has been modified in NDS and is waiting for the synchronization to occur, or waiting for the master node to communicate that synchronization event to all cluster nodes.

Node   A server in a cluster. Also known as a *cluster server* or *cluster node*.

Offline   The resource state where the resource is currently shut down and not running on any node.

Poison Pill   The command given to a misbehaving node or nodes on the losing side of the split brain vote, which causes that node to intentionally ABEND itself to prevent multiple servers from servicing the same resource.

Preferred Node (also known as Most Preferred Node)   The node in a cluster where a cluster resource is assigned to run when the resource is first started.

Preferred Nodes List   The list of all cluster nodes assigned as potential candidates to run a particular cluster resource.

Primary IP Address   The first TCP/IP address assigned to a server's network interface card via `INETCFG` or the `BIND` command.

Quorum   The minimum number of nodes that must join a cluster or the length of time the nodes must wait before they can start resources. Defining a quorum ensures that the first node that joins a cluster doesn't attempt to run all of the cluster's resources.

Quorum Wait   The resource state that occurs when the resource is waiting for the cluster to achieve quorum before it starts.

Resource Template   An NDS object that contains generic load and unload script commands for a specific type of resource such as GroupWise. Resource Templates allow you to quickly create a new resource of the application type and have all of the appropriate commands necessary for that resource.

Running   The resource state where a resource is currently active on a cluster node.

Secondary IP Address   A TCP/IP address that is added to the existing bindings on a network interface card (NIC), which must be on the same TCP/IP subnet as the primary IP address of the NIC.

Service Location Protocol (SLP)   An IETF standard protocol (RFC 2165) used to advertise service information across TCP/IP-based networks. SLP does for a TCP/IP network what SAP does for an IPX network, thus providing short name resolution of TCP/IP-based resources within your network.

Shared Disk   In the context of this book, a disk that can potentially be activated by more than one server, but not concurrently.

Single System Image   The concept of virtualizing services across multiple servers so they are presented to the user as a single service. By virtualizing these services, the user is not aware of the actual location where the service is running.

Slave Node   Any node that joins a cluster after the first (master) node.

Split Brain Condition   A situation when nodes in a cluster can no longer communicate with one another over the network (for example, when an Ethernet switch fails between nodes in the cluster). When a cluster experiences a split brain condition, each side of the cluster thinks that nodes on the other side of the condition have failed and will try to activate their resources, which can result in massive data corruption. Novell Cluster Services uses its Split Brain Detector (SBD) algorithm to make sure that split brain conditions are detected and dealt with properly so that no data corruption can occur.

Split Brain Detector (SBD)   An NLM that detects split brain conditions and deals with them before data corruption can occur.

Storage Area Network (SAN)   A network that connects multiple servers to a shared disk storage system via hubs or switches using either Fibre Channel technology or Serial Storage Architecture (SSA).

Transparent Client Reconnect   The process of automatically and transparently reconnecting NetWare clients to a surviving node in the cluster when the node from which they were accessing the resource fails. Transparent client reconnect preserves users' drive mappings when their volumes are remounted on a surviving server, and requires cluster-enabled volumes.

Trustee Migration (TRUSTMIG.NLM)   The process that migrates file system trustee rights associated with a cluster-enabled volume from a failed node to the surviving node that remounts the volume. Without this migration, users' rights assignments will be lost when the volume moves.

Two-Phase Commit   The communication process that occurs as follows:

1. The sender says to all receivers, "Are you ready?" (phase 1)

2. All receivers reply affirmative.

3. When sender receives replies from all, it says, "Okay, commit."

4. If the sender doesn't receive replies from all, it sends an abort, and the transaction is not committed anywhere.

Unassigned   The resource state where the resource is unable to run on any node in the cluster because the nodes in its preferred node list are not available.

Unload Script   The set of commands associated with a cluster resource that are executed any time the resource is brought offline, or migrated away from the current server.

Unloading   The state of a resource that is currently being brought offline or being migrated to a new node, before it has finished executing its unload script.

Virtual Disks   Disks that are configured using the hardware vendor's RAID array configuration utility to present one or more hard drives (typically using some level of fault tolerance) to the operating system as though they are a single hard drive, irrespective of how many physical drives exist in the system.

Virtual Server   The NCP server object that is created when you cluster enable a volume. The NDS volume object is then tied to the virtual server, and this virtual server can be hosted on any physical server within the cluster.

Volume Resource   The resource object representing a cluster-enabled volume, which is used to allow clients to retain their drive mappings when a resource is moved to another cluster node.

Zoning   The process of configuring a storage area network in such a manner that not all servers can see all of the SAN storage. Typically, zoning is used to prevent one operating system (OS) from seeing any storage that will be designated for use by another OS, or to prevent servers from seeing storage to be used for SYS volumes.

*I*ndex

NOVELL'S GUIDE TO STORAGE AREA NETWORKS AND NOVELL CLUSTER SERVICES

Fibre Channel (FC) (continued)
  versus arbitrated loops, 50
  versus SCSI over IP
    networks, 37–38
  very low bit error rate
    (BER), 25
  Wave Division Multiplexing
    (WDM) support, 36
  world wide name (WWN)
    conventions, 31
Fibre Channel disk interface,
  210–211
Fibre Channel standard,
  SANs, 6–7
Fibre-to-SCSI Bridge, 33
File ⇨ New ⇨ Cluster ⇨
  Cluster Resource
  command, 340
File ⇨ New ⇨ Cluster ⇨ Cluster
  Volume command, 609
File ⇨ New ⇨ Cluster ⇨
  New Cluster Volume
  command, 235
File ⇨ New ⇨ Cluster Resource
  command, 405
File ⇨ New Cluster Resource
  command, 413
File Copy on Write (COW),
  532–533
file corruption, duplicate
  volume names, 714–715
file system corruption,
  preventing, 699
file systems
  corrupting with duplicate
    volume names, 714–715
  LUN types, 47–48
  Novell Storage Services
    (NSS), 214–264
  NSS, 113, 127–128
  trustee assignments, 99
  trustee migration
    planning, 126

FileFlushTimer parameter
  described, 262
  NSS file system, 128
file-level backups
  cluster volumes, 518–519
  described, 517
files
  ADMSERV.NLM, 391
  AUTOEXEC.NCF, 127–128,
    150, 156, 217, 435
  backing up open cluster
    volumes, 532–536
  COMMGR.CFG, 366
  EWS startup, 404–405
  FTP_2.CFG, 433–434
  FTP_3.CFG, 435
  FTPSERV.CFG, 419, 426–428
  GroupWise 5.5 agent startup,
    325–326
  GroupWise 6 startup,
    633–634
  GWIA agent, 364–365
  GWTSA.NLM, 623–624
  HA_FTP.CFG, 427–428
  HOSTS, 118–119, 250,
    280–281, 308–309,
    314, 368
  MTA startup, 300–301
  node removal, 151
  NSHTTP.NLM, 391
  NSWEB.NCF, 391, 394–396,
    404–405
  NSWEBDN.NCF, 396
  NVXADMUP.NCF, 391
  NVXALLUP.NCF, 391
  NWCONFIG.NLM, 156
  NWFTPD.NLM, 418–419
  realtime virus scanning, 553
  SBD.NLM, 710
  startup, 339–340, 354–355
  TRUSTMIG.NLM, 126
firewalls
  BMEE, 488–490
  GWIA issues, 363–364

floating tape backups, 520, 526,
  529–530
floating volume backups, 520,
  526, 530–532
formulas, downtime cost, 65
forward slash (/) character,
  document root, 393
F-Port, fibre channel, 29–30
Frankfurt Airport, case study,
  685–686
free space, 219
frequency, defined, 65
FTP Server
  Active/Active FTP
    Servers, 426
  Active/Passive FTP Server,
    426–432
  anonymous user login
    support, 422–423
  client reconnect behavior,
    438–439
  cluster resource, 424
  described, 418
  failover testing, 437–439
  file access methods, 420–423
  FTPSERV.CFG file, 419,
    426–428
  home directory locations, 422
  installation, 424–425
  log ins, 422
  multiple Active/Active FTP
    Servers, 432–436
  multiple instances, 419
  node failure simulation, 438
  NWFTPD.NLM file, 418–419
  reasons for clustering, 423
  remote server access,
    419–420
  shared disk volumes versus
    remote server access, 421
FTP services, 418
FTP_2.CFG file, Active/Active
  FTP Server, 433–434

continued